Create a Business Letter

Print envelopes of various sizes.
See "Envelopes and Labels,"
page 282.

Use templates to create
documents with standard formats.
See "Using the Style Gallery,"
page 429.

Let Word enter
today's date for
you automatically.
See "DATE and
TIME Fields,"
page 696.

Insert pictures,
charts, and other
objects. See "Frames:
Positioning Text and
Graphics on the
Page,"
page 509.

Create a chart with
Word's Graph utility.
See "Creating Charts
with Microsoft Graph,"
page 572.

Store text or graphics
objects to insert as
AutoText entries. See
"Using AutoText,"
page 140.

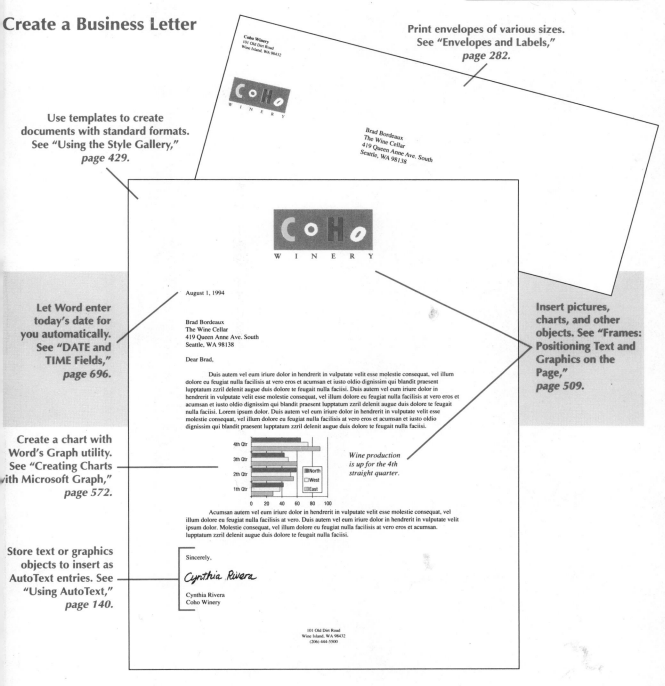

Coho Winery
101 Old Dirt Road
Wine Island, WA 98432

Brad Bordeaux
The Wine Cellar
419 Queen Anne Ave. South
Seattle, WA 98138

August 1, 1994

Brad Bordeaux
The Wine Cellar
419 Queen Anne Ave. South
Seattle, WA 98138

Dear Brad,

Duis autem vel eum iriure dolor in hendrerit in vulputate velit esse molestie consequat, vel illum dolore eu feugiat nulla facilisis at vero eros et accumsan et iusto oldio dignissim qui blandit praesent lupptatum zzril delenit augue duis dolore te feugait nulla faciisi. Duis autem vel eum iriure dolor in hendrerit in vulputate velit esse molestie consequat, vel illum dolore eu feugiat nulla facilisis at vero eros et accumsan et iusto oldio dignissim qui blandit praesent lupptatum zzril delenit augue duis dolore te feugait nulla faciisi. Lorem ipsum dolor. Duis autem vel eum iriure dolor in hendrerit in vulputate velit esse molestie consequat, vel illum dolore eu feugiat nulla facilisis at vero eros et accumsan et iusto oldio dignissim qui blandit praesent lupptatum zzril delenit augue duis dolore te feugait nulla faciisi.

Wine production
is up for the 4th
straight quarter.

Acumsan autem vel eum iriure dolor in hendrerit in vulputate velit esse molestie consequat, vel illum dolore eu feugiat nulla facilisis at vero. Duis autem vel eum iriure dolor in hendrerit in vulputate velit ipsum dolor. Molestie consequat, vel illum dolore eu feugiat nulla facilisis at vero eros et accumsan. lupptatum zzril delenit augue duis dolore te feugait nulla faciisi.

Sincerely,

Cynthia Rivera

Cynthia Rivera
Coho Winery

101 Old Dirt Road
Wine Island, WA 98432
(206) 444-5500

More ideas inside back cover...

Word 6
for Windows™
C o m p a n i o n

The Cobb Group
with M. David Stone & Alfred Poor
and Mark Crane

PUBLISHED BY
Microsoft Press
A Division of Microsoft Corporation
One Microsoft Way
Redmond, Washington 98052-6399

Library of Congress Cataloging-in-Publication Data
Word 6 for Windows companion / The Cobb Group with M. David Stone &
 Alfred Poor. -- 3rd ed.
  p. cm.
 Rev. ed. of: Word for Windows companion / Mark Crane, M. David
Stone & Alfred Poor. 2nd. ed. c1992.
 Includes index.
 ISBN 1-55615-575-1
 1. Microsoft Word for Windows. 2. Word processing. I. Stone, M.
David. II. Poor, Alfred E. III. Cobb Group. IV. Crane, Mark W.
Word for Windows companion.
Z52.5.M523W62 1992
652.5'536--dc20   93-37537
                CIP

Printed and bound in the United States of America.

1 2 3 4 5 6 7 8 9 AGAG 9 8 7 6 5 4

Distributed to the book trade in Canada by Macmillan of Canada, a division of Canada Publishing Corporation.

A CIP catalogue record for this book is available from the British Library.

Microsoft Press books are available through booksellers and distributors worldwide. For further information about international editions, contact your local Microsoft Corporation office. Or contact Microsoft Press International directly at fax (206) 936-7329.

Acquisitions Editors: Marjorie Schlaikjer, Lucinda Rowley
Project Editor: Rich Gold
Manuscript Editors: Ron Lamb, Mary Renaud, David Paul
Technical Editor: Stuart J. Stuple

For Bebe, Anna, and Alex,
who knew that we'd finish this eventually;
I owe you more than I could ever hope to repay.
—AEP

For Marie, again, and always.
—MDS

We want to thank all the folks at
Microsoft Press who worked so hard
to help get this book to you.

Contents

PART ONE: Getting Started

Chapter 1:   **A Brief Tour**   2

TOPIC FINDER   2

Starting Word for Windows   3
The Word Screen   9
Getting Help   28
Essential Customization Options   33

Chapter 2:   **File Handling**   42

TOPIC FINDER   42

Creating and Opening Documents   44
Saving Your Work   50
Deleting a File   62
Templates   63

Chapter 3:   **Essential Skills**   66

TOPIC FINDER   66

Entering Text   67
Displaying Special Marks   72
Basic Elements of a Document   73
Navigation   75
Selecting Text   84
Basic Editing Techniques   91
Canceling and Repeating Actions   94
Where We Go from Here   96

PART TWO: Basics

Chapter 4:   **Editing Text**   98

TOPIC FINDER   98

Copying and Moving Text   99
Using the Edit Find and Edit Replace Commands   109

Chapter 5:   Additional Editing Tools   130

TOPIC FINDER   130

Similarities and Differences
    Between AutoCorrect and AutoText   132
Using AutoCorrect   133
Using AutoText   140
Using the Spike   151
Using the Thesaurus   153
Using Symbols and Special Characters   156
Creating Headers and Footers   167

Chapter 6:   Proofing   178

TOPIC FINDER   178

Checking Spelling   179
Checking Grammar and Style   190
Hyphenation   198

Chapter 7:   Formatting   206

TOPIC FINDER   206

Top-Down Document Design   208
Document Formatting   209
Controlling Line and Page Breaks   219
Paragraph Formatting   221
Font Formatting   241
Copying and Moving Font and Paragraph Formats   248

Chapter 8:   Printing   252

TOPIC FINDER   252

The Windows Control Panel: Printers   253
Selecting a Printer from Within Word   262
Using the File Print Command   263
Previewing a Printed Document   273
Envelopes and Labels   282

Chapter 9:   Menu-Based Customization   292

TOPIC FINDER   292

Viewing Your Document   293

Word Defaults   309
Customizing Toolbars   316
The Tools Customize Menus and Keyboard Cards   322
Wizards: Automated Documents   322
An Introduction to Templates   325

PART THREE: Advanced Word

Chapter 10: Advanced Editing   332

T O P I C   F I N D E R   332

Bookmarks   333
Annotations   336
Footnotes and Endnotes   341
Advanced Go To Techniques   350
Revision Marks   353

Chapter 11: Building Tables   360

T O P I C   F I N D E R   360

Creating a Table   361
Using the Ruler with a Table   371
Entering Text in a Table   373
Navigating in a Table   374
Selecting Text in a Table   375
Changing the Layout of a Table   377
Deleting an Entire Table   398
Changing Table and Row Alignment   398
Entering Body Text Above or Between Table Rows   400
Working with Text in a Table   401
Adding Borders and Shading in a Table   407
Converting Existing Text to a Table   412
Converting All or Part of a Table to Text   416
Tables as Mini-Spreadsheets:
    Sorting and Calculating   417

Chapter 12: Styles & AutoFormat   418

T O P I C   F I N D E R   418

The AutoFormat Feature   420

Taking a Closer Look at Styles   427
Using the Style Gallery   429
Working with Styles   432
More About Built-In and Automatic Styles   445
More About Custom Styles   449
Applying Styles   454
Displaying the Style Area   457
Printing Lists of Styles and Shortcut Keys   459
Using Styles and Direct Formatting Together   460
Merging Styles from Another Document   462
Changing Defaults   465

Chapter 13: Bullets, Numbering, & Sections   468

TOPIC FINDER   468

Numbering Lines   470
Numbering Paragraphs and Creating Lists   475
Numbering Headings   483
Multisection Documents   485

Chapter 14: Columns, Frames, & Pictures   496

TOPIC FINDER   496

Multicolumn Formatting   497
Frames: Positioning Text and Graphics on the Page   509
Text Boxes and Callouts   525
Some Formatting Tricks with Frames and Text Boxes   531
Pictures   535

Chapter 15: Drawing, Graphics, & Other Objects   548

TOPIC FINDER   548

Using Word's Drawing Tools   550
Working with Word's Mini-Applications   559
Creating Font Effects with Microsoft WordArt   561
Creating Charts with Microsoft Graph   572
Inserting Other Objects   577

Chapter 16: Advanced Printing & Formatting   580

TOPIC FINDER   580

Understanding Screen Fonts and Printer Fonts   581

Setting Up Right and Left Pages   586
Defining the Position of a Header or Footer   588
Working with Long Documents   589
Using Special Fields for Formatting and Printing   595

Chapter 17: Advanced File Handling   598

TOPIC FINDER   598
Managing Files   600
Retrieving Documents   603

Chapter 18: Sharing Data with Other Programs   618

TOPIC FINDER   618
Some Thoughts on Exchanging Data   620
Opening Documents Stored in Other Formats   621
Importing Data   625
Moving Word Documents to Other Programs   632
Customizing the Conversion Process   634
Linking and Embedding   637

PART FOUR: Power Tools

Chapter 19: Outlining   650

TOPIC FINDER   650
Headings and Body Text   654
Building an Outline   654
Selection Techniques   660
Collapsing and Expanding an Outline   662
Editing in Outline View   664
Outline View and Styles   671
Printing an Outline   672
Outline Numbering   673
Master Documents   673

Chapter 20: Fields   674

TOPIC FINDER   674
What Is a Field?   675
The Format for Fields   676

Inserting Fields   679
Field Results vs. Field Codes   683
Editing Fields   689
Formatting Field Results   690
Nesting Fields   696
DATE and TIME Fields   696
Summary Information Fields   700
Statistical Fields   703
User Information Fields   707
Action Fields   707
Other Fields and Where to Find Them in This Book   713

Chapter 21: Form Letters, Labels, & Forms   714

TOPIC FINDER   714

Benefits of Using Mail Merge   716
Preliminaries: Database Definitions   716
Using the Tools Mail Merge Command   717
Using Special Fields for Mail Merging   737
Mail Merging Envelopes, Mailing Labels,
   and Catalogs   747
Creating Forms   752

Chapter 22: Tables of Contents & Indexes   760

TOPIC FINDER   760

A Note on Index-Related and Table-Related Fields   762
Creating a Table of Contents   762
Creating a Table of Figures   771
Creating an Index   775
Creating a Table of Authorities   783
Working with Long Documents   785

Chapter 23: Assorted Goodies   788

TOPIC FINDER   788

Sorting   789
Performing Mathematical Calculations   800
Setting up a Spreadsheet with a Table   812
Equation Editor   813

Character Formulas: The EQ Field   824
Numbering Items in Sequence   824
Creating Cross-References   832
The STYLEREF Field   835
The PRINT Field   838
Creating Special Characters   839

PART FIVE: Customizing Word

Chapter 24: Recording Macros   842

TOPIC FINDER   842

Recording a Macro   844
Running a Macro   857
Saving a Macro   860
Modifying a Macro's Properties   861
Editing a Macro   863

Chapter 25: An Introduction to Writing Macros   866

TOPIC FINDER   866

Limitations of the Record Macro Feature   868
Writing a Macro from Scratch   870
Some General Considerations for Macros   876
Testing, Modifying, and Debugging Macros   879
A Dozen Quick 'n Dirty (but Useful) Macros   890

Chapter 26: Dialog Boxes & Other Macro Magic   896

TOPIC FINDER   896

Interacting with Macros   897
Designing Custom Dialog Boxes with the
   Dialog Editor   910
Where to Go from Here   925

Chapter 27: Templates   928

TOPIC FINDER   928

Creating a New Document Template: The Mechanics   929
Editing a Document Template   937

Normal, Supplementary, and Global Templates   938
Why Use Supplementary and Global Templates?   943
Organizer: Moving Styles, AutoText,
   Toolbars, and Macros Among Templates   945

Chapter 28: Customizing Menus, Keys, & Templates   950

TOPIC FINDER   950

Customizing the Menus   952
Renaming, Adding, and Deleting Menus   964
Keyboard Customization   968
Another Macro Shortcut   975

PART SIX: Appendixes

Appendix A: Mouse & Keyboard Techniques   982

TOPIC FINDER   982

Mouse Fundamentals   983
Keyboard Fundamentals   984
Keyboard Shortcuts   985

Appendix B: ANSI & OEM Codes   995

Index   999

Introduction: Before You Begin

Welcome to the third edition of *Word for Windows Companion*. Tens of thousands of people have relied on the two previous editions to make the most of Microsoft Word for Windows. Since the second edition of this book appeared, both Windows and Word have grown and changed dramatically. Microsoft Windows 3.1 has made it possible for Windows-based programs to perform a host of new tricks. For example, you can create more powerful links between programs, making it easier to share the same information between Word and spreadsheet, graphics, and database programs.

The biggest changes of all have occurred in Word itself. After a few minor upgrades to Word 2.0 (we got up to version 2.0c in the end), Microsoft completely rebuilt the program and renumbered it to indicate that it is now in sync with the Macintosh version of Word. Welcome to Word 6.0!

What's New in Word 6.0 (and Where to Find It in This Book)

If you are already familiar with an earlier version of Word, you will find a lot of familiar features in Word 6.0. You'll also find hundreds of significant changes. Some are improvements to old features, some are replacements for features found in older versions, and some are new from the ground up. You'll find these new features discussed throughout the 28 chapters of this book, but to help you spot them, we've flagged the most significant changes with a "New!" symbol in the margin, just like the one next to this paragraph. We don't have room to list them all, but here's a quick look at some of the new and exciting features you will find.

More toolbars

You no longer get one toolbar with Word, you get more than a dozen. The Standard toolbar is similar to the Word 2.0 toolbar, and the Formatting toolbar is similar to the Word 2.0 ribbon. You also get specialized toolbars for specific functions, such as drawing, outlining, and adding borders. The ToolTips feature displays the name of a toolbar button so that you can see what the button does without clicking on it. You also have more options than ever for creating custom toolbars, giving you instant access to the commands and macros you use the most. You can even create your own toolbar buttons. Another new feature lets you place toolbars anywhere you want on the screen, not just within your Word window. (See Chapters 1 and 9.)

Wizards

Like many other recent versions of Microsoft Windows–based programs, Word 6.0 now has wizards. These are like "supertemplates" that guide you through the creation of complex document formats, from fax cover sheets to book layouts, from letterhead designs to calendars. All you have to do is fill in the blanks in a series of dialog boxes to create personalized document designs. And it's easy to use a wizard to create a template so that you can use your new layouts over and over again. (See Chapter 9.)

AutoCorrect and AutoText

Word 6.0 can automatically correct your typing errors as you type with the new AutoCorrect feature. And the Word 2.0 "glossary" feature has been replaced with AutoText, which you can use to enter everything from a company name to a signature at the touch of a key. (See Chapter 5.)

More help features

Word 6.0 has a new context-sensitive Help, which can provide specific help screens for menu commands or other items as well as display the paragraph and character formatting in use for a section of text. Word also has automated demos to step you through basic procedures and a How-To help feature that displays step-by-step instructions in a window on top of your document while you follow the steps. (See Chapter 1.)

Context-sensitive menus

The right button on your mouse becomes a handy tool with Word 6.0; press it and, in many situations, you get context-sensitive menus that list the commands you are most likely to need at that point. (See Chapter 1.)

Full Screen mode

Some people like to have all of Word's commands, toolbars, and other features visible while they work, while others prefer to work with nothing on the screen but their text. Word's new Full Screen mode lets you show as much or as little as you like on your screen while you're editing. (See Chapter 9.)

New template features

You can now attach more than one template to a given document. You can create templates that serve as tool kits, with macros and style definitions and other customized features, and then attach them to your documents as global templates to make their features available. You can also move style definitions, macros, and other customizations between templates using the new Organizer feature. (See Chapter 27.)

Multiple-level Undo

In Word 2.0, you could undo only the last editing change you made. With Word 6.0, you can undo multiple steps—either one at a time or all at once. And you can even change your mind and redo an action. (See Chapter 3.)

Forms

Word 6.0 lets you create on-screen forms that make it easy to collect information such as names and addresses. You can create custom prompts, default entries, and other features that most people associate only with sophisticated database programs. (See Chapter 21.)

AutoFormat

Let Word apply special formatting automatically to your documents with the new AutoFormat feature. (See Chapter 12.)

Character styles

In Word 2.0, you could define formatting styles for entire paragraphs, but if you wanted to apply formatting to just a portion of a paragraph, you had to apply it explicitly. Word 6.0 adds character styles, making it as easy to apply consistent formatting to certain words or phrases as it is to apply formatting to an entire paragraph. (See Chapter 12.)

Improved envelope and label features

Word 2.0 made it easy to print envelopes, but there were still some snags when it came to configuring the program to work with certain printers. Word 6.0 solves those problems with easy-to-use dialog boxes. You can also add U.S. Postal Service Postnet bar codes automatically to your addresses. A new label feature makes it easy to create labels in a variety of formats. (See Chapter 8.)

Improved mail merge

You can create complex documents based on lists of information from other programs, such as addresses, and merge this information with text to create form letters, catalogs, and other types of printed documents. New features make it easy to create mailing labels as well. (See Chapter 21.)

More page layout options

You can create complex page layouts with Word 6.0, including sophisticated multiple-column designs that include columns of different widths. (See Chapter 14.)

Improved Object Linking and Embedding (OLE 2)

Word 6.0 makes it easier than ever to create links with other applications written for Windows because of the addition of support for OLE 2. OLE 2 lets you open a linked file—such as a drawing or a Microsoft Excel spreadsheet—and edit it using the original program without leaving Word. Many of Word's mini-applications, such as WordArt, have been improved to include OLE 2 support. For example, WordArt 2 lets you use any TrueType font to create impressively formatted headlines and then link them to or embed them in your documents. (See Chapters 15 and 23.)

Improved Find File features

The Find File command has been expanded and improved. With it, you can use complex criteria to search across multiple directories, and then you can store your search specification to use again in the future. You can also perform a wide variety of useful file management tasks using Find File. (See Chapter 17.)

Easier field entry

You don't have to remember all the arcane details for controlling the behavior of Word's powerful fields. The Insert Field command will help you find the field you want and enter the correct codes to set field options and control formatting. Word can insert many of the fields automatically when you create a table of contents or index, making the task even easier. (See Chapters 20 and 22.)

Improved keyboard shortcuts

Word 2.0 limited you to single-keystroke combinations when you assigned a command, macro, or style to a keystroke. Word 6.0 lets you create multiple-keystroke assignments, making it easier to group similar commands, as well as giving you more combinations from which to choose. (See Chapter 28.)

A special note for WordPerfect users

It is easy to make the transition from WordPerfect to Word. Word 6.0 has special help features just for you. (See Chapter 1.)

Setting Up Word

Now we'll show you how to get ready to run Microsoft Word. First we'll describe the hardware you need to run the program, and we'll talk about some of the optional hardware accessories you might want for your system. Then we'll cover how to install the program on your hard disk.

Although the information in this chapter is sufficient to get you started with Word, we suggest that you also consult the *Quick Results* manual that comes with the Word for Windows package. You can call Microsoft for help if you have trouble installing and loading the program. The telephone number for Microsoft's Product Support is listed in the materials included with your Word for Windows package.

Hardware requirements

Word 6.0 requires Windows 3.1 or higher to run and, as a result, has similar system requirements. You need an IBM-compatible computer with an 80286, 80386, or 80486 processor. You need at least 4 megabytes (MB) of memory to run Word, but additional memory results in better performance.

Your computer must also have disk storage, and plenty of it. You'll need a floppy disk drive for loading the program. (The Word package comes with 1.4-MB, 3.5-inch floppy disks; you can request 5.25-inch disks instead if your system does not have a 3.5-inch drive.) Your hard disk must have at least 24 MB of free space to install the program and all its supporting files. (If you can do without all the extra features, including the Word Help files, you can install the program in less than 6 MB of hard-disk space.)

The Setup program will check to see that you have enough disk space available before it starts the installation, but you need to consider one potential problem before you start. If you are using a system with more than one hard disk (or more than one drive partition on a single disk) and you are planning to install Word on a drive other than the one on which your copy of Windows is installed, be aware that the Setup program will need about 6 MB of available space on your Windows drive for a complete installation. The remaining files will go on the drive where you install Word. This is because the Setup program places a number of utility programs and other files, such as the dictionary used for spelling checking, in your Windows directory rather than in the Word directory.

Finally, your computer must also have a graphics adapter card that is supported by Windows and a monitor that can display the card's video signal. This is a requirement of Windows, but it bears repeating because your choice of display can have a large impact on your experience with Word. A VGA display (or even an EGA display) works fine, but you may find that a higher-resolution image, such as a SuperVGA at a resolution of 800 by 600 or 1024 by 768, will provide more pleasing results and better detail.

Optional components

Although you can run Windows and Word on a bare-bones system, there are a number of additional components that can make your work easier, more efficient, and more productive. For many users, some of the following items are not optional but essential.

Mouse

There are many opinions about the appropriate role of a mouse in word processing. On the one hand, it is entirely possible to run Word without a mouse. On the other hand, the Windows interface is designed to take advantage of a mouse.

We believe that the process of entering text is primarily a task for the keyboard, and, as a result, we tend to use procedures that do not require us to take our hands away from the home keys. As professional writers who have been dealing with keyboards since before the first IBM PC appeared, we freely admit our bias on this topic. But even with this bias, we hasten to point out that certain editing and formatting tasks can be painfully slow and awkward without a mouse. And a few features do require a mouse—they can't be reached from the keyboard. So, while we do not recommend that you use a mouse for every command and operation that supports it, we still view the mouse as an essential system component for our computers. When you purchase a mouse, make sure it's supported by Windows.

Some computers have special mouse ports. With those that don't, you'll find that some mice attach to a serial port, while others come with an expansion card that includes a special bus mouse port. The serial models are a good choice if you have a serial port to spare since the bus mouse approach requires an expansion slot and has the potential to conflict with other expansion boards. If your serial ports are already tied up, you'll need a bus mouse.

Laser and ink-jet printers

As a Windows-based application, Word supports dozens of printers, ranging from state-of-the-art laser printers such as the Hewlett-Packard LaserJet to the venerable Epson FX-80 and IBM Proprinter dot-matrix printers. Since most people want to print their documents, we consider a printer to be an essential component for most systems. With the advent of the personal laser printer (with street prices around $500 to $800), most users will find that the speed, quietness, and print quality of a laser printer makes it the leading choice for word processing output. Also, a laser printer can give you easy access to different fonts to make your documents more attractive.

Ink-jet printers offer an attractive alternative if you want to take advantage of the many color output features of Windows and Word. A number of color ink-jet printers cost no more than many black-and-white laser printers and produce text output that is nearly as good as a laser. If you have a tight budget, some of the black-and-white ink-jets provide near-laser quality at a significantly lower cost. Finally, if you plan to use Word on the road with a laptop computer, a portable ink-jet printer can give you excellent output in a portable package.

Local area networks

You can install Word for Windows on a computer connected to a local area network, an option that lets two or more users share data stored on a common network drive. Word supports most major network software pack-ages, including Microsoft Windows for Workgroups and Novell Netware. For more information, see Appendix B, "Installing and Using Word on a Network" in the *Microsoft Word User's Guide,* which comes with the program.

Installing Word

Assuming that you have the appropriate hardware and the Word program itself, you're ready to install Word on your hard disk. Although Word's program files occupy several floppy disks, the installation process is straightforward.

You must have Windows 3.1 already installed on your system, and you must be running Windows before you install Word. The easiest way to start the installation process is to have the Program Manager active on your screen and then choose the File Run command (by clicking on the File menu name on the Program Manager's menu bar and then clicking on the Run command, or by holding down the Alt key while pressing F and then press-ing R by itself). When the Run dialog box appears, insert the first Word disk in the appropriate floppy disk drive and then type *a:setup* (or *b:setup*, as ap-propriate) in the Command Line text box. Then press Enter or click on the OK button to start the installation.

The Setup program will ask you to choose a drive and directory for your installation. The default is C:\WINWORD, but you can change it if you want. After checking to see that you have sufficient disk space, the program will ask whether you want to perform a Typical, Complete/Custom, Laptop (minimum), or Workstation installation. (A Workstation installation is an option only if you are running Setup from a network file server or shared directory.) If you do not have sufficient disk space for an installation option, it will be grayed and unavailable. We recommend that you choose the Complete/Custom installation option if you have enough disk space avail-able. Keep in mind that if you do not choose this option, the Setup program may not install all the files we refer to in the various sections of this book.

The Setup program will copy the various files to the appropriate places on your hard disk. A dialog box will keep you posted on the installation progress by reporting the percentage completed and showing the name of the file that is currently being installed. The Setup program also displays some "infomercials" about various Word features and reminds you to send in your registration card (which we recommend you do, by the way, to en-sure that you get notices of upgrades).

When all the files have been copied, the Setup program will offer to make some changes to your AUTOEXEC.BAT file. You should generally let it make the changes unless you have a good reason not to. The program will then return to the Program Manager and install a new program group for Microsoft Office with program item icons for Word, Word Dialog Editor, Word Readme Help, and Word Setup. At this point, you are ready to run Word.

Mininum installation

As we mentioned, the Setup program also offers a Laptop (minimum) installation option which installs essential files, including Word, its help files, and the spelling checker. This "minimum" installation will take up between 6 MB and 7 MB of disk space.

Fortunately, there is another approach for those with little disk space available. The Complete/Custom installation option in the Setup program lets you pick and choose which sets of files you want to install. The program provides a running total of the estimated disk space needed to accommodate your selections so that you can tailor the installation to match the space available. If you pick just the Word program files (and not the help files, spelling checker, sample files, or anything else), the installation will take about 6 MB.

Keep in mind that too little disk space can result in a severe performance loss for Windows-based applications, so if you're this tight on disk space, you should really consider adding more hard disk capacity if possible. On the other hand, if you're installing Word on a portable system with, say, a 40-MB hard disk, it's nice to know that you can keep the disk-space requirement relatively low.

Conventions Used in This Book

With Word installed, you are ready to put it to work. This book is designed to help you make the most of the program's power and flexibility, right from the start. Before we begin, however, let's take a moment to go over some of our assumptions and the conventions we'll use in the following chapters.

First, we assume that you have a basic understanding of how to work with Windows and Windows-based applications in general. We explain many of the fundamentals as we go along, but if you are not familiar with Windows, you may want to have a general reference handy.

We emphasize what you need to know in order to accomplish a specific task, and we have done our best to write our explanations in as readable and enjoyable a form as we can. In some cases, we have chosen not to use the official Windows or Word terminology because we feel those terms are misleading. When we do choose to substitute our own words, however, we are careful to explain how and why we are doing so. For example, Word has dialog boxes with multiple layers that look like index cards with tabs on their top edges to hold the labels. Word calls these different layers *tabs*, but we feel that this could be confusing since most people will think of the tab as the small label area at the top. Instead, we have chosen to call these layers *cards* because that's what they look like.

We already mentioned the "New!" symbols that appear in the margins next to features that are new or significantly changed in Word 6.0. You will also find two other marginal symbols. The "Note" symbol indicates information that may be a little tangential to the main discussion but that provides some important background, relates the discussion to other material, or supplies some details that can be essential in certain situations. And pay special attention to the "Tip" markers because they flag information you're not likely to find anywhere else. These tips can save you time by showing you some handy tricks or save you aggravation by helping you avoid some potential pitfalls.

We have also provided many cross-references between different sections of the book. This will make it easier and faster to find the information you need when you need it.

When discussing keyboard commands, we name the keys you are to press, such as Alt or Backspace or Right arrow. When you should press two keys at the same time, we'll combine the key names with a hyphen, as in Alt-F or Ctrl-Shift-C. When you should press a series of keys in sequence, we'll separate the key names with commas, as in Alt,O,O,K.

When you use the menu commands in any Windows-based application, you can make selections in several different ways:

- You can click on the menu name with the mouse and then click on a command within that menu.

- You can use the Alt key to activate the menu bar, and then you can use the arrow keys to navigate through the options, press Enter to open the drop-down menu, use the arrow keys to highlight a menu command, and then press Enter to choose the command.

- After pressing the Alt key to activate the menu bar, you can press the key corresponding to the letter that's underlined in the menu name to open the menu, and then you can press the key corresponding to the letter that's underlined in the menu command to choose the command.

- In many cases, you can use shortcut keys for choosing the same commands or buttons you can choose with the mouse. (You'll find a listing of the shortcut keys in Appendix A.)

Finally, we assume that you are starting with the default settings for Word as they are initially set by the Setup program. As we've already suggested and as you will see in later chapters, there are dozens of useful ways to customize the program: changing the menus and their options, adding new commands through macros, assigning new shortcut keys for commands, and more. At the start, however, we assume that you have not made any changes of this sort.

Now that we've gone over the ground rules, let's take a quick look at the program itself in Chapter 1.

PART ONE

GETTING STARTED

TOPIC FINDER

Starting Word for Windows   3

- How to start Word from Program Manager
- How to start Word and open a document simultaneously
- How to start Word from the MS-DOS prompt

The Word Screen   9

- The title bar
- The menu bar
- NEW! Context-sensitive menus
- The Standard toolbar
- The Formatting toolbar
- The ruler
- The scroll bars
- The status bar
- The mouse pointer

Getting Help   28

- How to use the Help menu
- How to get context-sensitive Help
- More about Help

Essential Customization Options   33

- The View menu
- The Options dialog box

A Brief Tour

his chapter provides an overview of Word for Windows. If you're new to Word, you'll want to read the chapter carefully because it lays the groundwork for everything that follows. If you've used earlier versions of Word, you might skim the chapter to be sure you know the basics of the program, especially new features or changes that you might otherwise overlook. New features are marked, so you can find them easily.

We'll start by showing how to load Word and by taking a tour of the screen and the help system. We'll end by discussing a few customization options that are critical to making you feel comfortable while working with the program.

Starting Word for Windows

As you'll soon discover, Word usually gives you more than one way to do things. In fact, that's one of the program's major strengths. You even have a number of choices for starting the program.

How to start Word from Program Manager

Most often you'll already be in Windows when you start Word. Depending on how your system is set up, it may start Windows automatically when it boots or you may have to start Windows manually. From the MS-DOS prompt, you can start Windows by typing *win* and pressing Enter. What happens next depends on how you have Windows set up; most likely, the Program Manager window will open. Because the Word installation program creates a separate Program Manager group for Word, you should see something similar to the screen in Figure 1-1.

When Windows starts, it usually opens the Program Manager window.

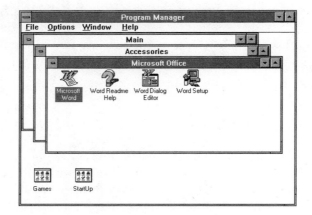

How to start Word using the Word for Windows icon

If you see the Microsoft Office group, you can use the mouse to click anywhere in the window to make it active. If you don't see the group, open the Window menu on the Program Manager menu bar. If you see Microsoft Office on the menu, choose it by pressing the number next to the item, by selecting (highlighting) the item and pressing Enter, or by clicking with the mouse. Alternatively, you can activate the window, whether you see it or not, by using Ctrl-Tab to cycle through the group windows until the Microsoft Office window is active. Note that if someone has installed Word and set up your system so that there is no Microsoft Office, you'll have to check the other groups in Program Manager or ask that person where the Word for Windows icon is.

After you select the appropriate group window, you can start the program. To start Word with the mouse, double-click on the icon. (In fact, you can start Word by double-clicking even if the window isn't active yet, as long as you can see the icon and move the mouse pointer to it.) If you prefer using the keyboard, you have to select the icon and then press Enter. You can tell which icon is selected by the colored block around the icon's title. If the Word icon isn't highlighted when you open its group window, you can select it with either the keyboard or the mouse. With the keyboard, use the arrow keys to move the highlight to the icon. With the mouse, click on the icon. When the icon is highlighted, you can start Word by pressing Enter.

Here's a quick way to select an icon within a group window: Type the first letter of the title of the icon. For example, to select the Word icon, which has the default title *Microsoft Word*, press M. If there is more than one icon with the same initial letter in its title, press the letter repeatedly. The highlight will cycle through all the icons with that initial letter.

How to start Word using the File Run command

If you'd rather not use the icon, you can start Word from either Program Manager or File Manager with the File Run command. Choose File Run, and you'll see a dialog box similar to the one in Figure 1-2. To start Word, type *winword* in the Command Line text box, as shown in the figure. Choose OK, and Word will start. (This assumes that you have the Word directory included in your MS-DOS PATH statement; if not, you need to specify the drive and directory in the Command Line text box, along with the WINWORD filename.)

FIGURE 1-2

You can start Word by entering *winword* in the Command Line text box.

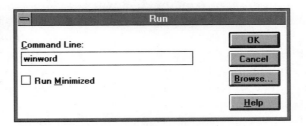

How to start Word and open a document simultaneously

Word normally opens a blank document named Document1 when you begin a new Word session. However, you can also start the program and open an existing document in one step.

How to start Word and open a document using the File Run command

One way to start Word and open a document is to choose File Run in Program Manager or File Manager. Add the full path and filename for the document to the *winword* command. For example, if you want to open the file BUDGET.DOC in the REPORTS directory on drive C, type the following command:

```
winword c:\reports\budget.doc
```

(This example assumes you have the Word directory included in your MS-DOS PATH statement. If not, add the full path for Word in front of *winword*.)

You can open multiple files at the same time with the File Run command. Simply list all the files you want to open, separating each name from the next one with a space. To open both BUDGET.DOC and ACTUAL.DOC, you could enter the following command:

```
winword c:\reports\budget.doc c:\reports\actual.doc
```

How to start Word and open a document using an icon

Having Word automatically load a particular document can be handy, especially if it's a document that you edit or reprint on a regular basis. There is a simple procedure in Windows that will make this task even easier by adding an icon for the document to a Program Manager group.

For example, suppose that you have a monthly report named C:\REPORTS\MONTHLY.DOC that stays much the same except that each month you change one or two paragraphs to enter some new numbers. You can assign an icon to the document so that you need only choose that icon to load both Word and the document.

To create the icon in Program Manager, first decide which group you want the icon to go in. Next select that group, choose File New, and press Enter to accept the default option: Program Item. Windows will display the Program Item Properties dialog box, as shown in Figure 1-3. Enter a description in the Description text box—for example, *MONTHLY REPORT*. Then, in the Command Line text box, enter the command for starting Word, along with the full path and filename for the document you want to open. In this example, to open the file MONTHLY.DOC you would use the following command:

```
winword c:\reports\monthly.doc
```

(This example once again assumes that you have the Word directory included in your MS-DOS PATH statement. If not, simply add the full path for Word in front of *winword.*)

If you choose OK at this point, Windows will insert a new item in the group you selected and assign a Word icon to this new item. If you'd prefer a different icon, choose the Change Icon button to open the Change Icon dialog box and then select an icon from the Current Icon window. Choose OK to close the dialog box, and choose OK again. Windows will insert the icon in the group window that was active when you chose the File New command. You can now use the icon in Program Manager, and Windows will load Word along with MONTHLY.DOC.

If Windows is set up appropriately and your filename ends with the extension DOC, as in MONTHLY.DOC, you can enter just the filename in the Command Line text box for the icon, omitting *winword* from the command line. However, this will work only with files whose names end with DOC and only if Windows is set up to assume that any file ending in DOC is a Word file. If you have other programs on your system that use the extension DOC, those programs may have set up Windows otherwise. Using the *winword* command as part of the command line ensures that the icon will load Word no matter how Windows is set up.

Note too that if Windows is set up to associate a DOC extension with Word, you can also take advantage of that association in File Manager. From File Manager, you can double-click on a filename ending in DOC to start Word and load the file. You can also highlight the file and then press Enter.

As with the File Run command, you can open multiple files at the same time by using an icon. This technique can be quite useful when you're working on a project with several document files that you need to open together on a regular basis. To create an icon that will open several files simultaneously, simply extend the command in the Command Line text box to list all the files you want opened. Separate each name from the next with a space. To open two documents—JANUARY.DOC and FEBRUARY.DOC— that are both in the REPORTS directory on drive C, for example, enter the following command:

```
winword c:\reports\january.doc c:\reports\february.doc
```

How to start Word from the MS-DOS prompt

You may occasionally want to go directly into Word from the MS-DOS prompt, bypassing Program Manager, where your program icons are located. Assuming your Word directory is included in your MS-DOS PATH statement, you can start Word from the MS-DOS prompt by typing the command *win winword* and then pressing the Enter key.

If your Word directory is not part of your MS-DOS PATH statement, you must either specify the full path for the directory or first change to the drive and directory where you've stored the program. For example, if you've installed the program in the directory WINWORD on drive D, you can type *win d:\winword\winword*. Or you can type *d:* and press Enter to make drive D your active drive; then type the command *cd \winword* and press Enter to move into the WINWORD directory; and, finally, type the command *win winword* and press Enter.

If you enter the *win winword* command at the MS-DOS prompt, Windows starts first, followed shortly by Word.

How to start Word and open a document from the MS-DOS prompt

If you're starting Word from the MS-DOS command line, you can load a file along with Word by adding the full path and filename to the *win winword* command. For example, to start Word and open the document BUDGET.DOC located in the REPORTS directory on drive C, enter the following command:

```
win winword c:\reports\budget.doc
```

The Word Screen

No matter which method you use to start Word, the first thing you'll see when Word is loaded will be the copyright notice. When it disappears, you'll see a screen similar to the one in Figure 1-4. (This discussion assumes that you are using the default settings. It's easy to change the appearance of this screen, however, as we'll discuss elsewhere in this chapter.)

If this is the first time you have run Word since installing the program, you will see a screen with the title *Quick Preview* instead of the screen shown in the figure. You may skip the preview by pressing Esc. To view the preview later, choose Help Quick Preview.

The window in the center of the screen in Figure 1-4 displays a "Tip of the Day" that points out useful tricks and shortcuts for using Word. You can press Enter (or click on OK) to close the box and proceed to the Word editing screen.

FIGURE 1-4

This screen will appear each time you begin a new Word session.

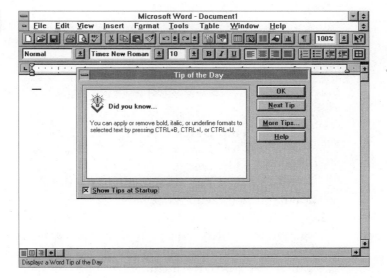

 The Tip of the Day tips are a painless way to learn a wide variety of tricks and shortcuts in Word. However, if you decide you don't want to see a Tip of the Day every time you start the program, click on the X next to "Show Tips at Startup" or press Alt-S, and the window will no longer appear each time the program starts.

As you can see from the name in the title bar in Figure 1-5, Word creates a new, blank document named Document1, ready for typing. (You can save the document under any name you like. We'll show you how in the next chapter.) If you've worked with other Windows programs, many of the screen elements will be familiar.

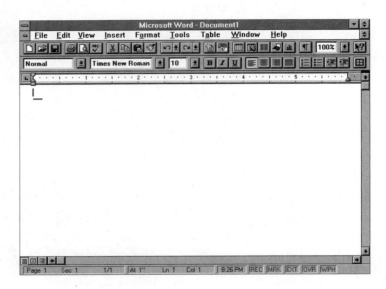

FIGURE 1-5

Word creates an empty document named Document1 when you first start the program.

The large, empty area that occupies the bulk of the screen is the document window—your workspace. This is where you will create, edit, format, and view your documents.

At this point, the document window will be empty except for a blinking vertical bar called the *insertion point,* or *cursor,* and a horizontal line below it called the *end-of-document marker.* Note that the cursor is different from the mouse pointer, which some people refer to as the *mouse cursor;* we'll discuss the mouse pointer later in this chapter. The cursor indicates your current position in the Word document. Each time you type a text character, the cursor moves one space to the right. You also use the cursor to specify the location you want to edit in existing text. If you have used other word processors, you'll find Word's cursor familiar.

The title bar

At the very top of your screen is the application title bar, shown in Figure 1-6.

| Microsoft Word - Document1 |

The application title bar.

Note that at the left end of the title bar is a box with a short horizontal bar. This is a menu box that you can use to open the Windows Application Control menu. To open the menu, you can either click on this box or press Alt-Spacebar. Note that two of the choices on the menu are Maximize and Minimize.

If your Word window is less than full screen, you'll see something slightly different from the figures in this book. To get a closer match, you can choose Maximize to change Word to a full-screen window. Also, if your Word window is less than full screen, you'll see a single upward-pointing arrow at the far right of the title bar, rather than an upward-pointing and a downward-pointing arrow as in our examples. The single arrow indicates the standard Windows Maximize button, and you can maximize the window by clicking on this button.

Note that in Figure 1-4 there is also a second set of upward-pointing and downward-pointing arrows on the menu bar, immediately below the set on the title bar. If you don't see these on your screen, it means that your document window is less than full size within the Word window. In that case, you'll see a separate document window with its own title bar showing the document name, as in Figure 1-7 on the next page. At the far right of this title bar, you'll see an upward-pointing arrow, indicating a Maximize button for the document window only. When you have more than one document open, each document appears in its own window. All of the document windows are maximized as a group.

At the left of the document title bar is the Document Control menu box, marked by a short horizontal bar. To open the menu, either click on the Control menu box or press Alt-Hyphen. You can maximize the document window within the Word window either by opening this menu and choosing Maximize or by clicking on the Maximize button. When you maximize the document window, the Document Control menu box and the Maximize button that were previously on the document title bar will show up on the menu bar. For the rest of this discussion, we'll assume that both the Word window and the document window are maximized.

Windows Application
Control menu box

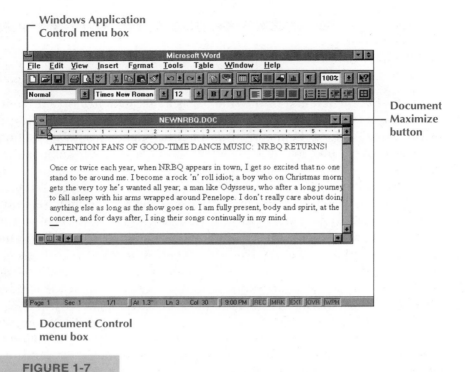

Document
Maximize
button

Document Control
menu box

FIGURE 1-7

A document window in Word.

 Word 2.0 had a Split command available on the Document Control
menu. In Word 6.0, this feature is included on the Window menu.

The title bar provides three important pieces of information. First, it displays the program name, Microsoft Word. Second, it changes color depending on whether or not the window is selected so that you can easily see which window is active if you have several windows showing. Third, it displays the name of the document in the document window. In general, this is the name Word will use when you choose the File Save command.

The menu bar

Immediately below the title bar is the menu bar, shown in Figure 1-8. You can use the menus on the menu bar to initiate many of the Word commands. You can redesign the menus if you want to add commands that aren't there; for now, however, we'll stay with Word's default menus. For details on customizing menus, see "Customizing the Menus" on page 952 and "Renaming, Adding, and Deleting Menus" on page 964.

| FIGURE 1-8 |

The menu bar.

There are nine menus in addition to the Document Control menu: File, Edit, View, Insert, Format, Tools, Table, Window, and Help. Each menu has its own set of commands, as shown in Figure 1-9 on the next page.

Briefly, you use the Document Control menu to control the size and position of the document window. The File menu concentrates on file-handling and printing commands. The Edit menu lets you copy and move text, search for text, replace text, and otherwise edit your document. The View menu lets you control some of the options for what appears on the screen; you can switch between Normal and Outline view, for example, and choose whether to see headers, footers, footnotes, and annotations. The Insert menu lets you insert page breaks, footnotes, page numbers, index entries, files, pictures, and more. The Format menu lets you control the way your text, pictures, and other elements of your document look. The Tools menu offers a wide range of ancillary tools, such as a spelling checker, a thesaurus, and a utility for handling envelopes, as well as tools for customizing the program. The Table menu is itself a powerful tool for creating and formatting tables within your document. The Window menu lets you rearrange and switch among document windows and create new windows to view different parts of a single document. The Help menu, finally, offers assistance when you need information on how to perform a task.

How to issue commands

Another feature for which Word offers you freedom of choice is the way in which you give commands. You can use either the mouse or the keyboard for most commands, and in each case you have a variety of choices.

To choose a command from a menu, you can use the mouse to point to the menu name on the menu bar and then click the left mouse button. When the full menu appears below the menu name, you can point to and click on the command you want. Alternatively, you can point to a menu name, hold the mouse button down, point to the choice on the menu, and give the command by releasing the mouse button.

To choose a menu command with the keyboard, press Alt or F10 to activate the menu bar; then open a menu either by typing the letter that's underlined in the name of the menu you want to use or by using the Left arrow and Right arrow keys to move to that menu and then pressing Enter or the Down

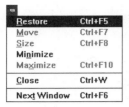

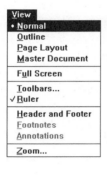

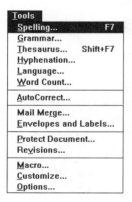

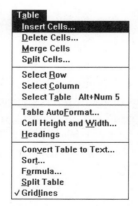

FIGURE 1-9

Each of Word's first-level menus offers its own set of commands.

arrow key. Alternatively, you can open the menu by holding the Alt key down while typing the appropriate letter. With the menu open, you can choose the command either by typing the letter that's underlined in the command name or by using the Up arrow and Down arrow keys to move to the command and then pressing Enter.

Keyboard shortcuts

As you glance through the Word menus, you'll notice that several key names, such as F7, Ctrl-X, and Shift-F7, appear to the right of some commands. These notations indicate shortcut keys you can press to choose commands without going through the menus. For example, the key combination Ctrl-S is next to the File Save command; you can press Ctrl-S to save a document. Similarly, you can press F7 instead of choosing Tools and then Spelling. Note that Word also has other such keyboard shortcuts that aren't listed on the menus. For example, pressing Ctrl-D opens the same dialog box as choosing Format Font. Pressing Shift-Ctrl-S twice opens the dialog box you would see by choosing Format Style. (The first Shift-Ctrl-S selects the Style list.) For a complete list of Word's default shortcut keys, see Appendix A, "Mouse & Keyboard Techniques," page 982.

Context-sensitive menus

In addition to drop-down menus on the menu bar, Word 6.0 offers context-sensitive menus at the click of a right mouse button. As shown in Figures 1-10A and 1-10B, these menus vary depending on what you're pointing at when you click on the right button. If you're pointing at a toolbar (and you have an arrow pointer), the menu appears with a set of commands

FIGURE 1-10A

Context-sensitive menus pop up at the click of the right mouse button. As shown here, and on the next page in Figure 1-10B, the menus vary depending on what the mouse is pointing at when you click.

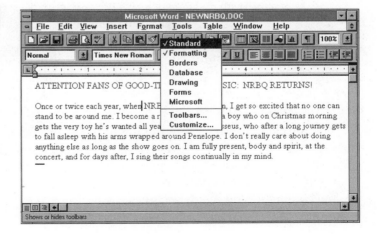

FIGURE 1-10B

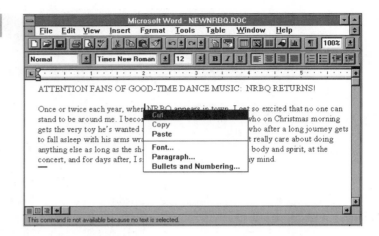

related to toolbars. If you're pointing to text in the document, the menu appears with a set of editing and formatting commands. The menu works just like the drop down menus, so you can choose commands with either the keyboard or the mouse, using the same techniques as for the drop-down menus. (On context-sensitive menus, there is no underlined letter in each command name—you simply type the first letter of the command to choose it. If two commands start with the same letter, you can press the initial letter a second time to move to the second command that starts with that letter.)

There are no commands on the context-sensitive menus that aren't also available through the drop-down menus. The advantage of the context-sensitive menus is that if you are working with your text, mouse in hand, you can click on the right mouse button to get to the commands you're most likely to need. For example, if you want to format a block of text and you prefer selecting text with the mouse rather than with the keyboard, you can select a block and immediately click on the right button to display the menu commands for Font, Paragraph, and Bullets and Numbering.

The Standard toolbar

The horizontal strip below the menu bar is the Standard toolbar, shown in Figure 1-11. This row of 22 buttons provides immediate access to such varied commands as Cut, Paste, Undo, and Spelling (spelling checking). To use the Standard toolbar, simply point with the mouse to the button that represents the command you want, and click.

FIGURE 1-11

The Standard toolbar.

In addition to the Standard toolbar, Word 6.0 comes with many other toolbars and lets you create more. You can customize each of the individual toolbars, and you can show or hide each one independently. For details on customizing toolbars, see "Customizing Toolbars" on page 316.

For now, we'll focus on the default settings for the Standard toolbar. Figure 1-12 lists the 22 buttons and the actions that they represent.

Button	Button Name	Action
	New	Creates a new document with default settings
	Open	Opens an existing document
	Save	Saves the current document
	Print	Prints the current document using current defaults
	Print Preview	Displays pages as they will be printed
	Spelling	Checks the spelling in the active document
	Cut	Cuts the current selection and puts it on the Clipboard
	Copy	Copies the current selection and puts in on the Clipboard
	Paste	Inserts a copy of the Clipboard's contents
	Format Painter	Copies the formatting of the current selection to a specified location

FIGURE 1-12

(continued)

Word's Standard toolbar buttons.

FIGURE 1-12. *continued*

Button	Button Name	Action
	Undo	Reverses, or undoes, the previous actions, one at a time
	Redo	Restores, or redoes, the previous actions that were undone, one at a time
	AutoFormat	Automatically formats a document
	InsertAutoText	Creates an AutoText entry if you've first selected some text, or inserts an entry
	Insert Table	Inserts a table, or lets you modify one that already exists
	Insert Microsoft Excel Worksheet	Inserts a worksheet from Microsoft Excel
	Columns	Changes the column format of the selected sections
	Drawing	Toggles between showing and hiding the Drawing toolbar
	Insert Chart	Inserts a Microsoft Graph object
	Show/Hide ¶	Toggles between showing all nonprinting characters (such as tabs) and hiding any nonprinting characters that are not specifically set to be visible
	Zoom Control	Scales the editing view
	Help	Provides Help information on a command, a screen region, or text properties

You don't need to refer to this list to find out what a given button does, however. Simply place the mouse pointer on a button, and within a second or so, you'll see a small box immediately below the pointer showing a one-word or two-word description of the button's function. You'll find a more complete explanation on the bottom line of the window. (This bottom line is called the *status bar*. If you turn off the status bar, the detailed message will not appear.)

The Formatting toolbar

If you installed Word with the default installation and haven't changed any settings, you'll see Word's Formatting toolbar immediately below the Standard toolbar, as shown in Figure 1-13. You can use the Formatting toolbar to choose the most commonly used formatting commands. As with all toolbars, you can point to a button with the mouse pointer to see an explanation of its function.

FIGURE 1-13

The Formatting toolbar.

The first text box in the Formatting toolbar shows the current paragraph style for the selected text. (The default style is Normal.) The second text box shows the current font. The third shows the font size in points. (A point is a typographical measurement that equals $1/72$ inch.) For more information on how font size is determined, see "Font Formatting" on page 241.

After the three text boxes come four groups of buttons. The three buttons in the first group are labeled with letters that stand for bold, italic, and underlined character formatting. The four buttons in the second group affect paragraph formatting: left aligned, centered, right aligned, and justified. The four buttons in the third group control other paragraph formatting features. The first adds automatic numbering to the paragraphs in the current selection of text or removes automatic numbering for text that's already numbered. The second button works much the same way except that it adds or removes bullets from bulleted lists. The next two buttons decrease and increase the amount of left indention for the current paragraph or paragraphs by one tab stop.

The last button on this toolbar looks like a window with four panes. This button displays (or hides) the Borders toolbar, which you can use to add borders around and between paragraphs or table cells, and to add shading.

The ruler

The horizontal strip below the Formatting toolbar is the ruler, shown in Figure 1-14 on the next page. The ruler serves two functions: You can use it to see the width of your text lines and also to format your text. The ruler shows the left and right margins, tab settings, and any indentions or extensions into the margin for a paragraph. You can move markers on the ruler to change these settings. For more information about how to use the ruler to change the appearance of your text, see "Paragraph Formatting" on page 221.

FIGURE 1-14

The ruler.

The scroll bars

The Word screen also has scroll bars—one horizontal and one vertical, as shown in Figure 1-15. These scroll bars indicate where you are in the document and give you a means of moving through it. As you move from the beginning of the document to the end, the box in the vertical scroll bar moves from the top of the bar to the bottom; its position is an indication of your relative location within the document.

FIGURE 1-15

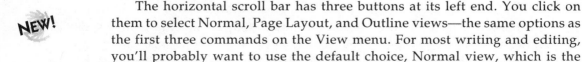

The scroll bars.

The horizontal scroll bar works in a similar way. When the left edge of your document is showing, the box in the horizontal scroll bar is at the far left. It moves to the right as the display shifts to the right.

You can use either scroll bar in three ways. You can click on the arrows at either end to move in small increments. You can point to the empty space on either side of the box and click to move in larger increments. Or you can drag the box to move it to the position you want. For more information about using the scroll bars for moving through your document, see "How to navigate with the mouse" on page 75.

How to change the View mode

The horizontal scroll bar has three buttons at its left end. You click on them to select Normal, Page Layout, and Outline views—the same options as the first three commands on the View menu. For most writing and editing, you'll probably want to use the default choice, Normal view, which is the leftmost button. For more information on these different views and when you might want to use them, see "Viewing your Document" on page 293.

How to split a window

There is a small black box, called the *split box*, just above the top arrow in the vertical scroll bar. You can use this to divide your document window into two parts, or panes. If you place the mouse pointer over this box, the pointer will change to the horizontal split pointer. See "The mouse pointer" on page 23 for more information on the different pointers. When you see the split pointer, click the left mouse button and hold it down. Drag the pointer downward until you've divided the window in the proportions you want, and then release the mouse button. You can also double-click on the split box to divide the window in half.

Alternatively, you can split your document window by choosing the Split command on the Window menu. You can then use the Up arrow and Down arrow keys (or the mouse) to position the split pointer. Then press Enter (or click the mouse) to set the split window in place. The current document will show in both panes of the window, but each pane will have its own vertical scroll bar. This means that you can look at two different sections of the document at the same time and scroll them independently. You can return to a single pane by double-clicking on the split box or by moving the pointer over the split box so that the split pointer shows and then holding the left button down while you drag the split pointer to the top or bottom outside the document window. If you prefer to use the keyboard, choose the Split command by using Alt-W and then P to return to a single pane.

The status bar

The horizontal strip at the bottom of the Word window is the status bar, shown in Figure 1-16. Word uses the status bar to show information about your document and to show prompts and messages when you use certain commands.

FIGURE 1-16

The status bar.

While you're writing or editing, Word uses the status bar to show both your position in the document and the settings for some features, such as Overtype mode. Figure 1-17 on the next page shows a typical Word document and its status bar. Figure 1-18 shows some of the codes you will see in the status bar as you work.

FIGURE 1-17

When you're writing or
editing, Word shows
information about your
document in the status
bar.

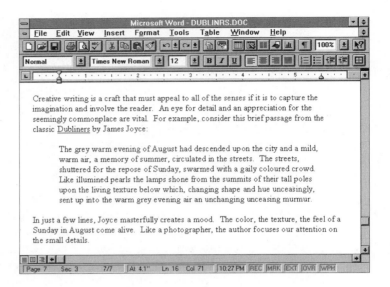

Indicator	Meaning
Page 7	Page 7 is currently displayed.
Sec 3	Section 3 is currently displayed.
7/7	Page 7 of a 7-page document is currently displayed.
At 4.1"	The cursor is 4.1 inches from the top edge of the page.
Ln 16	The cursor is in the sixteenth line of the current page.
Col 71	The cursor is 71 characters from the left margin.
REC	The macro recorder is on.
MRK	Word is in Mark Revisions mode.
EXT	Extend Selection (F8) is on.
COL	Column Selection (Ctrl-Shift-F8) is on.
OVR	Word is in Overtype mode.
WP	WordPerfect Help and Navigation are active.
WPH	WordPerfect Help is active.
WPN	WordPerfect Navigation is active.

FIGURE 1-18

Status bar messages and their meanings.

In some cases, more than one message may appear at a given spot. For
example, the EXT and COL messages both appear in the box to the right of
the Mark Revisions space. The WordPerfect Help messages all appear in the
far-right space.

Some of the status items in Word 6.0 do double duty by also letting you toggle a setting or open a dialog box. For example, you can turn on Extend Selection by double-clicking on the EXT indicator and turn on Overtype mode by double-clicking on OVR. In both cases, you can double-click again to turn the feature off. Similarly, you can open dialog boxes by double-clicking on MRK for marking revisions, REC for macro recording, and WPH for WordPerfect Help. Note that the text for each of these status items is grayed when the setting is off. When you turn the feature on, the item appears as solid text.

When you activate a menu, as shown in Figure 1-19, Word displays a short message in the status bar that explains the purpose of the highlighted menu item.

FIGURE 1-19

When you highlight a menu command, Word replaces the usual status bar information with a short message explaining the purpose of the command.

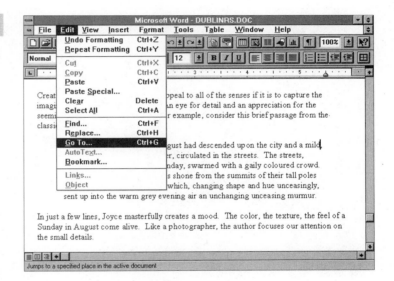

The mouse pointer

There is one more important element on the Word screen: the mouse pointer. Unlike the other elements, the pointer has no fixed location or shape. Rather, you can use the mouse to point to any location on the screen, and the pointer will take on different shapes in different locations.

If you position the pointer on one of the bars at the top of the screen or on a scroll bar, you'll see an arrow pointing up and to the left. We'll refer to this as the *left-arrow pointer*. You use this pointer to choose menu commands, click on toolbar buttons, use scroll bars, and place or move tab and margin markers on the ruler, among other tasks. If you move the pointer to the document window, it will change to look like a capital I; this called the *I-beam pointer*. It indicates that the mouse is set to work with text.

These are just two examples from the many pointers shown in Figure 1-20.
Each pointer indicates that the mouse is set to perform a different function.

Pointer	Name
I	I-beam pointer
 _I_	Italic I-beam pointer
 ▷	Left-arrow pointer
 ◁	Right-arrow pointer
 ⧗	Hourglass
+	Cross-hair pointer
÷	Horizontal split pointer
+‖+	Vertical split pointer
↓	Downward-pointing arrow
 ⟷	Double-headed horizontal sizing pointer
 ↕	Double-headed vertical sizing pointer
 ✛	Four-headed sizing pointer

FIGURE 1-20

(continued)

Pointers and their names.

FIGURE 1-20. *continued*

Pointer	Name
	Horizontal outline pointer
	Vertical outline pointer
	Four-headed outline pointer
	Magnifying pointer
	Graphics repositioning pointer
	Left diagonal pointer for frames
	Right diagonal pointer for frames
	Cropping pointer
	Drag-and-drop pointer for moving
	Drag-and-drop pointer for copying
	Format Painter pointer
	Macro-recording pointer
	Finger-pointing hand
	Arrow-and-question-mark pointer

The I-beam pointer appears when your cursor is over text and helps you select the proper insertion point. The italic I-beam appears whenever the cursor is over italic text and slants with the italic characters.

The arrow that points diagonally to the right appears only when you move the pointer into the invisible selection area at the left edge of the document window. When you see the right-pointing arrow, you can use the mouse to select lines, paragraphs, or the whole document. For details on this feature, see "How to select text by using the selection bar" on page 87.

The hourglass indicates that Word is busy. When you see it, you have to wait for Word to finish its current task before you can continue.

The cross-hair pointer appears when you insert a frame in your document; you can use it to define the size and position of the frame. For a discussion of frames, see "Frames: Positioning Text and Graphics on the Page" on page 509.

The horizontal split pointer appears when you choose the Split command from the Windows menu or when you position the pointer on the split box on the vertical scroll bar. For details on using this pointer, see "How to split a window" on page 21.

You'll see the vertical split pointer when the pointer is between the style area and the rest of the document window. For details about the style area and styles, see "Displaying the Style Area" on page 457.

The pointer takes on the downward-pointing arrow shape when you move it over the top of a table column. You can use this pointer to select an entire column of a table. For more information about this technique, see "Special table selection techniques for the mouse" on page 376.

A double-headed sizing pointer appears when you position the pointer on a window border. When the pointer is this shape, you can use the mouse to manually resize that window. Similarly, the pointer takes the shape of a four-headed sizing pointer when you choose the Move command on a window's Control menu.

The four-headed outline pointer (a thinner four-headed arrow than the four-headed sizing pointer) appears when you point to a heading or body-text icon while in Outline view. It changes to the vertical outline pointer when you drag the heading vertically. It changes to the horizontal outline pointer when you drag the heading left or right to promote or demote the heading. We'll cover Word's outlining features in Chapter 19.

The vertical and horizontal outline pointers also appear when you're moving or resizing graphics or frames, as do the two diagonal pointers and the graphics repositioning pointer. The cropping pointer is used to change how much of a graphic is visible. For a discussion of frames, see "Frames: Positioning Text and Graphics on the Page" on page 509.

The magnifying pointer appears in Print Preview mode and can be used to increase magnification of the document. We cover all of the Print Preview features in Chapter 8. One of the two drag-and-drop pointers appears when you drag a section of selected text or a framed object from one location to another. You can turn this feature off for text if you prefer. For details on turning the feature off and on, see "How to use the mouse to drag and drop text" on page 104.

The pointer for the Format Painter appears when you choose the Format Painter button on the Standard toolbar. The Format Painter enables you to copy character formatting, paragraph formatting, or both. We cover the use of this new feature in Chapter 7. The macro-recording pointer appears in the document window while you are recording a macro to remind you that Word doesn't record mouse movements as part of a macro. The pointer disappears when you start typing, but it reappears when you then move the mouse. We'll cover macros in detail in Chapter 24.

You'll see the finger-pointing hand when you position the pointer on an underlined term in a Help window. Clicking the mouse button when this hand shape is showing brings up information about that term.

Finally, you'll see the arrow-and-question-mark pointer when you press Shift-F1 to get context-sensitive help or when you click on the Help button on the Standard toolbar.

If you're concerned about how your text looks, you may find yourself going regularly to the Format menu, just to confirm that your text is formatted correctly. Word 6.0 can give you that information quickly. Display the arrow-and-question-mark pointer by pressing Shift-F1 or clicking on the Help button on the Standard toolbar. Then point to the text you want information about and click. Word will display the information in an information box similar to the one in Figure 1-21 on the next page.

FIGURE 1-21

Word can let you
see how your text
is formatted without
going to the Format
menu.

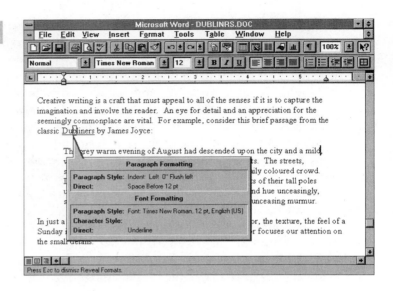

Getting Help

If you forget how to use a command or other feature (or haven't yet learned
it), you can use Word's online Help to get information about how the feature
works. There are two ways to get help. You can search through Word's extensive help information by using the Help menu. Alternatively, you can call
up context-sensitive Help by using the F1 key or the Shift-F1 key combination.

How to use the Help menu

If you display the Help menu, you'll see the nine commands shown in Figure
1-22. The Contents command opens a window, shown in Figure 1-23, that
lists the major topics available in the Help system. Search For Help On lets
you look up topics by using keywords. The Help Index command opens a
window, shown in Figure 1-24, that displays an alphabetic list that covers
most commands and procedures.

FIGURE 1-22

You can get help by
simply selecting the
commands on Word's
Help menu.

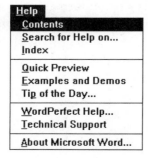

FIGURE 1-23

If you choose the Help Contents commmand, you'll see this window.

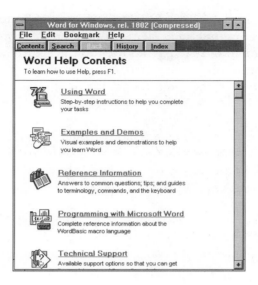

FIGURE 1-24

If you choose the Help Index command, you'll see this window.

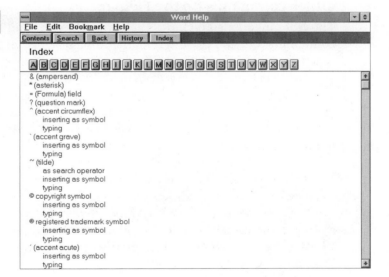

You can also use the row of buttons that show across the top of the window to jump to the contents page in Help; search for specific topics; step back through the last screens you viewed; see a list, or history, of the Help screens you've viewed (so that you can return to any of them directly); or go to the Help index.

On most Help screens, you'll see words and phrases that appear with a solid underline. Word calls these *jump terms*. You can think of jump terms as cross-references. When you point to one, the pointer will take on the shape of a pointing finger. (You can also use the Tab key to move to and highlight a term on the screen.) If you click on the mouse button or press Enter while pointing to a jump term, a Help window on that topic will open. After you read the jump term's Help window, you can return to the original Help window by either choosing the Back button or pressing the B key.

In addition to the jump terms, you'll also see words and phrases with dotted underlines. Word calls these *glossary terms.* As with jump terms, the pointer changes to a pointing-finger shape when it is on a glossary term. Click on the word to open a window containing the definition of that term. Click again, and the definition will disappear. To bring up a glossary term's definition from the keyboard, use the Tab key to highlight the appropriate term, and then press the Enter key. Press the Enter key again, and the definition will disappear.

You can close the Help window by double-clicking on the Control menu box in the upper left corner of the Help window, by pressing Alt-F4, or by pressing Alt-Spacebar to bring up the Control menu and then by pressing C for Close.

Other commands on the Help menu

The Help menu also includes the Quick Preview and Examples And Demos commands. Quick Preview runs the same interactive presentation that runs when you start Word for the first time after installing the program. It gives you an overview of many of Word's features. The Examples And Demos option offers an easy way to view dozens of on-screen examples of Word's features, along with instructions on how to apply them to your documents.

The next command is Tip Of The Day, which brings up the same Tip dialog box you see when the program is first loaded. This box shows you a useful tip or trick to make Word easier and faster to use. (Word chooses the day's tip at random.) If you want to see all the tips rather than wait for them to come up at random, choose More Tips for a list of tip topics.

Next on the menu is WordPerfect Help, which can help WordPerfect users make the transition from the character-based version of WordPerfect to Word. When you choose this item, the program opens the window shown in Figure 1-25.

The right side of the WordPerfect Help dialog box gives a description of the command that's highlighted in the Command Keys list on the left side. You select the WordPerfect command you want from the Command Keys list box. If you then choose the Demo button, Word will run the equivalent Word command (or series of commands) and display the Word commands. If you choose Help Text instead, Word will display a window that gives you instructions so that you can perform the steps yourself. The instruction window also includes a Demo Now button, so you can shift from manually

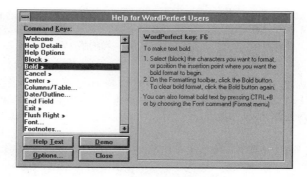

FIGURE 1-25

Word includes a special help system to make the transition from WordPerfect to Word for Windows easy.

entering the commands to the automated entry feature at any time. (Note that some commands open dialog boxes created especially for this WordPerfect Help system.)

The Options button in the lower right corner of the dialog box opens a dialog box, shown in Figure 1-26, in which you can choose the type of help and demos that Word provides and also activate the WordPerfect navigation keys.

FIGURE 1-26

The WordPerfect Help options let you customize the WordPerfect help features.

Note that, because WordPerfect features do not correspond to Word features one to one, some of these key assignments will yield somewhat different results with Word than they will with WordPerfect.

The Technical Support command on the Help menu provides information about Microsoft technical support, along with some hints and advice on solutions to try before you call the support lines.

The final command on the Help menu is About Microsoft Word, which opens a box containing information about Word, as shown in Figure 1-27 on the next page. The About dialog box displays the version of the program, copyright information, the name and company name of the person the copy is licensed to, and the serial number. Choose the System Info button at the bottom of this dialog box to run the MSINFO program, which displays lots of useful information about your system and how it is configured. For example, you can see a list of graphics filters or text file converters that are installed. System Info can give you information you need to diagnose and solve problems.

FIGURE 1-27

The About Microsoft Word dialog box has a button to display system statistics that can be helpful in troubleshooting a problem.

How to get context-sensitive Help

In addition to the Help menu screens, Word offers context-sensitive Help, which you can use with either the keyboard or the mouse.

Using the keyboard

To bring up context-sensitive Help with the keyboard, first either highlight the command on the appropriate Word menu, open the dialog box, or generate the message you want information on. Then press F1. Word will display the related Help screen. If you do not activate a command, dialog box, or message before you press F1, Word will display the Help window shown in Figure 1-24.

Using the mouse

To bring up context-sensitive Help with the mouse, first press Shift-F1 or click on the Help button at the right end of the Standard toolbar. The pointer will take the shape of a question mark over an arrow. Then click the command or screen area you want information on, and Word will display the related Help screen. If you change to the arrow-plus-question-mark pointer and then decide you don't want help after all, press the Esc key to return the pointer to its usual shape.

More about Help

The help system has still more features you may want to explore. The Edit Copy command on the Help window menu bar, for example, will copy help information to the Clipboard so that you can paste it into your documents. Even more useful, the Edit Annotate command lets you add your own annotations to the help system. Simply choose Edit Annotate, type in a note, and choose Save.

 If you add an annotation to a Help screen, Word will add a paper-clip icon to the screen to indicate that there's some information there. To see the note later, simply choose Edit Annotate or click on the paper-clip icon.

You can also print information from the help system with the File Print Topic command, and you can insert bookmarks with the Bookmark Define command. Bookmarks will let you quickly find a particular section later. The best way to learn more about the help system is to explore the menus in the Help window.

Essential Customization Options

There is one additional issue you should consider before you start working with Word.

Word's customization features give you the ability to match the program to the way you work. You can, in fact, change most of the features discussed in this chapter. You can rename the menu commands; redesign or hide the Standard and Formatting toolbars; hide the ruler, status bar, and scroll bars to display more text; reassign shortcut-key combinations; and even build your own commands.

Elsewhere in this book, you can learn how to use all of these features and more. For now, however, you shouldn't make too many changes to Word. The examples in this book use the default settings, and until you're familiar with the program, you should stay with the defaults so that your screen will look much like the illustrations in the book. Even so, there are several customization options you should know about now because they will affect how comfortable you are when using the program—particularly if you're used to another word processor and expect Word to behave in certain ways. Here, then, is a quick tour of the customization options you may want to consider right away.

The View menu

Start by opening the View menu, shown in Figure 1-28.

Notice that there is a check mark next to the Ruler command. This indicates that the command is active and that its associated screen element is displayed. You can display or hide the ruler by choosing the command.

The View menu has commands that control the appearance of the Word screen, including whether the ruler is visible.

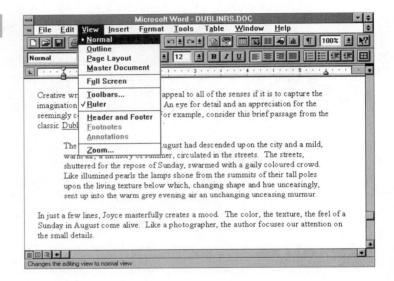

Notice also the command named Toolbars. This command opens a dialog box that lets you choose whether to display any (or all) of eight of the Word toolbars, including the Standard and Formatting toolbars that are displayed by default.

You can also display a shortcut menu controlling the toolbar features by clicking in the toolbar with the right mouse button.

You might want to hide the ruler or toolbars for either of two reasons: You don't use them—you might not use toolbars on a portable computer without a mouse, for example—or you want to see more text on your screen.

You can display or hide any of these items at any time, but note that some of our examples in later chapters use the ruler or toolbars and assume that they are showing.

The Options dialog box

Most of the menu-based customization choices are available through the Options dialog box. Choose Tools Options, and Word will display the dialog box shown in Figure 1-29. The Options dialog box looks much like a set of file cards with tabs showing. If you move from card to card, you'll find that the options in the box vary. The figure shows the View options.

FIGURE 1-29

When you choose the Tools Options command, Word will open the Options dialog box.

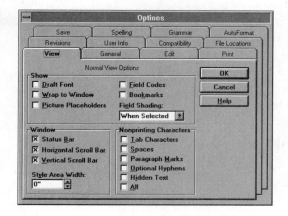

View options

If a card other than View is showing on your screen, click on the View tab or use the arrow keys to display the View card.

There are only a few items on the View card that you need to know about now. First, in the section labeled Window, are check boxes for the Horizontal Scroll Bar and the Vertical Scroll Bar. An X in a check box tells Word to display the item on your document screen. An empty, or *cleared,* check box tells Word not to display it. A check box toggles between checked and cleared each time you choose it. You can hide either or both of the scroll bars to give you more room on your screen for text.

Another important option, Draft Font, is listed in the Show box. When this check box is checked, Word will use a draft font that has little relationship to what your text will look like when printed. If you want the text on screen to be as close to the text on the printed page as possible, be sure that this check box is cleared (that is, there is no X in it). Word's default setting is for Draft Font off. For a thorough discussion on matching the screen and the printed page, see "Understanding Screen Fonts and Printer Fonts" on page 581.

If speed is a problem with your system and you don't need to see how text will look on the printed page while you're writing or editing, check the Draft Font check box on the View card. Word usually runs faster with this option turned on.

The Nonprinting Characters box includes check boxes for various items that don't appear on a printed page but that you might want to see on the screen while editing: tabs and spaces, paragraph marks, nonprinting characters, optional hyphens, and hidden text. If you check the Tab Characters and Spaces check boxes, Word will show tab characters on the screen as small arrows pointing to the right and spaces as small dots between words. This can help you distinguish tabbed spacing from sequences of character spaces. You can select either of these options independently.

If you check the Paragraph Marks check box, Word will display paragraph marks, showing you at a glance whether Word will treat a given line as a line within a paragraph or as a paragraph by itself. Checking the All check box is equivalent to checking all of the check boxes in the Nonprinting Characters box—Word will display all nonprinting items on the list. You can also toggle the All option by clicking on the Show All button at the right end of the Standard toolbar.

General options

The card after View is labeled General. Figure 1-30 shows the options included on this card.

FIGURE 1-30

The General card in the Options dialog box lets you change some basic Word settings.

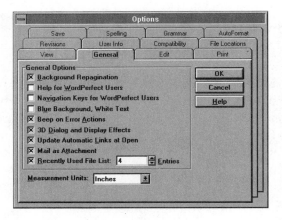

This screen has two check boxes of special interest to WordPerfect users—Help For WordPerfect Users and Navigation Keys For WordPerfect Users. If you check both, the effect is equivalent to choosing the navigation and Help options available through the Help WordPerfect Help command discussed earlier in this chapter. For details on the WordPerfect Help command, see "Other commands on the Help menu" on page 30.

Edit options

The card after General is labeled Edit, as shown in Figure 1-31.

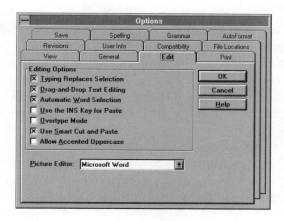

The Edit card in the Options dialog box lets you change some Word editing settings.

The first check box, Typing Replaces Selection, needs some explanation. If this box is checked (as it is by default) and you have highlighted some text in a document, Word will replace the highlighted text with the newly entered text when you start typing. If the check box is cleared, Word will not replace a highlighted block; instead, it will insert the new text before the highlighted block.

The second option is a bit safer, but the first approach also has advantages. If you want to replace one block of text with another, the Typing Replaces Selection option lets you do it in one step instead of two. Which option you choose is a matter of your preference.

If you have Word set so that typing will replace a selection and you accidentally delete a block of text, you can recover the text immediately after typing by choosing the Edit Undo command. Word 6.0 has a multiple-level Undo feature that can undo many previous steps. This feature will let you recover easily from accidentally replacing a section of text (or from other mistakes), even after you take other actions.

The Drag-And-Drop Text Editing option is another one that most people have strong preferences about, either for or against. If checked, this check box lets you drag a text selection to change its position. This feature is checked by default, and if you don't like it, you can clear it here.

For a discussion of drag-and-drop text editing, see "How to use the mouse to drag and drop text" on page 104.

The Automatic Word Selection check box affects how the highlight moves when you click and drag over text. Without it, the highlight moves one character at a time. With it, the highlight selects only complete words, and it will jump to include the entire next word as soon as the mouse pointer moves to the start of that word. For more details on this feature, see "How to extend a selection word by word" on page 86.

The next check box worth noting is Use The INS Key For Paste. If this is checked, you can use the Ins key to paste data from the Clipboard into your document. This choice is a favorite of Word for MS-DOS users, who are already accustomed to using the Ins key this way. Whether you select the Use The INS Key For Paste option or not, Ctrl-V or Shift-Ins will paste data from the Clipboard into your document.

The Overtype Mode check box sets Overtype as the default mode. Most users prefer to work in Insert mode, in which new text is inserted at the cursor, pushing the old text ahead of it. However, some prefer Overtype mode, in which new text replaces old text character by character, much like typing over a character on a typewriter.

 If you haven't selected the Use The INS Key For Paste option, you can use the Ins key to toggle between Insert and Overtype modes when you are working in a document.

Save options

The next card of immediate interest, labeled Save, is shown in Figure 1-32. There are four Save options you should be aware of from the start: Always Create Backup Copy, Allow Fast Saves, Prompt For Summary Info, and Automatic Save.

Checking the Always Create Backup Copy check box tells Word to save the old version of an existing file—a backup—before it saves a new version of that file. If a backup version already exists, it's replaced by the new backup version. This means you always have a one-generation-old version of a file available. This can be helpful if you decide you don't like a change that you made in the current version. It also gives you a recent version to go back to in case the current version is corrupted on disk.

The Allow Fast Saves option speeds document saving while you are creating or editing a document. Rather than save the entire file each time, Word

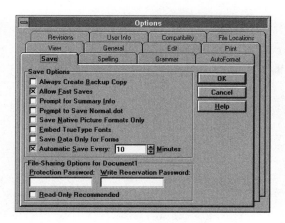

FIGURE 1-32

The Save options let you specify Word's actions when it saves document files.

attaches the changes to the end of the file. It will save the entire file only when you close the document. Checking this box makes the intermediate save operations faster, but the file will grow longer and longer until you finally close the document. This option is selected by default.

The Prompt For Summary Info check box, which is cleared by default, tells Word to ask for details about your document—title, subject, author, keywords, and comments—the first time you save a new document (or save an existing document with a new name). This information is useful for managing your documents. If you check this box, Word will always remind you to add the information to each file.

The Automatic Save option tells Word to save the current file at whatever interval you specify in the Minutes text box, although sometimes it might interrupt you while you're in the middle of writing a sentence, so you might find it distracting. We recommend using this feature and setting it to no more than 10 to 15 minutes.

The *Automatic Save* name for this feature is a little misleading because your work is not saved in the same way as it is when you choose the File Save command. Instead, the Automatic Save only protects you from losing information in the event of a system crash or power failure. All Automatic Save files are cleared when you exit Word normally. As a result, you should not rely solely on Automatic Save to protect your work; we recommend that you also save your work manually at regular intervals, such as every paragraph or every page.

User Info options

The User Info card is the last Tools Options card of immediate interest. As shown in Figure 1-33, this card displays basic information about the user.

FIGURE 1-33

The User Info options card displays information about the user that other features in Word can take advantage of.

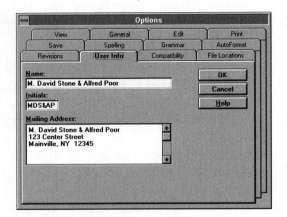

Word uses the entry in the Name text box to fill in the Author information in the Summary Info dialog box. It uses the entry in the Initials text box to mark annotations you insert in a document. And it uses the Mailing Address entry as the return address for the envelope-printing utility. If you entered this information properly when you installed Word, it will be correct here as well. If not, you'll want to make the corrections. If you need to change anything, simply type the changes in the appropriate text box. You'll also need to enter the rest of your address information, after your name and company name. The one tricky part about editing this screen is that you press Enter to start a new line in the Mailing Address box and use the Tab key or the mouse to move the cursor out of that box.

There are many other settings accessible through the Options dialog box. Browse through them and set any that you think are worthwhile. However, note that most of these options won't mean much to you until you're more familiar with Word. We'll come back to them later. Now it's time to begin working with documents.

TOPIC FINDER

Creating and Opening Documents   44

- How to create a new document
- How to open an existing document

Saving your work   50

- Filename rules
- File Save As options
- How to change a filename or directory
- Summary information
- How to save a document again
- How to save a read-only document
- How to save everything at once
- How to close files without leaving Word
- How to close files and exit Word

Deleting a File   62

- How to delete multiple files

Templates   63

- How to use templates

File Handling

earning how to use any word processor involves more than learning how to enter, edit, and format text. It also involves learning an entirely new filing system. When you enter text on your screen in Word—or in any other word processor, for that matter—your work isn't saved until you store it in a file on your computer's disk. And you'll find that you can quickly build up a large collection of files—so large that it can become unwieldy to keep track of them.

So before you invest time and energy in building a document, you'll want to be sure you understand how to open, close, and save files. You'll also want to be familiar with filling out the Summary Info dialog box. The information you supply in this dialog box can help you find specific files when you need them.

In this chapter, we'll look at the basic file-handling commands for creating new files, opening existing files, deleting files, and saving the files you're working on. For a discussion of Word's more sophisticated file-handling features, see Chapter 17.

Creating and Opening Documents

As we discussed in Chapter 1, there are several ways to start Word. If you simply double-click the Microsoft Word icon in the Windows Program Manager, for example, or if you select WINWORD.EXE in the Windows File Manager, Word will create a new, blank document and name it Document1. Alternatively, you can open one or more existing documents along with Word. For example, you can use Program Manager's File Run command and enter a document name or names along with the command for Word. Odds are good, however, that you'll be running Word already when you want to create or open a file. For more information on starting Word, see "Starting Word for Windows" on page 3.

How to create a new document

If you want to create a new document while running Word, simply choose File New. Word will open the dialog box shown in Figure 2-1.

FIGURE 2-1

Use the New dialog box to open a new document in Word.

The New dialog box lets you make two choices—one in the Template list box on the left and one in the New option box on the right—to designate the file as either a document or a template. Templates are useful for creating standard formats for your documents; we'll discuss them briefly at the end of this chapter and in more detail in Chapters 9 and 27.

As you can see in Figure 2-1, Word also has a large number of *wizards* listed in the Template list box. Wizards automate the creation of complex documents and even of customized templates. We'll ignore wizards in this discussion, but we'll cover specific wizards as appropriate throughout this book. For a discussion of wizards in general, see "Wizards: Automated Documents" on page 322.

For the moment, all you really need to know to start a new file is that you want to create a document rather than a template and that you want to use the template called Normal. Because Word defaults to both of these options in any case, you can open a new document by simply choosing OK.

> You can also create a new document that uses the Normal template by clicking on the leftmost button on the Standard toolbar.

As you create documents during any given session, Word will number them sequentially: Document1, Document2, Document3, and so on. Word will create a new document window for each new document.

How to open an existing document

If you want to retrieve an existing document from disk while you're in Word, choose File Open or click on the Open button—second from left on the Standard toolbar. Word will display a dialog box like that shown in Figure 2-2.

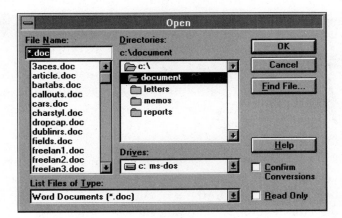

You can use the File Name text box at the top left both to look for a file and to specify the name of the file you want to open. The default entry is *.*doc*, which lists all files in the current directory that have a DOC filename extension. The list is displayed in the list box below the File Name text box. Note that by default, Word uses the DOC extension for both saving documents and opening them, although you can use other extensions if you prefer.

You can open the files in the current directory either by typing the filename in the File Name text box and pressing Enter or by selecting the name from the list box. (To select a name, double-click on it with the mouse, or highlight the name with the arrow keys and press Enter. You can also type just enough of the name to uniquely identify it. As you type each letter, Word will move the highlight to the first name in the list that matches the partial entry in the File Name text box.)

If you're in a different directory from the file you want to open, you can open it by typing the entire MS-DOS path and filename, and even the drive letter if the file is on a different drive. Typing *c:\data\report.doc*, for example, will load the file REPORT.DOC no matter which directory and drive are selected in the Directories list box.

If you can't remember the name of the file or directory, or if it's too much of a chore to type it in, you can easily move to a different drive and directory by selecting from the list boxes in the Open dialog box.

Word lists the name of the current directory just above the Directories list box. (The current directory in the sample dialog box is C:\DOCUMENT.) To change the current directory, you can type the name of the directory you want in the File Name text box and then choose OK, or you can select the directory in the Directories list box.

To select a directory with the mouse, double-click on it. To select it with the keyboard, press Tab or Alt-D to move the cursor into the Directories list box, use the arrow keys to highlight the directory you want, and press Enter.

With your cursor in the Directories list box, you can type the first letter of the directory name to highlight the name and then press Enter. If more than one directory has the same initial letter, you can cycle through the choices by repeatedly typing the letter.

The Directories list shows the current directory (highlighted unless you're in the process of choosing another directory to move to), the full directory path back to the root directory, and any subdirectories the current directory contains. Note that each level in the path is indicated by an additional indention in the Directories list. You can select any directory in the path and go directly to it. For example, you can go to the root directory to see other subdirectories of the root. If you prefer, however, you can move through the directory structure one step at a time.

If the cursor is in the File Name text box and you simply want to move one step back in the directory structure, the quickest way is to type two periods in the File Name text box and then press Enter to choose OK. This involves just three keystrokes: Period, Period, Enter. The two periods are MS-DOS shorthand for "the directory immediately above this one in the directory structure"—or what MS-DOS calls the *parent directory*.

As you navigate through the drives and directories on your system, Word will show you a list of those files in the current directory that match the filename entry in the File Name text box. By default, the entry is *.DOC files. However, you can change it at any time.

One choice is simply to type a name in the File Name text box to serve as a filter for the filenames you want to see. If you want to see all files, for example, type *.* (usually pronounced "star dot star") and choose OK. Note that the asterisk is the MS-DOS wildcard symbol, so *.* matches any filename (the part to the left of the period, or dot) and any filename extension (the part to the right of the dot).

You can use the wildcard feature in several ways. If you always use an LET extension for letters and an MEM extension for memos, for example, enter *.*let* to see a list of all letters or *.*mem* to see a list of all memos. If you always name your letters and memos for the recipient (BROWN01.LET, BROWN02.LET, and so on), enter *brown*.*.* to see all letters and memos you've sent to Brown.

You can also change the entry in the File Name text box by using the drop-down list labeled *List Files Of Type* at the bottom of the dialog box. If you open the list, you will see one similar to that shown in Figure 2-3.

FIGURE 2-3

The List Files Of Type list provides a choice of filenames to look for, based on the file-name extensions in parentheses.

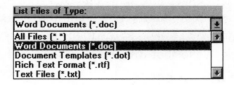

To look for a file type other than Word's *.DOC default, use the mouse or keyboard to select any file type from the list. Word will substitute that extension for the current entry in the File Name text box and list only files with the same extension. Figure 2-4 shows the List Files Of Type options.

Type of File	Extension
All files	*.*
Word documents	*.doc
Document templates	*.dot
Rich Text Format	*.rtf
Text files	*.txt

FIGURE 2-4

File types and extensions in the List Files Of Type list.

We'll discuss the details of importing and exporting files in Chapter 18, but for now, there are two important points to note. First, you'll find some file extensions associated with more than one file format. Second, many programs (including Word) let you use almost any extension when naming a file. Therefore, you can't depend completely on the extension to identify the format of a given file. This becomes important only when you import files stored in other formats, as we'll discuss in "Opening Documents Stored in Other Formats" on page 621.

Word will do its best to identify a file format created by a different program and convert it to Word format. If you check the Confirm Conversions check box in the File Open dialog box, Word will first display its guess and then give you the opportunity to change its selection if you know that the file is in a different format.

How to find a document

At times when you can't remember which directory a file is in, its exact name, or even the disk it's stored on, the Find File button on the right side of the Open dialog box can be helpful. For now, just be aware that this button is equivalent to the Find File command on the File menu. In either location, this feature provides a number of useful capabilities, including the ability to search for files in more than one directory as well as to print, delete, and copy multiple files. We'll discuss this feature in detail in "Retrieving Documents" on page 603.

How to access a network

If your computer is connected to a network, you can open a file stored on a network drive. When you connect to a network drive, you can access that drive as if it were a hard drive on your computer. Because you assign a drive letter to a network drive when you connect to it, you can switch to the network drive by selecting the drive from the Drives list in the Open dialog box.

You connect to a network drive by choosing the Network button, which is located below the Find File button in the Open dialog box. Word displays this button only if you have access to a network. When you click on the Network button, Word displays the Connect Network Drive dialog box. The contents of this dialog box varies according to the type of network you're connected to. An example of the dialog box is shown in Figure 2-5.

FIGURE 2-5

The Connect Network Drive dialog box gives you access to network drives.

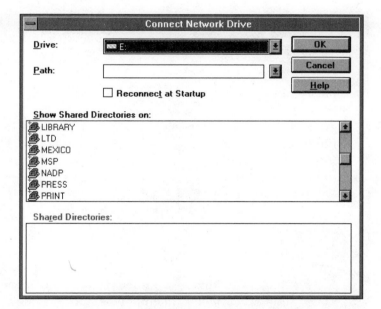

Select a drive letter, specify the network drive, and choose OK to make the network connection. Word returns you to the Open dialog box and displays the contents of the drive to which you connected. The connection will remain in effect even after you quit Word.

How to use the Read Only check box

In the lower right corner of the File Open dialog box is a check box labeled *Read Only*. If you check this box before you open a file, Word will let you browse through the document and even make changes to it, but it will not let you save the document under its original name. If you want to save any changes, you'll need to save the file under a new name, using the File Save As command. (We'll discuss the File Save and File Save As commands in a moment.) This Read Only feature gives you the ability to protect an important original from accidental changes but still use that original to create a revised version with a new name.

How to open recently used documents

If you create long documents, you'll often find yourself returning to Word to work with documents you worked on in a previous writing session. There's an easy way to reopen the documents you've used most recently. As you can see at the bottom of Figure 2-6, the File menu lists the last few document files you've opened. To reopen any of these, simply select the filename from the menu or type the number that appears to the left of the name.

FIGURE 2-6

The filenames at the bottom of the File menu provide an easy way to reopen the documents you've used most recently.

File	
New...	Ctrl+N
Open...	Ctrl+O
Close	
Save	Ctrl+S
Save As...	
Save All	
Find File...	
Summary Info...	
Templates...	
Page Setup...	
Print Preview	
Print...	Ctrl+P
Send...	
Add Routing Slip...	
1 C:\DOCUMENT\OLDDOCS\NRBQ.DOC	
2 C:\DOCUMENT\OLDDOCS\JAGGER.DOC	
3 C:\DOCUMENT\OLDDOCS\PROPOSAL.DOC	
4 C:\DOCUMENT\OLDDOCS\REPORT.DOC	
Exit	

You can change the number of recently opened files listed at the bottom of the File menu. By default, the File menu lists up to four names, but if you choose Tools Options and then choose the General card, you'll find an option labeled *Recently Used File List*. You can change this to any number from 1 through 9, or you can turn the feature off entirely.

Saving Your Work

As you work in Word, the documents you create reside in your computer's random access memory (RAM) and in temporary files on your disk. However, when you leave Word, the information held in RAM and the links to

the temporary files are both lost. To store a document so that you can retrieve it and work with it later, you must save it as a disk file. After it is
saved on disk, the file will remain there until you delete it.

Remember that even saved files are still at risk because you can
have a problem with your hard disk. As with all computer programs, you should protect the time and effort you invest in your
work by making frequent backups—that is, additional copies—of
any Word document files you can't afford to lose. There are many
strategies for creating backups—including adding a tape backup
system or additional hard disks to your computer. If you're new
to computers, however, the simplest approach is to save a second
copy of important files on a floppy disk, using Word's save feature. The extra work involved will pay off when (not if!) you lose a
file from your hard disk.

The tools you'll normally use to save a document are the File Save and
File Save As commands. The first time you use either command when working on a new document (or try to save changes to a Read Only file), Word
will display the Save As dialog box, shown in Figure 2-7. After you've
named and saved a document, you can bypass this dialog box by choosing
the File Save command. Note that clicking on the Save button—the third button from the left on the Standard toolbar—is equivalent to choosing the File
Save command.

FIGURE 2-7

Word displays the
Save As dialog box
when you choose File
Save As. It also shows
this dialog box when
you choose File Save
to save a file for the
first time.

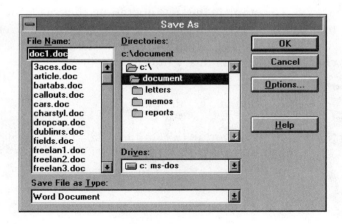

The first time you save a file, you must specify a filename. You can also
specify a drive and directory. By default, Word suggests the current drive
and directory (in our example, C:\DOCUMENT) and displays the directory

name above the Directories list box. If you want to store the document on a different drive, you can use the Drives drop-down list to choose a different drive, or you can change to that drive by typing the drive letter, followed by a colon, in the File Name text box and then pressing Enter.

If your computer is connected to a network drive, you can access the drive by choosing the drive letter from the Drives drop-down list. If you would like to save your file on a network drive that you haven't connected to yet, choose the Network button to connect to a new network drive. (The Network button appears below the Options button in the Save As dialog box only if you have access to a network.) Word displays the Connect Network Drive dialog box, whose contents depend on the type of network you have. An example of this dialog box is shown in Figure 2-5. Select a drive letter, specify the network drive, and choose OK to make the network connection. Word returns you to the Save As dialog box and displays the contents of the drive to which you connected.

Similarly, if you want to store the file in a different directory, you can use the Directories list box to select the directory you want, or you can type the directory path in the File Name text box. If you type the directory path, be sure to enter the full path, starting with the backslash (as in the path \DOCUMENT). Otherwise, Word may interpret the directory name as the name of a file to be saved in the current directory.

After you've specified the appropriate drive and directory, type the name for the file in the File Name text box and choose OK. (We'll ignore the Options button for the moment.) Depending on how you've set Word's save options, you may then see Word's Summary Info dialog box, shown in Figure 2-8. To complete the save operation, choose OK in this dialog box. (Note, in passing, that the Summary Info dialog box has several important features to help you manage your document files. We'll discuss them later in this chapter, under "Summary information.")

The Summary Info dialog box is displayed automatically only if you have checked the Prompt For Summary Info check box on the Save card in the Options dialog box. To check the setting, you can choose the Options button in the Save dialog box, or you can choose Tools Options and then choose Save.

FIGURE 2-8

The Summary Info
dialog box appears
when you choose OK
in the Save As dialog
box.

Summary Info		
File Name: Document2		OK
Directory:		Cancel
Title:		
Subject:		Statistics...
Author: M. David Stone & Alfred Poor		Help
Keywords:		
Comments:		

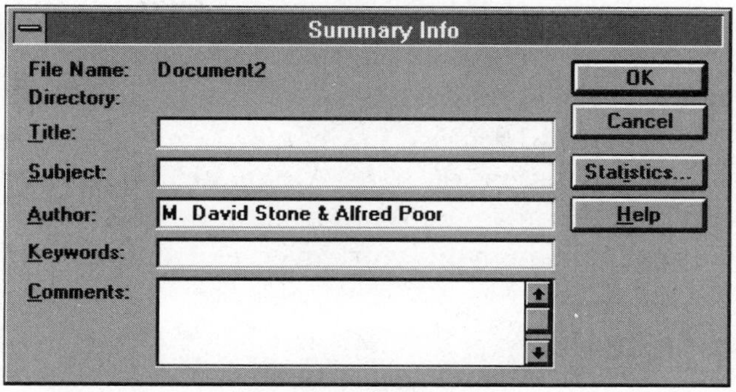

Filename rules

When naming Word documents, follow the standard MS-DOS naming conventions. You can specify a name that's one to eight characters long and an
optional extension up to three characters long. If you enter a filename by itself, Word will add the default DOC extension. However, you can enter any
extension you want by following the filename with a period and the extension. You can also specify no extension by entering a filename followed by a
period. We recommend that you accept the default, at least until you are
thoroughly familiar with the program, because the standard extension
makes it far easier to locate documents on your hard disk.

Filenames and extensions can include any letter of the alphabet, the digits 0 through 9, and many punctuation symbols. You cannot use blank spaces
or any of the following symbols:

    * ? + =] [; : " ¦ / \ < > ,

If you accidentally include any of these, Word will refuse to save the file.
Except for a few cases, which are MS-DOS special characters, Word will display a message box to tell you that you haven't entered a valid filename.

It doesn't matter whether you type uppercase or lowercase letters in
filenames; Word will treat report.doc and REPORT.DOC as the same filename.

File Save As options

In addition to the filename, directory, and drive, you can specify other options with the File Save As command. These options are available through
the Options button in the Save As dialog box.

The Options button in the Save As dialog box takes you to the Options
dialog box shown in Figure 2-9 on the next page. This is the same dialog box,

with the same Save card, that you can get to by using the Tools Options command, except that you can't change to any of the other cards as you can when you open the dialog box by choosing Tools Options. You'll find some of these options discussed in Chapter 1, but one option is important enough to repeat the discussion here: Automatic Save. We strongly recommend that you take advantage of Word's Automatic Save feature. It will minimize your chances of losing your work in case of a power outage or system failure.

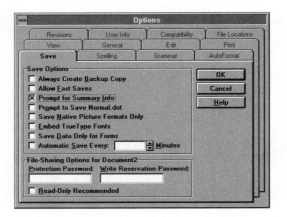

FIGURE 2-9

Choosing the Options button in the Save As dialog box lets you choose any of several saving options. It opens the same dialog box that is available through the Tools Options Save command.

For those who need to safeguard important files, Word's File Sharing Options group at the bottom of the Save card offers ways to protect a file from changes and from prying eyes. The File Sharing Options group includes two text boxes for passwords: the Protection Password text box and the Write Reservation Password text box. You can use each type of password independently of the other, but note that you can also use both together, with the protection password controlling who can see a file and the write reservation password controlling who can modify it.

Either password can be up to 15 characters long, using uppercase letters, lowercase letters, spaces, and punctuation. As you type, Word will substitute an asterisk for each character. To ensure that you typed the password correctly, Word will ask you to type it again after you choose OK. If the two entries match, the program will accept the password and return to the Save As dialog box. If you then choose OK to close the dialog box and finish saving, the password will take effect.

If you assign a protection password, you won't be able to open the file without entering the correct password. If you assign a write reservation password, you'll be able to read the file without knowing the write reservation password, but you won't be able to save changes to the file.

When opening a file that includes a write reservation password, you have a choice of entering the password, which will let you make changes to the file, or selecting the Read Only button in the Password dialog box. If you open the file as read-only, you can make changes and save the file under a new name. The new file will automatically inherit the same password or passwords as the original version unless you go to the Options dialog box and specifically remove the passwords.

Be careful when using protection passwords. Not only do you need the password to open the file in Word, but if you try looking at the file with another program or with the MS-DOS TYPE command, you'll find that your text is no longer stored as standard text (that is, as ASCII characters). If you don't know the password, there is no way to get to your text. This obviously makes for a secure system, but you need to be careful not to forget the password. Note also that the passwords are case sensitive, so that *hi there*, for example, will not match *Hi There* or *HI THERE*. When you enter a password, be sure to remember the case you used, as well as the characters themselves. We suggest maintaining a list of filenames and their corresponding passwords, but be sure to keep the list in a safe place. Too many security systems are defeated because users leave the passwords in an obvious location, such as in a desk drawer or even taped to the system monitor.

When used by itself, Word's protection password provides reasonably good security, as long as you don't give the password to anyone who might resave the file—or save a copy of the file—with the password removed. However, if you take advantage of the write reservation password to let some people read a file without being able to modify it, the security is limited at best. Using both types of passwords on the same file makes it more difficult for anyone to get to or change the file, but once you have a file open for reading, it's a simple matter to choose File Save As and then Options and remove the passwords to save an unprotected version of the file under another name. Write reservation passwords work well as a way to keep specific files intact, but don't rely on them if you want to keep information secret.

The third option in the File Sharing Options group is a Read-Only Recommended check box. If you select this option for a file, Word will display a dialog box similar to the one shown in Figure 2-10 on the next page each time the file is opened, recommending that the file be opened as read-only. If you choose Yes, Word will open the file as read-only. If you choose No, you'll be able to change the file and save the changes. Note, however, that if you have assigned a write reservation password to a file, the Read-Only Recommended check box will not bring up the dialog box shown in Figure 2-10.

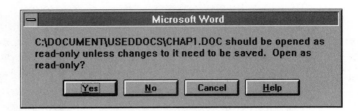

FIGURE 2-10

If you choose the Read-Only Recommended check box before saving a file, Word will display a dialog box similar to this whenever a user tries to open the file.

How to change a filename or directory

The File Save As command offers one other capability. Word has no direct way to change a filename or move a file to another directory from within the program. However, you can create a copy of the file under a different filename, in a different directory, or both, by using the File Save As command and specifying the appropriate directory and filename. You can then delete the original file, using any file-deletion technique you're comfortable with. This is a less than ideal workaround, but it yields the same effect as if you had simply renamed or moved the file.

Summary information

If the Prompt For Summary Info box is checked on the Save card in the Tools Options dialog box, the first time you save a document, Word will display a Summary Info dialog box similar to the ones shown in Figures 2-8 and 2-11. You can use this feature to make it easier to organize your documents and find files on your system.

It's a good habit to make sure you have appropriate entries in the Summary Info dialog box when you save a document for the first time. Alternatively, you can fill in the dialog box when you start a new document, before you actually create the document, by choosing the Summary button in the File New dialog box. You can also open the current document's Summary Info dialog box at any time by choosing File Summary Info.

How to enter summary information

Word automatically includes the filename and directory information at the top of the dialog box, and as already noted, you can't change these directly from within Word. However, all other entries in this dialog box are under your control.

You can enter a descriptive title in the Title text box. Unlike filenames in MS-DOS, which are restricted to 8 characters plus a 3-character extension, titles in the Title text box can be up to 255 characters long and can include any character or symbol that you can type on your keyboard, including spaces. For example, if you're writing a newspaper article about Mick Jagger of the Rolling Stones, you might save the document under the filename JAGGER.DOC but enter the title *Mick Jagger and the Rolling Stones Still Rocking* in the Title text box, as we've done in Figure 2-11.

FIGURE 2-11

We've entered some sample information in this Summary Info dialog box.

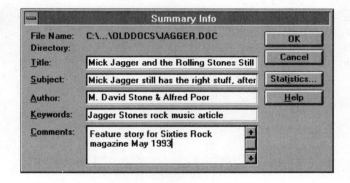

In addition to specifying a title, you can describe the subject of the document in the Subject text box. As with the Title text box, the Subject text box will accept up to 255 characters. For our sample, we've entered the text *Mick Jagger still has the right stuff, after 25 years.*

By default, Word fills in the Author text box using the name currently entered in the Name text box on the User Info card in the Tools Options dialog box. You can modify this entry, as we have here, to include additional authors, or you can change the name altogether. To change the default name, choose Tools Options, select User Info, and enter a new name.

You can create an index for your document by entering a list of keywords in the Keywords text box. The keywords should indicate the document's contents. For example, for our sample document, you might enter the words *Jagger, Stones, rock,* and *music.* Notice that in Figure 2-11 we've used a space between each keyword and the next keyword. You can enter up to 255 characters of keywords, including spaces. The main benefit of using keywords is that you can later find and open the document by searching for those words with the File Find File command. For information on the Find File command, see "Retrieving Documents" on page 603.

The last option in the Summary Info dialog box is the Comments text box. You can type any remarks you want in this text box. Here again, you can use up to 255 characters, including symbols. In our sample Comments text box, we've entered *Feature story for Sixties Rock magazine May 1993*.

How to get statistical information about a document

The Summary Info dialog box includes a button labeled *Statistics*. If you choose it, you'll see some useful information about your document, as shown in Figure 2-12.

FIGURE 2-12

The Document Statistics dialog box shows you information about your document.

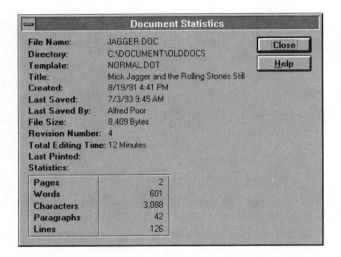

Document Statistics	
File Name:	JAGGER.DOC
Directory:	C:\DOCUMENT\OLDDOCS
Template:	NORMAL.DOT
Title:	Mick Jagger and the Rolling Stones Still
Created:	8/19/91 4:41 PM
Last Saved:	7/3/93 9:45 AM
Last Saved By:	Alfred Poor
File Size:	8,409 Bytes
Revision Number:	4
Total Editing Time:	12 Minutes
Last Printed:	
Statistics:	

Pages	2
Words	601
Characters	3,088
Paragraphs	42
Lines	126

The Document Statistics dialog box shows you the filename, directory, associated template, document title, date and time of creation and last revision, most recent author (or editor, or typist) to save the file, file size in bytes, revision number, total editing time, and date of last printing. It also shows the number of pages, words, characters, paragraphs, and lines in the document. You can't edit any of this information directly. To return to the Summary Info dialog box, choose Close. Word 2.0 users who are used to seeing an Update button in the Document Statistics box may notice that Word 6.0 does not include an Update button. Word 6.0 updates the information automatically.

Possible problems in saving

If you don't have enough room on the current disk to save your document, you'll see a message box like the one shown in Figure 2-13 when you try to save. If so, choose OK; Word will close the message and return you to the document window. Then you can choose the File Save As command to save the document on a different disk, or you can use the File Find File command to delete some of the files on the disk. (We'll show you how to do this shortly, in the section "Deleting a File.") Alternatively, you can open the Windows File Manager to delete files on your disk and free some space.

FIGURE 2-13

You'll see this message box if there isn't enough room to save your document on the active disk.

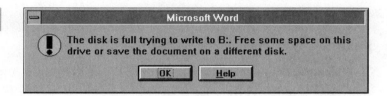

If the name you enter in the File Name text box duplicates a name that already exists in the current directory, you'll see a message box asking whether you want to replace the existing file. To replace the existing file with the document you're trying to save, choose Yes. Otherwise, choose No to return to the Save As dialog box, or choose Cancel to return to your document.

How to save a document again

After you save a document, you don't need to use the File Save As command again unless you want to save that file under a new name or change one of the file options. To save the changes to a file that you've previously saved, simply choose File Save or click the Save button on the Standard toolbar. Word will save the current version and let you continue editing.

Word provides shortcut keys for various tasks. You can use Ctrl-S to save the current file. (You can also use the shortcut from Word 2.0 for this task: Shift-F12.)

If you choose File Save As to save a file that you've previously saved, you'll see the Save As dialog box containing the current name in the File Name text box. If you meant to save the file under its original name, choose OK, and Word will save the file as if you had chosen File Save. If you want to save the document under a new name, however, type that name in the File

Name text box and choose OK. Word will then save the new version of the document under the new filename and leave the original file unchanged.

How to save a read-only document

If you try to save a file you opened with the Read Only option turned on, Word will display a message reminding you of the file's read-only status.

Choose OK, and Word will display the Save As dialog box. If you again try to assign the same name to the altered file, Word will again display the message box. To save your changes to the file, you must give the file a new name. As should be clear, the Read Only option is a convenient way to protect your files from unintended changes.

How to save everything at once

In addition to saving individual files one at a time, you can save everything that's open (including documents, templates, macros, and glossaries) by choosing File Save All. The File Save All command is particularly handy when you've split a single document into several files—as you might with long sections of a single report, for example—or when you're creating or editing AutoText entries or macros. We'll discuss AutoText in "Using AutoText" on page 140. We'll discuss macros in Chapters 24 through 26.

When you choose File Save All, Word will try to save all open documents and all changes in macros and AutoText entries. It will automatically save each open document (assuming the document isn't read-only), and for each additional item, it will display a dialog box like the one shown in Figure 2-14, asking whether to save that item. You can choose Yes or No for each item, or you can cancel the File Save All command by choosing Cancel.

FIGURE 2-14

When you choose File Save All, Word saves each open file that isn't read-only and displays a message box for each template that changed since the last save operation.

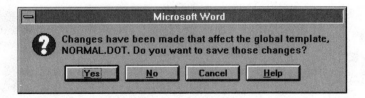

How to close files without leaving Word

The File Close command is meant to let you close files without leaving Word. For example, if you've opened three files to transfer data among them and you finish your work with one of the three, you can choose the File Close command so that you have only two windows left to work with. If you haven't made changes to the document since you last opened or saved it, Word will immediately close the file.

If you have made changes, however, or if you've entered anything in a new document, Word will display a message box asking whether you want to save the changes to the document. If you choose Yes and the current document has previously been saved, Word will save the document under its current name and then close it. If the document has never been saved, Word will display the Save As dialog box. If you choose No, Word will close the document without saving the changes. If you choose Cancel, Word will return you to the document without saving it or closing it.

The Close command on the Document Control menu is equivalent to the File Close command. To use it, type Alt-Hyphen to open the menu and then C to close the document window, or double-click on the Document Control box. (The shortcut key for closing a document window is Ctrl-W.)

How to close files and exit Word

The File Exit command tells Word to close everything that's currently open and return to the Windows Program Manager. If you haven't made any changes since the last time you saved the open files, Word will simply close up shop. If you have made changes or entered anything in a new document, however, you'll see a message box asking whether you want to save your changes. Word will try to save all documents and all changes in macros and glossaries, stopping to ask whether to save each item, *including* each document. You can save or discard your changes by choosing Yes or No for each item. You can also cancel the Exit command any time by choosing Cancel.

The Exit command on the Application Control menu, which you can open with Alt-Spacebar, is equivalent to the File Exit command. You can also close Word by double-clicking on the Application Control box or by pressing Alt-F4.

Deleting a File

To delete a file from within Word, first choose File Find File. Word will briefly display a message box titled *Building File List* as it searches through the files on your disk. When Word finishes, it will display a Find File dialog box similar to the one shown in Figure 2-15. (The first time you use this feature, Word may prompt you to enter a filename to search for and a location [a directory] in which to search; use *.DOC to search for all documents, and select the current drive to search the current directory on that drive.)

FIGURE 2-15

You can use the Find File dialog box for many tasks, including deleting a file.

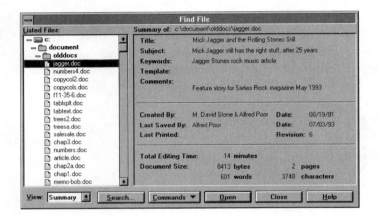

The Find File dialog box offers a wide range of sophisticated file search and file management functions, which we'll cover in detail in Chapter 17. For the moment, however, we're concerned only with the ability to delete files by using this dialog box. If you follow our earlier suggestion and use the *.DOC default extension to save document files, all Word files in the current directory will be included in the File Name list box. (If you don't see the file you want, even after scrolling through the choices, you can change the search specification with the Search button, as we'll discuss in Chapter 17.

To select a file to delete, simply click on the filename, or use the Up and Down arrow keys to move the highlight to the filename, or type the first letter in the filename. (If more than one filename starts with the same letter, you can type the same letter repeatedly to cycle through the choices.) When you've highlighted the file you want to delete, choose Commands and then choose Delete (or press the Del key). Word will display a message box asking whether you want to delete the file. Choose Yes to confirm the deletion or No to have Word return you to the Find File dialog box without deleting the file.

How to delete multiple files

If you want, you can delete more than one file at a time. To select multiple files with the keyboard, use the Up and Down arrow keys to highlight the first filename you want to delete, and then press Shift-F8. To add more names, use the arrow keys to move the highlight outline to the appropriate filename, and press the Spacebar to turn on the highlight. The Spacebar will toggle individual highlights on and off. However, if you have highlighted several names and want to remove the multiple highlights, you must press Shift-F8 again and then press an Up or Down arrow key to collapse the highlight to a single file. To select a group of adjacent files, highlight the first name and hold down the Shift key as you move over the list. To select multiple filenames with the mouse, hold down the mouse button as you extend the selection over adjacent files, or click on the first filename in the batch that you want to delete and then hold down the Shift key as you click on the last name in the list. Word will highlight all filenames between the two you selected. To select nonadjacent filenames with the mouse, hold down the Ctrl key while you click on each name. To remove a file from the list, hold down the Ctrl key and select the entry.

After you highlight the names of the files to delete, choose Commands and then choose Delete (or press the Del key). Word will prompt you to confirm the deletion. Watch out when deleting multiple files—you can easily highlight an extra name and delete the file accidentally. Pay careful attention to your selections because Word asks you only once to confirm all of the deletions.

Templates

There is one last topic related to file handling that you ought to be familiar with, if only on a superficial level: templates. We've mentioned templates in passing several times in this chapter. Word templates are a somewhat complex feature that we won't discuss in detail until much later. However, the concept of a template is so central to Word that you need to be aware of it, even at this early stage.

With most word processing programs, a template is a document that you create as a model for other documents. A letter template, for example, might include your return address, an automatic date entry, and some appropriate formatting commands. Depending on the program, you can use the template either by copying it to another file first and then loading that file or by opening a new file and loading the template.

Templates in Word are similar in concept. You can even create them and edit them in the same way you create and edit standard document files. The difference is that Word recognizes files with an extension of DOT as template files, and it requires that you designate a template for every document you create. (As with the DOC extension for documents, DOT is the default extension Word uses when saving a template. You can use other file extensions, but we strongly recommend that you accept the DOT extension unless you have a good reason for doing otherwise.)

To avoid being buried in a wealth of choices, we also strongly suggest that you use only the Normal template until you are thoroughly familiar with Word. However, note that Word templates also provide far more potential for customization than you would probably expect. As we'll discuss in Chapter 28, you can even create a different customized set of menus for each template. Note too, as mentioned elsewhere, that Word 6.0 comes with a large number of wizards that automate the process of creating complex templates and related documents. For a general discussion of wizards, see "Wizards: Automated Documents" on page 322.

How to use templates

Templates in Word work differently from how you might expect. When you attach a template other than the Normal template to an existing document, Word does not detach the Normal template—even though the program gives little indication that it is still attached. Similarly, if you open a new document and specify some other template, Word will still attach the Normal template.

In fact, the second template serves as an additional, or supplementary, template. In general, any customization that you saved in the Normal template is still available in a document that has a supplemental template attached, unless you've overridden the Normal template modifications by additional customization in the supplemental template.

If you've used Word 2.0, you may be aware of something called *context*, a confusing concept that Microsoft has, thankfully, dropped from Word 6.0. The manuals and dialog boxes now refer simply to storing customizations in specific templates. The underlying functionality of the different templates hasn't changed; only the terminology has changed—for the better, we think—to make templates easier to understand. However, you should be aware that Word 6.0 adds significant enhancements to the use of templates. For more information on templates, see "An Introduction to Templates," starting on page 325, and also Chapter 27.

Unless told otherwise, Word uses its default settings as the Normal template, which it uses to create a file named NORMAL.DOT. You can specify the Normal template with every file you create, or you can create a separate Letter template, Memo template, Report template, and so on for each kind of document you regularly use. In fact, Word comes with several sample templates that you can use as well.

If you don't fully follow this introduction to templates, don't let it throw you. Just be aware, for now, that templates exist. We'll come back to templates later in discussing features ranging from basic editing tools to some of Word's most sophisticated customization capabilities. Now we can move on to the basic skills for working with an actual document.

TOPIC FINDER

Entering Text   67

- A sample document

Displaying Special Marks   72

Basic Elements of a Document   73

- Characters
- Words
- Sentences
- Paragraphs
- Blocks
- Where the elements matter

Navigation   75

- How to navigate with the mouse
- How to navigate with the keyboard
- Other methods of moving through your document

Selecting Text   84

- How to select with the mouse
- How to select with the keyboard

Basic Editing Techniques   91

- How to insert new text
- How to delete text
- How to overwrite text
- How to cut text

Canceling and Repeating Actions   94

- NEW! How to undo an action or multiple actions
- How to repeat an action

Where We Go from Here   96

Essential Skills

fter you open a new document, you'll want to enter text, edit it, and format it to suit your needs. In this chapter, we'll show you how to enter text, and we'll introduce some navigation and selection techniques you'll need so you can view, edit, and format that text. We'll also cover some basic editing skills to set the stage for our discussion of Word's editing, proofing, and formatting features in Chapters 4 through 7.

You'll find many keyboard shortcuts in this chapter. We urge you to practice these; they will help you work more efficiently in Word because they let you keep your fingers on the keys rather than reach for the mouse all the time. For a summary of these and other keyboard shortcuts, see Appendix A, "Mouse & Keyboard Techniques," on page 982.

Entering Text

Entering text in Word is actually easier than typing on a typewriter. As with most word processing programs, the *wordwrap* feature lets you type continuously, without manually entering a carriage return at the end of each line. If you are new to word processing, you may be tempted to press the Enter key as you near the end of each line of text. Don't give in to the habit. If there's not enough room on the current line for the word you are typing, Word will move the entire word to the start of the next line automatically. The only time you need to press the Enter key while entering text is when you want to start a new paragraph.

More important than the fact that you don't have to enter the carriage return at the end of each line is the fact that you shouldn't. A carriage return at the end of each line makes it more difficult to edit and reformat text. You should press Enter only at the end of a paragraph (or a line that you want Word to treat as a paragraph).

A sample document

To illustrate some basic entry, selection, and editing techniques, we'll use the text in Figure 3-1. To work along with us, you can enter this text in a Word document yourself, or you can type in any other text. If you've just loaded Word, you can enter your text in the file titled Document1. If you need to open a new file, however, choose File New. When the New dialog box appears, choose OK to bring up the new, blank document.

FIGURE 3-1

We'll use this text as a sample document to illustrate text entry, selection, and editing techniques.

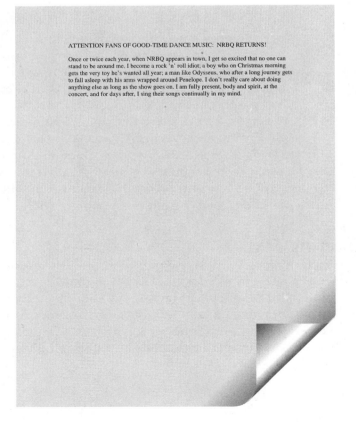

ATTENTION FANS OF GOOD-TIME DANCE MUSIC: NRBQ RETURNS!

Once or twice each year, when NRBQ appears in town, I get so excited that no one can stand to be around me. I become a rock 'n' roll idiot; a boy who on Christmas morning gets the very toy he's wanted all year; a man like Odysseus, who after a long journey gets to fall asleep with his arms wrapped around Penelope. I don't really care about doing anything else as long as the show goes on. I am fully present, body and spirit, at the concert, and for days after, I sing their songs continually in my mind.

What you'll see

Word displays your documents in one of four basic views: Normal, Page Layout, Outline, or Master Document (a variation of Outline view for long documents). Throughout this chapter, we will use Normal view. You'll find it easier to follow our examples if your screen is set the same way as ours. To verify that it is, open the View menu and make sure there is a bullet (a small dot) next to the Normal command. (The bullet indicates which of the four mutually exclusive choices is currently chosen.) If there isn't a dot, choose the Normal command to change to Normal view.

Next, choose Tools Options and select the View tab. Verify that the check box labeled Draft Font is cleared. If this check box is checked, the fonts and type sizes in your document will not be accurately displayed, nor will the line breaks appear as they will on the printed page. Although this can speed up performance a bit, you lose the ability to see how your document will look when it's printed, which is one of any Windows-based word processor's main strengths. To make sure that your screen matches our illustrations, do not use the Draft option.

You will also want to make sure that Word's zoom feature is set appropriately. If the zoom percentage is too high, the characters on your screen will be far larger, proportionately, than they'll appear in the illustrations. If the percentage is too low, the screen characters will be far smaller. Mouse users can open the Zoom Control drop-down list box on the Standard toolbar, as shown in Figure 3-2, and select 100%. Keyboard users can choose View Zoom to open the Zoom dialog box shown in Figure 3-3, choose 100% in the Zoom To box, and then choose OK.

FIGURE 3-2

You can tell Word to zoom in or out on a document by using the Zoom Control drop-down list box.

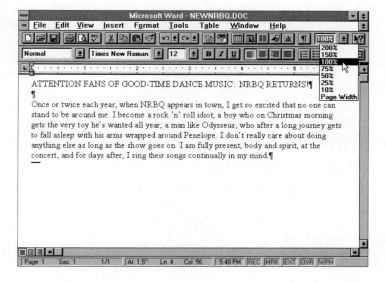

FIGURE 3-3

You can also tell Word to zoom in or out on a document by using the Zoom dialog box.

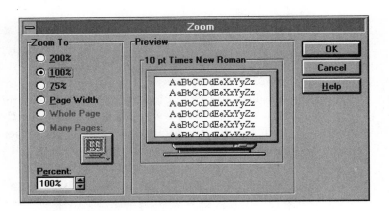

 If you want a zoom level different from those Word provides on its built-in list, you can simply type the level, either in the Zoom text box on the Standard toolbar or in the Percent text box in the Zoom dialog box.

The default font for a new document will depend on the printer you've installed, but it will typically be a 10-point version of Times New Roman, or something similar. (The issues of printer and screen fonts can get quite complex; we'll discuss them in more detail in Chapter 16.)

To make our text more legible, we'll enter it in 12-point type instead of in the default 10-point type. Make the change by opening the Font Size drop-down list on the Formatting toolbar, either with the mouse or with the shortcut keys (Shift-Ctrl-P, Down arrow). By the way, this and all other references to shortcut keys assume you are using the default settings for Word's keys. We strongly recommend that you not reassign any keys until you are thoroughly familiar with the program. (If you want to change keyboard assignments, however, we'll explain how to do so in Chapter 28.)

When you open the Font Size drop-down list, you should see a list similar to the one in Figure 3-4, although the actual choices will depend on your printer and other factors. If 12 is one of the choices on your list, select it. Any new text you enter at the cursor will now appear in 12-point type.

How to enter text

With 12-point type and Normal view selected, begin entering text. As you type, notice the blinking vertical cursor. The cursor moves one space to the right with each character you type, indicating your position in the document.

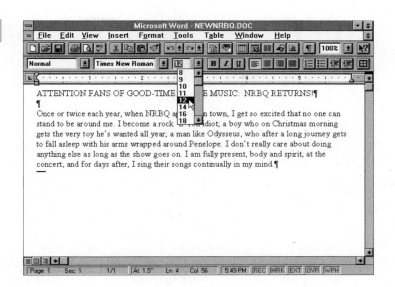

If you make an error, press the Backspace key to move the cursor back one space at a time and erase your mistakes. Then resume typing as usual. If you don't notice an error until you are well past it, don't worry about it at this point. We'll show you how to correct those mistakes later in this chapter.

You will notice that at the end of the first line in Figure 3-1 there is a symbol you won't find on your keyboard. It is shaped like a backwards P and is called the *paragraph symbol*. There's another on a line by itself below the first line. These paragraph symbols mark the points at which you should press the Enter key if you are entering our sample document. When you press Enter, the cursor will move to the start of the next line. Depending on how Word is configured, you may or may not see the paragraph symbols on your screen; as mentioned in Chapter 1, you can display and hide these by choosing Tools Options, then choosing View, and selecting the Paragraph Marks option. You can also click on the Show/Hide ¶ button on the Standard toolbar to show all nonprinting characters. For more information, see the next section, "Displaying Special Marks."

When you type text, press Enter only when you need to begin a new paragraph. If you like, you can emphasize paragraphs by pressing Enter twice between paragraphs or by pressing the Tab key at the beginning of each paragraph. However, be aware that there are easier ways to get the same effect, as we'll discuss in Chapter 7. Don't worry if some of the text scrolls off the top of the screen. As you'll see in a moment, you can use Word's scrolling features to bring text back into view.

Displaying Special Marks

One of Word's most striking features is its graphical interface, which can show a close approximation on the screen of what your text will look like on paper. This on-screen display is often referred to as WYSIWYG, an acronym for "What You See Is What You Get."

You might be surprised to learn that you actually enter special coding information every time you create a new paragraph or make a formatting change. Behind the scenes, Word keeps track of formatting changes with a series of nonprinting characters that indicate paragraphs, blank spaces, optional hyphens, and so forth.

As we discussed in Chapter 1, you can set Word to display some or all of these special marks. The Tools Options View card offers a set of check boxes for nonprinting characters, including one labeled All. Putting an X in the All check box displays all hidden formatting characters on the screen. The Show/Hide ¶ button, just to the left of the Zoom Control button on the Standard toolbar, has the same effect as the All check box.

There are times when it can be handy to see some or all of these nonprinting characters—to see whether you've used spaces or tabs, for example, for positioning. In general, though, whether you display some or all of the nonprinting characters is strictly a matter of taste. Figure 3-5 shows our sample with all nonprinting characters displayed.

The paragraph mark (¶) not only represents the end of a paragraph in your Word document, it also holds the formatting for the paragraph, as we'll discuss in Chapter 7.

FIGURE 3-5

We've turned on the display for all non-printing characters in our sample document.

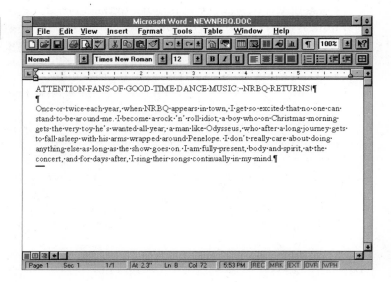

The dots (·) between words and sentences in Figure 3-5 represent blank spaces. It can be hard to distinguish space marks from periods, but if you look closely, you'll see that the space marks sit slightly higher on the line.

Basic Elements of a Document

Before we explain how to select, edit, and format, it's important that you understand how Word deals with text. Word has its own definitions for characters, words, sentences, paragraphs, and blocks, and you need to know what those are. The concepts aren't difficult to grasp, but they may differ from what you expect. And it's easy to become frustrated if you use one set of definitions while Word uses another.

Characters

The most basic element of text in Word is the character. A character can be any element you enter: a space, a tab, a letter, a number, a punctuation mark, or any of the nonprinting characters mentioned earlier. Blocks, words, sentences, and paragraphs are combinations of characters.

Words

To Microsoft Word, a word can be any combination of alphabetic and numeric characters—DOCUMENT1, for example, and ROOM2A are acceptable words. The program recognizes words as groups of characters that are set apart from other text by one or more blank spaces, by any punctuation mark other than an apostrophe, or by one of Word's nonprinting characters.

Word will treat some groups of characters as more than one word for purposes of moving the cursor or selecting text, but it will treat them as a single word in determining where to break a line. Consider, for example, a non-breaking space. A non-breaking space is a special character that you enter by pressing Ctrl-Shift-Spacebar. If you are displaying nonprinting characters, Word shows this as a small circle, similar to that used to denote "degrees" in mathematical notation. You might use a non-breaking space between ROOM and 2A, for example, to tell Word to treat ROOM 2A as a single word at the end of a line. Without the non-breaking space, Word might put ROOM as the last word in one line and 2A as the first word in the next. With the non-breaking space, Word will keep the two together. If you select the text one word at a time, however, you can select only ROOM; you have to select 2A separately.

For selecting text or moving through text, spaces don't count as words, but punctuation marks and symbols do. So Word considers *abc def* as two words, for example, but *abc=def* as three. The first line of our sample document (the title), in Figure 3-5, has 12 words, according to Word—including the hyphen between GOOD and TIME, the colon after MUSIC, and the exclamation point at the end.

Word does not use the same rules for counting words as for selecting them. Although *abc=def* is treated as three separate words for selection or navigation purposes, Word will count it as a single word if you ask for a word count by choosing Tools Word Count, or by choosing File Summary Info and then Statistics. For details, see "How to get statistical information about a document" on page 58.

Sentences

A sentence is a group of characters and words set apart by a period, exclamation point, or question mark. You can also use a paragraph mark or a forced line break to mark the end of a sentence. (A forced line break, entered with Shift-Enter, is represented on screen by the ⏎ symbol.) The character that marks the end of a sentence also marks the end of the last word in that sentence. For example, consider the first sentence in the first full paragraph in our sample. The sentence ends with "...to be around me." The period after the word *me* marks the end of the sentence, as well as the end of the word *me*.

Paragraphs

A paragraph can be any combination of characters, words, and symbols that are set apart by a paragraph mark. Keep in mind that the paragraph mark at the end of a paragraph is part of that paragraph. In fact, Word treats the paragraph mark as an individual word.

Blocks

In Word, a block of text is any group of characters—or even a single character—that you've highlighted. The highlight, or selection, tells Word to treat a group of characters as a single unit. Often a block of text will consist of a sentence, a paragraph, or several paragraphs. However, a block can be any arbitrary length and can start or end in the middle of a paragraph, sentence, or word.

Where the elements matter

These definitions for character, word, sentence, paragraph, and block may seem a bit esoteric at this point. However, they will become important when you begin moving around in your document and selecting blocks of text. If you select or move text and get unexpected results, referring to these definitions may help you understand what happened.

Navigation

Most documents are longer than the 20 or so lines that fit in a typical document window, so it's likely that most of your document won't be visible as you enter and edit text. If you are not familiar with this effect, it may help you to think of your words as written on a continuous scroll of paper that's wound on rollers hidden at the top and bottom of your screen. Text that comes before the section you're currently looking at has, in essence, scrolled off the top of the screen. If you move up in your document, the document will scroll down, revealing previous parts of the document, and subsequent parts of the document will scroll off the bottom of the screen. You can move down in your document to scroll these parts of the document back into view.

To move around in a large document, you'll need to use Word's navigation techniques. Some of these use the mouse; others use the keyboard. Which one you will prefer to use is largely a matter of taste, so we'll show both ways, starting with the mouse-based choices.

How to navigate with the mouse

When you navigate through a document with the mouse, there's one key point you'll need to keep firmly in mind: Your cursor will remain where it was before you moved unless you tell Word to move the cursor also. In fact, if you use the mouse to view another part of your document and then start typing, you'll find that Word returns you to your starting point and that anything you've typed is entered at the original cursor position.

You can use this feature as a convenient way to look at something elsewhere in your document and then return to the section you're currently working on. However, if you actually want to work on the other part of your document rather than just view it, place the I-beam pointer at the spot you want to move the cursor to, and then click the mouse button. You can also use this point-and-click technique to move the cursor anywhere within a single screenful of text.

The scroll bars

Among the most basic mouse-based navigation tools are the horizontal and vertical scroll bars. As we mentioned in Chapter 1, the boxes within the scroll bars are called scroll boxes, and the arrows at either end of each scroll bar are called scroll arrows.

You can turn the vertical and horizontal scroll bars on and off. If either or both scroll bars don't show on your screen, choose Tools Options, select the View tab, and make sure the Vertical Scroll Bars check box and the Horizontal Scroll Bars check box are checked. The scroll bars will also disappear—along with the Menu bar and most toolbars—if you choose View Full Screen to see more text. (To turn off the Full Screen option, press Esc.)

How to use the vertical scroll bar. To move through your document a line at a time with the vertical scroll bar, simply click on the scroll arrow at the top or bottom of the vertical scroll bar. Click the bottom arrow to scroll down—or forward—through a document and the top arrow to scroll up—or backward. To move through a document a full screen at a time, click anywhere within the scroll bar—above the scroll box to scroll up, or below the box to scroll down. Word will scroll the next screen into view and carry over two lines from the earlier screen to help you get your bearings. As shown in Figure 3-6, the distance that Word scrolls depends on the current size of the document window. If you've reduced the size, as in this figure, Word will still scroll one screen at a time, although there will be fewer lines per screen.

FIGURE 3-6

We've reduced the document window to four lines to show how window size affects scrolling. Note that the number of lines Word scrolls when you click below the scroll box is based on the size of the window. Note also the two lines carried over from the previous screen to help you keep track of where you are.

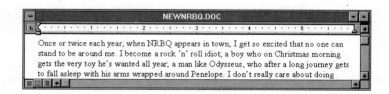

To move long distances through a document, you can drag the scroll box to the appropriate position in the scroll bar. The distance you travel by dragging the scroll box depends on the length of your document.

The scroll box position on the vertical scroll bar represents your relative position in the document. In a short document, the box will move a long distance if you scroll to the next screenful. In a long document, it will hardly move at all. Scrolling works the other way too: The distance you travel by dragging the scroll box depends on the length of your document. If you have a sense of where you want to move to, you can drag the scroll box to the appropriate position. For example, to move to page 25 in a 50-page document, drag the scroll box to the middle of the scroll bar. The screen will not change until you release the mouse button.

How to use the horizontal scroll bar. If you're working with a document that is too wide to fit on one screen—for example, if you're using a wide page width or a window that doesn't fill the entire screen—you can use the scroll arrows at either end of the horizontal scroll bar to move right and left. Horizontal scrolling is much like vertical scrolling: Use the scroll arrows to move short distances, click on either side of the scroll box to move by a full screen, or drag the scroll box to reposition the window manually.

Unlike the vertical scroll bar's relative positioning, which changes depending on how long the document is, the horizontal scroll bar's positioning is constant. Word allows a maximum document width of 22 inches and will let you scroll the full 22 inches with any document. If you drag the scroll box to the extreme right end of the horizontal scroll bar, you'll travel the full 22 inches; if you drag it to the middle of the scroll bar, you'll travel to the 11-inch mark—no matter where the right margin is in the current document.

How to navigate with the keyboard

For navigating, many people find the mouse easier to learn at first because of its straightforward point-and-click strategy; however, the keyboard commands are in many ways easier to use, once you've learned them. A little time invested in learning the keyboard commands can yield big dividends in efficiency because you can keep your fingers on the keyboard rather than reach for the mouse. Figure 3-7 summarizes the keystrokes we'll cover in this section.

One important difference between using the keyboard and using the mouse is that when you use the keyboard, the cursor will travel with you as you move through your document.

These Keys...	Move the Cursor...
Left arrow	Left one character
Right arrow	Right one character
Up arrow	Up one line
Down arrow	Down one line
Home	To the beginning of the current line
End	To the end of the current line
PgUp	Up one screen
PgDn	Down one screen
Ctrl-Left arrow	Left one word
Ctrl-Right arrow	Right one word
Ctrl-Up arrow	Up one paragraph
Ctrl-Down arrow	Down one paragraph
Ctrl-Home	To the top of the document
Ctrl-End	To the bottom of the document
Ctrl-PgUp	To the top of the screen
Ctrl-PgDn	To the bottom of the screen
Alt-Ctrl-PgUp	To previous page
Alt-Ctrl-PgDn	To next page
Shift-F5	To a previous location
F5	To a specified location

FIGURE 3-7

Keyboard navigation.

How to move short distances

The Left, Right, Up, and Down arrow keys are tremendously convenient for moving short distances. When you use the Up and Down arrow keys, your cursor will move more or less in a straight line. (Because line lengths vary and characters occupy different amounts of space, your cursor may jump around a bit as you move from line to line.) If you press the Up arrow key at the top of the document window or the Down arrow key at the bottom, Word will scroll the next lines of text into view.

When you press the Right or Left arrow key, the cursor will move one character to the left or right. (Be aware that a tab, which will show on screen as a right arrow ($\rightarrow$), is treated as a single character, no matter how much of a jump it represents.) Press the Left arrow key at the beginning of a line, and the cursor will move to the end of the previous line. If you press the Right arrow key at the end of a line, the cursor will move to the beginning of the next line.

If you press the Left arrow key when the cursor is at the beginning of the first line on the screen, or the Right arrow key when the cursor is in the bottom line, Word will scroll the document as well as move the cursor to the next line.

How to move by words or paragraphs

Word offers Ctrl-key shortcuts that you can use to move the cursor by words or paragraphs. To move from one word to the next, press Ctrl-Right arrow or Ctrl-Left arrow. The cursor will land immediately to the left of the next (or previous) word.

To move through your document a paragraph at a time, use Ctrl-Up arrow and Ctrl-Down arrow. If your cursor is currently in the middle of a paragraph, Ctrl-Up arrow jumps you to the beginning of that paragraph. If your cursor is already at the beginning of a paragraph, Ctrl-Up arrow will take you to the beginning of the previous paragraph. Similarly, pressing Ctrl-Down arrow will take you to the beginning of the next paragraph.

How to move by screenfuls

To move through your document a full screen at a time, you can use the Page Up and Page Down keys. To move up, press Page Up; to move down, press Page Down. The amount of text scrolled will depend on the size of the current document window; Word will carry over two lines from the previous screen to help you find your place. As you scroll new portions of the document into view, the cursor remains in the same relative screen position—unless the beginning or end of the document is already on screen. If the beginning of the document is on screen, the Page Up key will move the cursor to the beginning of the document. If the end is on screen, Page Down will move the cursor to the end.

How to move by pages

If your document is longer than one page, you can move forward one page at a time with Alt-Ctrl-PgDn. To move back a page, press Alt-Ctrl-PgUp.

How to move to the beginning or end of your document

You can also use the Ctrl key with the Home and End keys to move the cursor to the beginning or end of your document. Ctrl-Home will move it to the beginning of the document; Ctrl-End will move it to the end.

How to move the cursor to its previous location

When you edit text, you will likely find yourself skipping from one spot to another to move text, make minor changes, or remind yourself what you wrote elsewhere. Word offers a navigation feature to help streamline this process: the Shift-F5 keyboard shortcut.

When you press Shift-F5, the cursor will move to the last place where you made a change. (This is not necessarily the last place the cursor was located; you have to have made some editing change for this keyboard shortcut to work.) Word will keep track of the last three locations where you made changes and will let you cycle through those locations and your current position with Shift-F5, moving from the most recent change to the oldest one and then back to the place you started from.

The Shift-F5 technique is useful for toggling between two areas of your document when you need to compare two portions of text. For example, suppose you have a table on page 3 and a discussion of the table on page 4 and you want to keep moving between the text where you're discussing the table and the table itself. To tell Word to remember a point in the table, make a trivial change there, such as adding a space and then deleting it by pressing the Backspace key. Then you can move back and forth with Shift-F5.

How to use the Go To command

Moving by character, line, screen, and so forth is useful, but there will be times when you want to jump to a specific place. If you know the page or other specific location—or even if you don't—you can use the Go To command to get there. Start by either choosing Edit Go To or pressing F5. Word will respond with the Go To dialog box, shown in Figure 3-8.

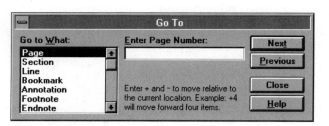

You can also bring up the Go To dialog box by double-clicking anywhere on the position information on the status bar—that is, anywhere in the box that includes page and section information or in the box that includes inch, line, and column information.

The Go To What list box shows the different kinds of items you can move to. By default, Word suggests Page unless you've used a different choice since you last loaded Word. If you want to go to the immediately following page—for example, page 4 when you're currently on page 3—you can simply choose Next. Word will move the cursor to the beginning of the first line on the next page. Notice, however, that Word will not close the dialog box unless you choose Close or press Escape.

Because Word keeps the Go To dialog box open until you explicitly close it, you can continue to move through the document one step at a time, choosing Next to move forward or Previous to move back. This technique will work with any of the items in the Go To What list box, taking you to the next or previous section, line, and so on. In effect, you can browse through your document until you find the item you're looking for.

If you know the page number you want to move to, you can simply type it in the Enter Page Number text box, as shown in Figure 3-9. Word will change the Next button to read Go To and will dim the Previous button. Choose Go To, and Word will move the cursor to the beginning of the first line on the specified page and display the page in the document window. It will also show the page number on the status bar to indicate the actual position of the cursor. (Note, in passing, that the status bar indicates the page numbers for the document as it will appear when it is printed.)

FIGURE 3-9

You can use the Go To dialog box to move quickly to a specified page or other location in your document.

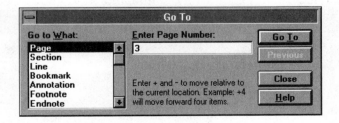

You can also specify relative position in the Enter Page Number text box. For example, enter *+2* to advance two pages or *–3* to move back three pages. You can enter *+* or *–* alone to move one page forward or back, but it's easier to use the Next and Previous buttons, as just described.

Moving through your document using any of the other choices in the Go To What box is similar to moving by pages. One of the few differences is that the heading over the text box labeled Enter Page Number in Figures 3-8 and 3-9 will change, depending on the item you've selected in the Go To What list box. If you select Bookmark, for example, the label will change to Enter Bookmark Name. (A bookmark is a kind of placeholder you can insert into your document by choosing Edit Bookmark, entering a name, and choosing Add.) With some choices, including bookmarks, the text box will become a drop-down list box containing all relevant items—bookmark names, for example. (For more information about bookmarks, see "Bookmarks" on page 333.)

Other methods of moving through your document

In addition to commands meant specifically for moving through your document, Word offers two navigation techniques that aren't usually thought of that way: the Edit Find command and the Outline view.

How to use the Edit Find command to navigate

You can use the Find dialog box, shown in Figure 3-10, to move to a location in your text defined by specific text; to a specific character, paragraph, or style formatting; or to any combination of these. You can begin a search from any point in your document and search forward from the cursor (by selecting

FIGURE 3-10

The Find dialog box lets you look for any combination of text and format.

Down in the Search box); backward from the cursor (by selecting Up); or through the entire document, starting at the cursor, going to the end of the document, and then starting again at the beginning (by selecting All). The ability to select All is a new feature in Microsoft Word 6.0.

After you define what to search for and choose Find Next, Word will highlight the first instance of the item that it finds. You can then choose Cancel to close the dialog box and remain at that location, or Find Next to look for another instance of the search item. If you begin the search in the middle of your document, Word will ask whether to continue searching from the beginning of the document when it reaches the end (if searching down) or continue searching from the end when it reaches the beginning (if searching up). For details about the Edit Find command and its companion, Edit Replace, see "Using the Edit Find and Edit Replace Commands" on page 109.

How to use Outline view to navigate

Word's Outline view is meant primarily for organizing your writing by using an outline. Outline view includes the ability to collapse an outline to show headings only, as shown in Figure 3-11. Collapsing the outline makes it easy to view the overall structure of your document and to move entire sections. It also gives you a way to move through your text quickly.

FIGURE 3-11

Word's collapsible outliner lets you see only your section headings and move through a document quickly by moving to a different heading.

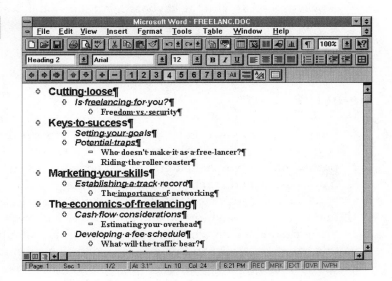

If you need to move through a long report or other document, you have only to choose View Outline to switch to Outline view. Then choose the lowest level of heading you want to see (by using Alt-Shift-1 for level 1 headings, Alt-Shift-2 for level 2 headings, and so forth, or by using the numbered buttons), move the cursor to the heading for the section you want to move to, expand the section by pressing the plus key on the numeric keypad, move the cursor to the part of the section you want to work with, and go back to Normal view by choosing View Normal. (This sounds more complicated than it really is. All the collapsing and expanding involves just six keystrokes.) Note that Word will not always expand the document to show you the current cursor position. However, you will move there immediately if you type any printing character, such as a letter of the alphabet or a number.

You can take advantage of this feature even if you use the outliner for nothing else. You have only to format your section titles with any arbitrary heading level. We'll show you how when we cover outlining later in this book, and we'll show you how to collapse and expand the outline with the mouse as well as with the keyboard. For the moment, simply be aware that it can be done. And you'll probably want to learn at least this much about the outline feature, even if outlining doesn't match the way you work. For details, see Chapter 19.

Selecting Text

Second in importance only to knowing how to move through your document is knowing how to select blocks of text. Before you can edit or format a given portion of text, you have to tell Word which text you want to work with. In most cases, you do that by selecting the text.

When you select text, Word will display the selected block of characters in inverse video—white text and graphics on a black background rather than the normal black on white (if you are using the default colors). Throughout this book, we'll refer to this inverse video as *highlighted text* or *selected text*. As with navigation techniques, Word offers many ways to select text, both with the mouse and with the keyboard. Each approach offers its own advantages. We strongly encourage you to explore all the methods discussed here so that you can find the ones that work best for you. Once again, we'll start with mouse-based techniques.

How to select with the mouse

As with navigation techniques, many people find it easier at first to use the mouse for selecting text. But you may be surprised at how many choices you have with the mouse alone.

How to drag across text

The most basic mouse selection technique is dragging across the text you want to select. For example, suppose you want to select the words *twice each year* in line 3 of the sample document. Begin by positioning the I-beam pointer just to the left of the letter *t* in the word *twice*. Next, press and hold down the left mouse button and, without releasing the button, drag to the right until you've highlighted the entire phrase, as shown in Figure 3-12. When you release the mouse button, the characters will remain highlighted. You can use dragging to select any size block of text, from a single character to an entire document.

FIGURE 3-12

You can select a block of text by dragging across the block.

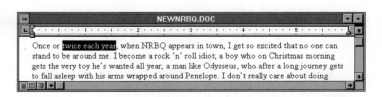

To select more text than appears on the screen, start your selection and drag past the top or bottom of the document window. Word will scroll the document and extend your selection until you re-lease the mouse button or until you move the cursor back into the document window. However, selecting text by dragging is best suited for relatively small blocks that fit on one screen. There are more efficient ways to select larger blocks.

How to select a word by double-clicking

To select an entire word with the mouse, simply double-click (press the mouse button twice in quick succession) anywhere on that word. Word will highlight the entire word and any space characters to its immediate right.

If you double-click on a word that is followed by a period, a comma, or some other delimiting character, you will not highlight the delimiting character. For example, if you double-click on the word *year* in the third line of our sample text, Word will highlight only the characters *year*—not the comma following that word or the space after the comma. Instead, punctuation characters are treated as separate words. In fact, if you double-click on the comma, Word will highlight the comma and the space.

How to extend a selection word by word

If you're familiar with selecting text by dragging in almost any Windows-based program, you probably know that when you extend a selection by dragging across text it's sometimes difficult to start and end the selection at the right place. The mouse is not a precision pointing device; sometimes you'll start a selection on the second or third character in a word when you wanted to start at the beginning, or you'll overshoot or undershoot the end of a word when you wanted to extend precisely to its end.

As we mentioned in Chapter 1, Word 6.0 includes a new option, Automatic Word Selection, that can make this selection task much easier. You can see the current setting for the option—and turn it on or off—by choosing Tools Options Edit. If you want the feature on, make sure the check box labeled Automatic Word Selection is checked. If you want it off, make sure it's not checked.

If Automatic Word Selection is on, you can start selecting text anywhere in a word. As soon as you extend past the end of that word, Word will select the entire word. In addition, each time you extend the selection into the next word, the program will select the full word.

If you don't always want to select complete words, you may well prefer to turn Automatic Word Selection off. Even with the feature off, however, you can get the same effect. Simply start by double-clicking on the first word you want in the selection, to highlight the whole word, and hold the button down on the second click. Then, as you drag the mouse to extend the selection, Word will extend it a full word at a time.

How to select a paragraph by triple-clicking

To select an entire paragraph with the mouse, simply triple-click (press the mouse button three times in quick succession) anywhere in the paragraph. Word will highlight the entire paragraph, including the paragraph mark.

You can continue to hold down the mouse button on the third click and drag to expand your selection a paragraph at a time.

How to select a sentence with Ctrl-click

Word also offers a simple technique for selecting an entire sentence. Just hold down Ctrl as you click anywhere in the sentence. Word will highlight the sentence, as well as the period and any blank characters after the sentence. If the sentence is the last one in a paragraph, Word will not highlight the paragraph mark, which it treats separately from the sentence.

You can continue to hold down the mouse button after a Ctrl-click and drag to expand your selection a sentence at a time.

How to select a block without dragging

Dragging the mouse to highlight line after line of text takes time. But Word offers a faster choice: the Shift-click method. First click at the beginning of the block you want to select. Then move the pointer to the end of the block, hold down the Shift key, and click. Word will highlight the entire block.

When you select a block with the Shift-Click technique, the end of the selection can be anywhere in the document and you can get there using any of the mouse navigation techniques we've discussed, as long as you don't click in the document window at any other position. You can also click at the end of the block first and then go to the beginning, and you can adjust the extent of the selection by holding down Shift and clicking again.

If the Automatic Word Selection on the Tools Options Edit card is cleared, Word will let you start and end the selection in midword. But if the check box is checked and you click in the middle of a word, your selection will automatically include the entire word.

How to select text by using the selection bar

Word has an invisible selection bar on the left side of the document window. Although you can't see it, you can use the selection bar to select a line, a paragraph, or the entire document. You will know you are in the selection bar when the mouse pointer changes to a right-pointing arrow.

To select an entire line of text, just move the pointer to the left side of the document window until it changes to the right-pointing arrow; then, with the arrow immediately to the left of the text, point to the line of text you want to select, and click. To select an entire paragraph, move your pointer to the selection bar and double-click.

To select the entire document, move the pointer to the selection bar and either triple-click or press the Ctrl key as you click once. This technique is particularly helpful when you need to make a global change to your document, such as changing the type style for all your text.

> You can set Word to show the formatting style for each paragraph at the left of the screen, in an area called the *style area*. To display the style area, choose Tools Options View and enter a setting in the Style Area Width text box. As Figure 3-13 shows, the selection bar lies between the left edge of the text and the right edge of the style area, indicated by the vertical line. If you move into the style area and click, you will select the entire paragraph. If you double-click, the Style dialog box will open. For details on styles and the style area, see Chapter 12.

FIGURE 3-13

You can use the style area to select a paragraph of text with the mouse.

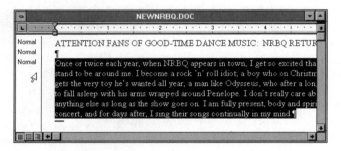

How to make column selections

Up to this point, all our selections have been for sequential blocks of characters—all the characters in a sentence, line, or paragraph. But there are times when you'll want to select only a vertical column of text, as with the table of text shown in Figure 3-14.

In Word 2.0, you could select a column of text by clicking the right mouse button. In Word 6.0, the right mouse button opens a context-sensitive menu. To select a column of text, position the pointer at one corner of the text you want to select. Next hold down the Alt key as you press the left mouse button, and drag to the opposite corner of the block. Word will highlight the text without regard for words, sentences, or paragraphs. If your document is in a proportional font, some of the characters in the selection may be only partially highlighted. When you make column selections, Word considers any character that is more than half highlighted to be part of the selection.

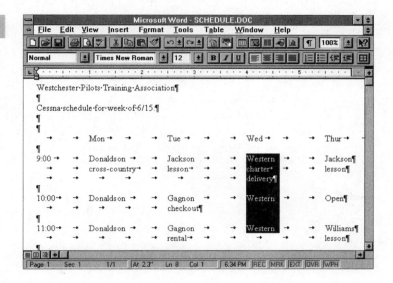

How to select with the keyboard

As with navigation, Word provides a full set of techniques for selecting text with the keyboard. And again, many people find it faster and easier to use the keyboard than to reach for the mouse.

How to use Extend Selection mode

One of the most useful selection tools is the Extend Selection key: F8. When you press F8, the letters *EXT* in the status bar turn solid and dark, indicating that Extend Selection mode is active. While you are in this mode, you can highlight text by using all the same keystrokes that you use for navigation, as listed in Figure 3-7 (except for Shift-F5, which cancels Extend mode). With Extend Selection active, however, these keystrokes will now select text as you move through your document. The initial position of the cursor serves as the anchor for one end of the selection. The cursor's current position marks the other end.

You can also turn Extend Selection mode on and off by double-clicking on the EXT indicator in the status bar at the bottom of the screen.

For example, if you press F8 and then press Ctrl-Right arrow, the cursor will move to the space following the current word and will highlight the text and the space simultaneously. Similarly, if you press F8 and then End, the

NEW!

cursor will move to the end of the current line, highlighting the text from the starting point to the end of the line. (You can also use the F8 key in combination with the mouse to extend a selection. Click at the beginning of the selection, press F8, and then click at the end of the selection.)

The F8 key has additional selection features. After you've pressed F8 once to turn on Extend Selection mode, you can press it a second time to highlight the word the cursor is currently in. Press it a third time to highlight the sentence the word is in, a fourth time to highlight the paragraph, and a fifth time to select the entire document. To cancel Extend Selection mode, press the Esc key and then any cursor-movement key to remove the highlight.

F8 has one more trick in its bag: searching for and extending the selection to a designated character. Press F8 once to activate Extend Selection mode; then press a key corresponding to any character: a letter, a number, or a punctuation mark. Word will search for the first occurrence of that character and highlight all text from the cursor through the character, including the character as part of the selection. At this point, you can press the key for the same character (or a different one) to extend the selection again.

For example, you can press F8 and then the period key to extend to the end of the current sentence; then repeatedly press the period key to extend the selection a sentence at a time. Similarly, you can press F8 and then the Enter key to extend to the end of the current paragraph; then repeatedly press Enter to extend the selection one paragraph at a time.

How to select with Shift-navigation keys

As an alternative to the Extend Selection method, you can hold down the Shift key to turn the navigation keys into selection keys. Place the cursor where you want to begin your selection, and then press and hold down Shift while using almost any of the keys listed in Figure 3-7. You will simultaneously move the cursor and highlight the text.

How to select the entire document

To select your entire document with the keyboard, press Ctrl-NumPad5 (the 5 key on the numeric keypad, found on the right side of most PC-compatible keyboards) or press the F8 key five times.

Basic Editing Techniques

The most common needs when you're editing text are inserting new characters, deleting existing characters, and overwriting the characters you want to change. These are also Word's most basic and most important editing techniques. Although we'll talk more about editing in Chapter 4, we'll introduce these techniques here because they relate closely to the selection and navigation techniques we've just explored.

As we mentioned earlier, Word wraps your text within a paragraph whenever you make editing or formatting changes. As you work with the insertion, deletion, and overwriting techniques, notice how Word reflows your text to adjust for the changes.

How to insert new text

Inserting text is as easy as typing, but first you have to be in Insert mode, not Overtype mode. In Insert mode, Word moves any text to the right of the cursor as you type. In Overtype mode, Word overwrites text to the right of the cursor. Press the Ins key several times; the OVR (for Overtype) flag should toggle on (dark text) and off (grayed) in the status bar with the repeated key presses. If it doesn't, you've probably set the Ins key for pasting. Choose Tools Options, choose the Edit tab, and clear the Use The INS Key For Paste check box. (If the status bar is not displayed, choose Tools Options, choose the View tab, and check the Status Bar check box.) Once you know how to turn the OVR flag on and off, make sure it is off.

Next, using keyboard or mouse, move the cursor to the spot where you want to insert the text. If you use the mouse, remember to reposition the cursor by moving the I-beam pointer to the desired spot and clicking. Then begin typing. As you type new characters, Word will push the existing characters to the right. Words at the end of the line will move to the beginning of the next line.

How to delete text

The easiest way to delete a character is to place the cursor to the right of it and press the Backspace key. Word will delete one character to the left of the cursor, pulling characters at the right of the cursor one space to the left. If you prefer, you can place the cursor to the left of the character you want to delete and press the Del key. In this case, Word will delete the character to the immediate right and move all following characters to the left.

To delete several characters at once, you can highlight them and then press either Backspace or Del. Word will delete the block and fill in the gap by pulling the remaining text in your document up and to the left.

If you press the Backspace key while your cursor is at the beginning of a line within a paragraph, Word will move the cursor to the end of the previous line and delete the last character in that line (usually a space). If this action joins two words, the newly joined word may be too long to fit on the previous line and may wrap to the line you started from. If you press Backspace while the cursor is at the beginning of a paragraph, Word will delete the paragraph mark at the end of the preceding paragraph and reflow your text to combine the two paragraphs.

 Word 2.0 would prevent you from deleting the paragraph marker between two paragraphs with different formatting. Word 6.0 no longer prevents this, however.

Deletion shortcuts

Word offers some keyboard shortcuts for deleting text. For example, instead of pressing the Backspace key to delete characters one at a time, you can press Ctrl-Backspace to delete everything from the cursor to the beginning of the word immediately left of the cursor. To delete the space to the right of the word as well, position the cursor to the right of that space before you press Ctrl-Backspace.

If you position the cursor in a word and press Ctrl-Backspace, Word will delete all the characters to the left of the cursor up to but not including the blank space that separates the current word from the previous word.

You can delete from the cursor to the end of the word at its *right* by pressing Ctrl-Del. If you position the cursor to the left of the first character of a word, Ctrl-Del will delete all of that word and the following space. If you position the cursor in the middle of a word, Ctrl-Del will delete all characters to the right of the cursor up to but not including the space that separates that word from the next.

How to overwrite text

Most users prefer to do all their editing in Insert mode and follow it up by deleting any text they mean to replace. In general, this is the safest procedure because you can easily retrieve the text you started with if you decide you want it back. However, you may prefer to write over the text you're replacing.

If so, you need to use Overtype mode, pressing the Ins key to toggle between it and Insert mode, as we discussed earlier in this chapter, in the section "How to Insert New Text."

After you toggle to Overtype mode (the OVR flag will appear as solid text in the status bar), all you need to do to overwrite text is move the cursor to the appropriate spot and start typing. The process is similar in concept to typing over characters on a typewriter except that Word fully replaces the existing characters you're typing over, leaving no telltale evidence that you've changed anything. Note that Word lets you overwrite text only within a paragraph. When you reach the end of the paragraph, anything more that you type stays in the same paragraph if you don't press Enter, or goes into a newly created paragraph if you do press Enter. Subsequent paragraphs move down, just as with Insert mode.

How to overwrite text by selecting it

Whether you are in Overtype mode or Insert mode, Word is set by default to delete any selected text when you start typing and replace it with the text you're typing. You can turn this option on or off by choosing Tools Options Edit and selecting or clearing the Typing Replaces Selection check box.

Be careful with the Typing Replaces Selection option. Unlike Overtype mode, which replaces one character at a time, the Typing Replaces Selection option immediately deletes all selected text as soon as you type a single character. If you are in Overtype mode as well, additional keystrokes will overtype additional text. But if you do accidentally delete a large block of text this way, don't panic. Word's multilevel undo feature will let you recover all the missing text. (We cover the undo feature later in this chapter, under "How to undo an action or multiple actions.")

Finally, be aware that you cannot overwrite a paragraph mark by selecting it and typing over it unless you select a block of text that ends after the paragraph mark. If you select a block that includes a paragraph mark and replace it by typing, Word will combine the current paragraph with the paragraph below it and will assign the paragraph formats from the second paragraph to the combined paragraph. For more details, see "Paragraph Formatting" on page 221.

How to cut text

In addition to the techniques we've discussed so far, Word provides the Edit Cut command, as well as the shortcut keys Shift-Del and Ctrl-X, for deleting text. You can also click on the Cut button—the one with the scissors icon—on the Standard toolbar to cut selected text. Unlike the deletion techniques, however, the Edit Cut command and equivalent shortcuts store the deleted text in a special place called the *Windows Clipboard*. Although the Clipboard is actually a large chunk of memory, you can think of it as a temporary storage place. For now, just note that after you place something on the Clipboard with the Edit Cut or Edit Copy command, you can paste the Clipboard's contents anywhere in your Word document (or, indeed, in documents in other programs) by using the Edit Paste command. We'll talk more about these commands and the Clipboard in the next chapter.

Canceling and Repeating Actions

When you insert, delete, or overwrite text, Word remembers your last set of keystrokes, as well as any text you deleted in the process. This short-term memory makes it possible to undo most editing changes or automatically repeat a command or another series of keystrokes.

How to undo an action or multiple actions

The Edit Undo command is one of the most important in Word because it gives you a second chance when you make a mistake or change your mind. To undo your most recent editing changes, simply choose Edit Undo, click the Undo button on the Standard toolbar, or press Ctrl-Z (or Alt-Backspace). Edit Undo can be a real lifesaver when you find that you have accidentally altered a critical passage of text.

Edit Undo is context sensitive; it changes to reflect your last action. If you insert new text or overtype selected text and then open the Edit menu, you'll see the Undo Typing command at the top of the menu. If you use the Del key to delete a selection, you'll see the Undo Clear command.

You can even undo an Edit Undo command. If you choose Edit Undo to undo some typing and then open the Edit menu again, the second menu command will be Redo Typing. Choose this command to restore the text.

One of the most powerful new features in Word 6.0 is its multiple-level Undo command. You can choose Edit Undo (or the Undo button on the Standard toolbar) repeatedly until you have completely reversed your edits.

There is also a drop-down list attached to the Undo button on the Standard toolbar. The list shows all the edits that can be undone. Simply pick the point you want to return to, click, and your work will be restored to its status at that point.

Be aware that the undo feature will undo *all* of your work back to the point you return to. If you realize you've made a mistake several steps earlier, however, you can still correct the mistake without losing the changes you've made since then.

Here's how to do it: Suppose, for example, that you've accidentally deleted a block of text and have since inserted additional text and added formatting. To retrieve the text, first give the Edit Undo command repeatedly until the deleted block of text reappears (or use the drop-down list to find the action you want to return to and go directly to that point). Then open a new document window with the File New command and copy the text to the new document, using any of Word's standard copy commands (such as Edit Copy and Edit Paste). Next return to the original document and use the Redo command to restore all of the changes you have just undone but wanted to keep. Finally copy the text back from the second document to the original.

The multiple-level undo feature can undo nearly any editing change, but keep in mind that there are other types of actions that can't be undone. For example, if you use the File Find File command to erase a file or you accidentally overwrite a file with the File Save As command, you won't be able to reverse those actions. The moral: Be careful when handling files.

How to repeat an action

As we've already mentioned, in addition to being able to undo your last action, you can also repeat it by using the Edit Repeat command.

Like the Edit Undo command, Edit Repeat is context sensitive, so it will change to reflect your last action. For example, if you use the Format Font command to change the format of some text, you'll see the command Repeat Font Formatting below the Undo Font Formatting command. You can then select blocks of widely separated text and reformat them one at a time by choosing Edit Repeat Font Formatting. The keyboard shortcut is Ctrl-Y or F4.

If your last action was an Undo operation, Edit Repeat becomes Edit Redo, and you can redo ("undo the undo" on) the operation that you've just undone. Like Undo, Redo (which is also available on the Standard toolbar, immediately to the right of the Undo button and drop-down list) can reverse multiple actions in sequence—which is handy in case you execute a number of Undo commands and overshoot the point where you wanted to stop. Unlike Undo, however, the Redo queue of commands is emptied as soon as you give a command other than Undo or Redo.

Where We Go from Here

The concepts and commands in this chapter form the basis for most of what you'll do when working with Word. If you learn nothing more than what's in this chapter, you'll be able to enter and edit text. In the next part of this book, we'll show you everything you need to know about entering and editing text, as well as about proofreading, formatting, and printing your text.

PART TWO

BASICS

TOPIC FINDER

Copying and Moving Text   99

- How to copy text
- How to move text
- How to use the mouse to drag and drop text
- How to replace text as you paste
- How to copy or move text between two documents
- Formatting issues
- NEW! How to use Smart Cut And Paste

Using the Edit Find and Edit Replace Commands   109

- How to search for text with the Edit Find command
- How to replace text with the Edit Replace command
- More on editing

4

Editing Text

n Chapter 3, we covered the most basic editing tasks: how to enter, select, delete, and overwrite text. However, there are at least two other editing tools that almost any Word user is likely to need on a daily basis.

These core tools are the cut-and-paste feature and the search-and-replace feature. We'll cover both in this chapter. Keep in mind that, as we discussed in Chapter 3, your first task in editing often is to select the text you want to change. As you practice with the features we'll discuss here, you may find it helpful to refer back to the selection and navigation techniques covered in Chapter 3; learning how to select text quickly will speed your editing significantly.

Copying and Moving Text

Word's Edit Cut, Edit Copy, and Edit Paste commands are the scissors and glue that make editing a snap. With just a few keystrokes or mouse clicks, you can reorganize your document or duplicate a block of text—perhaps to edit it experimentally or to add a copy of it elsewhere in a document. You can also copy or move items from one Word document to another, or even between Word and another program. In this chapter, we'll cover copying and moving text within Word. In Chapter 18, "Sharing Data with Other Programs," page 618, we'll show you how to share information with other programs.

In general, you copy or move text in Word by selecting the text and then choosing the location where you want to insert, or paste, it. You can also copy formats without text; we'll come back to formatting issues after we look at the Edit Cut, Edit Copy, and Edit Paste commands.

How to copy text

Rather than retyping a given block of text when you need a copy, you can use the Edit Copy command to copy the text to the Windows Clipboard, which is a temporary holding area for data, and then use the Edit Paste command to paste the text in one or more locations in your document. For obvious reasons, the Edit Copy command can save a great deal of time when you need to duplicate more than a word or two.

To copy a block of text, first select it, and then choose the Edit Copy command or click on the Copy button on the Standard toolbar. Next position the cursor where you want the copied block to appear, and choose Edit Paste or click on the Paste button on the Standard toolbar. Word will insert a copy of the text to the left of the cursor, leaving the cursor at the end of the pasted block. The original block of text will remain unchanged.

It's often a good idea to work on a copy of your text rather than on the original. Suppose, for example, that you're working with the document shown in Figure 4-1, and you're not happy with the first paragraph of body

FIGURE 4-1

You need a copy of the first paragraph to edit experimentally while leaving the original untouched.

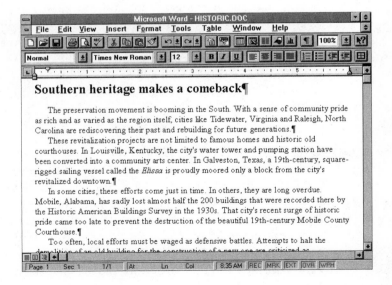

text. Instead of working with the existing paragraph, and perhaps needing to restore it to its original form if you decide you don't like your changes, you can select the entire paragraph, choose Edit Copy, position the cursor to the left of the first word in the paragraph, and choose Edit Paste. You can then work with the duplicate paragraph, as shown in Figure 4-2.

FIGURE 4-2

When you choose the Edit Paste command, Word will insert the copied paragraph just before the cursor. The copied paragraph in this case is the first paragraph of body text.

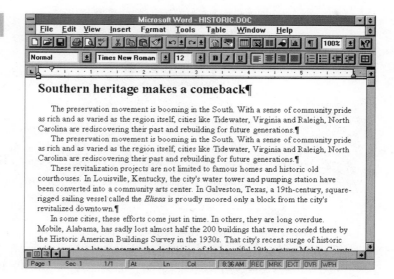

Keyboard shortcuts for copying text

Keyboard shortcuts make the copying process even easier. After you've selected a block of text, press Ctrl-C or Ctrl-Ins to copy the text to the Windows Clipboard. Then move to where you want the text to appear, and press Ctrl-V or Shift-Ins to paste. You'll also find a check box on the Tools Options Edit card that lets you designate the Ins key by itself for pasting.

The Windows Clipboard

We've mentioned the Windows Clipboard several times in describing the Edit Copy and Edit Paste commands. You can view the Clipboard's contents at any time by opening the Clipboard window. Simply choose the Clipboard Viewer icon, which will normally be in the Main group in the Windows Program Manager. Figure 4-3 on the next page shows the contents of the Clipboard after you copied the paragraph from the document shown in Figure 4-2.

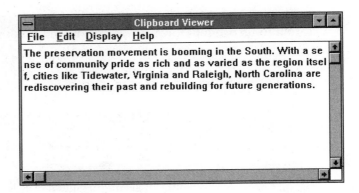

FIGURE 4-3

The Clipboard window contains the last selection you cut or copied.

If you've copied text to the Clipboard but you can't see it in the Clipboard Viewer, you may need to adjust the display option in the Viewer by choosing the Display Text command. If there is nothing on the Clipboard, the Display menu will be grayed on the menu bar.

You can also use the Clipboard's File Save As command to save the Clipboard's contents in a file with the CLP extension. You can open the file later, with the Clipboard's File Open command, to insert the contents in Word or another program.

Although the Clipboard can accommodate a text block of any size—from one character to an entire document (memory permitting)—it's important to understand that the Clipboard can hold only one selection at a time. If you select text and choose the Edit Copy or Edit Cut command (which we'll discuss shortly) and then make another selection and choose either command again, Word will erase the first selection from the Clipboard and replace it with the second. Of course, if you copied the first block of text, you have lost nothing but time. But if you cut the first block of text and then cut or copied another block of text before pasting the first one, you'll lose the first block. If you want to collect a series of items, see "Using the Spike" starting on page 151.

If you lose a block of text this way, you can recover it with the Edit Undo command. This command will not undo the changes to the Clipboard, but it will recover the lost text, placing the text back in your document in its original position, without affecting the contents of the Clipboard.

Once text is on the Clipboard, and until you overwrite it with another Edit Cut or Edit Copy command, you can paste it as many times as you like. Windows will remember the Clipboard contents even if you choose other commands or edit your document before you paste. You can also open and edit new documents (or even move to a different program) without losing the current contents of the Clipboard. However, the Clipboard contents are lost when you exit Windows or when you turn your computer off.

How to copy text without using the Clipboard

In some situations, you'll want to copy text without using the Clipboard. For example, the Clipboard may already contain text that you want to paste later, but you need to perform another copy operation first.

This is where Word's Copy To feature comes in handy. Start by highlighting the text you want to copy. Then place the mouse pointer where you want to paste a copy of the text, and hold down the Ctrl and Shift keys while you click the right mouse button.

If you prefer using the keyboard, highlight the text and press Shift-F2. Word displays a prompt in the status bar (assuming the status bar is showing) that asks *Copy to where?* Move the cursor to the new position (where it is displayed as a dotted line rather than the usual solid line), and press Enter to insert the copy.

If you like, you can designate the copy destination first. Place the cursor where you want the text to go, and then press Shift-F2. The prompt asks *Copy from where?* When you select the text, Word marks it with a dotted underline. Press Enter to complete the copy.

How to move text

Moving a block of text is similar to copying one, except that Word removes the block from its original location. To use the Clipboard to move text, select a block of text, choose Edit Cut, move to the new location, and then paste the text by choosing Edit Paste.

Keyboard shortcuts for moving text

The keyboard shortcuts for cutting text are Ctrl-X and Shift-Del; like Ctrl-C and Ctrl-Ins, both shortcuts give the same result. Pasting text that was cut to the Clipboard is the same as pasting text that was copied to the Clipboard. Move to where you want the text to appear, and press Ctrl-V or Shift-Ins to paste.

How to move text without using the Clipboard

As it does for copy operations, Word also has move options that bypass the Clipboard. Start by selecting the text you want to move. Then place the mouse pointer where you want to move the text, hold down the Ctrl key, and click the right mouse button. To use the keyboard instead, press F2 after selecting the text. Word will respond with a prompt in the status bar that asks *Move to where?* Position the cursor and press Enter to move the block.

As you can with the Copy To feature, you can designate the destination first, before pressing F2. Select the text in response to the *Move from where?* prompt, and press Enter to complete the move.

If you forget the shortcuts for the Clipboard operations, you can open the Edit menu and look at the keyboard shortcuts that appear to the right of the appropriate commands. Figure 4-4 summarizes the keyboard shortcuts for Edit Cut, Edit Copy, and Edit Paste and the shortcuts for copying and moving without the Clipboard.

Command	Keyboard Shortcut
With the Clipboard	
Cut	Ctrl-X or Shift-Del
Copy	Ctrl-C or Ctrl-Ins
Paste	Ctrl-V or Shift-Ins (or Ins when Use The INS KEY For Paste option is turned on)
Without the Clipboard	
Copy	Shift-F2
Move	F2

FIGURE 4-4

Keyboard shortcuts for cutting, copying, and pasting.

How to use the mouse to drag and drop text

For those who like to use the mouse, there is one more way to move or copy a block of text: by dragging with the mouse. First select the text you want to move or copy, and then place the mouse pointer anywhere in the selection. To move the text, click and hold down the left mouse button. A gray box appears at the bottom of the pointer, and a dotted vertical line is displayed in your text to the left or right of the pointer. Hold down the button while you drag to a new position, using the vertical line to indicate where Word should insert the text. When you release the button, Word will move the text, dropping it into place.

To copy text by dragging and dropping, follow the same procedure, but press the Ctrl key before releasing the mouse button and hold down the key until after you release the button.

Some users will find the drag-and-drop feature intuitive and useful. Others won't like it because it affects selection procedures: If you highlight text with the mouse when the drag-and-drop feature is active and then decide you want to select a smaller portion of that text, you must remove the highlight completely before changing the selection. Fortunately for both groups of users, you can turn this feature on and off by checking or clearing the Drag-And-Drop Text Editing check box on the Tools Options Edit card. For more details about the drag-and-drop feature, see "Essential Customization Options" starting on page 33.

How to replace text as you paste

Whether you are copying or moving text, you can have Word paste over, or replace, an existing block of text when you paste the copied or moved text. First be sure that the Typing Replaces Selection check box on the Tools Options Edit card is checked. Then cut or copy the text you want to paste. Select the text you want to replace, and choose the Edit Paste command.

Returning to the sample document shown in Figure 4-1 on page 100, suppose you want to replace the last sentence in the first paragraph of body text with the last two sentences from the second paragraph. Highlight the last two sentences of the second paragraph and choose Edit Copy. Next highlight the last sentence of the first paragraph and choose Edit Paste. As shown in Figure 4-5 on the next page, Word will overwrite the highlighted text with the copied text.

If the Typing Replaces Selection feature doesn't suit the way you work, remember that you can turn off the feature by clearing the Typing Replaces Selection check box on the Tools Options Edit card. For more information about using this feature, see "Essential Customization Options" starting on page 33.

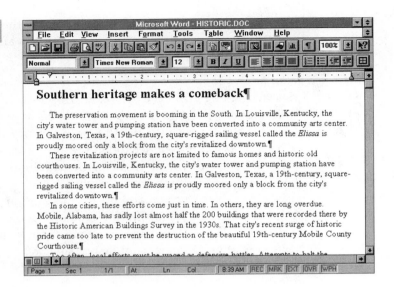

FIGURE 4-5

If you select a block of text before you paste and the Typing Replaces Selection option is on, Word will overwrite the selected text when you paste.

How to copy or move text between two documents

Occasionally you may want to use the same block of text in two or more Word documents or move text from one document to another—between two chapters of a book, for example. Rather than retyping the text, you can copy or move the original block. For example, consider the two document windows shown in Figure 4-6. Suppose you want to copy the paragraph that appears in the top document window (SALES1.DOC) and place it after the first paragraph in the second document (SALES2.DOC). (To display two documents at the same time, open both files and then choose Window Arrange All. This command splits the Word window horizontally to display both document windows.)

To copy the paragraph, first activate the SALES1 document window, highlight the paragraph, and choose Edit Copy or click on the Copy button. Next activate the SALES2 document window, move the cursor to the left of the word *As* in the second paragraph, and choose Edit Paste or click on the Paste button. As shown in Figure 4-7, Word will insert a copy of the paragraph in the SALES2 document window. When you want to move text rather than copy it, simply use Edit Cut instead of Edit Copy. Just as it does when you are working within a single document, Windows will remember your copied block until you choose Edit Cut or Edit Copy again or until you quit Windows.

FIGURE 4-6

You want to copy the paragraph from the top document window into the bottom document window.

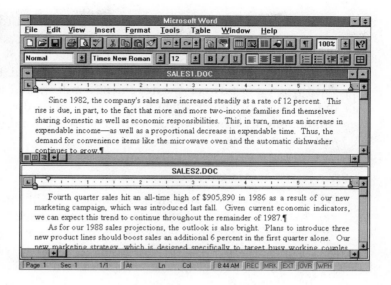

FIGURE 4-7

A copy of the paragraph now appears in the bottom document window as well.

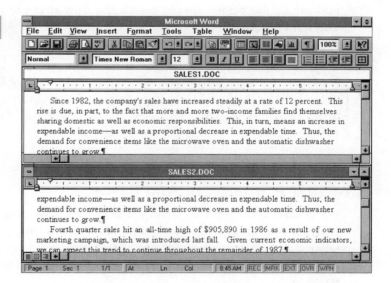

Note that you can use Word's File menu commands to open new documents and retrieve existing files in order to paste text into them or to cut or copy text from them. Similarly, you can use the Window menu commands to move to any open document window before pasting.

If you prefer to use the drag-and-drop method for copying or moving text, you'll find that Word 6.0 will also let you drag and drop between windows. Simply select the text you want to move or copy, and drag it from one document window to another. The mouse pointer will become a circle with a slash when it is between the document windows and will turn back into the drag-and-drop pointer when you move it into a document again. If you're running multiple instances of Word in separate windows, you can also drag and drop between these windows.

Formatting issues

When you copy or move a block of text, Word will generally retain the original character formatting of the text when it pastes the characters in the new location. Similarly, when you copy or move an entire paragraph, Word will retain the paragraph formatting of the copied or moved text, provided that you include the paragraph mark (¶) in the selection.

In either case, you may need to revise the character and paragraph formatting of the pasted text to match the formatting of the surrounding text. You'll find these formatting issues covered in Chapter 7, page 206, along with shortcuts for adjusting the formatting of pasted text.

Note that when you drag text between different instances of Word, changes in format follow somewhat different rules. In general, copied text will take on the same format as the paragraph into which you paste the text.

How to use Smart Cut And Paste

Word has an option that makes it easier to paste text into an existing sentence or paragraph. On the Tools Options Edit card, you'll find a check box labeled *Use Smart Cut And Paste*. If this option is checked, Word will do its best to preserve correct spacing between words and punctuation when you paste text.

For example, assume you've copied a block of text that has a space at the end, such as "block of text ". If Smart Cut And Paste is not turned on and you paste this block immediately after the first word of the phrase "paste here", you will get "pasteblock of text here"—with no space between *paste* and *block*, but with two spaces between *text* and *here*. When the Smart Cut And Paste option is turned on, however, Word will automatically insert a space between the first two words and remove the extra space between the last two. This feature can be a worthwhile time-saver, and we recommend that you use it.

Using the Edit Find and Edit Replace Commands

Like most word processors, Word lets you search through a document for a particular word or a sequence of characters. It also lets you search for a character sequence and replace it with a different one. Typically, the character sequence—often called a *string* of characters, or a *text string*—will be one or two words. It can, however, be several sentences long.

Searching and replacing are two of the most useful features in any word processing program. Word takes these features a step further than most by letting you look for and change formats and styles as well as characters. In this section, we'll show you how to use the Edit Find and Edit Replace commands. As you'll see, there are some less-than-obvious ways to use these features and some potential problems you need to be aware of.

How to search for text with the Edit Find command

To search for a character sequence, choose Edit Find to open the dialog box shown in Figure 4-8. When it first appears, you'll see a blinking cursor in the Find What text box. Type the characters you want to locate (we'll refer to this as your *search text*), and then choose Find Next to begin the search.

FIGURE 4-8

To search for a specific character sequence, enter your search text in the Find What text box.

The Find What text box can show only about 30 to 40 characters, depending on your display and the characters in the search text, although the search text itself can be as long as 255 characters. Text on the left side of the box will scroll out of view as you type beyond the right end of the text box, but you can bring the hidden portion into view by using the Left or Right arrow key (or the Ctrl-Left or Ctrl-Right key combination) to move left or right or by using the mouse to drag to the left or right. You can also jump to the beginning or end of the search text with the Home and End keys.

You can click on the down arrow at the right end of the Find What box (or press Alt-Down arrow key) to open a list box that shows the last four text strings you searched for during the current Word session.

Below the Find What text box is the Search text box, which defaults to All if no text is selected. The drop-down list for this box offers two other options: Down and Up. The All setting tells Word to begin the search at the current cursor location, scan forward to the end of the document, and then continue the search from the start of the document to the search's starting position. The Down setting tells Word to scan forward from the cursor location to the end of the document. The Up setting tells Word to search backward from the cursor location to the beginning of the document.

Choose Find Next to begin a search. If you're searching with the Down option selected and with the cursor located anywhere other than before the first character of the file, Word will display the message box shown in Figure 4-9 when it reaches the end of the document. If you're using the Up option, you'll see a similar message when you reach the beginning. In either case, if you want Word to jump to the other end of the document and continue the search, choose Yes. If you want to halt the search, choose No.

FIGURE 4-9

To continue a search from the beginning of your document, choose Yes in response to this message box.

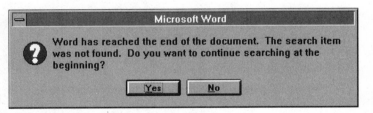

Regardless of the setting in the Search box, if Word reaches the starting point for the search without finding a match, it will halt and display the message box shown in Figure 4-10.

FIGURE 4-10

Word will display this message box if it cannot find the search text.

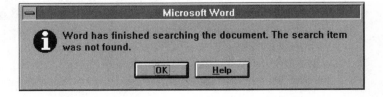

If Word does find your search text, it will scroll the found text into view, highlight the match on screen, and halt the search. You can then choose Cancel to close the Find dialog box, leaving the cursor at that location, or you can continue searching by choosing Find Next again. If you choose Cancel, you have two choices for continuing the search later: You can use the Edit Find command again and choose Find Next, or you can press Shift-F4 to repeat the search.

If you close the dialog box and then press Shift-F4 to continue searching, Word will not redisplay the Find dialog box. Rather, it will immediately scan for the search text you last typed in the Find What box. In fact, the search text will not change until you replace it, remove it, or quit Word. You can even open another document file to search for the same text in another document. However, the next time you choose the Edit Find command, Word will highlight the contents of the Find What text box so that you can overwrite the search text easily.

You can close the Find dialog box to edit the found text, but you don't have to. If you press Ctrl-Tab or point to the document with the mouse and click, Word will leave the Find dialog box on the screen but will activate the document so that you can edit it. If you need to edit a substantial amount of text, you can also use the standard Windows keystrokes or mouse actions to move the dialog box out of the way. When you finish editing, you can press Ctrl-Tab or click on the dialog box again to return to it.

If Word did not find the text you were searching for, but you're nevertheless convinced that the text is in the document, check the entry in the Find dialog box carefully. Keep in mind that unless you've told Word otherwise (in ways that we'll get to shortly) Word looks for exact matches. If you've entered extra blank spaces or typed a character incorrectly in the Find What text box, Word won't be able to locate the search text. (Capitalization doesn't matter unless you have checked the Match Case check box, which we'll also cover in a moment.)

Note that you can paste text into the Find What text box. If you spot one instance of your search text in your document, you can highlight it, copy it by pressing Ctrl-C, and paste it into the Find What box by pressing Ctrl-V or Shift-Ins. This should guarantee that the string is entered correctly. Of course, you may still have trouble finding a match if you have mistyped the text in your document.

You can also use the Edit Find command to jump quickly to any part of your document—to make revisions, for example. Suppose you want to edit a section of your text that comes immediately after the heading *Part II*. You can search for *Part II*, and Word will take you to that section heading, where you can revise the text as necessary.

How to use the options in the Find dialog box

The Find dialog box offers four check boxes: Match Case, Find Whole Words Only, Use Pattern Matching, and Sounds Like.

Match Case. With the Match Case option, you can limit your search to instances of the search text that exactly match the capitalization of what you enter in the Find What text box. If you don't check the Match Case check box, Word will ignore case (uppercase and lowercase) when it looks for the search text. For example, if you enter *Microsoft* as the search text and do not check Match Case, Word will also find *microsoft*, *MicroSoft*, and *MICROSOFT*. If you use Match Case, however, Word will find only *Microsoft*.

The Match Case option can be helpful when you're searching for a proper noun that has the same spelling as a common noun. Suppose, for example, you want to search for a reference to the Word program. To avoid stopping for the word *word*, simply enter *Word* as your search text and then be sure to check the Match Case check box. This option can also be useful if you're looking for a word or phrase that you know is at the beginning of a sentence.

Using the Match Case option has one possible disadvantage. If you've accidentally used the improper case in some instances in your text—typing the name of the software as *word* or *WOrd* instead of *Word*—the search will not find these occurrences. For the greatest assurance that you've found all the instances of a word—to check the correct case throughout the document, for example—it's safer to cast a wider net.

Find Whole Words Only. The Find Whole Words Only option is useful when you're searching for a short word, such as *action*, that is also likely to be contained within a larger word. Unless you check this check box, Word will also find text that occurs within another word. For example, if you search for *action*, Word will stop for such matches as *reactionary* and *actionable*. By checking the Find Whole Words Only check box, you're telling Word to ignore these matches.

On the other hand, performing a search without the Find Whole Words Only option can often be useful. For example, if you can't remember whether you wrote *We will look at...* or *We'll be looking at...,* you can search for *look* and find either phrase. Of course, if Word is finding many unwanted matches during a search, you can always turn on the Find Whole Words Only option at any time.

Use Pattern Matching. The Use Pattern Matching option determines whether Word looks for an exact match for the characters you enter in the Find What text box or interpret's them as pattern symbols. For example, the question mark is the MS-DOS wildcard character for matching any symbol. If you enter *th?* in the Find What text box and check the Use Pattern Matching check box, Word will treat *the* as a match as well as matching *th?* in a sentence such as *Did you finish fourth?* On the other hand, if you type *th?* and don't check the Use Pattern Matching check box, Word will look for a literal match, matching *th?* but not *the.*

There is much more to be said about pattern matching. We'll cover the feature in detail shortly.

Sounds Like. The fourth check box, Sounds Like, is one of Word's most sophisticated search options. It lets you match words even when their spelling differs from the spelling used in the search text. For example, if you type *nyff* or *nighf* in the Find What text box and check the Sounds Like check box, Word will treat *knife* as a match. The feature has its limitations, however; while *numona* will match *pneumonia,* for example, *numonya* will not (even though the spelling checker will correctly suggest *pneumonia* as the correct spelling for *numonya* but not *numona*). Note that Use Pattern Matching and Sounds Like are exclusive; you can have only one active at a time.

How to use pattern matching

Word's pattern-matching feature lets you cast a wider net when looking for matches. As we just discussed, Word will take advantage of pattern matching only if you have checked the Use Pattern Matching check box in the Find dialog box (or in the Replace dialog box, which we'll discuss later in this chapter).

Assuming you've checked the Use Pattern Matching check box, Word will recognize the question mark symbol (?) as a wildcard character, just as MS-DOS does. Each question mark in your search text will match any one character in a potential match. For example, if you enter *ba?e* as your search text, Word will find *bale, base, bane,* and *bake.*

Also as MS-DOS does, Word can use the asterisk (*) to match any number of characters. For example, the search text *ba*e* not only will find *bale, base, bane,* and *bake* but also will match *balance, backstage,* and *baccalaureate.*

Unlike the question mark, the asterisk will also match zero characters; in other words, the search text *ba*e* would match *bae* in the preceding example.

One minor problem with using the asterisk wildcard is that you can't then limit the search to whole words only. Look for *ba*e*, for example, and Word will also match the *base* in *baseball*. Nor can you limit the search to whole words by adding a space at the end of the search text. If you try, Word will then look for the next word that ends with *e*. For example, if you end one paragraph with the words *baseball park* and start the next with *Whatever happened to the...*, Word will match everything from *baseball* through *the*, including the period and the paragraph mark. The moral: You'll want to verify each match carefully when using the asterisk as a wildcard.

Square brackets ([ ]) serve a number of purposes. If you put two or more letters between the brackets, Word will match any one of the letters in that position. For example, *ba[lr]e* will match *bale* and *bare*. Put two letters separated by a hyphen within the brackets to define a range; *ba[k-n]* will match *bake*, *bale*, and *bane*. Put an exclamation mark before the first character within the brackets to match any word that does *not* have the specified characters in that position. For example, *ba[!rs]e* will not match *bare* or *base* but will match *bake* and *bale*. Similarly, you can put an exclamation mark before a range of characters within the brackets (indicated by a hyphen), and Word will match any word that does *not* contain any of the characters in the range in that position. For example, *ba[!m-z]e* will not match *bare* or *base* but will match *bake* and *bale*.

Curly brackets ({}) indicate numeric patterns. A number within the brackets will match any word with exactly that number of adjacent occurrences of the prior character; *be{2}*, for example, will match *beers* and *bee* but not *bed*. Including a number and a comma requires at least that many occurrences of the prior character; *be{1,}*, for example, will match *beers*, *bee*, and *bed*. Two numbers separated by a comma indicate a range of occurrences of the prior character; *10{1,3}* will match *10*, *100*, or *1000* but not *1*. (It will also match *10000*, which is *1000* plus an extra *0*.)

The @ symbol signals one or more occurrences of the prior character. For example, *be@r* will match *berry* or *beer*.

The less than (<) and greater than (>) symbols will let you match characters at the beginning or end of a word. Type *<ho* in the Find What box to match *how*, *house*, and *hose* but not *roughhouse*. Type *ge>* in the Find What box to match *huge*, *rouge*, and *page* but not *get*.

Finally, you can use parentheses to group characters and to control the sequence of matching, in much the same way you use parentheses to control the order of processing in arithmetic or algebraic expressions.

How to search for a pattern-matching character

If you have checked the Use Pattern Matching check box and you need to use one or more of the pattern-matching characters (or *operators*) as a literal match, simply precede the character with a backslash (\). For example, to search for a question mark when the pattern-matching feature is turned on, type \? to have Word match literal question marks rather than matching any character.

If you want to search for a question that begins with *Why*, you can turn on pattern matching and type *(Why)*\? in the Find What box. To search for a literal backslash character when the Use Pattern Matching check box is checked, you need to type a second backslash (like this: \\).

If you're familiar with Word 2.0, you may be familiar with using the caret (^) to designate a literal interpretation of a pattern-matching character. Word 6.0 does not recognize the caret for this purpose, but, like Word 2.0, it recognizes the caret as an indicator of special characters, such as ^t to indicate a tab. To search for a caret when pattern matching is turned on, you must type ^^.

How to find special characters

Another useful feature of the Edit Find command is that it can find special characters such as paragraph marks, non-breaking spaces, and optional hyphens. Word even provides a feature that will automatically insert most of the relevant codes for special characters into the Find What text box for you.

Figure 4-11 shows the list that opens when you choose the Special button at the bottom of the Find dialog box without checking the Use Pattern

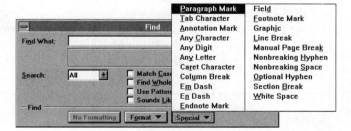

FIGURE 4-11

When you choose the Special button in the Find dialog box without pattern matching, Word will display this list of special characters whose codes can be added to the Find What text box.

Matching check box. The location and shape of this box can vary, depending on the position of the Find dialog box on your screen when you choose Special. To insert a special search code in the Find What text box, simply select the element you want to find from the selection box, and Word will insert the appropriate code.

When the Use Pattern Matching feature is turned on, Word will not recognize certain codes for special characters—those for paragraph marks or for blank space, for example. It will recognize others, however, such as ^t for tab. Note that choosing the Special button when pattern matching is turned on produces a different set of entries in the selection box, as shown in Figure 4-12.

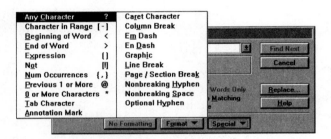

If you know the code for the special character you want to find, you can type the code directly into the Find What text box. The table in Figure 4-13 lists the characters you can search for and gives the corresponding keyboard code for each. At the risk of getting ahead of ourselves, but to make this a more useful reference, we've also listed several codes that you can use only when replacing text. We'll come back to these codes later in this chapter, in "How to replace text with the Edit Replace command" on page 121, which covers Word's search-and-replace feature.

This Code...	Represents This Character...
Codes that work in the Find What or Replace With box	
^t	Tab mark (→)
^0nnn	ANSI character in *nnn* (decimal) form (case-sensitive when pattern matching is on)
^nnn	OEM character in *nnn* (decimal) form (case-sensitive when pattern matching is on)

(continued)

FIGURE 4-13

Search-and-replace codes for special characters.

FIGURE 4-13 *continued*

This Code...	Represents This Character...
Codes that work in the Find What or Replace With box *(continued)*	
^^	Caret character (single caret also finds a single caret whenpattern matching is not on; to find two carets, you must enter four carets)
^n	Column break (dotted line across a column)
^l	Line-break character (⏎)
^m	Manual page break (also matches section breaks when pattern matching is on)
^-	Em dash
^=	En dash
^s	Non-breaking space (°)
^~	Non-breaking hyphen
^-	Optional hyphen (¬)
^p	Paragraph mark (¶) (only works in the Find What text box when pattern matching is not on)
Codes that work in the Find What box only	
^a	Annotation reference
^g	Any graphic
Codes that work in the Find What box only and work only when pattern matching is on	
?	Question mark (treated as a character otherwise)
*	Asterisk (treated as a character otherwise)
Codes that work in the Find What box only and work only when pattern matching is off	
^e	Endnote
^d	Field
^f	Footnote
^b	Section break (when pattern matching is on, *^m* matches both page and section breaks)
^w	White space (any combination of normal spaces, non-breaking spaces, and tab marks)
^?	Any character (equivalent to *?* used by itself when pattern matching is on)
^#	Any digit
^$	Any letter
Codes that work in the Replace With box only	
^c	Clipboard contents
^&	Find What text box contents

The codes used to search for special characters are case-sensitive; you must use lowercase letters. If you're moving to Word 6.0 from Word 2.0, note also that some of these codes in Word 6.0 differ from those in Word 2.0.

Several codes listed in Figure 4-13, such as ^w, need further explanation. When you specify ^w as your search text, Word will find the blank space that appears between any two printing characters in your document, including the single spaces between words, as well as tabs. This ^w code will not treat paragraph marks as white space.

The codes for ANSI and OEM characters in decimal form also require some explanation. You can search for any ANSI character by entering a caret followed by a zero and the character's three-digit ANSI code. For example, if you enter ^0097 as your search text, Word will find every occurrence of the letter *a*. Even though 097 is the ANSI code for a lowercase *a* and 065 is the code for an uppercase *A*, Word will find every *a*, regardless of case, unless you check either the Match Case check box or the Use Pattern Matching check box.

To search for an OEM character, enter a caret followed by the character's three-digit OEM code—without the extra zero needed when searching by ANSI code. Searching by OEM codes will treat case the same way as searching by ANSI codes. Note too that the first 126 character codes are the same for both the OEM and ANSI character sets. For a list of ANSI and OEM codes, see Appendix B, page 995.

Word can find many special characters even when they're not visible on the screen. For example, if you haven't checked the Paragraph Marks check box on the Tools Options View card, the paragraph mark at the end of each paragraph will not be displayed on your screen. However, if you search for the code ^p, Word will highlight the space following each paragraph. Similarly, Word can find tab marks, optional hyphens, and end-of-line markers even when they aren't displayed.

Be aware that your search text can include any combination of special characters and other text. For example, to find every instance of a paragraph that begins with *For*, you can choose the Edit Find command and enter ^pFor in the Find What text box. When you choose OK, Word will highlight the paragraph mark at the end of the preceding paragraph as well as the word *For* at the beginning of the following paragraph.

How to find hidden text

Word cannot find matches in text that has been formatted as hidden unless you first set the program to display the hidden text. If hidden text is currently hidden from view, you can display it either by clicking on the Show/Hide ¶ button on the Standard toolbar or by checking the Hidden Text check box on the Tools Options View card. You can then begin the search.

How to find formatting attributes and styles

As mentioned earlier in this chapter, Word lets you search not only for a character sequence but for font, paragraph, and style formats as well. You even have the choice of searching for a format by itself or in combination with a particular character sequence. For example, suppose you use the Heading 3 style at the start of each section in a document. By searching for the style, you can rapidly move from section to section using Shift-F4 to repeat the last Edit Find command. Similarly, you can go to a particular heading by searching for both the style and a keyword in that heading. For information about styles, see Chapter 12, "Styles & AutoFormat," starting on page 418.

At the bottom of the Find dialog box, shown in Figure 4-8 on page 109, are the No Formatting and Format buttons. Until you specify some formatting as part of your search text, the No Formatting button will remain grayed. If you specify a format as part of the search text, however, the button will become available, and you can choose it to remove the format from the search criteria.

Choose the Format button, and Word will offer a menu with four choices: Font, Paragraph, Language, and Style. The Font, Paragraph, and Style choices open the Find Font, Find Paragraph, and Find Style dialog boxes, which are similar to the formatting dialog boxes you'll see when you choose the Format Font, Format Paragraph, and Format Style commands. The Language choice opens the Find Language dialog box, which is similar to the dialog box available when you choose Tools Language. In all of the dialog boxes available through the Format button, you can specify which format and language attributes to search for, using essentially the same procedure you would use to assign those attributes to your text.

Because these dialog boxes are essentially identical to the dialog boxes used for applying formats, we won't work through each one here. Note, however, that when designating formats to search for or replace, you have three choices, as opposed to the two you have when assigning formats. For example, when you assign formats, you must define text as either bold or not bold. But when searching or replacing, you can specify that the text must be bold, that it must not be bold, or that it can be either. Unless you specify otherwise, Word will assume that any given type of format—bold, italic, typeface, font size, and so on—is irrelevant. But if you open the various dialog boxes available through the Format button, you can specify those formats you want to look for.

Note too that in these dialog boxes, the check boxes can toggle through three states: gray (the default) to indicate that the state for that format option doesn't matter; blank to indicate that you want to match only text that lacks that format; or checked to indicate that you want to match only text that has that format. In much the same way, you can leave text boxes blank to tell Word to ignore the setting for that format; any entry in a text box will restrict matches to matching formats. For details on the various formats and on how to use the formatting dialog boxes, take a look at "Paragraph formatting" on page 221 and "Font formatting" on page 241. You'll also want to refer to all of Chapter 12, "Styles & AutoFormat," starting on page 418, which includes a discussion of the Language dialog box.

Keyboard shortcuts for format attributes and styles in Find. For those who prefer keyboard shortcuts, Word offers shortcuts for specifying most common formatting attributes in the Find dialog box. For example, pressing Ctrl-B when the Find dialog box is open lets you cycle through the attributes Bold, Not Bold, or either, without opening the Find Font dialog box. Figure 4-14 lists all these shortcut keys. (You can use the same shortcuts to specify formats for replacement text, as we'll describe in the next section.)

If you're familiar with the shortcut keys in Word 2.0, you'll find that some of the keys listed in Figure 4-14, such as Ctrl-B for bold, are the same as the shortcuts you're used to. But you'll also find that some have changed, so be sure to look over the list.

Press This...	To Specify This Format...
Keys that do not toggle the setting off	
Ctrl-Shift-A	All caps
Ctrl-Shift-K	Small caps
Ctrl-Shift-F	Font name—each keypress scrolls forward through the list of available fonts
Ctrl-Shift-P	Font size—each keypress displays the next font size in half-point increments, starting at 1 point

(continued)

FIGURE 4-14

Keyboard shortcuts for specifying formats when searching or replacing.

FIGURE 4-14 *continued*

Press This...	To Specify This Format...
Keys that do not toggle the setting off *(continued)*	
Ctrl-1	Single spacing
Ctrl-2	Double spacing
Ctrl-5	1½ spacing
Keys that toggle the setting on and off	
Ctrl-E	Centered alignment
Ctrl-J	Justified alignment
Ctrl-L	Left alignment
Ctrl-R	Right alignment
Keys that toggle between three states: attribute included in the search, attribute excluded, and attribute ignored	
Ctrl-=	Subscript
Ctrl-Shift-=	Superscript
Ctrl-B	Bold
Ctrl-Shift-D	Double underline
Ctrl-Shift-H	Hidden
Ctrl-I	Italic
Ctrl-N	New text entered while Word was in Mark Revisions mode
Ctrl-U	Underline
Ctrl-Shift-W	Word underline
Keys that remove formatting	
Ctrl-Spacebar	Remove only character-level formatting from the specification
Ctrl-Q	Remove only paragraph-level formatting from the specification
Alt-T	Remove all paragraph and character formatting from the specification

How to replace text with the Edit Replace command

The Edit Replace command is closely related to the Edit Find command. In fact, if you choose the Replace button in the Find dialog box, Word will expand the dialog box and rename it Replace. This Replace dialog box, shown in Figure 4-15 on the next page, is identical to the Replace dialog box you can open by choosing Edit Replace. As the name implies, it differs from the Find dialog box primarily in that it lets you automatically replace found text with new text rather than simply searching for text. You can also use it to search for and replace styles and other formats.

FIGURE 4-15

FIGURE 4-15

The Replace dialog box lets you find and replace text, formats, and styles in a single step.

The options and operation of the Replace dialog box are nearly identical to those of the Find dialog box, except for the addition of a Replace With text box. At its simplest, you use the replace feature by typing the search text in the Find What text box and the replacement text in the Replace With text box. If you leave the Replace With box blank, Word will replace the search text with nothing—that is, it will simply delete the search text.

Like the Find What box, the Replace With text box can display only about 30 to 40 characters but can hold up to 255 characters. You can scroll the text left or right with the Left or Right arrow key (or Ctrl-Left or Ctrl-Right arrow key) or by using the mouse to drag to the left or right. You can also jump to the beginning or end of the search text by using the Home and End keys.

As is the case with Edit Find, after you choose the Edit Replace command and specify settings, Word will remember the entries in the text boxes, and those entries will be the new defaults until you delete them, replace them, or quit the program.

After you enter the search text and the replacement text, choose Find Next if you want to see each match before replacing it, or choose Replace All to change every match without reviewing any of them. If you choose Find Next, Word will stop at each match and scroll the match into view with the text highlighted, as shown in Figure 4-16. Choose Replace to overwrite the found text with the replacement text. When Word pastes the replacement text into your document, the new text will take the same format as the search text it replaces unless you've specified a new format in one of the dialog boxes available through the Format button. Word will also attempt to match the capitalization of the text you replace, as explained more fully later in this chapter.

FIGURE 4-16

When Word finds
the search text using
Find Next, it highlights
the match in your
document.

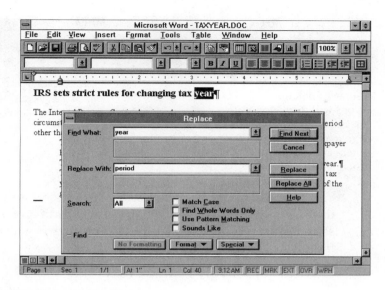

How to use the Replace All option

Suppose you're working in the document shown in Figure 4-16 and you decide to change every occurrence of the word *year* to the word *period*. Assume that the cursor is at the beginning of the third paragraph (the second paragraph of body text) when you open the Replace dialog box. Type *year* in the Find What text box and *period* in the Replace With text box. Then choose Replace All. Word will start the replace procedure. If you've set the Search box to All, rather than Up or Down, Word will make all the replacements and then display the message box shown in Figure 4-17.

FIGURE 4-17

Word has replaced all
seven occurrences of
the word *year* with the
word *period*.

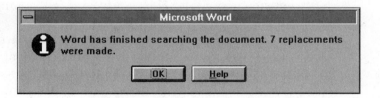

If you select either Up or Down for the Search setting, Word will start replacing at the cursor position and then pause at the beginning or the end of the document to ask whether you want to continue the replacement for the remainder of the document. Figure 4-18 on the next page shows the message you'll see for searching Down.

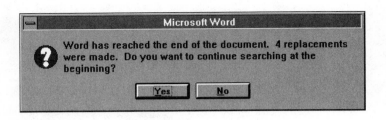

If you choose Yes in the message box to continue the replacement procedure, Word will continue making changes until it reaches the point where it
started. When Word completes all the changes, it will display a message box
indicating the number of changes it made.

How to selectively replace text

In many cases, you won't want to replace every occurrence of your search
text. Sometimes you'll want to examine each match before you tell Word it's
OK to change the text. At other times you'll want to confine the replacement
to a selected portion of your document. Word lets you use either of these
strategies.

Single replacements. If you want to see each match before deciding whether to
change it, use the Replace button instead of Replace All. After you choose the
Find Next button the first time, Word will highlight the first match and then
wait. If you choose Replace, Word will make the replacement and move on to
highlight the next occurrence of the search text. If you don't want to make the
replacement, choose Find Next, and Word will continue the search without
replacing.

Using the Replace button rather than the Replace All button is particularly helpful when you believe that your document might contain several
variations of the search text. For example, suppose you are changing the
word *walk* to *run*. As you go through the document, Word may match the
past-tense form *walked*. If you have chosen Replace All, *walked* would become
runed. When you check each match, however, you can click in your document with the mouse or press Ctrl-Tab to switch to the document, replace
the word *walked* with *ran*, and then click on the Replace dialog box or press
Ctrl-Tab to return to the dialog box and continue the search.

Replacements within a selected block of text. To change all matches within a
specific block of text, simply select the text before you choose the Edit Replace
command. If you want to change the word *year* to *period* within only the first
paragraph of body text, for example, select that paragraph before choosing

Edit Replace. You can then type *year* in the Find What text box and *period* in the Replace With text box. When you choose the Replace All button, Word will change every occurrence of the search text within the selected paragraph and will indicate the number of changes in the subsequent message box.

How to use the Match Case option

When you check the Match Case check box in the Find dialog box, Word will find only that text whose capitalization exactly matches that of the search text. This same rule applies when you use the Edit Replace command. In this case, however, the Match Case option also affects your replacement text.

If you do not turn on the Match Case option and you type your replacement text in lowercase letters, Word will replace all instances of the search text, regardless of case, and will follow the existing capitalization of each occurrence to determine the capitalization of the replacement. If you use uppercase in your replacement text, however, Word will follow this capitalization. If you use the Match Case option, Word will match case for both the search text and the replacement text.

For example, suppose you want to replace the word *May* with the word *April* throughout the sample document shown in Figure 4-19. If you type your search text and your replacement text in all lowercase letters and do not turn on Match Case, Word will find all occurrences of *may*, ignoring case, and replace them with the word *april* when you choose Replace All, as shown in Figure 4-20 on the next page.

FIGURE 4-19

You want to change the word *May* to *April* throughout this document.

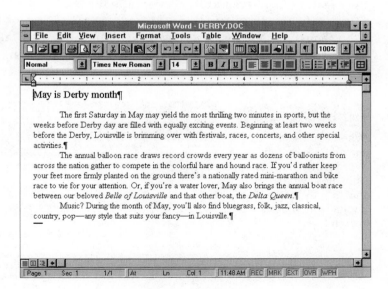

FIGURE 4-20

If you type your
search text and your
replacement text in all
lowercase letters and
do not use the Match
Case option, Word will
retain the document's
existing capitalization.

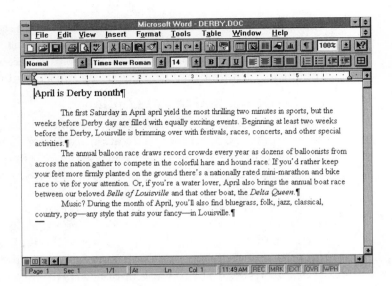

Notice that in every instance where the word *may* was capitalized, Word
also capitalized the replacement text *april*. But if you want to ensure that
April will be capitalized in every instance, you should type it that way in the
Replace With text box. This feature is handy when you've inadvertently
capitalized a word incorrectly throughout your text—typing *MicroSoft*, for
example, rather than *Microsoft*—and you want to use the search-and-replace
feature to automatically fix the capitalization.

In the first paragraph of body text in Figure 4-20, notice that Word
changed the phrase *May may yield* to *April april yield*, although you obviously
want to change only the month names. You can avoid this by using
the Match Case option. Figure 4-21 shows the effect of the Edit Replace

FIGURE 4-21

When you use the
Match Case option,
Word will change
only those words
that exactly match the
capitalization of the
search text.

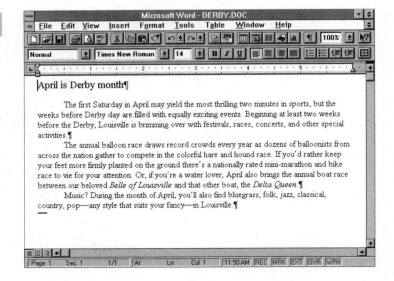

command—replacing *May* with *April*—on our original sample document with the Match Case option turned on. Notice that the phrase *May may yield* is now changed, correctly, to *April may yield*.

At the risk of repeating ourselves, the rule is this: With the Match Case box checked, Word will find only those instances of the search text whose capitalization exactly matches the capitalization of the text you type in the Find What text box. In addition, with the Match Case box checked, Word will always paste your replacement text into your document exactly as you typed it in the Replace With text box.

How to use wildcards with Edit Replace

As we detailed earlier in Figure 4-13, you cannot use wildcards in the Replace With box. If you use pattern-matching characters in the Find What box, however, Word will replace all matches with the text in the Replace With text box.

For example, suppose that you want to replace every occurrence of the words *software* and *hardware* with the phrase *computer supplies*. Choose Edit Replace, type *????ware* as your search text, and check the Use Pattern Matching check box (or type *^? ^? ^? ^?ware* without using pattern matching). Then type *computer supplies* as your replacement text, and choose the Replace All button. Word will look for all words that begin with four letters followed by *ware* and will replace those words with *computer supplies*.

How to replace hidden text

The Edit Replace command will affect hidden text only if the text is displayed on screen. By default, Word won't display any text that is formatted as hidden, and it will ignore that text during a search-and-replace operation. If you want to change hidden text, check the Hidden Text check box on the Tools Options View card or click on the Show/Hide ¶ button on the Standard toolbar before you begin the search-and-replace operation.

How to replace formatting attributes and styles

The Edit Replace command can search for and replace formats using exactly the same search capabilities that we discussed for the Edit Find command.

You can specify formatting for the replacement text using the same procedures and keyboard shortcuts that you use for the search text. The position of the cursor—in either the Find What or the Replace With text box—determines whether the attribute is applied to the search text or the replacement text. When you specify a format, it's easy to confirm that you specified it correctly by looking at the settings below each text box.

As we noted when discussing the Find feature, it's often useful to look for specific text based on its formatting. It's sometimes even more useful to specify the formatting and style of the replacement text. For example, suppose you've been using the term *widget* as the name of a new product. The marketing department has now decided that the official name is *WidJet* and that it should always be printed in bold italics. Word's ability to specify formatting for the replacement string makes replacing *widget* a simple task. Similarly, you might have a document in which you need to replace all bold text with italics. Here again, the ability to search for and replace formats makes replacing *widget* a simple matter of specifying bold for the search text and specifying italic and not bold for the replacement text.

How to use special characters with Edit Replace

Earlier in this chapter, we discussed the special codes you can use in the Find What text box to search for special characters in a document. For example, if you want to include a paragraph mark as part of your search text, you can type *^p*. You can use many of these same codes, and some others, in the Replace With text box as part of your replacement text. If you want an extra carriage return after each paragraph, for example, you can search for *^p* and replace it with *^p ^p*.

Figure 4-13 starting on page 116 lists the codes available for both the Find What box and the Replace With box. You·cannot use some of these codes in the Replace With text box; the codes for white space and for any field, for example, would make no sense as part of replacement text. Other codes, such as *^b* for section break, would make sense as replacement text, but they work only for finding text. As you can with Find What, you can click on the Special button to display a list of available characters.

Figure 4-13 also includes two codes that work only in the Replace With box: *^c*, which inserts the Clipboard contents; and *^&*, which uses the search text as part of the replacement text. Both of these are worth a closer look.

How to replace from the Clipboard. Word provides an unusual option for search-and-replace operations by letting you store the replacement text on the Clipboard. Storing replacement text on the Clipboard offers two advantages: First, the Clipboard is not bound by the 255-character maximum that applies in the dialog box, so you can use the Clipboard when the replacement text is unusually long. Second, replacement text pasted from the Clipboard is pasted into your document with formatting intact. This makes the Clipboard the preferred choice when you have a mix of formats in the replacement text. (This is true only for text that is formatted directly. If you are formatting with styles, the replacement text will not retain its formatting. For a discussion of style formats, see Chapter 12, "Styles & AutoFormat," page 418.

To use the Clipboard's contents as the replacement text, be sure that the cursor is in the Replace With text box, choose the Special button, and then select Clipboard Contents from the list. You can also simply type the characters ^c in the Replace With text box.

How to use search text as part of the replacement text. The second code that works only in the Replace With box is ^&, which inserts the search text as part of the replacement text. This code can save you time and effort for certain kinds of search-and-replace operations. For example, if you've been referring to someone by his or her last name throughout your text and you want to add a title, you need to type the last name only once, in the Find What box. To change *Schlagenhauffer* to *Dr. Schlagenhauffer* throughout your text, enter *Schlagenhauffer* in the Find What text box and *Dr.* ^& in the Replace With text box.

A more interesting use for the ^& code involves combining this code in the Replace With box with the wildcard codes in the Find What box. Suppose, for example, you've written a report that includes the phrases *hardware sources*, *software sources*, and *information sources*. To avoid confusion, you want to change the first two references to *hardware vendors* and *software vendors*. By taking advantage of the wildcard character with pattern matching selected, you can search for *????ware sources* to find instances of both *hardware sources* and *software sources*. If you type ^& *vendors* as replacement text, Word will replace *hardware sources* with *hardware sources vendors* and replace *software sources* with *software sources vendors*. You can then replace all occurrences of *sources vendors* with *vendors* alone to complete the change.

More on editing

As we've demonstrated in this chapter, you can use Word's Edit Find and Edit Replace commands to make rapid changes in your text. Part of the flexibility comes from the generalized nature of these features. However, Word offers other, more specialized, editing tools as well for altering text in your documents. We'll cover some of these in the next chapter.

Topic Finder

NEW! **Similarities and Differences Between AutoCorrect and AutoText**   132

NEW! **Using AutoCorrect**   133
- How to use AutoCorrect
- NEW! Replace Text As You Type
- How to override AutoCorrect changes

Using AutoText   140
- How to use AutoText
- How to add a new AutoText entry
- How to revise an existing AutoText entry
- How to delete an AutoText entry
- How to rename an AutoText entry
- How to insert an AutoText definition with the AUTOTEXT field
- How to store pictures as AutoText
- How to choose a template
- How to save the AutoText entries on disk
- How to print the AutoText entries

Using the Spike   151
- What is the Spike?
- How to place text or pictures on the Spike
- How to insert the Spike's contents

Using the Thesaurus   153
- How to find the right synonym
- How to recall other words
- How to replace the old word with a new one

Using Symbols and Special Characters   156
- How to insert special characters
- Special characters

Creating Headers and Footers   167
- How to add page numbers to your printed document
- The View Header And Footer command
- How to create a header or footer
- How to format and position the header text
- How to delete headers and footers
- How to use editing and proofing tools in headers and footers

5

Additional Editing Tools

ord has a number of specialized tools that make certain kinds of text entry and editing tasks easier. Some of these—such as the tool for footnotes—are so specialized that you may find them indispensable, or you may use them rarely, if at all, depending on your personal taste and the kind of writing you do. However, there are several tools that most people will need at least occasionally. These include the AutoCorrect and AutoText features, the Thesaurus, special characters and symbols, and tools to create and edit headers and footers.

In many ways, these tools are more sophisticated than the basic editing features we discussed in Chapter 4. Where Word's search-and-replace feature, for example, is best described as a sophisticated version of a basic word processing function, the program's AutoCorrect and AutoText features are sophisticated in concept as well as in implementation. They are, in fact, supremely elegant tools for entering text and other data. Much the same can be said of the other tools we'll discuss in this chapter.

Similarities and Differences
Between AutoCorrect and AutoText

AutoText and one of the AutoCorrect options perform similar functions: They both store frequently used text and graphics so you can insert them in your document with minimal effort. In both cases, the stored text can be as short as a single character or as long as several pages. The entries may be signature blocks, long passages of boilerplate text, specially formatted phrases such as a company trademark, graphics (such as a company logo), pre-formatted tables, or just about any other kind of data that you may need to enter repeatedly.

Both AutoText and AutoCorrect can speed text entry by reducing the number of keystrokes it takes to type a block of boilerplate text or other item you use often. In addition, both features offer the significant benefit of im-proving accuracy; you can use them to make certain that you never again misspell the name of an important client or an important person in your or-ganization. And in both cases, once the new text (or other data) is inserted into your document, you can edit and format it.

Although the two features share similar functions, they are also quite different. Both have *auto* in their names, but AutoCorrect is more automatic. Specifically, AutoCorrect will replace an abbreviation with its full text, or *definition*, as soon as you enter a space, tab, or carriage return to signal the end of the abbreviation. (This also happens when you have one or more

Whether you choose AutoCorrect or AutoText to store a given definition will depend partly on how often you intend to use the definition, partly on the abbreviation you intend to use, and partly on the reason you need it. For abbreviations that you use frequently—and that you're not likely to type for some other pur-pose—AutoCorrect is the preferred choice because it doesn't wait for you to give a specific command before it expands the abbrevia-tion into the full definition. Similarly, if there are any typing er-rors you habitually make, AutoCorrect is the better choice, since you're likely to make the errors without being aware of them.

For abbreviations that you use infrequently, you'll generally be better off using AutoText so that having to give a command isn't bothersome. AutoText is also better for abbreviations that you might use for another purpose—for example, *pc* used as an abbreviation for *personal computer*.

punctuation characters—such as a comma or a period—after the abbreviation; AutoCorrect makes the replacement and retains the punctuation.) In contrast, AutoText works only when you tell Word to replace the abbreviation, and only when the cursor is within or immediately follows the abbreviation.

Also, as the name implies, AutoCorrect is meant to help you catch and correct common typing mistakes. For example, it can automatically convert *teh* to *the* without your having to notice the mistake or even think about it. And AutoCorrect offers several options that turn some elementary correction features on and off without your having to define any special abbreviations or definitions. We'll cover these in the section immediately after this.

Using AutoCorrect

AutoCorrect is designed to correct mistakes automatically. If you've set any of the AutoCorrect options to work (some are on by default when you first install Word), they'll be watching over your typing from the time you start the program; Word will correct the specified mistakes as you make them. If none of the AutoCorrect options are set to work, it's simple enough to activate them.

How to use AutoCorrect

To see the current settings for the AutoCorrect options, choose Tools AutoCorrect. Word will display the AutoCorrect dialog box, shown in Figure 5-1. The figure shows the dialog box as it appears with the default settings. The first four check boxes govern some straightforward correction features.

FIGURE 5-1

Use the AutoCorrect dialog box to select options that make Word identify and correct mistakes as you type.

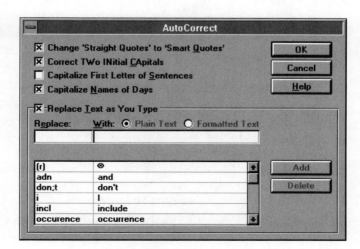

The Change 'Straight Quotes' To 'Smart Quotes' option will automatically change quotation-mark characters as you type. If you're not familiar with typographic conventions, you might not be aware that there are different kinds of quotation marks. Many people simply use the *straight quotes:* ' and ". From a typographical viewpoint, however, these should be used only to signify certain units of measure, such as ' for feet and " for inches. For dialog or for quoted excerpts and terms, the preferred choices are pairs of opening and closing quotation marks, such as

'this'

and

"this"

These are widely known as *curly quotes.* The reference to Smart Quotes means that the feature can automatically determine whether a given curly quote should be the opening or closing quotation mark. If there's a check in this check box, Word will convert all quotation marks in your documents to curly quotes.

Word's approach to Smart Quotes doesn't always make the right choice between opening and closing quotation marks. In particular, if you have a quotation within a quotation, as in

"I said, 'What kind of quotes do you want?'"

Word will sometimes choose the wrong quotation marks. In this example, if you don't add a space between the final single quotation mark and the final double quotation mark, Word will end with a closing double quotation mark—as it should. But if you add a space, Word's Smart Quotes feature will guess wrong and insert an opening double quotation mark instead of a closing one. In general, whether or not you add a space depends on whether you feel the particular font crowds the three quotation marks together. So although there is no hard-and-fast typographical rule about whether to add a space or not, you may well prefer to add one.

There are several ways around this problem, including some that take advantage of macros—an advanced feature that we'll cover in the last section of this book (but without dealing with this particular problem). If you use the Smart Quote feature, however, you should at least be aware of the problem. And note that the simplest fix is to type all combinations of single and double quotation marks without spaces and then use Word's search-and-replace feature to search for '" and replace them with ' ". If you need to re-place curly quotes, note that to insert them into the Find or Re-place dialog box, you need to use special shortcut keys. The opening quotes use the grave accent (generally found on the up-per left of the keyboard) and are Ctrl-`, " for " and Ctrl-`, ` for '. The closing quotes use the single straight quote (next to the Enter key) and are Ctrl-', " for " and Ctrl-', ' for '. Finally, when using the Find or Replace feature, curly quotes match exactly (an opening quote matches only an opening quote), but the straight quotes in-serted from the keyboard match any quote (" matches ", ", or ").

The second check box is Correct TWo INitial CApitals. This is one of our favorite additions to Word version 6.0, since we both occasionally fail to re-lease the Shift key quickly enough to prevent the second letter of a word from being capitalized by accident. If you check this check box, Word will correct such typos—for example, it will change *WOrd* to *Word*—even if you don't notice the mistake. At the same time, it will leave recognizable abbre-viations, such as NY and CA, alone.

The next check box, Capitalize First Letter Of Sentences, will automati-cally capitalize the first word of a sentence. By default, this box is not checked, on the assumption that most people shift case on their own at the start of a sentence and there are times when they may not want to. But if you sometimes forget to capitalize the first letter in a sentence, or you find it a chore, you can check this check box and Word will take care of the capitaliza-tion for you.

The Capitalize Names Of Days check box controls the last of the four ba-sic AutoCorrect options. This feature can recognize the days of the week. Add a check here, and if you forget to capitalize *friday*, Word will automati-cally turn it into *Friday* for you.

Replace Text As You Type

The last check box in the AutoCorrect dialog box—the Replace Text As You Type check box—determines whether Word pays any attention to the rest of the AutoCorrect dialog box. If the check box is checked, Word will watch for words or abbreviations listed in the Replace column, and when you type one, it will swap that text for the text (or other data) in the With column.

The Replace Text As You Type option is the AutoCorrect feature that's similar to AutoText—that is, you can use it to store frequently used text and other data. The list in the Replace column shows the abbreviations, or names, for the complete entries. For our purposes, we'll use *AutoCorrect name* to refer to an item that AutoCorrect puts in the Replace list. The

AutoCorrect definition is the full text that's represented by the AutoCorrect name. In contrast, an *AutoCorrect entry* refers to the complete item—both the AutoCorrect name and the text it represents.

How to name AutoCorrect entries

For obvious reasons, it helps to use AutoCorrect names that are easy to remember. Word provides plenty of flexibility for names; you can create names up to 31 characters long. This should be plenty—you'll want to keep the abbreviations as short as possible so that you can type them quickly. On the other hand, you won't want to make them so short that you can't remember which is which.

There are a few rules to keep in mind for AutoCorrect names. They must be single words, which means they cannot contain any spaces. They can use virtually any character you can type at the keyboard, including numbers and punctuation characters. AutoCorrect names are not case-sensitive, at least in the sense that Word will treat *teh* and *TEH* as the same abbreviation; however, the capitalization of the abbreviation will affect how Word inserts the AutoCorrect text, as we'll explain in the next section.

The AutoCorrect definition can be text or graphics or both. If it's text, you can type up to 255 characters into the With text box directly. You can insert much larger selections—several pages long—or graphics by entering the text or graphics in a document, selecting what you've entered, and then choosing Tools AutoText. Word will assume you want to create a new definition and will insert the text or graphic into the With text box. You need only add an abbreviation in the Replace box and choose Add.

Capitalization complications

The way the AutoCorrect feature treats case is a bit complex, but you can use the feature to your advantage. If you create an AutoCorrect name in lowercase, Word will recognize text exactly as you type it in your document if you type it in lowercase, with an initial capital, or in all capitals. So if you enter *teh* as an AutoCorrect name, Word will match the case of each letter when you type *TEH*, *Teh*, or *teh*; Word will not match the cases, however, if you type *teH* or *tEh*. If you put one or more capital letters in the name when you create it, Word will match words you type in your document only if they have exactly the same capitalization.

Word also follows some complex rules about case when it replaces the AutoCorrect name with the full text of the definition. If the name, as shown in the Replace column of the AutoCorrect dialog box, has any capital letters in it, Word will replace it without making any changes to the capitalization of the full definition as you stored it in the AutoCorrect dialog box. On the other hand, if the name is stored in lowercase, Word will, under some conditions, change the capitalization of the text it inserts. For example, Word will capitalize the first word if you type the name in your document with the first letter capitalized; or Word will capitalize every letter in the definition if you type the name in your document in all caps. There is an important exception to this rule, however: If the first word of the stored definition is capitalized, Word will not alter the case of any of the text under any circumstances when it inserts it in your document. If a letter in any word other than the first word of the definition is capitalized, that capital will be preserved no matter how the name is entered.

Given the complexity of capitalization with the AutoCorrect feature, it helps to follow a simple rule of thumb: If you want Word to follow the capitalization of the name as you type it in your document, be sure to type your AutoCorrect names and definitions in lowercase in the AutoCorrect dialog box. If you want Word to always insert text with a specific capitalization, you should include a capital letter in the name as you store it in the AutoCorrect dialog box and be sure to type it in your document with the same capitalization.

How to add AutoCorrect entries

Word comes with a number of predefined AutoCorrect entries, some of which are illustrated in Figure 5-1. You will likely want to add your own, however.

For example, you might have a colleague whose name you have to write frequently, such as *M. David Stone*. You could type the complete name each time you use it. Or you could let Word type it for you, by assigning an AutoCorrect name—using, for example, the initials *mds*—to a definition consisting of the entire name.

Word provides several ways to define this combination. One of the easiest is to choose Tools AutoCorrect and then type *mds* in the Replace text box and *M. David Stone* in the With text box. As soon as you type an acceptable entry in each text box, the Add button in the dialog box will change from grayed to active. You can then choose the Add button to add the entry to the list at the bottom of the dialog box.

 Word arranges the AutoCorrect entries in alphabetic order, as determined by the Replace abbreviation. If there are more entries than will fit in the list box at one time, Word will display a scroll bar at the right of the list so that you can scroll through the list.

As mentioned already, you can also enter text or other data directly in your document, then select a block, and then choose Tools AutoCorrect. Word will insert the selected block in the With text box. All you have to do then is type a word in the Replace text box and choose the Add button to create the AutoCorrect entry. This approach is particularly handy when you want to define a large block—from a paragraph to several pages—as an AutoCorrect item. It also works for pictures and similar objects other than text. We'll discuss additional aspects of pictures and other objects in Chapter 15, "Drawing, Graphics, & Other Objects," page 548.

When you use this block method with text, the Plain Text and Formatted Text radio buttons in the dialog box will not be grayed the way they are if you type the definition text in the With text box directly. You use these buttons to retain the formatting of the With text.

If you want your AutoCorrect text to include specific formatting when Word inserts it into your document—as you would with a letterhead or company logo, for example—choose the Formatted Text option when defining the AutoCorrect entry. Otherwise, choose the Plain Text option, and the inserted text will take on the same formatting as the name it replaces. Be aware, however, that you cannot store plain text definitions longer than 255 characters. For longer entries, you *must* use formatted text.

Finally, you can use the Clipboard to paste text into the With text box. This makes it possible for you to paste text copied from programs other than Word. When you're using text that originated in Word, however, the Clipboard is not as useful as selecting text on the screen because it won't give you the option of storing the definition as formatted text.

How to change AutoCorrect names and definitions

After you've created an AutoCorrect entry, you may want to change its name or definition.

To change an AutoCorrect name. First choose Tools AutoCorrect to open the dialog box. Then select the entry you want to change in the list box. Word will insert that entry in the text boxes above the list box. Make the changes in the Replace text box, choose Add, and Word will add the new item to the list box. Then select the original item, and choose Delete. Word will remove the item from the list box without asking for confirmation.

To change an AutoCorrect definition that's short enough to fit in the With text box. Follow the steps described for changing an AutoCorrect name to place the name and definition in the text boxes. Make any changes desired to the definition and choose Replace. (The Add button changes to Replace whenever you edit a definition.) Word will display the message shown in Figure 5-2 asking you to confirm that you want to replace the definition. Choose Yes to proceed with changing the definition.

To change the formatting for the definition. If the definition is too long to fit in the text box, or you want to change the formatting of the definition, start by inserting the definition in your document. Then make whatever changes you want. When you finish modifying (or creating) the new text, select the text in your document and choose Tools AutoCorrect to open the dialog box; Word will insert the selection in the With text box. Next you type the name for the entry you want to change and then choose the Replace button. Word will display the message shown in Figure 5-2 asking you to confirm that you want to redefine the entry. Choose Yes to proceed with the change.

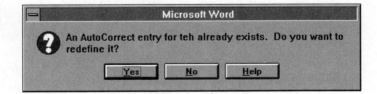

FIGURE 5-2

Word will warn you with this message before you change the definition of an AutoCorrect item.

How to delete AutoCorrect combinations

To get rid of an AutoCorrect item, highlight the item in the list box at the bottom of the AutoCorrect dialog box, and then choose the Delete button.

Be careful when using the Delete button. Word will delete the highlighted item from the list box without asking for confirmation first. You cannot recover the deleted entry with the Undo feature.

How to override AutoCorrect changes

There may be times when you don't want Word to replace an abbreviation with AutoCorrect text. For example, assume you're writing a technical paper that refers to a device with the acronym *TEH*. To prevent Word from replacing the acronym with *THE* each time you type it, you could turn off the AutoCorrect Replace Text As You Type feature. But that would mean having to do without the feature entirely.

There's a better way. Word treats the AutoCorrect process as an editing step, in the same way as it treats typing, deleting, or moving text. As a result, you can undo an automatic correction. If Word applies any of the AutoCorrect features to an exception that you don't want changed, simply choose the Undo command with Ctrl-Z (or any other method you prefer) and continue typing. If you plan to use a given exception often, however, you may want to remove the abbreviation from your AutoCorrect list and re-create it as AutoText.

Using AutoText

As we discussed at the beginning of this chapter, AutoText works much like the Replace Text As You Type option in the AutoCorrect feature. The key difference is that with AutoText, Word does not replace the AutoText name with the full definition until you tell it to. As with AutoCorrect, however, you can create an AutoText definition as text, pictures, or a combination of the two.

We'll discuss how to create AutoText entries shortly, but first we'll look at how to insert an AutoText entry. This will help clarify the difference between the semiautomatic AutoText and the fully automatic AutoCorrect.

Users familiar with Word versions 1.0 and 2.0 may recognize AutoText as a new name for the Glossary feature from those earlier versions of the program. Although the feature is essentially unchanged, the new name is a more immediately understandable description of what the feature does.

How to use AutoText

There are two ways to use an AutoText entry. Which approach you choose is largely a matter of taste. Of course, for either method to work, you must first create an entry.

One approach is to pick the entry from a list. If you choose Edit AutoText (with nothing selected in your document), Word will open the AutoText dialog box, shown in Figure 5-3. You can then select the name you want from the list box in the top half of the dialog box. For our purposes, and in parallel with our definitions for the AutoCorrect feature, the *AutoText name* refers to an item in this list box. The *AutoText definition* is the full text that is represented by the name. An *Autotext entry* refers to the complete AutoText item—both the name and the text it represents. Notice that the list box shows only the AutoText names—the abbreviations for the actual entries.

FIGURE 5-3

You can use the AutoText dialog box to select an AutoText entry from a list of names.

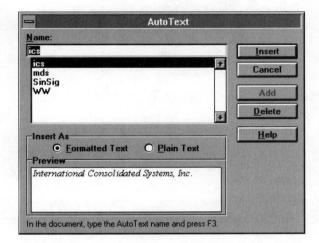

If there are more AutoText names than can fit in the list box at once, the vertical scroll bar at the right of the list box will become active, and you can scroll though the list. As you select each one, you can see as much of the text for that entry as will fit—in the box labeled Preview in Figure 5-3. When you find the item you want, choose the Insert button to insert the text in your document.

If you know the AutoText name for an entry, you can use either a keyboard or a mouse shortcut instead of choosing from a list. Suppose, for example, that you regularly type your company name, *International Consolidated Systems, Inc.*, but you sometimes need to use the abbreviation *ICS* as well. This is a good candidate for an AutoText, rather than AutoCorrect, entry because it's a long name that you need to use repeatedly, and its obvious abbreviation—*ICS*—is also something that you'll occasionally need to use. We'll discuss how to create the entry shortly. For the moment, assume that it already exists, with *ICS* as the AutoText name.

To use the entry, you first type the abbreviation *ICS* in your document. If you want the abbreviation only, you can continue typing; Word will leave the *ICS* as is. If you want to replace the abbreviation with the full definition, however, you can simply give a shortcut command to replace it. For keyboard users, the command is F3 or Ctrl-Alt-V. If you prefer using the mouse,

you can point to the AutoText button on the Standard toolbar—the icon
resembles a hand pointing to a keyboard—and click.

The primary difference between AutoCorrect and AutoText is that
AutoCorrect replaces an entry's name without needing a command, whereas AutoText waits until you tell it to replace the
name with a definition. That frees you to use abbreviations that
are meaningful and that you might use as words by themselves—
as in the example in this section.

How to add a new AutoText entry

Before you can use an AutoText entry, of course, you have to create one. The
first step for creating a new entry is to create the AutoText definition anywhere in your document and then select the definition. (As with
AutoCorrect entries, you can highlight any part of your document to create
an entry, including pictures and other objects.) Next choose Edit AutoText to
open the AutoText dialog box, shown in Figure 5-4. You can use the menu or
click on the AutoText button on the Standard toolbar.

FIGURE 5-4

The AutoText dialog
box contains options
for creating, modifying,
and deleting AutoText
entries.

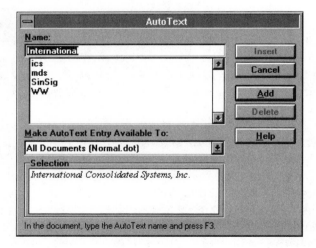

Word will show as much of the selected text, picture, or other object as
will fit in the Selection box at the bottom of the dialog box, and it will display
the first few words in the Name box at the top. (If the selected item does not
contain any text or other characters you can type at the keyboard, or if it
includes certain special characters such as paragraph marks, Word might

use asterisks in the Name box.) At this point, you can edit the text in the Name box to change the name to anything you prefer. Finish by choosing the Add button to add the item to the list of AutoText entries.

When you type an AutoText name, there are a few rules to keep in mind. First, if you enter a name that already exists, Word will display a message box, as shown in Figure 5-5, that asks whether you want to redefine the AutoText entry. Choose Yes to replace the old entry with the new text that you've selected or No to return to the AutoText dialog box without changing the entry.

FIGURE 5-5

If you try to assign an existing name to a new AutoText entry, Word will ask whether you want to redefine the entry.

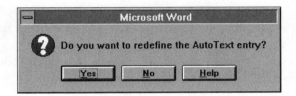

You can also use the Clipboard to create the AutoText name. Copy the text you want for the name to the Clipboard, and then highlight the block of text you want for the definition. Next choose Tools AutoText. Word will insert the selected text as the AutoText definition. You can then simply press Ctrl-V or Shift-Ins to paste the text from the Clipboard into the Name text box, and you can choose Add to finish adding the item.

Naming the entries

AutoText, unlike AutoCorrect, lets you include spaces in an entry's name. In fact, you can use any characters you want, including punctuation marks, that you can generate with the keyboard. Being able to contain spaces means the AutoText name can consist of two or more words—for example, *Sig Sin* instead of *SigSin* for a signature block using *Sincerely Yours*. However, the name cannot exceed 32 characters (including spaces). This shouldn't be an issue, since, as with AutoCorrect entries, you'll want to keep the AutoText names as short as possible so that you can type them quickly. As with AutoText names, also, you'll want to avoid making the names so short that you can't remember what each one is for.

> Try to use meaningful AutoText names. Also, try to group similar entries to make them easier to remember. If you use *HeadLtr* to store the heading boilerplate for letters, *HeadMem* is a good choice for memos, and *HeadRep*, for reports. And because Word lists AutoText entries in alphabetic order based on their names, you can group related entries such as these together simply by adding the same prefix to each of their names.

Unlike AutoCorrect, AutoText pays no attention to the capitalization of either the AutoText name itself or the way you type it in your document; Word will match the two regardless of case. Also unlike AutoCorrect, the AutoText feature will not change the capitalization of the AutoText definition under any circumstances when it inserts the text into your document. This means that Word will interpret any attempt to define the AutoText name *ICS* as redefining *ics*. It also means that you can use capitalization to help increase the readability of AutoText names without making it harder to type the names when you want to use them. For example, you can create the AutoText name *SigSin* and insert its definition into your text by typing *sigsin* and pressing F3.

Although you can change the entry in the Name box while adding an AutoText item, you cannot change the contents in the Selection box. To change the AutoText definition, you have to choose Cancel to close the AutoText dialog box, make the changes in the text within the document, highlight the modified block of text, and reopen the AutoText dialog box.

Formatted AutoText entries

When you select text for a new AutoText entry, Word stores the current format for that text along with the entry. Using an earlier example, if you italicize the words *International Consolidated Systems, Inc.*, before defining them as an AutoText entry, Word will insert them with italic formatting, by default, whenever you use the AutoText name *ics* (combining it with any formatting of the AutoText name). If you want to insert the text without the original formatting, you have to insert it from the AutoText dialog box, rather than using a shortcut; before choosing the Insert button, choose Insert As Plain Text. (In a case like this, however, you may find it just as easy to reformat the text after it is inserted by AutoText.)

In addition to storing formats such as bold or italic, Word will store fonts, point size, superscript, subscript, and any other character formats you assigned to the text before defining it as AutoText. If your AutoText definition includes one or more paragraph marks, Word will store the paragraph formatting as well—including line spacing, indention, and so forth.

When you open the AutoText dialog box and select a name in the Name box, Word will show you as much of the definition for that name as will fit in the Preview box. The Preview box always shows the text formatted the way Word will insert it. By default, Word sets the option for Formatted Text, so the text in the Preview box will match the text as formatted when you defined the entry plus any format you've applied to the name. If you choose the Plain Text option instead, the text will match the format currently applied to the point where you are about to insert the entry. In other words, if you choose the Plain Text option, the entry will take on the format applied to the AutoText name.

How to revise an existing AutoText entry

If you use the AutoText feature often, you will occasionally need to change the definition for a given entry. Changing the definition is similar to creating a new entry. Rather than editing the definition within the AutoText dialog box, you have to replace it with new text. For a short entry, you can simply type the new text anywhere in a document. For a longer entry, you will probably want to insert the text as AutoText and then edit it.

After you edit the definition, you can highlight it, open the AutoText dialog box, and select the AutoText name whose definition you want to replace. At this point, the Preview box will show the currently stored definition for the entry. After confirming that you've selected the correct entry, choose the Add button. When Word asks whether you want to redefine the entry, choose Yes to redefine it and return to the document.

How to delete an AutoText entry

You might also occasionally need to delete an AutoText entry. To delete an entry, open the AutoText dialog box, select the AutoText name you want to get rid of, and choose the Delete button. Word will remove the selected entry and leave the dialog box open so that you can insert or delete other entries.

Word will let you delete only one AutoText entry at a time. This is an important safety feature, since the program doesn't stop to ask for permission before deleting. If you need to delete several entries, you have to delete each one individually.

How to rename an AutoText entry

If you want to change the name of an AutoText entry, you must use the Organizer. We will discuss the Organizer in detail in "Organizer: Moving Styles, AutoText, Toolbars, and Macros Among Templates" starting on page 945.

For now, just follow these steps to open the Organizer and change an AutoText entry's name. Choose File Templates to open the Templates And Add-Ins dialog box, and then choose the Organizer button. Word will open the Organizer dialog box. Choose the AutoText card, as shown in Figure 5-6. In this example, the current document is attached only to the Normal template, which is why the figure shows the entries for NORMAL.DOT on both sides of the Organizer dialog box. (We'll touch on saving AutoText entries in other templates elsewhere in this chapter.)

FIGURE 5-6

You can use the Organizer's AutoText card to change the name of an AutoText entry.

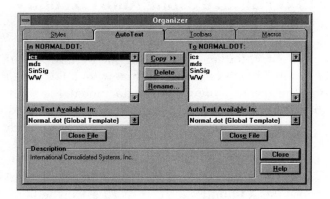

You can highlight the appropriate AutoText entry in either NORMAL.DOT list box, and Word will display its text in the Description box at the bottom of the card. Then choose the Rename button. Word will display a Rename dialog box, in which you can enter a new name for that entry. Type the new name, and then choose the OK button; Word will return you to the AutoText card in the Organizer dialog box. Choose the Close button to return to your document.

How to insert an AutoText definition with the AUTOTEXT field

We've already mentioned three ways to insert AutoText definitions into your document: by typing the AutoText name and pressing F3 or Ctrl-Alt-V, by typing the name and then clicking on the AutoText button on the Standard toolbar, and by choosing the entry in the AutoText dialog box.

Still another way to insert an AutoText definition is with the AUTOTEXT field. Although fields are an advanced subject that we won't examine in detail until Chapter 20, it makes sense to look at the AUTOTEXT field with other AutoText issues.

Briefly, the AUTOTEXT field is a marker that takes the place of the actual AutoText definition. When you insert the field, the marker maintains a permanent link to the AutoText entry it refers to. If you then change the AutoText definition for that entry, Word can automatically update all instances of the entry in your document.

To create an AUTOTEXT field, press Ctrl-F9 to insert a pair of curly brackets in your document, like this:

{}

The cursor will appear within the brackets. Do not enter these brackets by typing them. The resulting brackets may look the same on the screen, but Word will not recognize them as indicating a field.

The AUTOTEXT field takes the form {AUTOTEXT *AutoTextName*}, where *AutoTextName* is the name of the entry you want to insert. With the cursor inside the curly brackets, type the word AUTOTEXT, a space, and the appropriate AutoText name. Then press F9 to update the field with AutoText's current text. If necessary, press Shift-F9, and Word will show the field results rather than the field code.

After you have inserted an AUTOTEXT field in your document, you can update it whenever you modify the text for that entry. Simply select the entire document, pressing Ctrl-A or Ctrl-NumPad5, and then press F9. Word will update all fields in the selection to match the new text.

Note that you can also store other kinds of fields as part of your AutoText definition, so you can enter and easily update such items as date, time, or page number. We'll cover fields in more depth in Chapter 20.

How to store pictures as AutoText

Although you'll probably use AutoText mainly for text, you can also use it for pictures. As we've already mentioned in passing, the mechanics of storing pictures as AutoText are essentially identical to the mechanics of storing text. But before you can use pictures for AutoText entries, you have to know how to work with them in your documents directly. For details on working with pictures and other objects, see Chapters 14 and 15.

How to choose a template

One last important difference between the AutoCorrect and AutoText features is that with AutoCorrect, all entries are available to all documents in Word. AutoText entries, in contrast, may not be.

Word stores its AutoText entries in special files, called *templates*. Unless you tell Word otherwise, it stores all AutoText entries in the standard template, NORMAL.DOT. In general, the NORMAL.DOT settings amount to your default settings for the program; they are available while you work in any Word document—not just documents based on the template NORMAL.DOT—unless you override the settings with supplementary templates.

If you're working with a document that's based on a template other than NORMAL.DOT, you can tell Word to save an AutoText entry in that document's supplementary template instead of NORMAL.DOT. When you save the entry in any template besides NORMAL.DOT, however, you can use that entry only with documents that are based on that supplementary template.

As a concrete example, suppose you are working with a document that is based on the supplementary template MEMO.DOT. If you save an AutoText entry in NORMAL.DOT and then open any other document, you will be able to use that AutoText entry. But if you save the entry in MEMO.DOT and then open a document that isn't based on MEMO.DOT, you will not be able to use the AutoText entry while working with the second document.

There is one further complication. In addition to the Normal template and supplementary templates, Word version 6.0 will also let you designate so-called global templates. (If you're familiar with Word 2.0, be forewarned that a global template in Word 6.0 is not the same thing as the Normal template in version 2.0.) To avoid getting bogged down in detail here, simply note that if you designate a template as a global template, its AutoText entries will be available to all open files. However, you won't be able to save new entries to the template directly. For a detailed discussion of this and other template issues, see Chapter 27.

When you add an AutoText entry with the AutoText dialog box, you can indicate your choice of template for storing the entry in the Make AutoText

Entry Available To text box. This text box appears only when you are creating a new entry. If you open the drop-down list in this box, you will see a list of templates (other than global templates) that are attached to the document, as shown in Figure 5-7. You can then select the template in which to store the AutoText entry before you choose the Add button.

FIGURE 5-7

The drop-down list box attached to the Make AutoText Entry Available To box shows the templates attached to the current document.

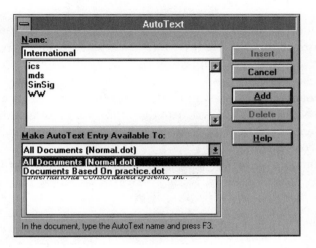

 Until you become thoroughly familiar with templates, we recommend that you store all changes in NORMAL.DOT, which Word will suggest by default. When you are familiar with templates, you can move AutoText entries to any template you like. For details on moving entries, see "Organizer: Moving Styles, AutoText, Toolbars, and Macros Among Templates" starting on page 945.

How to save the AutoText entries on disk

Word doesn't actually save your AutoText entries on disk when you define or change them. Left to its own devices, it simply keeps the AutoText entries in memory, eventually saving the changes in one of two ways. If you make changes to the entries in NORMAL.DOT, Word won't make any effort to save the changes on disk until you exit from Word. When you choose the File Exit command, however, Word will ask whether you want to save the changes, by way of the message box shown in Figure 5-8. You can then choose Yes to save the changes, No to throw them away, or Cancel to go back to Word.

FIGURE 5-8

Word will ask whether
to save your AutoText
entry changes to
NORMAL.DOT when
you exit from Word.

Word treats changes to a supplementary template somewhat differently
from changes to NORMAL.DOT. If you've made any AutoText changes in a
supplementary template, Word will ask whether to save them when you
close the document that's based on that template. When you choose File
Close, Word displays the message box shown in Figure 5-9. As with changes
to NORMAL.DOT, you can then choose Yes to save the changes, No to throw
them away, or Cancel to go back to the document rather than close it.

FIGURE 5-9

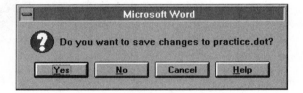

Choose Yes in this
message box if you
want to update the
changes you've made
to the template's
AutoText entries.

How to save AutoText entries
with the File Save All command

As anyone who has ever lost work to a power blackout or a system crash can
tell you, leaving a large amount of data in memory without saving it on disk
is a good way to lose your work. Fortunately, Word provides a simple way
to save the AutoText changes on command. Choose File Save All, and Word
will try to save all open files with any changes since the last save, as well as
any changes to the AutoText entries in both NORMAL.DOT and any supplemental templates currently open. For each template, Word will display a
message box asking whether you want to save your changes. You can choose
Yes or No for each one, or you can return to your document without saving
by choosing Cancel.

How to print the AutoText entries

If you use a lot of AutoText entries, you'll find that it can quickly become
difficult to remember them all. Fortunately, Word provides a straightforward way to print your AutoText entries so that you can keep a handy refer-

ence near your computer. First open a document that's attached to the template containing the AutoText list you want to print. (Any document will do for those in NORMAL.DOT.) Next choose File Print, select AutoText Entries from the Print What drop-down list, and choose OK. Word will print a list containing each AutoText name and its definition. Figure 5-10 shows a sample AutoText list.

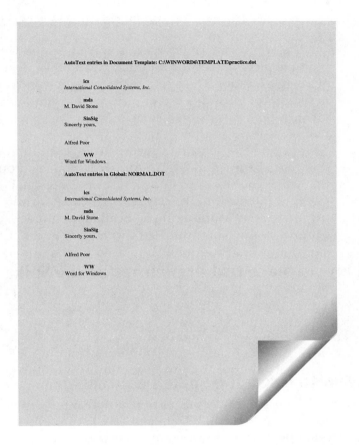

AutoText entries in Document Template: C:\WINWORD6\TEMPLATE\practice.dot

ics
International Consolidated Systems, Inc.

mds
M. David Stone

SinSig
Sincerly yours,

Alfred Poor

WW
Word for Windows

AutoText entries in Global: NORMAL.DOT

ics
International Consolidated Systems, Inc.

mds
M. David Stone

SinSig
Sincerly yours,

Alfred Poor

WW
Word for Windows

Using the Spike

Word offers a special AutoText entry called the Spike. The Spike gets its name by analogy to the physical spike that some businesses use to hold bills, receipts, and other loose pieces of paper.

What is the Spike?

To understand how the Spike works, imagine you own and operate a small hardware store. Next to your cash register, you keep a spike to hold copies of your sales receipts. Each time a customer buys something in the store, you hand one copy of the receipt to the customer and place the store's copy on the spike. At the end of the day, you take all the receipts off the spike and log each sale in a journal. When business begins the next day, the spike is empty, ready for a new day's receipts.

Like a physical spike, Word's Spike is useful for collecting and storing multiple pieces of related information and then depositing that information at a single location. Of course, the information on Word's Spike isn't a group of receipts or bills—it's text or pictures that you want to insert in your document. After you've stored something on the Spike, you can insert the contents at a single location in your text.

The Spike is actually a special AutoText entry named Spike. The main difference between the Spike AutoText name and other AutoText names is that when you store text or a picture on the Spike, Word doesn't replace the current contents with the new text or picture; instead, it adds the new text or picture to what's already there. In all other respects, the built-in Spike entry behaves as any other AutoText entry does.

How to place text or pictures on the Spike

To move an item to the Spike, first select the text or picture you want to move, and then press Ctrl-F3. Word will remove the selected item from the document and add it to the Spike. To add another item, simply repeat the process. Each time you press Ctrl-F3, Word will add the current selection.

How to insert the Spike's contents

You have two choices for inserting the contents of the Spike: You can empty the contents into your document, or you can copy the contents without emptying the Spike. (You cannot insert a portion of the Spike's contents into a document.)

How to empty the Spike

To empty the Spike into a document, place the cursor in the appropriate spot and press Ctrl-Shift-F3. Word will transfer the contents from the Spike to the document, emptying the Spike in the process. Word inserts a paragraph mark following each item that you add to the Spike's contents.

How to copy from the Spike

To copy the Spike's contents into a document without emptying the Spike, you can use any of the three standard commands for inserting AutoText entries. Type the word *spike* and then press F3 or Ctrl-Alt-V; or type *spike* and then choose the AutoText button; or choose the Edit AutoText command, select Spike in the list box, and then choose Insert. In each case, Word will insert a copy of the Spike's contents but leave the Spike unchanged so that you can either continue adding to it or insert additional copies elsewhere.

Techniques for using the Spike

Occasionally, you may want to add text to the Spike but not delete the text from your document. Unfortunately, Word does not have a built-in command to copy text directly to the Spike. But there is a simple technique that will serve the same purpose. Select the text you want to add to the Spike, and then, before you press Ctrl-F3, copy the selection to the Clipboard. (Ctrl-C is a handy way of copying to the Clipboard.) Next add the selection to the Spike by pressing Ctrl-F3. This procedure will delete the selection, but you can now replace it by using the Edit Paste command if you do so before copying anything else to the Clipboard. (You may find the Ctrl-V keyboard shortcut the most convenient way of pasting.)

Another technique that isn't immediately obvious is to clear the Spike if you decide you don't want to insert the accumulated text anywhere after all. Of course, you can always use Ctrl-Shift-F3 to empty the Spike, and then delete the text from your document. But a more elegant choice is to choose Edit AutoText, select Spike in the Name list box, and choose Delete. Word will clear the Spike and remove Spike from the list of AutoText names.

You can define an AutoText entry named Spike with the standard AutoText procedures. The AutoText entry you define this way will act as if it were the initial entry for the Spike, and it will clear any text or other data already stored in the Spike. Word will ask for confirmation before clearing the current text or other data in the Spike, but it's still best to use this technique with care.

Using the Thesaurus

The Word Thesaurus provides a storehouse of synonyms—as well as some antonyms—that you can use much like you use a book-bound thesaurus. In particular, you may find the feature helpful for avoiding unnecessary repetition in your writing. And if you're a careful writer who cares about word choice, the Thesaurus can be invaluable when you are looking for just the right word to say precisely what you mean.

To use the Thesaurus, first type the word for which you want a synonym or an antonym. Then highlight the word, or put the cursor anywhere on the word, or leave it on the space immediately after the word. Next press Shift-F7, or choose Tools Thesaurus. Word will open the Thesaurus dialog box. As shown in Figure 5-11, Word will display the currently selected word in the Looked Up text box. (In some cases, such as when the cursor is between two paragraph marks, Word will not consider any text selected and will display the Thesaurus dialog box without any text entered.) If you highlight more than one word before choosing Tools Thesaurus, Word will try to match the entire phrase, as shown in Figure 5-12. In either case, if the Thesaurus does not find a match, it will show the label of the text box as Not Found and provide an alphabetic list of possible words to choose from, as in Figure 5-13.

FIGURE 5-11

The Thesaurus dialog box displays the current selection in the Looked Up text box.

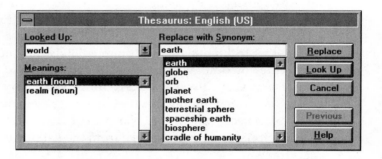

FIGURE 5-12

If you highlight more than one word, the Thesaurus will try to match the entire phrase.

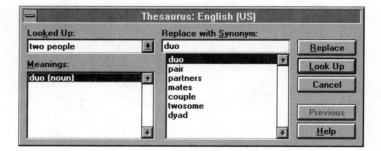

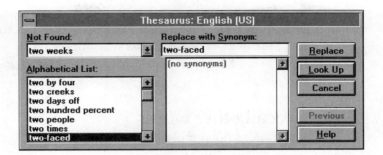

FIGURE 5-13

If the Thesaurus does not find a match, it will show you a list of similarly spelled words to choose from.

How to find the right synonym

Note that the Replace With Synonym list box shows the synonyms for the definition currently selected in the Meanings list box. In Figure 5-11, for example, it shows the synonyms of *world* (the word we looked up) for the definition *earth*. If you highlight a different definition in the Meanings list box, Word will change the list in the Replace With Synonym box to match it. In this case, if you select *realm* in the Meanings list box, you will get the list shown in Figure 5-14. Notice that both definitions in the Meanings list box show the part of speech in the context of the definition.

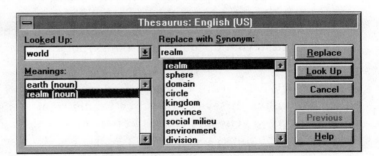

FIGURE 5-14

The list of synonyms in the Replace With Synonym list box depends on which definition you select in the Meanings list box.

Often you will want to see synonyms for a word that shows up in the Replace With Synonym box. For example, after you open the dialog box shown in Figure 5-11, you may want to see synonyms for the word *orb*. Simply highlight the word and choose the Look Up button (or double-click on the word). Word will respond by putting the selected word in the Looked Up text box, and it will show you the appropriate entries in the Meanings and Replace With Synonym list boxes.

Some words will also show an item labeled *Antonyms* in the Meanings box. Select this word to see a list of antonyms in the list box where Word normally displays synonyms.

How to recall other words

You can review the full list of words you've looked up during any Thesaurus search by opening the Looked Up list. For example, after browsing through synonyms for *earth* and *orb*, you can return to the original list of synonyms by selecting *world* from the Looked Up list. You can also step back through the words you have looked up by choosing the Previous button. This button will be grayed when there are no more previously looked-up words to recall.

Word will retain the list of looked-up words only as long as the Thesaurus dialog box is open. When you close it, the list is emptied.

How to replace the old word with a new one

After you identify a suitable synonym, simply select that word in the Meanings or Replace With Synonym list box. Word will place the selected word in the text box at the top of the Replace With Synonym list. Choose the Replace button, and Word will close the Thesaurus dialog box and replace the original word in your document with the synonym you specified.

When you're trying to find an appropriate word and you can think of several that aren't quite right, it's sometimes useful to type your near misses in the Thesaurus dialog box and have the Thesaurus look up each word. The Thesaurus can manage this task easily enough, but not the way you might expect. Rather than entering your near miss in the Looked Up text box, you need to enter it in the Replace With Synonym text box and choose the Look Up button. Word will move the word to the Looked Up text box and look up the word. If it finds a match, it will show the appropriate synonyms and definitions.

Using Symbols and Special Characters

There are times during the creation of a document when your problem isn't a matter of finding the right word—it's a matter of finding the right character. Word offers several special formatting characters you can insert along with your text. These characters include nonbreaking spaces, optional hyphens, nonbreaking hyphens, and characters such as curly quotes. In addition, Word offers a wide range of symbols, such as copyright marks and foreign language characters.

How to insert special characters

There are two built-in ways to add symbols and special characters to your documents with Word: through the Symbol dialog box and through keyboard shortcuts. The keyboard is quicker, but the dialog box is easier until you learn the shortcut keys. And because the dialog box will show you the shortcut keys as you choose each symbol, you can use it as a tool to learn the keyboard shortcuts as well.

The Insert Symbol command

To use the Symbol dialog box, start by placing the cursor at the point in your document where you want to insert a symbol or a special character. Then choose Insert Symbol. Word will open the Symbol dialog box, which has two cards labeled Symbols and Special Characters. Figure 5-15 shows the dialog box, with the Symbols card showing.

FIGURE 5-15

The Symbols card makes it simple to put special symbols in your documents.

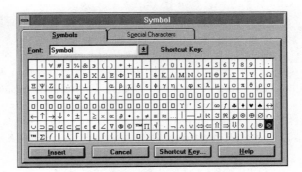

Symbols. At the top of the Symbols card is the Font text box, which in Figure 5-15 shows that the currently selected font is Symbol. The majority of the card is filled with a grid showing the 223 printable characters available in the Symbol font's character set. You can choose from other available fonts by opening the Font drop-down list box; the list of fonts will vary depending on how your copy of Windows is set up and which printer you've installed. In general, your choices will include Wingdings, Symbol, and MS Line Draw, which are all TrueType fonts, plus the choice (normal text) that shows the characters available in most other Windows fonts.

When you first open the dialog box, one square on the grid will be high-lighted to indicate that it's the currently selected character. To see an en-larged view of a character, you can point to it with the mouse and click the left mouse button, or you can use the arrow keys to move around the table. After the first keypress, Word will show an enlarged view of each symbol as you highlight it.

As you can see in Figure 5-15, there are several buttons along the bottom of the Symbols card. Choose the Insert button, or double-click on any character in the grid, and Word will insert the selected symbol at your cursor location.

After you insert a character with the Insert button or by double-clicking, Word will not close the Symbol dialog box. This lets you easily insert several symbols without the chore of having to re-open the dialog box repeatedly. You can click on your document and then move the cursor position—or even edit the document—before inserting each symbol. Word will make the document ac-tive while leaving the Symbol dialog box on top of the document on the screen. After you move the cursor to the new position, click on the dialog box to make it active.

After you insert the first symbol, Word will rename the Cancel button to Close, and after each insertion it will select the Close button as the highlighted choice; you can either press Enter or choose Close to return to your document easily. If you prefer se-lecting the symbols from the keyboard rather than with the mouse, note that once Word selects the Close button, you'll have to tab back to the grid of characters before you can use the arrow keys to move the character selection again. This leaves the Insert button as the highlighted choice.

How to assign a shortcut key to a symbol

You can use the Shortcut Key button to assign a keystroke combination so that, in subsequent usage, you can insert a symbol without opening the Sym-bol dialog box. First select the symbol and then choose the Shortcut Key but-ton, and Word will open the Customize dialog box with the Keyboard card showing, as in Figure 5-16.

We've arranged the figure so that you can see the Symbol dialog box be-hind the Customize dialog box. In this example, we have chosen the Wingdings font and selected the third box from the right in the third row. This symbol is a shaded box that's particularly useful for creating checklists and survey forms. That makes it a prime candidate for a character that you might use repeatedly.

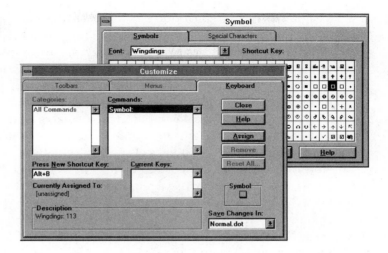

FIGURE 5-16

The Customize
Keyboard feature lets
you assign shortcut
keys to symbols.

When you open the Customize dialog box this way, Word limits
the possibilities for customization. Specifically, you can use only
the Keyboard card, and only to assign a keystroke to the character
you selected before opening the Customize dialog box. Notice that
the Categories list box is grayed, with only one choice—All Commands—available in any case, and the Commands list box is limited to one choice as well—Symbol—with the actual symbol
showing in the lower right corner of the card, just above the Save
Changes In box. As you might suspect, you can use this dialog box
for far more sophisticated customizing as well. We'll cover the
keyboard customizations in depth in Chapter 28.

In Figure 5-16, we have pressed Alt-B (as a mnemonic for *box*), and Word
displays the key combination in the Press New Shortcut Key text box. The
Current Keys list box is empty, indicating that there are no shortcut keys
currently assigned to this symbol, and the Currently Assigned To area, just
under Alt-B, indicates that this shortcut key is not assigned to any other
character or command. If it were already assigned, Word would show you
the assignment. You could then backspace to remove Alt-B from the text box
and then press another key combination for the new shortcut key. Alternatively,
you could go ahead and assign Alt-B to the box, overriding the previous

assignment. The Description box indicates that this is character number 113 in the font that's named Wingdings.

As with AutoText entries, shortcut keys are stored in templates, and all of the same considerations about templates apply. Briefly, the Save Changes In box lists the templates to which the current document is attached. NORMAL.DOT is the default selection, and storing a shortcut key in NORMAL.DOT will make the shortcut available to all documents you create. Until you're familiar with templates, and unless you have a specific reason for storing your shortcut keys elsewhere even then, we recommend that you store your shortcut key customizations in NORMAL.DOT. For more on templates, see "How to choose a template" on page 148.

When you're satisfied with the settings, choose the Assign button to assign the shortcut key. Word will remove the keystroke combination from the Press New Shortcut Key text box and add it to the Current Keys box. Should you change your mind and decide that you want to remove the key assignment, simply select the key combination in the Current Keys box, and then choose the Remove button.

To close the Customize dialog box, choose the Close button, and Word will return you to the Symbols dialog box. The shortcut key is now assigned to the symbol, and when you're working in your document you'll be able to insert the shaded box from the Wingdings font simply by pressing Alt-B. Note also that Word will show you the shortcut key for any character as you select it from the grid on the Symbols card. The keystroke is displayed after the words *Shortcut Key*, to the left of the Font box at the top of the card.

You can define more than one shortcut key for the same symbol. You might want multiple shortcut keys for any of several reasons. For example, if more than one person uses the same computer and each user prefers different keystrokes, each user can use the keystroke he or she prefers. To define additional shortcut keys, simply repeat the procedure just described. As you assign each one, Word will add the new key to the Current Keys box.

If you want to insert a symbol several times in a given document but don't expect to use it again in future documents, you don't need to assign a shortcut key. After you insert the symbol once, close the Symbol dialog box, and use the Edit Repeat command (this is fastest with the F4 shortcut) to repeat the Insert Symbol operation wherever you need that symbol in your document. The drawback to this technique is that you'll need to insert all the symbols before performing any other editing task: Your next editing operation will change the Edit Repeat function.

Special Characters

The second card in the Symbol dialog box is labeled *Special Characters*. Select it, and the dialog box will look like the one in Figure 5-17.

The Special Characters card in the Symbol dialog box makes it easy to select a special character to insert in your document.

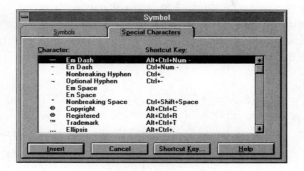

The card shows a list of characters, their names, and their shortcut keys (if any are assigned). The buttons along the bottom of the card are the same as for the Symbols card, and they work the same way. To insert one of the special characters, for example, you select it in the list and choose the Insert button (or double-click on the entry to be inserted). Word will insert the selected character and keep the dialog box open until you choose the Close button. Similarly, the Shortcut Key button will open the Customize dialog box, in which you can assign or remove a shortcut key as just described.

If you browse through the list box on the Special Characters card, you can see that there is some overlap with the characters on the Symbols card— with choices, for example, that include the Copyright, Registered, and Trademark symbols. However, you'll also find characters that aren't available on the Symbols card. For the most part, these are meant for typesetting or desktop publishing needs, so you may not be familiar with them.

Depending on your needs, you may want to take advantage of these typesetting characters, or you may want to stay with the typewriter-style equivalents. However, there are also some characters that you may find helpful even if all you're interested in is typewriter-style output. Here's a quick rundown of the characters and their uses, in their order within the Character list. You'll also find a list of the keyboard shortcuts for easy reference, following the discussion of the various characters.

Em dashes and en dashes

Many people use a hyphen, or two hyphens together, when they want to insert a dash in their text. From a typographical viewpoint, however, the hyphen should be used only for hyphenated words or to mark the break in a word at the end of a line. At other times, you should use an em dash or an en dash. The em dash is defined as a line that is as long as an uppercase *M* is wide, whereas an en dash is defined as a line that is as long as an uppercase *N* is wide. You can use either one to replace a hyphen or a double hyphen in your text. The en dash is meant for use with large fonts, where the em dash would take up too much space. The shortcut keys for both use the minus key located on the numeric keypad. The shortcut for the em dash is Alt-Ctrl-NumPad -, and for the en dash, Ctrl-NumPad -.

 If you're used to typing two hyphens in a row but prefer the way an em dash looks, use Word's AutoCorrect feature, covered in the first part of this chapter, to replace two hyphens with an em dash whenever you type them.

Hyphens

Word offers three kinds of hyphens: regular, optional, and nonbreaking. For the most part, Word treats a regular hyphen, which you enter by pressing the hyphen key, like any other character in your document. If the hyphenated word falls at the end of a line, however, Word will split the word between two lines, keeping the hyphen and all characters to the left of the hyphen on the first line.

Nonbreaking hyphens

Use a nonbreaking hyphen when you don't want a word to break at the hyphen under any conditions. For example, suppose you're writing about the software program Lotus 1-2-3. To prevent Word from breaking *1-2-3* at the end of a line, use nonbreaking hyphens. The shortcut key for a nonbreaking hyphen is Ctrl-Shift-hyphen (not the minus key on the numeric keypad). Nonbreaking hyphens are always displayed on your screen, but their format changes depending on whether or not optional hyphens are being displayed. To display optional hyphens (discussed in the next paragraph)—as well as to change the display of nonbreaking hyphens—choose Tools Options and then the View card, and add a check to either the Optional Hyphens or the All check box in the Nonprinting Characters section. Alternatively, you can click on the Show All button on the Standard toolbar. When Word is set to display optional hyphens, nonbreaking hyphens appear slightly longer and slightly higher than regular hyphens; otherwise, they appear identical. On your printouts, however, nonbreaking hyphens always look exactly like regular hyphens.

Optional hyphens

An optional hyphen is printed only when the hyphenated word is broken at the end of a line. When you use the Tools Hyphenation command to insert hyphens automatically, Word will insert only optional hyphens. (We'll discuss the Tools Hyphenation command in the next chapter.) To create an optional hyphen manually, press Ctrl-hyphen (not the minus key on the numeric keypad). If Word is set to display all optional hyphens (as discussed previously), optional hyphens are displayed on the screen as ¬. If you choose not to display optional hyphens, Word will show only the ones that happen to fall at line breaks. These will look exactly like regular hyphens.

We recommend that you use an optional hyphen whenever you hyphenate a word at the end of a line. If you later revise your document, Word will not print the hyphen if the word has moved to the middle of a line.

Em spaces and en spaces

The em space and en space are similar to the em and en dash, in that their widths match the widths of the uppercase letters *M* and *N*. Use these when you need extra space between a pair of letters or words but do not want to change the spacing for all letters or words. There is no default shortcut key for either of these.

Nonbreaking spaces

A nonbreaking space is a space that Word treats like a printing character in some ways. If you place one or more nonbreaking spaces between two words, Word will not put the words on different lines when they fall at a line break. Rather, Word will treat the two words and the nonbreaking space as a single unit when wrapping text.

To create a nonbreaking space, press Ctrl-Shift-Spacebar. If Word is set to display spaces, each nonbreaking space will look like a degree character (°) on your screen. These special characters will not appear in your printed document; Word will print a blank space.

Nonbreaking spaces can be useful when you want to keep two or more words together on the same line. For example, when you enter a date, such as July 23, 1992, you may want to enter nonbreaking spaces between July, 23, and 1992. You might also use nonbreaking spaces between the different portions of a multipart number, such as a social security number.

One important characteristic of a nonbreaking space is that it maintains a specific width. You may have noticed that in a justified paragraph the width of a regular space will vary as Word adjusts the space between words. A nonbreaking space, on the other hand, is always about as wide as a lowercase *n*. However, Word adjusts the width of nonbreaking spaces according to the point size and character formatting of your text (just as the size of the lowercase *n* would change). For example, a nonbreaking space in the middle of boldface text will be slightly larger than one that falls in the middle of plain text.

Copyright, registered, and trademark symbols

These three characters are available on both the Symbols card and the Special Characters card. The versions available on the Special Characters card are drawn from the character set of the current font in your document—meaning the font Word will use if you close the dialog box and simply type text at the cursor position. This is also the same version of the symbols that you'll find on the Symbol card if you select (Normal Text) in the Font box. However, they are different from the similar symbols available in other specific fonts, such as the Symbol font. The shortcut keys for these three symbols are Alt-Ctrl-C for Copyright, Alt-Ctrl-R for Registered, and Alt-Ctrl-T for Trademark.

Ellipses

An ellipsis, which looks like a sequence of three periods in a row, is generally used to represent text that has been omitted. In fact, you can get a nearly identical effect by entering three periods. The advantage of using the special character is that Word treats it as a single character and will not break it into two parts if it falls at the end of a line. The shortcut key is Alt-Ctrl-period.

Single and double opening and closing quotation marks

As we discussed in the AutoCorrect section earlier in this chapter, opening and closing curly quotes (' ' and " ") are much preferred over straight quotes (' and ") for those who care about such things, except for a few special purposes that require straight quotes, such as ' for feet and " for inches. In general, it's easier to use the AutoCorrect feature for curly quotes, but you can use these choices on the Special Characters card to get the same effect.

You can also use keyboard shortcuts to insert these characters into a document. See Figure 5-18.

Keyboard shortcuts

Although you can create your own shortcut key assignments for any symbol or special character, as we described earlier in this chapter, Word comes with a large number of shortcut keys already defined for special characters. These include the shortcuts we've mentioned while describing the characters available on the Special Characters card. For reference, Figure 5-18 lists these characters and their default shortcut key assignments.

Special Character	Shortcut Key
Em dash	Alt-Ctrl-NumPad - (minus key on numeric keypad)
En dash	Ctrl-NumPad - (minus key on numeric keypad)
Nonbreaking hyphen	Ctrl-underscore (Shift-hyphen)
Optional hyphen	Ctrl-hyphen
Nonbreaking space	Ctrl-Shift-space
Copyright symbol	Alt-Ctrl-C
Registered symbol	Alt-Ctrl-R
Trademark symbol	Alt-Ctrl-T
Ellipsis	Ctrl-period
Single opening quote	Ctrl-grave accent, grave accent
Single closing quote	Ctrl-apostrophe, apostrophe
Double opening quote	Ctrl-grave accent, double quotation mark
Double closing quote	Ctrl-apostrophe, double quotation mark

FIGURE 5-18

Word provides predefined shortcut keys for certain special characters.

Foreign language characters

Word also offers a wide range of foreign language characters that you can insert by pressing predefined shortcut keys. These include letters with various diacritical marks, as well as diphthongs, such as æ, as shown in Figure 5-19.

Character(s)	Shortcut Key
à, è, ì, ò, ù	Ctrl-grave accent, *letter*
À, È, Ì, Ò, Ù	Ctrl-grave accent, Shift-*letter*
á, é, í, ó, ú, ý	Ctrl-apostrophe, *letter*
Á, É, Í, Ó, Ú, Ý	Ctrl-apostrophe, Shift-*letter*
â, ê, î, ô, û	Ctrl-Shift-^, *letter*
Â, Ê, Î, Ô, Û	Ctrl-Shift-^, Shift-*letter*
ã, ñ, õ	Ctrl-Shift-~, *letter*
Ã, Ñ, Õ	Ctrl-Shift-~, Shift-*letter*
ä, ë, ï, ö, ü, ÿ	Ctrl-Shift-colon, *letter*
Ä, Ë, Ï, Ö, Ü, Ÿ	Ctrl-Shift-colon, Shift-*letter*
å, Å	Ctrl-Shift-@, a *or* A
æ, Æ	Ctrl-Shift-&, a *or* A
œ, Œ	Ctrl-Shift-&, o *or* O
ç, Ç	Ctrl-comma, c *or* C
ð, Ð	Ctrl-apostrophe, d *or* D
ø, Ø	Ctrl-/, o *or* O
¿	Ctrl-Alt-Shift-?
¡	Ctrl-Alt-Shift-!
ß	Ctrl-Shift-&, s

FIGURE 5-19

These shortcut keys make it easy to insert foreign language characters in your documents.

How to insert any character from the keyboard

If all else fails, note that you can insert any character from the current font without using the Insert Symbol command or specially assigned keyboard shortcuts. If you know the ANSI or OEM code for the character you want, you can insert these by holding down the Alt key and typing the numeric code with the numeric keypad. For details on how to use the ANSI and OEM codes, take a look at the section "How to find special characters" on page 115. You can find the codes themselves in Appendix B, "ANSI & OEM Codes."

Creating Headers and Footers

There is one other kind of text that you're likely to need at least occasionally: headers and footers. As the names imply, headers normally go at the top of each page in your document and footers go at the bottom. In general, both headers and footers serve as guideposts for the reader. In magazines, for example, they offer information such as the name, volume, issue, and date of the publication. In books, they often include a chapter or section name. But even in something as short as a two-page letter, a header or footer can be useful for showing the page number if nothing else.

Word's system for creating, formatting, and editing headers and footers is one of the most flexible of any word processor's. You can create headers and footers that range from a single character to multiple paragraphs. You can format them using many of the same features you use for body text. And you can also add graphics, such as a logo, to headers and footers. You can define different sets of headers and footers for odd and even pages, and a different set for the first page of a section or document. You can even control the position of headers and footers to place them anywhere on the printed page. We will cover some of the advanced techniques in later chapters. For now, we'll stick to the basics.

Except when you check spelling, Word doesn't display headers or footers in Normal or Outline view. If you're in either of these views when you choose a command to work with a header or footer, Word will switch to Page Layout view, in which it will show the headers and footers—and let you edit them—in their proper positions as they will be printed. You can also see the layout of headers and footers with the Print Preview command.

Because headers and footers are essentially identical in behavior, differing only in where they are located on the page, we'll concentrate on headers in this discussion. Except where explicitly stated otherwise, however, the following comments apply to footers as well as headers.

How to add page numbers to your printed document

Probably the most common need with headers and footers is that they contain the page number for each page. The need is so common, in fact, that Word offers an Insert Page Numbers command that you can think of as a kind of minimal header-and-footer feature. More important, if all you want in your header or footer is a page number and (optionally) a chapter number, Insert Page Numbers is the easiest way to put it there.

If you are a Word 2.0 user who has learned to ignore Insert Page Numbers in favor of the View Header and Footer command, you will want to take another look at the feature. Insert Page Numbers in version 6.0 offers a number of important new capabilities—including, for example, the option to print the page number starting with the first page of your document.

You can choose Insert Page Numbers from Normal or Page Layout view. Word will respond with the dialog box shown in Figure 5-20.

FIGURE 5-20

The Page Numbers dialog box helps you add page numbers to your document quickly and easily.

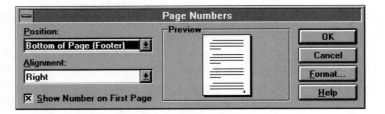

As Figure 5-20 shows, the Page Numbers dialog box has two list boxes, for Position and Alignment, plus a check box labeled Show Number On First Page. You can use these to tell Word where to print the page numbers. The Preview box will show the effects of your choices on a thumbnail sketch of a page.

The Position list box has two choices: Top Of Page (Header) and Bottom Of Page (Footer). These mean just what they say; you use them to assign the vertical position of the number.

The Alignment list box is a bit more complex, with five choices. The first three choices—Left, Center, and Right—will position the page number at the left side, the center, or the right side of the page, whichever you select. The remaining two—Inside and Outside—are not quite self-explanatory. These two are meant for documents that are to be printed on both sides of the paper and bound along one edge, as in a book. Choose either of these, and the preview box will change to show two pages so that you can see the layout of the page numbers on a pair of facing pages, as shown in Figure 5-21.

FIGURE 5-21

In the Page Numbers dialog box, you can format page numbers for facing pages.

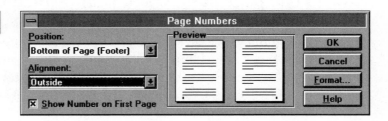

The Show Number On First Page setting is not reflected in the Preview box, but if you check this box, the first page number will appear on the first page of the document. This is frequently the preferred choice for a report, but most people do not number the first page of a letter or memo. If you don't want the first page numbered, verify that the box is cleared.

In addition to setting position, alignment, and first-page numbering in the Page Numbers Dialog box, you can choose the Format button to display the Page Number Format dialog box, shown in Figure 5-22.

FIGURE 5-22

Use the Page Number Format dialog box to tell Word how to number your pages.

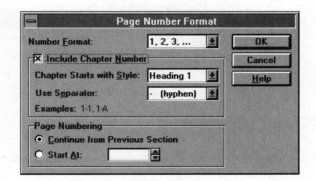

The Page Number Format dialog box has three sections. The top section contains a single item: Number Format. If you open this drop-down list box, you'll see examples of different numbering formats: Arabic numbers, upper-case or lowercase alphabetic characters, and uppercase or lowercase Roman numerals. Most often you'll probably want the default selection of Arabic numbers. Simply choose the format to use in any case.

In the bottom section of the dialog box, you tell Word to start numbering at a number of your choice, using the Start At text box, or to continue numbering from the preceding document section. This feature is useful if you have a long document, such as a book, broken into several files because it lets you set the starting page number for each file in order to maintain a continuous numbering scheme. (Note, however, that any changes in page length in one file will throw off the numbering in other files.) For a better way to handle page numbering over multiple files, see "Working with long documents" on page 589. You can also use Start At to return the page count to 1 at the beginning of each section of your text. You create new sections with the Insert Break command, which we'll cover in Chapter 13.

Between the top and bottom sections of the dialog box is a section that starts with a check box labeled Include Chapter Number. If the box is cleared, the rest of this section will be grayed. If the box is checked, however, the remaining options are available. As the name suggests, you can use this option to add a chapter number to your numbering system; for example, you can number pages in Chapter 1 as 1-1, 1-2, 1-3..., pages in chapter 2 as 2-1, 2-2, 2-3..., and so on.

Simply adding a check in the Include Chapter Number check box will not add chapter numbers to your headers—even with appropriate settings for the rest of the entries in this section of the dialog box. To have Word add chapter numbers along with Page Numbers in the headers or footers, you also have to add heading numbers with the Format Heading Numbering command. In addition, if you want to start the page numbering at 1 for each new chapter, you'll have to put each chapter in its own section. For details on adding numbers to headers, see "Numbering Headings" on page 483. For details on dividing documents into sections and making use of those sections, see "Multisection Documents" on page 485.

You use the Chapter Starts With Style list box to specify which style you've used to format the chapter headings. We'll discuss styles in Chapter 12. For now, simply be aware that if you want to include a chapter number in your header, you must be consistent about using a specific style—from Heading 1 to Heading 9—to format your chapter headings, and you cannot use the style for anything else. If you've used the Format Heading Numbering command to number the headings, then each time Word encounters a paragraph formatted with the specified style, it will advance the chapter count by one.

You use the remaining option in this section, Use Separator, to specify the character that will separate the chapter from the page number; the choices are hyphen, period, colon, em dash, and en dash. For a more detailed discussion of adding chapter numbers to headings, take a look, once again, at "Multisection Documents" on page 485.

When you finish with the Page Number Format dialog box, choose OK to close it and return to the Page Numbers dialog box. To create the header, select Top Of Page (Header) in the Position box. Choose OK to close the dialog box and return to your document.

When Word returns you to your text, it will also insert the {PAGE} field into your header. We'll discuss fields in detail in Chapter 20. For the moment, it's enough to know that the field is a marker that tells Word to put the current page number at that spot. If the program is set to view field codes, when you look at your document in Page Layout view you will see the field {PAGE}. If the program is set to show field results, you will see a page number. In either case, when you print your text, Word will insert the page number.

If you have already defined a header, using the techniques that we'll explain in the next section, and you give the Insert Page Number command, Word will not warn you about the potential conflict with the header that's already there. In fact, the conflict is more apparent than real. Word inserts page numbers in the header (or footer) area within a frame, without deleting or otherwise affecting any text already in the header. You may have to adjust the position of the page number frame or adjust the position of the text to make the layout of the two elements visually attractive, but you won't accidentally replace the old header with a page number and then have to re-create it.

The View Header And Footer command

Although you can use the Insert Page Numbers command for some header and footer functions, you'll need to use Word's View Header And Footer command to add information such as the document name or the current date. If you like, you can also use the View Header And Footer command simply to insert a page number.

The Header And Footer toolbar

When you choose View Header And Footer, Word opens the Header And Footer toolbar, shown in Figure 5-23 on the next page. In addition, if you are in Normal or Outline view, the program switches to Page Layout view. When you choose the Close button on the Header And Footer toolbar, Word will remove the toolbar from your screen and switch back to the view you were using when you started.

When you choose View Header And Footer, Word moves your cursor to the header. To move to the footer, you can either scroll to the bottom of the current page or click the leftmost button on the Header And Footer toolbar (the Switch Between Header And Footer button).

You can use the next two buttons on the toolbar—Next and Previous—for switching to the next or previous header defined within the document. This may mean moving between even and odd headers, moving to the first page header, or even moving between headers in different sections. The fourth button is used for controlling whether the current header is linked to the previous section. When headers are linked, changes in one section are duplicated in all linked sections. When the button is pressed, the Same As Previous message appears on the upper right border of the header. When the button is raised, the header is not linked and can be changed independently of headers in other sections. Of course, when you are viewing the footer, the Next and Previous buttons move between footers and the Same As Previous button links between footers. See "Multisection Documents" on page 485.

FIGURE 5-23

You create and edit headers and footers in Page Layout view, as shown here.

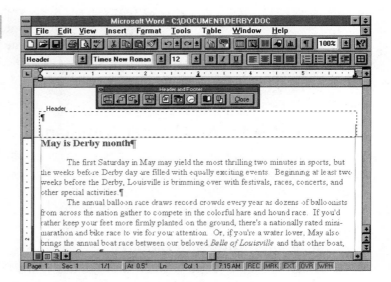

How to add page, date, and time to a header

In addition to header text such as a report title, which will stay the same on each page, you'll usually put some information in a header or footer that will change. The page number is the most likely candidate in this category. You may also want to include the current date and time when printing.

As we mentioned when discussing Word's Insert Page Numbers command, Word provides a special kind of entry for this kind of variable information. The entries are called fields. You can press Shift-F9 to toggle between seeing the fields themselves—such as {PAGE}, {DATE}, and {TIME}, for example—and seeing the results of those fields, such as the actual page number, date, and time. Alternatively, you can switch between field codes and field code results by checking and clearing the Field Codes check box on the Tools Options View card. (See Chapter 20 for more information on how to change the format of the information displayed by these fields.)

The next three buttons on the Header And Footer toolbar—starting with the fifth button from the left—will insert the field codes for page numbers, date, and time. If you want to add these to a header, you can simply position the cursor where you want the information to appear, and choose the appropriate button.

If you prefer, you can insert any of these fields from the keyboard. Start by pressing Ctrl-F9 to insert Word's field marker, a pair of curly brackets, which will appear on the screen with the cursor between them. You can then simply type *page* or *date* or *time* and then press F9 to update the code. Press Shift-F9 to display field results rather than the field codes. When you finish, the result will be exactly the same as using the buttons in the Header And Footer toolbar.

The fields that Word inserts when you choose the date and time buttons from the Header And Footer Toolbar (or type those same fields in directly, as just described) give the current date and time as registered in your system. These can serve as a date and time stamp for the document each time you print it; however, you may prefer to show a specific date and time that will remain constant. To convert a date or time field to text that won't change as the system date and time change, select the date and time field (or field results), and then press Ctrl-Shift-F9.

Also be aware that Word offers other date and time fields, including the date and time the document was created; both of these use the information in the MS-DOS date stamp on the file itself. For details on using these and other fields, see Chapter 20.

How to get different headers and footers on odd and even pages

To the right of the Time button on the Header And Footer toolbar is the Page Setup button. Click this to open the Page Setup dialog box with the Layout card showing, as in Figure 5-24 on the next page.

For the moment, the only section of interest on this card is the center section on the left side, labeled Headers And Footers. Your choices will affect the thumbnail sketch of a document in the Preview section of the card. We will discuss the rest of the Page Setup dialog box options in Chapter 17.

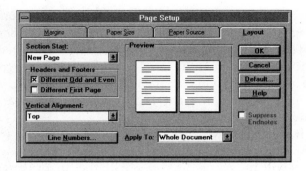

FIGURE 5-24

You can use the Page Setup Layout card to create different headers and footers for facing pages, as well as special first-page headers and footers.

You use the Different Odd And Even check box to create different sets of headers and footers on facing pages. For example, you might want to have the page numbers and a report title on the odd (right-hand) pages, and the date on the even (left-hand) pages.

How to print a different header and footer on the first page

You use the Different First Page option to specify a different header and footer for the first page only. Check this box if you want the header on the first page to be different from those in the rest of the document. You also check this box if you want no header on the first page but are using a header in the rest of the document.

How to hide the body text while editing a header or footer

The next button on the Header And Footer toolbar is the Show/Hide Document Text button. There are times when you might want to focus on the contents of a header or footer and not be distracted by the body text of your document. Click on this button to switch between displaying the full page and displaying only the header or footer.

How to leave the header or footer area

The last button, labeled Close, will close the Header And Footer toolbar, leaving the header and footer areas so that you cannot edit them. If you were in Page Layout view when you chose View Header And Footer, choosing the Close button will return the cursor to your body text and gray the header or footer text. If you were in Normal or Outline view, choosing the Close button will return you to the view you started in. You can choose the Close button either by clicking on it or by pressing Alt-Shift-C.

You can also close the Toolbar and hide the header or footer by double-clicking on the body text area in the document. This will have exactly the same effect as choosing the Close button. If you're used to Word version 2.0, you may be surprised to find that you cannot simply use the arrow keys to move between the header and the body text. You must choose Close, either by choosing the Close button with keyboard or mouse or by double-clicking on the body text.

How to create a header or footer

When you first choose the View Header And Footer command for a document that doesn't already have a header, Word positions your cursor at the first character space in the header area, much as it does when you open a new document window. In fact, the header area functions much like the standard document area in most ways. You can, for example, use the Formatting toolbar and the Ruler to control formatting.

Just above the header area, Word displays the label Header. For a footer area, it displays Footer. Other possible labels include First Page Header, First Page Footer, Even Page Header, Even Page Footer, Odd Page Header, and Odd Page Footer, depending on the settings you have chosen on the Page Setup Layout card and which page you are editing. (You can use the Show Next and Show Previous buttons to move between areas.) In a multisection document, the label will also indicate which section of the document the header is in, adding the word *Section* and the section number. (Once again, we will cover multisection documents, along with even and odd page layouts, in detail in Chapter 13.)

Whenever the cursor is in the header area, you can create the header simply by typing and formatting the text you want. For example, suppose you're writing an article about the Kentucky Derby and you want *Off to the Races* printed at the top of each page. You have only to type the phrase in the empty header area, as shown in Figure 5-25.

Press the Tab key to separate elements in a header or footer. By default, Word defines tab stops for the center and flush-right positions.

As the ruler in Figure 5-25 shows, the header is initially set flush left, with a centered tab at 3 inches and a right-aligned tab at 6 inches. If you are using Word's default settings, the header area's right-indent marker will fall at the 6-inch mark. Of course, the ruler settings will vary according to the formatting options you specify, just as they do in the body of your document.

FIGURE 5-25

To create a header, just type the text you want in the header area.

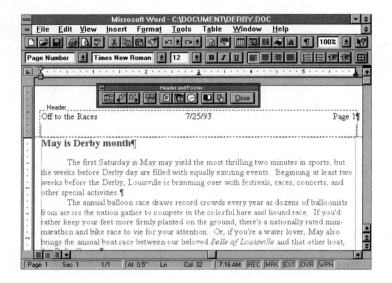

How to format and position the header text

Word's default positioning for a header is 0.5 inch from the top of the page, with the body text 0.5 inch below the header (1 inch from the top of the page). It's also 1.25 inches from the left side of the page, aligned with the body text.

You can use almost all of Word's formatting features—which we will discuss in detail in Chapter 7, "Formatting"—on your header text. For example, you can right-align the text, right-align a multiline header, or use borders to visually separate headers from body text.

Word also has options, such as the From Edge settings on the Page Setup Margins card, that change the spacing and location of your headers and footers. We will discuss these in Chapter 16.

How to delete headers and footers

To delete a header or footer, simply move the cursor to the header or footer area, select all of the text, and then press the Del key or choose Edit Cut.

How to use editing and proofing tools in headers and footers

If you start the spelling check with the cursor in the body text of your document, Word will check the body text first and then the headers and footers. If you start the spelling check from the header area, however, Word will check only the header. If you start from the footer area, Word will check only the footer.

Interestingly, if you are in Normal or Outline view when you start a spelling or grammar check, Word will remain in that view and open a separate pane at the bottom of the document window. This split into two panes looks similar to the result of using the Window Split command except that the lower pane contains either a header or a footer.

When you finish the spelling check, Word will close the second pane for you. If you choose the Cancel button during the spelling check, however, Word will leave the extra pane open. You can then edit the header or footer in the pane, and when you finish, you can either choose the Close button or press Alt-Shift-C to close the pane. If you're familiar with Word version 2.0, you'll recognize this pane as the only way version 2.0 provided for editing a header or a footer in Normal or Outline view.

Now that we've covered the basics of typing and editing text, we're ready to explore the three proofing tools—for checking spelling, grammar, and hyphenation—in the next chapter.

TOPIC FINDER

Checking Spelling   179

- A quick tour of the Spelling dialog box
- The Tools Options Spelling card
- How to find and correct misspelled words
- Custom dictionaries
- How to exclude words
- The (no proofing) language option

Checking Grammar and Style   190

- A quick tour of the Grammar dialog box
- Readability measures and how to use them
- How to use the grammar-checking options

Hyphenation   198

- How to use the Tools Hyphenation command
- Manual hyphenation
- Save hyphenation for last
- How to delete unwanted optional hyphens

Proofing

O nce you have entered and edited your text, Word stands ready to help provide a final polish to your words with three proofing tools. The spelling checker will help you locate and change misspelled words. The grammar checker will help you check common usage and grammar errors. Automatic hyphenation will help you hyphenate words correctly at the ends of lines. Each of these three tools can help you make a better impression with your writing.

Checking Spelling

Spelling errors are among the more distracting mistakes you can make. Misspell a common word, and it makes your work look sloppy. Misspell an unusual word, and you appear unfamiliar with it. Misspell someone's name, company, or product, and you stand a good chance of offending the reader. Word's spelling checker can help you avoid all of these mistakes.

Word identifies misspelled words by comparing them to one or more lists of correctly spelled words. The program comes with a dictionary of 106,000 words. In addition to this main dictionary, you can also develop custom dictionaries to locate and correct misspellings. Typically, these user-created custom dictionaries will contain proper nouns, technical terms, and other specialized words that match your needs. You may find also that Word's standard dictionary is missing quite a few nontechnical words that you use frequently. Fortunately, you can build these dictionaries painlessly over time as you use the spelling checker.

To check spelling, open the document you want to check, and choose Tools Spelling or click on the Spelling button on the Standard toolbar or press the F7 shortcut key. Word will begin the spelling check. When it encounters the first questionable spelling, Word will select the word in the text and open the Spelling dialog box, shown in Figure 6-1.

FIGURE 6-1

The Spelling dialog box.

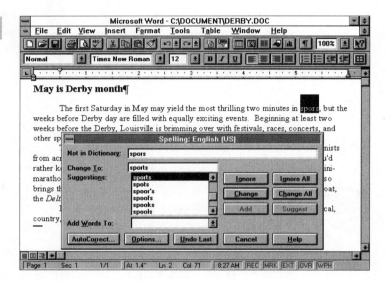

A quick tour of the Spelling dialog box

A tour of the Spelling dialog box will tell you most of what you need to know about the spelling checker. The title bar shows the dictionary currently in use—in this case, it is English (US), the dictionary with American spellings (*color*, for example, rather than *colour*). At the top of the Spelling dialog box is the Not In Dictionary text box, where Word will show you any word that it can't find in its dictionary. Below that text box is another text box with an attached list box. The second text box is labeled Change To, and the list box is labeled Suggestions. By default, when Word can't identify a word in your text, it suggests alternative spellings. This is an option you can turn off, as we will discuss shortly.

Ignore and Ignore All

There are six buttons along the right side of the dialog box, plus another five along the bottom. The top two on the right side are labeled Ignore and Ignore

All. If you don't want to change a word that the spelling checker considers suspect (as might be the case with someone's name or the name of a product, for example), you can tell the spelling checker to ignore that word. The Ignore button tells Word to skip just the one instance. The Ignore All button tells Word to skip all occurrences for the rest of the current editing session.

> That last point is worth special emphasis: Once you choose the Ignore All command for a given word, the spelling checker will continue to ignore that word even during later spelling checks during the same session. You can tell Word to stop ignoring words, however, with the Reset Ignore All button available on the Tools Options Spelling card, which we'll discuss later in this chapter. Word will also stop ignoring the words if you exit from Word and restart it.

Change and Change All

Below the Ignore and Ignore All buttons are the Change and Change All buttons. You can select a replacement for a suspect word from the Suggestions list box, or you can type the correct spelling directly in the Change To text box. If you choose Change, the spelling checker will replace the suspect word for the single instance that is currently highlighted in the document. If you choose Change All, the spelling checker will make the same change for any identically misspelled words it finds.

Add and Suggest

If you choose the Add button, the spelling checker will add the suspect word to the custom dictionary currently in the Add Words To box. If no custom dictionary is selected in the Add Words To box, the Add button will be grayed. (We'll show how to create and use a custom dictionary shortly.)

> In general, you should add words that are correctly spelled but not recognized if you expect to use them in other documents and if you're sure you'll never type the word accidentally when you mean something else. If you write about computer software, for example, you may often use a term like *.txt. But if you add txt to your dictionary, you risk missing a misspelling of *text*.

The Suggest button next to the Add button will be grayed by default; Word makes suggestions automatically unless you change a setting on the Tools Options Spelling card, as we'll discuss in a moment.

Auto Correct

The first of the five buttons across the bottom is labeled AutoCorrect. When Word finds a word with questionable spelling or capitalization, this button will be active. (When Word finds a repeated word in your text, the AutoCorrect button will be grayed.) If you choose AutoCorrect, Word will store the words currently in the Not In Dictionary box and the Change To box as an AutoCorrect entry. This feature makes it easy for you to build up AutoCorrect entries for your most common spelling and typing mistakes.

Think twice when adding AutoCorrect entries from the spelling checker. If the questioned word is actually spelled correctly but isn't the word you meant to use, adding it as an AutoCorrect entry will tell Word to change it for you even when you do intend to use it. For example, you might type *ti* instead of *it*, but if you designate these as an AutoCorrect entry, Word will change a passage about musical notes from *sol la ti do* to read *sol la it do*—which significantly alters the meaning (not to mention the fact that it makes the passage more difficult to sing).

Options

Choosing the Options button takes you to the Tools Options Spelling card. We'll skip that for now, but we'll discuss the Spelling card as soon as we finish looking at the remaining buttons.

Undo Last

The Undo Last button lets you back up if you realize you've accidentally chosen the wrong button. When you choose it, the spelling checker returns to the previous suspect word and undoes whatever instructions you gave the spelling checker about that word.

As with Word's Edit Undo feature, you can back up multiple steps to reverse spelling changes. In general, you can undo changes back to and

Even if the Undo Last button is grayed, you can still undo other spelling changes in the document so long as they were made during the current editing session—meaning since the document was opened for editing. Because Word treats spelling changes as editing actions, you can use the Edit Undo feature to reverse them. For details on the Edit Undo command, see "How to undo an action or multiple actions" on page 94.

including the first change since you started the current spelling check. If you undo all changes you've made during the current spelling check, the Undo Last button will be grayed.

Cancel and Help

The Cancel button aborts the spelling check, closes the Spelling dialog box, and leaves the last suspect word highlighted. This changes to the Close button after you use the Change or the Change All button.

The Help button takes you directly to help for the Spelling command.

The Tools Options Spelling card

Choosing the Options button takes you to the same screen that choosing Tools Options Spelling does, as shown in Figure 6-2.

FIGURE 6-2

Choosing the Options button displays the Tools Options Spelling card.

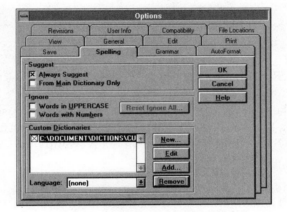

The Suggest options

In the area labeled Suggest, you'll see two check boxes, both of which are checked by default. The first is Always Suggest. If this box is checked, Word will always look for and display suggested corrections for words it cannot find in its dictionaries. The second box is From Main Dictionary Only. As the name suggests, using this option limits Word's search for suggestions to the main dictionary only.

As we've already mentioned, Word checks the Always Suggest check box by default; however, you may want to clear it to speed performance. Searching for suggestions can take time, and you must wait while Word displays its list of alternative spellings. If most of your misspellings tend to be typing errors, you may find you can spell most words correctly when Word brings the error to your attention. (Don't worry about mistakes. Word checks your corrections as well.) And you can always resort to the Suggest button to find the spelling for any individual word you really need help with. If spelling is not one of your strong points, however, you probably won't gain anything by clearing the Always Suggest check box.

The Ignore options

The next section, labeled Ignore, contains two check boxes and a button.

The two check box options are Words In UPPERCASE and Words With Numbers. By default, these are not checked. If you check the first of these, the spelling checker will ignore words that appear entirely in capital letters, on the grounds that these are likely to be trademarks, acronyms, or other special-purpose words with unusual spellings. If you check the second choice, the spelling checker will skip words that contain numerals, for the same reason.

We strongly suggest that you use these options sparingly; it is better to add your acronyms and other special-purpose words to the custom dictionary than to risk missing misspelled words.

The Reset Ignore All button will be grayed unless you've used the Ignore All button in the Spelling dialog box during the current editing session. When the Reset Ignore All button is active, you can use it to tell Word to stop ignoring the words you've designated with Ignore All. This feature comes in handy when you discover you've inadvertently told Word to ignore a word that is misspelled.

The combination of the Ignore All and Reset Ignore All features can help speed spelling checks on a rough draft of a document. If you are working with a draft that's filled with abbreviations, notes, the initials of the person who wrote each note, and other items that the spelling checker will question, you can tell it to ignore them during preliminary spelling checks with the Ignore All button. When you're ready for the final version and you want to be sure you've cleaned out all the notes from the rough draft, use the Reset Ignore All button to tell Word to stop ignoring those items.

The Custom Dictionaries options

You use the Custom Dictionaries section at the bottom of the card to manage custom dictionaries.

This section contains a list box that shows the available custom dictionaries and which of them are active. You can activate up to 10 dictionaries simply by adding a check in each dictionary's check box. (Toggle the check on or off by pointing with the mouse and clicking, or by highlighting the choice and pressing the Spacebar.)

Four command buttons along the right side of this section let you create and manage custom dictionaries. You can use the New button to create a new dictionary file. Choose it, and Word will open a dialog box in which you can specify a path and a name for the file. Dictionary files have the default extension DIC. You can store them in any directory on your disk.

You use the Edit button to open and edit the currently highlighted dictionary file as a Word document—a process that we'll discuss in a moment. This button is grayed if you opened the card from the Spelling dialog box. If you want to edit a custom dictionary with this command, you need to open the dialog box with Tools Options Spelling.

The Add button will open a dialog box in which you can specify a dictionary file to add to the Custom Dictionaries list. Note that you can add only files that already exist. If you want to create and add a new dictionary, you'll have to do it in two steps, creating it first with the New button.

The Remove button will remove a file from the list. Simply highlight the file you want to remove, and then choose the Remove button. Word will not stop to ask for confirmation. If you accidentally remove the wrong file, it's easy enough to add it back to the list by choosing the Add button.

You use the Language box to choose a language setting for the currently highlighted custom dictionary. As is the case with the Edit button, this option is grayed unless you opened the dialog box with the Tools Options command (Spelling card).

How to close the Tools Options Spelling card

After you make the changes you want on the Spelling card, choose OK to save your changes, or choose Cancel to discard any changes to the check boxes. (Reset Ignore All and changes to the list of custom dictionaries are not restored.) If you opened the dialog box by using the Options button in the Spelling dialog box, Word will return you to that dialog box.

How to find and correct misspelled words

You now know most of what you need to about spelling checker basics except how to designate the text to check. You have two choices, depending on whether you want to check your entire document or just a portion of it.

Most often you'll want to check all of your text (including annotations and footnotes, even if they are not displayed). With the cursor anywhere in your document and no text selected, simply choose Tools Spelling or press F7 or click on the Spelling button on the Standard toolbar. Word will check the entire document starting from the cursor's current position to the end of the document; then it will check from the start of the document to the cursor's current position. When the spelling checker reaches the point where you started, Word will display a message telling you the spelling check is complete.

How to check the spelling in a selection

You can choose to check only a portion of your text. Simply select the text you want to check; the selection can be as small as a single word. Then either choose Tools Spelling, press F7, or click on the Spelling button on the Standard toolbar. If Word finds a suspect word in the selection, it will display the word in the Spelling dialog box. When it finishes checking the selection, Word will display a message asking whether or not to continue checking the rest of the document. Choose Yes or No as appropriate.

Custom dictionaries

To use the spelling checker efficiently, you will almost certainly want to create one or more custom dictionaries to supplement the main dictionary. No matter what business you're in or what type of writing you do, chances are that you frequently use a specialized vocabulary that isn't in the main dictionary. At the very least, you probably use a specialized set of proper nouns, product names, and acronyms. It can quickly become annoying to have Word flag these words as unknown every time you use them. If you add them to a custom dictionary, however, Word will recognize them as legitimate words.

The easiest way to add words to a custom dictionary is with the Add button in the Spelling dialog box, which we described earlier in this chapter. However, there are some issues you should know about when you add words to a custom dictionary. First, Word provides a way to edit a dictionary entry should you make an incorrect entry. There is a way around the problem of incorrect entry, as we'll show you in a moment, but the easiest solution is to avoid it in the first place. As much as possible, be sure to type a new word correctly the first time.

Capitalization

Capitalization is another issue to be aware of. If you add a word to a dictionary in all lowercase letters, the spelling checker will accept that word in your text as long as it is all lowercase, all uppercase, or lowercase with an initial capital letter.

If you capitalize the first letter in the word when you add it, however, Word will recognize only occurrences that are capitalized the same way or are in all capital letters. For example, suppose you add the name *Cesarini* to a custom dictionary. When it checks spelling, Word will flag any occurrence of this name where the *C* is not capitalized or where not all of the letters are capitalized; *cesarini*, *CEsarini*, and *cEsarini* would all be flagged, but *Cesarini* and *CESARINI* would be accepted. If the dictionary entry has two or more letters capitalized, as in *McDonald*, the capitalization must match exactly in order for Word to accept it.

As much as possible, then, you'll want to add common terms in all lowercase letters. Use uppercase letters when you want the spelling checker to use capitalization as part of the basis for recognizing a word, as in the case of proper names. If the word is at the beginning of a sentence the first time the spelling checker finds it, you can add it with the initial capital letter if you like, but you'll have to add it again later in all lowercase if it shows up in the middle of a sentence.

Capitalization also affects the way Word shows alternatives in the Suggestions list box. If the suspect word is capitalized, Word will show the alternatives as capitalized also, and it will capitalize any replacement word you accept.

How to edit a custom dictionary

As mentioned earlier, Word offers an optional way to delete mistakes from a custom dictionary. You can edit a dictionary's contents using the Edit button on the Spelling card.

Custom dictionaries are simply text files, with each word on a separate line in alphabetic order. The Edit button on the Spelling card will open the highlighted dictionary for editing in Word.

After you open a custom dictionary file, you can add, edit, or delete words at will. Note that you do not need to keep the file in alphabetic order; Word will reorder it for you the next time you add a new word from within the Spelling dialog box.

You can also use this technique to add words from other lists or from dictionaries created in other programs. If you can edit the other file so that it contains one word per line, you can use the Insert File command to add those words to an existing custom dictionary. After merging the files, you should use the Table Sort Text command with the Case Sensitive option cleared; that way, you can scan through the file and look for duplicate entries. Then save the file. Your custom dictionary will contain all the added words. We'll discuss the Table Sort command in "Sorting" on page 789.

How to exclude words

There are times when you may want the spelling checker to question words it would ordinarily accept. For example, if you have a habit of transposing letters, you might type *teh* or *fro* when you intend to type *the* or *for*. While *teh* is not a word, *fro* is, as in *moving to and fro*.

You can tell Word not to accept *fro* by creating a new file called an *exclude dictionary*. Before you can create it, however, you need to know the name of the main spelling dictionary Word is using. You can find the name in the WIN.INI file, which Windows stores in the Windows directory. Open the file using Word or any other editor, and look for a line beginning with the word *Spelling*, in a section of the file labeled *[MS Proofing Tools]*. Figure 6-3 shows a sample WIN.INI file, with the single *Spelling* entry wrapping to three lines, as it will with most text editors. Note that at the end of the *Spelling* entry, you will find the path and name of the main dictionary file—in this example, C:\WINDOWS\MSAPPS\PROOF\MSSP2_EN.LEX. In any case, the file will end with the file extension LEX.

FIGURE 6-3

Your WIN.INI file should have a *Spelling* entry with the name of the main dictionary Word is using.

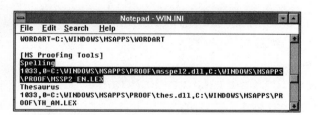

When you find the name for the main dictionary, write it down; you'll need it for naming the exclude dictionary. Be careful to close the WIN.INI file without saving any changes to the file. Next open a new document and type the words you don't want Word to recognize, using one line per word. Save this file in Text Only format, giving it the same name as the main dictionary but with the extension EXC instead of LEX. Be sure to store it in the same directory as the main dictionary. For example, if your main dictionary file is

```
C:\WINDOWS\MSAPPS\PROOF\MSSP2_EN.LEX
```

the exception dictionary must be saved as

```
C:\WINDOWS\MSAPPS\PROOF\MSSP2_EN.EXC
```

Word will then refer to this file whenever it performs a spelling check, and if it finds one of the words in the EXC file, it will treat that word as if it were not in the dictionary file.

The (no proofing) language option

After Word finishes a spelling check, you may see the message shown in Figure 6-4, indicating that Word found text formatted with the (no proofing) language option.

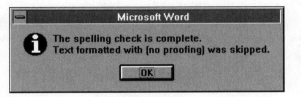

FIGURE 6-4

Word notifies you that it found text formatted with the (no proofing) language option.

The point of the message is to tell you that some or all of your text was skipped over during the spelling check—a valuable piece of information if you applied the (no proofing) format by accident. Unless you are already working with styles, the most common way you might make this mistake is by accidentally defining the Normal style with (no proofing). We will discuss styles in more detail in Chapter 12, but for now, you can check the setting by choosing Format Style and selecting Normal in the Styles list. If the Description box includes the words *(no proofing)*, you should change it. Choose the Modify button, and then choose the Format button. From the drop-down list, select Language, and then select an option from the Mark Selected Text As list box. This defines which dictionary to use; most American English speakers will want the English (US) option. Choose OK to close the language dialog box, OK again to close the Modify Style dialog box, and Close to close the Style dialog box.

You can use the (no proofing) format option to advantage. For example, you might have a table of organization names with their acronyms. To keep the spelling checker from stopping at each one, you could select the table, choose the Tools Language command, and select the (no proofing) option.

Checking Grammar and Style

It's one thing to know whether you've spelled your words correctly. It's another thing entirely to know whether you've put them together in a readable combination. Word helps you solve this problem with a second tool: the grammar checker. This tool will identify possible errors in grammar and style, suggest improvements, and provide a readability rating for your text. What's more, you have a great deal of control over the kinds of issues the grammar checker will flag for you.

A quick tour of the Grammar dialog box

You can start the grammar checker by choosing the Tools Grammar command. Word will then scan your entire document sentence by sentence, starting with the sentence the cursor is in.

Like the spelling checker, the grammar checker will ignore any text that is formatted with the (no proofing) option.

In its default setting, Word will also check spelling at the same time that it checks grammar. Spelling comes first, so if Word does not recognize a word in a sentence, you'll see the Spelling dialog box before you see the Grammar dialog box for that sentence. (If you like, you can turn off the spelling check, as we will explain later in this chapter.) After the program checks the spelling in a sentence, it checks for grammar. If it finds any suspect grammar, it displays the Grammar dialog box, shown in Figure 6-5.

FIGURE 6-5

The Grammar dialog box notifies you of possible grammar and style errors.

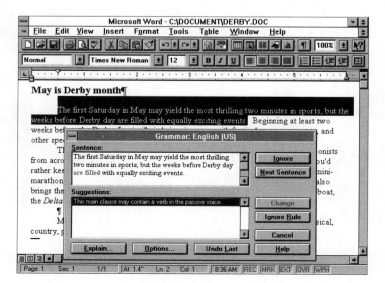

When the grammar checker flags a possible problem, it shows you the current sentence in the Sentence text box. You can edit the text in this box if you want to make changes.

Suggestions and explanations

Below the Sentence text box is the Suggestions box, where Word will offer suggestions for changes that might improve the sentence. Be careful about taking the program's advice. Remember that the English language is complex, and no one has yet written a grammar checker that has a real understanding of grammar or syntax.

Basically, the grammar checker follows rules that tell it when to flag something as being suspicious. And although the grammar checker is extremely sophisticated compared to a spelling checker, it will often make suggestions that are blatantly wrong. Even more often, the suggestions will be arguable. For example, Word will flag a sentence that starts with *And* or *But* and will tell you that it is preferable to avoid a sentence beginning with either. But there are times when breaking the rule makes for stronger writing. In short, you need to evaluate the sentence yourself and decide whether the suggestions make sense.

If you don't understand why Word is making a given suggestion, choose the Explain button at the bottom left of the Grammar dialog box. As shown in Figure 6-6, Word will offer an explanation of the rule and sometimes even suggest when it's OK to break the rule. These explanations can help you decide whether the suggestion applies to your sentence.

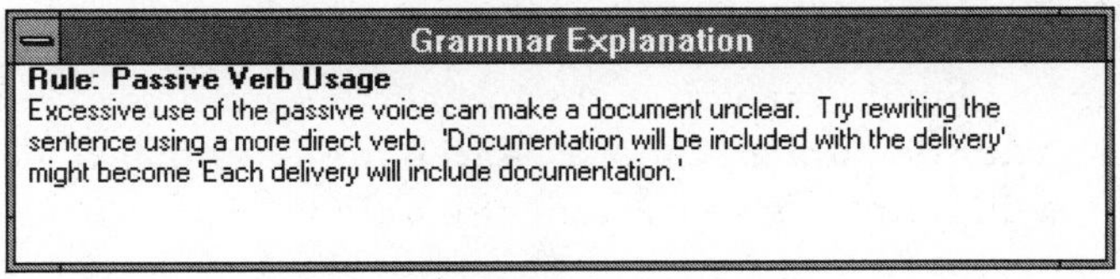

FIGURE 6-6

When you select the Explain button in the Grammar dialog box, Word will provide an explanation of the rule it used to make a suggestion.

Grammar Explanation

Rule: Passive Verb Usage

Excessive use of the passive voice can make a document unclear. Try rewriting the sentence using a more direct verb. 'Documentation will be included with the delivery' might become 'Each delivery will include documentation.'

How to find and fix the problem

When the grammar checker finds a possible problem, as in Figure 6-5, it highlights the relevant word or phrase in the Sentence text box (by presenting it in a second color). It also highlights any corresponding words in the Suggestions box. This makes it easier to locate the problem in the original sentence. If the suggestion includes a possible text change, Word may offer to make the change for you. In these instances, the Change button will be active so that you can select it. If there is more than one suggestion, you can choose one before making the change. You can also double-click on a suggestion—the equivalent of highlighting it and choosing the Change button. You also choose the Change button to apply to your document any changes you make to the text in the Sentence text box.

> You can also make edits directly in the document window if you prefer. To get to your text, you can use the mouse to click in the window, or you can switch to the window with Alt-F6 or Ctrl-Tab. In either case, the Grammar dialog box will remain visible. When you've completed your changes, you can return to the Grammar dialog box by clicking on the box or pressing Ctrl-Tab, and you can continue the grammar check by choosing the Start button.

If you make a change and then decide you shouldn't have, you can choose the Undo Last button at the bottom of the Grammar dialog box. This will reverse the last change made by the program. You can also use the Edit Undo feature to reverse the changes after closing the Grammar dialog box.

How to tell Word to move on without making a change

If you decide not to take Word's suggestion (as will frequently be the case), you can skip the suggestion by choosing the Ignore button. If you think the sentence is correct as it stands and you don't want Word to check it for any other possible errors, choose the Next Sentence button. If you completely disagree with the rule Word is using to make the suggestion, you can select the Ignore Rule button. You can also exclude rules on a permanent basis with the Grammar configuration options available through the Options button; we'll discuss these in a moment.

Finally, if you want to halt the grammar check entirely and return to your document, choose Cancel; the Grammar dialog box will close, and you will return to the document window.

Readability measures and how to use them

If you let Word complete a grammar check, assuming you're using the default settings, the grammar checker will display a Readability Statistics dialog box for your document, as in Figure 6-7.

These statistics are based only on the section of the document covered by the grammar checker in its most recent session. If you close the Grammar dialog box to edit your text and then restart the grammar checker, the statistics restart as well. Also, any text formatted with the (no proofing) option will be excluded from the results.

The first section of the Readability Statistics dialog box lists some basic information: the number of words, characters, paragraphs, and sentences.

The middle section uses these numbers to calculate average sentences per paragraph, words per sentence, and characters per word.

FIGURE 6-7

After it completes a grammar check, Word will display statistics about the readability of your document.

Readability Statistics

Counts:
Words	157
Characters	773
Paragraphs	6
Sentences	6

Averages:
Sentences per Paragraph	1.0
Words per Sentence	26.2
Characters per Word	4.7

Readability:
Passive Sentences	16%
Flesch Reading Ease	51.6
Flesch-Kincaid Grade Level	12.1
Coleman-Liau Grade Level	13.5
Bormuth Grade Level	11.2

OK   Help

The bottom third of the box reports some readability ratings. The first is the percentage of sentences containing constructions in the passive voice. Note that some sentences may be mistakenly flagged as passive.

In general, you should avoid passive voice where possible because it can make your writing seem stuffy and will definitely make it harder to read. For example, *He wrote the book* is livelier and easier to read than the passive construction *The book was written by him*. Some people insist it sounds more objective to write *It has been determined that...*, rather than *I discovered that....* In truth, the second form is not only stronger and easier to read, it's more honest because it tells the reader *who* determined whatever you are about to say.

The other four readability ratings are based on formulas that analyze sentence length and the number of multisyllable words. Text with longer sentences and bigger words is typically more difficult to read and therefore rates higher on these scales. The Flesch Reading Ease score is based on a 100-point scale; a lower-rated text is easier to read than a higher-rated one. Standard writing typically falls within the 70-to-80-point range.

The other three scores, Flesch-Kincaid, Coleman-Liau, and Bormuth Grade Levels, are reported in U.S. school grade levels. Text that scores between 7th and 8th grade level is considered easily readable by most adults. Note, however, that these measures will usually report different grade levels. Lower scores are theoretically easier to read; higher scores, more difficult.

These measures aren't absolute. The following selection scores between 11th and 15th (college-level) grades according to the Readability Statistics criteria:

The National Football League Championship is called the Superbowl, and the Philadelphia Eagles are one of the favorites this year.

In contrast, the next selection rates between 3d and 8th grade levels:

The bit count starts with the hex offset address. The first 2 bytes point to the last register in the FIFO segment.

All three readability scores rate the first sentence as more difficult to read, but most people will find the second much more difficult to understand. One of the reasons is that the second sentence relies heavily on specialized terms—jargon. These small words make the selection more readable according to the grammar checker formulas, but not in real life. The moral: Take the Readability Statistics results with a large grain of salt.

How to use the grammar-checking options

As we mentioned earlier in this chapter, you can change the way the grammar checker works by specifying which rules it uses. You can change these settings on the Grammar card of the Tools Options dialog box, shown in Figure 6-8. To reach the card, choose the Options button in the Grammar dialog box; alternatively, choose Tools Options and then Grammar. Notice that by default, Word checks both the Check Spelling and Show Readability Statistics check boxes. You can turn either of these features off if you like by clearing the appropriate check box.

FIGURE 6-8

You can use the Grammar card of the Tools Options dialog box to configure the grammar checker.

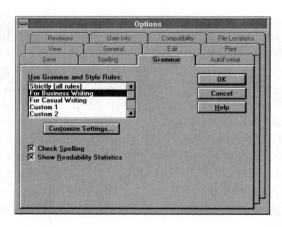

In the list box labeled Use Grammar And Style Rules, you can select a set of grammar rules for the Grammar checker to follow. Word can store six sets of rules; you can define any of them however you like. Until you change it, the Strictly (All Rules) option is set to use all grammar rules available to the program. The For Business Writing option, which is the default choice, uses fewer rules, and the For Casual Writing option uses the fewest rules. The other three sets are simply named Custom 1, Custom 2, and Custom 3. Choose the Customize Settings button to open the Customize Grammar Settings dialog box, in which you can specify the rules to use in each set, on a rule-by-rule basis. Figure 6-9 on the next page shows the Customize Grammar Settings dialog box.

The top item in the dialog box—the Use Grammar And Style Rules box—includes an attached drop-down list box from which you can pick which set of rules to modify. The example in the figure is set for business writing.

Second from the top are the Grammar and Style option buttons. These determine which types of rules Word will display in the list box immediately below the option buttons.

Most of Word's grammar rules, such as agreement between subject and verb, are clear-cut issues of right and wrong. Most style rules, such as the acceptability of starting a sentence with *And* or *But*, are open to debate (and are regularly broken by writers of the highest caliber). However, this distinction is not strictly true. For example, Word lists homonyms (words that sound alike but mean something different, such as *affect* and *effect)* as a style rule. But using the right word is not a matter of taste. Similarly, Word lists informal usage as a grammar rule. But usage is, in fact, normally considered an issue of style.

As you can see in Figure 6-9, each rule has a check box. The scroll bar on the side of the list box indicates that there are more rules than the list box can display at once. You can scroll through the list for each kind of rule.

If you are not sure what one of the rules refers to, you can select the rule in the list box and then choose the Explain button. Word will open a Grammar Explanation message box similar to the one shown in Figure 6-10 on the next page. You can then go back to the rules boxes, by clicking with the mouse or using Ctrl-Tab, to scroll through the list. As you highlight each rule, Word will show the explanation for it in the Grammar Explanation box. Note that if you highlight the rule by clicking with the mouse, the rule will toggle on or off. Click the rule again to reset it.

FIGURE 6-9

Use the Customize Grammar Settings dialog box to fine-tune the grammar checker rules to your needs.

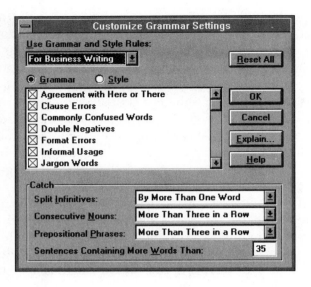

FIGURE 6-10

Word can provide explanations for the rules listed in the Customize Grammar Settings dialog box.

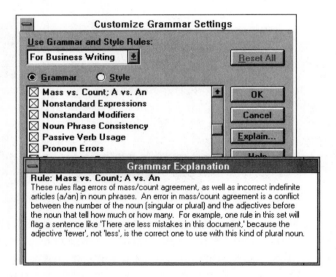

The default setting For Business Writing (the choice showing in the Use Grammar And Style Rules box in Figures 6-9 and 6-10) activates most, but not all, of the rules listed in the box under the Grammar and Style option buttons. More important, you can add or clear specific rules to customize the grammar checker. For example, if you know you tend to use weak modifiers such as *nice*, you might add the Weak Modifiers rule to the business writing configuration. Simply choose the Style option button, and check the Weak Modifiers check box in the Style list box.

As already mentioned, you can redefine all six sets of rules: Strictly (All Rules), For Business Writing, For Casual Writing, and the three Custom choices. If you go to the Use Grammar And Style Rules drop-down list, you'll see that the selected choice of rules changes as you change the selection. More important, you can define your personalized profile for each one independently of the others. The Strictly (All Rules) choice becomes something of a misnomer if you choose to leave out some rules, but you can still use the choice to include the maximum number of rules you want to follow.

> If you have made changes to any set of rules, you can choose the Reset All button at any time to tell Word to return the set to its default rules. Simply open the Customize Grammar Settings box and choose Reset All. Note that this will change only the set of rules currently shown in the Use Grammar And Style Rules box.

Finally, note the Catch section at the bottom of the dialog box. You can use the three drop-down lists to tell the grammar checker to point out split infinitives, strings of nouns, and consecutive prepositional phrases. More important, you can customize these to suit your taste. The choices in the Split Infinitives drop-down list are Always, Never, By More Than One Word, By More Than Two Words, and By More Than Three Words. The default For Business Writing choice is By More Than One Word. The choices for Consecutive Nouns and for Prepositional Phrases are Never, More Than Two In A Row, More Than Three In A Row, and More Than Four In A Row. The default For Business Writing choice for both is More Than Three In A Row.

The final item in the Catch section is a text box labeled Sentences Containing More Words Than. Word will flag any sentence with more words than the number in this box; the default setting in all cases is 35 words.

A strategy for using the grammar checker

Word's grammar checker is certainly not one of the program's strongest features, but that's the nature of all grammar checkers today. While it can catch mistakes that you might miss when proofreading, and while you can configure it to suit your needs and tastes, it is slow and not completely reliable. Used on well-written text, it suggests more mistakes than actually exist, a tendency that can quickly become tiresome. On the other hand, one mistake in a document can be too many, and if the program catches just one error, the improvement can be worth the time and effort.

In truth, the grammar checker's most valuable feature is simply that it will help make you aware of your writing. But for actually checking grammar, the grammar checker works best if you already know how to write well and you've taken the time to customize it. You'll want to turn off rules for mistakes you don't make, to avoid bothersome false alarms. And be sure to turn on the rules for mistakes that you do make. You will do well, also, to make the grammar check the last step (with the possible exception of hyphenation) in preparing your text.

Hyphenation

Word's hyphenation feature is another tool you can use to improve the final appearance of your text. Hyphenation is particularly helpful when you are using justified paragraphs or narrow columns. By hyphenating words, you can avoid the unsightly extra spaces that Word occasionally inserts to maintain a justified right margin. If you are using left-aligned paragraphs instead of justified paragraphs, hyphenation helps give lines somewhat more nearly equal lengths.

Word can hyphenate words as you enter text. If you find that distracting, you can use the Tools Hyphenation command on text you've already created. Either choice is far more efficient than manually inserting optional hyphens with Ctrl-Hyphen, and either one frees you to concentrate on your writing while you type or edit text. You can choose Tools Hyphenation to hyphenate an entire document or a selected portion of text.

As with the Spelling and Grammar checkers, hyphenation will skip over any text formatted with the (no proofing) Tools Language option. Although you can use this feature to good advantage, be careful not to format text for no proofing unless that's really what you want. If you simply want Word's hyphenation feature to ignore a section of text but you still want the spelling checker and grammar checker to check that section, you should format the text with Word's Don't Hyphenate option.

To format one or more paragraphs as Don't Hyphenate, first place the cursor in the paragraph you want to format; if you want to format more than one paragraph, extend the selection to all the paragraphs you want to format. Then choose Format Paragraph, select the Text Flow card, check the

Don't Hyphenate check box, and choose OK.

We'll cover paragraph formatting in detail in Chapter 7 on page 206.

How to use the Tools Hyphenation command

Before looking at the mechanics of Word's hyphenation feature, it's important to understand that Word actually has two different hyphenation features, both of which are available through the Tools Hyphenation command. The fully automatic hyphenation feature will insert all hyphens in a document without asking for your approval. The so-called *manual hyphenation* feature is semiautomatic. Choose manual hyphenation, and Word will prompt you to accept, reject, or change the position for each hyphen that it proposes.

If you want to hyphenate your text with the semiautomatic feature, first select the portion you want to hyphenate. If you want to hyphenate the entire document, make sure no text is selected. In the latter case, Word will check the entire document, no matter where the cursor is located. The selection, or lack of selection, will have no effect on the fully automatic feature.

To start the hyphenation, choose Tools Hyphenation. Word will show you the Hyphenation dialog box, illustrated in Figure 6-11.

FIGURE 6-11

The Tools Hyphenation command opens the Hyphenation dialog box, in which you can make configuration changes or start the hyphenation process.

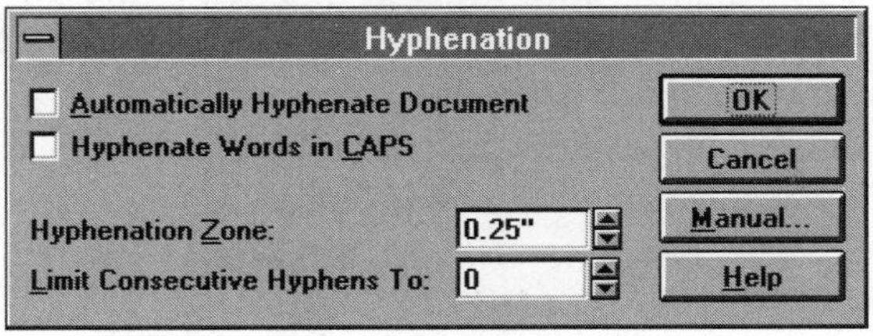

If you check the Automatically Hyphenate Document check box at the top of the Hyphenation dialog box, Word will do all of the work for you. (Word will make its decisions based on the settings in the dialog box for the Hyphenation Zone and Limit Consecutive Hyphens To boxes, which we'll explain in a moment.) If you prefer to make your own choices, use the Manual button—which we'll also explain shortly. If the Automatically Hyphenate Document check box is cleared and you choose the OK button, Word will return to your document without making any changes—just as if you had chosen Cancel.

Automatic hyphenation has a distinct advantage over other methods of hyphenation in that it will readjust the hyphenation if you change the font or size of your text or if you change other formatting settings. It will also enable you to undo all hyphenation in a single stroke. You can remove hyphenation by simply clearing the Automatically Hyphenate Document check box. Word stores the automatic hyphenation setting with each file.

The two disadvantages of automatic hyphenation are that you lose control over where the hyphens go and that your computer's performance can slow down because of the extra work Word does to determine where the hyphens should go. If your system is fast enough, the second disadvantage is not an issue. In general, if you use hyphenation, we recommend using the automatic choice unless you absolutely insist on controlling the position for each hyphen.

The Hyphenate Words In CAPS option

You use the Hyphenate Words In CAPS check box in the Hyphenation dialog box to tell Word either to hyphenate or to ignore capitalized words. If you don't want to hyphenate words that are in all caps, make sure this check box is cleared.

In general, you will not want this box checked if you are letting Word hyphenate automatically. The danger is that you could end up hyphenating a person's name, a place name, or an acronym in all caps. All of these possibilities are generally best avoided.

The Hyphenation Zone text box

Use the Hyphenation Zone text box to set the allowable distance between the right indent and the end of the line, an area that Word calls the *hyphenation zone*. By adjusting the width of the zone, you can adjust the unevenness of lines along the right margin in a ragged-right format. This setting also affects the number of words that will be hyphenated overall. The larger the zone, the fewer the words that will be hyphenated.

If the distance between the indention and the end of the line is greater than the value in the Hyphenation Zone text box, Word will try to hyphenate the first word on the next line so that part of the word will appear on the preceding line. The default measurement is 0.25 inch. If you want to decrease the raggedness of the words along the right margin, or if you want to reduce the amount of space that appears between words in justified text, enter a smaller Hyphenation Zone setting. On the other hand, if you want to hyphenate as few words as possible, or if you dislike seeing short single syllables at the beginnings of lines, enter a larger Hyphenation Zone setting.

Limit Consecutive Hyphens To

The Limit Consecutive Hyphens To text box controls how many consecutive lines can end in hyphens when Word hyphenates automatically. A value of 0 allows a hyphen on every line. Most people, however, prefer to limit the number of successive hyphenated lines to one or two. To limit the number, simply enter 1 or 2 in the text box. (The limit for the box is 32,767 lines, but anything over 3 or 4 in this text box will be effectively the same as entering a 0.)

Manual hyphenation

If, instead of using automatic hyphenation, you choose the Manual button in the Hyphenation dialog box, Word will search for the first candidate for hyphenation. It will then display the Manual Hyphenation dialog box, shown in Figure 6-12 on the next page.

When you use manual hyphenation, Word switches to Page Layout view.

As you can see in Figure 6-12, at this point Word shows the word broken into syllables in the Hyphenate At text box. You cannot see it in the figure, but Word positions a blinking cursor at the proposed location for a hyphen. Word will also highlight the suggested word break in your document, where it will show the recommended hyphenation in its context.

FIGURE 6-12

When Word finds a
candidate for hyphen-
ation, it will suggest a
word break.

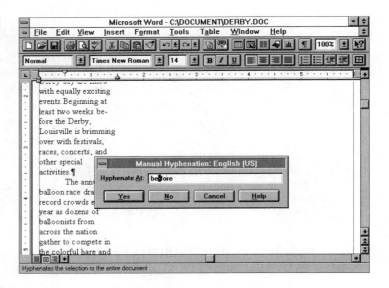

If you want to accept the hyphenation Word suggests, simply choose Yes. If you want to change the hyphenation, use the Left or Right arrow key or the mouse to move the blinking cursor to a new hyphenation point in the Hyphenate At text box, and then choose Yes. When you choose Yes, Word inserts an optional hyphen character at that point. For more information on optional hyphens and other special characters, see "Special Characters" on page 161.

If you don't want to hyphenate the word, choose No to skip it, or choose the Cancel button to end hyphenation and return to the document. Note that if you specify a hyphenation point that comes after the line break (marked by a dotted vertical line in the Hyphenate At text box), Word will add an optional hyphen at that point, but the word will wrap to the next line. If you edit or reformat your text later, however, so that the word's position shifts in the line, Word may be able to take advantage of the optional hyphen.

Word will let you hyphenate a word between any two letters—you do not have to break the word between syllables. If you place the cursor somewhere other than at a syllable break in the text box, Word will display a vertical cursor at that point rather than highlighting the break. You will find this flexibility in controlling word breaks very helpful in those few situations in which Word's syllable breaks are unacceptable.

If you start hyphenation for an entire document from the middle of a document, Word begins at the start of the current paragraph and proceeds to the end of the document. Then it starts hyphenating at the beginning of the document again and continues to the original cursor position. If you selected a block of text before starting hyphenation, Word will first hyphenate the selected block and then display a message asking whether you also want to hyphenate the rest of the document. After you have hyphenated the full document, Word will display a message telling you that the hyphenation is complete.

Save hyphenation for last

If you use Word's manual (semiautomatic) hyphenation feature, you will generally be better off if you complete your writing, editing, and formatting before you hyphenate. In particular, if you make substantial changes to a document after you've hyphenated it, you will almost certainly change the location of any number of hyphenated words, moving them to the middles of lines. In addition, you'll probably need to hyphenate a number of words that have moved to the ends of lines. Because hyphenation affects only the appearance of the final printed document, it is a waste of time to run the hyphenation feature repeatedly.

Having to rehyphenate is not an issue with automatic hyphenation, of course, because Word will adjust the hyphens for you as you change your text. Even with automatic hyphenation, however, you may be better off waiting until you've finished writing, editing, and formatting before starting the feature. Having automatic hyphenation break a word as you're typing it, and having it adjust line breaks as you write or edit, can be distracting. Depending on your system, you might also find that it slows your computer's performance noticeably.

Most important, if you wait until you're finished and then check the Automatically Hyphenate Document check box, you'll get the same result as if you had had the feature on from the moment you started writing the document. If you take this route, however, we recommend that you look through your document before printing it because hyphenation will affect line breaks and can therefore affect page breaks.

How to delete unwanted optional hyphens

Note that if you use manual hyphenation, you don't have to remove unnecessary optional hyphens from your text because Word doesn't print them unless they appear at line breaks. Even if you don't delete them, they won't affect the appearance of your printed text in any way. However, if you work with nonprinting characters displayed, we recommend that you delete unnecessary optional hyphens before you rehyphenate. Otherwise, your screen will be cluttered with optional hyphens.

The easiest way to remove optional hyphens is with the search-and-replace procedure described in Chapter 4. Use ^- (caret, hyphen) as the Find What text, and leave the Replace With text box blank to replace the hyphens with nothing. (The ^- is a special search-character combination that will find only optional hyphens. It will not find standard hyphens or nonbreaking hyphens.) If you've hyphenated your text recently, you also have the option of using the Edit Undo command.

The spelling and hyphenation tools covered in this chapter can play an important part in making your documents look better from a mechanical point of view, and the grammar tool can help make them read better. If you want to dress up your words visually, however, you'll need to format them to take advantage of your system's—and particularly your printer's—capabilities. In the next chapter, we'll cover fundamental formatting techniques.

TOPIC FINDER

Top-Down Document Design   208

Document Formatting   209
- How to determine the size of the text area
- The horizontal ruler
- How to change left and right margins
- NEW! The vertical ruler
- NEW! How to change top and bottom margins

Controlling Line and Page Breaks   219
- How to force line breaks
- Page breaks and repagination

Paragraph Formatting   221
- The defaults
- How to apply paragraph formats with the mouse
- How to apply paragraph formats with the keyboard
- The Paragraph dialog box: Indents And Spacing
- The Paragraph dialog box: Text Flow
- Tabs
- Paragraph borders and shading

Font Formatting   241
- How to apply font formats with the mouse
- How to apply font formats with shortcut keys
- The Font dialog box

Copying and moving font and paragraph formats   248
- How to copy a paragraph mark
- NEW! How to use the Format Painter

Formatting

s a full-featured word processor, Word for Windows offers you far more features than an ordinary text editor, but it stops short of equaling a desktop publishing program. Word gives you control over many formatting aspects of a document—page size, margins, text size, font, and line spacing, to name just a few. And the Windows interface lets you see what a formatted page will look like before you print it. Word doesn't offer quite the sophisticated formatting and typographic control of a high-end desktop publishing program, but it is capable of just about any desktop publishing task most users will ever need.

We'll discuss Word's advanced formatting features in later chapters. For now, we'll stick to basics. Be forewarned that even the basic features can get a bit intimidating, but one concept can make them easier to understand.

Formatting in Word takes place at four levels: the overall document, the section, the paragraph, and the character. (Note that Word 6.0, unlike earlier versions, refers to character formatting as *font* formatting.)

There is a distinction between formatting directly and formatting by style. We'll stay strictly with direct formatting in this chapter and save styles for Chapter 12.

Top-Down Document Design

Most formatting changes made at one level can affect the formatting at lower levels. For example, if you change the margins for your whole document (a document-level formatting change), you'll affect the width of every paragraph in the document. Because the different levels are interrelated, it makes sense to design your documents from the top down.

To design your document from the top down, decide first on the most general aspects of your document layout—paper size and margins, for example—and then fine-tune such factors as paragraph and font formats. You'll find that this approach simplifies document design and eliminates a lot of backtracking. Figure 7-1 lists some of the features you can set at each formatting level.

FIGURE 7-1

You can simplify document design by moving from the general to the specific.

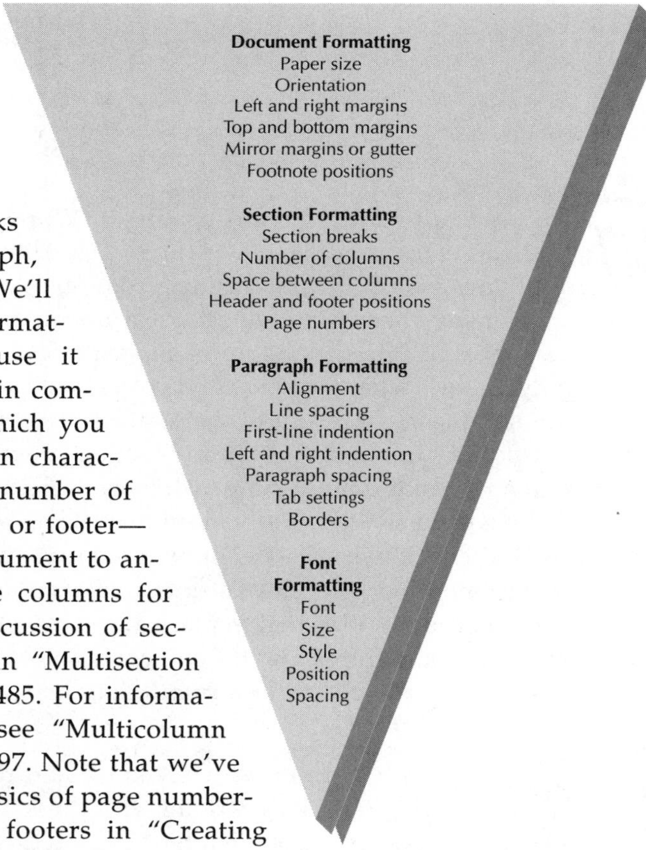

This chapter looks at document, paragraph, and font formatting. We'll save section-level formatting for later, because it comes into play only in complex documents in which you need to change certain characteristics—such as the number of columns or the header or footer—from one part of a document to another. We'll also save columns for later. You'll find a discussion of section-level formatting in "Multisection Documents" on page 485. For information about columns, see "Multicolumn Formatting" on page 497. Note that we've already covered the basics of page numbering and headers and footers in "Creating Headers and Footers" on page 167.

Document Formatting
Paper size
Orientation
Left and right margins
Top and bottom margins
Mirror margins or gutter
Footnote positions

Section Formatting
Section breaks
Number of columns
Space between columns
Header and footer positions
Page numbers

Paragraph Formatting
Alignment
Line spacing
First-line indention
Left and right indention
Paragraph spacing
Tab settings
Borders

Font Formatting
Font
Size
Style
Position
Spacing

Document Formatting

The first step is to establish your page layout. In most documents, the only factors that affect the layout are paper size, margins, and print orientation. Since the size of your available text area will affect the appearance of every paragraph, you should establish these three settings before any other formatting. If you change the size of your text area after you've changed paragraph or font formats, you may have to go back and reapply your paragraph or font formats.

How to determine the size of the text area

Figure 7-2 shows Word's default page layout. Word assumes that you're using 8½-by-11-inch pages in portrait orientation—that is, positioned so that

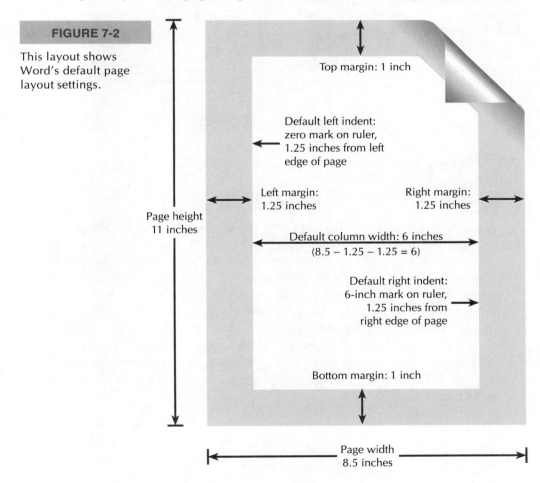

FIGURE 7-2

This layout shows Word's default page layout settings.

Top margin: 1 inch

Default left indent: zero mark on ruler, 1.25 inches from left edge of page

Left margin: 1.25 inches

Right margin: 1.25 inches

Page height 11 inches

Default column width: 6 inches
(8.5 − 1.25 − 1.25 = 6)

Default right indent: 6-inch mark on ruler, 1.25 inches from right edge of page

Bottom margin: 1 inch

Page width 8.5 inches

the lines of text print running parallel to the short sides of the paper. The default left and right margins are 1.25 inches each. The top and bottom margins are 1 inch each. These margins define the amount of blank space between the edge of the paper and the edge of your text.

The combination of paper size, margins, and page orientation delimits your available text area. The width of the text area, for example, is the width of the paper minus the left and right margins. With Word's default settings, the text area on each page is 6 inches wide (8.5 minus 1.25 minus 1.25) and 9 inches high (11 minus 1 minus 1).

You can change paper size and margin settings by choosing File Page Setup, which will open the Page Setup dialog box, as shown in Figure 7-3.

FIGURE 7-3

The Margins card in the Page Setup dialog box contains options for adjusting the margins of your document.

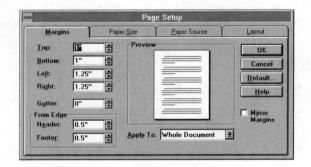

The Page Setup dialog box contains four cards: Margins, Paper Size, Paper Source, and Layout. You'll find a button labeled *Default* on each of the four cards. Choose this button, and Word will make the current settings on the card the default settings for the attached template. First, however, Word will ask you to confirm that you want to change the default settings, and it will show you the name of the template in which the changes will be stored. Answer Yes or No, as appropriate. Note that if you are using the Normal template, Word will not ask again whether to save the changes. If you are using a supplementary template, however, Word will ask whether to save those changes—and any others that you've made—on disk when you close the files that are using that template or when you leave Word. For details on using templates, see Chapter 27.

Margins

As you can see in Figure 7-3, the Margins card contains options for adjusting the top, bottom, left, and right margins. You need only enter a new setting in the appropriate text boxes along the left side of the card.

The Preview box in the center shows a thumbnail sketch of a formatted page. As you change the margin settings, the sketch will change to show the effect of the new settings.

The Mirror Margins check box in the lower right lets you set different inside and outside—rather than left and right—margins. This is a common requirement if you plan to print your document on both sides of the paper and you want the text area on both sides to match up, even if the left and right margins are different. If you check this box, the Left and Right margin labels will change to Inside and Outside, and the Preview box will change to represent a pair of facing pages.

Binding margins. You use the Gutter setting if you want to create a binding margin, which is important for pages that you plan to bind in a booklet, for example. (Do not confuse this Gutter setting with the concept of a gutter between columns, which Word refers to as the *space* between columns.)

If you enter a Gutter setting without checking the Mirror Margins check box, the binding margin will go on the left side of each page. If you check Mirror Margins, the binding margin will go along the inside edge of the facing pages, as shown in Figure 7-4.

FIGURE 7-4

Check the Mirror Margins check box, and Word will change the Left and Right margin labels to Inside and Outside. It will also show two facing pages and the effect of the Gutter settings along the inside of both pages.

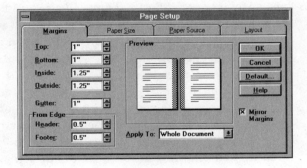

In a sense, the Gutter setting is redundant; you can get the same result on your printed page with or without it. For example, say that you want a 1-inch binding margin plus an additional inside margin of 1.25 inches and an outside margin of 1.25 inches. To get it, you can check the Mirror Margins check box and set the Inside margin to 2.25 inches, the Outside margin to 1.25 inches, and the Gutter to 0 inches. Or you can set the Inside margin to 1.25 inches, the Outside margin to 1.25 inches, and the Gutter to 1.0 inch. The two combinations of settings are equivalent.

You use the Apply To drop-down list in the lower right corner of the Margins card to specify whether the settings will affect the whole document (the default) or everything from the current cursor position to the end of the document. Word may offer other options depending on your document's contents and whether a block of text is highlighted when you open the dialog box.

Finally, note the Header and Footer text boxes in the From Edge box. These help determine the placement of headers and footers, but we'll ignore them for now. For details, see "Defining the Position of a Header or Footer" on page 588.

The text boxes in Figures 7-3 and 7-4 use Word's default units of measure: inches. You can change the unit of measure to centimeters, points, or picas, if you prefer, in the Measurement Units list box on the Tools Options General card. Even if you don't change that setting, you can still use any of the units that Word recognizes. To set a margin of 2.54 centimeters, for example, simply type *2.54 cm* in the appropriate text box and then choose OK. Word will convert the entry to inches, and the next time you open the Page Setup dialog box, the setting will read 1". Note that when you increase the top or bottom margin, you decrease your text area and, therefore, the number of lines that fit on each page. When you decrease a margin, you increase the text area.

Paper Size

Figure 7-5 shows the Paper Size card in the Page Setup dialog box. Note that this card includes the same Apply To drop-down list as the Margins card.

The operative word here is "same," not similar. You can't have one setting in this box for margins and another for size. As with the Margins card, the Preview thumbnail sketch will show you the effects of your current choices for both margins and paper size.

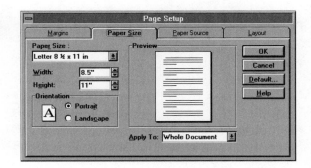

You use the Paper Size card in the Page Setup dialog box to define your page size and paper orientation.

The Paper Size drop-down list already defines a number of standard paper sizes. These will vary depending on which printer or printers you've installed and which is currently selected. (You can change the current printer by choosing File Print and then the Printer button.) When you select any of these predefined sizes, Word enters the dimensions in the Width and Height text boxes. If you are using an unusual page size, you can type the dimensions into the text boxes. Word will automatically change the Paper Size option to Custom Size.

Orientation. The Orientation box has two option buttons: Portrait and Landscape. Not all printers can take advantage of these options, but many can. With portrait (vertical) orientation, Word will format your lines of text to print them parallel to the short edges of the page. With landscape (horizontal) orientation, Word will format your text to be printed parallel to the long edges of the page. Figure 7-6 on the next page shows a layout sketch of a page that uses Word's default page size and margin settings but uses landscape orientation. Choose the Portrait or Landscape option button, and Word will adjust both the preview and the width and height settings appropriately.

When you format a document for landscape orientation, the text area may be wider than will fit on the screen. If the text doesn't fit, you can then use the horizontal scroll bar or the cursor-movement keys to scroll left and right, or you can adjust the text size with the View Zoom command, which we will discuss in Chapter 9.

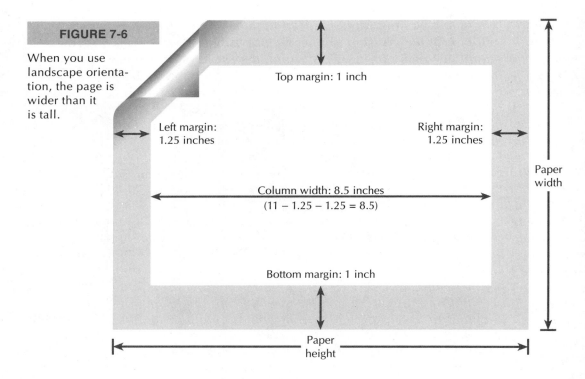

FIGURE 7-6

When you use
landscape orienta-
tion, the page is
wider than it
is tall.

Top margin: 1 inch

Left margin:
1.25 inches

Right margin:
1.25 inches

Column width: 8.5 inches
(11 − 1.25 − 1.25 = 8.5)

Bottom margin: 1 inch

Paper
width

Paper
height

For some printers, there are also Portrait and Landscape settings
in the Setup dialog box. If you've installed the HP LaserJet III, for
example, you can choose File Print, then Printer, then Options, to
open the LaserJet III's Options dialog box, where you can change
the orientation. Be aware, however, that changing the orientation
in the printer's Options dialog box does not affect the page layout
settings in Word; in fact, the setting will be ignored when you
print. To format the page correctly, you must choose Word's File
Page Setup command and use the settings on the Paper Size card.

Paper Source

The third card in the Page Setup dialog box is Paper Source. It contains options similar to those shown in Figure 7-7, although the choices in the list
boxes vary depending on which printer you have installed and designated as
the default printer. Note that you can specify one paper source for the first
page and a different one for all later pages—provided that your printer has
two paper sources. If so, you can use preprinted letterhead for the first page,
for example, and regular sheets for the rest of the document.

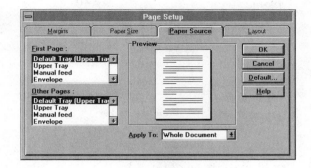

FIGURE 7-7

The Paper Source card in the Page Setup dialog box will vary depending on the printer that's installed and selected.

Layout

The Layout card, shown in Figure 7-8, contains some options that we've covered earlier and others that belong in a discussion of advanced features. We'll ignore this card for now. For a discussion of the Headers And Footers options, take a look at "Creating Headers and Footers" on page 167. For a discussion of the advanced features on this card, see "Multisection Documents" on page 485.

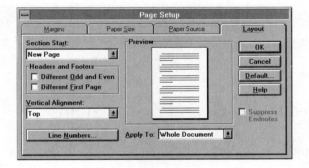

FIGURE 7-8

The Layout card in the Page Setup dialog box contains more options that affect your document's format.

The horizontal ruler

Word's horizontal ruler contains several symbols that indicate your current page and paragraph formats. The symbols double as tools that you can use to adjust these formats. For the moment, we'll concentrate on the symbols related to page format. Note that Word also contains a vertical ruler, which we'll discuss shortly.

If you're using Word's default settings and you're working in Normal view, the ruler will look like Figure 7-9 on the next page. The zero point is at the left edge of the white section of the ruler, and it always indicates the left edge of your text column—regardless of your left margin setting, paper size, or page orientation. For example, Word's default left margin setting is 1.25 inches from the left edge of the paper. If you change the margin setting to 3, the zero point on the ruler will represent a position 3 inches from the left edge of the paper.

FIGURE 7-9

This is the horizontal ruler with Word's default settings in Normal view.

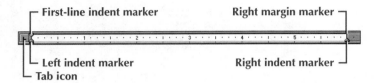

First-line indent marker   Right margin marker

Left indent marker   Right indent marker
Tab icon

The right margin, as defined by the Format Page Setup command, is indicated by the right edge of the white section of the ruler. This edge may not be visible, depending on several factors including the settings for your side margins, your Zoom setting, and your monitor type. In Figure 7-9, the zero point is at the left, and the right margin is at the 6-inch mark on the ruler.

Unless told otherwise, Word will align the right indent marker for your paragraph with the right margin. Similarly, Word will align the first-line and left indent markers with the zero point unless instructed otherwise. Do not confuse the indent markers with the left and right margins. The key point: You can change the indent markers to affect one or more paragraphs without affecting the overall margins for your document. To put it another way, changing the indents merely changes the position of text relative to the margins. (We'll say more about this when we discuss paragraph formatting later in this chapter.)

How to change left and right margins

Word provides two approaches for changing margins: through the ruler and through the Page Setup dialog box. If you like, you can use the mouse for this task; change to Page Layout view by choosing View Page Layout, or change to Print Preview by choosing File Print Preview. Then move the mouse pointer to the edge of the margin, on the horizontal ruler. The pointer will change to a left-and-right-pointing arrow, as shown in Figure 7-10. To move the margin, hold down the left mouse button and drag in either direction. Note that when you hold down the mouse button, Word will display a vertical dotted line down the entire page, as in Figure 7-11, to show where the new margin will fall. To accept the new margin setting, simply release the button.

If you prefer using the keyboard to change the margins, choose File Page Setup, and select the Margins tab. Then change the left and right margin settings (or the inside and outside settings if the Mirror Margins option is active) in the appropriate text boxes.

FIGURE 7-10

When you move the
mouse pointer over
the margin edge on the
horizontal ruler in Page
Layout view or Print
Preview, the pointer
will change to a left-
and-right-pointing
arrow, indicating that
you can drag the
margin indicator.

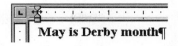

FIGURE 7-11

When you're dragging
the margin marker with
the mouse, Word dis-
plays a vertical dashed
line to indicate where
the margin boundary
will fall in relation to
the text.

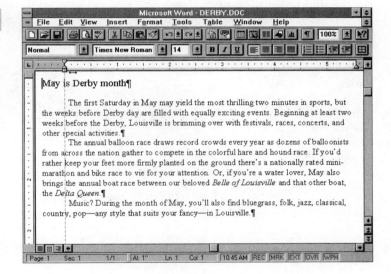

You can adjust margins with the mouse and ruler only when in
Page Layout view or Print Preview. If you work mostly in Normal
view, you can usually change the margin settings more quickly
through the Page Setup dialog box. Note, too, that changing the
settings through the dialog box is generally more accurate in any
case because you type precise measurements rather than judge
margin size by eye.

The vertical ruler

When you switch to Page Layout view or Print Preview, Word adds a vertical ruler to the left side of the screen. As Figure 7-11 shows, the vertical ruler is similar to the horizontal ruler; its white section delineates the body text area for a page, and the gray represents the margin. (More precisely, the white section will represent the currently active text area on the page, which will be the header or footer if that's what you're working with.)

How to change top and bottom margins

You can use the vertical ruler to adjust the top and bottom margins by dragging with the mouse, much as you can use the horizontal ruler to adjust the side margins. Figure 7-12 shows the top margin in the process of being adjusted, with the horizontal dashed line indicating the current position of the margin.

FIGURE 7-12

In Page Layout view or Print Preview, you can use the vertical ruler to change top and bottom margins by dragging.

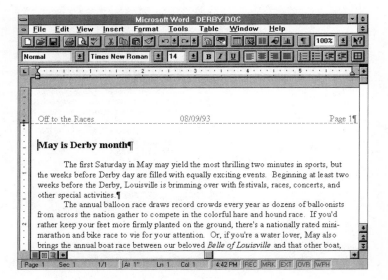

Again, if you prefer using the keyboard to change the margins, choose File Page Setup and then select the Margins tab. Change the top and bottom margin settings in the appropriate text boxes. As with side margins, changing the settings through the dialog box is generally more accurate than dragging.

You can also use the vertical ruler to adjust the header and footer positions. For details on adjusting header and footer placement, see "Defining the Position of a Header or Footer" on page 588.

Controlling Line and Page Breaks

The size of the text area usually determines how long individual lines of text can be and how many lines can fit on a page. There are times when you might want to override these settings, however, and make a line or a page end earlier.

How to force line breaks

Word automatically breaks lines at the right margin; however, you can also force line breaks. You can, of course, press the Enter key to start a new paragraph. However, you will sometimes want to start a new line without starting a new paragraph. To start a new line without starting a new paragraph, press Shift-Enter. Word will mark the line break on your screen with a ⏎ symbol. The new line will still be a part of the same paragraph as the line preceding it and will be treated that way for all formatting purposes.

Page breaks and repagination

Word also automatically calculates where page breaks will fall. If you like, you can have Word calculate page breaks only when you tell it to, by clearing the Background Repagination check box on the Tools Options General card. Doing so may increase your computer's speed slightly when you work in Normal or Outline view. Word will automatically repaginate when you print or when you're working in Page Layout view or Print Preview.

On the status bar, Word displays the page number of the cursor's current location. This page number will be accurate if you've selected the Background Repagination option. If Background Repagination is off, however, you shouldn't trust the page number on the status bar except when you're in Page Layout view or Print Preview.

Manual page breaks

Sometimes you'll want to force a page break at a particular position in your document. You might, for example, want to ensure that some material stays together on the same page. To insert a page break, move the cursor to the spot where you want the new page to begin, and press Ctrl-Enter. Alternatively, choose Insert Break, select Page Break, and choose OK. Either technique will insert a manual page-break marker at the cursor position.

Notice that the dots in the horizontal line marking a manual page break are closer together than those in a line marking an automatic page break. (The former may even appear as a solid line, depending on your screen and resolution.) And, in case that's too subtle a distinction for you, the manual break is marked in the middle with the label *Page Break*. Figure 7-13 compares the automatic and manual page-break markers.

FIGURE 7-13

The dots in a manual page-break marker are more closely spaced than those in an automatic page-break marker. The manual break is also clearly labeled *Page Break*.

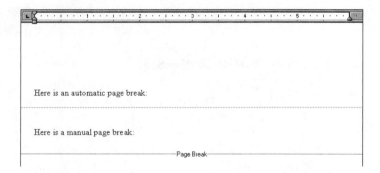

Here is an automatic page break:

Here is a manual page break:

Page Break

Keep in mind that automatic page-break markers will change position each time you repaginate your document. Manual page breaks, however, will stay at the location where you inserted them. Because of this, we suggest you use manual page breaks sparingly. Otherwise, if you reformat or otherwise change your document, the manual page breaks could cause unwanted gaps and awkward breaks on your printed page. Note that a manual page break is a single character to Word, and you can delete it like any other character.

If you want to force a new page so that a certain paragraph is always at the top of a page, you may want to assign the Page Break Before formatting option to that paragraph rather than insert a manual page break. We'll discuss that possibility later in this chapter, when we discuss the Paragraph dialog box.

Other factors that affect page breaks

Other factors affect where a page will end. Widows and orphans—that is, single lines that get stranded at the top or bottom of a page—are one such factor; Word has a way to prevent these automatically, as we will discuss shortly. Headers and footers can also affect page breaks. In addition to the simple headers and footers discussed in Chapter 5, you can create multiline headers or footers that can have an even greater effect. Multisection documents and footnotes are also factors in where pages break. We'll discuss these topics in later chapters.

Paragraph Formatting

After you establish a document's page layout, you're in a better position to format individual paragraphs. Word's paragraph formatting options cover a lot of territory, including indentions, alignment, line spacing, and before-and-after spacing. In many documents, your paragraphs may all conform to one or two formats, so you won't need to format many individual paragraphs. In other documents, however, you may need a variety of paragraph formats.

Word's paragraph formatting commands always apply to whole paragraphs. To indicate which paragraph you want to format, place the cursor anywhere in that paragraph or select any or all of its text. If you want to format two or more paragraphs at once, first you must extend the selection to include some text in each of those paragraphs.

In this section, we'll cover direct paragraph formatting only. As we mentioned earlier, Word also provides formatting by styles, which we'll cover in Chapter 12. Styles are a powerful formatting tool, particularly for complex documents. We firmly recommend that you learn to format by styles, and the present discussion is important as a foundation for moving on to styles.

Word also has a feature called AutoFormat, which you'll find on the Tools menu. AutoFormat analyzes your document and automatically applies paragraph and font formatting. This is a useful tool, but since it relies on predefined styles for the actual paragraph and font settings that it applies, we'll postpone our discussion of AutoFormat to Chapter 12.

The defaults

Word's default settings for a paragraph are flush left and single spaced (based on the tallest character), with no first-line, left, or right indent. Flush left refers to how the text is aligned—with an even left margin and a ragged right margin. Single spacing refers to the amount of leading (pronounced "ledding") between lines of text. Word automatically adds 2 points of space (approximately $1/36$ inch) between lines to create buffers between the ascenders and descenders of characters on adjacent lines. You can increase or decrease this line spacing as needed.

The default indent settings of no left, right, or first-line indent mean that all text is aligned within the text area established by your page margins. However, you can increase or decrease the width of one or more paragraphs as needed. For example, if you want to set a quotation off from the rest of your text, you first put it in its own paragraph and then adjust the left and right indent markers to narrow that paragraph. You can also format a paragraph to indent its first line automatically, and then you won't need to press the Tab key at the beginning of each paragraph.

 A note of warning: You may be tempted to change your margin settings by moving the indent markers on the horizontal ruler. We strongly urge you to resist this temptation. As we've pointed out earlier, if you later make any changes to your page size, margins, or print orientation, Word will move the indent markers on the ruler to reflect the new settings, thereby scrambling the "margins" you set with the indent markers.

How to apply paragraph formats with the mouse

There are a wealth of options for formatting paragraphs. You can use the mouse or the keyboard. The Formatting toolbar and the horizontal ruler are especially handy if you use the mouse. Figure 7-14 shows the Standard and Formatting toolbars and the horizontal ruler.

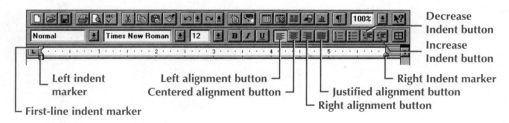

FIGURE 7-14

You can use the Standard and Formatting toolbars and the horizontal ruler to format your paragraphs.

The Formatting toolbar contains drop-down lists for styles, fonts, and font sizes. We'll cover styles in Chapter 12 and the two font list boxes later in this chapter. The first three buttons to the right of the drop-down lists are for font formatting, which we'll cover toward the end of this chapter. The next set of four buttons relates to paragraph alignment.

 Keep in mind that all of the techniques described in the following discussion change only the current paragraph or paragraphs—that is, the paragraph containing the cursor, or all paragraphs in which some text is selected. To change all paragraphs in a document, you need to select the entire document first.

Alignment

The Formatting toolbar's four paragraph alignment buttons are labeled with thumbnail sketches of what they do, as shown in this table:

Button	Alignment	Button	Alignment
▤	Left	▤	Right
▤	Centered	▤	Justified

To use these buttons, place the cursor or selection anywhere in the target paragraph and click on the button for the format you want to apply. Notice that you can tell the alignment of any paragraph from these toolbar buttons; when the cursor is in the paragraph, the appropriate alignment button will appear depressed. In Figures 7-15 and 7-16 on the next page, for example, you can see that the left alignment button is depressed.

Indents

As we discussed earlier, document margins are controlled by the margin settings in the Page Setup dialog box or by the margin markers on the ruler in Page Layout view or Print Preview. By default, Word will align the first-line and left indent markers with the left margin and the right indent marker with the right margin. (See Figure 7-14.) You can move these markers to change the width of the text in one or more paragraphs.

How to change indents with the mouse and the ruler

To change the width of a paragraph with the mouse, first make sure that the cursor or current selection is somewhere in the paragraph or paragraphs you want to change. Then drag the left or right indent marker as appropriate.

For example, the second paragraph in Figure 7-15 is a quotation from James Joyce's *Dubliners*. To set it off by indenting, first move the cursor to the

FIGURE 7-15

The second paragraph in this sample document is a quotation.

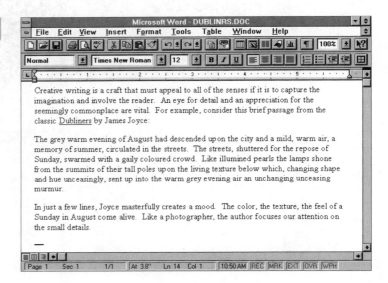

FIGURE 7-16

To indent the left and right edges of a paragraph, move the indent markers on the ruler.

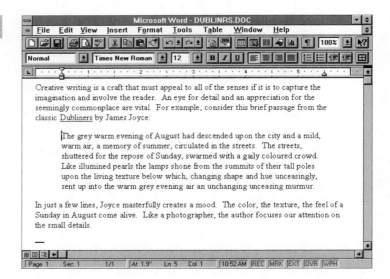

paragraph or select any portion of it. Then move the mouse pointer to the rectangle below the left indent marker (the bottom of the two indent markers on the left side of the horizontal ruler), hold down the left mouse button, and drag the marker to the 0.5-inch position. (Dragging the rectangle will move both the top and bottom markers at the same time.) To indent the right edge of the paragraph, drag the right indent marker to the 5.5-inch position. Figure 7-16 shows the result.

The left indent marker is split into two triangles. The top triangle controls the indent for just the first line of a paragraph, and the bottom triangle indents all subsequent lines in the paragraph. You can use this feature to indent the first line of a paragraph or to create a hanging indent, in which the first line extends to the left of the rest of the paragraph. Note that when you drag the rectangle below the bottom triangle, as in our example, the top triangle moves with it. But if you drag either the top or bottom triangle by itself, the other will not move.

How to change indents with the Formatting toolbar

You can also move the left indent to the next tab setting by clicking on the Increase Indent and Decrease Indent buttons on the Formatting toolbar:

Button	Action
	Increase Indent
	Decrease Indent

By default, these are the second and third buttons from the right on the Formatting toolbar. Each click on the Increase Indent button will move the left indent one tab stop to the right. (Tab stops are 0.5 inches apart in Word's default settings.) Each click on the Decrease Indent button will move the left indent one tab stop to the left. Note that you cannot use the Decrease Indent button to move the left indent beyond the left margin.

How to set tabs with the mouse

Although Word has a sophisticated table feature (which we will cover in Chapter 11), you can also create columns of tabular information simply by using tab stops. As with a typewriter, you set the places where the cursor will stop when you press the Tab key. Unlike a typewriter, Word offers four different kinds of tab settings, allowing you to easily align numbers, names, or other data in columns.

These tab stops are controlled by the button at the left end of the horizontal ruler. The shape of the icon indicates which kind of tab will be inserted when you click on the ruler.

Button	Tab Alignment	Button	Tab Alignment
L	Left	⌐	Right
⊥	Centered	⊥	Decimal

A left-aligned tab aligns the left edge of text with the tab stop. A right-aligned tab aligns the right edge of text with the tab stop. Centered tabs center text on the tab stop. Decimal tabs—usually the best choice for a column of numbers—align numbers on the decimal point (or after the last digit if there is no decimal).

To set a tab stop with the mouse, start by clicking on the Tab button at the left side of the ruler until it displays the type of tab you want. If you need to enter a column of numbers, for example, click until you see the decimal tab icon. Then click on the ruler at the position where you want the tab stop. To change the position, you can drag the tab stop to a new position. To delete a tab, simply drag it down and off the ruler.

How to apply paragraph formats with the keyboard

There are keyboard shortcuts for some, but not all, of the mouse techniques we have just described. There are also some keyboard shortcuts for paragraph formatting features that aren't readily accessible with the mouse.

 Unlike Word 2.0, Word 6.0 does not offer any way to take advantage of the ruler from the keyboard.

Paragraph formatting shortcut keys

Word offers a number of shortcut keys for paragraph formatting. Several are mnemonic (Ctrl-L for left-aligned and Ctrl-R for right-aligned, for example), making them easy to remember. Figure 7-17 lists these shortcuts.

This Key Combination...	Moves...
Ctrl-M	Left indent and first-line indent one tab stop to the right
Ctrl-Shift-M	Left indent and first-line indent one tab stop to the left
Ctrl-T	Left indent but not first-line indent one tab stop to the right (hanging paragraph)
Ctrl-Shift-T	Left indent but not first-line indent one tab stop to the left

This Key Combination...	Sets Paragraph To...
Ctrl-L	Left alignment
Ctrl-E	Centered alignment
Ctrl-R	Right alignment
Ctrl-J	Justified alignment
Ctrl-1	Single spacing
Ctrl-5	$1^1/_2$ spacing
Ctrl-2	Double spacing
Ctrl-0 (digit 0)	Adds or deletes a line of space before the paragraph

FIGURE 7-17

Shortcut keys for paragraph formatting.

Left indent shortcut keys

The left indent shortcuts work similarly to the Formatting toolbar's Increase Indent and Decrease Indent buttons. Ctrl-M moves the left indent and the first-line indent one tab stop to the right; Ctrl-Shift-M moves them both one tab stop to the left. (By default, Word sets tab stops every $^1/_2$ inch along the ruler.) As with the equivalent toolbar button, you cannot use Ctrl-Shift-M to move the indent marker beyond the left margin. Note that you can also move the left indent without moving the first-line indent. Ctrl-T moves the left indent to the right; Ctrl-Shift-T moves it to the left.

Paragraph alignment shortcut keys

Using the shortcut keys for paragraph alignment is equivalent to clicking on the Formatting toolbar paragraph alignment buttons. Ctrl-L formats to left alignment, Ctrl-R to right alignment, Ctrl-J to justified alignment, and Ctrl-E to centered alignment.

Three of these four shortcut keys are easily remembered mnemonics. It may help you to think of Ctrl-E as Entered Centered. Alternatively, if you're willing to give up Ctrl-C for copying text to the Clipboard, you could redefine Ctrl-C for centering, using the techniques we'll describe in Chapter 28.

Line-spacing shortcut keys

By default, Word automatically adds 2 points of leading (spacing) between lines of text. This results in single spacing based on the tallest character in the line. More precisely, for point sizes typically used in body text (10–12 points), Word allows 2 points of space between the tallest ascender on one line and the lowest descender on the line immediately above. For example, if you're using 10-point Times New Roman type, Word will allow 12 points from the bottom of one line to the bottom of the next line, creating 2 points of separator space between lines.

In addition to single-spaced lines, you can easily create double-spaced and $1^1/_2$-spaced lines. The first format is standard for manuscript pages because it gives you extra room on the printed page for writing notes and corrections. The second is often useful for making a long report easier to read. With double spacing, Word will insert a full line of blank space above each line of text. For 10-point Times New Roman type, this means 12 points of leading. With $1^1/_2$-spaced lines, Word will insert one half-line of blank space above each line of text, or about 6 points of leading. Figure 7-18 shows examples of single spacing, $1^1/_2$ spacing, and double spacing.

FIGURE 7-18

You can set single spacing, $1^1/_2$ spacing, or double spacing with keyboard shortcuts.

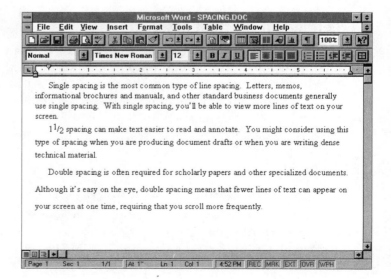

Word's shortcut keys for spacing are Ctrl-1 for single spacing, Ctrl-2 for double spacing, and Ctrl-5 for $1^1/_2$ spacing.

You can use the Paragraph dialog box to control the line spacing more precisely, and with many more options. You can create line spacing that's larger than double spacing or smaller than single spacing. We'll discuss this later in this chapter.

Paragraph-spacing shortcut keys

Paragraph spacing is similar to line spacing except that the spacing applies only to the space above the top line of the paragraph, as shown in Figure 7-19. There are two settings available with keyboard shortcuts: Ctrl-0 (the digit 0) toggles between one extra line of space before the paragraph and no extra space.

FIGURE 7-19

Use paragraph spacing to create extra space between paragraphs. The top two paragraphs have no extra spacing; the bottom one has.

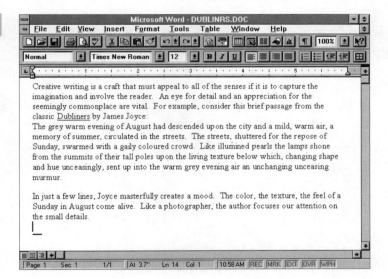

If you set paragraph spacing with the Paragraph dialog box (which we'll discuss shortly), you can insert space before or after the paragraph and specify precisely how much space to insert.

About paragraph spacing

If you generally use single spacing and you separate paragraphs by a blank line, you're probably used to creating the blank line manually by pressing the Enter key twice at the end of each paragraph. This technique is inferior in at least one important way to using the Before or After setting in the Spacing group.

These settings make it easier to reformat if you decide to change the amount of space between paragraphs. With Before or After, you need only select the paragraphs and then change the Before or After setting. This one change will reformat all of the selected paragraphs at once. (You can also use style sheets to make this type of wholesale formatting change even easier, as we'll discuss in Chapter 12.)

The Paragraph dialog box: Indents And Spacing

To exercise full control over your paragraph formats, you need to use the Format Paragraph command. Format Paragraph opens a dialog box with two cards: Indents And Spacing and Text Flow. Figure 7-20 shows the Indents And Spacing card.

FIGURE 7-20

The Paragraph dialog box controls the format of the current paragraph.

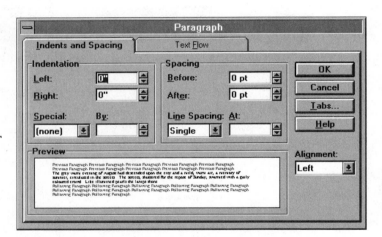

Both cards share a Preview area with a thumbnail sample of your text. The paragraph marked in bold in the sample will reflect any changes you make to the settings in this dialog box. Both cards also share a Tabs button that opens the Tabs dialog box, which we will explore later.

You can open the Paragraph dialog box by choosing the Format Paragraph command or by popping up a context-sensitive menu. To use the context-sensitive menu, place the cursor or selection in the paragraph or paragraphs you want to format; then press Shift-F10, or move the mouse pointer anywhere within the paragraph or selection and click the right mouse button. Choose Paragraph to open the same Paragraph dialog box as with the Format Paragraph command.

Indentation

The first two Indentation text boxes define the paragraphs's indention from the left and right margins. The default measurement is inches, but you can use any other unit of measure that Word recognizes. These are the same indentions you can set with the Increase Indent and Decrease Indent toolbar buttons and the equivalent keyboard shortcuts. With the Paragraph dialog box, however, you can specify indents more precisely.

You can specify a measurement by typing it in the appropriate text box or by clicking on the arrows at the right side of each box. Note that you can create a negative indent—to start the lines in the margins—by specifying a negative (minus) number in either box.

You use the Special text box to define a first-line indent or a hanging indent. These settings affect the starting position of the paragraph's first line relative to the remaining lines. If you choose First Line, the first line of the paragraph will be indented by the amount displayed in the By text box. If you choose Hanging, the first line will start at the point indicated by the Left indentation setting, and the remaining lines will be indented farther to the right by the amount shown in the By text box.

Spacing

You use the Spacing options to specify the amount of space between paragraphs and between the lines within paragraphs.

The Before and After text boxes control the amount of spacing between paragraphs. The default is no extra space, but you can specify any amount from 0 through 1584 points. The default unit of measure is points, but you can use any other unit Word recognizes, provided that you add the correct abbreviation for the units: *cm* for centimeters, *in* or " for inches, *li* for lines, *pi* for picas, and *pt* for points.

The Line Spacing list box has a number of predefined settings. Single, Double, and 1.5 Lines match the settings for the keyboard shortcuts we discussed earlier. The Multiple setting, last on the list, lets you define any line spacing by entering a number in the At text box (default is 3 lines). If you choose At Least, Word adjusts the spacing as required for different fonts but lets you specify a minimum spacing in the At text box. (Note that single, double, 1.5, and multiple line spacing are treated as At Least settings.) If you prefer, you can specify a precise spacing by selecting Exactly and entering a value in the At text box—but keep in mind that this will prevent Word from making any automatic adjustments should you change text size.

As with the Before and After text boxes, you can specify any unit of measurement that Word recognizes, as long as you use the correct abbreviation for the units. You cannot specify a negative value.

Alignment

The Alignment drop-down list in the lower right corner offers the same four options as the toolbar buttons and the equivalent shortcut keys: left aligned, center aligned, right aligned, and justified.

The Paragraph dialog box: Text Flow

The Text Flow card in the Paragraph dialog box, shown in Figure 7-21, controls where Word will break text to start a new line or a new page.

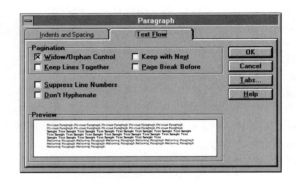

The Text Flow card in the Paragraph dialog box controls line breaks and page breaks.

Pagination

The Pagination box has four check boxes that help Word determine where to place automatic page breaks.

Widow/Orphan Control. Although it is none-too-progressive jargon, the term *widow* refers to those straggling single lines of text that sometimes appear at the top of a printed page, separated from the rest of their paragraph. The first line of a paragraph left alone at the bottom of a page is called an *orphan*.

In general, you should keep at least two lines of a paragraph on a given page. If there isn't room for two lines, you should push the entire paragraph to the beginning of the next page. And if there is room at the bottom of a page for all but one line of a paragraph, you should push an extra line to the top of the second page.

When checked, the Widow/Orphan Control check box on the Text Flow card ensures that no single line of text from a paragraph stands alone on a page, unless it is a single-line paragraph. If you use this option, Word will adjust your page breaks so that at least two lines of a paragraph always appear on a page. In some cases, this means that Word will print fewer than the maximum number of lines on a page, making your bottom margin slightly larger.

Keep Lines Together. This option tells Word not to allow a page break within a paragraph. Use it when you want to keep an entire paragraph together. For example, if you've formatted tabular columns with forced line breaks so that the entire table is one paragraph, checking the Keep Lines Together check box will ensure that the table will be printed on a single page.

Keep With Next. This option tells Word not to break a page between the current paragraph and the next so that at least a portion of each will appear on the same page. This is useful for section headings, to make sure that the heading will not be printed at the bottom of a page separately from the next paragraph.

Page Break Before. This option tells Word to place the current paragraph at the top of a new page, no matter how much empty space that would leave on the preceding page. You might want to use this option for a paragraph (such as a chapter title or other heading) that marks the beginning of a new topic or section.

Suppress Line Numbers

We will discuss line numbering in Chapter 13. For now, simply be aware that if you have Word set to add line numbers to a document, you can turn this feature off for any paragraph or paragraphs by checking the Suppress Line Numbers check box.

Don't Hyphenate

Checking the Don't Hyphenate check box tells Word not to apply hyphenation to the current paragraph when Word is set to hyphenate the document automatically. We discussed hyphenation in "Hyphenation" on page 198.

Tabs

To open the Tabs dialog box, shown in Figure 7-22, choose the Tabs button on either card in the Paragraph dialog box. When the Paragraph dialog box is not open, you can open the Tabs dialog box by choosing Format Tabs.

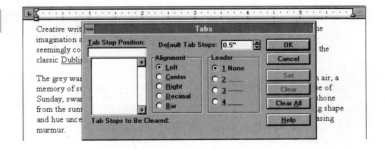

FIGURE 7-22

You can use the Tabs dialog box to add, delete, and modify tab settings for a paragraph.

Figure 7-22 shows the default Word settings for the Tabs dialog box. In the Default Tab Stops text box, at the top center, you can specify a set of evenly spaced tabs for the paragraph. By default, this is set to 0.5".

As you define custom tab settings for a paragraph, they appear in the Tab Stop Position list box at the left of the dialog box, as shown in Figure 7-23. You can also see the tabs on the ruler in the background. Note that when you create custom tab stops, you clear all of the default tab stops to the left of those you create.

FIGURE 7-23

Word lists custom tab stops in the Tab Stop Position list box by their location on the horizontal ruler, measured in inches.

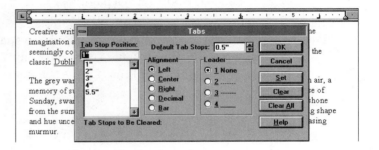

The Alignment and Leader areas show the definition for the tab stop position currently displayed in the Tab Stop Position text box. The ruler shows the specifications for all tab stops set for the current paragraph. In Figure 7-23, for example, the marker on the ruler indicates that the tab stop at 4 inches is decimal aligned and has a dotted-line leader.

The first four options in the Alignment area are the same as those controlled by the four tab-stop markers on the ruler. The fifth option, Bar, is not a tab in the usual sense. A bar tab by itself doesn't function as a tab stop; you can't tab to it, and inserting it doesn't clear any of the default tab stops to its left. Instead, the bar tab creates a solid vertical line that runs through the text of a paragraph at that position.

The bar tab can be quite helpful if you are building a table by using tabs, rather than Word's table feature, and you want to separate the columns with vertical lines. Build the table by using left, right, centered, and decimal tabs, as appropriate. Then insert the bar tabs between columns. The result will look similar to Figure 7-24.

FIGURE 7-24

The bar tab adds vertical lines to tables you build with tabs.

Sales by Region for the Past Four Months

Region	Aug	Sept	Oct	Nov
East	123	273	251	342
Central	432	325	234	435
West	341	287	246	141

A leader on a tab is a pattern of characters—usually alternating periods and spaces—that fills the space between the points where the tab begins and ends. The default is to have no leader, but a leader can help make lists of names or numbers easier to read. Figure 7-25 shows a table of contents that uses a leader between chapter titles and the starting page numbers.

FIGURE 7-25

A tab leader can make it easier to read formatted lists, such as this table of contents.

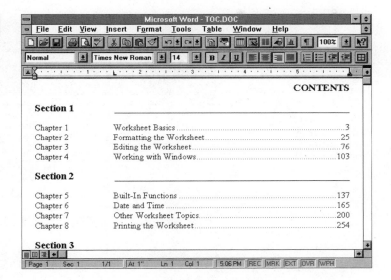

You can add a new tab stop by typing a value in the Tab Stop Position text box, setting the Alignment and Leader options, and choosing the Set button or OK. You can also modify the alignment and leader settings for any tab stop by selecting the tab in the Tab Stop Position list box, changing the options in the Alignment and Leader boxes, and then choosing Set or OK. In both cases, if you choose Set, Word will leave the dialog box open. If you choose OK, Word will close the dialog box.

To delete a tab stop, select it in the Tab Stop Position box, and then choose the Clear button. If necessary, you can delete all tab stops at once by choosing the Clear All button. In either case, Word will delete the tab stops from the list box but will not throw them away completely. Instead, it will either maintain a list of each tab stop to clear, titled Tab Stops To Be Cleared, or display the notation All at the bottom of the Tabs dialog box. If you decide you don't want to clear those tabs after all, choose Cancel, and Word will close the dialog box without deleting the tab stops. To close the dialog box and accept the changes you've made, choose OK.

Paragraph borders and shading

You can make individual paragraphs or groups of paragraphs stand out from the rest of your text by adding a border like the one shown in Figure 7-26. You can add borders with the Border toolbar or with the Paragraph Borders And Shading dialog box, which you open by choosing Format Borders And Shading.

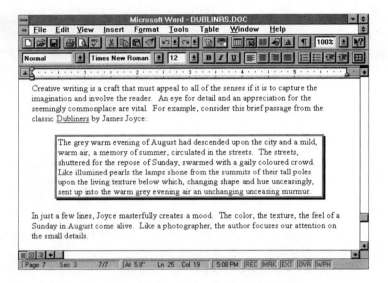

FIGURE 7-26

You can use borders, like the shaded border here, to make individual paragraphs stand out from surrounding text.

Before you can format a border, you must first decide whether you want the border to go around a single paragraph or several. If you extend a selection to include more than one paragraph before opening the dialog box or using the Borders toolbar, any border you define will include all of the paragraphs with text selected. If all paragraphs in the selection have the same indent settings, Word will enclose them in a single border. If the indents vary, however, Word will start a separate border outline each time an indent changes.

If a page break occurs between two paragraphs enclosed by a single border, Word will automatically add a bottom line to the border on the first page and a top line to the border on the second. If the page break falls in the middle of a paragraph, Word will break the border, so it will be missing a bottom line on the first page and a top line on the second. If you edit the text so that the page break changes, Word will continue to adjust the borders, following this same rule.

You can control whether Word will create full borders on both pages when a page break falls within a bordered area. If you want the border to break, delete any paragraph returns within the text surrounded by the border. To create text that looks like multiple paragraphs but is actually one long paragraph, use Shift-Enter when you want to force a new line. If you want a complete border on each page, you can either make each line its own paragraph—which will work well for lists or tables created with tabs—or you can format the paragraphs with the Keep Lines Together option on the Text Flow card in the Paragraph dialog box.

How to add a border using a dialog box

To add a border, place the cursor in the paragraph you want to add it to, or make a selection that extends from the first to the last paragraph you want to surround. Then choose the Format Borders And Shading command to open the Paragraph Borders And Shading dialog box. The dialog box has two cards, Borders and Shading. The Borders card is shown in Figure 7-27.

FIGURE 7-27

You can use the Borders card to add borders to one or more paragraphs.

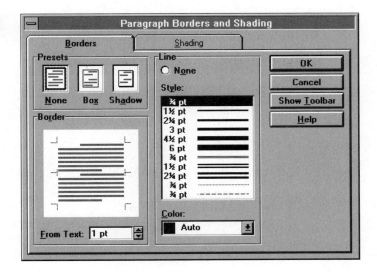

The Presets box displays the three options for borders: None, Box, and Shadow. (The Shadow option provides a slight 3-D effect.) These make it easy to quickly create a standard border. But you can also create your own settings if you prefer.

The thumbnail sketch in the Border box shows what your border will look like. The From Text box controls how far (in points) the border will be from the text in the paragraph or paragraphs.

Word requires a single From Text entry for all four sides of a border. If you need uneven spacing between the border and the text, you can adjust spacing manually. First set the From Text entry to match the setting you want for the right side of the text. Next, to adjust the top or bottom spacing, press Enter to add a blank line in its own paragraph above or below the text, and adjust the height of the line by putting the cursor in that paragraph and choosing Format Paragraph. Set the line spacing option to Exactly, and enter the appropriate height in the At text box. To adjust the spacing at the left side of the text, choose Format Paragraph and format the text with the Hanging option in the Special box, using the By text box to adjust the space. Then add a tab in front of the first line to indent the first line by the same amount as the rest of the paragraph. We covered each of these settings in "The Paragraph dialog box: Indents And Spacing" on page 230.

Note that when you increase the setting in the From Text box, the size of the text area will shrink within the Border box. This can give you the wrong impression of how your page will look. In fact, the text for the paragraph or paragraphs stays constant, while the border around the text gets larger. The thumbnail sketch shows you the increase in space between text and border, not the increase in the border size.

The Line box displays the different line types you can select—thin lines, thick lines, single or double. You can also specify a dotted or dashed line. The Line box contains a Color drop-down list that you can use to apply a color to the border. (The shadow in a shadowed border is always black regardless of the color of the lines.)

If you don't want to use any of the predefined choices in the Presets box, you can create custom borders in the Border box. Guidelines at the corners of the thumbnail sketch indicate the allowable positions for border lines, and triangle-shaped handles indicate which border lines are active at any given moment. You can use the mouse to click on the guidelines and toggle the handles on or off, or you can press Alt-R and then any of the arrow keys to cycle through different sets of lines. A line is active when the black triangles appear at the two ends of its handles; you can redefine all active lines at once by choosing a different style, color, or both in the Style and Color list boxes. By setting different lines as active, you can define any border you like. You can, for example, create a border with a single line at the top and bottom and a double line down the left and right side, using blue for the top and left, and green for the bottom and right. Simply turn the individual lines on and off, and define the format for each separately.

Note, too, that there is an allowable line in the middle of the Border box that is not active in the default setting. You can activate this with the mouse or the keyboard. If you define a line for this position, it will surround each paragraph in a selection with its own border, rather than including all of the selected paragraphs within a single border.

How to format a paragraph with shading

You can add any of various patterns and colors of shading to selected paragraphs with the Shading card, shown in Figure 7-28. The Preview box shows the effect of the settings as you select them. By default, Word selects the None button, meaning no shading. To add shading, choose the Custom button, and then define the shading you want before choosing OK to apply it.

FIGURE 7-28

Use the Shading dialog box to add a shaded pattern to a paragraph.

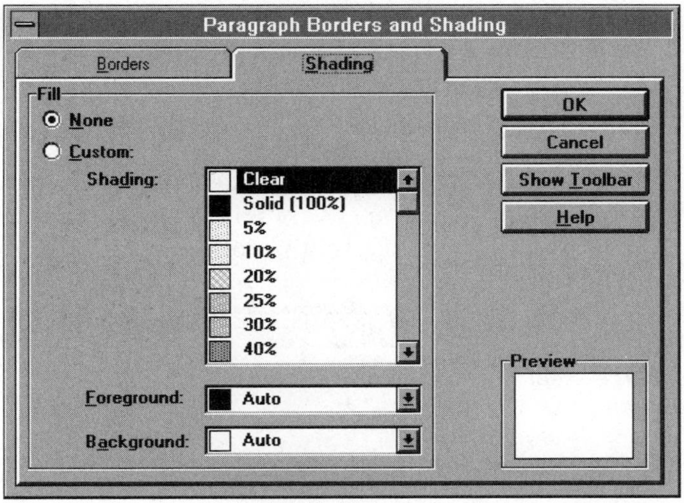

Start by choosing a pattern from the Shading list, shown in Figure 7-29 on the next page. The top of the list is organized by percent of foreground color. The bottom of the list contains dark and light patterns of lines. Then choose a color for the pattern and its background from the Foreground and Background drop-down lists.

FIGURE 7-29

The Shading list offers
various shading and
crosshatched patterns
to choose from.

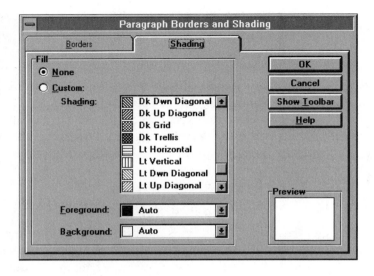

Make test printouts of the different shading patterns and colors
so that you know what your printer's output will look like. Even
with a monochrome printer, your color choices can produce
different effects depending on your printer.

How to add a border and shading with the Borders toolbar

Both cards in the Paragraph Borders And Shading dialog box have a Show
Toolbar button. If you choose this, or the Borders button on the Formatting
toolbar, Word will display the Borders toolbar, shown in Figure 7-30.

FIGURE 7-30

The Borders toolbar
gives you quick access
to most of the borders
and shading options.

The Borders toolbar provides easy access to a subset of the features
available on the Borders and Shading cards. The left drop-down box contains line style options for the border. The buttons in the middle of the
toolbar let you designate which edges you want the line to apply to: top,
bottom, left, right, inside, outside, and none. The right drop-down box
contains shading pattern options. You cannot change line or shading colors
from this toolbar; for that, you must choose the Format Borders And Shading
command.

Font Formatting

The third level of direct formatting is font formatting. Font formatting defines how text characters will look: the font you want to use; the size of the font; any special emphasis such as boldface, italics, and underlining; the position of the characters relative to each other; and the amount of space between characters. In the following section, we'll show you how to control these factors.

You can apply font formats as you type your text or afterward. If you've already entered the text, you will need to select the text before you apply formats to it. The text selection can be as small as a single character or as large as your entire document. Word will format only the text that you've highlighted.

If you prefer, you can format text as you create it. When you type new text in a Word document, it takes on the formatting characteristics of the text immediately preceding it. For example, if you move the cursor to the middle of a line formatted in 18-point boldface type, any new characters you type will also appear in 18-point bold. If you want to change formats in midstream, you can choose new formatting options without selecting any text; Word will apply those new formats to any text you type from that point forward. As you continue to type, the formatting characteristics will stay the same unless you apply new formats or move the cursor to another part of your document.

As with paragraph formats, you can change font formats with the mouse or the keyboard, and there are shortcuts for each. We'll start, as before, with the mouse shortcuts.

How to apply font formats with the mouse

You can use the mouse to apply the font formats available on the Formatting toolbar. The choices you are likely to use most often are these three buttons:

Button	Format
B	Boldface
I	Italic
U	Underline

To change existing text, select the text and click on the button you want. To apply formatting to new text, position the cursor and then click on the button; any new characters you type will use the chosen format. You can apply more than one format to the same text; for example, you can apply both boldface and underline formats simply by clicking on both buttons.

When text containing one or more of these formats is highlighted, the corresponding button will appear as if it were pressed. You can then remove the format by clicking on the button. Similarly, as you type text, you can toggle formatting on and off at the cursor position.

To the left of these three buttons are three drop-down lists. The leftmost is the Style list, which we will cover in Chapter 12. The next two lists are the Font and Font Size lists.

An aside: What's a font?

At one time, the term *font* referred to all characters of a given typeface in a given size—a definition from the days of movable type and printing presses, when each font was stored in a separate drawer. With the advent of personal computers, laser printers, and software that offers sophisticated formatting, the definition of this term has become fuzzy. In Word's context, a font is a family of type styles, including different sizes as well as medium, boldface, and italic versions of a given typeface.

In *monospaced* fonts, each letter is assigned the same amount of space on a line. Courier, for example, which has long been one of the most widely used fonts for typewriters, is a monospaced font. *Proportionally spaced* fonts, or simply *proportional* fonts, assign different amounts of space to different characters. These fonts give more space to a capital *M* than to a lowercase *i*, for example. You'll find them in most books, magazines, and newspapers.

Many fonts, such as the popular Times New Roman font, have little tails on the strokes of their letters. These tails are called *serifs*, and fonts that have them are called *serif fonts*. American readers tend to prefer serif fonts for the main text of documents. Fonts without the tails, such as Arial, are called *sans serif* fonts; these are better suited for headlines and tables. Figure 7-31 shows a sample of Times New Roman and a sample of Arial.

FIGURE 7-31

The serif font Times New Roman is popular for body text. The sans serif font Arial is well suited for headlines and tables.

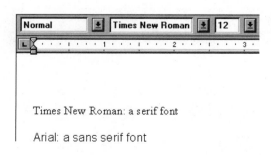

Times New Roman: a serif font

Arial: a sans serif font

How to select a font and a font size with the mouse and the Formatting toolbar

You can use the mouse and the Formatting toolbar to change fonts and font size. To change the font, just select the text whose font you want to change, or position the cursor where you want to begin typing a new font. Then open the Formatting toolbar's Font list box, as shown in Figure 7-32, and choose the font you want to use. Note that the font names in this list will vary depending on which printers you've installed and which printer you have selected with the File Print Setup command. Note that Windows and Word may not be able to display the characters on screen as they will look when printed; see "Understanding Screen Fonts and Printer Fonts" page 581.

FIGURE 7-32

The Formatting toolbar's Font drop-down list lists the fonts available for your currently chosen printer.

The Points drop-down list works similarly; select some text or reposition the cursor, and then open the list and choose the font size you want (in points). If you want text the same size as Pica type from a typewriter (six lines per inch), you should select a 10-point font. (Note that font size defines the height—but not necessarily the width—of characters.)

If you format your paragraphs with a Line Spacing of anything but Exactly, Word will automatically adjust the line spacing to match larger or smaller font sizes.

How to apply font formats with shortcut keys

Shortcut keys can duplicate all the formatting features of the Formatting toolbar and more. Many users will find shortcut keys the quickest method of formatting text. Figure 7-33 on the next page lists the shortcut keys for font formatting.

Toggle shortcuts

The first set of commands in the table in Figure 7-33 are toggles. You press the keystroke combination once to apply the format and press the keys a second time to remove it. For example, if you highlight some text and press Ctrl-B once, the text will be boldface. Press Ctrl-B again, and the boldface format will be removed.

This Key Combination...	Toggles This Font Format...
Ctrl-B	Boldface
Ctrl-I	Italic
Ctrl-Shift-D	Double underline
Ctrl-U	Single underline (words and spaces)
Ctrl-Shift-W	Single underline (words only)
Ctrl-Shift-A	All capital letters
Ctrl-Shift-K	Small capital letters
Shift-F3	Cycle the case of letters
Ctrl-=	Subscript (down 3 points)
Ctrl-Shift-=	Superscript (up 3 points)
Ctrl-Shift-H	Hidden text
Ctrl-Shift-* (not NumPad)	Display nonprinting characters

This Key Combination...	Applies This Font Format Feature...
Ctrl-Shift-F	Formatting toolbar Font list
Ctrl-Shift-P	Formatting toolbar Points list
Ctrl-Shift->	Grow font (increase to next available size on the Formatting toolbar Points list)
Ctrl-Shift-<	Shrink font (decrease to next available size on the Formatting toolbar Points list)
Ctrl-]	Increase font size by 1 point
Ctrl-[	Shrink font size by 1 point
Ctrl-Spacebar or Ctrl-Shift-Z	Remove all direct font formatting
Ctrl-Shift-Q	Use Symbol font

FIGURE 7-33

Shortcut keys for font formatting.

Most of the toggle commands are self-explanatory; the underline options, however, deserve explanation. Ctrl-Shift-D puts a double underline under all characters in the selected text. Ctrl-U does the same, except that it uses a single underline. Ctrl-Shift-W does something a little bit different; it uses a single underline, but only under the printable characters in the selection—not under the spaces.

Note, too, that Shift-F3 (Change Case) is not a toggle, because it cycles through three states instead of two. Shift-F3 will change the case of the selected text each time you press it: for example, from all lowercase, to initial capitals, to all capitals, and then back to all lowercase again.

Shift-F3 will work differently depending on the text you've highlighted. If the text includes periods or other punctuation to indicate that it contains full sentences, Word will try to find and capitalize the first letter of each sentence for the initial capitals part of the cycle. If there's no indication that the text consists of sentences, Word will capitalize the first letter of each word instead.

Two other shortcut keys need further explanation: Ctrl-Shift-H (Hidden Text) and Ctrl-Shift-* (Nonprinting Characters). Word will not normally print text formatted as hidden, but you can set Word to print hidden text with the Tools Options Print card. Similarly, Word will not display hidden text unless you check the Hidden Text check box on the Tools Options View card or, alternatively, set Word to display all nonprinting characters; you can do the latter either by checking the All option on the View card, by clicking on the Show/Hide ¶ button on the Standard toolbar, or by pressing Ctrl-Shift-*.

How to change fonts and font sizes from the keyboard

The next six keyboard shortcuts in Figure 7-33, beginning with Ctrl-Shift-F, cover fonts and font sizes. If you have the Formatting toolbar displayed, you can use Ctrl-Shift-F to activate the Font list box and Ctrl-Shift-P to activate the Points list box. Once the list boxes are activated, you can then choose a font or size, as appropriate, by using the Up and Down arrow keys and then pressing Enter to complete the selection.

If the Formatting toolbar is not displayed, Word will open the Font dialog box when you press Ctrl-Shift-F or Ctrl-Shift-P. If the Formatting toolbar is displayed, Word will open the Font dialog box if you press Ctrl-Shift-F or Ctrl-Shift-P a second time—after the Font list box or Points list box is active. (We will look at the Font dialog box immediately after this discussion of the shortcut keys.)

Both Ctrl-Shift-> (Grow Font) and Ctrl-] (Increase Font By 1 Point) will increase the font size of the currently selected text, but they take different approaches to increasing font size. Ctrl-Shift-> will increase the font to the next size, as specified in the Points list box, so if the list box shows point sizes of 10, 11, 12, 14, 16, 18, 20, 22, 24, 26, 28, 36, 48, 72, the Grow Font shortcut key will change font size using just those choices, changing in steps of 1,

2, 8, 12, or 24 points. On the other hand, Ctrl-Shift-] (Increase Font By 1 Point) will change size by 1 point, in all cases, no matter what the current setting. The same considerations apply to the Ctrl-Shift-< (Shrink Font) and Ctrl-[(Shrink Font By 1 Point) keys.

How to remove direct font formatting

There may be times when you want all characters within a selection to revert to their default settings. Simply select the text and press Ctrl-Spacebar or Ctrl-Shift-Z.

How to switch to Symbol font

The Ctrl-Shift-Q shortcut key is simply a quick and easy way to switch to Symbol font so that you can type Greek letters, mathematical symbols, and other special symbols directly from the keyboard. Pressing Ctrl-Shift-Q is equivalent to choosing Symbol from the Font list box, but only for the next character you type. After you type one character, Word will switch you back to the default format for the text.

The Font dialog box

As with paragraph formatting, you can apply font formats by way of a dialog box. This approach can give you more precise control over some of the features. You can open the Font dialog box by choosing Format Font or by pressing the shortcut key Ctrl-D. The Font dialog box has two cards: Font and Character Spacing. The Font card is shown in Figure 7-34.

FIGURE 7-34

Use the Font card in the Font dialog box to specify formatting features for the selected text.

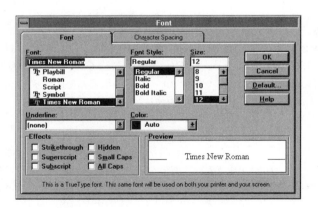

Notice the Preview box in the lower right corner of the card. If you have some text selected, a portion of it will appear here, complete with any formatting you've applied to the text. If no text is selected, Word will use the font name as a sample. As you change the formatting choices in the Font dialog box, the Preview sample shows the effects of your settings.

The Font, Font Style, and Size text boxes have list boxes underneath them. You can choose a typeface and font size using the Font and Size lists. The Font Style box lists the available font styles—Regular, Italic, Bold, and Bold Italic. When you choose any item from one of these list boxes, Word displays it in the appropriate text box.

The Underline drop-down list offers five choices: four types of underlining plus None. In addition to the three underlining types we discussed in the shortcut key section, you can also choose a dotted underline.

The Color drop-down list lets you add color to your text. The default (Auto) is black. If you don't have a color printer, Word will print all of your text in black or a gray interpretation of any colors.

Even if you don't have a color printer but you do have a color monitor, you can still see the colors on the screen. For example, if you write notes to yourself in your text, you might define them with a distinct color so that you won't miss them later. Similarly, if you create on-screen forms, as we'll discuss in Chapter 23, you can use color to differentiate some parts of a form from others.

The Effects box offers a set of check boxes for additional formatting choices. Strikethrough puts a line through the middle of each character. Superscript and Subscript move the text to a position higher or lower than other text on the same line. By default, Superscript and Subscript move text up or down by 3 points and automatically convert the characters to a smaller size (although the setting in the Size box will not change). Superscript and Subscript are mutually exclusive, so you can apply only one at a time. Small Caps and All Caps are self-explanatory and, as with Superscript and Subscript, are mutually exclusive. We described the Hidden attribute in "Toggle shortcuts" on page 243.

Figure 7-35 on the next page shows the Character Spacing card. This controls some finer details of letter spacing, such as kerning. These features let you control the appearance of the text, and how many characters fit on a line. Unless you have some specific need for these features—such as crafted formatting for desktop publishing—you will probably leave these at their default settings.

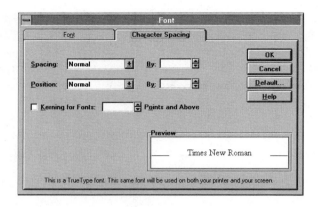

FIGURE 7-35

The Character Spacing card controls advanced spacing features that many users will never need.

How to change your default font format

The Default button that is present on both the Font and Character Spacing cards will make the current settings on both cards the default for the current template. If you choose this button, Word will display a dialog box asking whether you want to make the change to the template. If you are working in a document that is based on the NORMAL.DOT template, this will reset the default for font formatting, so be careful before you make the change.

If you change your mind about applying a font format, you can choose the Cancel button to go back to your document without making any changes. Choosing the OK button will apply any settings that you've chosen.

How to change more than one selection of text

If you need to change more than one selection of text to the same new settings, remember the Edit Repeat command (and its shortcut key, F4). You can use it to apply the same formatting repeatedly to different selections. After you've formatted the first selection, simply select the next and press F4. You can repeat this as many times as necessary. Also remember that you can use the Edit Replace command to change font formatting for specific strings of text.

Copying and Moving Font and Paragraph Formats

When you copy or move a block of text, Word will generally retain any font formats you assigned directly to that text when it pastes the characters into the new location. (This is not true for formats applied through styles. In Chapter 12, we'll talk about the effects of editing text that's formatted with styles.) If you copy or move an entire paragraph, including the paragraph mark, Word will also retain the paragraph formats of the copied selection when you paste. However, if you copy or move any part of the paragraph and don't include the paragraph mark in your selection, Word will use the paragraph formats assigned to the text in the paste area.

In any case, you may need to revise the formats of the pasted text to match those of the surrounding text. Word provides both keyboard and mouse shortcuts to copy character or paragraph formats without copying any text.

How to copy a paragraph mark

One easy way to copy a paragraph format—with either the mouse or the keyboard—is to copy just the paragraph mark from the end of one paragraph and then either paste it over the mark at the end of another paragraph or insert it before the old paragraph mark and then delete the old one. Because all paragraph formatting information is stored with the paragraph mark, Word will reformat the paragraph. Note that to use this technique, you'll need to display paragraph marks in your document either by choosing the Show/Hide ¶ button on the Formatting toolbar, by pressing Ctrl-Shift-*, or by activating the Paragraph Marks or All option on the Tools Options View card. (Note also, in passing, that if the source paragraph is formatted with a named style, Word will apply that style to the destination paragraph. We'll talk about styles in Chapter 12.)

If you've moved a paragraph formatted with one set of paragraph formats to a section of text that's formatted with a different set, the easiest way to change formatting will often be to go to the end of the paragraph you've moved, delete the paragraph mark, and then press Enter. Because Word stores all formatting with the paragraph mark, deleting the marker at the end of the first paragraph not only joins the two paragraphs but formats all of its text to match the second paragraph. When you press Enter to create a new paragraph mark, the first paragraph retains the format it had when the text was joined. Also note that if you place the cursor at the end of the first paragraph and use the Del key to delete the paragraph mark, Word will delete the paragraph mark whether or not it is currently showing on the screen.

How to use the Format Painter

Perhaps the easiest way to use a block of text as the model for other text is to use the Format Painter. The feature is available both on the Standard toolbar, using the button with an icon that looks like a paintbrush, and through the shortcut key Ctrl-Shift-C.

How to use the Format Painter with the mouse

Start by highlighting a portion of text whose format you want to apply else-where in your document. Then click on the Format Painter button. Your mouse pointer will change to look like the normal I-beam with a paintbrush to its left. Hold down the mouse button and drag across the section of text that you want to apply the formatting to. Word will highlight the selection as you paint. When you release the mouse button, the text will take on the formatting of the source selection, and the mouse pointer will revert to the normal I-beam.

If you want to apply the same formatting to several sections, double-click the Format Painter button. Having started with a double click, you'll find that when you finish highlighting a section and release the mouse button, the mouse pointer will remain in the Format Painter mode so that you can repeat the process as many times as you want. To turn off the feature, press any key. Esc is probably the safest and most convenient choice; if you had text highlighted and pressed a character key, the highlighted text would be replaced with that character.

How to use the Format Painter with the keyboard

You can also use essentially the same method to copy formats with the key-board. Once again, start by selecting a block of text that has the format you want to apply elsewhere. Then press Ctrl-Shift-C. Next highlight the desti-nation text and press Ctrl-Shift-V to apply the formatting to the new text.

Copying formats with these shortcut keys is similar to using the Edit Copy and Edit Paste commands except that you're copying formatting only. In fact, the Word commands attached to these keystrokes are CopyFormat and PasteFormat, and it may help you remember the shortcut keys if you think of this as copying and pasting formats. As with the Edit Paste command, you can use Ctrl-Shift-V to apply formatting to successive selections of text.

Some general comments about the Format Painter

Whether you use the mouse or the keyboard to copy formats with the Format Painter, there are several points you should be aware of. Most important is that you can copy font formatting, paragraph formatting, or both. To copy font formatting only, select source text without a paragraph mark.

To copy paragraph formatting only (including any font formats applied to the paragraph as a whole), select only the paragraph mark as the source. For example, if you've applied boldface to an entire paragraph but not to the paragraph mark and you select the paragraph mark as the source, you will apply only the paragraph formatting to the target text. If you've applied the boldface format to the paragraph mark itself at the source, however, you'll also apply boldface to the target text.

To copy paragraph and font formatting together, select both the text and the paragraph mark. If the font formatting of the text is different from that of the paragraph mark, Word will copy the paragraph-level formats—for indentions, for example—but will use the font formatting from the source text.

If your selected text has more than one type of font formatting applied to it, Word will recognize only the first formatting that it encounters. For example, if the first word in the selection is bold and the second is italic and you attempt to copy the formatting to a different two-word selection, both words will be bold.

At this point, if you've read everything from the beginning of this book, you've covered everything you need to know to create documents and format them attractively. All that is left is getting the product onto paper. We'll cover that subject in the next chapter.

TOPIC FINDER

The Windows Control Panel: Printers   253

- How to install a printer
- How to configure a printer

Selecting a Printer from Within Word   262

Using the File Print Command   263

- How to work with the Print Manager
- File Print command options

Previewing a Printed Document   273

- Print Preview
- How to use Page Layout view

Envelopes and Labels   282

- How to create an envelope
- *NEW!* Labels

Printing

ord's printing features are straightforward if you want to accept the default settings. However, there are many options you may want to use. Before you can print with Word, you have to be sure your printer is correctly installed and configured. Even then, the results may not always be precisely what you had in mind. You may have to fine-tune the Print Manager, the font selection, or the formatting before your pages are printed the way you want.

We'll start with setting up your printer. This process actually breaks into two procedures: printer installation and printer selection.

The Windows Control Panel: Printers

Before you can print anything with Word—or any other program in Windows—you need to tell Windows about the printer (or printers) you have installed on your system. Typically, you install one or more printers when you first run the SETUP program to install Windows on your computer. You can also install additional printers or alter the information about those you've already installed by using the Windows Control Panel. Assuming that your printer and computer are hooked up properly, we'll take a quick look at how to install and configure printers within Windows. For further details, refer to your Windows manuals or contact your printer manufacturer.

This discussion assumes that you are using Windows 3.1. If you are using Windows 3.0, the Control Panel and other screens will differ from those described here.

How to install a printer

To install a printer, start by running the Windows Control Panel: Double-click on its icon, located by default in the Main group in Program Manager. Alternatively, you can find the file CONTROL.EXE, which should be in your Windows directory, and then choose Program Manager's File Run command to run it. After the Control Panel opens, double-click on the Printers icon to open a dialog box similar to the one in Figure 8-1.

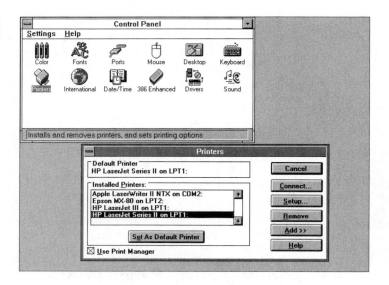

FIGURE 8-1

Use the Printers dialog box, available through the Windows Control Panel, to install and configure Windows for your printer or printers.

The Installed Printers box lists all printers you've installed for Windows. You can install multiple printers, and you can have more than one printer installed for any given port.

How to designate the default printer

To designate which is the default printer, highlight the printer in the Installed Printers list and choose the Set As Default Printer button. Alternatively, you can double-click on the name in the Installed Printers list. Windows will change the entry in the Default Printer box to match your choice.

Only one printer can be designated as the default printer. Word
will assume this is the printer you want to use, but you can choose
a different printer from within Word if you want.

Print Manager

At the bottom of the Printers dialog box, you'll see the Use Print Manager
check box (checked by default). The Print Manager is the Windows print
spooler, a utility that lets Windows applications print to temporary files on
disk and then sends them to the printer. This feature offers advantages because printing to disk is faster than printing to a printer. The result is that
you'll be able to return to using Word sooner. Your document will be printed
while you go on to other tasks. Bypassing the Print Manager will generally
speed the actual printing, but you will wait longer to regain control of your
system.

The Print Manager operates in the background while you continue to
work. You can clear the Print Manager check box, but we don't recommend it
unless you find that printing in the background makes your system so unre-
sponsive that it's essentially unusable.

How to add a printer

If you need to install another printer, choose the Add button in the lower
right corner of the Printers dialog box. The dialog box will expand, as shown
in Figure 8-2.

FIGURE 8-2

You'll use the
expanded Printers
dialog box to choose
from the list of
additional printers to
install.

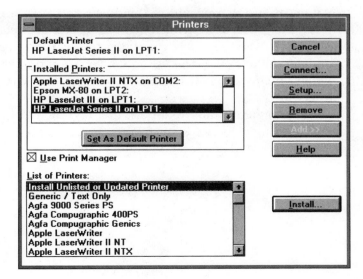

Select the printer you want from the List Of Printers list box, and choose the Install button. If Windows can't find a driver for the printer on your hard disk, it will prompt you to insert the appropriate Windows disk in your floppy disk drive. (However, if the driver is stored in another directory on your hard disk, you can specify the drive and directory name to tell Windows where it can find the driver.)

Although Windows comes with drivers that support a wide range of printers, you might have a printer that comes with its own driver instead. This is most likely to happen with a relatively recent printer model that Windows doesn't support fully with any of its own drivers. Most such drivers follow Windows conventions, requiring that you install them through the Printers dialog box, where you choose the Install Unlisted Or Updated Printer option. However, an increasing number of printers that include their own drivers also provide their own installation programs, which you have to run separately—by choosing File Run from within Program Manager, for example. Often it will seem as if the driver is being properly installed as you follow the usual Windows procedures, but the printer will refuse to print. The moral: If your printer comes equipped with its own driver, be sure to follow the installation instructions that come with the driver.

How to configure a printer

After you install a printer in Windows, you still need to configure it properly. The configuration includes basic settings (such as port assignment) and setup issues (such as specifying the available fonts, default paper size, and default paper source). Although you should be sure to check these items when you first install a printer, you can also change them at any time afterward.

To assign a printer to a port, first highlight the printer name in the Installed Printers list, and then choose the Connect button. Windows will open the Connect dialog box, shown in Figure 8-3.

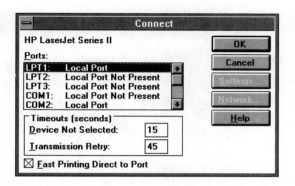

FIGURE 8-3

Use the Connect dialog box to specify the port assignment and timeout settings for an installed printer.

How to specify a printer port

To configure the printer, you need to know the designation of the port the printer is attached to. You can then assign the printer to a port by highlighting the port name in the Ports list box and choosing OK.

The most common type of connection is a parallel interface—referred to as LPT. If you have only one printer, odds are that it is attached to LPT1 (although some computers have second and third parallel ports installed, which would be LPT2 and LPT3). The other common choice for attaching a printer is through a serial port. Serial ports are called COM; the first is named COM1. You can have as many as four serial ports installed under Windows. The Ports box will indicate which ports Windows recognizes in your system.

If your system has more than one port and you don't know which one the printer is attached to, you may simply have to try each possibility. If you're reduced to this brute force method, start with LPT1, the most common choice; then try COM1, then LPT2, and so on.

There are other options in the Ports list besides the parallel and serial ports. In particular, there is the FILE setting, which you can use with any printer, no matter what port it's physically attached to—or even if your computer isn't connected to a printer. Rather than send the printed output through a port, the FILE setting captures the output in a file on disk; Windows will ask you the name to use for the file each time. You can print the file later by copying it to a printer with the MS-DOS COPY command. If the printer is attached to LPT1, for example, the command to type at the MS-DOS prompt would be:

copy *filename* lpt1

> Printing a file to disk can be particularly handy if you're creating a file on one system that you want to print on a printer that's attached to another system. But if you select FILE as the output port, note that you can later trick Word into printing directly to a printer on LPT1 by specifying PRN as the destination filename. Word will ask whether you want to overwrite the existing file. If you choose Yes, it will print to your printer.

Word also has an option for sending a print job to a file. We'll cover it later in this chapter. In Windows, your best bet normally is to assign your printer to the port where it is attached and use Word for sending the occasional print job to a file.

The other choices in the Ports list box—EPT, LPT1.DOS and LPT2.DOS—are rarely used. The EPT port, for example, is for a few printers that need a special expansion interface card in your computer. Your printer's documentation should indicate whether you need this setting.

Timeout settings

The timeout settings determine how long Windows will try a given print operation before giving up and displaying an error message. The default settings for most printers are 15 seconds for Device Not Selected (meaning the printer appears to be off line) and 45 seconds for Transmission Retry (meaning Windows thinks the output hasn't been received and is notifying you that it cannot print to that device). These settings will serve most cases with most monochrome printers. However, you may need to increase the Transmission Retry time if you are printing to a serial port, printing complicated graphics (particularly to a PostScript printer), printing to a network with heavy traffic, or printing to a color printer. Before changing either of these settings, consult your Windows manuals for more information.

The Settings button will be grayed unless you have selected one of the COM ports. With a COM port selected, this button will open a dialog box in which you set the communications specifications for the port—such as baud rate and flow control protocol. Consult your printer documentation for information on the settings required by your printer.

The Network button will be grayed unless you have a network installed. If the button is available, you can use it to open the Network Connections dialog box, which gives you access to shared printers on the network.

The Setup options

Choose the Setup button in the Printers dialog box to see configuration options that are specific to the currently highlighted printer. As Figures 8-4, 8-5, and 8-6 show, the available options will vary with different printer drivers.

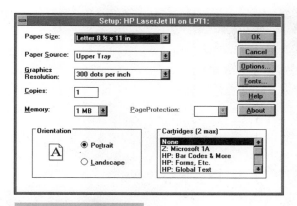
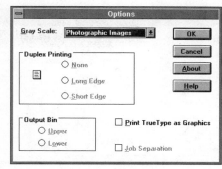

FIGURE 8-4

These are the configuration options available with the PCL/HP LaserJet III printer driver.

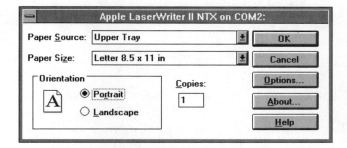

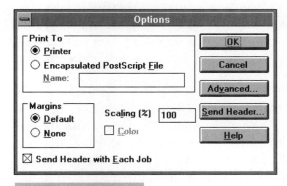

FIGURE 8-5

These are the configuration options available with the Apple LaserWriter II NTX printer driver.

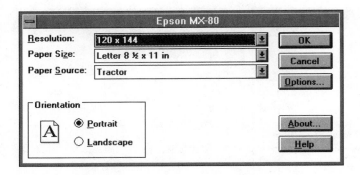

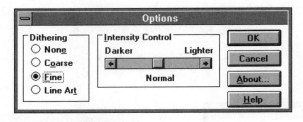

FIGURE 8-6

These are the configuration options available with the Epson MX-80 printer driver.

Choose from the available options for graphics resolution, page orienta-tion, paper source, and so on. As we mentioned in Chapter 7, the page orien-tation settings for most laser printers will not affect printing from Word; you have to change those settings with Word's File Page Setup dialog box.

Be aware that you won't have all options available for every printer. For example, of the three printers in the figures above, only the Epson printer has Tractor as an option for Paper Source. Since almost all laser printers use cut-sheet paper, there is no point in offering a tractor-feed paper option for them.

Of the three driver dialog boxes in Figures 8-4, 8-5, and 8-6, only the LaserJet driver has a Cartridges list box and a Fonts button. That's because with LaserJet printers (and many compatible models), you install additional fonts with either a removable font cartridge or downloadable soft fonts. If you choose the Fonts button in the HP LaserJet III dialog box, Windows can find the soft fonts on your computer's disks and configure the printer to use them. This will make these soft fonts available to almost all of your Windows applications. Word, in particular, will automatically add the names of the soft fonts to its font lists.

Be aware that there are some complex issues involving printer memory, downloadable fonts, and the on-screen display of downloadable and cartridge fonts, most of which are beyond the scope of this book. As we'll discuss in Chapter 16, Windows TrueType fonts can simplify these issues for most printers. In addition to reading our discussion in that chapter, we suggest that you investigate font utilities, consult your Windows manuals, or contact your printer manufacturer for more information about printer and screen fonts under Windows.

One option worth particular mention is the Copies text box in some printer drivers' configuration dialog boxes. Many printers offer a feature that will print multiple copies of the same page without having the computer send the page several times. If you are printing a document that requires multiple copies, particularly one that includes complex formatting or graphics, this feature can save a lot of time. The copies will not be collated; rather, each set of duplicate pages will be printed as a group. But the savings in print time can more than offset the time it takes to collate the pages manually.

For printer drivers that offer this choice, you can use the Copies setting to configure your printer for a specific number of copies. However, you don't need to set the option here; as we'll discuss later in this chapter, Word offers its own settings for you to take advantage of a printer's multiple-copy feature. You should leave this option set to one copy and use Word to set printing for multiple copies.

You should also investigate other buttons contained in your printer driver's configuration dialog box, such as the Advanced button shown in Figure 8-5. Since these vary from one printer to the next, we won't cover them here.

After you choose the settings you want, choose OK. If you choose Cancel or press Esc, the settings will not be stored in the Windows configuration file. Choose Close in the Printers dialog box to save the changes.

How to delete an installed printer

To "uninstall" a printer—after you change the printer on your system, for example—open the Printers dialog box, using the Printers icon in the Control Panel; highlight the printer you want to delete in the Installed Printers list box, and choose the Remove button. Windows asks for confirmation before it deletes the printer from your configuration. Choose Yes to remove the printer.

Selecting a Printer from Within Word

After you have installed and configured one or more printers in Windows, you can use them with Word. You will have some of the same configuration control within Word as in the Windows Control Panel, but there are some features that you cannot change without going back to the Control Panel.

To see or modify the current printer settings from within Word, choose File Print to open the Print dialog box, and then choose Printer to open a Print Setup dialog box similar to Figure 8-7. Note that the Printers box lists all installed printers, with the Default Printer indicated at the top of the box. You can make any printer on the list the new default printer by highlighting the name on the list and choosing the Set As Default Printer button.

FIGURE 8-7

Word's Print Setup dialog box lists all installed printers.

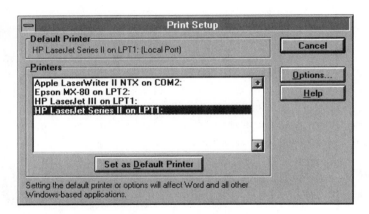

There are several reasons why you might want to change to a different printer. For example, you might be working on a document that you plan to print on another system. Installing the driver for the final printer will let you format your document for the fonts and other features supported by that printer; it will also give you a good idea of how the document will look when you print it. However, be aware that when you change the default printer with the Print Setup dialog box, you're changing it for all programs in Windows, and Windows will stay set for the new printer until you change it back. If this is not the printer that you want other programs in Windows to use, be sure to reset the printer when you've finished with it.

After highlighting a printer in the Printers list, you can choose the Options button to see the options available for that printer. For some printers, choosing this button will open the same dialog box you'll see if you go to the Windows Control Panel, open the Printers dialog box, and choose Setup. For other printers, however, choosing this button will open the Options dialog box that's available if you choose the Options button from that printer's Setup dialog box. More generally, choosing this button will let you see whatever options you can change for this printer from within Word. The actual dialog boxes will vary depending on the printer.

Using the File Print Command

After you've installed and selected your printer, you can print in Word by choosing File Print, typing the keyboard shortcut Ctrl-P, or clicking on the Print button on the Standard toolbar—fourth from the left, with an icon that resembles a printer.

When you choose the Print command, Word will always print the active document. It will not print any other documents that happen to be open unless you activate those windows individually and choose the print command for each. You can print more than one document at a time with the File Find File command; for details, see "How to print, delete, or copy one or more documents" on page 616.

If you click on the Print button, Word will immediately start printing without giving you a chance to change settings. If you choose File Print or type the shortcut key, Word will display the Print dialog box, shown in Figure 8-8. Notice that Word identifies the current printer and its port assignment at the top of the dialog box. If you want to change the printer, you must choose the Printer button to open the Print Setup dialog box. If you want to change the port assignment for the current printer, you'll have to go to the Windows Control Panel, as we discussed earlier in this chapter.

FIGURE 8-8

Choose File Print to open the Print dialog box.

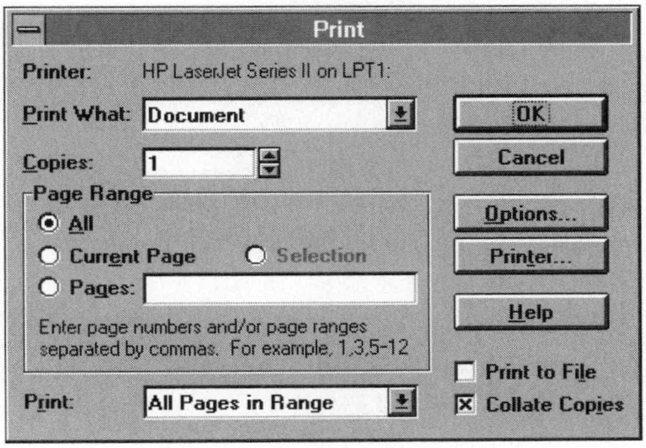

Print

Printer: HP LaserJet Series II on LPT1:

Print What: Document

Copies: 1

Page Range
○ All
○ Current Page   ○ Selection
○ Pages:

Enter page numbers and/or page ranges
separated by commas. For example, 1,3,5-12

Print: All Pages in Range

OK
Cancel
Options...
Printer...
Help

☐ Print to File
☒ Collate Copies

To print from the Print dialog box, choose OK to accept the default settings and send your entire document to the printer. (We'll cover the rest of the choices in this dialog box in a moment.)

If the Background Printing option—which you'll find on the Tools Options Print card—is active, Word will immediately start printing in the background. It will indicate its progress by displaying in the status bar an animated icon of a printer and the number of the current page being printed. Even while Word is printing, it will return you to the active document so that you can continue editing. If background printing is not active, however, Word will display a message box to indicate progress.

If the background printing option is not active, you can interrupt printing at any time by pressing Esc or choosing the Cancel button in the Printing message box. If background printing is active, however, there is no way to interrupt printing from Word once it has started. Instead, you'll need to go to the Windows Print Manager. If background printing is not active but the print job has already been handed over to the Print Manager, you'll need to go to the Print Manager to halt the printing. Note, too, that Word's background printing feature works along with the Windows Print Manager. In fact, if Windows is set not to use the Print Manager and you check the Background Printing check box on Word's Tools Options Print card and then choose OK, Word will ask whether you would like to enable the Print Manager. If you choose Yes, Word will turn the Print Manager on.

How to work with the Print Manager

If, for any reason, Word can't communicate with your printer while you are using the Print Manager, Word will display a message box similar to the one in Figure 8-9.

FIGURE 8-9

The Print Manager shows this message box if Windows cannot communicate with your printer.

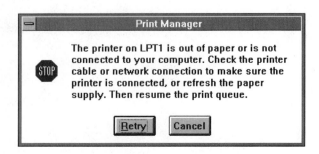

If this message box appears, verify that the printer is turned on, is on line, and is loaded with paper, and that the cable is firmly seated in both the printer and your computer. After you correct the problem, open the Print Manager program. Figure 8-10 shows the Print Manager screen.

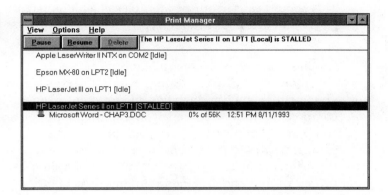

FIGURE 8-10

The Print Manager lists all current print jobs and their status.

Because it is the Windows print spooler program, the Print Manager accepts print jobs from programs, saves the information in temporary files on disk, and then prints in the background while you go about your work. If the Print Manager displays the message box in Figure 8-9 and you choose Cancel, it will show the printer as stalled, as demonstrated in Figure 8-10. To restart the print job, choose the Resume button. To cancel the print job, select the job on the Print Manager's screen, and choose Delete. The Print Manager will display a message asking for confirmation before deleting the job from the print queue. Choosing OK deletes the print job. Choosing Cancel aborts the deletion. Either way, Windows returns you to the Print Manager screen.

How to troubleshoot printer problems

If you still can't get Word to print your document after following these steps, verify that you can print from MS-DOS or an MS-DOS program, to confirm that your printer and computer are hooked up properly. For example, if you are using a non-PostScript printer and your printer is plugged into LPT1, you should be able to print from MS-DOS (but not from Windows, and not from an MS-DOS window running in Windows) by pressing either the PrtSc (Print Screen) key or Shift-PrtSc, depending on your system.

If you have a non-PostScript printer plugged into any other port, you can use the MS-DOS ECHO command to send a form feed command to that port. If the printer is plugged into COM1, for example, go to the MS-DOS prompt and type *echo* followed by a space, and then press Ctrl-L followed by a space, and then type > *com1:* and press Enter. The command should look like the following:

```
echo ^L > com1:
```

This should cause your printer to eject a blank page.

For a PostScript printer, type

```
echo showpage > com1:
```

which should also produce a blank sheet.

If you can't print anything, even from MS-DOS or an MS-DOS program, your printer may be installed incorrectly, or one or more of your system components may need repair or replacement. For assistance, contact your company's support staff, or your printer or computer vendor. If you can print from MS-DOS but not from Windows, you probably haven't installed the printer choices correctly in Windows. Be sure that you have installed the proper printer and assigned it to the correct port.

File Print command options

Assuming you can successfully print a document, you can now explore the options in the Print dialog box, shown earlier in Figure 8-8. If all you ever want to print is your entire document, one copy at a time, you will never need any of these additional features. We expect, however, that you will use other options at least occasionally. We'll start with the most commonly used options.

Multiple copies and collating

You use the Copies text box in the Print dialog box to specify the number of copies to print. Notice the Collate Copies check box in the lower right corner of the dialog box. If this is checked and you specify multiple copies, Word will send the print job to the printer repeatedly to make the requested number of copies. As we mentioned earlier, however, many printers can print multiple copies of a single page after receiving the data once. This approach saves time but yields uncollated sets of pages. If your printer works like this and speed is more important than collating the pages, be sure the Collate Copies check box is cleared.

Print Range: How to print the entire document, specific pages, the current page, or a selection

By default, Word prints your entire document; however, you can choose to print only parts of it if you prefer. As shown in Figure 8-8, the Page Range box contains four option buttons: All, Current Page, Selection, and Pages.

Current Page refers to the page where the cursor is currently located; note that this isn't necessarily the same as the page that is currently displayed on the screen. If you have any question about the cursor's location, close the dialog box and check the page number in the status bar. Note that you can't check the location with the dialog box because Word uses the status bar for a message while the dialog box is open.

The Selection option button will be grayed unless you selected some text before opening the Print dialog box. If you choose this option, Word will print only the selected text.

If you print a selection, the text will be correctly formatted, but any automatic page breaks will be ignored. This means that Word will print your selection starting at the top of the sheet of paper, no matter where it falls on the page displayed on the screen. Similarly, if your selection starts in the middle of a paragraph, Word will print the selection with the correct formatting for that paragraph, but it will format the first printed line as the start of a new paragraph, no matter where in the paragraph the text selection actually starts. Other page formatting features, such as headers and footers, may also be printed differently from how they otherwise would.

The Pages option includes a text box in which you can specify a set of pages to print. Simply enter the numbers of the pages in the text box. You can list individual pages, a range of pages (separate the starting and ending pages with a hyphen), or a combination of the two. Separate each page number or range from the following one with a comma. For example, to print pages 1, 3, 4, 5, and 7, you can enter *1,3-5,7*.

How to simulate duplex printing: Odd Pages and Even Pages

Some printers are equipped with a duplex printing option. Each sheet of paper makes two passes through the printer, so that you can print one image on the front of the sheet and another on the back. Duplex printing can save lots of paper and make the finished document look more professional.

Even if your printer does not support duplex printing, it's easy to get equivalent results. The Print box at the bottom of the Print dialog box lists three options: All Pages In Range (the default), Odd Pages, and Even Pages. To print a document on both sides of the paper, print the odd pages first; then put the stack of pages back in the input tray and print the even pages.

Note that you will need to feed the pages in reverse order the second time. With a typical laser printer, for example, this means the pages need to be face down, with page one on top, followed by three, five, and so on.

If your printer doesn't have an optional paper path that will stack the output in this order, you can use the Reverse Print Order option on the Options Print card, which we will discuss later in this chapter.

Some laser printers have a difficult time when printing on the back of a page that was recently printed. For best results when printing odd and then even pages, be sure to use fresh paper that hasn't been moistened by exposure to high humidity. After printing the odd pages, give the paper a little time to dissipate some of the heat from the fuser rollers, and fan the stack to help eliminate static electricity. These steps should help reduce paper-feeding problems that can ruin a duplex print job.

How to print to a file

By checking the Print To File check box, you can save the print job in a disk file rather than sending it to the printer. The file will contain all of the printer commands and text for your document, and you can print the file later by copying it to a printer with the MS-DOS COPY command. The file you print to disk will include commands from the printer language used by the active printer. If you want the pages to be printed correctly, you can use this file only with a compatible printer.

If you check the Print To File check box and then choose OK, Word will ask for an output filename by way of a Print To File dialog box. Give the file any filename that conforms to MS-DOS filename rules, and choose OK to print. You can cancel the Print To File operation from this dialog box by choosing the Cancel button.

How to print supplementary information

We skipped over one item near the top of the Print dialog box: the Print What drop-down list. The default selection is Document, but there are other choices—as you can see in Figure 8-11, which shows the opened list.

The Summary Info choice prints the information from the File Summary Info and Document Statistics dialog boxes, both of which we covered in Chapter 2. Annotations prints a list of all annotations in the document, in order, along with the page number each annotation refers to. (We'll cover annotations in Chapter 10. Annotations are similar to footnotes except that they are comments about the document rather than a part of the document.) Styles prints the definitions of all style formats for the document. (We'll cover styles in Chapter 12.) AutoText Entries prints all AutoText entries, including any in the Normal template and the current supplementary template if there's one attached. Key Assignments is similar to the AutoText Entries choice: It prints any key assignments in the Normal and supplementary templates that are changed from the default settings.

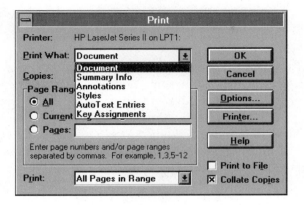

FIGURE 8-11

The Print What drop-down list in the Print dialog box enables you to print items other than your document.

You can print any one of these items by choosing it in the Print What drop-down list. Note that you can also tell Word to print the Summary Info and Annotations with every document by using the Options settings.

The Printer and Options buttons

There are two buttons in the Print dialog box worth mention. The Printer button opens the Print Setup dialog box, which we covered earlier in this chapter. The Options button takes you to the Print card in the Options dialog box, shown in Figure 8-12. This is the same card that you see when you choose Tools Options and then choose Print.

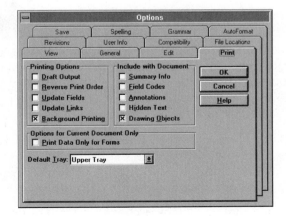

FIGURE 8-12

The Options button in the Print dialog box opens the Options dialog box.

The card is divided into three group boxes and a separate text box: Printing Options, Include With Document, Options For Current Document Only, and the Default Tray list box. Here's a look at each.

Printing Options

Your choices in the Printing Options box define how you print—in draft, for example, or in reverse order—and whether to update information while printing.

Draft Output. Checking the Draft Output check box will, in general, speed printing by leaving out some features. The differences between draft and higher-quality output depend on your printer. For example, some printers won't show all text formatting in draft mode, but others will; some will print graphics when in draft mode, but others won't. To see the effects with your printer, simply print a heavily formatted document with and without the Draft Output check box checked.

Reverse Print Order. Checking the Reverse Print Order check box tells Word to print the document starting with the last page first. This is useful if you have a printer that stacks its output face up rather than face down; in this case, you'll have your pages in the correct order immediately upon printing.

This option can also be helpful if you need to print in reverse order to simulate duplex printing, which we discussed earlier in this chapter. If your printer doesn't offer an option to stack pages in reverse order when you print the first side of the pages, checking the Reverse Print Order check box in Word will serve the same purpose.

Update Fields. Checking the Update Fields check box makes sure that all fields in the document are updated before they are printed. As we mentioned in Chapter 5, when discussing the PAGE, DATE, TIME, and AUTOTEXT fields, you can update fields at any time by selecting a block of text and pressing F9. If you make sure the Update Fields check box is checked, however, you don't have to remember to update fields manually before printing. Unless you have a specific reason for not wanting to update your fields each time you print, we suggest you check this box. We'll discuss fields in detail in Chapter 20, page 674.

Update Links. Similar to the Update Fields option, Update Links will update any linked objects before printing. For more information on linked objects, see Chapter 15, "Drawing, Graphics, & Other Objects," page 548, and Chapter 18, "Sharing Data with Other Programs," page 618.

Background Printing. This check box is checked by default. Background printing lets you continue working on your document while a print job is being formatted and sent to the Print Manager. For faster printing, clear this check box. Note that you cannot halt a print job from within Word if Background Printing is active, but you can if the option is not active.

Include With Document

In the Include With Document box, you can specify additional items to print with documents.

Earlier in this chapter, we described how you can tell Word to print the summary information or annotations, among other choices, from within the Print dialog box. When you specify these choices in the Print dialog box, however, Word prints only the specified item. By adding a check to the appropriate check box here, you can tell Word to print these items automatically *along with* any document. Note that if you check the Annotations option, Word will check the Hidden Text option as well.

Summary Info. Check the Summary Info check box, and Word will print the information stored in the Summary Info and Document Statistics dialog boxes on a page by itself. The document will start on its own page (page 1 unless you've assigned a different number to the document's first page).

Field Codes. If this box is checked, Word will print the *field codes* instead of the *field results* for any fields in your document. In the majority of cases, you will probably not want to check this box. We will discuss fields in depth in Chapter 20.

Annotations. Annotations are notes, formatted as hidden text, that you can store in your document. Checking this box tells Word to print the notes. Word will print them after the document, starting on a separate page. If you check the Annotations check box, Word will also automatically check the Hidden Text check box. This makes sense; the markers for annotations are formatted as hidden text, and you need to print the markers as well—much as you need to see footnote references in your text to know what the footnotes refer to. For more information about annotations, including how to display them on your screen, see "Annotations" starting on page 336.

Hidden Text. Check the Hidden Text check box if you want Word to print text that you've formatted as hidden. Normally, of course, the point of formatting text as hidden is to hide it. For example, you might write yourself a note within a document to remind you to check a fact or identify the source of some information. Occasionally, however, you may want to print hidden text.

If you print a document complete with hidden text, keep in mind that this will result in a longer document. It will also change the pagination, throwing off page breaks. Note, too, that you can select Hidden Text without selecting Annotations, but not vice versa.

Drawing Objects. Word checks this check box by default. Clear the check box to tell Word not to print drawing objects along with the document. For more information about drawing objects, see Chapter 15, "Drawing, Graphics, & Other Objects," page 548.

Options For Current Document Only

The only item in the Options For Current Document Only box is Print Data Only For Forms. If this check box is checked and the document you're printing is a form, Word will print only the information in the form fields, and not the form itself. Unlike the other options on this card, which affect all documents you print with Word, the setting for this option is stored as part of each individual document file. For information on forms and how to create them, see Chapter 21, "Form Letters, Labels, & Forms," page 714.

Default Tray

You use the Default Tray list box by opening the drop-down list, as shown in Figure 8-13, and selecting the paper feed option you want to use.

FIGURE 8-13

The Default Tray list box lists the available paper feed options for the currently chosen printer.

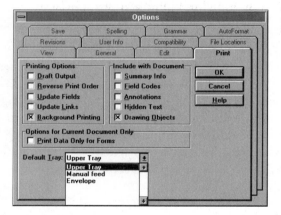

The options in the Default Tray list box will vary depending on the printer currently set as the default printer. The choices for the HP LaserJet III, for example, are Upper Tray, Manual Feed, and Envelope; the choices for the Epson FX-80 are Tractor, Manual Feed, and Upper Tray; and the choices for the Canon LBP-8 III are Upper, Lower, Manual, Envelope, and Automatic. In most cases, the meanings of the choices are obvious. If they are not, you can try printing with each option and see which paper source your printer uses.

Previewing a Printed Document

Given all of the formatting choices and printing options, it can be difficult to predict how all these elements will work together. To help avoid unpleasant surprises with the appearance of your printed document, Word offers two features that show you how your printed document will look before you print it: Page Layout view and Print Preview.

Both features let you see and work with anything from a bird's-eye view of multiple pages on up to a bigger-than-life-size view of part of a single page. With either feature, you see what amounts to a preview of your printed document, complete with headers, footers, and other special elements in place. And both features can help you avoid wasted time and effort on print runs that don't produce the results you have in mind. We'll look at the File Print Preview command first.

Print Preview

When you choose File Print Preview (or click on the Print Preview button on the Standard toolbar), Word displays a screen like the one in Figure 8-14. Notice the word *(Preview)* following the filename on the title bar. Also notice the Print Preview toolbar, immediately below the menu bar. The text on the preview screen may or may not be readable, depending on the font size, the current resolution setting for your video card, and the current Zoom setting.

FIGURE 8-14

You can choose the Print Preview command to preview and alter your page layout.

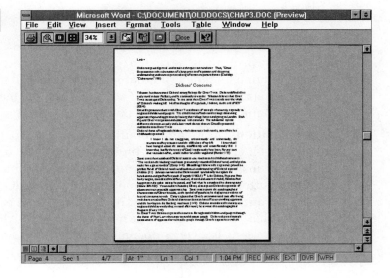

The Print Preview toolbar

The Print Preview toolbar makes it easy to adjust your screen display and use the special features available in Print Preview. Here's a look at the toolbar buttons and their functions.

Button	Function
	Print
	Magnifier
	One Page
	Multiple Pages
	View Rulers
	Shrink To Fit
	Full Screen

Print button. As with the Print button on the Standard toolbar, you can choose this button to print all of the current document using the existing print settings and without opening the Print dialog box. (Note that you can also print from Print Preview mode by choosing File Print from the menu bar. If you use the File Print commmand, Word will open the Print dialog box before printing.)

Magnifier button. The Magnifier button is actually a toggle that primarily controls the effect of a mouse click on the screen. Click on the button to toggle between the magnifier mode and normal text editing mode.

If this button is inactive, the mouse will behave just as it does in Normal or Page Layout view. However, if the button is active—in which case it will look as if it has been pressed—the mouse pointer will look like a magnifying glass whenever it is over a document, and it will have either a plus or a minus sign in the magnifying glass. This shape indicates that the mouse will provide a shortcut for zooming in (magnifying a page) or zooming out (making a page smaller) on the screen.

When the screen shows one or more full pages at a time, the magnifying glass will include a plus sign. If you click on a page to enlarge it, Word will zoom the page to the 100% zoom setting and position the image to show the portion of the page that you clicked on. When the image is displayed at a zoom size larger than 100% (or if you clicked to zoom to 100%), the mouse pointer will contain a minus sign, and if you click on the page, Word will zoom out to full page view.

> The page size Word uses when it zooms out to show a full page in response to a mouse click depends on the last setting you've used to show one or more full pages. For example, if you last set Word to show one full page, which works out to a 34% zoom setting in standard VGA, clicking with the mouse will zoom out to a 34% zoom setting. If you last set Word to see several pages at once, however, with, say, a 16% zoom setting, clicking to zoom out will result in a 16% setting. The only settings that count for this purpose, however, are those that you make through the One Page and Multiple Pages toolbar buttons, which we'll describe shortly.

You can edit your document in Print Preview just as if you were in Normal or Page Layout view. The key differences between Print Preview and Page Layout view are that in Page Layout view, the toolbars are the same as in Normal view—that is, you don't have the Print Preview toolbar. As a result, in Page Layout view, the magnifier button isn't available for zooming in and out. In both Page Layout view and Print Preview, however, you can see what amounts to a print preview with all formatting visible; and in both views you can make changes, deletions, and additions to your document and Word will reformat the document to reflect those changes. In both Page Layout view and Print Preview, your computer's performance will be slower than in Normal view.

If you like, you can add a Magnifier button to your Standard toolbar that's similar in function to the Magnifier button on the Print Preview toolbar. Once you've done that, the difference between Page Layout view and Print Preview is almost nonexistent (except that Word doesn't display the Standard and Formatting toolbars in Print Preview). You'll find details on how to add this—or any other—button to a toolbar in "Customizing Toolbars" starting on page 316.

NEW!

One Page button. Clicking the One Page button will set the zoom setting to display a single page—a 34% zoom setting with standard VGA. It will also set Word to use the same setting for the zoom-out shortcut with a mouse click if you use the Magnifier button as described earlier.

Multiple Pages button. This button displays more than one page at a time. If you simply click on this button, you'll see the grid shown in Figure 8-15.

FIGURE 8-15

Click on the Multiple Pages button on the Print Preview toolbar, and you can then specify how many pages you will see on the screen at one time.

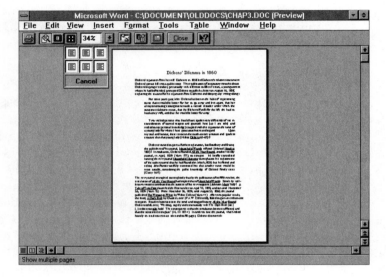

If you point to the Multiple pages button and hold the mouse button down while you drag across the grid, you'll find that the grid will grow to as large as four rows of eight columns each (if you are using 1024-by-768 resolution) or to three rows by seven columns (in standard VGA, as shown in Figure 8-16). (Note that you can also click the Multiple Pages button, point anywhere on the grid, and then hold down the mouse button and drag.)

If you have checked the mirror margins check box in the Page Setup dialog box (Margins card), the pages will be displayed as two-page spreads with a binding between the paired pages, as shown in Figure 8-17. For more information on mirrored margins, see "Margins" on page 211.

FIGURE 8-16

If you drag across the
Multiple Pages grid,
it will grow as you
drag—to as large as
three rows of seven
columns in standard
VGA.

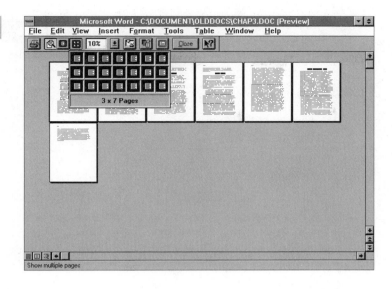

FIGURE 8-17

If you have specified
mirrored margins as
part of your page setup,
the Print Preview
screen will show pairs
of facing pages when
you zoom out enough
to see multiple pages.

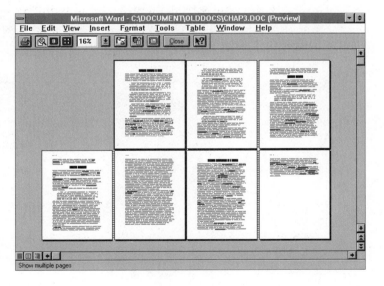

Zoom Control text box. The Zoom Control text box on the Print Preview
toolbar shows the current scale—or zoom percentage setting—for the view; the
smaller the percentage setting, the smaller the page on screen. Word sets this
percentage when you use the Magnifier or click on the One Page or Multiple
Page button. But you can also set the zoom to other percentages.

The drop-down list that goes with this box, shown in Figure 8-18, offers a range of predefined settings, from 10% to 200% and from one-page width to two pages. You can also enter any zoom percentage you prefer, from 10 to 200.

FIGURE 8-18

The Zoom Control box includes a drop-down list of options.

View Ruler button. The View Ruler button toggles the rulers on and off. When the option is active, the View Ruler button will look as if it's pressed down. More important, you'll see the vertical and horizontal rulers for the current page, as shown in Figure 8-19. If Word is set to display more than one page at a time, you can move from page to page by clicking on a page with the mouse. The only way to move from page to page with the keyboard is to use the arrow keys to move through the text or use the Edit Go To command. When you move to a different page, the ruler positions will change to match the page you're on.

FIGURE 8-19

You can display rulers with your document in Page Preview.

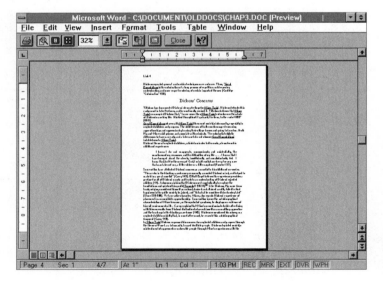

Note that the top (horizontal) ruler indicates left and right margins, as well as the left, right, and first-line indent markers for the paragraph containing the cursor—just as in Normal view. And the tab icon in the left corner of the ruler also functions as in Normal view. We covered the horizontal ruler and tabs in Chapter 7.

Shrink To Fit button. Suppose you've written a letter or a memo, only to discover that a few lines—such as a signature block by itself—spill onto the last page. To fit those lines onto the next-to-last page, you could try moving the margins out a little or shrinking the fonts a bit; or you could click on the Shrink To Fit button, and Word will automatically reduce the font size in an effort to fit the document on one fewer page. Word will not remove manual (hard) page breaks, however. If there are any in your document, you may not be able to eliminate that extra page by clicking the Shrink To Fit button.

Use this feature with caution. Word shrinks the document by reducing the font size. And it will try to comply with the command even if you choose it more than once. You could end up with text that is too small to read comfortably. Be sure to check the results before you decide to stick with them. And be prepared to use the Undo command.

Full Screen button. The Full Screen button is exactly equivalent to choosing the View Full Screen command. If you click on this button, Word will switch to Full Screen view, hiding the title, menu, and status bars—and, indeed, everything but the Page Preview toolbar. (The View Ruler button acts independently in these two views; you can click it on in one view and off in the other if you choose.) The whole point of Full Screen view is to display as much of the page at one time as possible. You can toggle back to the default version of Print Preview, with the additional items displayed, by clicking on the Full Screen button again.

Close and Help buttons. The Close button will return you to the view your document was in when you chose the File Print Preview command. (Note, however, that if you are in Full Screen view when you choose the Close button, you will still be in Full Screen view when you return to the prior view.)

The last button on the Print Preview toolbar provides access to context-sensitive Help, much like the Help button on the Standard toolbar. See "Getting Help" starting on page 28 for more information about online Help.

How to navigate in Print Preview

When you choose Print Preview, Word will always display the page that was currently visible on your editing screen—either as the only page (if Print Preview is set to show a single full page) or as one of multiple pages (when Print Preview is set to show more than one page). Before it displays the page, however, Word will automatically repaginate your document up to and including the pages it will preview on the screen.

If more than one page is displayed, the current page will be highlighted with a border around it. You can position the mouse pointer on a different page and click it to make that page active.

You can move through your document while in the Print Preview screen with the arrow keys, the Page Up and Page Down keys, or the vertical scroll bar. As in Page Layout view, the scroll bar buttons with two triangles move you a page at a time through your document if Word is set to show one full page at a time. If more than one page is displayed, these buttons will take you to the next screenful of pages. You can also press Ctrl-Home and Ctrl-End to jump to the first and last pages.

How to change formats within Print Preview

As mentioned earlier, you can edit text in Print Preview. In fact, if you drop the Word menus down, you'll find that most choices are still available—including File Page Setup to adjust the margins and other page setup options. You can also use the rulers and the mouse to change other settings, such as indents and margins.

You can move the horizontal ruler's indent markers with a mouse while in Print Preview, exactly as you would in Page Layout or Normal views, by pointing to the appropriate marker, holding down the mouse button, and dragging the marker. You can also add, delete, or move tabs just as in Page Layout or Normal view. Keep in mind that changes to indents and tabs will affect only the current paragraph or paragraphs—meaning the paragraph or paragraphs containing the cursor or selection.

You can also adjust the margins with the rulers and the mouse exactly as you can in Page Layout view, by pointing to the margin marker on the appropriate ruler, holding down the mouse button, and dragging the marker. We discussed how to use Word's rulers to adjust indents and margins in "The horizontal ruler" starting on page 215, and tabs in the section "Tabs" starting on page 233.

Note that if you're working in a multisection document, your changes to the margins made with the mouse will apply to the current section only. If you want to change the format in more than one section, you can highlight some text that crosses the section breaks and then make your changes. We'll discuss multisection documents in detail in Chapter 13, "Bullets, Numbering, & Sections," page 468.

The ruler scale is too small for precise adjustment of margins, tabs, and indents when you are viewing one or more full pages on the screen. You will find that such changes are easier if you zoom in for a close-up view of your page, which will also give you a more detailed ruler to work with. Don't forget that you can reverse changes with the Undo command if the result isn't what you wanted.

Headers and footers

Although you can edit the text of your document in Page Preview, you cannot make changes to headers or footers. All you need to do, however, is either choose View Header And Footer or double-click on a header or footer. Word will switch to Page Layout view with the header or footer area active and the Header And Footer toolbar displayed. When you finish editing, choose Close on the Header And Footer toolbar. Word will leave you in either Page Layout or Normal view, whichever one you were in when you first switched to Print Preview.

You can also adjust the position and size of headers and footers. For details, see "Defining the Position of a Header or Footer" starting on page 588.

How to use Page Layout view

Like Print Preview, Page Layout view displays a close approximation of your printed pages complete with margins, headers, page numbers, footnotes, and other assorted elements in place. The main difference is that in Page Layout view Word, by default, displays the Formatting and Standard toolbars rather than the Print Preview toolbar. In addition, you can edit headers and footers in Page Layout view.

In essence, Page Layout view offers a middle ground between Normal view and Print Preview, although it's closer to Print Preview. We'll cover the differences between Normal and Page Layout views in the next chapter, along with Word's other View menu commands. For the moment, it's enough to know that, as with Print Preview, Page Layout view displays all of the elements on your page while you edit and format your text.

There are several ways to switch to Page Layout view. We'll save most of these for the next chapter as well. For now, simply choose View Page Layout. And note that to change from Page Layout view to another view (such as Normal), you can, once again, choose the appropriate View menu command. If you're not sure which view you are currently in, take a look at the View menu. Word always indicates the active view by displaying a dot next to the appropriate command. (If you are currently in Print Preview, the active view, as indicated by the dot, is the one you will return to when you close Print Preview.)

Limitations of Page Layout view

Page Layout view doesn't provide quite as accurate a representation of your printed document as Print Preview. In particular, if you've checked the Hidden Text check box on the Tools Options View card, any text formatted as hidden will appear in Page Layout view. This will be true even if you've set hidden text not to print, on the Tools Options Print card. In contrast, hidden text will show on the screen in Print Preview only if the Hidden Text check box on the Tools Options Print card is checked. And it will show even if Word is set not to show hidden text in Page Layout and Normal views.

Envelopes and Labels

There is one last printing-related issue that virtually everyone has to deal with at least occasionally: envelopes and labels. Printing and formatting envelopes have traditionally caused problems for even the best word processors, and many offices equipped with the highest-quality laser printers and the latest software were obliged to keep typewriters within reach, just for addressing envelopes. Although such problems have not quite become a thing of the past, much progress has been made in envelope-printing with word processors—and Word 6.0 goes a long way toward making this chore quick and easy.

You can use the envelope-and-label feature without opening a document that includes the address you want, but if you do, you'll miss half the fun. When you choose Tools Envelopes And Labels (or click the Envelope icon on the Word For Windows 2.0 toolbar if you have that toolbar showing), Word will first look at the current cursor position in the active document. If it doesn't see what looks like an address there, it will start at the top of the document and work its way downward, searching for anything that looks like an address. It will then open the Envelopes And Labels dialog box, as shown in Figure 8-20, with the Envelopes card displayed.

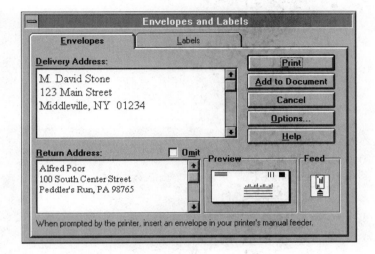

FIGURE 8-20

With the Envelopes And Labels dialog box, you can edit and print envelopes and labels from within your document.

How to create an envelope

If Word doesn't find anything it recognizes as an address, it will leave the Delivery Address text box empty. But if it finds text that looks like an address, it fills in the box.

Word shows quite a lot of intelligence in identifying the address. A series of short lines can confuse it, but it generally finds an address if one exists. If you want to make certain that Word finds the address, you can select the text or place the cursor in the address. But if you're curious, you might experiment a bit to see just how clever the program is at discovering an address on your page.

Word also inserts information in the Return Address text box. This is the Mailing Address entry currently stored on the Tools Options User Info card, but you can edit it in the Envelopes And Labels dialog box if you need to. If you make changes to the return address, Word will ask whether you want to use the revised address as your default return address when you print the envelope. Answer Yes, and Word will modify the information on the Tools Options User Info card. You can also check the Omit check box to have Word print only the Delivery Address. Use this option if you have preprinted envelopes that already include the return address.

The Preview and Feed areas show how your envelope will look when printed and how the blank envelope should be oriented when fed into your printer. To change these settings, choose the Options button on the Envelopes card.

How to change the format for an envelope

Figure 8-21 shows the Envelope Options dialog box, which Word will open when you choose the Options button on the Envelopes card. The box has two tabbed cards: Envelope Options and Printing Options; the Envelope Options card is illustrated in the figure.

FIGURE 8-21

The Envelope Options card contains a variety of options controlling how your envelope will appear when printed.

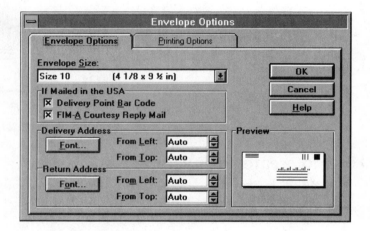

The first item on the Envelope Options card is the Envelope Size text box. The default setting is the standard Size 10 business envelope, but you can open the attached drop-down list to find 10 additional predefined sizes. You'll also find a Custom Size option; choosing this will open a dialog box in which you can enter the height and width of the envelope you want to use.

If you plan on using large envelopes (larger than 8.5 by 11 inches), make certain that your printer's paper path can handle the larger paper size. Most laser printers cannot take paper wider than 8.5 inches. If your envelope is too wide for your printer, you may find it convenient to print the address on a label instead. We'll cover Word's label-printing feature immediately after the envelope-printing feature.

How to add Postnet and FIM bar codes. The If Mailed In The USA box contains two check boxes. Check the Delivery Point Bar Code check box if you want Word to add a Postnet bar code to the envelope face. This bar code contains the ZIP code information from the delivery address in a machine-readable code that the U.S. Postal Service's automated mail-handling equipment can read. (Note, in passing, that if you tell Word to add the envelope to your file, it adds the Postnet bar code as a field, called the BARCODE field. You can also add a BARCODE field manually if you like. We will discuss fields in more detail in Chapter 20, page 674.)

NEW!

The FIM-A Courtesy Reply Mail check box will be grayed unless the Delivery Point Bar Code check box is checked. If you check this second check box, Word will print a different bar code along the top of the envelope. This helps the mail-handling equipment locate both the postage and the Postnet code. Check with your local post office for more information on FIM bar codes.

How to format addresses. Both the Delivery Address and Return Address boxes have a Font button and From Left and From Top text boxes. The Font buttons will open an Envelope Address dialog box for the delivery address and an Envelope Return Address dialog box for the return address. You can use these dialog boxes to modify the font formats for the address and return address, as appropriate. Use the From Left and From Top boxes to position the address blocks precisely. The default setting for all four is Auto, which will take care of placement for you.

NEW!

Note that there is no way to control the font format for individual words or lines in an address block. However, you can change these formats if you choose the Add To Document button on the Envelopes card and then format the individual words and lines within the document. We'll discuss the Add To Document button in a moment.

How to set the envelope feed options. Figure 8-22 on the next page shows the Printing Options card for envelopes. The items and choices on this screen will vary depending on your default printer. Word displays the printer name after the word *Printer* at the top of the card.

NEW!

The Feed Method box in the middle of the card shows the available options for feeding envelopes into the current default printer. For most laser printers, the choices will include left-aligned, centered, and right-aligned positioning, with either the long or the short edge of the envelope being fed into the printer.

The Face Up, Face Down, and Clockwise Rotation buttons will appear on the Printing Options card for only some printers. You choose the Face Up or

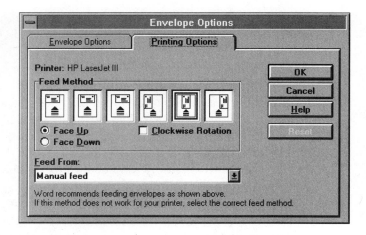

FIGURE 8-22

The Printing Options card contains envelope feed options for your selected printer.

Face Down button to match the orientation of the envelope with your printer, as appropriate. Clockwise Rotation shifts the orientation for envelopes that are fed short edge first.

The Feed From text box includes a drop-down list of available paper sources. For a laser printer, these might include Manual Feed and Default Tray, among other choices.

By default, Word will highlight the recommended Feed Method and Feed From options for the current printer. If you change any of these, you'll see a message at the bottom of the card warning that you have made a change that might not work. You can use the Reset button to return to Word's recommended settings.

How to print the envelope

After you finish setting the envelope options, you can choose OK to return to the Envelopes And Labels dialog box. If you're satisfied with your settings, you can either print the envelope immediately by choosing the Print button or add the envelope to your document for later printing by choosing the Add To Document button.

If you print the envelope immediately, Word doesn't save it anywhere. If you add it to the document, Word will save it with the document and won't print it until you choose a print command. This option is particularly useful when you want to apply some special font formatting or when you want to edit the envelope further in some other way, such as by adding a picture or other object.

When you add the envelope to your document, Word adds a new section at the beginning of the file. We will discuss sections in Chapter 13; for now, it's enough to know that the envelope must be in a separate section because it's formatted with a page size and margins that differ from the rest of your document. (When Word changes these formats, the changes must apply to an entire section.)

Along the bottom of the Envelopes And Labels dialog box is a message that will vary depending on the printer and paper source that are currently selected. If you have a dot-matrix printer, for example, and the Feed From choice on the Envelope Options Printing Options card is set to Tractor, the message will generally tell you to verify that an envelope is loaded before printing. Similarly, if you have a laser printer with an automatic envelope feeder and the Feed From box is set to Envelope, the program will remind you to insert envelopes into your printer's envelope tray. These reminders are always worth paying attention to.

Labels

The Labels card, shown in Figure 8-23, is similar to the Envelopes card. You can use it to print one label or many labels.

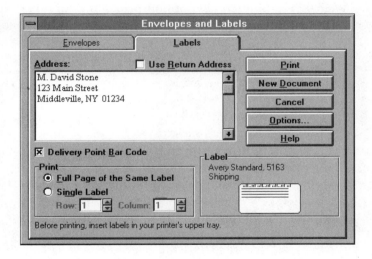

FIGURE 8-23

With the Labels card, you can quickly print one or more labels.

To display the Labels card, choose Tools Envelopes And Labels and then choose the Labels card. Assuming that Word is able to identify an address in the current document, the Address box will contain the same address block as the Delivery Address on the Envelopes card. Instead of a return address, the Labels card contains a check box labeled Use Return Address, immediately above the Address box. If you check this box, Word will replace the destination address taken from your current document with the address from the Tools Options User Info card. In other words, the only address Word will print on the label is your return address.

The return address feature on the Labels card makes it easy to print one or more return address labels, but it isn't much help if you are trying to create a shipping label with both a return and a destination address on it. If you need to create a shipping label and the label comes in a one-across format, define the format as an envelope rather than a label. Choose the Custom Size option on the Envelope Options card for the envelope size, and specify the appropriate height and width. For details, see the discussion of printing envelopes, earlier in this chapter.

The Delivery Point Bar Code check box on the Labels card works the same way as on the Envelope card. The Label box displays a preview of the label and includes the label type, as defined in the Label options card, which we'll discuss in a moment.

The Print box, which contains two option buttons, is unique to the Labels card. The Full Page Of The Same Label option prints a full sheet of the same label. The Single Label option prints an individual label and also specifies the row and column position of the label on the sheet. The choices available for row and column number will vary depending on the type of label.

Note that the ability to specify a row and a column for printing a single label implies the ability to run the same label sheet through your laser printer any number of times, printing one label each time. Be aware that most printer label manufacturers do not recommend using a label sheet more than once. Each time you run the sheet through your printer, you increase the odds of having a label come off and stick to something inside the printer. That's particularly true if you've already used the label at the leading edge of the sheet such that the label in the next row presents an edge to the printer. If a label comes off, it may cause serious damage—and, at the very least, will be a chore to find and remove. Some people use partially filled label sheets without any problems, but you may want to be more cautious and use this feature sparingly if at all. If you do try using partial sheets, print your labels so that you remove them from the bottom of the page first.

If you choose not to use partially filled sheets, you can minimize the number of wasted labels by dividing the sheets into smaller sheets. If you start with a sheet of 20 labels, for example, with two columns of 10, you can cut the sheet in half lengthwise and then cut each of the two halves in half. The final result is four sheets of five labels each. And each one will have a proper leading edge.

Instead of the Envelope card's Add To Document button, the Label card has a New Document button. Choosing this button creates a new document, formatted to produce the specified label (or page of labels). As with the equivalent option for envelopes, use this option if you want to edit the label further—to add font formatting to individual words or lines, for example, or to add graphics. You will also want to use this option if you plan to reprint the same page of labels at some later time, as with a sheet of return address labels.

How to define the label to use: The Label Options dialog box

The Options button on the Labels card opens the Label Options dialog box, shown in Figure 8-24. You use this box to specify the type of labels being used.

FIGURE 8-24

The Label Options dialog box contains settings that control how your labels will appear when printed.

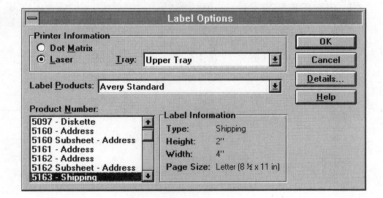

In the Printer Information box you choose a printer type (Dot Matrix or Laser) and a paper source. (Even though the list box is labeled Tray, it will show the available paper sources for the current default printer.)

You can select Dot Matrix even if your default printer is a laser printer. If you do however, you may not get the results you want since the laser printer versions of labels in various sizes use a format different from that of the dot matrix versions. In addition, when you choose Dot Matrix, you lose the option to specify a paper source in the Tray box. So be careful about changing the label type.

The Label Products box has a drop-down list of supported label brands, including Avery Standard, Avery Pan European, and Other. If you cannot find a choice that matches the labels you use, you can create your own custom format, as we will discuss in a moment.

The Product Number box lists the supported label formats for the Label Products group you specified. The majority of the available types are Avery products, and they cover everything from mailing labels to Rolodex cards. The Label Information box to the right of the Product Number box displays the type, width, height, and page size for the label that's currently highlighted in the Product Number list.

If you want to change the settings for a label or create your own custom settings, choose the Details button. This will open a dialog box, similar to the one in either Figure 8-25 or Figure 8-26, in which you can specify a custom format for a label sheet or tractor feed labels.

FIGURE 8-25

Choosing the Details button on the Label Options card will open a dialog box similar to this one and the one in Figure 8-26. This dialog box is typical for laser printers.

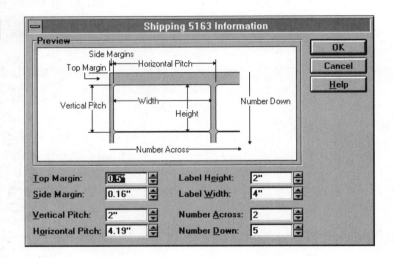

FIGURE 8-26

This dialog box is typical for dot matrix printers.

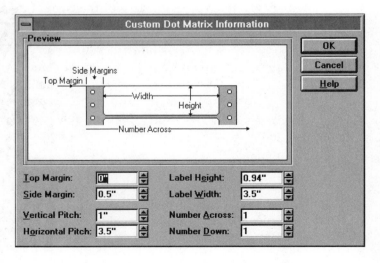

As you can see in the figures, the dialog box will vary depending on the setting for Printer Information in the Label Options dialog box. Figure 8-25 is an example of what you'll see for laser printers, Figure 8-26 for dot matrix printers.

For laser printers, you can define the top margin (distance from the top of a sheet to the top of the first label on the sheet), side margin (distance from the side of the sheet to the edge of the first label), vertical pitch (distance from the top of one label to the top of the next label), horizontal pitch (distance from the left edge of one label in a row to the left edge of the next), label height, label width, and number of labels in each row and column of a sheet. For dot matrix printers, you can define most of the same measurements. In both cases, these choices are enough to let you easily create custom settings for virtually any label.

If you've been following along from the beginning of the book, by now you know enough about Word to go from a blank screen to final printed output. Unless you have specialized requirements such as footnotes and multiple columns, you know most of what you need to know. But we haven't covered everything that every Word user should know.

There are a number of ways in which you can reconfigure the Word program to suit your own needs and preferences, and so far we've barely touched on them. In fact, there are some straightforward settings that we haven't even looked at yet. In the next chapter, we'll show you some of the more straightforward ways of customizing Word to meet your needs.

TOPIC FINDER

Viewing Your Document 293

- • Normal view
- • Normal view with the draft font
- • Outline view
- • Page Layout view
- NEW! Master Document view
- NEW! View Full Screen
- • Zoom settings

Word Defaults 309

- • The View card
- NEW! The General card
- • The Edit card
- • The File Locations card
- • The Save card
- • The other Tools Options cards

Customizing Toolbars 316

- NEW! Floating toolbars
- NEW! How to change or create a toolbar

The Tools Customize Menus and Keyboard Cards 322

NEW! ## Wizards: Automated Documents 322

An Introduction to Templates 325

- • What is a template?
- • Normal, document (supplementary), and global templates
- • How to edit a template
- • How to create a new template
- • How to attach and detach templates
- • More about templates

Menu-Based Customization

f you've been following the discussion from the beginning of the book, you now know how to go from a blank Word screen to final printed output, unless you have some specialized requirements such as footnotes or multiple columns. Up to now, however, we have done most things Word's way, using most of the program defaults.

By now, you should have a sense of which defaults you'd prefer to change. In the final section of this book, we'll show you some sophisticated tricks for redesigning menus, reassigning keystrokes, and building macros. For now, we'll look at some relatively simple ways you can change Word to better match your tastes.

Viewing Your Document

Among the most fundamental settings for Word is the way it displays your document on the screen. Depending on how you count them, there are at least five basic choices for viewing a document, and even more when you consider the scaling options. The basic views for editing are Normal, Outline, Page Layout, and Master Document views, plus Print Preview. In addition, Normal, Outline, and Master Document views can appear with or without Draft mode turned on, and you can choose a Full Screen option for any view.

Some of these choices—Print Preview and Page Layout view, for example—are better suited to certain editing or formatting tasks than others. But you are likely to find each of the choices useful at some time or other. We've already mentioned some of these, and we covered Print Preview in depth in Chapter 8. Here's a look at the rest, starting with the one you have seen most often: Normal view, without Draft mode.

Normal view

As the name implies, Normal is the view most people normally use for most of their work. And it's the view we've used for most of our examples up to this point. Normal view is generally considered to be WYSIWYG (What You See Is What You Get) because what you see on the screen is a close approximation of what you'll get on a printed page. By default, Normal view will show you all character and paragraph formatting, tab-stop alignment, line breaks, and page breaks (as a dotted line across the screen page).

Normal view has some limitations to its WYSIWYG features. It doesn't show headers, footers, footnotes, or side-by-side snaking columns as they'll appear on the printed page. Nor will Normal view show how text wraps around fixed-position paragraphs, tables, and pictures.

However, there are advantages to using Normal view as well. Because Word does not spend time calculating such details as headers and footers while in Normal view, working in Normal view is faster than working in the more fully WYSIWYG Page Layout view. In addition, because it doesn't show top and bottom margins on a page, Normal view will let you see the text at the bottom of one page and the top of another at the same time, as shown in Figure 9-1. This can be an important advantage when you're writing or editing and a page break falls in the middle of a sentence. For all of these reasons, you'll probably want to use Normal view most of the time.

To set your screen for Normal view, open the View menu, and make sure that a dot appears next to Normal. If you see a dot next to a different view choice, simply choose Normal. Alternatively, you can press the Alt-Ctrl-N shortcut keys to set Word for Normal view. Mouse users can click on the Normal View button, which is the leftmost of the three buttons that appear beside the horizontal scroll bar.

FIGURE 9-1

FIGURE 9-1

Normal view offers a useful balance between WYSIWYG features and system speed. It also lets you see the bottom of one page and the top of another at the same time.

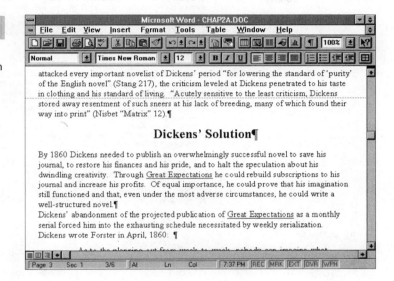

Normal view with the draft font

As your documents grow longer and more complex, it will take Word longer to display them and move through them. If you feel frustrated at the lack of speed, you may want to use Word's draft font when displaying your document. You can toggle the draft font on and off in Normal view with the Draft Font check box on the Tools Options View card.

Word operates much faster when displaying the draft font because it doesn't bother to show most character formatting on the screen. Word will display all of your text in the Microsoft Windows System font (the font used in the menu bar). If you've added any character formatting such as boldface or italics, that text will display as underlined.

Figure 9-2 on the next page shows a sample document displayed using the draft font. Although this document is formatted with the Times New Roman font, as you can see by the Formatting toolbar, it's displayed with the System font.

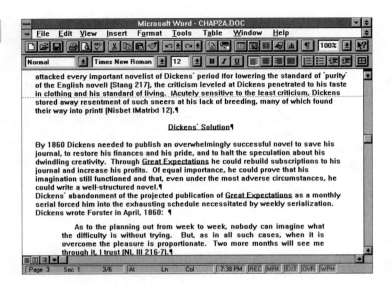

FIGURE 9-2

Draft mode trades
WYSIWYG capabilities
for speed.

If you're familiar with Word 2.0, you may know that Draft mode in version 2.0 displayed imported pictures as empty boxes in addition to showing text in the draft font. Word now offers this option as a separate check box, Picture Placeholders, on the Tools Options View card, as we'll describe later in this chapter. By dividing the Draft mode features into two separate settings, Word not only lets you use Picture Placeholders within Normal view but also enables you to view your pictures when using the draft font. In many cases, using Picture Placeholders rather than the Draft Font setting in Normal view will be the best compromise between speed and being able to see the formatting of your document.

One instance where the draft font comes in handy is when you're editing text in a small font size. By working with the draft font, you will probably find it easier to read and select the small text. (You can also use Word's View Zoom command, however, which we will discuss later in this chapter.)

Keep in mind that the Draft Font setting controls only the way Word displays the document on your screen; it does not affect the way the document will look when you print it. If you want to print a draft version of your document, choose File Print, choose the Options button in the Print dialog box, and check the Draft Output check box. Then choose OK. The appearance of a draft printout will vary depending on the printer you have installed.

Outline view

Word's Outline view is what's known as a collapsible outliner. If your document has headings of various levels defined (using styles, which we will discuss in Chapter 12), you can collapse the document to see only the headings. You can also choose to see headings up to a specified level. And you can move sections of your document around with ease, collapsing an entire section to a single line and then moving all of the text in that section by moving the one line. You can also use Outline view to collapse the document so that you can move through it quickly.

We'll cover the outlining features in Chapter 19. For now, it's enough to know that even if you don't generally use outlines, you may find Outline view helpful for such tasks as creating a table of contents.

You can switch to Outline view by choosing View Outline, pressing Alt-Ctrl-O, or clicking on the Outline View button next to the horizontal scroll bar. (Note that the same button will switch you to Outline view or Master Document view, depending on which of the two views you were in most recently.)

Word will display a dot next to Outline on the View menu to indicate that it's set for Outline view. Figure 9-3 shows our sample document (uncollapsed) in Outline view. Notice the plus sign next to the title, indicating that the title is defined as a heading paragraph and that there is text under the heading. The indention of the other paragraphs indicates that they come under the heading. The small box next to each one indicates that they are defined as normal text, rather than headings.

FIGURE 9-3

Outline view shows the structure of your document. It is useful for creating a table of contents, moving through long documents, and rearranging large blocks of text.

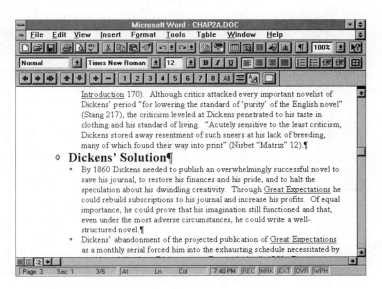

Outline view, like Normal view, works with or without Draft mode. You can use Draft mode in Outline view to gain the same speed advantage as in Normal view.

Page Layout view

Page Layout view provides an on-screen representation of your printed document, yielding something very close to full WYSIWYG. In addition to the WYSIWYG features in Normal view, Page Layout view shows headers, footers, and footnotes as they will appear on the printed page. It also displays snaking columns side by side and shows how text will wrap around fixed-position objects.

There is one important performance issue to consider with Page Layout view. Compared with Normal view, Page Layout view requires Word to work much harder—making complex calculations to determine the line and page formatting, and then creating the images to display on your screen. Given a complicated format, this can be a taxing load, even for a fast computer. As a result, you will probably find that you're best off typing and editing in Normal view, with or without Draft mode. We recommend that you reserve Page Layout view for when you absolutely need it.

You switch to Page Layout view by choosing View Page Layout, pressing Alt-Ctrl-P, or clicking on the Page Layout View button (the middle button in the group of three beside the horizontal scroll bar). There are also a few commands, such as Insert Frame, that either automatically switch to Page Layout view or ask whether you want to. Whenever you're in Page Layout view, Word displays a dot next to the Page Layout command on the View menu.

When you're in Page Layout view, Word displays the top and bottom margins of each page, as well as the body text. For example, if your document has a 1-inch top margin with a header, the margin and header will appear at the top of each page. Similarly, the bottom margin will show at the bottom of each page, along with any footer you've created.

When you scroll vertically in Page Layout view, Word will also display the top and bottom edges of each page instead of marking page breaks with a dotted horizontal line as in Normal view. When you scroll horizontally, it will display the left and right edges of each page. For example, Figure 9-4 shows the bottom of one page and the top of another in Page Layout view after we've scrolled to bring the left edge of the pages into view. Notice the margins on both pages and the header at the top of the second page. The paragraph is broken in midsentence, making it clumsy to work with if you are writing or editing.

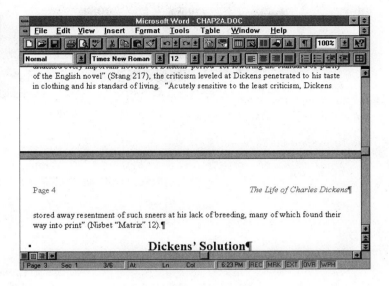

FIGURE 9-4

Page Layout view lets you see the elements of your document on the page, positioned as they will print.

When you are viewing the bottom of one page and the top of the next in Page Layout view, as shown in Figure 9-4, your page margins take up much of the available screen space. To see more of the pages without reducing the image size, you can use Full Screen mode, which we will cover later in this chapter.

Text areas

In Page Layout view, Word treats different elements of your page layout as separate text areas. A simple document has only one text area—the single column of text that's bounded by the left, right, top, and bottom margins. In a multicolumn layout, each column is a separate text area. Each header and footer is also a text area.

The concept of text areas becomes significant as you move around and select text in Page Layout view. For example, each text area has its own ruler. Before we look at these issues, however, let's identify the separate text areas on a page.

Boundary lines

To help you keep your bearings and distinguish text areas while in Page Layout view, Word can display boundaries, or dotted lines, around the different text

areas of a document. To activate this feature, choose Tools Options, select
the View card, and check the Text Boundaries check box in the Show group
box. Figure 9-5 shows the same document you saw in Figure 9-4, but with
text boundaries displayed.

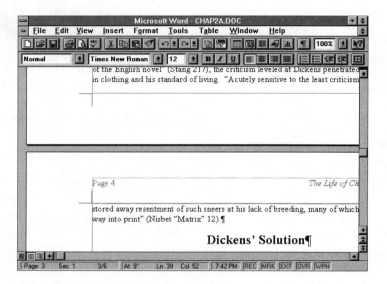

FIGURE 9-5

You can tell Word to
display boundary lines
by selecting the Text
Boundaries option on
the Tools Options View
card.

The View card shows a slightly different set of options in Page
Layout view than it does in Normal view. In addition to the Text
Boundaries check box, the card in Page Layout view contains a
Drawings check box, an Object Anchors check box, and a Vertical
Ruler check box. Choices available in Normal view (but not in
Page Layout view) are the Draft Font and Wrap To Window check
boxes and the Style Area Width option. In general, the choices that
aren't available in one view aren't meaningful in that view. We'll
cover each of these options later in this chapter.

Figure 9-5 shows two kinds of boundary lines. The vertical and horizontal lines that intersect below the header in the upper left corner of the page
are the margin boundaries. If you scroll to any corner of the page, you will
see similar intersecting lines. Above the header is the top of the header
boundary. This top line is 0.5 inch from the top edge of the page—the position specified as the From Edge setting for the header, on the File Page Setup
Margins card. If a page contains a footer, the bottom boundary of the footer
will be marked by a similar line. There are also short horizontal and vertical

lines that meet just outside the corner of the text area; these marks are similar to crop marks that layout artists use to mark the corners of a page.

How to navigate in Page Layout view

In addition to the usual commands for navigating in Page Layout view, you can use the Page Back and Page Forward buttons at the bottom of the vertical scroll bar.

Button	Name
⯭	Page Back
⯯	Page Forward

When you click on the Page Back button, Word will move back one full page. If you start with the top of the current page showing, Word will move back to show the top of the previous page; if you start with the bottom of the current page showing, Word will move you back to the bottom of the previous page. Similarly, clicking on the Page Forward button will move you forward one full page.

Word also offers shortcut keys for moving around in Page Layout view. Alt-Down arrow moves the cursor to the beginning of the next frame, object, or column on the current page; Alt-Up arrow moves to the beginning of the previous frame, object, or column on the current page. Note that Word's idea of what comes next might not always match yours. For example, if you have a page with two frames surrounded by text, and you start at the bottom of the page, Alt-Up arrow may move you in a continuous cycle to the columns on either side of the frame, then to the top of the page, then to the frame, and then to the columns surrounding the frame. If you're at the top or bottom of one page and want to move to the next, the Up and Down arrow keys by themselves will move you from the current page. Note also that if you use the arrow keys by themselves to move around in a multicolumn document in Page Layout view, you have to use the Left and Right arrow keys to move from the end of one column to the beginning of the next. Pressing the Down arrow key while you're in the last line of the first column, for example, will take you to the next page, not the next column.

As you navigate through your document in Page Layout view, you'll notice that Word always aligns the zero point of the horizontal ruler with the left boundary of the current text area. For example, consider the two-column document in Figures 9-6 and 9-7. With the cursor in the left column (as shown in Figure 9-6), Word aligns the zero point of the horizontal ruler with the left boundary of that text area. With the cursor in the right column (as shown in Figure 9-7), the ruler's zero point is the left boundary of that text area.

FIGURE 9-6

Word aligns the horizontal ruler's zero point with the left boundary of the current text area. Here the cursor is in the left text column.

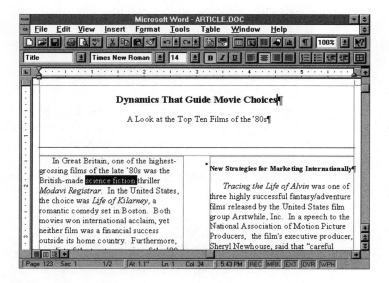

FIGURE 9-7

Now the cursor is in the right text column; the zero point on the horizontal ruler has also moved.

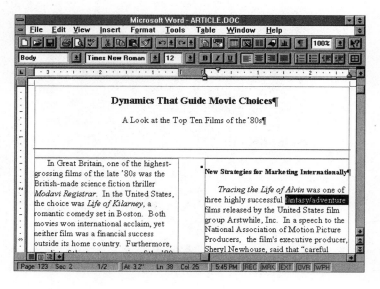

How to select text in Page Layout view

Each text area in Page Layout view has its own selection bar. You can see evidence of this as you move the pointer around. When the pointer moves over the selection bar for a text area, it changes shape to a right-arrow pointer. For example, suppose you are working with a two-column layout. Your document window will have a selection bar on the far left, as it normally does. However, this selection bar is for the left column only. If you want to select text in the right column, you can use the right column's selection bar, located just to the left of the right column.

If you want to select all of the text in a document, move the pointer to any selection bar other than one for a header or footer and press the Ctrl key as you click the mouse button. You can also use all of Word's usual selection techniques. And you can select text on two or more pages by dragging to extend a selection beyond the top or bottom border of the text window. (You may find that this is much slower in Page Layout view than in Normal view.)

How to edit and format in Page Layout view

Although you'll probably want to use Normal view for most of your editing and formatting, you'll often need to make minor changes while in Page Layout view as well. Of course, you can do everything in Page Layout view if you have a fast enough system and decide that you prefer to work this way. To make any changes, choose the same editing or formatting commands that you would choose in Normal view.

Headers and footers in Page Layout view

Page Layout view shows you the position of each page's header and footer as they will appear when printed. To add new headers or footers, use the View Header And Footer command, as we discussed in Chapter 5. If you select the Different Odd And Even or Different First Page option for headers and footers on the File Page Setup Layout card, Word will label each header or footer—as Odd Page or Even Page, for example—but only while you are editing it. The labels will not show when you work with body text.

If you want to edit a header or footer that already exists, either choose View Header And Footer or double-click on the header or footer area. Word will activate the header or footer itself so that you can make changes, and it will display the Header And Footer toolbar. Word will apply any change you make to all appropriate headers or footers—meaning all headers on odd pages or even pages, for example, or all those in the current section. If your document has multiple sections, changing a header or footer on one page will affect any linked headers or footers in subsequent sections. We'll explain sectional headers and footers in "Section headers and footers" on page 492.

Footnotes in Page Layout view

Footnotes function very much like headers and footers when you're in Page Layout view. When you choose Insert Footnote, Word will insert the footnote reference mark in the document's text and move the cursor to the footnote area at the bottom of the page. You can then type the footnote. If the footnote already exists, you can move to it with the keyboard or mouse any time you're in Page Layout view and edit it as needed. We will discuss footnotes in more detail in "Footnotes and Endnotes" on page 341.

Master Document view

Master Document view is closely related to Outline view, except that it gives you a way to view, open, and manage many related files at once. This is particularly useful when you are working with a large document made up of many separate files—such as chapters of a book or sections of a long report. We will discuss Master Document view in more detail in "How to use Master Document view" on page 590.

View Full Screen

The View menu offers a command called Full Screen. This is available no matter which view you're in—even Print Preview.

Full Screen mode hides almost all of Word's on-screen window dressing. Switching to Full Screen mode will always remove the title bar and menu bar. It may also remove toolbars, rulers, scroll bars, and so on, depending on how you've set Word. In any case, the point is to display on one screen as much of your document as possible. Some users will prefer this over the regular Word display because it removes potentially distracting items and makes it easier to focus on writing. Figure 9-8 shows a document in Page Layout view in Full Screen mode.

FIGURE 9-8

Word's Full Screen mode makes it easy to hide everything but your text.

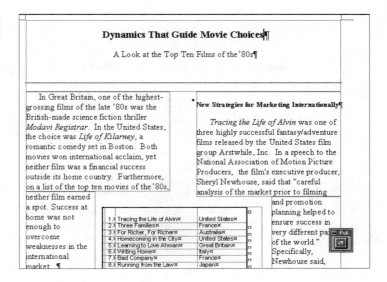

Word remembers the settings you make in Full Screen mode for what to display and what to hide. You can change these settings the same way you change them when not in Full Screen mode—by choosing View Ruler to hide or display the rulers, choosing View Toolbars to open the Toolbars dialog box and hide or display individual toolbars, and checking or clearing the check boxes in the Window group box on the Tools Options View card.

More important, Word remembers separate sets of settings for Full Screen mode and non–Full Screen mode. So even if you don't want to use Full Screen mode for its obvious purpose—providing an uncluttered screen that shows more text—you might want to use it to toggle between two states, such as one that shows one set of toolbars and one that shows a different set. This can be quite useful if, for example, you've created some custom toolbars and want them available when you're formatting your document but not when you're writing or editing.

How to turn Full Screen mode off

When you switch to Full Screen mode, Word will, by default, display a special Full Screen toolbar (although you can set Word not to show this either). The toolbar holds only one button, so it's only large enough to show the word "Full" on its title bar. This name is a bit misleading, however, because you click on the button to *leave* Full Screen mode. Alternatively, you can press the Esc key to leave Full Screen mode, or choose View Full Screen to toggle Full Screen off.

Note that even though the menu bar is not visible in Full Screen mode, it's still active. You can use any keystroke method to choose a command. Alt-V, for example, will open the View menu.

Zoom settings

The Zoom command, at the bottom of the View menu, affects what you'll see in Normal, Outline, and Page Layout views, with the Draft Font option on or off, and whether you are in Full Screen mode or not. The Zoom command is one of Word's most useful viewing tools; it gives you control over how much of a page you can see at one time and how large the text characters and graphics will be on screen. The feature has much the same effect as a zoom lens on a camera, enabling you to zoom in for a close look or zoom out for a more sweeping view of your page.

You can treat the View Zoom command both as an aid to formatting and as a way to adjust text size for comfortable viewing. As a formatting aid, the feature will let you zoom out to see all or most of a page at once (or more than one page in Page Layout view) so that you can judge larger formatting issues, such as page and column breaks. It will also let you zoom in on your page so that you can see and control the precise placement of a picture or other graphic element.

Most of the time you'll probably want to see text in approximately the same size as it will be printed. With most programs, the size of text on the screen varies with the type of monitor and screen driver you have installed in Windows. With Word's View Zoom command, however, you can precisely control the text size by choosing a setting that's appropriate for your particular monitor and your individual taste.

Word will remember different zoom settings for Normal, Page Layout, and Outline views (with Outline and Master Document views sharing the same zoom setting). You can use this to good effect. For example, if you are creating a newsletter, you'll often need to make small changes in your text strictly for formatting purposes—as when you have to cut lines because a story doesn't quite fit the allotted space. By setting Page Layout view to show an overall view of the page and Normal view to display the text large enough to read easily, you can toggle back and forth between the two views—to Normal view so that you can quickly and easily make changes, and to Page Layout view so that you can see the effect of the changes on the overall layout.

How to change zoom settings with the Zoom dialog box

To change the zoom setting in Word, you can choose View Zoom. Word will open the Zoom dialog box, shown in Figure 9-9.

FIGURE 9-9

The Zoom dialog box gives you control over the enlargement or reduction of your document on screen.

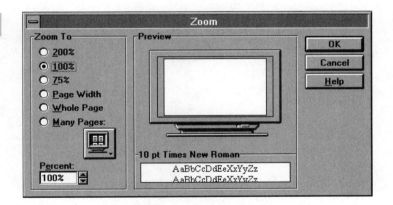

The Zoom To group box on the left side of the Zoom dialog box contains six option buttons, a text box, and a rather large toolbar-style button. The Preview box to the right of the Zoom To box will show the effect of your settings as you make them. If you're in Normal or Outline view, the small screen displayed within the monitor graphic will show the Normal style text as the text appears at that scale. If you are in Page Layout view, the box will show the outline of a page (or multiple pages) as the pages appear at that scale. In Page Layout view, Word adds a second preview area below the small monitor screen to show how the text will look.

Three of the option buttons in the Zoom To box are for preset zoom levels: 200% (useful for precise placement of graphics or text), 100% ("full size," appropriate for most writing and editing), and 75% (still large enough to be readable on many monitors, but showing more text than the 100% level).

The next three options are given in terms of a page rather than a percentage. Page Width will adjust the zoom scale to be large enough that the left and right margins both show on the screen. (Note, however, that if the style area is displayed at the left side of the screen, Word will not take it into account in adjusting the page width.)

The Whole Page and Many Pages options are available only if you are in Page Layout view or Print Preview. Whole Page will fit a single page on the screen. The Many Pages option will activate the large button just below it. This button works like the Multiple Pages button on the Print Preview toolbar, which we discussed in Chapter 8. When you click on the button, a grid opens. As shown in Figure 9-10, you can click and drag on the grid to indicate how many rows and columns of pages you want to see on the screen at one time. (Alternatively, you can simply click on the button and immediately drag over the grid.) These thumbnail views of pages are handy when you want to see the overall layout or form of a document.

FIGURE 9-10

You can set Word to display multiple pages in Page Layout view.

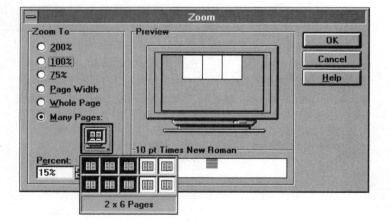

 You can also use the Many Pages option with the keyboard. Press the arrow keys or Alt-M to select the Many Pages option, press Tab to move to the toolbar-style button, press Enter to open the configuration box, and use the arrow keys to highlight the rows and columns on the grid. Press Enter to finish.

If none of the preset zoom choices serves your needs, you can specify any zoom level from 10% to 200% in the Percent text box. Word will use the setting until you either change it or choose one of the preset options.

How to change zoom settings with the Standard toolbar's Zoom Control box

Word provides the Zoom Control box on the Standard toolbar for changing the zoom setting quickly with a mouse. When you click on the down arrow next to the box, you'll see a drop-down list of zoom setting choices, as shown in Figure 9-11.

FIGURE 9-11

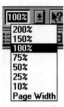 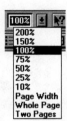

The Zoom Control box on the Standard toolbar gives mouse users a quick way to change the zoom setting. The list on the left shows the choices available in Normal and Outline views; the one on the right shows the choices in Page Layout view.

As you can see from Figure 9-11, the choices available on the drop-down list depend on the view. In Normal or Outline view, the choices are 10%, 25%, 50%, 75%, 100%, 150%, 200%, and Page Width. In Page Layout view, Word adds Whole Page and Two Pages to the list.

Word Defaults

You can switch from one of Word's various views to another as often as you need to. However, Word also has a number of settings that you're likely to set once and then leave pretty much alone. These settings provide control over options that range from screen defaults to printing defaults to your default data directory. When you installed Word, all of these settings were predefined. But you can change any of them.

As we discussed at the end of Chapter 1, you can change many of the default settings from the various Tools Options cards. We've covered some of these settings in Chapter 1 and elsewhere; we'll discuss most of the rest now and refer back to those we've already looked at.

To open the Options dialog box, choose the Tools Options command. To display any card within the dialog box, choose the appropriate tab at the top of the dialog box.

The View card

As shown in Figure 9-12, Word has a number of View settings that affect your screen display. We covered most of the Window options and the Nonprinting Characters options in Chapter 1, but we need to mention a few here.

FIGURE 9-12

The View card in the Options dialog box offers settings that affect how Word displays your document.

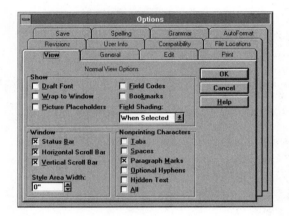

The options on the View card will change somewhat, depending on what view Word is currently set for. The options for Normal view and Outline view are the same, but those for Page Layout view are different. Note that in Figure 9-12, Word is set for Normal view, and the text at the top of the card reads *Normal View Options.* This text will change to reflect the view you're in.

When you're in Page Layout view, the View card contains several options that apply to features affecting only Page Layout view—for example, the Text Boundaries option (which adds dotted lines to indicate text areas on the page, such as body text and headers). The options contained only on the Normal and Outline versions of the card apply to features that affect only Normal and Outline views—for example, the Style Area Width option, which we'll discuss in a moment.

The Status Bar option in the Window group box on both cards determines whether the status bar will be displayed at the bottom of your screen. If you choose not to display it, you will still see most prompts and messages on the bottom line of your screen, but most of the time this line will be used as part of the document window. You will not see the brief help comments displayed when a command is highlighted.

The Style Area Width text box—available only in Normal, Outline, or Master Document view—lets you reserve a portion of the left side of the document window for displaying style names. Enter any measurement to have Word display the name of the current style for each paragraph while you are in Normal or Outline view. You can then adjust the size of the style area to see all or just part of each style name. We will discuss styles in Chapter 12, "Styles & AutoFormat," page 418.

The Vertical Ruler check box—available only in Page Layout view—displays or hides the vertical ruler.

We covered most of the choices in the Nonprinting Characters group box in Chapter 1. Note that except for the All check box, which is equivalent to checking all of the other boxes, the choices in this group box let you selectively display or hide specific nonprinting characters, such as paragraph marks. Checking All is equivalent to clicking on the Standard toolbar's Show/Hide ¶ button.

If you choose to display tab characters, they will appear as small arrows pointing to the right. Spaces appear as dots that look much like periods but are raised off the text baseline to about the same level as the center of an uppercase O. We covered optional hyphens in Chapter 6. If you choose to display them, they will appear as hyphenlike lines with a short vertical segment (¬).

Hidden text, a font formatting option, is text that you don't usually want to see or print—notes to yourself, for example. If you display hidden text, it will appear with a dotted underline.

The check boxes in the Show group box control some finer points of how Word displays your document. Picture Placeholders speeds up display performance by using a box placeholder in a document instead of a picture's actual image. The Field Codes check box toggles Word between displaying fields themselves—for example, {DATE} or {TIME}—and displaying what Word calls the field results, such as *10/12/93* or *7:58 PM*. We'll discuss fields in detail in Chapter 20. For now, simply note that there are many more field codes that you might want to include in your document. At times, you'll want to see the field codes; at other times, the results.

If you check the Bookmarks check box, Word will add square brackets around sections you've designated as bookmarks with the Edit Bookmark command. We'll discuss the Edit Bookmark command in Chapter 10. For now, just note that the Bookmarks check box will make it easy to visually identify the bookmarks in your documents.

The Field Shading option provides a similar feature for fields, adding shading to fields to help you identify them. We'll explain how to use the field shading option when we cover fields in Chapter 20.

The Draft Font and Wrap To Window check boxes are available only on the Normal and Outline view versions of the View card. As we discussed earlier in this chapter, the Draft Font choice displays text in the System font, rather than the font the text is formatted in.

Checking the Wrap To Window check box tells Word to adjust line breaks on screen to match the width of the document window rather than the actual margins of the document. This can come in handy if you're viewing one or more documents in partial screen windows, or if you're working with a document that's too wide to fit on screen. Figure 9-13 shows two windows, side by side, each with its own document. The one on the left is set with the Wrap To Window check box checked; the one on the right is set with the check box cleared. The text in the left window is fully visible, wrapping at the edge of the window. The text in the right window is cut off at the edge of the window. We recommend that you check the Wrap To Window check box if you're working with partial screen windows or wide documents but that you leave it cleared otherwise.

FIGURE 9-13

The Wrap To Window check box, which is checked for the document window on the left in this figure and cleared for the window on the right, will wrap lines at the window edge rather than at the document margins.

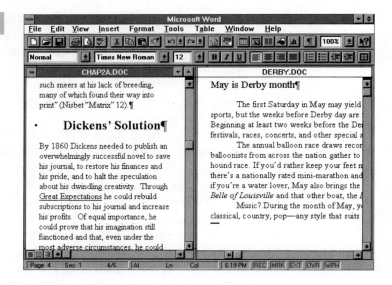

The Drawings, Object Anchors, and Text Boundaries check boxes are available only on the Page Layout view version of the View card. As discussed earlier in this chapter, the Text Boundaries option will display lines around text areas when Word is in Page Layout view. The Drawings check box causes Word to display Word drawings as boxes, which can speed up display performance. The Object Anchors check box causes Word to display the location of each frame's anchor—the paragraph to which it is attached.

For more details about frames, see Chapter 14, "Columns, Frames, & Pictures," page 496. For more about Word drawings, see Chapter 15, "Drawing, Graphics, & Other Objects," page 548.

The General card

The General options affect the way certain commands and keys work. As with the View options, we covered some of these in Chapter 1; here's a look at the rest.

Checking the Background Repagination check box tells Word to continually recalculate the automatic page breaks in your document while you work on it. If you want to increase the program's speed, you can turn this option off; Word will still repaginate whenever you switch to Page Layout view or Print Preview, or when you print your document.

Two options affect the appearance of the screen: Blue Background, White Text and 3D Dialog And Display Effects. The first gives you an alternative to the typical Windows black text on a white background display. You still don't have much control over the color of your display, but at least you now have two choices. Check the check box to see the blue background alternative.

The 3D Dialog And Display Effects check box toggles the shaded effects of dialog boxes and other interface features on and off. These are on by default. You may prefer the simpler image you get without them; to see the effect, clear the check box.

The Beep On Error Actions check box controls whether Word makes a sound when indicating an error. To hear a beep, make sure the box is checked. If you don't want to hear a beep, clear the check box.

The Update Automatic Links At Open check box controls whether Word automatically updates information that's linked to other files every time you open the document. We'll discuss this in the context of the features it affects in Chapter 18.

The Mail As Attachment check box enables you to attach documents to an electronic mail message. This is meaningful if your computer is on a local area network and has a supported electronic mail program installed. For more information on networks and mail, see your network administrator.

The last option in the General Options group box lets you choose how many of the most recently opened document files will be listed at the bottom of the File menu. The default is four, but you can set this option from zero to nine.

Finally, you can use the Measurement Units box to set the default measurements that Word will use. The choices in the attached list box are Inches, Centimeters, Points, and Picas.

The Edit card

We discussed all but three of the options on the Edit card in Chapter 1, and the Use Smart Cut And Paste option in Chapter 4. The only two we haven't covered yet are the Allow Accented Uppercase and Picture Editor options.

The Allow Accented Uppercase option applies only to text formatted as another language, such as French. Add a check to this check box, and Word's proofing tool and change case features will suggest adding accents to upper-case letters where appropriate.

You use the Picture Editor option to designate the application you want to use for editing pictures. We'll discuss this in the context of working with pictures in Chapter 15.

The File Locations card

The File Locations card has a two-column list; one column is File Types and the other is Location. Location refers to where Word will look for the type of file indicated unless told otherwise; you can always instruct Word to use a file of a given type from some other directory.

You probably won't need to make many changes to these settings, but there is at least one that you should change. By default, Word saves new documents in the same directory in which the program was installed. But this is a little like organizing your file cabinets by throwing all your docu-ments—office supply catalogs, incoming and outgoing letters, check stubs, reports, and so on—into one file folder without sorting them. You can use the options on the File Locations card to impose some order on your files.

We recommend that you create a separate directory specifically for your Word documents. Or, better yet, create a main data direc-tory with a set of subdirectories under it. Use any organizational scheme that makes sense to you. You might, for example, create a separate directory for each client and, within each client directory, a separate subdirectory for each project. Alternatively, you might create a separate directory for each kind of document—one for let-ters, one for reports, and so on. Use an organizational scheme that can be easily extended as needed and will readily guide you to a file you're looking for.

When you've decided on a main data directory, set the Documents file type to that directory. Highlight Documents in the File Types list, choose the Modify button, and then choose the directory you want in the Directories box. Notice that you can also create a new directory from the Modify Location dialog box: Choose the New button, and type a new directory name in the Create Directory dialog box. Now, whenever you choose File Save for a new file or choose File Open, Word will, by default, look in the main data directory you've specified, and you need only change from the main directory to the appropriate subdirectory. (Be aware, however, that once you tell Word to use some other directory, Word will continue to use that directory during the current editing session until you tell it otherwise.)

The same principles that apply to organizing your data files apply to other files as well. You should also consider taking advantage of the other file type choices on the File Locations card to sort your files into different directories. Here again, separating the files will make it easier to find a file when you're looking for it.

The Save card

We discussed most of the choices on the Save card in Chapter 1, and we discussed the file-sharing options in Chapter 2. Of the four remaining choices, we'll save three for discussing in the context of the features they affect. The fourth, Prompt To Save Normal.dot, determines whether Word asks you if you want to save changes such as AutoText entries to the Normal template when you close the program, or whether it automatically saves them. To have Word prompt you, make sure this box is checked. To have Word save the changes automatically, clear the check box.

The other Tools Options cards

We've covered only five of the twelve cards in the Options dialog box here; however, we've already covered some of the others. For details on the Print card, see "Printing Options" on page 270; on the User Info card, see "User Info options" starting on page 40; on the Spelling card, see "The Tools Options Spelling card" on page 183; and on the Grammar card, see "How to use the grammar-checking options" on page 194.

The remaining three cards affect features we haven't looked at yet. We will cover these cards in the context of the features they affect. For details on the AutoFormat card, see "The AutoFormat Feature" on page 420; on the Compatibility card, see "How to use the Tools Options Compatibility card" on page 634; and on the Revisions card, see "Revision Marks" on page 353.

Customizing Toolbars

If you use a mouse, Word's toolbars are one of the program's most powerful and attractive features. They provide instant access to a wide range of commands—and also macros, if you care to add them to toolbars. In fact, you can think of the toolbars as "shortcut keys" for the mouse. As with many of Word's most attractive features, a large part of the appeal lies in the fact that you can easily customize the toolbars to suit the way you work.

Floating toolbars

As you may have noticed, not all toolbars are displayed neatly below the menu bar. Some of the specialized toolbars, such as the Full Screen and the Header And Footer toolbars, show up by default as floating toolbars that you can drag and place anywhere on the screen.

Less obvious is that you can also move the Standard and Formatting toolbars anywhere you like. You can even place a toolbar outside the Word window altogether. Figure 9-14 shows a Word window reduced to less than full screen, with the Standard toolbar moved into the document window and the Formatting toolbar outside the Word window.

FIGURE 9-14

You can drag toolbars to new positions on the screen—even outside the Word window itself, if you like.

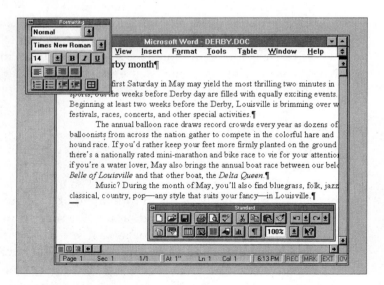

To move a toolbar from the top of the Word window, simply click on a space between buttons and drag the toolbar to a new location. Once a toolbar is floating, you can grab it and move it by pointing either to an empty space between buttons or to the toolbar's title bar and then dragging. To put any toolbar—including toolbars that float by default—at the top of the window, drag it to the position where you want it and drop it. Alternatively, you can simply double-click on the toolbar background or on the title bar.

You can even change the shape of a floating toolbar. Point to anywhere on the toolbar border, and the mouse pointer will change to a two-headed arrow. Drag the side to make the window bigger or smaller; Word will automatically resize the other dimension and arrange the buttons to fit within the new space. (Notice that the toolbar snaps into place for its new positions, with the allowable dimensions determined by the number and size of buttons on the toolbar.) You can make a toolbar tall and thin or short and wide so that it will block the least amount of information on your screen while you're working.

In general, when you drop a floating toolbar at the top of the Word window, Word will try to insert it based on the position of the floating outline just before you dropped it. If the outline straddles two toolbar rows, for example, Word will generally insert it between the two. Occasionally, you may misjudge. For example, you can easily position the toolbar in such a way that instead of pushing an existing toolbar down, Word inserts the new toolbar on the left side and pushes part or all of the original toolbar off the screen to the right. To recover the original toolbar, move the new one up or down so that it's on its own line, and then move the original toolbar back to the left to take its original position. With a little practice, you should consistently be able to place the toolbars where you want them.

How to change or create a toolbar

You can do much more than just move toolbars around the screen; you can also change the buttons on any toolbar, or even create new toolbars to suit your needs.

To create or change a toolbar, start by choosing the View Toolbars command, and then choose the Customize button; alternatively, choose Tools Customize and then choose the Toolbars card. In either case, you'll see a dialog box similar to the one shown in Figure 9-15 on the next page.

FIGURE 9-15

The Tools Customize
Toolbars card enables
you to change Word's
toolbars by adding or
removing buttons for
commands or macros.

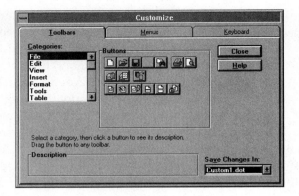

Note the Save Changes In list box in the lower right corner of the card. We've chosen the Custom1 template, which is the supplemental template for the current document. You could also store the changes as part of the Normal template. We'll discuss templates later in this chapter; for the moment, it's enough to know that Word always attaches the Normal template to each document and that you can optionally attach a supplementary template as well. If you're using only the Normal template, it will be the only choice available in the Save Changes In list box.

How to delete a button

Whenever the Customize dialog box is open, toolbars and toolbar buttons are not active: Clicking on a button will not execute a command.

You can remove any button from a toolbar to reduce the clutter or make room for a different button. With the Customize dialog box open and the Toolbars card displayed, click on the toolbar button that you want to remove, drag it off the toolbar, and release it anywhere over the document window or over the Customize dialog box. That's all there is to it.

How to add a button

Adding a new button to an existing toolbar is nearly as easy as deleting one. The Categories box on the Toolbars card lists various types of items that you can add to the toolbar—all of the standard menu names (File, Edit, View, Insert, Format, Tools, Table, and Window and Help) plus choices for Drawing, Borders, Mail Merge, All Commands, Macros, Fonts, AutoText, and Styles. Figure 9-16 shows the Toolbars card with the Categories list scrolled down partway.

Your choice in the Categories list box determines the options available in the second box. If you choose any of the categories that match a name on

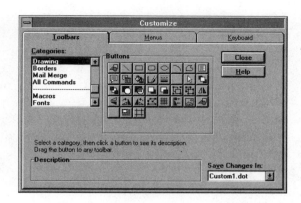

FIGURE 9-16

The Categories box lists categories of items to add as toolbar buttons.

the menu bar (or choose Mail Merge), for example, Word will label the second box as Buttons and show a group of predefined buttons that you can choose from. To see a short description of any button's function, click on the button; Word will display the description in the Description box at the bottom of the card. To add a button to a toolbar, simply drag it to the toolbar and drop it in place. Word will automatically shift other buttons to the right, if necessary, to make room for the new one.

The last five items in the Categories list—All Commands, Macros, Fonts, AutoText, and Styles—do not display predefined buttons. Choose one of these, and Word will label the second box to match the category. Choose All Commands, for example, and Word will label the box as Commands. And instead of buttons, the second box will contain a scroll box filled with a list of commands (or other items). If you then drag an item that does not have a default button into the toolbar area, Word will open the Custom Button dialog box, shown in Figure 9-17, and you can choose a button for the particular item.

FIGURE 9-17

The Custom Button dialog box lets you choose an icon for a toolbar button.

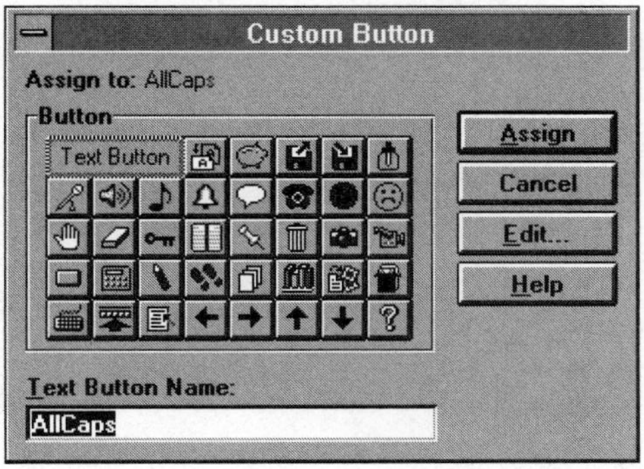

The first choice in the Custom Button dialog box is Text Button. If you prefer buttons to be labeled in words instead of using icons that are often hard to remember, you can use this choice to create a button with a text label instead of an icon; you type the text in the Text Button Name box at the bottom of the dialog box. If you also define a shortcut key that uses the first letter of the button label, you'll be able to choose the item with either the mouse (by clicking on the button) or the keyboard (by using the keyboard shortcut). We'll show you how to define (or redefine) shortcut keys in "Keyboard Customization" on page 968. For now, simply be aware that it can be done.

Choose the Edit button in the Custom Button dialog box to alter an existing icon or create a new one. Figure 9-18 shows the Button Editor dialog box. To edit a button icon, click on the color you want to use—or click on the Erase pattern if you want to use that—and then draw the image, pixel by pixel, either by clicking the appropriate locations in the grid within the Picture box or by holding down the left mouse button and dragging over the grid. The Clear button will replace the entire image with the Erase pattern. The Move buttons move the image up, down, left, or right by one row or one column of pixels.

FIGURE 9-18

Use the Button Editor to create your own button icons for toolbars.

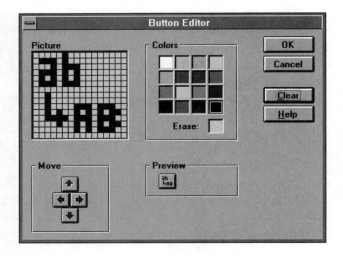

You can edit any button's icon—not just the ones in the Custom Button dialog box. With the Customize Toolbars card showing, place the mouse pointer on any button on a toolbar and click the right mouse button. This will open a context-sensitive menu. Choose Edit Button Image to open the Button Editor with the button's icon already loaded. Note, too, that the context-sensitive menu also includes options for copying and pasting a button image, resetting a button to its original setting, and choosing a different button image. The first three choices are self-explanatory. The Choose Button Image choice opens the Custom Button dialog box, in which you can choose a different button icon to replace the icon of the button you clicked on.

How to create a new toolbar

To create a new toolbar of your own design, simply drag a button or other item from the Toolbars card and drop it in the document window or on any part of the toolbars area that isn't already covered by a toolbar. Word will automatically create a new toolbar around the new button and will expand the toolbar as you add more buttons to it. If you start with an item other than a button, such as a style name, Word will also open the Custom Button dialog box when it creates the new toolbar so that you can define the icon or text for the button.

Word will treat your custom toolbars just like Word's default toolbars; they can either float or sit at one of the edges of the screen. And you can change their position and shape at will by dragging and dropping.

Word automatically names new toolbars in sequence, starting with *Toolbar 1*. While this is functional, it hardly describes the toolbar's designed purpose. You can change the name with the Template Organizer. From the editing screen, choose File Templates and then the Organizer button; then choose the Toolbars card in the Organizer dialog box, as shown in Figure 9-19 on the next page. Highlight the toolbar whose name you want to change. Then choose the Rename button to open the Rename dialog box. You can then give the toolbar a more meaningful name, such as *Set Styles* for a toolbar with buttons that apply particular styles to paragraphs. When you've finished, choose OK to accept the new name, and then choose the Close button.

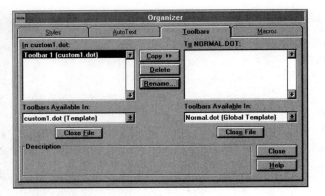

FIGURE 9-19

You can give toolbars more meaningful names with the Rename feature on the Toolbars card in the Organizer dialog box.

The Tools Customize Menus and Keyboard Cards

The Customize dialog box has two more cards: Menus and Keyboard. You can use the Menus options to modify the Word menus, whether you want to rename a single command or completely restructure the entire Word menu system. You use the Keyboard options to assign new keyboard shortcuts to commands and macros. These are advanced features that we'll cover in detail in Chapter 28.

Wizards: Automated Documents

Your documents themselves represent another category of important objects for customization. By using Word's wizards, you can automatically add complex, custom formats to some of the more common kinds of documents you create.

A *wizard* is a special type of file that can automatically create a document (or template) that uses sophisticated formatting. The essence of a wizard is that it will customize the result for you by prompting you for your formatting and text choices.

To create a new document with a wizard, choose File New, and then select one of the wizards in the Template list. For this example, we'll use the Fax Wizard, which will create a fax cover sheet.

In general, a wizard presents one or more dialog boxes with options that offer you choices for customizing the format of the document. The first dialog box in the Fax Wizard is shown in Figure 9-20, asking whether you want to format the page for portrait or landscape orientation. The unlabeled preview box on the left displays the effect of your choice.

FIGURE 9-20

A wizard prompts you for information about how you want to customize a new document.

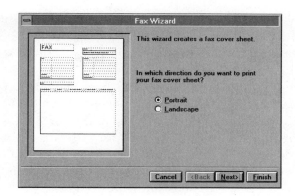

At the bottom of the screen are four buttons: Cancel, Back, Next, and Finish. The Cancel button cancels the creation of the new document; the Finish button tells Word to go ahead and create the new document using the information you've given to this point. The Back and Next buttons move you backward and forward through the wizard's dialog boxes, one step at a time. In the wizard's first dialog box, the Back button is grayed; when you reach the final dialog box, the Next button will be grayed.

Generally, you will want to go through all of a wizard's dialog boxes before choosing the Finish button. The only other time you should use this button is when you are certain that all questions in all of the dialog boxes have been answered as you want them.

The remaining dialog boxes for this particular wizard ask you to choose a style for your cover sheet (contemporary, modern, or jazzy); to enter or confirm your name, company, and address; and to enter or confirm your voice and fax phone numbers. When you've worked through all of these, Word will display a Finish dialog box, shown in Figure 9-21.

FIGURE 9-21

Word will present a Finish dialog box when you have answered all questions in a wizard's dialog boxes.

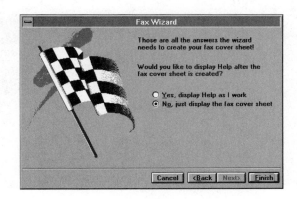

The final dialog box contains an option button called Yes, Display Help As I Work. If you select this before you choose Finish, Word will open a How To file that gives useful information such as how to work with the tables that make up the new fax cover sheet.

We won't cover other wizards here; the whole point of wizards is that they are fully self-explanatory. They give even the beginning Word user the benefit of elaborate formatting capabilities. Even the names of the wizards are self-explanatory: Fax Wizard for creating a fax cover letter, Calendar Wizard for creating a monthly, weekly, or yearly calendar, and so on. However, we firmly recommend that you take the time to experiment with the wizards to see which ones suit your needs.

When you create a document with a wizard, Word stores your answers to use as defaults the next time you use the same wizard. The answers for all wizards are stored in a single file named WORDWIZ.INI, which Word puts in the Windows directory. After you've used a given wizard at least once, you can use it again without having to go through the dialog boxes. If you use only one format for a fax cover sheet, for example, you can simply start the wizard and choose the Finish button in the first dialog box.

If you've used a given wizard but you want to use it again with a clean slate, you can open WORDWIZ.INI in Word or any other text editor and erase the corresponding section of the INI file. Or, if you prefer, you can type the defaults you want to use into the WORDWIZ.INI file. The settings are reasonably self-explanatory. The first line for the return address, for example, is shown as

```
ReturnAddress1=X
```

where X is the first line as you want it to appear.

You can also build up a collection of alternative answers to the wizard questions by copying the WORDWIZ.INI file to a file with a different extension, such as WORDWIZ.BUS for business settings or WORDWIZ.PER for personal settings. You can then copy the appropriate file to WORDWIZ.INI before you use a wizard. Alternatively, you can use the wizards to create templates for each format you use frequently. We'll discuss that possibility in "How to create a template using a wizard" starting on page 936.

An Introduction to Templates

To take fullest advantage of Word's flexibility and customizability—and even to take fullest advantage of wizards—it's important to understand the concept of templates. As we've mentioned earlier, templates hold information about your preferences for particular kinds of documents—allowing, for example, defaults for a letter that are different from those for a manuscript. The underlying concept of templates is simple. Learn to use templates, and you can unlock much of Word's power.

What is a template?

A template is a special type of Word document that serves as a pattern for other documents. Just as a shoemaker uses templates to make shoes of different sizes, so too can you use templates to create documents of different types.

Suppose, for example, that you print many of your Word documents on preprinted letterhead. Each time you begin a letter, you change the left margin from 1.25 inches to 1 inch and the top margin from 1 inch to 3 inches.

Instead of changing margins manually each time, you can create a template that automatically handles the task for you. After you've created the template, all you have to do is choose File New, choose the name of the template in the Template list box, and choose OK. Word will create a new document that has the correct margins. You can then begin typing the new letter.

A template can contain a lot more than margin settings. Among other possibilities, it can contain boilerplate text—blocks of text that you use in every document of the same type. These blocks can contain fields, such as a date field, which Word will automatically update for each new document. Templates can also have their own style settings (so that all documents created with the same template will have the same formatting and appearance) and their own AutoText entries (so that you can have different sets of AutoText entries in different kinds of documents), as well as specific macros, menus, and shortcut keys (so that each kind of document can have its own customized commands).

Normal, document (supplementary), and global templates

Although Word now has three types of templates, only one is attached to all documents—the Normal template. Settings stored in the Normal template are available to all documents unless they are overridden by the settings in an attached template. In Word 2.0, a document could have at most two templates: the Normal template and a supplementary template (any template attached to the document other than the Normal template). In Word 6.0, however, it is possible to have several templates attached to the same document: the Normal template, the attached *document template* (or *supplementary template*), and multiple *global templates*. We will reserve the term *supplementary template* to refer only to a template that has been attached as the current document template. (You can also designate a third level of templates, called *global templates*. For now, it's enough to know that a global template makes its AutoText entries, macros, and customized features available to all open documents. We'll cover the subject in "Normal, Supplementary, and Global Templates" starting on page 938.)

If you attach a supplementary template, either by selecting it as the document template when creating the new file or by using the File Templates command, its name will be shown in the Document Template text box in the Templates And Add-Ins dialog box. If no supplementary template has been selected, you'll see the word *normal* in the Document Template text box.

The supplementary template works in addition to, not instead of, the Normal template. Any settings stored in a supplementary template take precedence over those in the Normal template, but anything not specified in the supplementary template will follow the settings in the Normal template. That means that any AutoText entries, macros, keystroke assignments, or any other customized feature stored in a supplementary template will be available whenever you have that template attached to the file you're currently working in. Any such items that you've stored in the Normal template will be available as well—except for settings that conflict with the current supplementary template.

By default, all Word template files use a DOT filename extension (not counting wizards as templates)—hence the filename for the Normal template, NORMAL.DOT. As we'll discuss in Chapter 27, you can assign a different extension if you like, but under most conditions you'll want to stay with the default.

When you first install Word, there is no NORMAL.DOT file on your disk. Word simply uses the default settings that are part of the program to create a new NORMAL.DOT file the first time you open Word. This means that you can return to Word's document default settings by deleting NORMAL.DOT from your Word template directory or by renaming it with standard Windows or MS-DOS commands. (Word's options are set by entries in a separate file, called WINWORD.OPT.)

So much for the general introduction to templates. To use templates, there are some specific techniques you need to understand: how to edit and create templates, how to create a new document based on any given supplementary template, and how to attach a template to and detach a template from an existing document.

How to edit a template

There are two ways to change any template. You can create or modify features such as AutoText entries while working on a document; you can then save those changes in the Normal template or in the current supplementary template, if there is one. Alternatively, you can load the template and edit it directly. If you want to add boilerplate text to the template, editing the template is the only choice.

To open an existing template file for editing, choose File Open, select Document Templates (*.dot) in the List Files Of Type drop-down list, and choose the appropriate filename in the File Name list box. You can then edit the file and change its settings just as you would with any document file. When you're done, simply save the file by choosing File Save.

How to create a new template

Word comes with a starter set of templates and wizards that you can use to create new documents or templates. You'll be able to use some of these for your own work, but you'll probably want to create your own templates as well. To create a new template, choose the File New command, choose the Template option button in the New box, and then choose OK. Word will open a document window, but instead of using the name *Document1* in the title bar, it will use the name *Template1*. Make whatever changes you like to styles, margins, and other settings. Also add any text, headers, or footers that you want to define as part of this template. Word will automatically apply these settings to, and enter the text in, any documents you later create with this template attached.

You can save a template file using the same commands you would for saving a document. Word will prompt you for a filename; note that the program will assume that you want to assign a DOT extension, since this is a template file. We suggest you accept the DOT extension, unless you have a specific reason for doing otherwise. Enter a name, and then choose OK to finish saving. When you're done making changes, choose File Close. Once the template is created, you can use it as the basis for new documents or attach it to existing document files, as we'll discuss next.

How to attach and detach templates

To attach any template to a new document, choose the template from the Template list box in the New dialog box. Keep in mind that the default is the Normal template; if you accept the default, you'll be using the Normal template only. If you choose a different template from the list, Word will attach that template. Word will treat this template as the document template, and it will also use the Normal template.

If you've already created a document with a supplementary template or with the Normal template alone, and you decide later that you want to use a different supplementary template or add one, use the File Templates command. With the document open and active on your screen, choose File Templates. Word will display a dialog box like the one shown in Figure 9-22.

FIGURE 9-22

Choose the File Templates command to attach a different template to an existing document.

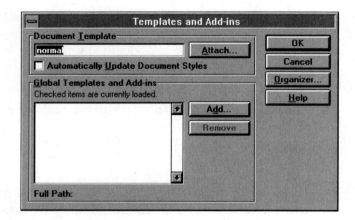

To see a list of available templates, choose the Attach button. The resulting Attach Template dialog box looks and functions just like the File Open dialog box. You can use it to find a particular template file and attach it.

If you choose the Normal template, Word will detach any template that's attached and will thereafter refer to the Normal template as the document template. If you choose any other template, Word will detach any supplementary template that's currently attached and replace it with the newly chosen template. Word will now refer to this newly chosen template as the document template. The Normal template will remain attached in any case.

As we mentioned earlier, you can tell Word whether to add customized features such as macros and AutoText entries to the Normal template or to the current supplementary template. In fact, you'll find a text box called something like Make AutoText Entry Available To in each item that you can assign to your choice of currently active templates. In general, unless you have a specific reason for doing otherwise, you should save customizations to the Normal template so that they will be available at all times.

More about templates

This is the barest of introductions to templates. We can't cover most of the possibilities for customizing templates yet because we haven't covered the features themselves. As you learn new customization features, from styles (Chapter 12) to macros (Chapters 24–26), you can experiment with adding them to templates as it seems appropriate.

In the rest of this book, starting with the next chapter, we'll explore Word's advanced features. After we finish with them, we'll take a more detailed look at templates in Chapter 27.

PART THREE

ADVANCED
WORD

TOPIC FINDER

Bookmarks   333

- How to define a bookmark
- How to redefine a bookmark
- How to delete a bookmark
- How to go to a bookmark

Annotations   336

- How to insert an annotation
- How to work with annotations
- How to lock a document for annotations
- How to print annotations

Footnotes and Endnotes   341

- How to create a footnote
- How to edit footnotes
- How to format footnotes

Advanced Go To Techniques   350

- How to use the Go To command to move to specific kinds of items

Revision Marks   353

- How to mark a document
- How to review the revisions
- *New!* How to compare two versions of a document
- How to merge multiple sets of revisions

10

Advanced Editing

hen you're fully comfortable with Word, you'll want to explore some of its advanced editing features. In this chapter, we'll discuss bookmarks, annotations, revision marks, and advanced Go To features, all of which will help you work with long and complex documents and help coordinate writing and editing tasks that involve more than one person. We will also cover a specialized type of editing, namely footnotes.

Bookmarks

Word's bookmark feature gets its name by analogy to a real bookmark because it serves a similar purpose. After you define a bookmark, you can use the Go To command to move to that spot from anywhere in the document.

Word also uses bookmarks for other purposes. You can, for example, use them in references to number items automatically. We'll cover these other uses elsewhere, in the context of advanced techniques.

How to define a bookmark

Defining a bookmark is similar to creating a new AutoText entry. Suppose you've created the document shown in Figure 10-1 on the next page, and you want a bookmark at the beginning of the introduction so that you can return to that section easily. First position the cursor or selection at the start of the introduction. Then choose Edit Bookmark to open the Bookmark dialog box, shown in Figure 10-2, and enter *Intro* in the Bookmark Name text box. Your screen should look like Figure 10-2. Choose Add to finish.

FIGURE 10-1

We'll use this document to demonstrate some bookmark basics.

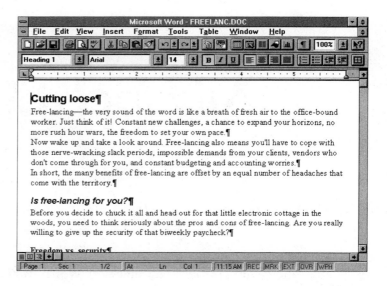

FIGURE 10-2

To define a bookmark, position the cursor or selection in the text you want the bookmark to mark. Then open the Bookmark dialog box to assign a bookmark name.

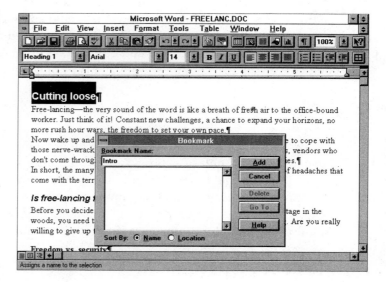

Bookmark names

Bookmark names follow a few simple rules. The name cannot exceed 40 characters, it must begin with a letter of the alphabet, and it can contain only letters, numbers, and the underline character. If you type an invalid character in the Bookmark Name text box, the Add button will be grayed. You'll have to change the name before the Add button will become active again.

How to redefine a bookmark

Although you can't move or modify a bookmark, you can achieve the same effect by redefining the bookmark name to refer to a different location. Simply move the cursor or selection to the new location. Then choose Edit Bookmark and assign the bookmark name, either by typing it in the Bookmark Name box or by choosing it from the list. Finally, choose Add to close the dialog box and redefine the name. The bookmark feature is not case sensitive, so typing *INTRO*, *Intro*, or *intro* will all produce the same effect.

How to delete a bookmark

To delete a bookmark, first choose Edit Bookmark. Then type the name to delete in the Bookmark Name text box (or choose it from the list), and choose the Delete button. Word will delete the bookmark and remove its name from the list box without asking for confirmation.

 If you delete text that includes a bookmark, you will also delete that bookmark.

How to go to a bookmark

One of the advantages of bookmarks is that they make it easy to go to a specific place in a document. After you've defined a bookmark, you can move to it by using the Go To dialog box, shown in Figure 10-3. To open the dialog box, choose Edit Go To, press F5, or double-click on the status bar anywhere to the left of the time display.

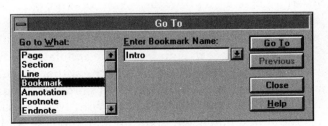

The Go To What list displays the kinds of items you can move to from this dialog box. If you highlight Bookmark, the label on the text box to the right will read Enter Bookmark Name, and the attached drop-down list will display all bookmarks in the current document. You can then enter the bookmark name in the text box (or choose it from the list) and choose the Go To button. If the bookmark you've specified marks a place in the document, Word will move the cursor to that position. If it defines a block of text, Word will move to that point and highlight the entire block. We'll cover the other choices later in this chapter.

Annotations

Annotations are hidden text that you can add as notes to a document without cluttering up the text. Word numbers each annotation automatically and marks it with its author's initials (based on information on the User Info card). If you have a document that a number of people are reviewing, annotations make it easy to keep track of who wrote what. You can also use annotations for notes to yourself—to remind you where you got certain information, for example, or to remind you to check your facts before printing or circulating the document.

As we'll discuss, you can lock a document for annotations, which means you can let others insert annotations while keeping them from making any changes to the document itself. And you can print a document's annotations.

How to insert an annotation

To insert an annotation, move the cursor to the appropriate location or highlight the text you want to comment on; then choose Insert Annotation, and write your note. For example, suppose you want to insert the following annotation into the document shown in Figure 10-4:

Additionally, total expenditures for the month were well under budget.

Simply position the cursor where you want the annotation reference (or highlight the text you are annotating), and choose Insert Annotation. Word will insert a reference mark at the cursor location, open the annotation pane at the bottom of the window, as shown in Figure 10-4, and move the cursor to the pane. You can then type the text, just as you would in a document window.

As you can see in Figure 10-4, the annotation reference mark consists of a pair of brackets ([ ]). These enclose the author's initials (in this case, AP) and a number that marks the annotation's order in the document. (In this case, it is the first annotation.) Note that Word uses the same reference mark both for the annotation itself, in the annotation pane, and for the annotation's position in your text.

The Insert Annotation command opens the annotation pane so that you can type your annotation.

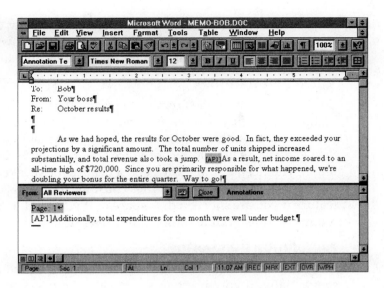

Word automatically formats the the reference mark in your document as hidden text. However, the reference marks will be displayed whenever the annotation pane is open, whether you've set Word to show hidden text or not. When you are editing an annotation in the annotation pane, Word will highlight the corresponding mark in the document (and any associated text you selected when you created the annotation).

If you use annotations, we recommend that you either keep the annotation pane open while editing (by choosing the View Annotations command) or set Word to display hidden text (by checking the Hidden Text check box on the Tools Options View card). Being able to see the reference marks will keep you from accidentally deleting an annotation that you didn't know was there.

You can use the From list box at the top of the annotation pane to specify which annotations you want to view. If you are creating a new document, the only choices in the drop-down list will be All Reviewers and the current user as defined on the Tools Options User Info card. If the document has annotations from other users, however, the list will also include the name of each user. You can specify All Reviewers or select a specific reviewer to see notes only from that reviewer.

When you finish typing a note, you can close the annotation pane by choosing the Close button. (Click on it with the mouse, or press Alt-Shift-C.) Alternatively, you can choose View Annotations to toggle the feature off.

Any time you want to see your annotations, simply choose View Annotations again. If the annotation reference mark is showing, mouse users can double-click on the reference mark to open the annotation pane.

Voice annotations

The button between the From text box and the Close button has an icon of an audio cassette. If you have a sound card in your system and a microphone, you can click on this button—or choose Insert Object and pick Sound from the Object Type list—to record voice annotations. To listen to a sound annotation, you need a sound card and a headset or speakers.

Keep in mind that sound files consume lots of disk space. Don't use this feature if you are short on disk space or if you need to keep file sizes small to minimize transfer time across phone lines or local area network connections.

Annotation numbering

As you add annotations to a document, Word numbers the reference marks sequentially. If you insert an annotation above existing ones, Word will renumber annotations that come later. For example, if you insert an annotation at the top of the document, as shown in Figure 10-5, Word will number the new annotation 1 and will renumber the existing annotation 2.

FIGURE 10-5

Word marks each annotation reference with the initials stored on the Tools Options User Info card. It numbers the reference marks sequentially.

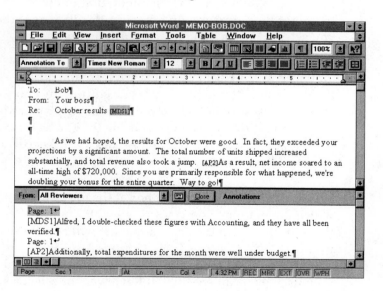

When you insert an annotation, Word creates the reference mark by using the initials currently stored on the Tools Options User Info card. If more than one person uses the same installed copy of Word to add annotations, all reference marks will have the same initials (unless each user remembers to change the information on the User Info card). However, if each individual adds the annotations on his or her own computer, each annotation will include that individual's initials. Figure 10-5 shows an annotation pane with notes written by two different people, MDS and AP. Notice that the reference marks are numbered sequentially, so [AP2] refers to the second annotation in the document, not the second one by AP.

How to size the annotation pane

As you may have noticed, Word separates the document pane from the annotation pane with a split bar. You can adjust the size of the pane by adjusting the position of the split bar, using the techniques we covered in Chapter 1.

How to move between the annotation and document panes

You can move between the annotation and document panes by either clicking on the pane you want to move to or pressing F6. Notice that if you scroll through either pane, Word will scroll the other so that you can see both an annotation and the text it refers to.

In addition to using annotations to write notes to yourself or to others, you can use them for any text you don't want in the document itself. For example, you might want to draft an alternative version of a given paragraph.

How to work with annotations

Whatever you use annotations for, there will be times when you want to insert all or part of an annotation into your document and other times when you simply want to get rid of an annotation altogether. There may also be times when you want to move some text from your document to an annotation.

How to move an annotation to or from the document pane

If you want to include text from an annotation in your document, cut or copy the text in the annotation and paste it into your document. (You can use any of the usual Word commands for cutting and pasting, such as Edit Cut and Edit Paste.) You can then delete the annotation reference mark by selecting the annotation mark in the document pane—so that it shows as black, not gray—and pressing Del.

You may also want to move text from the document to an annotation. For example, you may be considering deletion of a paragraph, but you have enough doubts that you aren't ready to throw the paragraph away yet. To move text to an annotation, first insert the annotation; then move back to the document, cut the text, move back to the annotation pane, and paste the text into the annotation.

How to delete an annotation

You can delete all of the text in an annotation from within the annotation pane, but you can't delete the annotation itself in this pane. To delete an annotation, select the appropriate reference mark in the document so that it shows as black rather than gray, and press Del. Word will remove the annotation mark and annotation entirely and automatically renumber subsequent annotations.

How to lock a document for annotations

As we mentioned earlier, you can prevent others from making changes to your document but still let them insert annotations. To take advantage of Word's document protection feature, choose Tools Protect Document to open the Protect Document dialog box, shown in Figure 10-6.

FIGURE 10-6

The document protection feature lets you control the type of changes that can be made to a document.

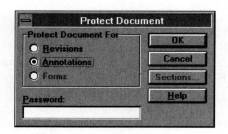

The Protect Document For box contains three options: Revisions, Annotations, and Forms. We'll discuss the Revisions option later in this chapter and the Forms option in Chapter 21. For the moment, we're concerned only with the Annotations option.

If you choose Annotations and then choose OK, the only changes Word will let anyone make to the document will be the addition, deletion, and modification of annotations. If you add or change an annotation, Word will mark the changes as inserted text, using the current revision mark settings. (We'll cover these later in this chapter.) Note that Word will let you delete an annotation, but it won't necessarily erase it. More precisely, if you try to delete an annotation that you've added after applying document protection to the document, Word will erase the annotation. But if you try to delete one that you added before protecting the document, or one that some other user has added, Word will mark the annotation as deleted text using the current revision marks. (Here again, we'll discuss these later in this chapter.)

The Protect Document dialog box also includes a Password text box. If you type a password in it, Word will show only asterisks and will prompt you to retype the password to confirm it. If you want to remove the protection from the document later, you'll be prompted to give the password.

How to unlock a document

After you add protection to a document, the Tools menu command name changes to Unprotect Document. Choose this command to remove protection and allow normal editing of the document. If you defined a password when you protected the document, you'll be prompted to enter the password to remove protection.

How to print annotations

To print a document's annotations by themselves, choose File Print to open the Print dialog box, choose Annotations from the Print What drop-down list box, and choose OK. Word will print all of the annotations, showing each reference mark, associated text (if any), and the page each applies to.

If you want Word to print annotations along with a document, choose Tools Options and then the Print card (or choose File Print and then the Options button to display the Tools Options Print card). Make sure the Annotations check box is checked. Word will print your annotations at the end of the document, much like endnotes.

Footnotes and Endnotes

The mere mention of footnotes can strike fear in the heart of anyone who has ever struggled through a term paper. Footnotes are cumbersome to deal with on typewriters and on many word processors. But Word's footnote feature, which is similar to its annotation feature, makes the job easy. You can add footnote text while you're working on the body of the document or later. Word will automatically number your footnotes and renumber them—even if you modify the document by adding and deleting footnotes or text or by inserting new footnotes between existing ones.

You can place footnotes at the bottom of each page, or you can make them endnotes located at the end of the document. You can also control how they are separated from the rest of your text. We'll start by showing you how to create a footnote.

How to create a footnote

In the sample document shown in Figure 10-7 on the next page, we'll add a footnote reference mark at the end of the first paragraph of body text.

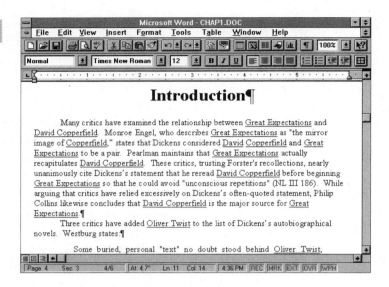

FIGURE 10-7

We'll insert a footnote reference mark into this document.

The first step is to position your cursor where you want the footnote reference mark. Then choose Insert Footnote to open the Footnote And Endnote dialog box, shown in Figure 10-8.

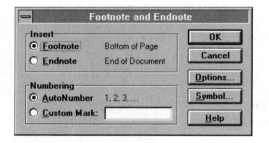

FIGURE 10-8

Use the Footnote And Endnote dialog box to insert footnotes into a document.

In the Insert group box, you specify whether you are inserting a footnote or an endnote. Either choice will insert a reference mark in the document. Choose Footnote to print the note at the bottom of the same page. Choose Endnote to print it on a separate page (or pages) at the end of the document. Note that you can create both footnotes and endnotes in the same document. Word will maintain a separate numbering scheme for each.

The Numbering box contains two options: AutoNumber and Custom Mark. If you choose AutoNumber, Word will number all of the footnotes or endnotes in sequence, and it will automatically renumber them for you as needed. (We'll show how you can choose the numbering scheme you want in a moment.)

If you'd rather use a custom footnote reference mark, such as an asterisk, type the character you want in the Custom Mark text box. By default, the character (or characters) will be inserted in the same font as the adjacent text but in a smaller size and formatted as a superscript. You can type a character directly from the keyboard, or you can choose the Symbol button to open the Symbol dialog box and insert a symbol. The latter approach works similarly to the procedure we discussed in "The Insert Symbols command" starting on page 157.

> You are not limited to single-character entries in the Custom Mark text box. Word will use up to 10 characters, including letters, spaces, and punctuation marks.

Footnote options. If you choose the Options button in the Footnote And Endnote dialog box, Word will open the Note Options dialog box, shown in Figure 10-9.

FIGURE 10-9

Use the Note Options dialog box to control how Word numbers and formats footnotes and endnotes.

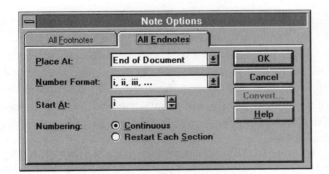

The Place At list box on the All Footnotes card offers two choices: Bottom Of Page and Beneath Text. Choose Bottom Of Page to put footnotes at the bottom margin of the page even if the body text ends above the bottom margin. Choose Beneath Text to put the footnotes just below the last line of body text on a page, regardless of where the body text ends.

The Number Format list box offers six predefined numbering schemes for the footnote reference marks: Arabic numbers, uppercase or lowercase letters, uppercase or lowercase Roman numerals, and a series of typographic symbols commonly used for footnotes.

In the Start At box, you can specify the number, letter, or symbol for the first footnote mark. The default choice is the first item in the sequence you chose in the Number Format box.

The three Numbering option buttons are Continuous, Restart Each Section, and Restart Each Page.

For most documents, you will probably want continuous numbering; this will number all footnotes sequentially for the entire document. If you've divided a document into sections, however, and those sections represent separate parts—such as chapters—you might want to use Restart At Each Section. This will reset the numbering to the beginning of the sequence at the start of each section.

If you use the typographic symbol sequence, you might want to choose Restart For Each Page because this is the conventional usage for these symbols. Choosing another numbering option for such symbols could yield an unexpected result; Word can number continuously using these symbols, but only by using multiples of the symbols—one of each the first time through, two of each the second time through, and so on. Since there are only four symbols, these multiple marks can easily become distracting if your document has many footnotes.

Endnote options. The options on the All Endnotes card, also shown in Figure 10-9 on the previous page, are similar to those on the All Footnotes card.

The Place At list box contains two choices: End Of Section and End Of Document. If you choose End Of Section, Word will place the endnote text after the last line of a section and before the first line of the next section. If you choose End Of Document, the endnotes will appear after the last line of the document. The Number Format and Start At options are the same as for footnotes.

There are two Numbering options: Continuous and Restart Each Section. The Continuous option works exactly as for footnotes, as does the Restart Each Section option when combined with the End Of Section placement option. However, if you've selected End Of Document in the Place At box, selecting Restart Each Section places all notes at the end of the document and numbers them sequentially by section. This is a useful feature for books in which endnotes are printed in a separate section subdivided by headings such as *Notes to Chapter 1*, *Notes to Chapter 2*, and so on.

Footnote and endnote options. Both cards include a Convert button that opens the same Convert Notes dialog box, which contains three options: You can convert all footnotes in the document to endnotes; you can convert all endnotes to footnotes; or you can swap the two, so that all footnotes become endnotes and all endnotes become footnotes. This feature can be handy if you change your mind about how you want your notes formatted.

Finishing up. When you close the Convert Notes dialog box, you will return to the Note Options dialog box. Close this, and you will return to the Footnote And Endnote dialog box.

If you choose OK at this point, Word will insert the footnote reference mark at the cursor position in your document (or the leftmost position of a selection). If you're in Normal or Outline view, Word will split your document window into two panes, as shown in Figure 10-10, with a corresponding footnote reference mark in the footnote pane at the bottom. The cursor will move to the footnote pane, just to the right of the footnote reference mark. If you're in Page Layout view or Print Preview, Word will insert the reference mark into the text and move the cursor to the area of the page where the footnote text will be printed.

FIGURE 10-10

When you choose OK in the Footnote And Endnote dialog box, Word will add a footnote reference mark and, if you're in Normal or Outline view, open a footnote pane.

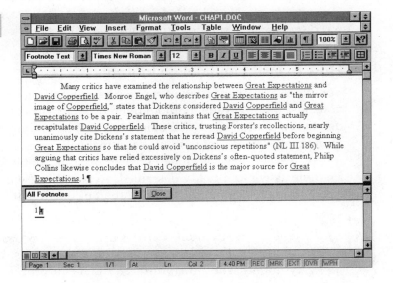

How to work in the footnote pane

Now you can type your footnote in the footnote pane, just as if you were working in the document pane. If the footnote is too long to view in its entirety,

Word will scroll the pane as you type. You can also use the vertical scroll bar in that pane to bring additional text into view, or you can move the split bar to make the pane larger. See "How to split a window" starting on page 21 for details on how to move the split bar.

How to move between the footnote and document panes

You can move between the footnote and document panes with the same techniques you use to move between the document and annotation panes: Press F6, or use the mouse to click anywhere in the pane you want to move to.

When you leave the footnote pane, Word will keep it open until you choose the Close button (with the mouse or with Alt-Shift-C) or by choosing View Footnotes. You can reopen the footnote pane anytime by choosing View Footnotes again. Note, too, that you can quickly open the footnote pane with the mouse by double-clicking on a footnote reference mark. If you scroll through either pane, Word will scroll the other, and you will see both a footnote and the text it refers to.

How to edit footnotes

After you've created a footnote, you can use Word's standard editing techniques to edit it. You can also find and replace footnotes, and you can use the Spelling, Thesaurus, and Hyphenate commands on them. We discussed finding and replacing in "How to find special characters" starting on page 115, and we discussed the spelling, thesaurus, and hyphenation tools in Chapter 6, "Proofing," page 178.

How to insert and delete footnotes

You insert and delete footnotes much as you do annotations. To delete a footnote, just highlight the footnote reference mark in your document pane and delete the mark. Word will delete the corresponding footnote text and re-number all subsequent footnotes automatically.

To insert a new footnote between existing footnotes, simply create the footnote as we've already described. Again, Word will renumber all subsequent footnotes automatically in both your document and footnote panes.

There are two keyboard shortcuts for inserting footnotes and endnotes. These bypass all of the dialog boxes we've discussed, so you may want to go through the menu process first to adjust the format settings. You can then use Alt-Ctrl-F to insert a footnote, or Alt-Ctrl-E to insert an endnote, at the current cursor position.

How to copy footnotes

Here's a handy shortcut for repeating a footnote entry or copying it to another document. Select a footnote reference mark in the document, choose Edit Copy, and then paste the reference mark where you want the copy. Word will copy the reference mark for the footnote and insert the text in proper sequence in the footnote pane. If you copied an automatically numbered reference mark, Word will also renumber all footnotes appropriately.

How to change a footnote's custom reference mark

If you've inserted a custom footnote reference mark (an asterisk, for example), and you decide to use a different reference mark, you'll need to change the mark in your document. If you try to edit the reference mark directly, Word will delete the entire footnote—both reference mark and text. To change the reference mark, select it in your document, choose Insert Footnote, and either type the new custom reference mark in the Custom Mark text box or choose the AutoNumber footnote option, as appropriate. Word will change the reference mark in both the document and the footnote pane.

How to format footnotes

One of the most difficult aspects of manually inserting footnotes—whether with a typewriter or with a word processor that lacks a footnote feature—is formatting. Trying to determine how much space to leave at the bottom of the page, for example, can be a real problem, and dealing with a footnote that spills over to the bottom of the next page can be a headache. Word handles all these issues automatically.

How to format footnote text and reference marks

When you insert a footnote in your document, Word adds two styles to the document's list of styles in use: Footnote Reference and Footnote Text. Similarly, when you insert an endnote, you'll find two other styles: Endnote Reference and Endnote Text. We will discuss styles in Chapter 12. For now, simply be aware that you can change the appearance of the footnote text, footnote reference marks, endnote text, or endnote reference marks by changing the style definitions. You can also use all of Word's direct formatting tools. Select the reference mark in the document text, or select the text you want to format in the footnote pane, and use the formatting commands just as you would for any other text in your document.

How to change footnote and endnote separators

Unless told otherwise, Word will add a short horizontal line between the document text and footnote text to separate the two when you print a document that includes footnotes. Also, when a footnote is too long to fit entirely on the same page as the referenced text, or when all the footnotes for a page won't fit at the bottom of that page, Word will automatically place the remaining text on the next page. To indicate that the footnote text on the second page is a continuation, Word uses a horizontal line that extends from margin to margin. Similar separators are used for endnotes.

If you prefer, you can create custom separators. First make sure you're in Normal view with the footnote pane open. (Choose View Footnotes if necessary.)

The list box in the upper left corner of the footnote pane should be displaying *All Footnotes* or *All Endnotes*, depending on which kind of notes you're working with. If you open the drop-down list, however, you'll see other choices.

If the box says *All Footnotes*—and assuming you have both footnotes and endnotes in the document—the drop-down list will contain five choices: All Footnotes, All Endnotes, Footnote Separator, Footnote Continuation Separator, and Footnote Continuation Notice. If the box shows *All Endnotes*, the last three choices will be for endnotes instead of footnotes.

Choose the item you want to change, and Word will display the current version of that item in the footnote pane. If the current item is still the default line that Word normally uses, as shown in Figure 10-11, you can't edit it; however, you can add to it, delete it, or replace it.

FIGURE 10-11

From within the footnote pane, you can customize the separator that divides footnotes from body text.

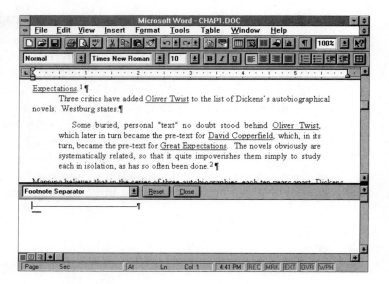

To add anything before or after the default line, position the cursor and type any characters you want to add. To delete the line, select the entire line and press Del. To replace the line, highlight the line and type the replacement. When you type the first character, Word will delete the line. You can then type any additional characters. If you like, you can open Microsoft Draw (which we will discuss in Chapter 15) and create a custom separator as a drawing object. And you can insert fields so that you can add a dynamic page number to your separator, for example.

The Footnote Continuation Notice and Endnote Continuation Notice are blank by default. You can create any message you like; however, keep in mind that the continuation notice will be visible only when the footnote or endnote continues onto the next page.

Figures 10-12, 10-13, and 10-14 show custom versions of the footnote separator, footnote continuation separator, and footnote continuation notice. Figure 10-15 on the next page shows how the custom separator and continuation notice appear in Page Layout view.

FIGURE 10-12

In this custom footnote separator, the word *Footnotes* replaces Word's default separator.

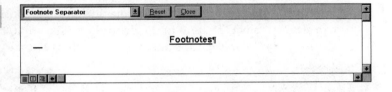

FIGURE 10-13

This custom footnote continuation separator is defined as *Footnotes (continued)*.

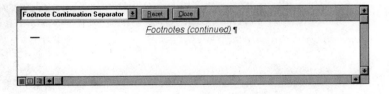

FIGURE 10-14

You can also add a footnote continuation notice.

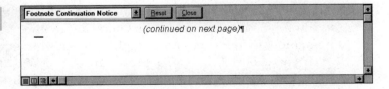

FIGURE 10-15

Page Layout view
shows the custom
footnote separator and
continuation notice.

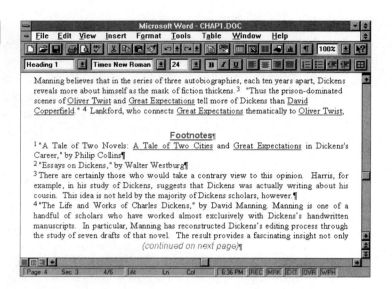

To go back to the default setting for any of these items—the footnote or endnote separators, continuation separators, or continuation notices—you can simply select the item in the drop-down list so that the current version of the item shows in the footnote pane, and choose the Reset button.

Any customizations you make for the footnote or endnote separators, continuation separators, or continuation notices are document specific. However, you can copy these to another document by copying between windows. You can also store customized separators as AutoText entries so that you can easily insert them in any document.

Advanced Go To Techniques

We've discussed using the Edit Go To command to jump to a bookmark. In addition, you can use the Go To command to jump to a page, section, line, annotation, footnote, endnote, field, table, graphic, equation, or object.

If you choose Edit Go To, press Ctrl-G, press F5, or double-click on any of the positional information in the status bar, Word will display a Go To dialog box like the one shown in Figure 10-16. The Go To What list box contains the types of items you can jump to. The label for the text box to the right of the list box changes depending on which type you choose. With some types of items, the text box offers an attached drop-down list containing, for example, a list of bookmark names.

FIGURE 10-16

You can navigate through long documents by using the Go To dialog box.

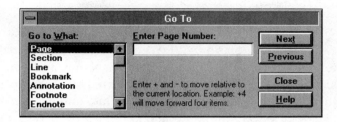

After you choose the item in the Go To What list, you can use the Next and Previous buttons to move through your document. You can also type numbers in the middle text box to go directly to a particular item—or, for most kinds of items, enter a plus or minus sign along with a number to go forward or backward that number of items: Typing *+4* and then choosing the Go To button will take you forward four pages, four lines, four sections, and so forth. And don't forget that after using the Go To command, you can use Shift-F5 to return to a previous position.

How to use the Go To command to move to specific kinds of items

Although the Go To command works similarly for all types of items, there are some differences you should be aware of. Here are some points to keep in mind for specific items.

Going to a page. To go to a particular page in the document, simply enter the page number in the Enter Page Number text box.

The page number specifies the number of pages from the beginning of the document—not necessarily the number assigned to the page. If you're working with a two-section document with two pages in section 1 and four separately numbered pages in section 2, entering *4* will jump you to the second page in section 2. Remember also to repaginate before jumping to a page. Word repaginates your document whenever you switch to Page Layout view or Print Preview; repagination will take place continuously if you've checked the Background Repagination check box on the Tools Options General card.

Going to a bookmark. If you choose Bookmark in the Go To What list, you must select a specific bookmark to go to. If you try entering a relative number, such as *+5*, to go forward that number of bookmarks, Word will interpret the entry as a bookmark name and display an error message stating that the bookmark does not exist.

Going to an annotation. When you pick Annotation in the Go To What list, the text box changes to Enter Reviewer's Name, and you can choose among all annotations or choose only those inserted by a specific user. You can also enter the annotation's number or use the plus/minus notation.

Going to a footnote or an endnote. To go to a specific footnote or endnote, choose Footnote or Endnote in the Go To What list and type a number in the text box. As it does for page numbers, Word counts the actual footnotes or endnotes. If you started numbering at some number other than 1, for example, entering *6* will jump you to the sixth footnote or endnote in sequence, regardless of the number that designates it in your numbering scheme.

Going to a field. When you pick Field in the Go To What list, the text box changes to Enter Field Name, with a drop-down list that includes every kind of field Word uses. You can choose between moving to a field of any type and moving to a specific kind of field. We'll discuss fields in Chapter 20; for now, just be aware that you can move to a specific kind of field if you know which kind you're looking for.

If you find it awkward to choose a type of item first and then move to the text box to type a specific item, note that there's a shortcut you can use instead. Choose Page in the Go To What list. Then, in the Enter Page Number text box, type a code plus a number to tell Word to go to a specific section, line, and so on. The available codes are as follows:

Item	Code	Item	Code
Page	P	Endnote	E
Section	S	Table	T
Line	L	Graphic	G
Annotation	A	Any Object	O
Footnote	F		

The Go To command also provides a somewhat hidden keyboard equivalent to using the mouse and scroll bar for moving through a document. To move to the document's halfway point, for example, first choose Page in the Go To What list. Then type *50%* or *%50* and choose the Go To button. To jump to approximately three-fourths of the way through the document, type *75%* instead of *50%*; and so on. Note that Word figures the position based on number of characters, not pages. So if you have forced page breaks, for example, going to the 50% position may not take you to the middle page of your document.

Revision Marks

As with annotations, Word's revision marks feature is designed for documents that are reviewed and edited by more than one person. It can also be useful if you simply want to keep track of changes from one draft to the next.

When you use the revision marks feature, you will be able to edit text and see exactly what has changed. For example, if you delete text, Word will strike through that text and change its color rather than remove it from the document. And if you add text, Word will underline it and change its color. In addition, Word adds vertical bars, called revision bars, alongside the revised lines of text.

As an alternative to adding revision marks while you edit, you can tell Word to compare a revised version of a document to an original version. Word will mark the entire document.

However you add the revision markings, you can review the document to see the revisions and undo or accept them. You can make the final decision case by case, reviewing each revision individually, or you can accept or undo all revisions in one fell swoop. Here's a look at each of these possibilities, starting with marking the revisions as you make them.

How to mark a document

To add revision marks as you revise a document, choose Tools Revisions to open the Revisions dialog box, shown in Figure 10-17 on the next page. Alternatively, you can double-click on the MRK indicator on the status bar. Check the Mark Revisions While Editing check box, and choose OK. As shown in Figure 10-18 (also on the next page), the MRK indicator will no longer be grayed, indicating that the revision marks feature is active.

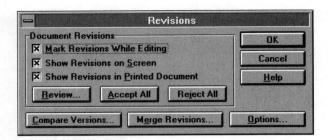

Figure 10-18 shows some text with strikethrough formatting and some with underlining. The strikethrough indicates text that has been deleted with revision marking active; the underlining indicates text that has been added. The deleted text and the special marking for added text will show on screen only if the Show Revisions On Screen check box in the Revisions dialog box is checked. The third check box in the Revisions dialog box, Show Revisions In Printed Document, determines whether the marked revisions will be printed.

FIGURE 10-18

When you edit text
with Mark Revisions
turned on, Word will
strike through any
deleted text and mark
new text in your choice
of formats—using
underlining, in this
case.

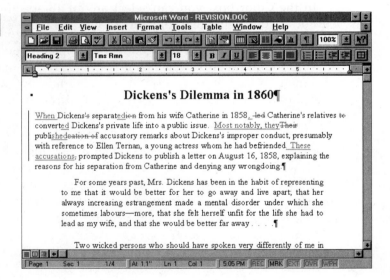

How to change the format of inserted and deleted text

By default, Word uses the strikethrough format for deletions and uses underlining for insertions, but you can change this if you like. Although you cannot see it in Figure 10-18, the revisions are marked in color, which you also can control.

To change the format for revisions, choose the Options button in the Revisions dialog box, or choose Tools Options and then the Revisions card. Either way, the Tools Options Revisions card, shown in Figure 10-19, will open.

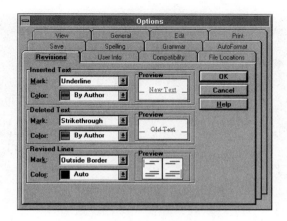

FIGURE 10-19

Use the Tools Options Revisions card to control how Word marks revisions in your document.

The Inserted Text group box includes drop-down list boxes and a Preview box to show a sample of how the current settings will affect inserted text. In the Mark box, you choose the format for new text: None, Bold, Italic, Underline, or Double Underline.

In the Color box, you can select any of 16 specific colors, Auto, or By Author. If you choose one color, Word will always use that color for inserted text. Choose Auto to use the default Windows text color, which you can set through the Color icon in the Windows Control Panel.

By Author (the default) tells Word to use a different color for each of the first eight authors who edit the document, with authors defined by the settings on the Tools Options User Info card. The colors stand out from the original text, making it obvious who made which changes.

The choices in the Deleted Text group box work almost identically except that the only options available in the Mark drop-down list are Hidden and Strikethrough.

How to move the revision bars

The Tools Options Revisions card also contains a group box labeled Revised Lines. This controls how Word adds the vertical revision bars alongside the text, to help you spot revisions more easily. Your options are None (no bars), Left Border (bars in the left margin), Right Border (bars in the right margin), and Outside Border. The Outside Border option tells Word to print the bars in the left margin of even-numbered pages and in the right margin of odd-numbered pages. In Normal or Outline view, the revision bars will always be displayed in the left margin; however, they will be displayed in their specified positions in Page Layout view or Print Preview, as well as on the printed page.

Any changes you make on the Tools Options Revisions card will affect the entire document, including any revisions already made with the revision marks feature active. This means that you can't change settings as a way to track different generations of edits. However, you can track different sets of changes by using the default By Author settings for colors and changing the Name entry on the Tools Options User Info card. Change the name, and Word will treat you as a different user, assigning a different color to your edits for each new name. If you use this trick, however, be sure to change the entry back to the correct name when you finish.

How to review the revisions

At some point you have to decide whether or not to keep your revisions. Word provides tools that will let you accept or undo any revision. Accept it, and Word will delete text marked for deletion and remove the revision marks from new text. If you undo a revision, however, Word will restore text to its original form, removing the strikethrough format from text marked for deletion and deleting new text. You can update or undo all revisions in a single step, or you can update them one at a time.

How to update or undo all revisions at once

To accept or undo all revisions in a document at once, choose Tools Revisions to open the Revisions dialog box. As shown in Figure 10-17, there are three buttons along the bottom of the Document Revisions group box: Review, Accept All, and Reject All.

You can accept all revisions to the document by choosing Accept All, or you can undo all of them by choosing Reject All. With either choice, Word will display a message box asking for confirmation.

  If you choose Accept All or Reject All and then answer Yes by mistake, you can use Edit Undo to undo the changes. To be safe, however, you should save a copy of your marked-up document under a different filename before working on it. That way, you can always come back to the original should you change your mind later.

How to update revisions individually

Most often you'll want to review each revision individually rather than update an entire document at once. With the cursor anywhere in the document, choose Tools Revisions to open the Revisions dialog box. Then choose the Review button in the Document Revisions group box to open the Review Revisions dialog box, shown in Figure 10-20.

The Review Revisions dialog box makes it easy to review individual changes to a document.

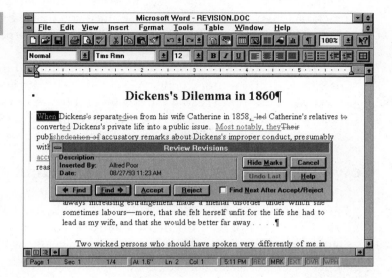

Notice the two Find buttons, one with an arrow pointing left (toward the beginning of the document), and one with an arrow pointing right. Choose either button, and Word will search for and highlight the first instance of revised text it finds in the direction the arrow indicates. When it finds a revision, it will add two lines to the Description box above the Find buttons, showing what kind of change is highlighted (Inserted, Deleted, or Replaced), who made it, and the date and time the change was made. Word will do its best to display the revision where you can see it. If necessary, though, you can move the dialog box when it obstructs some of the text.

At this point, you can choose either the Accept or the Reject button to update the revised text. You can also move between the document window—to edit further—and the dialog box by pressing Ctrl-Tab or by clicking on the window or the dialog box with the mouse. If you prefer not to make a decision for the moment, you can choose one of the Find buttons to move to the next revision.

Checking the Find Next After Accept/Reject check box tells Word to move immediately to the next revision each time you choose the Accept or the Reject button.

The Hide Marks button turns off the revision marking, showing the text as it would appear if all current revisions were accepted. This can be useful to clarify the current state of text that's cluttered with a great many revisions. If you choose the Hide Marks button, the label changes to Show Marks. Choose Show Marks to display the revision markings again.

The Review Revisions dialog box also contains an Undo Last button. You can use this to undo any Accept or Reject choice you've made, and you can backtrack to undo all changes made since you opened the Review Revisions dialog box. However, Word will not display all the parts of the document that would let you see each Undo take place.

You can continue using the Find buttons until you reach the beginning or the end of the document. Word will then display a message asking whether you want to search the header and footer (if they exist). If you proceed, Word will ask whether you want to continue searching from the other end of the document. Choose Yes or No as appropriate.

How to compare two versions of a document

In addition to marking revisions while editing, Word can compare two versions of a document in different files and add revision marks to indicate differences. This can be particularly handy when one of the files was revised with a word processor other than Word.

If you've used Word 2.0, you may be aware that it contained a wimpy compare feature that would mark an entire paragraph if there was so much as an extra space in the paragraph in one of the versions. Word 6.0's compare feature does a much better job of marking just the parts that are different.

To compare two versions of a document, first open the most recent version. Next choose Tools Revisions, choose the Compare Versions button, and enter the name of the original file in the Original File Name box. The dialog box in which this appears, shown in Figure 10-21, looks and works much like the Open dialog box Word displays when you choose File Open.

After you specify the original file, choose OK to start the comparison. Word will add revision marks in the currently active document and keep you posted on progress by means of a graphic display on the status bar much like the display it uses when saving a file.

When Word finishes comparing the documents, you can review the comparisons, using the same techniques as for reviewing revisions.

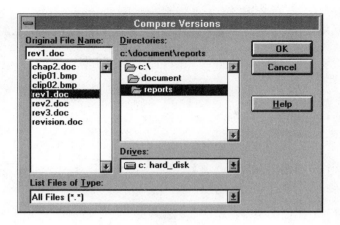

FIGURE 10-21

The Compare Versions dialog box is similar to the Open dialog box.

How to merge multiple sets of revisions

You can also merge the marked revisions from one document into another. This can be extremely useful if you've circulated the same file to several people and need to integrate all of their revisions into one document file. Note that you can merge only revisions that are already marked.

To merge revisions from a file, open the revised version of the document, choose Tools Revisions, and choose the Merge Revisions button to open the Merge Revisions dialog box. Again, this dialog box looks and works like the Open dialog box. Choose the original document, and then choose OK. Word will merge revisions—and annotations—into the original document. If you are combining revisions from several copies of the document, simply repeat this procedure for each copy.

The revision merging feature is much more useful if you also take advantage of Word's document protection feature before distributing the file. To do so, choose Tools Protect Document and then Revisions; specify a password if you want. If you choose Tools Revisions to open the Revisions dialog box while protection is applied, you'll see that the Mark Revisions While Editing check box is checked, and the option is grayed so that you can't clear it— unless you choose Tools Unprotect Document. By applying document protection before distributing the file, you are, in short, guaranteeing that all changes will come back marked as revisions.

TOPIC FINDER

Creating a Table   361
- How to create a table with menu commands
- How to create a table with a toolbar button
- Getting your bearings
- NEW! How to create and format a table with the Table Wizard
- NEW! How to use Table AutoFormat—with or without the Table Wizard

Using the Ruler with a Table   371

Entering Text in a Table   373

Navigating in a Table   374

Selecting Text in a Table   375
- Special table selection techniques for the mouse
- Special table selection techniques for the keyboard

Changing the Layout of a Table   377
- How to adjust cell and column width
- How to adjust row height
- NEW! How to control whether rows can break across pages
- How to add rows
- How to delete rows
- How to insert and delete columns
- How to add and delete cells
- How to merge and split cells

Deleting an Entire Table   398

Changing Table and Row Alignment   398
- How to indent rows

Entering Body Text Above or Between Table Rows   400
- How to change part of a table to text
- How to split a table vertically

Working with Text in a Table   401
- How to edit text in a table
- How to format text in a table

Adding Borders and Shading in a Table   407
- How to define a single table to look like two tables side by side
- How to redefine or delete borders and shading

Converting Existing Text to a Table   412
- The rules Word uses for converting text to a table

Converting All or Part of a Table to Text   416

Tables as Mini-Spreadsheets: Sorting and Calculating   417

11

Building Tables

n addition to creating tabular columns with tabs, you can create a table in Word in either of two ways: You can create a blank table and then fill it in, or you can convert existing text to a table. Both approaches use Word's Table menu commands. If you use tables often, or if you ever need more than the most minimal of tables, you'll find the table feature to be among Word's most useful capabilities. You can use it for anything from a simple two-column list to complex page designs for elaborate forms.

We'll start by explaining how to create a blank table and how to edit and format it. At the end of this chapter, we'll show you how to create a table from existing text.

Creating a Table

Suppose you need to create a two-column table like the one shown in Figure 11-1 on the next page. Although this is a simple table, notice that the text in the second column wraps to the next line. You could create this effect using tabs, but the table feature makes this type of formatting much easier.

FIGURE 11-1

The Table menu
commands make it
easy to create tables
like this one.

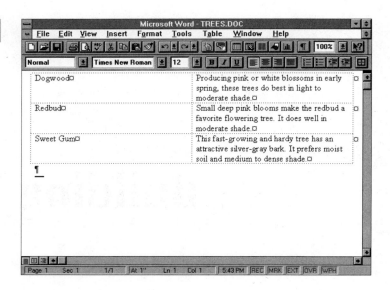

How to create a table with menu commands

To create a table, place the cursor where you want the table to appear, and
choose Table Insert Table. Word will open the Insert Table dialog box,
shown in Figure 11-2. As you can see, Word suggests two columns and two
rows. For our sample table, two columns is the right number, but you'll need
to change the Number Of Rows setting to 3.

FIGURE 11-2

When you choose
Table Insert Table,
Word displays this
dialog box.

Before you choose the Table Insert Table command, be sure that
you haven't highlighted any text—not even a space or a paragraph mark. If you have made a selection, Word will assume that
you want to convert the selection to a table (a topic we'll discuss
later in this chapter) and will create a table that will probably not
be what you want.

The Insert Table dialog box also lets you specify a column width. The default setting, Auto, tells Word to determine column width by dividing the total width of the text area by the number of columns. If you're using Word's default settings, with a 6-inch width for single-column text, each column in a two-column table will be approximately 3 inches wide. For now, you can use the Auto setting. To accept the settings in the Insert Table dialog box, choose OK. Word will close the dialog box and insert a table in your document, as shown in Figure 11-3.

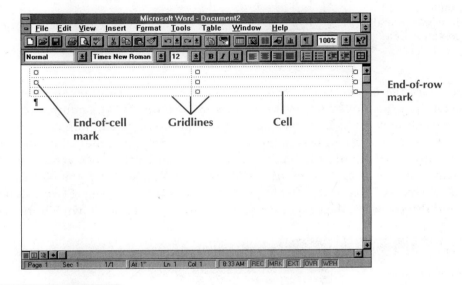

FIGURE 11-3

We used the Table Insert Table command to create this blank table.

If you insert a table into a document that itself has a multicolumn format, Word will determine the table's column width by dividing the width of the current text area by the number of columns in the table. For example, if you're working in a three-column document whose columns are 2 inches wide and you insert a two-column table using the Auto setting, Word will insert a table with two 1-inch-wide columns.

How to create a table with a toolbar button

For mouse users, there's an even easier way to insert a table. If you click on the Table button on the Standard toolbar to create a new table, Word will display a small representation of a table, as shown in Figure 11-4.

When you click on the Table button, Word will show you a small representation of a table.

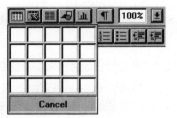

Use the mouse to select the number of rows and columns to create. As you drag the mouse across the grid, Word will display the number of rows and columns (in RxC format) below the grid. If you need more rows or columns than Word displays in the initial grid, simply drag the pointer beyond the grid, and Word will expand it, as shown in Figure 11-5. When you release the mouse button, Word will insert the table, just as if you had chosen Table Insert Table and set Column Width to Auto. If you select two columns and three rows in the grid, the result will match the table shown Figure 11-3.

If you need a table larger than the grid Word initially displays, simply drag the pointer beyond the grid.

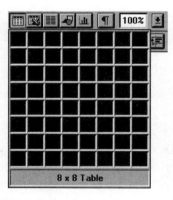

Getting your bearings

There's another way to insert a table, but it will be easier to understand certain aspects of it if we first take a look at the table you've just inserted. The blank table shown in Figure 11-3 includes *gridlines* that show the rows and columns of the table. These gridlines also define a set of boxes, or *cells*—a term borrowed from spreadsheet programs. Each cell is defined by both the row and the column in which it is located.

Although you can turn the gridlines on or off, you'll most often want them on while you're working with a table. Without them, it can be difficult to visualize some important characteristics of the table, such as column width, row alignment, and row height. If your screen isn't showing these gridlines, choose Table Gridlines. (Alternatively, if you're working in Page Layout view, you can check the Text Boundaries check box on the Tools Options View card. But this option will show all text boundaries, not only the table gridlines.)

As you can see in Figure 11-3, each cell in the table contains an *end-of-cell mark*. The mark is similar in concept to a paragraph mark in that it shows how far the text in that cell extends. It's also similar in that Word will display the end-of-cell mark only if you've set the program to display paragraph marks, either by clicking on the Show/Hide ¶ button on the Standard toolbar or by choosing Tools Options View and then checking the Paragraph Marks check box. When there is no text in a cell, the end-of-cell mark appears at the left side of the cell. An identical character, the *end-of-row mark*, appears at the right of each row. As we'll demonstrate later in this chapter, this mark becomes important when you want to add a new column to the right edge of a table.

Word will not display a paragraph mark in a cell unless you add one by pressing Enter. Nevertheless, Word treats the text in separate cells as separate paragraphs for formatting and navigation purposes. The end-of-cell mark, then, defines both the end of the cell and the end of the last paragraph of text in a cell.

Word will not include the gridlines, end-of-cell marks, or end-of-row marks in a printed document. However, if you want to print gridlines with a table, you can do so by adding borders. We'll show you how later in this chapter; see "Adding Borders and Shading in a Table" on page 407.

How to create and format a table with the Table Wizard

The third way to create a table is with Word's Table Wizard. This wizard is an automated tool for creating tables complete with standard layouts and the most common row and column headings, such as years, months, or days of the week.

To use the Table Wizard, you can choose File New and choose Table Wizard as the template. Word will then open a new file and start the wizard. Most often, however, you'll want to create a table in an existing file. To do this, simply position the cursor where you want the table to appear, choose Table Insert Table, and then choose the Wizard button in the Insert Table dialog box to start the Table Wizard. Figure 11-6 shows the wizard's first dialog box.

FIGURE 11-6

The Table Wizard's first dialog box lets you choose a layout for the table grid.

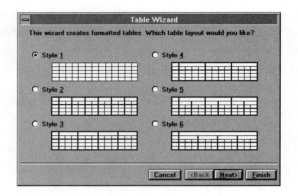

Although at first glance the choices in this dialog box might seem to be among various patterns of borders you might use in a table, in fact none of these choices adds borders. Rather, they offer various arrangements of columns in which two or more columns in the body of the table can be grouped under a single cell in the table header.

Style 1 in the dialog box, for example, doesn't group columns together (and is the appropriate choice for our sample table). Style 3 groups three columns together—columns 2, 3, and 4; columns 5, 6, and 7; and so on—with each group under a single cell in the first row. You might use this layout to show monthly figures grouped by quarters, with headings in the first row specifying 1st Quarter, 2d Quarter, and so on, and headings in the second row indicating months. Style 6 is similar to Style 3, but it groups four sets of three columns under each cell in the first row, with each trio of columns grouped under one cell in the second row. You can use this layout to indicate a year in the first row, a quarter in the second, and a month in the third.

The rest of the Table Wizard is self-explanatory. After you pick a style and choose the Next button to go to the next dialog box, the choices are straightforward. Briefly, you can decide the following:

- Whether to include column headings, with possible choices for months, quarters, days of the week, numbers, or years, depending on the table style

- Whether to repeat column headings on each page if the table is longer than one page

- How to align column headings (left, right, or center)
- Whether to include row headings, with the same set of choices available for column headings
- How to align row headings
- How to format cells in the body of the table (as right-aligned or decimal-aligned numbers or as left-aligned or centered text)
- Whether to print the table in portrait or in landscape mode

You simply move through the dialog boxes and make your choices. Note that the specific set of dialog boxes and options Word displays can vary. For example, if you choose not to include column headings, the Table Wizard will not ask you how to align them.

To create our sample table, pick Style 1 in the Table Wizard's first dialog box. Then choose no column headings and set the number of columns to 2. Choose no row headings and set the number of rows to 3. Specify that most table cells will be left-aligned text, and specify portrait orientation.

> The Table Wizard will be most helpful for creating tables that can take advantage of the standard layouts or the wizard's ability to automatically enter such headings as quarters, months, or days of the week. If you're using Style 1 and simply entering the number of columns and rows, however, it's more efficient to use the Insert Table dialog box or the Table button on the Standard toolbar.

If you use a particular table layout very often—for a monthly report, for example—you might want to store it as AutoText rather than generating it from scratch each time. You can store any table as an AutoText entry, not only those you generate with the wizard. For details on Word's AutoText feature, see "Using AutoText" on page 140.

How to use Table AutoFormat— with or without the Table Wizard

After you finish defining a table with the Table Wizard, but before the wizard inserts the table into your document, the wizard will start Word's Table AutoFormat feature, which opens the dialog box shown in Figure 11-7 on the next page.

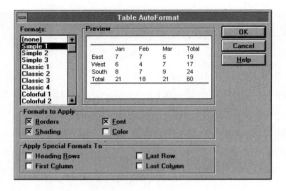

FIGURE 11-7

The Table AutoFormat dialog box will let you add a wide range of attractive formats to your table with minimum work.

Whether you prefer adding such formatting as borders, shading, and font enhancements to your table as a first step or as a final flourish—or whether you choose to make these additions at all—is strictly a matter of taste. Word will let you ignore the Table AutoFormat feature altogether, even when you are using the Table Wizard; simply choose Cancel to close the dialog box without adding formatting. You can also take advantage of the feature—to add, change, or remove formatting—at any time.

You can open the Table AutoFormat dialog box from the Insert Table dialog box by choosing the AutoFormat button. When you finish with AutoFormat, Word will return you to the Insert Table dialog box, where you can choose OK to insert the table, complete with the format you've defined. In addition, you can open the Table AutoFormat dialog box at any time by placing your cursor or selection in a table and choosing Table Table AutoFormat. When you use either of these two methods, the dialog box will contain an additional button—the AutoFit button—in the Formats To Apply group.

Using the Table AutoFormat feature is extremely straightforward. The Formats list box in the upper left portion of the dialog box lists 34 predefined formats. When you highlight a format name from the list, the Preview box shows what that choice will look like, using sample data. If you select None, Word formats your table with no borders or shading.

You can't add custom choices to the Formats list, but you actually get far more than 34 formats since you can vary each one by using the check boxes in the bottom half of the dialog box. To give you some sense of the variety of choices, Figure 11-8 shows the Preview box for several predefined formats, with all check boxes checked. Figure 11-9 on page 370 shows the Preview box for a single format, with different combinations of check boxes checked.

FIGURE 11-8

These sample previews indicate the range of predefined table formats Word offers.

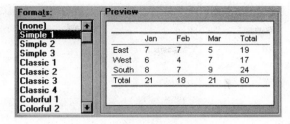

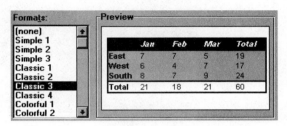

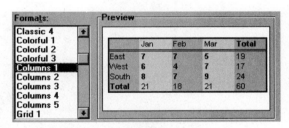

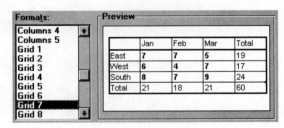

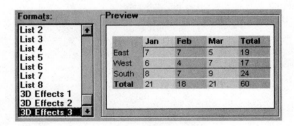

FIGURE 11-9

These sample previews
indicate the variety
available when you
check different com-
binations of check
boxes with a single
predefined table
format.

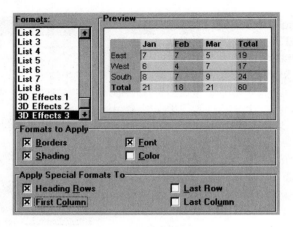

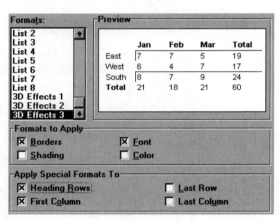

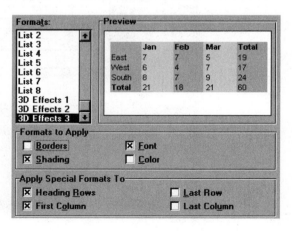

The check boxes are divided into two groups. The choices in the Apply Special Formats To group toggle formatting on or off for a specific part of the table: Heading Rows, First Column, Last Row, or Last Column. For example, if the format defines both bold and shading for the heading rows (the rows Word identifies as part of the table heading) and you clear the Heading Rows check box, you'll turn off both shading and bold for the heading rows without removing shading or bold from any other part of the table.

The choices in the Formats To Apply group toggle specific kinds of formatting on or off for the entire table. The Borders (lines around or between cells), Shading, and Font (enhancements such as bold and italic) options are self-explanatory. Color is of interest only if you have a color printer.

AutoFit, which is not available if you're creating a table with the Table Wizard, adjusts column width. If there isn't much text in any cell in a given column, this option will set the column to be just wide enough for the widest line of text. If there's a great deal of text, AutoFit will adjust the column to use as few lines as possible.

The formatting you add with the Table AutoFormat feature is automatically applied, but it will not automatically change as you change the table in your document. If you apply the AutoFit option, for example, and then change the text in the table, the column width will not change. However, it is easy enough to move your cursor to the table and choose Table Table AutoFormat at any time to reapply a format.

Note too that you can take advantage of AutoFit even if you don't want to add borders or shading. AutoFit is also available on the Column card in the Cell Height And Width dialog box, which is opened from the Table menu.

Using the Ruler with a Table

As you work with tables, you'll probably want to use Word's ruler. You'll need to know about some special features of the ruler as it applies to tables.

If you're familiar with Word 2.0, you'll quickly find that Word 6.0 uses the ruler in tables in a somewhat different fashion. But most of the differences are cosmetic rather than functional, so you shouldn't find the new ruler features difficult to learn. For those few cases in which the behavior of the ruler has changed—for example, when adjusting cell width—we've marked the appropriate paragraphs as new features.

Figure 11-10 shows the same blank table you saw in Figure 11-3, with the ruler displayed and the cursor in the first cell of the first row. When you move the cursor to a table, Word will automatically set the ruler for the table, as shown in Figure 11-10.

FIGURE 11-10

When the cursor is in a table, the ruler marks the table and cell boundaries.

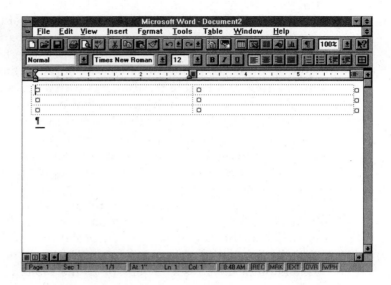

The ruler works much the same way for a table as it does for standard text. When you're working in a table, the ruler scale shows the width of the text area, with the left edge of the text area beginning at the zero point on the ruler and the right edge marked by a vertical line and by a change in color from white to gray (assuming the Windows default colors). In addition, the ruler marks the boundary of each column with a crosshatch pattern that looks like small bumps. For most columns, these boundary markers are contained in a small rectangle. For the rightmost column, the marker appears just to the right of the right margin boundary. For the leftmost column, the marker is just to the left of the left margin boundary and will usually be hidden in Normal view (although visible in Page Layout view) unless you scroll the page horizontally.

When you move the mouse pointer over these markers or just to the left of the leftmost boundary, the pointer will change to an arrow pointing left and right, and you can drag to change column width, as we'll discuss later. (If you drag the left-and-right arrow, the left indent marker, or the first-line indent marker to the left edge of the Word window, Word will scroll the screen to the right and you'll be able to see the boundary marker.)

In Figure 11-10, for example, the cursor is in the first cell of the table. The text area of this cell begins at the zero point on the ruler, which is 0.075 inch from the left edge of the cell as defined by the gridlines. The marker for the right side of the current cell is at 2.925 inches, or 0.075 inch from the beginning of the text area in the second column. This 0.075-inch offset on each side results from Word automatically adding space to create what amounts to a gutter between columns. We'll talk more about this space later, but for now note that the small rectangles containing the boundary markers on the ruler indicate the size of these gutters. Also notice that the left, right, and first-line indent markers in Figure 11-10 indicate the text area for the cell in which the cursor is located. If you move the cursor to the second column, the ruler will show the indent markers for the cell in that column instead.

Entering Text in a Table

Entering text in a table is just like entering any other text: Simply move the cursor where you want to place the text, and start typing. The text will appear in the Normal style for the current document unless you've assigned a different format. (In our sample table, the Normal style calls for a 12-point Times Roman font, aligned flush left.)

To create the sample table shown in Figure 11-1 and again here in Figure 11-11, use the arrow keys or the mouse to move the cursor to the first cell of the blank table you inserted earlier in this chapter (shown in Figure 11-10), and type *Dogwood*. Then move to the second cell by pressing the Right arrow key or the Tab key or by pointing and clicking with the mouse, and type the text for that cell. (We'll talk more about navigation techniques in the following section.) To finish, simply repeat these steps until you've filled in the table to match the sample shown in Figure 11-11.

FIGURE 11-11

Word will wrap text within each cell of a table.

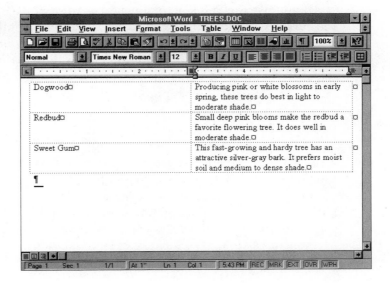

If the text you enter is longer than the width of the current cell, Word will wrap the text within the cell, as you can see in Figure 11-11, and will increase the height of the cell to accommodate multiple lines of text. Notice that Word automatically increases the height of the adjacent cell in the first column as well, even though it contains only one line of text.

Navigating in a Table

You have several choices for moving around in a table. In addition to using the mouse to click on the cell you want to work in, you can use the Tab key or the arrow keys to move from cell to cell. If you use the Left or Right arrow key, the cursor will move through the text in each cell, going to the next cell in the same row when it reaches the beginning or end of the text in the current cell. When the cursor reaches the end of a row, it will make an extra stop at the end-of-row mark before moving to a cell in the next row.

If you use the Up or Down arrow key, the cursor will move through the lines of text in the current cell, going to the next cell above or below after the last line of text in the current cell.

Since Word treats each end-of-cell mark as a paragraph, you can also press Ctrl-Up arrow key or Ctrl-Down arrow key to move between cells. If a cell contains more than one paragraph, Word will move the cursor one paragraph at a time within the cell before it moves to the next paragraph in the next cell. If each cell contains only one paragraph, the cursor will move forward or backward one cell with each keystroke. Here again, the cursor will make an extra stop at the end-of-row mark in each row, treating it as a separate paragraph.

If you use the Tab key to move forward or Shift-Tab to move backward, the cursor will move from cell to cell, highlighting all the text in the cell it moves to and skipping over the end-of-row marks when moving between the last cell in one row and the first cell in the next. When you're in a cell with selected text, pressing the Left arrow key will remove the highlight and leave the cursor at the beginning of the text in that cell. Pressing the Right arrow key will remove the highlight and leave the cursor at the end of the text in that cell.

If you're in the last cell of the last row of the table, pressing Tab will add a new row to the end of the table. However, if the cursor is in the first cell of the first row of the table, pressing Shift-Tab will have no effect.

Figure 11-12 summarizes the keyboard shortcuts for moving around in a table, including some navigation shortcuts we haven't mentioned here and some other kinds of shortcuts we'll cover later in this chapter.

This Key Combination...	Does This...
Tab	Moves right one cell *or* moves to the first cell in the next row if currently in the last cell of a row *or* creates a new row if currently in the last cell of the last row of the table. Selects all text in the cell it moves to.
Shift-Tab	Moves left one cell *or* moves to the last cell in the previous row if currently in the first cell of a row *or* does nothing if currently in the first cell of the table. Selects all text in the cell it moves to.
Ctrl-Up arrow key	Moves to the next cell (or next paragraph within the current cell).
Ctrl-Down arrow key	Moves to the previous cell (or the previous paragraph within the current cell).
Alt-Home	Moves to the first cell in the current row.
Alt-End	Moves to the last cell in the current row.
Alt-PgUp	Moves to the first cell in the current column.
Alt-PgDn	Moves to the last cell in the current column.
Alt-NumPad5 (5 on the numeric keypad)	Selects the entire table. (Use Alt-Shift-NumPad5 if Num Lock is active.)
Ctrl-Shift-Enter	Splits the table into two tables, inserting a paragraph mark above the row in which the cursor is currently located.

FIGURE 11-12

Keyboard shortcuts for navigating in and working with a table.

Selecting Text in a Table

In most ways, selecting text in a table is just like selecting text in any other part of a document. For example, you can use mouse techniques such as dragging to select text, double-clicking on a word, and so on. With the keyboard, you can hold down the Shift key or press F8 (Extend Selection) and then define the selection with the arrow keys.

Whenever you select text in two or more cells, Word will highlight those cells in their entirety. If you highlight the last word in a cell, for example, and extend the selection to the next cell, Word will select all the text in both cells as soon as you cross the cell boundary.

With any of these techniques, if you start and end the selection in two cells in the same column, Word will select text in that column only. If you want to select text in two or more columns, you need to start the selection in one column and end it in another. The cells you start and end with will define opposite corners for the selected block—either the upper left and lower right corners or the upper right and lower left. Word will select all text in all cells in a rectangle defined by that block.

Word also provides menu commands for selecting text in a table. With the cursor anywhere in the row or column you want to select, choose Table Select Row or Table Select Column, as appropriate. If you select several cells in a column before choosing Table Select Row, Word will select all the rows in which you've selected cells. Similarly, if you select several cells in a row before choosing Table Select Column, Word will select all the columns in which you've selected cells. Choose Table Select Table to select the entire table.

Special table selection techniques for the mouse

Word also offers several special mouse techniques for selecting text in a table. These all take advantage of the same underlying feature: Each cell, row, or column in a table has its own invisible selection bar, just as each paragraph outside a table has its own invisible selection bar.

If you move the mouse pointer to the left edge of a cell, it changes to a right-arrow pointer, as shown in Figure 11-13, indicating that the pointer is in the cell's selection bar. Similarly, if you move the pointer to the left of the leftmost boundary of the table, it also changes to a right-arrow pointer, indicating that it is in the row's selection bar. If you move the pointer to the top of a column, it changes to a down-arrow pointer, as shown in Figure 11-14, indicating that it is in the column's selection bar.

FIGURE 11-13

You can select a row in a table by double-clicking in the selection bar for any cell in that row. The right-arrow pointer in column 2 indicates that the mouse pointer is in the cell's selection bar.

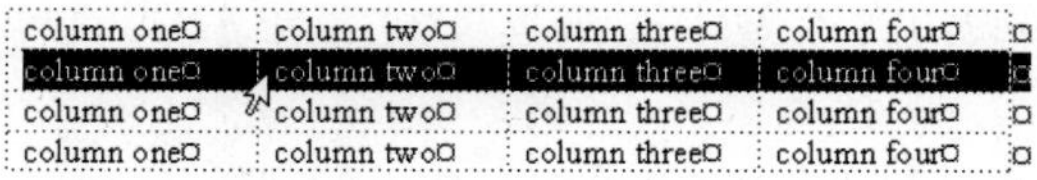

FIGURE 11-14

The down-arrow pointer indicates that the pointer is in the selection bar for the second column.

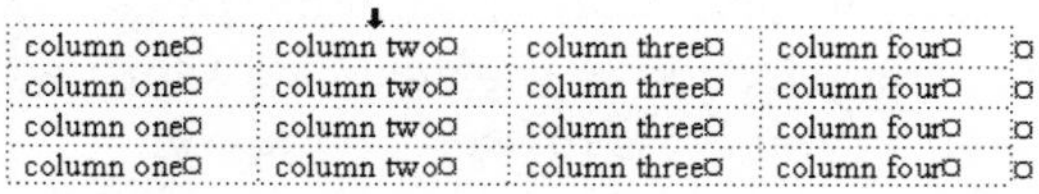

You can select the contents of a cell by clicking once anywhere in the cell's selection bar. To select an entire row, click once in the row selection bar, or double-click in the selection bar for any cell in that row. To select an entire column, place the pointer in the column selection bar and click. To select an entire table, position the pointer in any cell or row selection bar, hold down the Ctrl key, and click.

Special table selection techniques for the keyboard

As already mentioned, when you move to a cell with the Tab key, Word highlights the text in that cell. In addition, the standard keyboard techniques for selecting text work well within a table, especially if you combine them with the shortcut navigation techniques for tables.

For example, to select an entire column, you can press Alt-PgUp to move to the beginning of the first cell in a column, F8 to turn on the Extend Selection feature, and then Alt-PgDn to highlight the entire column. Similarly, you can press Alt-Home to move to the leftmost cell in a row, F8 to turn on Extend Selection, and then Alt-End to select the entire row. In either case, after the row or column is selected, Extend Selection is still turned on, so you can move left and right, or up and down, to make the selection larger or smaller. To select the entire table, be sure that Num Lock is off and press Alt-NumPad5 (5 on the numeric keypad); if Num Lock is on, press Alt-Shift-NumPad5.

Changing the Layout of a Table

After you create a table, you will often want to change its appearance by altering the width of one or more columns, changing the spacing between columns, or adding and deleting rows and columns. In fact, you may want to use a different number of columns in different parts of the table. You may also want to change the alignment of some of the rows. Word will let you make any of these changes. We'll start with a look at how to change width.

How to adjust cell and column width

The techniques for changing the width of a cell and those for changing the width of a column are essentially the same. Changing the width of an entire column is simply a matter of changing the width of all the cells it contains.

How to change cell or column width with the mouse

To change cell width using the mouse, first select the cell you want to change. Next move the pointer over the left or right cell boundary, as appropriate, until it changes to a vertical split pointer. Then hold down the left mouse button and drag the gridline to a new position. Alternatively, you can highlight the cell, move the pointer to the cell's boundary marker on the ruler, and drag the marker to the new position. In either case, Word will ignore other cells in the column and will adjust width only for the row of the highlighted cell. What happens within that row is a bit more complicated.

If you drag to the left, you'll be able to move only to the maximum position in the next cell to the left. (Note that the maximum position is defined by the text area of the cell rather than by the cell boundary or the gridline.) The only change in width will be for the highlighted cell and the cell to the immediate left or right of the boundary you are moving.

If you drag the left boundary to the right, you'll get much the same effect, adjusting only the single boundary. When you reach the maximum position for the right side of the highlighted cell, however, you'll find that you can move past that point. If you do so, the highlighted cell will be at its minimum possible size when you stop and release the mouse button, and all the cells to the right will simply be pushed to the right, maintaining their previous widths.

If you drag the right boundary to the right, you will once again adjust only the one boundary between two cells until you reach the maximum position in the cell to the right. If you drag farther, the width of the highlighted cell will be extended to the position where you stop, the cell to the right will be at its minimum possible size, and all cells farther to the right will be pushed to the right while maintaining their previous widths.

Figure 11-15 shows a four-column table. We've widened the first cell in the second row so that its right boundary falls just a little to the right of most of the cells in the first column. Notice that the rightmost cell in the second row is still even with most of the rest of the table. We've also widened the first cell in the fifth row so that its right boundary falls to the right of the cells in the second column. Notice that the second cell in the fifth row is at its minimum size and that the rightmost cell has been pushed to the right of the rest of the table.

If you want to change the width of two or more cells in a column, but not the width of the entire column, select the cells you want to change before you adjust the size.

FIGURE 11-15

When you adjust the
width of a single cell,
Word will reposition
other cells in that row if
you drag beyond the
maximum position of
the next cell to the right.

To adjust the width of the entire column following the set of rules we just
described, select the entire column before dragging. You can also adjust column width using a slightly different set of rules if you simply drag any
column boundary, with nothing selected. Word will leave the right edge of the
table unchanged and will adjust all columns to the right proportionately. If you
drag to the right until all the columns are at their minimum size, however, Word
will then push the right edge of the table to the right as you drag still farther.

> If you've selected a column containing cells of different widths,
> Word will adjust all cells whose boundaries are in the same or
> nearly the same position as the boundary you're dragging. If you
> haven't selected any cells in the table, Word will adjust all bound-
> aries to the right of the one you move, whether the boundaries are
> in the same position or not.

How to change cell or column width with the Table Cell Height And Width command

You can also adjust cell or column width with the Table Cell Height And
Width command. Like many other formatting commands, this command allows more precise control than dragging with the mouse.

Before choosing the Table Cell Height And Width command, you need to
indicate which cells or columns will be affected by the settings. If you want
to adjust one column only, you can select the column or simply place the
cursor in any cell in that column. If you want to adjust specific cells only or
to adjust more than one column, highlight the cell, cells, or columns you
want to adjust. After you've indicated the cells or columns to change, choose
Table Cell Height And Width to open the dialog box shown in Figure 11-16
on the next page. You can also open this dialog box by double-clicking on
a boundary marker.

Choose Table Cell
Height And Width to
open the Cell Height
And Width dialog box.

Cell Height and Width

Row   Column

Width of Column 2: `1"`

Space Between Columns: `0.15"`

OK

Cancel

AutoFit

Previous Column   Next Column   Help

As the name implies, you can adjust both height and width in this dialog
box. For the moment, we're concerned only with column width, so the relevant settings are on the Column card. Notice that the first text box is labeled
Width Of Column 2. The column number in this label will change depending
on where the cursor or selection is located. If you've selected cells in columns 1 and 2, for example, the label will become Width Of Columns 1–2.

Normally, the Width Of Column text box will show the width of the current cell or cells. However, if you've selected two or more cells of different
widths, the text box will be blank.

To change the width of the column, cell, or cells you've indicated, enter a
measurement in the Width Of Column text box. You can type the measurement, you can click on the arrows at the right of the text box, or you can
move to the text box and press the Up or Down arrow key to change the
setting in increments of 0.1 inch. When you're finished, choose OK. You can
type the measurement in inches, centimeters, points, or picas. If you don't
specify a unit of measure (by typing *in* or *"*, *cm*, *pt*, or *pi*), Word will use
whatever unit you've chosen as your default measurement unit on the Tools
Options General card.

If you select Auto for the width, with cells in more than one column selected (but not including the last column), Word will leave the left and right
boundaries of the selection in place and adjust the cells within the selection
so that the cells are of equal width. If the left and right boundaries vary for
rows within the selection, Word will make the adjustment independently for
each row. If you include cells from the last column, Word will move the right
boundary of the table to the right indent and then adjust the width of the
cells so that they are equal within the new boundaries.

The AutoFit button. The AutoFit button, located below the OK and Cancel
buttons, works essentially the same way as the AutoFit button in the Table
AutoFormat dialog box that we've already discussed. Briefly, if you choose
this button, Word will adjust the column widths based on the contents of
the cells. Note that the automatic adjustment will vary depending on how

much of the table, and which parts of the table, you've selected. For consistently predictable results, we suggest that you use the AutoFit button only when you've selected the entire table.

The Previous Column and Next Column buttons. At the bottom of the Column card in the Cell Height And Width dialog box are two buttons labeled Previous Column and Next Column. You can use these to set the size for other columns without leaving the dialog box. When you choose the Next Column button, Word will set the width for the current column (or the currently highlighted cell or cells), move one column to the right, and display the new width in the Width Of Column text box. Similarly, when you choose the Previous Column button, Word will set the width for the current column (or the currently highlighted cell or cells), move the selection one column to the left, and display the new width.

If you have selected two or more cells in a column and you choose the Next Column or the Previous Column button, Word will select cells in the same rows when you move to the next or previous column. For example, if you've selected the second and third cells in column 2, Word will select the second and third cells in column 1 or column 3. If you select an entire column before opening the dialog box, choosing Previous Column or Next Column will select the entire neighboring column.

If you choose the Next Column button when you're in the last column of the table, Word will move to the first column of the table. Similarly, if you choose Previous Column when you're in the first column, Word will move to the last column in the table. In all cases, the selection, if any, will remain in the same row or rows.

How to adjust the space between columns

The Column card of the Cell Height And Width dialog box contains one other text box, labeled Space Between Columns. As we've already mentioned, Word automatically defines some space between the text in each column of a table when you create the table. This space is indicated on your screen by the distance between the left cell boundary and the beginning of your text, or between the cell boundary and the end-of-cell mark. As you enter text, you'll see that Word also leaves blank space between the last character on each line and the right cell boundary.

Word's default spacing between columns is 0.15 inch, as you can see when you create a new table, choose Table Cell Height And Width, and then the Column card to see the setting in the Space Between Columns text box.

This setting can be confusing. It affects entire rows, not only the currently selected cells. And because it always affects the leftmost cell in a row, it has the effect of changing the position of the row's gridlines, as well as leaving more room between the edge of the text and the gridlines. If you increase the setting, for example, you won't see any change in the width of your table cells, but you will notice that Word shifts the cell boundaries to the left and repositions the text within the cell, changing the way the text wraps.

The way Word allocates the space between columns is also a little different from what you might expect. Word divides the value in the text box between the two ends of each cell in a row. For example, if you've specified 0.5 inch as your Space Between Columns setting for a given row, Word will assign 0.25 inch to each side of each cell in that row. And you won't be able to enter text in these areas unless you change the indents for that text. (More on this subject later.) Note that Word inserts a 0.25-inch space at the left edge of the first cell in the row and at the right edge of the last cell. Obviously, this space does not fall between columns, despite the name of the setting.

To get a better handle on the Space Between Columns setting, look at the ruler shown in Figure 11-17. The four-column table in the figure contains four 1-inch-wide columns and is formatted with the default Space Between Columns setting of 0.15 inch.

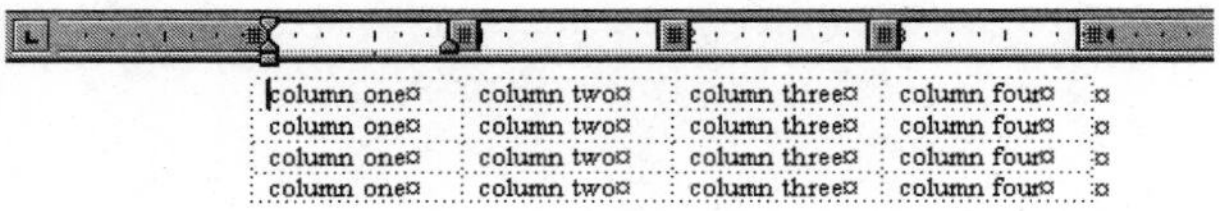

FIGURE 11-17

This table is formatted with the default Space Between Columns setting of 0.15 inch.

As the ruler in Figure 11-17 shows, the width of the text area in the current cell is slightly less than 1 inch, extending from the zero point on the ruler to the vertical line on the ruler and the end of the white area. This width reflects the width of the cell (1.1 inches) minus the default space between columns (0.15 inch).

As Figure 11-17 also shows, the gridline marking the left boundary of the table falls to the left of the zero point on the ruler. However, the cursor (and the text in the first column of the table) is aligned with the zero point. The space between the table's left boundary line and the left edge of the text in each cell is half of the 0.15-inch setting for Space Between Columns—the space that Word has allotted to the left end of the cell.

Now consider what happens when you increase the Space Between Columns setting to 0.5 inch. If you select all the cells in one column, open the Cell Height And Width dialog box, enter *.5"* in the Space Between Columns text box, and choose OK, you'll get the result shown in Figure 11-18. As you can see, the left boundary of the table is shifted farther left. With the increased Space Between Columns setting, Word allocates 0.25 inch of space to each end of each cell and shifts all column boundaries to the left.

FIGURE 11-18

This is the table shown in Figure 11-17, after the Space Between Columns setting is increased to 0.5 inch.

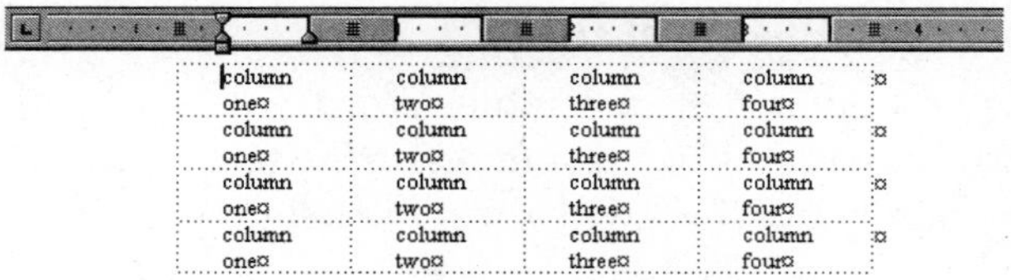

When you increase the space between columns, Word does not change the relative alignment of the text in the table. Notice that the cursor and the leftmost text in the first cell are still aligned with the zero point on the ruler. Similarly, the left edge of the text in each column has retained its original alignment. However, the text area on the ruler is now only 0.5 inch wide for each cell, reflecting the 1-inch column width minus the 0.5-inch space between columns. As a result, Word had to wrap the text in each cell to a new line. Notice also how much larger the gray rectangles between columns on the ruler have become in Figure 11-18.

Key points about table column spacing. If you're finding this discussion of column spacing confusing, you're not alone. But if you keep just a few key points in mind, you should be able to adjust the space between columns to suit your needs:

- Remember that Word subtracts the Space Between Columns setting from the cell width. The text area is the remaining space in the cell.

- Word creates space between columns by allotting blank space at both ends of each cell in a row. This space appears at the beginning of the first cell in a row as well as at the end of the last cell in a row.

- Changing the Space Between Columns setting does not affect the horizontal alignment of text in a row. It may, however, change the way Word wraps text and breaks lines within each cell as the text area increases or decreases when you change the setting.

- Keep in mind that the setting Space Between Columns is a bit of a misnomer. In truth, the measurement used for this setting is not the spacing between columns but rather is twice the distance between the text and either the left or the right cell boundary.

As you'll see later in this chapter, you can use paragraph formatting to change the alignment of text within cells (and of individual paragraphs in the same cell). And by changing the paragraph indents, you can also move text into the blank area that Word allots at each end of a cell.

How to adjust row height

As you enter text in a table, Word will automatically adjust the height of individual rows to accommodate the text. Both the size of the characters and the number of lines will affect the height of a row. In the sample table shown in both Figure 11-1 and Figure 11-11, notice how Word adjusts the height for all the cells in each row to accommodate the second column. If you reformatted the text with a larger point size, Word would increase the row height even more.

Word also lets you increase the height of rows manually to allow more space between the text in adjacent rows. For example, to increase the height of the second row in our sample table, select either or both cells in row 2, choose Table Cell Height And Width, and choose the Row card, shown in Figure 11-19.

Notice that the Height Of Row drop-down list is labeled to indicate the row or rows that the settings will affect. If the cursor is located anywhere in the table (with no selection), the settings will apply to all rows, and the label will reflect that. If the cursor is located in our sample table, for instance, the label will read Height Of Rows 1–3. If you select a cell in one or more rows before opening the dialog box, the list box label will indicate those rows— select a cell in row 2 only, for example, and the label will read Height Of Row 2; select cells in rows 1 and 2, and the label will read Height Of Rows 1–2.

When you open the Height Of Row drop-down list, you'll see three choices for specifying row height: Auto, At Least, and Exactly. Auto, the default setting, lets Word determine row height. At Least sets a minimum size that Word will not go below but tells Word to automatically increase row height if needed. Exactly tells Word to use the setting exactly as given, even if some of the text in the cell won't be displayed or printed.

For this example (in which you've selected one or both cells in row 2), you can select the At Least setting, enter .75" in the At text box, and choose OK. Figure 11-20 shows the result of the new setting for row 2. You can set the height by typing the measurement, by clicking on the arrows at the right of the text box, or by moving to the text box and pressing the Up or Down arrow key to change the height in increments of 1 point. You can type any measurement that Word recognizes: *in* or " for inches, *cm* for centimeters, *pt* for points, or *pi* for picas. The next time you open the Row card, however, Word will show the setting in points.

FIGURE 11-19

Choose Table Cell
Height And Width, and
then choose the Row
card to see the settings
for row height.

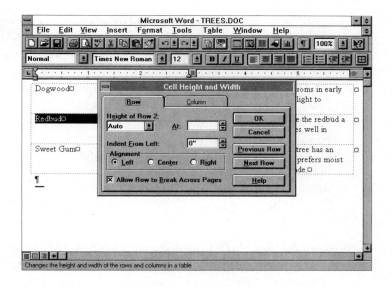

FIGURE 11-20

This is our sample table
of tree information
after the height is
increased for the
second row.

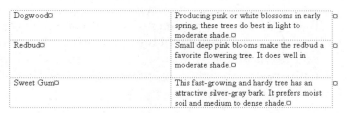

When Word increases row height, it inserts the additional space
below the text. If you want space above the text, use the Before
setting in the Paragraph dialog box. (We'll discuss spacing later in
this chapter.) Notice also that the Height Of Row setting affects all
the cells in a row. Word does not allow cells of different heights in
the same row. To return a row to its default height, choose Table
Cell Height And Width, choose the Row card, and set Height Of
Row to Auto.

How to use the Previous Row and Next Row buttons

On the right side of the Row card in the Cell Height And Width dialog box
are the Previous Row and Next Row buttons. Like the Previous Column and
Next Column buttons on the Column card, these two buttons let you enter
settings for additional rows without leaving the dialog box. When you
choose the Next Row button, Word will set the row height or other settings
for the current row or rows so that you can see the results on the screen.

Word will then move down one row and display the settings for that row in the various text boxes. Similarly, when you choose the Previous Row button, Word will set the changed settings for the current row or rows and move the selection up one row.

If you choose the Next Row button when the cursor is in the bottom row of the table, Word will move to the first row. If you choose the Previous Row button when the cursor is in the top row, Word will move to the last row. If you select two or more rows before opening the Cell Height And Width dialog box, Word will select only a single row when you choose Next Row or Previous Row. After you adjust the settings, you can choose OK to accept all settings and close the dialog box. If you choose Cancel after entering a setting but before moving to a different row, Word will ignore that setting.

How to control whether rows can break across pages

At the bottom of the Row card in the Cell Height And Width dialog box is a check box labeled Allow Row To Break Across Pages. This option determines where Word will position a row if a page break falls in the middle of a row that includes multiple lines of text. If you format any given row by checking this check box, Word will break the text within the row at the page break. If you format the row without checking this check box, Word will move the entire row to the next page when a page break would otherwise fall horizontally within the row.

This setting affects only page breaks that fall within rows, not page breaks that fall between rows. If you want the entire table to stay together, select the table, and choose Format Paragraph. Choose the Text Flow card, and check the Keep Lines Together and Keep With Next check boxes.

How to add rows

As we've already mentioned, you can add a new blank row to the end of a table by placing the cursor anywhere in the rightmost cell of the last row and pressing Tab. The new row will have the same formatting as the last row of the table.

To add a row in any other part of a table, you use either the Table Insert Rows command or the Table Insert Cells command. The difference between inserting a row and inserting an entire row of cells is subtle but real. We'll start with the Table Insert Rows command.

How to add rows with the Table Insert Rows command

NEW!

Suppose you want to add a row between the second and third rows of the table shown in Figure 11-21. Begin by moving to the third row and either selecting nothing or selecting the entire row including the end-of-row mark. Then open the Table menu. As you can see in Figure 11-21, the Insert Rows command has now become the first item on the menu. Choose Insert Rows, and Word will add a new row. You can also add a row by clicking on the Table button on the Standard toolbar. (This button's ToolTip name in fact changes to Insert Rows when the cursor is in a row or when a row is selected.) You can use the context-sensitive menu by pointing to the third row, clicking the right mouse button, and then choosing Insert Rows. Regardless of how you create a new row, Word will insert it just above the row you indicated and will give it the same formatting as that row.

FIGURE 11-21

If you select an entire row or simply place the cursor in a row, the Insert Rows command becomes the first item on the Table menu.

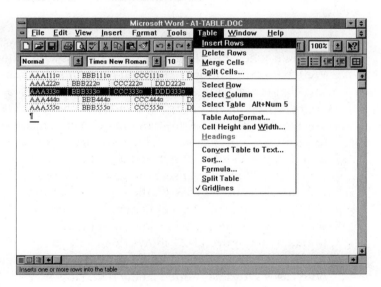

How to add multiple rows

NEW!

You can add two or more rows to a table in one step. First select as many rows—including the end-of-row marks—as you want to insert. For example, if you want to insert three rows, select three. Keep in mind that Word will insert the new rows above the first row you select. After making the selection, choose Table Insert Rows or click on the Table button (whose ToolTip name is now Insert Rows) or use the right mouse button. The new rows will have the same formatting as the top row in your selection.

How to add rows with the Table Insert Cells command

You can also add rows by inserting cells. Once again, suppose you want to add a row between the second and third rows of the table shown in Figure 11-21. This time, begin by selecting the leftmost cell in the third row. Then choose Table Insert Cells or click on the Table toolbar button (whose ToolTip name now becomes Insert Cells). Word will respond with the Insert Cells dialog box, shown in Figure 11-22.

FIGURE 11-22

With the Insert Cells dialog box, you can shift cells right or down or insert entire rows or columns.

```
┌─────────────────────────────────────┐
│ ▭              Insert Cells          │
├─────────────────────────────────────┤
│  ○  Shift Cells Right     ┌────────┐ │
│  ◉  Shift Cells Down      │   OK   │ │
│  ○  Insert Entire Row     ├────────┤ │
│  ○  Insert Entire Column  │ Cancel │ │
│                           ├────────┤ │
│                           │  Help  │ │
│                           └────────┘ │
└─────────────────────────────────────┘
```

As you can see, the Insert Cells dialog box allows you to shift cells right or down when inserting cells. You can also insert entire rows or columns. We'll cover the options of shifting right and inserting columns a little later in this chapter; for now, we'll focus on the other two options.

Selecting Insert Entire Row and then choosing OK is equivalent to choosing the Table Insert Rows command. You can insert rows from the Insert Cells dialog box without having to return to the table and change your selection if you accidentally selected a partial row or rows rather than full rows. As before, Word will insert the new row or rows just above the top row in the selection and will assign the same formatting as that used in the top row.

If you select Shift Cells Down, however, and then choose OK, you will wind up with the top table shown in Figure 11-23. For comparison, the bottom table in Figure 11-23 shows the result you get if you use the Table Insert Rows command instead. If you count the rows in each table, you'll see that in both cases Word has added a new row. However, in the table in which we've inserted cells rather than rows, there are still only two rows—2 and 3—that have a different format from the rest of the rows. When you insert cells rather than rows, Word creates new rows at the *end* of the table, following the format of the last row or rows in the table. In this particular example, if you inserted three rows rather than one, Word would repeat the formats for rows 3, 4, and 5 in the new rows 6, 7, and 8.

Also notice that Word pushes all the text down by as many rows as you've just inserted—but only for those columns in which you selected cells. In the example in Figure 11-23, we had selected a cell only in the first column, so the only text Word pushed down was in the first column.

FIGURE 11-23

If you insert rows with Table Insert Cells and tell Word to shift cells down, as in the top table shown here, Word will add new rows at the end of the table and push the text down for columns where you had selected text.

Row added with Table Insert Cells:¶
¶

AAA111¤	BBB111¤	CCC111¤	DDD111¤	¤
AAA222¤	BBB222¤	CCC222¤	DDD222¤	¤
¤	BBB333¤	CCC333¤	DDD333¤	¤
AAA333¤	BBB444¤	CCC444¤	DDD444¤	¤
AAA444¤	BBB555¤	CCC555¤	DDD555¤	¤
AAA555¤	¤	¤	¤	¤

¶
Row added with Table Insert Rows:¶
¶

AAA111¤	BBB111¤	CCC111¤	DDD111¤	¤
AAA222¤	BBB222¤	CCC222¤	DDD222¤	¤
¤	¤	¤	¤	¤
AAA333¤	BBB333¤	CCC333¤	DDD333¤	¤
AAA444¤	BBB444¤	CCC444¤	DDD444¤	¤
AAA555¤	BBB555¤	CCC555¤	DDD555¤	¤

Like some other issues involved with tables, this difference between inserting rows as rows and inserting rows as cells can be confusing. Just note that in most cases you'll want to insert rows as rows so that you can match the existing rows. Also be aware that you can move and copy rows by using Word's drag-and-drop feature.

How to delete rows

You can delete rows at the beginning, middle, or end of a table.

To delete rows at the beginning or end of a table, simply extend a selection across the top or bottom boundary line of the table into the adjacent body text, and then delete the rows with any of Word's usual deletion commands. If you start by selecting one cell in each row you want to delete, Word will automatically select entire rows as soon as you cross the top or bottom boundary line.

If you want to delete rows from elsewhere in a table, you need to use the Table Delete Rows or the Table Delete Cells command. As is the case when inserting rows and cells, there are some differences between deleting rows and deleting cells. We'll start with the Table Delete Rows command.

How to delete and move rows with the Table Delete Rows command

Deleting rows with the Table Delete Rows command is straightforward. First select the row or rows you want to delete, including the end-of-row marks, and choose Table Delete Rows. Word will delete the selection and will move up any rows below to avoid a gap in the table.

If you accidentally delete rows that you want to keep, you can recover them with the Edit Undo command. However, be aware that Word does not store rows that you delete with the Table Delete Rows command or the contents of rows that you delete by using the Del key or Edit Clear, so you cannot recover these rows by pasting them back into your document from the Clipboard.

In contrast, if you select an entire row (including the end-of-row mark) and choose Edit Cut, Word will delete the row and place it on the Clipboard. (If you don't include the end-of-row mark, Word will delete only the contents of the row.) After you place rows on the Clipboard, you can paste them into another section of the table, or elsewhere in your document, by choosing the Edit Paste Rows command. Note that if you select every cell in the table and then choose Edit Cut, Word will delete the entire table and place it on the Clipboard. This can be handy if you want to move a table. We'll discuss all these possibilities in more depth a little later in this chapter.

There's an easier way to move rows than cutting and pasting. Place the cursor or selection anywhere in the row or rows you want to move, and press Alt-Shift-Up arrow key or Alt-Shift-Down arrow key. Word will select the rows and move them up or down. You can even move rows out of the table this way. Once the selected rows are at the top or bottom of the table, press the key combination one more time to move the rows past the next paragraph immediately above or below the table.

This technique for moving rows also works for moving paragraphs of body text and is related to Word's outlining feature. For this trick to work properly, the Show All toolbar button in Word's Outline view must be selected whether you're using the Outline view or not. This is the default setting, but if you've changed it, you can reset it easily enough: Choose View Outline, and either press Alt-Shift-A or click on the Show All button on the Outlining toolbar. Then return to the view you were working in.

How to delete rows with the Table Delete Cells command

The difference between Table Delete Rows and Table Delete Cells is, fortunately, less confusing than the difference between Table Insert Rows and Table Insert Cells. If you place the cursor or selection in the row or rows you want to delete and then choose Table Delete Cells, you'll see the Delete Cells dialog box, shown in Figure 11-24. Selecting the Delete Entire Row option and choosing OK is equivalent to selecting a row (including the end-of-row mark) and choosing Table Delete Rows. Somewhat surprisingly, you can also get the same result by selecting all the cells in a row or rows without the end-of-row mark, choosing Table Delete Cells, Shift Cells Left, and then OK.

FIGURE 11-24

In the Delete Cells dialog box, you can tell Word to shift cells left or up or to delete entire rows or columns.

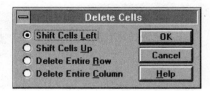

In contrast, if you select all the cells in a row or rows without the end-of-row mark, choose Table Delete Cells, Shift Cells Up, and then OK, Word will not delete any rows. Rather, it will delete the text in the selected cells and move all text up to fill in the now-empty cells. Figure 11-25 shows the results of using the Shift Cells Up option after highlighting the cells in row 3. Notice the newly empty row at the bottom of the table.

FIGURE 11-25

If you select a row (without the end-of-row mark), choose Table Delete Cells, and select Shift Cells Up, Word will delete the text and shift all text up by one row.

AAA111□	BBB111□	CCC111□	DDD111□	□
AAA222□	BBB222□	CCC222□	DDD222□	□
AAA444□	BBB444□	CCC444□	DDD444□	□
AAA555□	BBB555□	CCC555□	DDD555□	□
□	□	□	□	□

How to insert and delete columns

Inserting and deleting columns is similar to inserting and deleting rows. In particular, just as you can add rows to the end of the table or insert them above selected rows, so too can you add columns to the right of the table or insert them before (to the left of) a selected column. We'll start with inserting columns within a table.

How to add a column within a table or to the left side

Suppose you want to insert a new column between the AAA column and the BBB column in the sample table shown in Figure 11-26 on the next page. First select the entire second column. Then open the Table menu. As Figure 11-26 shows, the first two menu items are now the Insert Columns and the Delete Columns commands. Choose Insert Columns, and Word will insert a column to the left of the column you selected.

FIGURE 11-26

When you select one or more columns, Word will display the Insert Columns and the Delete Columns commands on the Table menu.

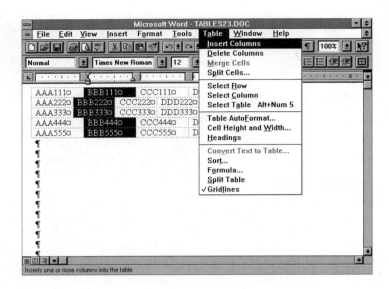

Alternatively, with the column selected, you can insert a new column by clicking on the Table button on the Standard toolbar. (The ToolTip name of this button changes to Insert Columns.) Yet another alternative is to select any part of the column (in this case, simply placing the cursor in the column won't display the proper command), choose Table Insert Cells, Insert Entire Column, and then OK. All of these strategies insert a column to the left of the originally indicated column, which means you can use this technique to add a column to the left side of the table by selecting the first column in the table.

Each cell in the new column will initially have the same width as the cell to its right, as shown in Figure 11-27. However, you can change the width of the cells using any of the techniques described earlier in this chapter. See "How to adjust cell and column width" on page 377.

FIGURE 11-27

When you insert a new column, each cell in the new column will have the same width as the cell in the same row and column that you originally highlighted.

How to add a column to the right side of a table

To add a column to the right side of a table, select the end-of-row marks, as shown in Figure 11-28. Then choose Table Insert Columns or click on the Table button (now named Insert Columns) on the Standard toolbar. Word will add a new column on the right side of the table—or to the left of the end-of-row marks—as shown in Figure 11-29. Each cell in the column will be the same width as the cell to its immediate left.

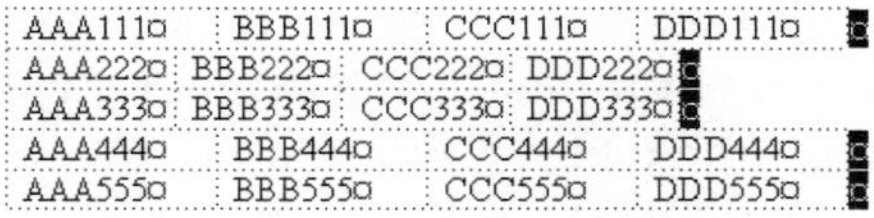

AAA111	BBB111	CCC111	DDD111
AAA222	BBB222	CCC222	DDD222
AAA333	BBB333	CCC333	DDD333
AAA444	BBB444	CCC444	DDD444
AAA555	BBB555	CCC555	DDD555

FIGURE 11-28

To add a column to the right side of a table, first select the end-of-row marks.

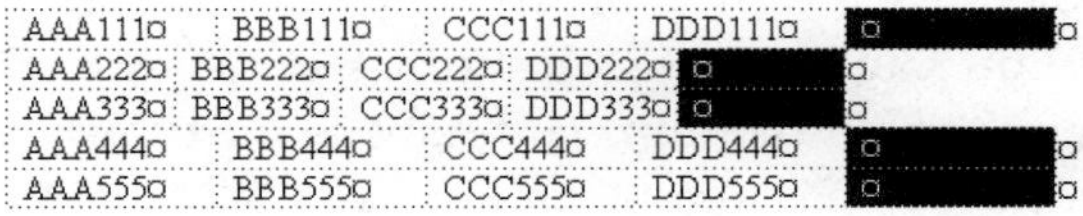

AAA111	BBB111	CCC111	DDD111	
AAA222	BBB222	CCC222	DDD222	
AAA333	BBB333	CCC333	DDD333	
AAA444	BBB444	CCC444	DDD444	
AAA555	BBB555	CCC555	DDD555	

FIGURE 11-29

When adding a column to the right side of a table, Word will set each new cell to the same width as the cell to its immediate left.

How to add multiple columns

You can add multiple adjacent columns much as you add multiple rows. To add multiple columns within a table, first select the number of columns you want to add. If you want to add two new columns, for example, select two existing columns. (If you want to add more columns than you have in the current table, you can select the end-of-row marks to add an extra column.) Next choose Table Insert Columns or click on the Table (Insert Columns) button on the Standard toolbar. Word will insert the columns to the left of the leftmost column you originally selected. Each cell in the new columns will have the same width as the cell to its immediate right.

You cannot append multiple columns to the right edge of a table with a single command. However, since Word leaves the inserted column highlighted, you can first add one column as described in the preceding section and then add more columns by repeatedly choosing Table Insert Columns or repeatedly clicking on the Table (Insert Columns) button on the toolbar.

How to delete and move columns

Deleting a column or columns is straightforward. If you want to get rid of the columns entirely, simply select them and choose Table Delete Columns. Alternatively, you can select one or more cells in the column or columns you want to delete, choose Table Delete Cells, Delete Entire Column, and then OK. Word will delete the selected columns and shift the remaining columns to the left to close any gaps in the table.

If you delete any columns accidentally with these techniques, you can choose Edit Undo to recover them. As is the case with rows, Word does not place deleted columns on the Clipboard when you use these techniques, so you cannot recover the columns by pasting them back into your document. However, if you use Word's Edit Cut command to delete a column, Word does put the column on the Clipboard.

This ability to use the Clipboard comes in handy when you need to move a column to a different place in a table. For example, to move the first column in a four-column table to the third column position, select the column, choose Edit Cut, position the cursor anywhere in the first cell of what will now be the third column, and choose Edit Paste Columns. If Word's drag-and-drop feature is active, you can also select the column, drag it to the new position, and release the mouse button. You can move multiple columns with either of these methods.

How to add and delete cells

You can use the Table Insert Cells and the Table Delete Cells commands for parts of a table that are smaller than an entire row or column. The Shift Cells Right and Shift Cells Down options in the Insert Cells dialog box and the Shift Cells Left and Shift Cells Up options in the Delete Cells dialog box tell Word how to adjust the table when you insert or delete partial rows and columns.

Consider, for example, Figure 11-30, which shows a simple four-column-by-five-row table. To delete the two cells selected in the second row, choose Table Delete Cells to open the Delete Cells dialog box, with the Shift Cells Left option already selected. Choose OK to have the remaining cells in that row shift to the left, resulting in the table shown in Figure 11-31. If you select Shift Cells Up instead, the result is the table shown in Figure 11-32. Notice that in this second case two blank cells appear in the sixth row of the table. Word doesn't disturb the basic shape of the table when you shift cells up.

If you start with the table shown in Figure 11-30 and you insert cells rather than delete them, shifting cells right will insert two blank cells to the

FIGURE 11-30

We'll use this table to illustrate deleting cells.

AAA111◻	BBB111◻	CCC111◻	DDD111◻	◻
AAA222◻	BBB222◻	CCC222◻	DDD222◻	◻
AAA333◻	BBB333◻	CCC333◻	DDD333◻	◻
AAA444◻	BBB444◻	CCC444◻	DDD444◻	◻
AAA555◻	BBB555◻	CCC555◻	DDD555◻	◻

FIGURE 11-31

If you select Shift Cells Left when deleting the two highlighted cells shown in Figure 11-30, this table is the result.

AAA111◻	BBB111◻	CCC111◻	DDD111◻	◻
CCC222◻	DDD222◻	◻		
AAA333◻	BBB333◻	CCC333◻	DDD333◻	◻
AAA444◻	BBB444◻	CCC444◻	DDD444◻	◻
AAA555◻	BBB555◻	CCC555◻	DDD555◻	◻

FIGURE 11-32

If you select Shift Cells Up when deleting the two highlighted cells shown in Figure 11-30, this table is the result.

AAA111◻	BBB111◻	CCC111◻	DDD111◻	◻
AAA333◻	BBB333◻	CCC222◻	DDD222◻	◻
AAA444◻	BBB444◻	CCC333◻	DDD333◻	◻
AAA555◻	BBB555◻	CCC444◻	DDD444◻	◻
◻	◻	CCC555◻	DDD555◻	◻

left of the originally selected cells, making the second row two cells wider than the rest of the table. Shifting cells down will push the text in the first two columns down one row, will leave the first two cells in the second row blank, and will add a new row at the end of the table (with its last two cells blank) to handle the shifted cells.

How to merge and split cells

Word will let you merge two or more cells in the same row. (You cannot merge cells in the same column.) To merge cells, simply select the cells you want to combine, and choose Table Merge Cells. Word will remove the boundaries between the selected cells and create one cell whose width is equal to the combined widths of the merged cells. It will also convert the end-of-cell marks in each cell into paragraph marks (except for the last cell being merged) and will treat each cell's text as a separate paragraph in the new cell.

A newly merged cell is treated just like any other cell. You can, for example, merge it with still other cells. If you merge the first three cells in a row and then decide that you should have merged the first four instead, you can simply merge what is now the first cell with what is now the second.

Word 6.0 also offers a Table Split Cells command (which, not so incidentally, works differently than the Table Split Cells command in Word 2.0). If you want more cells in a given row, you can choose Table Split Cells as an alternative to the Table Insert Cells command. Simply select the cells you want to split, and choose Table Split Cells. Word will open the dialog box shown in Figure 11-33. By default, Word enters 2 in the Number Of Columns box, which means it will split each cell you've selected into two cells. You can increase this number, but if the total number of cells in the row would then exceed 31 (the maximum number of cells allowable), Word will respond with a message telling you that you have exceeded the maximum number of columns.

FIGURE 11-33

When you choose Table Split Cells, Word opens the Split Cells dialog box to let you specify how many split cells to create from each selected cell.

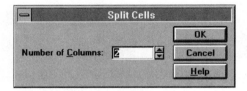

When you split a cell that contains text, Word will move the text into different cells based on the position of paragraph marks, if any. If the original cell contains more paragraphs than the final number of cells, Word will put the last paragraph in the last split cell, the next-to-last paragraph in the next-to-last cell, and so on, leaving the remaining paragraphs in the first cell. If the original cell contains fewer paragraphs than the final number of cells, Word will put the first paragraph in the first cell, the second in the second cell, and so on, and will leave the remaining cells empty.

If you want all the text to stay in one cell, be sure to replace any paragraph marks with line-break characters (entered by pressing Shift-Enter). (And, to make it easier to see what's happening, be sure to set your screen so that you can see paragraph marks. To do so, check the Paragraph Marks check box on the Tools Options View card.)

How to work with different numbers of cells in different rows

One reason for merging cells is to create a title that stretches across two or more columns in a table. You can find examples of such titles in the heading rows of the standard table layouts offered by the Table Wizard; see "How to create and format a table with the Table Wizard" on page 365.

The effect of merging two empty cells is the equivalent of deleting one cell in the row (using the Shift Cells Left option) and then resizing the remaining cells. If you're familiar with Word 2.0, you may know that Word 2.0 treated these visually equivalent situations differently, keeping track of the original position of merged cells so that you could still select columns easily. Word 6.0, however, does not recognize such a difference.

Figure 11-34, for example, shows two three-column tables. We produced the top table by merging the first two cells in the first row. We produced the bottom table by widening the first cell in the first row so that its right boundary is even with the right boundary of the second cell in the other rows. We then deleted the second cell in the top row so that all rows in the table end at the same place on the ruler. In either table, if you try to select a column starting with the rightmost cell in the first row, Word will select the offset column as shown in the figure, highlighting the second cell in each row.

FIGURE 11-34

When you create a wide cell from a single cell or by merging two cells, Word's idea of a column will not necessarily match the way the cells line up visually, as shown in this selection of a single column.

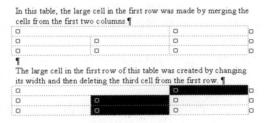

In this table, the large cell in the first row was made by merging the cells from the first two columns.¶

The large cell in the first row of this table was created by changing its width and then deleting the third cell from the first row. ¶

The offset selection of a column can make life difficult when you want to select columns to format them. For example, in Figure 11-34, you might want to select all cells in the far right column to format them with a particular shading, but there's no way to select them all at one time. To avoid this sort of problem, we recommend that when possible you create tables by approximation first, adjusting to minimum width any cells you plan to remove. Then add text and formatting so that you can work with complete columns. When you're satisfied with the approximate formatting, you can merge or delete cells you don't want and adjust the final cell width as necessary. Note that if you use the Table Cell Height And Width command, Word will track columns by the position of each cell in its row. But if you adjust columns using the mouse, Word will let you move all cell borders on the same vertical line at the same time.

Deleting an Entire Table

Occasionally you'll want to delete an entire table. Given that you can approach a table as the sum of all its rows, columns, or cells, you can use any of the techniques we've discussed for deleting rows, columns, or cells. However, we strongly advise that you get in the habit, when deleting an entire table, of using deletion techniques that place the table on the Clipboard. That way, if you delete the table accidentally, it will be available for pasting. The simplest choice for placing the table on the Clipboard is to select the entire table, with or without surrounding text, and choose Edit Cut.

Changing Table and Row Alignment

As we've already pointed out, when you create a table, Word aligns the left edge of the text area in the first column with the left edge of your document's text column. Assuming that you're working in a single-column layout and you haven't moved the first-line or left indent marker on the ruler, the position of the left edge of the table text will correspond to the zero point on the ruler. However, the left boundary of the table itself will appear to the left of the zero point.

As you may recall, we haven't yet discussed two settings on the Row card of the Cell Height And Width dialog box (shown in Figure 11-19): the Indent From Left text box and the Alignment box, which contains buttons for Left, Center, and Right alignment.

The alignment setting becomes noticeable only if the width of a table is less than the width of the current text column. Assuming that the table is narrower than the text, however, you can use this setting to change the alignment of the entire table or of individual rows.

The Left alignment option, which is the default, will align the left boundary of the table with the left edge of the text column. More precisely, it will align the left edge of the text in the leftmost column of the table with the left edge of the body text in the document. All the tables we've looked at in this chapter so far use left alignment.

The Center option centers the table within the document's text column. The Right option aligns the right edge of the table with the right edge of a document's text column; more precisely, Word aligns the right edge of the text area in a table's rightmost column with the right edge of the document's text column. Figure 11-35 shows three tables, each with a different alignment.

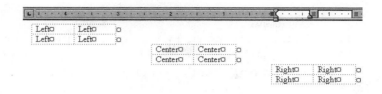

FIGURE 11-35

The three tables shown here demonstrate, from top to bottom, left, center, and right alignment.

In most tables, you'll want to align all the rows alike. However, at times you might need a different alignment in different rows to create a special effect. For example, if you use a table to design a complex form, you may want to change the alignment of one or more rows. In these situations, you can apply the alignment to selected rows as needed. For information about the rules for selecting rows before choosing Table Cell Height And Width and for moving through the rows with the Next Row and Previous Row buttons, see "How to adjust row height" on page 384.

> The alignment of a table or row has nothing to do with the alignment of text within individual cells. As we'll demonstrate shortly, Word lets you change the alignment of text in a table without changing overall table alignment.

How to indent rows

The Cell Height And Width dialog box also includes an Indent From Left setting on the Row card that can give you precise control over shifting anything—from one row to the entire table—to the left or right. For example, suppose you're using the default left alignment and you want to shift the entire table 0.5 inch to the right. You can simply place the cursor anywhere in the table (or select one or more columns), choose Table Cell Height And Width, choose the Row card, enter .5" in the Indent From Left text box, and choose OK. Word will close the dialog box and move the table 0.5 inch to the right. To shift one or more rows to the left and into the page margin, you can enter a negative number in the Indent From Left text box.

> You can use the Indent From Left setting in combination with alignment settings. Any change from the default setting of 0 will shift the table or rows by the designated amount from the left, center, or right position.

Mouse shortcuts for positioning rows

You can use the mouse to position the leftmost boundary of one or more rows in a table but not to indent the entire row in a single step. As we pointed out earlier in this chapter, if you move the mouse pointer over the left boundary marker on the ruler, the pointer will change to an arrow pointing left and right. You can then click the left mouse button and drag the boundary. If you have first selected one or more cells in the first column, Word will change the leftmost position for those rows only. You'll get the same effect if you select cells in the first column, position the mouse pointer over the leftmost boundary of the table itself, and then drag when the pointer changes to the vertical split pointer.

This technique is *not* equivalent to indenting rows with the Table Cell Height And Width command. When you change the Indent From Left setting on the Row card of the Cell Height And Width dialog box, Word shifts the entire table to the left or right. When you drag the left boundary, you are actually adjusting the position of the left boundary of the leftmost cell, and Word will follow the rules described earlier in this chapter for changing cell or column width. For details, see "How to change cell or column width with the mouse" on page 378.

Entering Body Text Above or Between Table Rows

When working with tables, you may find that you need to enter some text above a table that you've inserted at the top of a new document. Or you may decide that you want to split a table in two. In either case, you need to enter a blank paragraph—above the table or between two rows.

To enter a new paragraph above a table that's located at the top of a document, simply move the cursor to the beginning of the first cell in the first row, and press Enter. If the table is at the very beginning of the document, Word will add a new paragraph above the table. If the table is located anywhere else in a document, Word will add a new paragraph within the cell. To enter a new paragraph before a table that is not at the top of the document, simply move to the end of the paragraph that precedes the table and press Enter.

To split a table, place the cursor or selection below the point where you want to insert the break—that is, in the first row of what will become the bottom table—and press Ctrl-Shift-Enter or choose Table Split Table. Word will split the table and insert a blank paragraph just above the row in which you placed the cursor or selection.

How to change part of a table to text

You may sometimes want to split a table because you want to convert part of it to text. To split a table and convert rows to text at the same time, start by selecting the row or rows you want to convert. Then choose Table Convert Table To Text. Word will open the Convert Table To Text dialog box, in which you can choose to separate the text that currently appears in different cells with paragraph marks, tabs, commas, or some other symbol, as appropriate. Choose OK, and Word will convert your selected rows to normal text, splitting the table in the process. Toward the end of this chapter, we'll explain how to use this dialog box to convert an entire table to text; see "Converting All or Part of a Table to Text" on page 416.

How to split a table vertically

Word will not let you split a table vertically between columns because you can't create two tables side by side in a single text column (unless you put one or both in a separate frame). However, you can create the same visual effect by inserting one or more new columns in the middle of a table. Choose Table Insert Columns, as we've already described, to insert a new, blank column where you want the visual split. As we'll show you later in this chapter, you can then use borders to make the result look like two separate tables. (You can also create side-by-side tables by using a two-column format and Word's section formatting features to create balanced columns. We'll cover columns in Chapter 14.)

Working with Text in a Table

You can work with the text in a table much as you can with any other document text, with only a few differences. We've already shown you how to select text in a table. Here are some notes on how to edit and format text.

How to edit text in a table

You can use most of the same editing tools in a table that you use in normal document text, including all the basic editing techniques described in Chapter 4. However, there are a few issues to keep in mind.

When you press the Enter key while the cursor is in a table, Word will generally begin a new paragraph in the cell that contains the cursor, rather than move the cursor to the next row of cells.

Also, when you use Word's Edit Cut, Edit Copy, and Edit Paste commands within a cell, you'll get different results depending on whether the selection you copied or cut includes an end-of-cell mark. If it does include an end-of-cell mark, the Paste command on the Edit menu will read Paste Cells, and when you paste the selection into another cell, Word will replace the entire contents of that cell. If the selection does not include an end-of-cell mark, the name of the Paste command will not change, and Word will follow its usual behavior, inserting the selection at the cursor or replacing the current selection (depending on whether the Typing Replaces Selection option on the Tools Options Edit card is selected).

Keep in mind that you cannot select text from two or more cells without also selecting the end-of-cell marks. If you want to paste text from two or more cells without deleting the current contents of the target cells, you must cut or copy the text from each cell separately, being careful not to include the end-of-cell mark when you select the text.

How to select a paste area within a table

When you move or copy text from more than one cell in a table, the paste area will correspond in number of rows and columns to the area that you cut or copied. The cells in the paste area need not be the same width or height as the cells you copied from.

For example, suppose you want to copy the text in the four cells in the bottom two rows and first two columns of the table shown in Figure 11-36 and paste it into the cells in the last two columns and first two rows of that table. First select the cells you want to copy from, as shown in the figure. Choose Edit Copy (or the equivalent, using any of the copy commands you're comfortable with). Next select the target cells, as shown in Figure 11-37. Choose Edit Paste Cells, and Word will paste the text into the cells.

FIGURE 11-36

To copy a block of cells, first select the block to copy, and then choose Edit Copy.

AAA111□	BBB111□	CCC111□	DDD111□	□
AAA222□	BBB222□	CCC222□	DDD222□	□
AAA333□	BBB333□	CCC333□	DDD333□	□
AAA444□	BBB444□	CCC444□	DDD444□	□
AAA555□	BBB555□	CCC555□	DDD555□	□

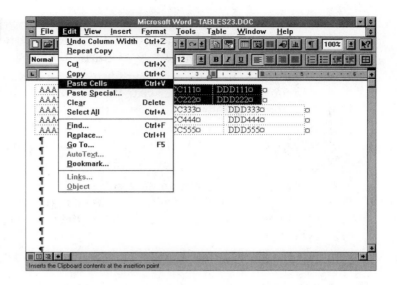

FIGURE 11-37

To paste a block of cells, select the target cells, and then choose Edit Paste Cells.

If the block of cells you select as the paste area doesn't match the shape of the block you copied, Word will not paste the cells. Instead, it will display a message telling you that the Paste command failed because the copy and paste areas are different shapes. Figure 11-38 shows the message Word displayed after we copied a block of two rows by two columns and then defined the paste area as two rows by three columns. If you see this message, simply choose OK, redefine the paste area, and paste the cells again.

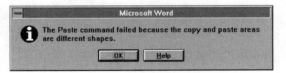

FIGURE 11-38

If you define the paste area with a different shape than the block you copied, Word will not paste the cells.

There are exceptions to this rule. If you place the cursor or selection in a cell without selecting the end-of-cell mark, Word will treat that cell as the upper left corner of the paste area and will paste without complaint. This can be dangerous because you can accidentally overwrite more cells than you meant to. However, if you use this feature with care and check the results immediately afterward, you can always recover from mistakes by choosing Edit Undo.

You can use this feature to create new columns and rows as you paste. In the sample table shown in Figure 11-39, select the four cells in the lower left corner of the table, and try these pasting variations:

- If you place the cursor in the rightmost cell in the top row and paste the four cells, you'll overwrite the top two cells in that column and add two new cells to the right of those cells.

- If you place the cursor between the right side of the table boundary and the end-of-row mark for the first row, you'll add two new cells to each of the top two rows in the table.

- If you place the cursor in the rightmost cell on the bottom row, you'll replace the text in that cell, create a cell to the right of that cell, and add a new row. The cells to the left of the pasted cells in the new row will be blank.

Figure 11-39 shows the original table and all three of these examples.

FIGURE 11-39

Depending on the shape and size of the pasted block of cells, Word may add new rows and cells to a table.

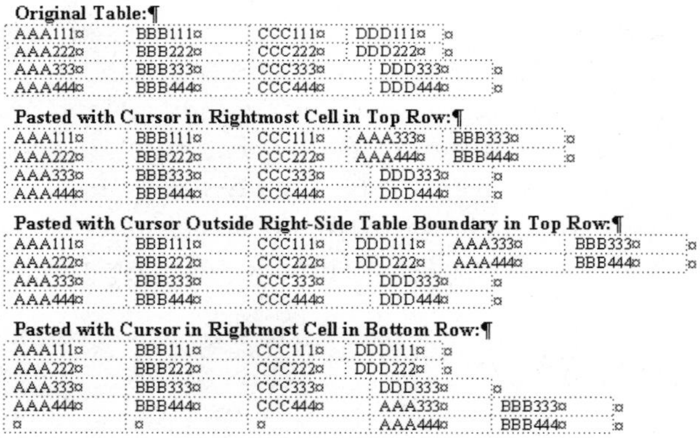

Original Table:¶

AAA111¤	BBB111¤	CCC111¤	DDD111¤	¤
AAA222¤	BBB222¤	CCC222¤	DDD222¤	
AAA333¤	BBB333¤	CCC333¤	DDD333¤	¤
AAA444¤	BBB444¤	CCC444¤	DDD444¤	¤

Pasted with Cursor in Rightmost Cell in Top Row:¶

AAA111¤	BBB111¤	CCC111¤	AAA333¤	BBB333¤	¤
AAA222¤	BBB222¤	CCC222¤	AAA444¤	BBB444¤	
AAA333¤	BBB333¤	CCC333¤	DDD333¤	¤	
AAA444¤	BBB444¤	CCC444¤	DDD444¤	¤	

Pasted with Cursor Outside Right-Side Table Boundary in Top Row:¶

AAA111¤	BBB111¤	CCC111¤	DDD111¤	AAA333¤	BBB333¤	¤
AAA222¤	BBB222¤	CCC222¤	DDD222¤	AAA444¤	BBB444¤	¤
AAA333¤	BBB333¤	CCC333¤	DDD333¤	¤		
AAA444¤	BBB444¤	CCC444¤	DDD444¤	¤		

Pasted with Cursor in Rightmost Cell in Bottom Row:¶

AAA111¤	BBB111¤	CCC111¤	DDD111¤	¤	
AAA222¤	BBB222¤	CCC222¤	DDD222¤	¤	
AAA333¤	BBB333¤	CCC333¤	DDD333¤	¤	
AAA444¤	BBB444¤	CCC444¤	AAA333¤	BBB333¤	¤
¤	¤	¤	AAA444¤	BBB444¤	¤

How to paste text outside a table

There is another exception to the general rule that you have to match the paste area to the area you copied from. As we mentioned earlier, you can paste copied cells anywhere outside a table to create a new table, complete with the text and cell formatting that you copied. More precisely, you will be able to paste a new table elsewhere in your document if the original selection included any end-of-cell marks. If the selection did not include an end-of-cell mark, Word will paste only the text.

If you want to create a new table this way, you must have at least one paragraph mark (or blank line, or line of text, if you prefer to think of it that way) between the original table and the cells that you paste. Otherwise, Word will simply add the newly pasted cells to the end of the current table.

How to format text in a table

In addition to entering and editing text in a table, you'll want to format it, an issue quite separate from that of formatting the table itself.

Word lets you use just about any formatting feature inside a table that you can use outside one. You can apply any combination of character and paragraph formatting. You can also use styles, which we'll cover in detail in Chapter 12. (Styles let you apply any combination of paragraph and character formats to a paragraph, or any combination of character formats to selected text, in a single step.) In addition, you can format each paragraph in a table independently of the others—a particularly useful feature that frees you to use different indents, alignments, line spacing, tabs, and so on for any paragraph in your table.

There are a few restrictions for formatting. You cannot force table text to flow across a cell boundary, and you cannot create a table within a table. Also note that every cell in a table will take on the character and paragraph formatting of the text in which the cursor was located when you inserted the table. For example, if you insert the table while the cursor is located in text formatted as 14-point Arial bold, with centered alignment, each cell in the table will be formatted that way.

To change the format, select one or more cells, and choose the appropriate formatting commands. You can select as many cells as you like and reformat them all at one time.

To demonstrate what you can do with formatting in a table, we took a sample table that we used earlier in this chapter, added some information to it, and formatted it as shown in Figure 11-40.

FIGURE 11-40

Paragraph and character formatting can give your tables a more professional look.

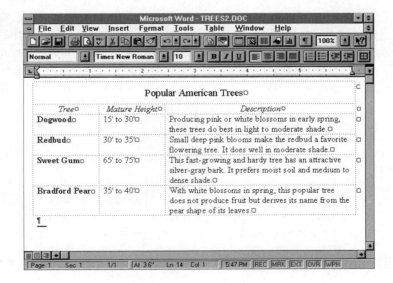

In addition to adding boldface for the tree names, we created a title as a single merged cell across the top of the table and formatted it in 14-point bold type. We also added 8 points of space before and after the title (using the Before and After text boxes in the Paragraph dialog box), and we set the heading for each column in italics with centered alignment and with 2 points of space before and after. These are straightforward applications of formatting techniques covered in Chapter 7. Here are a few tips for less obvious ways to use standard formatting within tables.

How to indent table text

Changing the indents of paragraphs of text in a table will have an effect similar to that of adjusting the Space Between Columns setting on the Columns card of the Cell Height And Width dialog box. In either case, the text will move closer to or farther from the left and right boundaries of the cell. However, the Space Between Columns setting applies to every cell in a row, while you can change paragraph indents on a selective basis. In effect, by adjusting paragraph indents, you can override the Space Between Columns setting for one or more cells.

How to add space before and after table text

As we've already mentioned, if you choose Format Paragraph and adjust the Before and After settings in the Paragraph dialog box, you can add space between the text in a cell and the top and bottom boundaries of that cell. When you add space this way, Word will adjust the row height as necessary to accommodate the additional space. (This assumes that you haven't set the Height Of Row option to Exactly on the Row card of the Cell Height And Width dialog box; for details, see "How to adjust row height" on page 384.)

In some ways, adding space before and after table text is similar to choosing Table Cell Height And Width, choosing the Row card, setting the Height Of Rows option to At Least, and then entering a row height setting that's larger than needed to show all the text. There is one important difference, however: When you adjust height on the Row card, Word adds any extra space below the text in each cell. When you adjust the Before and After settings in the Paragraph dialog box, you can specify how much space to put above the text and how much below.

How to use tabs in a table

Given the tremendous advantages of the table feature over creating tabular columns, you might wonder why anyone would want to use tabs within a table. As it happens, there are at least two situations in which using tabs makes sense. First, tabs can provide an easy way to align text within a cell.

Second, and more important, decimal tabs are the easiest way to create decimal alignment for a column of numbers in a table. For more on creating and using tabs, see "Paragraph Formatting" on page 221.

Because the Tab key functions as a navigation key in a table, you can't use it to insert a tab in a table and move to the next tab stop as you can in other parts of a document. Rather, you have to move the cursor to the cell and then press Ctrl-Tab. Note that Ctrl-Tab will toggle between some open dialog boxes, such as Find, so you cannot insert a tab in a cell when one of these dialog boxes is open.

Adding Borders and Shading in a Table

As we've mentioned, the gridlines that define the rows and columns in a table on the screen don't print. But if you want a printed table to include gridlines, you can format the table with borders. When you use borders, you don't need to display lines between every row and every column. You can apply borders selectively to specific rows, columns, cells, or the entire table, to produce many different effects. You can also add different kinds of borders to different parts of the table.

To add a border to a table, first select the portion of the table to which you want to add the border. Then choose Format Borders And Shading to open a Borders And Shading dialog box similar to the one shown in Figure 11-41 on the next page. This dialog box is essentially identical to the Paragraph Borders And Shading dialog box we discussed in Chapter 7 except that the From Text text box is grayed. When you are working in tables, the function that is usually performed by this text box is handled by the Space Between Columns setting on the Column card of the Cell Height And Width dialog box.

Note that the title of the dialog box will be Table Borders And Shading if the borders will be applied to the entire table (the cursor is in a single cell or all of the table is highlighted). If only some of the cells are highlighted, the title of the dialog box will be Cell Borders And Shading.

What you'll see in the Borders And Shading dialog box will vary slightly depending on the block of cells you've selected. You can see the differences in the thumbnail sketch that appears in the Border box and in the choices displayed in the Presets box. Figure 11-41 shows the Borders card as you'll see it if you have simply placed the cursor in the table without selecting anything (in which case any changes will apply to the entire table) or you have selected a block of cells that includes at least two rows and two columns (in which case any changes will apply only to your selection). We'll discuss this version of the dialog box first.

FIGURE 11-41

Select the portion of the table to which you want to add a border, and then choose Format Borders And Shading to open a Borders And Shading dialog box.

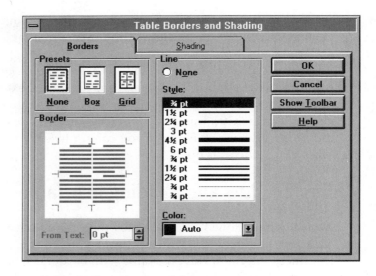

The thumbnail sketch of four cells in the Border box lets you define different borders (or no border at all) for the whole area you selected (the outside of the thumbnail sketch), for vertical lines between cells, and for horizontal lines between cells. The Presets choices are None, Box (outline the selection only), and Grid. In most cases, you'll want to use one of the Presets choices and select a line style in the Style list box. However, you can also use the techniques we discussed in Chapter 7 to define a custom set of borders. You may also want to move to the Shading card, shown in Figure 11-42, and apply shading to the selection. For details on using the Borders and Shading cards, see "Paragraph borders and shading" on page 236.

FIGURE 11-42

The Shading card in the Borders And Shading dialog box is identical to the Shading card for paragraphs.

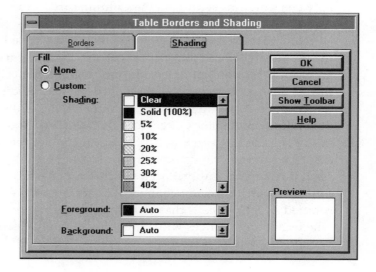

If you make any changes on either the Borders or the Shading card, choose OK to close the dialog box and accept the changes and have Word apply the new settings to the selection. Choose Cancel to close the dialog box without accepting any changes.

Figure 11-43 shows the Border and Presets portions of the Borders card as you'll see them when you've selected multiple cells in a single row, multiple cells in a single column, or a single cell.

FIGURE 11-43

The Border and Presets portions of the Cell Borders And Shading dialog box change depending on the selection. These three dialog boxes represent what you'll see when you've selected multiple cells in a single row, multiple cells in a single column, and a single cell.

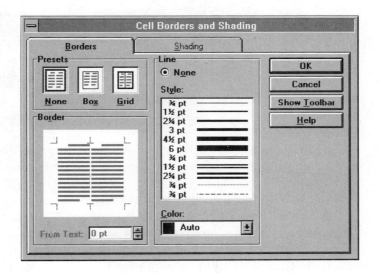

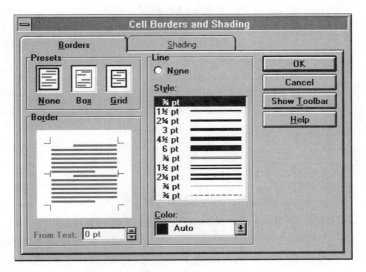

(continued)

FIGURE 11-43 *cont.*

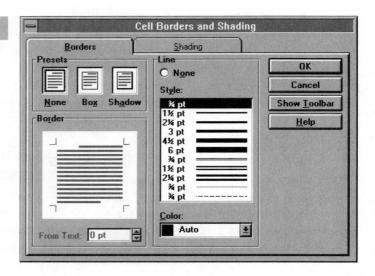

As you can see in Figure 11-43, Word supplies thumbnail sketches that match the current selection when you choose Format Borders And Shading. If you've selected multiple cells in a single row, you can define the outline for the selection and the vertical lines between adjacent cells. If you've selected multiple cells in a single column, you can define the outline for the selection and the horizontal lines between adjacent cells. (This is the same information for the Border and Presets portions that you will see in the Table Borders And Shading dialog box if your table contains a row with a single column.) If you've selected a single cell, you can define any or all of the lines around the cell. The mechanics of defining the borders are the same in each case, and, in each case, you can also move to the Shading card to define shading.

Finally, if you select text within a cell without including the end-of-cell mark, Word will display the Paragraph Borders And Shading dialog box, and you can define borders for the paragraphs within the cell. Word positions the borders for the paragraph by using the first-line indent and the right indent within the cell; the borders for the cell are positioned at the cell boundaries.

How to define a single table to look like two tables side by side

Earlier in this chapter, we mentioned that you could not place two tables side by side in a single text area (unless you used one or more frames) but that you could get the same visual effect by creating a single table and using borders to make it look like two.

Consider, for example, Figure 11-44, which appears to show two tables side by side in Print Preview. The table on the left reports sales by quarter; the table on the right reports sales by region. In fact, these two apparently separate tables are one.

With careful use of borders, you can make one table look like two tables side by side.

Sales by Quarter	
First Quarter	$16,008.93
Second Quarter	$14,567.30
Third Quarter	$18,301.98
Fourth Quarter	$16,489.79

Sales by Region	
Northeast	$12,321.32
South	$6,528.12
Southwest	$24,658.89
West	$21,859.67

Figure 11-45 shows the same table in Normal view before we added the borders. As you can see, we've really created one table whose different sections are separated by a column of blank cells.

This is how the table shown in Figure 11-44 looked before we added borders.

Sales by Quarter¤		¤	Sales by Region¤		¤
First Quarter¤	$16,008.93¤	¤	Northeast¤	$12,321.32¤	¤
Second Quarter¤	$14,567.30¤	¤	South¤	$6,528.12¤	¤
Third Quarter¤	$18,301.98¤	¤	Southwest¤	$24,658.89¤	¤
Fourth Quarter¤	$16,489.79¤	¤	West¤	$21,859.67¤	¤

To create the table shown in Figure 11-45, we used several of the formatting techniques discussed earlier in this chapter. The titles for each portion of the table are in merged cells and are centered over the appropriate columns. The two columns of numbers are aligned with decimal tabs. We've added a little extra spacing above and below some of the text by choosing Format Paragraph and entering settings for Before and After. And, finally, we've formatted the titles in boldface.

To turn the table shown in Figure 11-45 into the tables you see in Figure 11-44, start by highlighting the body of the "first table." Then choose Format Borders And Shading, and select the Borders tab. Select Grid in the Presets box. In the Style box, select the fourth line down (3 pt). Choose OK, and Word will close the Cell Borders And Shading dialog box. Repeat these steps for the title of the "first table." When you remove the highlight from the table, you should see a screen much like the one shown in Figure 11-46 on the next page.

When you return to the
document and remove
the highlight from the
table, Word will
display the border
you've just defined.

Sales by Quarter¤		¤	¤	Sales by Region¤		¤
First Quarter¤	$16,008.93¤	¤		Northeast¤	$12,321.32¤	¤
Second Quarter¤	$14,567.30¤	¤		South¤	$6,528.12¤	¤
Third Quarter¤	$18,301.98¤	¤		Southwest¤	$24,658.89¤	¤
Fourth Quarter¤	$16,489.79¤	¤		West¤	$21,859.67¤	¤

To add the border to the other section of the table (the "second table"),
select that section and repeat the same steps. Finally, choose File Print Preview to see the table as it appears in Figure 11-44.

Note that you can use these same techniques to build anything from a
single box around a table to complicated forms complete with shaded areas
and lines of different thicknesses.

How to redefine or delete borders and shading

Deleting borders or shading from a table is a simple matter of redefining the
format using the same techniques you use for adding borders and shading.
Select the section that you want to change, and choose Format Borders And
Shading to open the dialog box. You can remove all the borders from the
selection at once by selecting None in the Presets box and then choosing OK.
Similarly, you can change or delete specific borders as needed. When you're
satisfied with your redefinition, choose OK to close the dialog box. To redefine shading, select the section that you want to change, choose Format Borders And Shading, select the Shading card, and change the settings on the
card as appropriate.

Converting Existing Text to a Table

As we mentioned near the beginning of this chapter, Word will let you convert existing text to a table. Most often the text you'll want to convert will
already be in columnar format, arranged with tabs. However, you can also
convert comma-delimited text (text that is separated by commas instead of
tabs), which is a common format for data that you've imported from another
program, particularly a database program. (We'll discuss exchanging data
with other programs in Chapter 18.)

To convert existing text to a table, select the text, and then choose Table Convert Text To Table. Word will respond by opening the Convert Text To Table dialog box, shown in Figure 11-47. Note that this dialog box and its functions have been considerably expanded in comparison to the dialog box of the same name in Word 2.0.

The Convert Text To Table dialog box lets you tell Word how many rows and columns to use as well as what symbol to use to designate the end of a cell.

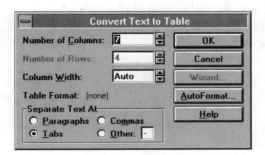

As you can see, Word makes its best guess about the number of rows and columns the new table should contain and about which symbol should indicate the end of a cell—paragraph marks, tabs, commas, or any other single character you want to specify as a separator character. If you've followed a consistent scheme for designating each column and each row for the table (or each field and record, to use database terminology), Word's best guess will usually be right. If not, adjust the settings as necessary before choosing OK.

If you need to change any settings in the Convert Text To Table dialog box, start with the Separate Text At box because this setting will automatically adjust the Number Of Columns and Number Of Rows boxes. You can then make further changes in the two text boxes if necessary, and you can set a specific width in the Column Width box—although the Auto setting will usually provide suitable widths. You can also choose the AutoFormat button to open the Table AutoFormat dialog box, which you can use to add a format to the table. For details about the Table AutoFormat feature, see "How to use Table AutoFormat—with or without the Table Wizard" on page 367.

Once you're satisfied with the settings in the Convert Text To Table dialog box, choose OK, and Word will convert the selected text to a table. Figure 11-48 on the next page shows text in both tabular (columnar) and comma-delimited formats, with the same name and address information listed in each. The tabular format represents the kind of simple column setup you might create using tabs. The comma-delimited format is a standard format that many database and spreadsheet programs use, or at least can import from and export to. Figure 11-49 shows the same document after we've converted both sets of information to tables (and made room to display the tables by choosing View Full Screen). Word converted both sets of text to tables using the default settings in the Convert Text To Table dialog box.

FIGURE 11-48

The tabular format is representative of a simple column setup you might create with tabs. The comma-delimited format is a standard database format.

TABULAR FORMAT¶
LastName→FirstName→Address1 → Address2→City → ST → Zip¶
Girard → Mike → 302 Sunshine Street→ → Redmond→WA→ 90201¶
Petrey → John → 3945 Medical Street→Suite 45 → Louisville→KY → 40222¶
Hambaugh→Jerry → 893 Hoosier Lane → → Carmel → IN → 40201¶
¶
¶
COMMA-DELIMITED FORMAT¶
LastName, FirstName, Address1, Address2, City, ST, Zip¶
Girard, Mike, 302 Sunshine Street, , Redmond, WA, 90201¶
Petrey, John, 3945 Medical Street, Suite 45, Louisville, KY, 40222¶
Hambaugh, Jerry, 893 Hoosier Lane, , Carmel, IN, 40201¶

FIGURE 11-49

Although the column widths are somewhat different in these two tables, the version converted from tabular format is otherwise identical to the version converted from comma-delimited format.

TABULAR FORMAT¶

LastName¤	FirstName¤	Address1¤	Address 2¤	City¤	ST¤	Zip¤	¤
Girard¤	Mike¤	302 Sunshine Street¤	¤	Redmond¤	WA¤	90201¤	¤
Petrey¤	John¤	3945 Medical Street¤	Suite 45¤	Louisville¤	KY¤	40222¤	¤
Hambaugh¤	Jerry¤	893 Hoosier Lane¤	¤	Carmel¤	IN¤	40201¤	¤

¶
¶
COMMA-DELIMITED FORMAT¶

LastName¤	FirstName¤	Address1¤	Address2¤	City¤	ST¤	Zip¤	¤
Girard¤	Mike¤	302 Sunshine Street¤	¤	Redmond¤	WA¤	90201¤	¤
Petrey¤	John¤	3945 Medical Street¤	Suite 45¤	Louisville¤	KY¤	40222¤	¤
Hambaugh¤	Jerry¤	893 Hoosier Lane¤	¤	Carmel¤	IN¤	40201¤	¤

To get from the screen shown in Figure 11-48 to the one shown in Figure 11-49, we had to convert the two sets of information separately. Word can convert text by using commas, tabs, or other symbols to indicate where each cell starts, but it can't convert using more than one separator character at a time. Word's ability to split text into cells based on only one separator character has some advantages. In particular, it means that you can use commas as part of the text in tabular columns and still convert the columns to tables.

The rules Word uses for converting text to a table

To best use Word's conversion capabilities, it helps to understand the rules Word follows for settings in the Convert Text To Table dialog box:

■ When creating a table based on tabs, commas, or any symbol you've entered in the Other text box, Word will assume that you want to create a separate row in the table for each paragraph mark or line break in the text. If a line wraps to the left side of the screen because of wordwrap, Word will still consider the line as part of the same row in the table and will assume that you want to add cells to each row until it finds a line break or paragraph mark.

This means you have to be sure that each line in the text you're converting does, in fact, end with a paragraph mark or line break. It also means that any blank lines in your text will be assigned their own rows. You can use this feature to create blank rows in the table. But if you don't want a blank row at a given position, you should delete any paragraph mark or line break that's on a line by itself.

■ Word will base the number of columns in the table on the row with the most commas, tabs, or other separator character. This means that if you have an extra comma, tab, or other separator character in one line, you could wind up with a table that's one column too long and that has the data in the one line offset from similar data in other lines. Extra commas are hard to spot in comma-delimited text, but extra tabs are relatively easy to find if you have checked the Tab Characters check box on the Tools Options View card to have Word display tab characters. On the other hand, you can also adjust the table after creating it by inserting or deleting cells.

■ The rules for converting text based on paragraph marks are a little different from the rules for converting text that uses other separator characters. When you tell Word to convert text to a table based only on paragraph marks, the program always suggests a single-column table, and it puts each paragraph in its own cell. If you create a table with more than one column, the paragraphs are placed in cells from left to right, top to bottom. Also, when converting text based on paragraph marks, Word does not count line breaks as indicating the end of a cell. Converting text to a table based on paragraph marks is the least useful of the four options, but you can use it as the first step in building a table.

You can also use the Convert Text To Table dialog box to spot problems in how you've formatted the text and, optionally, to override Word's assumptions. For example, if you have created text with six rows of seven fields each and have inadvertently omitted the paragraph mark from one row because it happens to wrap at the right place, Word will display 13 as the Number Of Columns setting, to match the longest record it finds. (In Word's count, the last field in the row with the missing paragraph mark is combined with the first field in the next row because Word finds no separator between them.) If you know that the number of columns should actually be 7, the setting in the dialog box should warn you that something is wrong. Choose Cancel, and look for the mistake to correct it.

Alternatively, you can change the Number Of Columns setting to 7, which will force Word to create the table you want. You'll still have to find and fix the problem rows, since Word will combine the two fields where you left out the paragraph mark, but the rest of the table will be the way you want it if—and it's a big if—you haven't made other mistakes in the way you've set up the text.

In general, you're better off finding and fixing mistakes before you convert the text to a table. That way, the settings in the Convert Text To Table dialog box are a confirmation that you located and corrected all the mistakes. Admittedly, however, it's usually easier to spot mistakes after the text is converted to a table, so you may decide to go ahead with the conversion in any case.

Converting All or Part of a Table to Text

Word will also let you convert a table to text. To convert the table, begin by selecting one or more rows or selecting the entire table. (You cannot convert partial rows to text.) Next choose Table Convert Table To Text, and Word will display the dialog box shown in Figure 11-50, in which you can choose whether to separate the contents of cells in each row with paragraph marks, tabs, commas, or another separator character that you enter in the Other text box. Choose Tabs for a tabular format, Commas for a comma-delimited format, Other for any other character-delimited format, or Paragraph Marks to put the information from each cell in a paragraph of its own. As in the case when you convert text to a table, the Paragraph Marks option is generally the least useful of the four.

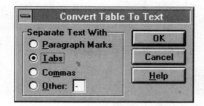

FIGURE 11-50

Word opens this dialog box when you select one or more rows and choose Table Convert Table To Text.

Tables as Mini-Spreadsheets: Sorting and Calculating

If you've read through this entire chapter, you now have a pretty good idea of what Word's table feature can do, and you should be able to build as complex a table as you need. You should be aware of two other features of tables, however, even though we won't cover them in this chapter.

If you've ever worked with a spreadsheet program such as Borland's Quattro Pro, Lotus 1-2-3, or Microsoft Excel, you've probably noticed a more than passing resemblance between spreadsheets and the tables you can create in Word. In truth, the similarity goes further than mere resemblance; you can build a surprisingly sophisticated spreadsheet in Word. You can, for example, enter calculation fields in table cells that will automatically calculate the totals of columns. You can also use Word's sorting feature to sort tables by the entries in a column and therefore to change the order of the rows. We'll cover both of these features in Chapter 23. For now, simply be aware that they are available if you need them. More immediately, we'll now turn to issues of advanced formatting and a discussion of styles.

Topic Finder

NEW! **The AutoFormat Feature   420**
- How to set the AutoFormat options
- How to use AutoFormat

Taking a Closer Look at Styles   427
- Types of styles
- Where styles are stored

NEW! **Using the Style Gallery   429**

Working with Styles   432
- How to see a list of styles in your document
- How to use the Format Style command and its dialog boxes
- How to create and change styles

More About Built-In and Automatic Styles   445
- Built-in styles other than Normal
- How to add an automatic style to a document manually
- The relationship between Normal and other built-in styles

More About Custom Styles   449
- How to create and modify styles by example
- How to use based-on styles when defining by example
- Notes about based-on styles
- Notes about related styles

Applying Styles   454
- How to use shortcut keys with styles
- How to use a list or a text box to apply a style

Displaying the Style Area   457
- How to resize the style area
- How to close the style area

Printing Lists of Styles and Shortcut Keys   459

Using Styles and Direct Formatting Together   460
- Resetting paragraph-level and character-level formatting

Merging Styles from Another Document   462
- NEW! How to copy one style
- How to import styles with Word's Organizer

Changing Defaults   465
- The effect of changing a style in a template
- How to modify styles in the Normal template from a document
- How to save changes to styles in a template
- How to return to Word's original default settings

12

Styles &
AutoFormat

ord has a number of advanced features, such as tables, that are helpful for anyone who needs those specific capabilities. But few advanced features are as potentially helpful to as many users as styles. Styles let you define a set of formats—including font, paragraph, tab, border, language, frame, and numbering format—and apply the entire set to text all at once by applying the style. By changing the definition of a style, you can quickly reformat all text in a document that's formatted with the same style. And styles make it easy to maintain a consistent format within a document—or a category of documents, for example, when you want to maintain a corporatewide standard.

Using styles differs a great deal from using direct formatting, however, and the concepts take some time to learn. So Word also provides the AutoFormat feature, as an easy way to get started with styles. AutoFormat can apply styles for you, even if you know nothing about styles beyond the fact that they exist. In this chapter, we'll look first at AutoFormat, which you can think of as an aid for working with styles, though it does a bit more as well. Then we'll take a closer look at styles themselves.

The AutoFormat Feature

As its name implies, AutoFormat can handle any number of formatting tasks automatically. In fact, if you simply type your text and ignore formatting, or if you import unformatted text created in another program, you'll find that you can run AutoFormat and usually wind up with a close approximation of an acceptably formatted document. If you take the time to add some clues to your text—using minimal formatting such as bold for headings, for example—AutoFormat does an even better job of applying the right formats.

Because this feature can also add the wrong formats, Word lets you put on the brakes by giving you lots of control over the kinds of changes AutoFormat makes. As we'll discuss later, you also have the option of reviewing each change before accepting or rejecting it.

AutoFormat works with the formatting of the headings and text of your document. To format information that has been organized as tables, you should use the Table Table AutoFormat command. See "How to use Table AutoFormat—with or without the Table Wizard" on page 367.

How to set the AutoFormat options

To give AutoFormat its marching orders, choose Tools Options and select the AutoFormat card, shown in Figure 12-1. The AutoFormat card contains

FIGURE 12-1

The Tools Options AutoFormat card lets you control the formatting changes AutoFormat can make.

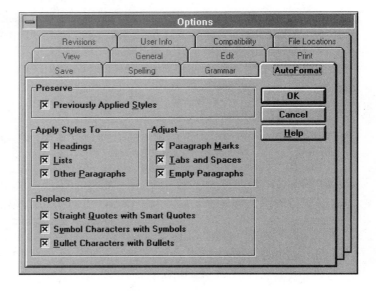

four group boxes: Preserve, Apply Styles To, Adjust, and Replace. Together, they offer 10 check boxes that give you plenty of control over the AutoFormat feature. All 10 are checked by default.

The Preserve group box

The Preserve group box contains one option: the Previously Applied Styles check box. Checking this box tells Word to retain any styles that you have already applied to the text instead of changing them with AutoFormat. Keep in mind that Normal is the default style for any paragraph that isn't formatted with another style. When you check this check box, Word will reformat any paragraphs that are formatted as Normal, even if you have explicitly applied the Normal style.

You can get around this limitation by creating another style that is based on Normal but includes no additional formatting. (We'll explain how later in this chapter.) Give the second style an appropriate name, such as NormalToo. AutoFormat will then ignore paragraphs formatted with the NormalToo style.

The Apply Styles To group box

The Apply Styles To group box has three choices, representing the three categories of text that AutoFormat recognizes.

If the Headings check box is checked, Word will assign a heading level from 1 through 9 to paragraphs it identifies as headings. The program uses several rules of thumb to recognize headings. For example, if it finds a one-line paragraph that starts with a capital letter, does not end with a period or a question mark, and is followed by a blank line, it will recognize the paragraph as a heading. But it will not recognize the same line as a heading if no blank line follows it, unless you've formatted the line in bold. If Word finds two sizes of headings, it will mark the larger as Heading 1 and the smaller as Heading 2. In short, Word works hard to recognize headings, although you may not agree with its conclusions.

The Lists option tells Word to add appropriate list and bullet styles to any paragraphs it identifies as part of a bulleted or numbered list. Here again, Word uses certain rules to recognize list items. For example, it will recognize paragraphs that start with a hyphen, a plus sign, or an asterisk plus space as bulleted paragraphs. It will also recognize numbered lists based on numbers you've typed, and it will recognize bullets and numbers you've added with Word's bullets and numbering feature.

The third option in this group box, Other Paragraphs, is a catchall. When this box is checked, Word will assign styles such as the Body Text style or the Body Text Indent style to a paragraph that it does not identify as either a heading or a list.

The Adjust group box

The options in the Adjust group box are designed to let you control the changes AutoFormat will make to several elements in your document that control spacing and line-break features. Unfortunately, they do not work as designed, at least in the initially shipping version.

For example, if you check the Paragraph Marks check box, Word is supposed to eliminate paragraph marks at the end of lines when these lines should be joined into one paragraph and should not exist as separate paragraphs by themselves. These extra paragraph marks often show up in text that originated elsewhere and has been imported into Word. (You would get the same effect in Word by pressing Enter at the end of each line you type rather than depending on wordwrap.)

The Tabs And Spaces option is supposed to change spaces to a tab character where appropriate and will strip out any extra spaces at the start of a paragraph. The third option, Empty Paragraphs, is supposed to tell Word to remove blank lines consisting only of paragraph marks.

Of the three options, only Empty Paragraphs works, and even that is limited. It will remove only one empty paragraph in a sequence at a time, so you must use AutoFormat repeatedly to remove multiple empty paragraphs.

The Replace group box

The fourth group box, Replace, covers a number of character replacements AutoFormat can handle.

Check the Straight Quotes With Smart Quotes check box if you want AutoFormat to automatically replace the straight quote marks you type (inch marks) with curved opening and closing quotation marks (curly quotes). Word can usually determine in which direction Smart Quotes should curve.

The Symbol Characters With Symbols option will replace the common typed representations of certain symbols with the actual symbol, as shown in the following list:

If You've Typed This Text	AutoFormat Inserts This Symbol
(TM) *or* (tm)	™
(C) *or* (c)	©
(R) *or* (r)	®

With its AutoCorrect feature, Word can replace straight quotes with curly quotes and symbol representations with actual symbols *as* you type. At first glance, then, you might think that AutoFormat's corresponding Replace options are superfluous. But the AutoFormat options are useful for making these replacements *after* you've typed your text—and they are particularly handy for documents that you've imported into Word.

Bullet Characters With Bullets determines whether AutoFormat will replace a character such as an asterisk, a hyphen, or a plus sign with a bullet. If this check box isn't checked, Word will not replace the typed character when it detects a bulleted paragraph.

How to use AutoFormat

To use AutoFormat, simply choose the Format AutoFormat command. (We'll discuss keyboard and mouse shortcuts later.) If you want to format the entire document, you can position the cursor anywhere, without selecting text. If you want to format only a portion of the document, select that portion before choosing the command, and Word will format the selection only.

Don't worry about the possibility of ruining your document's formatting with AutoFormat. If you don't like the results of AutoFormat, you can use Word's Undo feature and return to the starting point by pressing Ctrl-Z or clicking on the Undo button on the Standard toolbar. (Click on Undo twice if you chose Format AutoFormat; click once if you used the shortcuts we'll cover later.) However, it's a not a bad idea to save your work before initiating major changes, including AutoFormat.

When you choose Format AutoFormat, Word will display the dialog box shown in Figure 12-2 on the next page. If you choose the Options button, you'll go to the Tools Options AutoFormat card described in the preceding section. When you're satisfied with the option settings, close the card to return to the AutoFormat dialog box in Figure 12-2. Choose OK, and Word will automatically format the document or selection.

FIGURE 12-2

Word will display this
dialog box before it
starts to automatically
format a document.

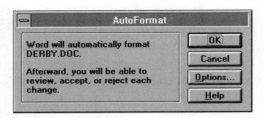

After the document is formatted, Word will display the AutoFormat dialog box shown in Figure 12-3. In this dialog box, you have the choice of accepting, rejecting, modifying, or reviewing the format changes Word has just
made. To accept or reject all the changes, you can choose the Accept or the
Reject All button, but you will usually want to review the changes first to be
sure that they make sense.

FIGURE 12-3

After AutoFormat has
finished its work, this
dialog box lets you
accept, reject, or
modify the changes.

How to review and modify AutoFormat changes

Word provides two approaches for reviewing and modifying the changes
AutoFormat makes.

First, you can move to your document by clicking on it or by pressing
Ctrl-Tab. You can then scroll through it, looking for format changes, modifying them, adding more formatting, or even editing the document. The
AutoFormat dialog box will remain visible so that you can toggle back and
forth between the dialog box and the document with Ctrl-Tab or the mouse.
When you're satisfied with the result, you can choose the Accept button to
accept all the changes.

The second approach is to choose the Review Changes button in the
lower left corner of the dialog box. This will open the Review AutoFormat
Changes dialog box, shown in Figure 12-4. This dialog box is very similar to
the Review Revisions dialog box that we discussed in Chapter 10, except that
it lacks an Accept button. In fact, the two dialog boxes are closely related,
since Word treats the AutoFormat changes as revisions and will show you
both inserted and deleted format information.

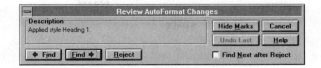

The Review AutoFormat Changes dialog box is a sophisticated tool that will help you find all the changes that AutoFormat made. The two Find buttons—one with a right-pointing (forward) arrow and the other with a left-pointing (backward) arrow—let you move forward and backward within the document. Choose either one, and Word will search in the appropriate direction for the next change.

When Word finds a change, it will highlight the affected text—highlighting a paragraph to indicate a change in paragraph style, for example. In the Description box, Word will also describe the change AutoFormat made to the highlighted text. You can then choose the Reject button to return the highlighted text to its original format or choose one of the Find buttons to continue to the next change. You can also press Ctrl-Tab or click with the mouse to move between your text and the dialog box to edit or reformat the text.

If you check the Find Next After Reject check box, Word will automatically move forward to the next change whenever you choose Reject. If you change your mind about a rejection, you can choose the Undo Last button (or use Word's standard Undo command) to undo the rejection.

When you first open the Review AutoFormat Changes dialog box, notice that Word modifies your document to show all changes on screen. If you have a color monitor, Word will by default indicate deletions with red and insertions with blue. It will also add revision bars in the left margin to indicate lines where AutoFormat has changed the format or text. And it will display paragraph marks even if Word is not set to show them. If you have set Word to show paragraph marks, style changes will be displayed as two paragraph marks (one deleted, one inserted). Where Word has changed the style of a paragraph, for example, you'll see a blue paragraph mark at the end of the paragraph and a red paragraph mark by itself on the next line. The red paragraph mark represents the old, replaced style. If Word is not set to show paragraph marks, you will see only the inserted paragraph mark for a changed paragraph.

If seeing both the insertions and deletions at the same time makes it diffi-cult to judge whether you want to keep a given change, you can choose the Hide Marks button in the Review AutoFormat Changes dialog box. Word will show you the text as it will appear if you accept the changed format. The Hide Marks button will also change its name to Show Marks, and the Find and Reject buttons will become unavailable. To continue reviewing the changes, choose Show Marks.

When you first open the dialog box, the upper right button will be la-beled Cancel. As soon as you reject a change or use the Hide Marks button, the Cancel button will change its name to Close. In either case, it performs the same function: Use it to close the Review AutoFormat Changes dialog box and return to the AutoFormat dialog box.

If you choose the Accept button in the AutoFormat dialog box and then immediately spot something in your document that makes you want to review the changes after all, you have another alter-native for reviewing AutoFormat changes. You can give the Undo command once—by pressing Ctrl-Z, choosing Edit Undo, or click-ing on the Undo button on the Standard toolbar. You can then choose Tools Revisions and click on the Review button to open the Review Revisions dialog box and work your way through the document in essentially the same way as you do with the Review AutoFormat Changes dialog box. In this case, however, you'll have to choose the Accept button for each item rather than accept-ing all items at once. For a long document, this trick can save a great deal of time compared to choosing Undo twice to undo all the formatting and running AutoFormat again just so you can re-open the Review AutoFormat Changes dialog box.

Notice too that if you have a color monitor, Word will display all changes in color when you choose Undo once but, by default, will use the same color for both insertions and deletions. You can use different colors for each by choosing Tools Revisions, clicking on the Options button, and changing the Color option in either the Inserted Text or the Deleted Text group box.

You can modify AutoFormat changes in yet another way, by using the Style Gallery button in the AutoFormat dialog box to open the Style Gallery dialog box. You can also get the same results by choosing Format Style Gal-lery from the document itself. We'll cover this choice later in the chapter; see "Using the Style Gallery" on page 429.

How to use AutoFormat shortcuts

As we mentioned earlier, Word also provides shortcuts for using the AutoFormat feature. Specifically, you can press Ctrl-K, or you can click on the AutoFormat button, which is just to the right of the Redo button on the Standard toolbar. (The AutoFormat button's icon looks a bit like a page with a star sparkle in the upper left corner.)

If you use either of the shortcuts, Word will automatically format your document—but without displaying the AutoFormat dialog boxes, without giving you a chance to change the options, and without giving you a chance to review the changes. While this makes the process more automatic, it also gives the feature an opportunity to run amok. And although you can undo all the changes with the Undo command, you must undo everything in a single step instead of giving the Undo command once and then using Word's revision features to review the changes. Given all these drawbacks, we recommend that you not use these shortcuts until you're extremely familiar with AutoFormat and are satisfied that it does what you want it to do. Even then, be sure to look over the formatted result before you accept it as final.

Taking a Closer Look at Styles

As we've already suggested, you can use AutoFormat without knowing much about styles. But you can take better advantage of AutoFormat if you do understand a little about styles. As you learn more about them, you'll find that you can go well beyond AutoFormat's capabilities.

Briefly, a style is a set of formatting instructions. Apply the style, and in one step you apply all the formatting defined by that style. For example, you might create a style called Indented Quotes with all the formatting features you want to apply to each quote. The style might perform three separate formatting tasks: switch the font to italic, change left and right indents, and even change font size. After you define the style, you can format each quote as you create it simply by applying the style. At base, it's that easy.

Although formatting a paragraph with one command instead of three is an obvious timesaver, the real beauty of styles is that they make it much easier to modify the format later. Once you've applied the style to widely separated selections of text, you can, in a single step, alter the format of all those selections—changing every figure caption, for example, from 10-point Arial italic type to 12-point Times New Roman bold.

One actual example should make the case for how useful styles can be. In writing this book, we set the Normal style to single spacing. That let us see as much text as possible on screen at once, a valuable feature when writing and editing. When we printed the text, however, we needed double-spaced output to make the text easier to read on paper. To get the format we needed, we simply changed the Normal style to double spacing. It took about 10 seconds to give the commands that changed the style, and every paragraph throughout the file was set to double spacing simultaneously. When we finished printing, we reset the Normal style to single spacing so that we could continue working with greatest efficiency.

Styles can get pretty complex if you want to learn all their nuances. But you can work with them in useful ways even if you learn only a little about them. And you'll find that the time they save makes them well worth mastering. In fact, they are one of the most valuable features in Word.

Types of styles

There are several ways to categorize styles. One difference, for example, is between paragraph and character styles. Another is between built-in and custom styles. And yet another is between automatic and manually applied styles. Here's a look at each.

Paragraph and character styles

The difference between these two kinds of styles is the same as the difference between paragraph-level and character-level formatting. Paragraph styles can define font, indents, tabs, borders, language, frames, and numbering. Regardless of the format, the style applies to the paragraph as a whole. All paragraphs in a Word document are formatted with a paragraph style, even if you never go anywhere near the style or AutoFormat feature. The default paragraph style for most text in your document, for example, is Normal. And you can change the default settings for font, paragraph indent, and so on by changing the definition of the Normal style.

Character styles are limited to font and language options, and they can apply to any arbitrary selection of text. Word comes with several predefined character styles, including, for example, a style that it automatically applies to footnote references. Character styles let you define a format for specific text that must be different from the rest of the paragraph, without having to resort to direct formatting.

Built-in and custom styles

As the name implies, a built-in style is one that Word supplies by default, one that is literally built into the program. A custom style is one that you define, using a name that differs from the names of the styles provided by Word. For the most part, Word treats built-in styles and custom styles the same way; you won't see any differences between them when you use them or redefine them. However, you can't delete a built-in style such as Normal. You can redefine it—essentially overlaying it with a custom style of the same name—but you can't get rid of it.

Automatic and manually applied styles

You can apply any style manually, using techniques we'll discuss later in this chapter. But Word also applies certain styles automatically. Insert a footnote, for example, and Word will automatically format the footnote with the Footnote Text style and the footnote reference with the Footnote Reference style. All of the automatic styles are also built-in styles. However, not all built-in styles are automatic. In general, you'll find automatic styles for most of the common elements in a document—such as headers, footers, footnotes, and annotations—that Word can identify unambiguously when you enter the text.

Where styles are stored

One of the most critical issues for understanding styles is knowing how they're stored. Briefly, Word stores styles in templates—the same templates that you attach to a file when you give the File New command and choose a template in the New dialog box. However, Word does not store styles in templates only.

Most important—and this is the tricky part—once you create a document, Word does not directly use the styles as stored in the template. Rather, the templates serve as a kind of reservoir for the styles. When you first create a document and tell Word which template to base it on, Word adds all the style information to the document for the entire set of styles in that template. But the document simply stores the information as it exists at that moment. If you attach a different template or make changes to the original template—adding new styles or redefining old ones—the document styles won't change unless you specifically update them. And, in fact, you can update the styles in the document based on the styles in *any* template.

Using the Style Gallery

The Format Style Gallery command lets you update all the style definitions in the current document at one time, copying the updated definitions from a template to the current document. You can use the Style Gallery feature at any time, but you'll find it most useful if you've already added styles to your document, either with the AutoFormat feature or by applying the styles manually.

To use the Style Gallery, you can choose Format Style Gallery from within your document, or you can choose the Style Gallery button in the AutoFormat dialog box. Either way, you'll see the Style Gallery dialog box, shown in Figure 12-5.

FIGURE 12-5

The Style Gallery dialog box lets you import a new set of styles into a document.

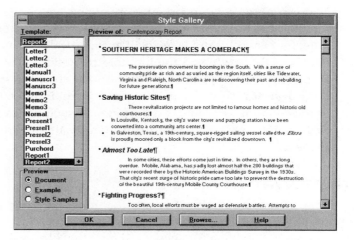

On the left side of the Style Gallery dialog box is the Template text box, with a list box containing a list of available templates. Figure 12-5 shows only the templates that come with Word, but if you've created your own templates, those will be available as well. By far the largest part of the dialog box is the Preview Of box to the right. This box lets you preview the effects of the styles stored in the template currently entered in the Template text box.

Just below the list of templates is the Preview group box with three options. Choose Document to see how your document will look if you import the styles from the currently highlighted template to replace styles of the same name currently in your document. Choose Example if you'd rather see the effects of the template on a sample document. Select Style Samples if you want to see an alphabetical list of all the styles in the template, along with samples of the format for each. Note that not all templates have examples or samples.

If you've already applied styles to your document and want to see how the styles in a different template will affect it, the Document option is the obvious choice. But to use this option to full advantage, you have to use the same names for the same functions in all templates. For example, if you have a style named Long Quotes for paragraph-length quotes in the template you used to create your document, Word will look for a Long Quotes style in the template you're using for the preview and will apply that style. This is easy with Word's built-in styles, since all templates must share the same names for the same built-in styles. You should keep this in mind when you create your own styles too.

You can look through the templates until you find a set of styles you want to use or decide to keep the set you started with. Then choose OK to import styles from the currently highlighted template, or choose Cancel to close the dialog box without changing the styles in the current document. The Browse button opens the Select Template Directory dialog box, which works much like the Open dialog box, allowing you to change directories to look for a particular template file.

When you are looking for the right template, it may help to know that Word comes with several templates designed for various purposes. The categories include brochures, directories, fax cover sheets, invoices, letters, manuals, manuscripts, memos, presentations, press releases, purchase orders, reports, resumes, theses, and a weekly time sheet. The names of the template files themselves are similar to these category names.

In addition, Word designates so-called families of templates. Whatever the purpose of a given template, 1 at the end of its name indicates that it is using Word's classic set of styles, 2 indicates the contemporary set, 3 indicates the typewriter set (styles that make text look as if it was created on a typewriter), and 4 indicates the elegant set. Once you know which families you like, you can ignore any you don't like. You may also want to follow this same numbering scheme, or add to it, when you create your own templates.

When you select the template you want for your document and choose OK in the Style Gallery dialog box, any styles in your document with the same name as styles in the selected template will be replaced by new definitions copied from that template. Word adds to your document any styles in the template that have different names. And any styles in your document whose names differ from styles in the template will remain unchanged.

After you create a document, if you later change the template it is based on, you can use the Style Gallery dialog box to update the document to match the current styles in the template. Simply open the document, choose Format Style Gallery, enter the template name in the Template text box, and choose OK.

Working with Styles

As we've already suggested, there is a lot more to learn about styles. We'll start by focusing on how to use styles within a single document, which is the way you'll usually work with them.

You can create as many styles for a document as you care to add, with each one formatted in any way that meets your needs. You might, for example, have styles for figure captions, indented quotes, bulleted lists, and so on. And keep in mind that you can create either paragraph styles or character styles.

Character styles open the possibility of creating such things as an Emphasis style. You could, for example, define the Emphasis style as bold and apply it to scattered text in paragraphs throughout your document. If you later change your mind and decide you want to use italic for emphasis instead, you could redefine the style and change all the isolated emphasized text throughout your document at one time.

How to see a list of styles in your document

If you want to see the list of styles that Word considers to be actively in use for a document, you can open the Style drop-down list on the Formatting toolbar, as shown in Figure 12-6, by clicking on the down arrow next to the box or by pressing Ctrl-Shift-S and then the Down arrow key. Alternatively, you can choose Format Style (or press Ctrl-Shift-S twice) to display the Style dialog box and set the List box to Styles In Use, to have Word list the active styles in the Styles box, as shown in Figure 12-7.

FIGURE 12-6

The Style drop-down list on the Formatting toolbar contains a list of the styles currently used in your document.

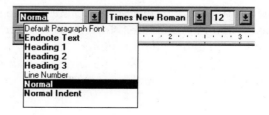

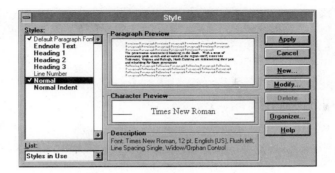

To see the styles currently in use, choose Format Style to open the Style dialog box, and set the List box to Styles In Use.

You can use either of these lists to apply styles to the current paragraph or paragraphs in your document (by which we mean the paragraph or paragraphs in which your cursor or selection is located). First highlight the name of the style you want to use. Then, if you're using the drop-down list, either click on the name or press Enter; if you're using the Style dialog box, double-click on the name or choose the Apply button. As you can see in Figures 12-6 and 12-7, Word shows paragraph styles in bold, but not character styles, so that you can easily see which category a given style falls into. Note too that in Figure 12-7 Word puts a check next to the paragraph and character styles of the current selection or cursor location. If the selection includes more than one style of either category, Word will not add the check.

One advantage of using the Style dialog box instead of the drop-down list on the Formatting toolbar is that you can easily move to an expanded list of styles. The drop-down list is limited to the same styles you'll see in the Style dialog box when you select Styles In Use.

If you're using the Normal template, haven't added or redefined any styles, and haven't yet added any text to your document, the styles in use will consist of the paragraph styles Normal and Heading 1 though Heading 3, plus the Default Paragraph Font character style. Later on, this list will also include any custom styles you've defined, any built-in styles you've redefined, and any other styles you've applied to text in the document.

Clearly, most styles do not, by default, appear on the Styles In Use list. However, you can see them and easily apply them to your text if you choose All Styles in the List box of the Style dialog box. The third choice for this box, User-Defined Styles, is handy when you want to see a list containing only those styles you've created or modified.

How to view a style definition

Another advantage of choosing the Format Style command to see the list of styles is that Word will display a definition in the Description box for each style you highlight, as shown in Figure 12-7. You can also see a preview of the paragraph-level formatting in the Paragraph Preview box and character-level formatting in the Character Preview box. Together, these features make it easy to find the style you want even if you're not sure of its name.

How to use the Format Style command and its dialog boxes

Word provides several methods for applying styles. Before we discuss how to apply styles, however, we'll show you how to create alternative styles so that you'll have more styles to apply. We'll also take a closer look at what a style is and explain how to change the default Normal style. Along the way, we'll touch on some of the methods you can use to take advantage of styles.

In this section, we'll begin by taking a detailed look at the choices available to you through the Format Style command. Specifically, we'll examine some of the options you'll find in the Style, New Style, and Modify Style dialog boxes.

In addition to the Styles list and the List, Description, and Preview boxes, the Style dialog box has seven buttons: Apply, Cancel, New, Modify, Delete, Organizer, and Help. If you choose Apply, Word will apply the currently highlighted style to the current paragraph or paragraphs and will close the dialog box. If you choose Cancel, Word will close the dialog box without applying a style. The remaining buttons and the choices they provide need a little more explanation.

As you might guess, you can choose New in the Style dialog box to define a new style or choose Modify to redefine an existing style. In fact, the two procedures are almost identical. In this discussion, we'll focus on the choices available for defining a new style, but keep in mind that all of these comments also apply to modifying an existing style. We'll provide some specific examples of defining and modifying styles later in this chapter; see "How to create and change styles" on page 441.

To define a new style, choose the New button in the Style dialog box to open the New Style dialog box, shown in Figure 12-8. The New Style dialog

FIGURE 12-8

Choose the New button from the Style dialog box to open the New Style dialog box.

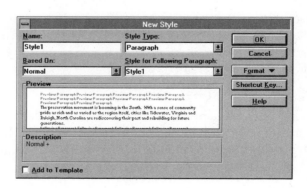

box includes Description and Preview boxes that serve the same purpose as the Description and Paragraph Preview boxes in the Style dialog box. It also includes a text box; three boxes with drop-down lists; two buttons in addition to the usual OK, Cancel, and Help buttons; and a check box.

The Name text box lets you enter a name for the style. By default, Word suggests Style1, Style2, and so on, but if you don't use a descriptive name, odds are you'll soon forget what the style is for. You can simply type the name you want to use in the text box.

Each style must have a unique name. You can use mixed uppercase and lowercase letters to vary style names and to make them easier to read. You can include letters, spaces, numbers, and any punctuation in a style name except a backslash (\), a semicolon (;), or curly brackets ({}). Names can be up to 253 characters, although we recommend keeping them short enough to fit completely in the Styles list box of the Style dialog box so that you can read the name easily.

In general, you'll want to use names that will help you remember the purpose of each style, and you'll want the names to describe the kind of text the style is meant for, rather than the formatting it applies, in case you decide to change the formatting later. In short, function-related names such as Long Quote and Emphasis are preferable to format-related names such as Indented Italic and Bold Italic Caps. Using functional descriptions will make it easier for you to change your mind about the formats you want to use.

Because Word distinguishes between uppercase and lowercase letters, you can create two style names that differ only in case. In general, you will want to avoid doing this. But you might consider taking advantage of this feature if you're disciplined enough to follow a clear convention, such as capitalizing the first letter of all paragraph styles and using all lowercase for character styles. You could then create, say, an *Emphasis* paragraph style that adds bold, italic, and a border to paragraphs, plus an *emphasis* character style that adds bold and italic to shorter selections. If you take this route, however, we recommend that you use it sparingly and that you follow whatever convention you choose as strictly as possible.

The Style Type drop-down list in the New Style dialog box offers two choices: Paragraph and Character. Simply choose Paragraph to define a paragraph style and Character to define a character style. We'll come back to the other two drop-down lists a little later.

Notice also the Add To Template check box in the lower left corner of the dialog box. You can check it when you want to tell Word to store a new style in a template as well as in the document you're currently working in. We'll cover this feature later in this chapter; for the moment, however, we'll ignore it, since we are focusing on working within a single document.

Style formatting choices

If you click on the Format button in the New Style dialog box, you'll open a menu with seven choices: Font, Paragraph, Tabs, Border, Language, Frame, and Numbering. Each one opens an additional dialog box. These closely resemble the dialog boxes Word opens when you choose the menu items of the same, or similar, names on the Format or Tools menu. The primary difference is that the definitions apply to the style you're defining rather than to a specific selection of text.

 If you click on the Format button when you're defining a character style, the only two choices available on the menu will be Font and Language. All the other choices will be grayed because they are all paragraph-level formatting features.

Some options in these dialog boxes will not be available when you open them through the New Style dialog box. The Default Tab Stops text box, for example, is missing from the Tabs dialog box. Similarly, the Default buttons in the Font and Language dialog boxes are grayed. None of these options would make much sense when you're defining a style. Remember that when you redefine the Normal style, you are in fact defining the default for the document, so there's no need to define defaults while defining other styles as well. Note too that you'll find two cards, rather than three, in the Bullets And Numbering dialog box. (The multilevel card is not available.)

If you need details on how to use any of these dialog boxes, you'll find that we cover the Font, Paragraph, Tabs, and Border dialog boxes in Chapter 7, the Bullets And Numbering dialog box in Chapter 13, and the Frame dialog box in Chapter 14. We touched on the Language dialog box in Chapter 6 when discussing the spelling checker.

The Language dialog box, shown in Figure 12-9, warrants a quick look here. Its most prominent feature is the Mark Selected Text As list box, which lists a number of languages, including a choice at the start of the list labeled (no proofing), which isn't visible in the figure. The spelling checker and Word's other proofing tools automatically use the dictionary for the language that's highlighted in the list box, if that dictionary is available.

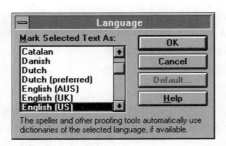

FIGURE 12-9

In the Language dialog box, you can choose the language for Word's proofing tools to use.

Most users in the United States will usually format most of their text with the English (US) choice. However, if you include some paragraphs written in another language—and if you have the dictionary and other proofing tools for that language—you will likely want to format that text for the other language. Similarly, if your text includes a list of trademarks, proper names, or other unusual material, you may want to format it with the (no proofing) choice.

You can format such text directly, of course, but you can create special "no proofing" or foreign language styles instead. We highly recommend using a style rather than direct formatting, since you can then easily change the language format throughout your document by changing the style. You might, for example, format lists of trademarks and proper names as (no proofing) until your final pass. That will tell Word to ignore them most of the time when proofing but will let you proof them easily when you want simply by changing the Language setting in the style.

How to specify the next style

The two drop-down lists just above the Preview box in the New Style dialog box are labeled Based On and Style For Following Paragraph. If you open either one, you'll see a list of all styles available in the document. (Note, however, that if you're modifying the Normal style, you can't open the Based On list box because the Normal style can't be based on any other style.)

The Style For Following Paragraph list box applies only to paragraph styles and will be grayed if you're defining a character style. This list box lets you tell Word what style to use immediately after the style you're currently defining. When you enter a section heading, for example, you'll almost always want the next paragraph to be body text, formatted with the Normal style. By specifying Normal as the next style, you're telling Word that when you start the next paragraph after a section heading by pressing Enter, that paragraph should be formatted as Normal.

This ability to define a style for the following paragraph is a nice touch. When you know that a given style will always (or almost always) follow some other specific style, you can avoid the extra steps it would take to format that next paragraph.

For Word to change styles for the next paragraph as instructed, the cursor must be located just before the paragraph mark when you press Enter. Otherwise, the new paragraph will keep the same style as the preceding one. You can take advantage of this behavior to split a paragraph and keep the same style in both the resulting paragraphs. You can also use it to advantage if you don't want to change styles in a given situation—simply type an extra space and move one character to the left before pressing Enter.

Keep one constraint in mind when you specify the next style: You must choose the style name from a list of existing styles. This can be a problem if you haven't yet created the style you want to use as the next style. For example, if you are about to create a list of names and telephone numbers, and you want to move automatically from a bold Name style to an italic Phone style and back to the bold Name style, you can't fully define either style until you've defined the other. In this case, you might define either one first, starting with Name, say, and selecting Normal in the Style For Following Paragraph box. Then define the Phone style, selecting Name as the next style. Finally, redefine Name and select Phone as the next style.

In a longer repetitive list, you'll want to define the styles in reverse order—that is, the first style you define should be the last style you need in the sequence. When you've defined the entire sequence, you can redefine the last style to use the first one as the next style.

How to base one style on another

The Based On drop-down list in the New Style dialog box lets you use the formatting characteristics you have defined for one style as the starting point for other styles. That, in turn, lets you redefine whole groups of styles by redefining a single style.

For example, suppose that you define the Normal style for a document as single-spaced text in a 10-point Arial font and that you then define all your other styles as based on Normal. Heading 1, for example, might be Normal plus bold and 12-point text. Later you decide you want to use double-spaced text in Times New Roman throughout your document. If all your styles are based on Normal, you need only change these settings in the Normal style definition. All the text formatted in the other styles will adopt the new font and spacing automatically. If you haven't used the based-on feature, you'll have to redefine the settings in each individual style.

> Some of Word's styles use fonts that are different from the fonts used in the Normal style, even though these styles are otherwise based on Normal. If you want a style to follow any font changes you make in Normal, you'll first need to modify that style to use the same font as Normal. Your first step must be to modify the style to match Normal even if you plan later to change Normal to the style's current font. If you change Normal to match the style instead, the style still won't be based on Normal. If you then change Normal again, you'll find that the other style retains its original font. The general rule is that if you want a style to follow changes in a style on which it is based (the based-on style), you must change the format in the first style to match the format in the based-on style before making other changes.

When you base one style on another, the description for the style you are defining begins with the name of the style you've based it on. The description also includes only those characteristics that differ from the based-on style.

In much the same way, if you look at the description of the Normal style shown in Figure 12-7, you'll see that this definition doesn't spell out every formatting characteristic. For example, the Normal style uses no indents, but this is not specifically stated in the definition. Except for the font, font size, paragraph alignment, line spacing, and language for proofing, the definition of any style that isn't based on another style will specify only those formatting characteristics that differ from Word's defaults.

Styles based on styles that are based on styles

You can also base a style on another style that is itself based on another style. In other words, you can link styles in multiple steps.

Suppose, for example, that you've created a character style called Emphasis that is based on the Default Paragraph Font style and adds bold. You can then create another character style called Serious Emphasis that's based on Emphasis and adds double underlining and all caps. Figure 12-10 on the next page shows examples of these two styles. Each is applied to a block of text within a paragraph that is formatted as Normal, with Normal defined here as 12-point Times New Roman. If you change the font in the Normal style to Arial, the change will affect the font in the Emphasis and Serious

Emphasis styles as well, as shown in Figure 12-11. Similarly, if you change the Emphasis style to bold plus italic, you'll also get bold plus italic when you format with the Serious Emphasis style, as shown in Figure 12-12.

FIGURE 12-10

This paragraph includes text formatted with the Emphasis character style as well as text formatted with the Serious Emphasis style, which is based on the Emphasis style.

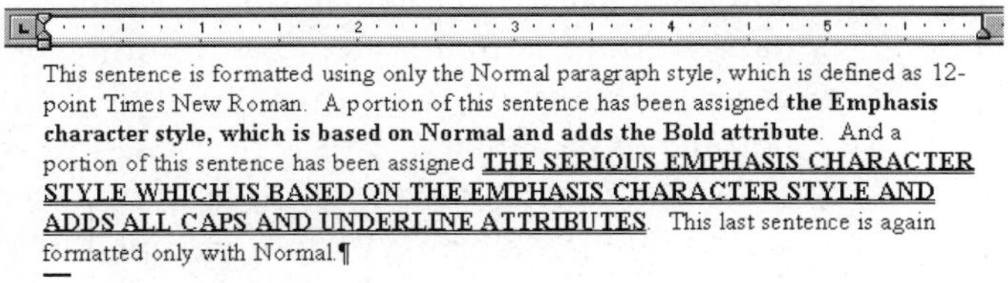

This sentence is formatted using only the Normal paragraph style, which is defined as 12-point Times New Roman. A portion of this sentence has been assigned **the Emphasis character style, which is based on Normal and adds the Bold attribute**. And a portion of this sentence has been assigned <u>THE SERIOUS EMPHASIS CHARACTER STYLE WHICH IS BASED ON THE EMPHASIS CHARACTER STYLE AND ADDS ALL CAPS AND UNDERLINE ATTRIBUTES</u>. This last sentence is again formatted only with Normal.¶

FIGURE 12-11

The document shown in Figure 12-10 looks like this after we change the Normal style from Times New Roman to Arial.

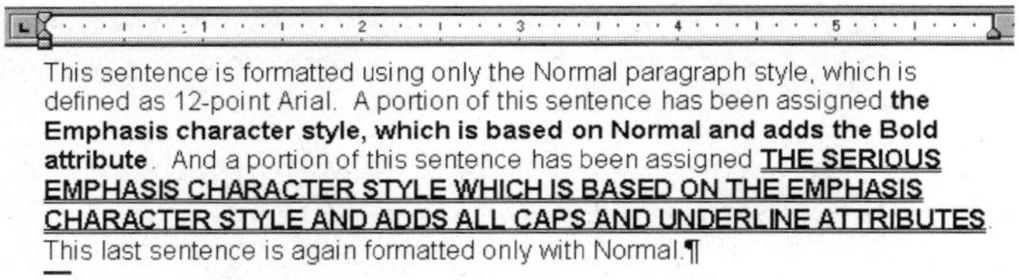

This sentence is formatted using only the Normal paragraph style, which is defined as 12-point Arial. A portion of this sentence has been assigned **the Emphasis character style, which is based on Normal and adds the Bold attribute**. And a portion of this sentence has been assigned <u>THE SERIOUS EMPHASIS CHARACTER STYLE WHICH IS BASED ON THE EMPHASIS CHARACTER STYLE AND ADDS ALL CAPS AND UNDERLINE ATTRIBUTES</u>. This last sentence is again formatted only with Normal.¶

FIGURE 12-12

The document shown in Figure 12-11 looks like this after we change the Emphasis style from bold to bold plus italic.

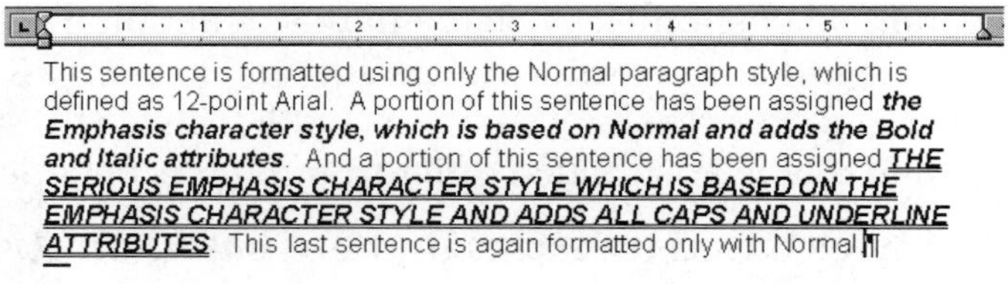

This sentence is formatted using only the Normal paragraph style, which is defined as 12-point Arial. A portion of this sentence has been assigned *the Emphasis character style, which is based on Normal and adds the Bold and Italic attributes*. And a portion of this sentence has been assigned <u>*THE SERIOUS EMPHASIS CHARACTER STYLE WHICH IS BASED ON THE EMPHASIS CHARACTER STYLE AND ADDS ALL CAPS AND UNDERLINE ATTRIBUTES*</u>. This last sentence is again formatted only with Normal.¶

This boils down to one simple rule: If there are any differences between the current style and the style you've based it on, the definition for the current style will always take priority. If you keep this rule in mind, you can design your styles so that if you decide to change styles—standardizing on a different font, for example—the change will require minimal work. There is more to be said about based-on styles; we'll come back to this subject after we finish discussing how to create and change styles. See "How to use based-on styles when defining by example" on page 450 and "Notes about based-on styles" starting on page 451.

Special considerations for character styles

The only character style that Word always considers to be in use is Default Paragraph Font. If you highlight this style in the Style dialog box, you'll see that it's defined as using the font of the underlying paragraph style. Because this is the only built-in style that you can't modify, the Modify button in the dialog box will be grayed.

Somewhat confusingly, the Character Preview box in the Style dialog box will display the default paragraph font as Times New Roman (or the equivalent font for the printer you have installed) regardless of the actual font for the paragraph or paragraphs the cursor or selection is in. This remains true even if you don't have a single paragraph style in the document defined to use Times New Roman. In fact, Word will display all character styles in Times New Roman in the Character Preview box, unless you specifically define them otherwise. Don't let this throw you. Word simply uses Times New Roman—or the equivalent for your printer—as a sample font. When you apply the style to text, you'll get the correct font (the font of the underlying paragraph style) unless you've defined the style otherwise.

All of Word's other built-in character styles are based on the Default Paragraph Font style. Since you can't modify this style, that's equivalent to saying that each of these styles is defined as matching the underlying paragraph style, plus whatever modifications you add. When you define your own character styles in the New Style dialog box, you'll also find a choice called (underlying properties) in the Based On drop-down list. Given that Default Paragraph Font is defined as following (underlying properties), these two choices are fully equivalent.

How to create and change styles

At this point, you know a great deal about creating and modifying styles, but we need to look at the actual mechanics of the process. You can take either of two approaches. We'll start with the more straightforward one. We'll cover the second approach later; see "How to create and modify styles by example" on page 449.

How to add a style

To add, or create, a style, choose Format Style. Choose the New button to open the New Style dialog box, and then type a name for the style in the

Name text box. For this example, we'll create the Emphasis character style discussed in the preceding section. Type *Emphasis* in the text box, as shown in Figure 12-13.

FIGURE 12-13

To create a new style, open the New Style dialog box.

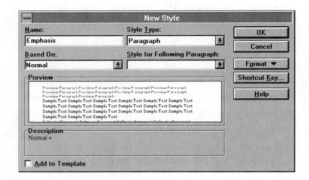

As you can see in Figure 12-13, Word assumes that you want to create a paragraph style and that you want to base the new style on the style in which the current paragraph was formatted when you opened the Style dialog box—Normal in this example. In this case, however, you want to create a character style instead. If you choose Character in the Style Type box, as shown in Figure 12-14, Word will automatically change the entry in the Based On box.

FIGURE 12-14

When you change the style type to Character, Word will enter an appropriate style in the Based On box.

If, when you gave the Format Style command, the cursor or selection was located in text that was formatted with a character style, Word will enter that style in the Based On box when you set the style type to Character. Otherwise, as shown in Figure 12-14, it will enter Default Paragraph Font, which happens to be the choice you want in this case. If you want to base the new style on a different style, you can open the Based On drop-down list and select the appropriate style. Note that when you set the style type to

Character, the Style For Following Paragraph choice is grayed because the option is meaningless for character styles.

Next use the menu available through the Format button to define the format for the new style. Remember that when you define a character style, the only choices available will be Font and Language. (If you were defining a paragraph style, you could open additional dialog boxes for paragraph-level formatting such as indents or tabs.) For this example, choose Font from the Format button's menu to display the Font dialog box. Highlight Bold in the Font Style list, and choose OK. Then choose OK again to return to the Style dialog box.

At this point, you can choose Apply to apply the style to currently selected text, or you can choose Close to return to your document. In either case, Word will add the style to the Style drop-down list on the Formatting toolbar and to the list of styles in use in the Style dialog box.

How to modify a style

As we've mentioned, the procedure for modifying a style is nearly identical to the procedure for creating one. Suppose, for example, that in addition to the Emphasis style you've created a second style called Emphasis 2 and that you want to change it to match the Serious Emphasis style of our earlier example. To keep the steps simple, we'll assume that you've defined Emphasis 2 as the Default Paragraph Font style plus italic.

To modify Emphasis 2, choose Format Style, highlight Emphasis 2 in the Styles list, and choose the Modify button to open the Modify Style dialog box, shown in Figure 12-15.

FIGURE 12-15

To modify a style, open the Modify Style dialog box.

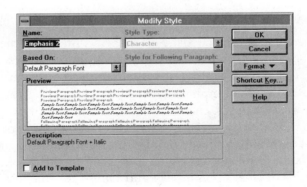

The Modify Style dialog box is almost identical to the New Style dialog box, but with an important difference: When you open the Modify Style dialog box, Word limits you to changing the style that was highlighted in the Style dialog box when you chose the Modify button. If you try to type a different style name in the Name text box, for example, you will rename the style rather than create a new style. Note too that Word grays the Style Type box because you cannot change one kind of style to the other. (In Figure 12-15, Word has also grayed the Style For Following Paragraph box, but that's because Emphasis 2 is a character style. When you modify a paragraph style, the Style For Following Paragraph box is available.)

The Modify Style dialog box works essentially the same way as the New Style dialog box. To eliminate italic from the Emphasis 2 definition and add the all-caps and double-underline formatting, choose Font from the Format button's menu to open the Font dialog box. Delete the Italic entry from the Font Style box on the Font card (or select Regular), check the All Caps check box, and choose Double from the Underline drop-down list. Then choose OK to return to the Modify Style dialog box.

The description for Emphasis 2 should now read *Default Paragraph Font + Double Underline, All Caps*. If you then choose Emphasis from the Based On list, the description will change to *Emphasis + Double Underline, All Caps*. Choose OK to close the Modify Style box, redefine the style, and return to the Style dialog box. Alternatively, you can choose Cancel to return to the Style dialog box without accepting the redefinition.

> Keep in mind that if you accept the new definition of the style, Word will reformat not only text to which you apply the changed style but also any other text in the document already formatted with that style.

How to rename a style

To rename a style, choose Format Style, highlight the name in the Style dialog box, choose the Modify button, and enter the new name in the Name text box. To continue with our earlier example, you might rename the Emphasis 2 style to Serious Emphasis. After you change the name and make any other necessary changes, choose OK. Word will accept the new name and will update it on the Styles list and wherever else it appears.

You can give a style more than one name by using Word's alias feature. If you enter two or more names in the Name text box, separated by commas, Word will treat them all as valid names for that style. This can be useful if you want a fully descriptive name for a style, such as Serious Emphasis, but also want to designate it with a shortcut term, such as SE, in the Style box on the Formatting toolbar.

How to modify Normal and other built-in styles

Modifying a built-in style such as Normal is essentially identical to modifying a custom style except that you can't rename a built-in style. If you try to do so, Word will simply add the new text as an alias for the existing style name. If you try to change Normal to Norm, for example, Word will show the style name as Normal,Norm, treating the new name as an alias.

Remember that the Normal style is a special case in that redefining it redefines the default format settings for your document. Note too that if you open a template file and redefine the Normal settings in the template, the result will define the default format settings for all new files based on that template (although not for existing files unless you specifically copy the new definition to each existing file).

How to save style changes

It's important to realize that when you change a style, Word is saving your changes to memory only, not on disk. However, Word will automatically save the style changes the next time you save the document.

How to delete a style

The Style dialog box offers a Delete button, which you can use to delete custom styles. Simply highlight the style that you want to delete in the Styles list, and choose Delete. Word will stop and ask for confirmation. If you choose Yes, it will both delete the style from the list and remove the style formatting from any text that has been formatted with that style.

More About Built-In and Automatic Styles

Word offers 73 built-in styles in the Normal template: 6 character styles and 67 paragraph styles. Of these, 33 are identified as automatic styles—that is, they are styles that Word automatically applies when you use certain features. For example, when you use the Insert Footnote feature, Word automatically applies the Footnote Text and Footnote Reference styles. Other templates contain additional built-in styles.

There are some additional styles, such as the Heading styles or even the Normal style, that Word doesn't classify as automatic but that it applies automatically in some situations. We've already covered the Normal style, which defines the default settings for text in your document, and we've shown you how to change it. Here's a closer look at the other built-in styles.

Built-in styles other than Normal

Although most of Word's automatic styles won't appear in a document's active style list until you add the type of text element the style applies to or until you manually apply the style, it's helpful to know what the automatic styles are so that you aren't surprised by them. Figure 12-16 lists the name and purpose of each automatic style. Figure 12-17 lists the additional built-in styles that Word doesn't classify as automatic. You should also be aware that many of Word's templates include custom styles that are defined within those templates.

Word Uses This Style	To Format This Element
Annotation Reference	The annotation reference mark that appears in a document (a character style)
Annotation Text	Text in an annotation
Caption	Captions inserted by the Insert Caption command
Default Paragraph Font	Text (matches the default font setting of the paragraph style)
Endnote Reference	The endnote reference that appears in the document (a character style)
Endnote Text	Text in an endnote
Footer	Text in a footer
Footnote Reference	The footnote reference mark that appears in a document (a character style)
Footnote Text	Text in a footnote
Header	Text in a header
Index 1–Index 9	Levels of entries in an index
Line Number	Automatic line numbers (a character style)
Macro Text	Text of a WordBasic macro
Page Number	Automatic page numbers (a character style)
Table of Authorities	Entries in a table of authorities
Table of Figures	Entries in a table of figures
TOC 1–TOC 9	Entries in a table of contents

FIGURE 12-16

Word's automatic styles.

Word Provides This Style	To Format This Element	
Body Text	Body text in documents	NEW!
Body Text Indent	Text formatted based on the Body Text style but with a left indent	
Closing	The closing of a letter, above the signature	NEW!
Envelope Address	The address on an envelope	NEW!
Envelope Return	The return address on an envelope	NEW!
Heading 1–Heading 9	Heading levels for section headings and for Outline view	
Index Heading	Heading separators in an index	
List and List 2–5	List items with a hanging indent; each subsequent List style indents an entire item further	NEW!
List Bullet and List Bullet 2–5	List items with bullets; each subsequent List Bullet style indents an entire item further	NEW!
List Continue and List Continue 2–5	Additional paragraphs in a numbered or bulleted list item; each subsequent List Continue style indents the paragraph further	NEW!
List Number and List Number 2–5	List items with numbering; each subsequent List Number style indents an entire item further	NEW!
Normal	All text not assigned another style (the default format)	
Normal Indent	Text formatted based on the Normal style but with a left indent	
Signature	The signature on a letter	NEW!
Subtitle	A subtitle within a document	NEW!
Title	The title of a document	NEW!
TOA Heading	Table of authorities heading	

FIGURE 12-17

Word's additional built-in styles.

How to add an automatic style to a document manually

As we've already pointed out, Word will add an automatic style to a document whenever you add the appropriate text element to that document. For example, when you add a footnote, Word will automatically format the footnote and add two styles to the list of styles in use: Footnote Reference, to format the number or symbol you use as a footnote reference mark; and Footnote Text, to format the footnote itself.

If you want to use an automatic style for some other element in a document, keep in mind that you can see a list of all styles—not just those in use—by choosing Format Style and setting the List box to All Styles. You can then select and apply the style. Once you've applied it, Word will recognize the style as being in use and will add it to the drop-down list on the Formatting toolbar and to the list that appears in the Style dialog box when the dialog box is set to show styles in use.

The relationship between Normal and other built-in styles

All of Word's built-in styles (in the Normal template, at least) are by default based on the Normal style—or on another style that is based on Normal. This has two important consequences.

First, the format specified by each built-in style will include all the characteristics of the Normal style except those that are explicitly defined otherwise.

Second, as you know, any change you make to the Normal style will affect the other built-in styles. For example, if you change the font for the Normal style from Times New Roman to Arial, most of the other built-in styles will use the Arial font as well. The whole point of the based-on link is to help you maintain consistency among the different parts of a document.

We suggest that whenever you need to make wholesale changes to a document, you start by adjusting the Normal style as appropriate. This is another variation on a top-down formatting strategy. It will minimize the number of changes you have to make in styles that are based on Normal.

For example, suppose you create a document and directly format the main body text in 12-point Arial type, rather than modifying the definition of the Normal style. You then decide to add a header to the document. Since you formatted the body text in this document with direct formatting, the header, which is based on the Normal style, will still use the default 10-point Times New Roman font rather than the 12-point Arial you're using for body text.

As a result, if you want the font in the header to be consistent with the rest of the document, you must either manually reformat the header text, modify the header style, or modify the Normal style (as you should have in the first place). You'll face the same choice if you add a footer, a footnote, or any other element for which Word supplies an automatic style.

You can avoid this problem entirely by applying styles instead of direct formatting. It's far easier to redefine the Normal style for a document than to reformat each element or each automatic style as it shows up.

More About Custom Styles

Earlier in this chapter, when we explained how to create a new custom style by defining it from scratch, we also mentioned a second way to create and modify styles. With this other approach, you first format a block of text the way you want it and then tell Word to use the formatted text as an example for the style you are defining or modifying.

How to create and modify styles by example

To create a custom style by example, place the cursor in the formatted text (or highlight the text) that you want to use as a model. Then move to the Style box on the Formatting toolbar (by clicking with the mouse or pressing Ctrl-Shift-S). Alternatively, choose Format Style, choose the New button to open the New Style dialog box, and go to the Name text box. In either case, type the new style name in the text box, and press Enter. Word will create a new style using the format of the text surrounding the cursor (or highlighted text). (Note that if the Formatting toolbar isn't displayed, pressing Ctrl-Shift-S will open the Style dialog box.)

If you use the Style box on the toolbar to create a style, Word will always create it as a paragraph style. If you open the New Style dialog box, you can define the new style as either a paragraph style or a character style.

To modify a style by example, start by formatting some text with the style you want to change and then reformat the text with direct formatting. With the cursor or selection still in the text, move to the Style box on the Formatting toolbar. Make sure the style name is highlighted and then press Enter, or open the drop-down list and click on the style name. Word will respond with a dialog box asking whether you want to redefine the style using the selection as an example or whether you want to return the formatting of the selection to match the style. Select the first option and then choose OK to make the change and return to the document window. Choose Cancel to return to the document window without making any changes.

Note that you cannot use the style-by-example approach to modify a style with the Format Style command.

Advantages and disadvantages of creating a style by example

The main difference between creating a style by defining it in the New Style dialog box and creating it by example is that when you create by example, you define the format before you name the style. It's an advantage to see the effects of your formatting before you actually create the style. This is especially helpful with a complicated format that requires fine-tuning to get exactly the result you want.

In addition, creating a style by example can come in handy when you've manually formatted a paragraph and then decide later that you want to use the same format in other locations in your document. Rather than manually reformatting the other text, you can use the first paragraph as an example to define a new style and then apply the style to all the paragraphs you want to format the same way.

Creating a new style by example can also have disadvantages, however. For example, Word assumes that the style for the following paragraph should be the same as the style you just created. Since that will often not be what you want, you'll have to choose Format Style, choose the Modify button, and set the Style For Following Paragraph box in the Modify Style dialog box to match your needs.

When using the style-by-example approach, you may get unexpected results if you accidentally select example text that includes varying formats. When you use this technique, be sure to confine the selection only to text with the formatting you actually want. Better yet, simply place the cursor in appropriately formatted text.

How to use based-on styles when defining by example

Whenever you define a new style, Word assumes that you want it to be based on an existing style. If you define a new paragraph style by example using the Format Style command and the New Style dialog box, Word will automatically set the Based On box to the style that was previously applied to the example paragraph. Similarly, when you define a new character style by example, Word will automatically set the Based On box to the character style that was previously applied to the example (or will set it to Default Paragraph Font if the text did not have an explicit character style). This means that it's a good idea to decide which style you want to use as your based-on style before you begin to define a new style by example. You can then use that style as your starting point.

For example, suppose you want to create a new paragraph style with all the characteristics of the Normal style except that the first line of each paragraph will be indented ¾ inch. Because this new style is so similar to Normal, it would make sense to start with an example paragraph that's formatted with the Normal style. This will save work in formatting the new style, and Word will automatically make Normal the based-on style. If necessary, you can change the based-on style later.

Notes about based-on styles

Because specifying a new based-on style changes the foundation of a style, it can drastically change the attributes of the current style. Suppose, for example, that the document you're working with contains styles named Normal, Style1, and Style2. The Normal style specifies 10-point Times New Roman type with flush-left alignment and no indents. Style1 is based on Normal, and its definition reads *Normal + Bold, Italic, Indent: Left 0.5" Right 0.5" Justified, Space Before 10 pt*. Style2 is based on Style1 and is identical to Style1 except that it specifies 12-point type. Figure 12-18 shows the definition and previews for Style2.

FIGURE 12-18

Style2 is identical to Style1 (its based-on style) except for font size.

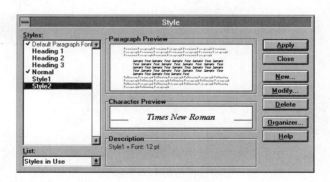

Suppose you want to change the based-on style for Style2 to Normal. Choose Format Style, and highlight Style2 in the Styles list. Then choose the Modify button to open the Modify Style dialog box and enter *Normal* in the Based On box. The result should match Figure 12-19 on the next page.

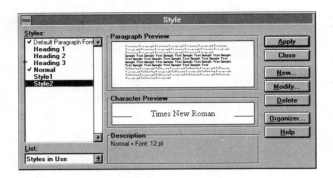

FIGURE 12-19

If you replace a based-on style, the current style will lose all the formatting characteristics defined in the previous based-on style.

With Style2 based on the Normal style, as shown in Figure 12-19, the formatting instructions for Style2 now build only on the Normal style, without the instructions you had added to Style1. As a result, text formatted with Style2 will resemble text formatted with Normal, rather than text formatted with Style1, except that it will have 12-point rather than 10-point characters.

It's best to avoid basing styles on unrelated styles. For example, you may have based an Indented Quote style on one of your heading styles because the two happen to have some similar formatting, although quotations and headings are not closely related document elements (as, for instance, a group of headings would be). If you then decide to change your headings to another format, you may not want the change to affect the Indented Quote style. In that case, you'll need to redefine the Indented Quote style, basing it on another style. If you base your styles on related styles, you're more likely to avoid this sort of situation.

When you change a style that serves as the based-on style for other styles, keep in mind that most changes will affect those other styles. For example, changing the font for the Normal style will change the font for most styles based on Normal; the only exceptions will be those styles that have a different font defined as part of the style or as part of an intermediate based-on style. The moral is simple: Be careful with changes, and watch out for a cascading effect.

Styles that are not based on other styles

If you want to create a style that's completely independent of the other styles in your document, you can select (no style) from the Based On drop-down list. The resulting style definition will consist of Word's default settings, plus any changes you've defined in the style.

However, in most cases you'll want to avoid creating a style independent of any other style. Remember that one of the biggest advantages of using based-on styles is precisely that you can change a feature in an underlying style, such as Normal, and have that change automatically reflected in all styles that are based on that style. You can avoid having to make the same change in each style if you change the font in the Normal style, for example, or change the line spacing.

In short, don't create an independent style unless you have good reason to. Typically, that means you want to ensure that its format remains unchanged no matter how you modify other styles in your document.

Notes about related styles

A style can be directly based on only one style, but any given style can be indirectly related to several styles, through a chain of based-on styles. In our earlier example, for instance, Style2 was based on Style1, which was in turn based on Normal. Style2 was thus indirectly related to Normal and directly related to Style1.

Word will not let you create circular style references. For example, suppose you create a Style3 and base it on Style2. If you then try to redefine Style1 to base it on Style3, Word will refuse to make the change and will display a message telling you that this style has a circular based-on list. You can then choose OK in the message box and enter a different based-on style.

Word will also refuse to let you create more than 11 levels of based-on styles (with 10 connections). For example, you can create a set of styles in which Style10 is based on Style9, which is based on Style8, and so forth, through Style1, based on Normal. However, if you try to create a Style11 that is based on Style10, Word will not accept it because it is based on too many styles. Fortunately, it's unlikely that you'll ever need as many as 11 levels for your styles.

Applying Styles

Most of this chapter up to now has been concerned with creating and modifying styles. In fact, we've mentioned only a few techniques for applying styles. Now it's time to remedy that situation.

How to use shortcut keys with styles

We'll begin with one of the most important techniques for applying styles: attaching them to shortcut keys. By assigning a particular set of shortcut keys to a style, you can create a handy way to quickly apply the style in your document.

How to assign shortcut keys to a style

You can attach styles to shortcut keys by way of the Keyboard card in the Customize dialog box. You can reach the Keyboard card by choosing Tools Customize and selecting the card or by choosing the Shortcut Key button that's available in both the New Style and Modify Style dialog boxes. Using the Tools Customize command will give you full access to all of Word's keyboard customization features. In contrast, if you choose the Shortcut Key button, Word restricts you to adding shortcuts only for the one style you're currently defining. For now, we'll look only at the more restricted capability available through the Modify Style and New Style dialog boxes. We'll cover the full-blown use of the Customize Keyboard card in Chapter 28, "Customizing Menus, Keys, & Templates," starting on page 950.

When you open the Customize dialog box through the Modify Style or New Style dialog box, Word will automatically take you to the Keyboard card, shown in Figure 12-20. It will not let you move to the other cards or even pick another style to assign a key to. Quite the contrary, in fact; you'll be able to assign a shortcut key only to the style you were defining before you chose the Shortcut Key button. That style—Normal in this case—will be displayed in the Commands list box as the only choice in that list.

FIGURE 12-20

Choose the Shortcut Key button in the Modify Style or New Style dialog box to open the Keyboard card in the Customize dialog box.

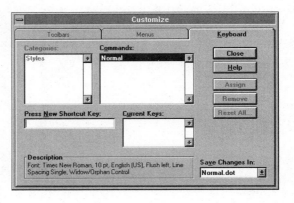

For the moment, the only two items you need to be concerned with on this card are the Press New Shortcut Key text box and the Current Keys list box. The Current Keys list box will list any shortcut keys currently assigned to the style you're working with. (As you'll see, you can assign more than one key combination.) The Press New Shortcut Key box is where you specify the keys you want to use.

Word will let you assign shortcut keys that use two keystrokes rather than one. This makes it far easier to use mnemonics rather than arbitrary combinations of easily forgotten keys. The first keystroke must be either a function key or a combination of Alt, Ctrl, Alt-Shift, Ctrl-Shift, Alt-Ctrl, or Alt-Ctrl-Shift with nearly any alphanumeric, punctuation, or function key on the keyboard. The second keystroke can be any one of the allowable alphanumeric, punctuation, or function keys by itself or in combination with the shift key.

Word initially places the cursor in the Press New Shortcut Key box. To enter the shortcut keys, simply press the appropriate keys. If you want a two-keystroke shortcut consisting of Alt-Shift-P followed by N, for example, press Alt-Shift-P and then press N. Word will display this in the Press New Shortcut Key box as *Alt+Shift+P,n*. It will also add a note below the box either indicating that these keys are currently unassigned or telling you the name of any command, macro, style, or other item to which the keys are currently assigned. If you want to change the shortcut key assignment, you can press Backspace to back up and start again.

As soon as you enter anything in the Press New Shortcut Key box, Word will make the Assign button available. Choose it to assign the shortcut key (or keys) to the style, and Word will add the shortcut to the Current Keys list, even if it was previously assigned to another item. Word will also gray the Assign button and wait. Figure 12-21 shows the Keyboard card after we've defined the Normal style as Alt-Shift-P,N.

FIGURE 12-21

After you define shortcut keys for a style, Word will wait to let you define additional shortcuts.

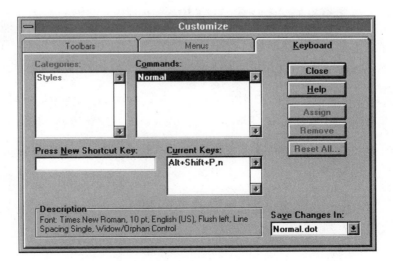

Once you've assigned shortcut keys to a style, you can define additional shortcuts with the same procedure. The ability to define additional shortcuts can be handy if more than one person is working on your system and each prefers a different set of shortcuts. You can also delete shortcut keys by moving to the Current Keys list, highlighting the shortcut keys you want to delete, and choosing the Remove button. When you've finished assigning shortcut keys, choose Close to close the dialog box and return to the Modify Style or New Style dialog box.

We strongly recommend that you take advantage of Word's two-keystroke capability and that you divide shortcut key mnemonics into groups to make them even easier to remember. You might, for example, use Alt-Shift for all style-related shortcut keys, reserving Alt-Shift-P for paragraph styles and Alt-Shift-C for character styles. Alternatively, if you depend heavily on styles and on shortcut keys, you might use a scheme such as Alt-Ctrl for paragraph styles and Alt-Shift for character styles. This would free you to use such mnemonics as Alt-Ctrl-H,1 for the Heading 1 style, Alt-Ctrl-H,2 for the Heading 2 style, Alt-Ctrl-E,A for the Envelope Address style, and so on.

How to apply a style with shortcut keys

Once you've attached a shortcut key to a style, applying the style is simple. To apply a paragraph style, place the cursor or selection in the paragraph or paragraphs you want to apply the style to and press the shortcut key. To apply a character style to any selection of text—and only to that selection, even if it stops in the middle of a word—select the text and press the shortcut key. To apply the style to a word, place the cursor anywhere in the word and press the shortcut key. To apply the style to text you are about to type, place the cursor where you want to insert the text—being careful to make sure it is not within a word—press the shortcut key, and start typing.

How to use a list or a text box to apply a style

If you don't like using shortcut keys, or if you find you can't remember the keys for styles you use infrequently, you can take advantage of several other methods Word offers for applying styles. Most of these let you choose the style name from a list. All assume that you've already positioned the cursor or selected the text you want to format, following the rules we just described for applying a style with shortcut keys. Since that's a universal requirement, we won't bother mentioning that step for the rest of this discussion.

How to apply a style from the Formatting toolbar

If you can recognize the name of the style you want, and if the style is already in use in the document, one of the simplest options is to use the Formatting toolbar (assuming that the toolbar is displayed on screen). Move to the Style box and open the drop-down list with the mouse or by pressing Ctrl-Shift-S and then the Up or Down arrow key. Scroll through the list until you see the style name you want, and either click on the name with the mouse or highlight it with arrow keys and press Enter.

Alternatively, if you already know the style name, you can simply type it in the Style box and press Enter. (You can also type part of the name and press the Down arrow key to have Word jump to the first style name in the list that matches the letters you typed. For example, typing *in* and then pressing the Down arrow key might move the highlight to Indented Quote or Index 1, if either name is in the list.)

When you designate the style with any of these methods, Word will immediately apply it to the current paragraph or paragraphs.

How to apply a style from the Style dialog box

If the Formatting toolbar is not displayed when you press Ctrl-Shift-S, Word will take you to the Style dialog box, just as if you had chosen Format Style. In the Style dialog box, you can set the List option to All Styles, Styles In Use, or User-Defined Styles to display the Styles list you need. You can then scroll through the Styles list, reading the description for each style as you highlight it, until you see the style you want. Once you find it, be sure that it is highlighted in the Styles list. Then choose Apply to apply the style and close the dialog box, or simply double-click on the style name.

Displaying the Style Area

As you become more comfortable with using styles, you'll find that it's often useful to know the style for the paragraphs you're currently looking at. Although the Style box on the Formatting toolbar always displays the name of the current style where the cursor is located, that style will sometimes be the current character style rather than the paragraph style.

In any case, it's even more helpful to see the style names for all the paragraphs on screen. You can see the names by opening the style area, which runs vertically along the left edge of the document window. When you open the style area, Word will display the name of the style used for each paragraph at the first line of the paragraph. (Note that you can open the Style dialog box quickly by double-clicking anywhere in the style area.)

Word will display the style area only when you're in Normal, Outline, or Master Document view. To see the area, first make sure you are not in Page Layout view. Next choose Tools Options, choose the View card, and enter a setting between 0.1 and 4.27 inches in the Style Area Width box. For this discussion, we'll use a setting of 0.6 inch. After you move to the Style Area Width box, you can type the number, or you can press the Up and Down arrow keys or click on the arrows at the right of the box to change the setting in 0.1-inch increments. Choose OK to accept the new setting and close the dialog box.

Your screen should now look similar to the one shown in Figure 12-22, assuming you have some text on your screen. Word will separate the style area from the text area with a vertical line and will display the style names in the style area for each paragraph.

FIGURE 12-22

When you open the style area, Word will show you the style for each paragraph, putting the style name at the beginning of each paragraph.

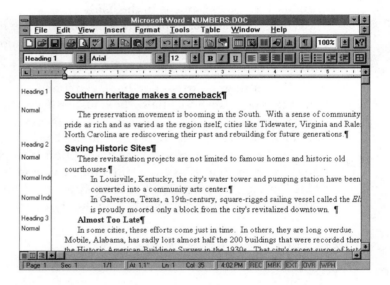

When you pick a size for the style area, your first thought will probably be to make it wide enough to show the longest style name in your document. If you make the style area too wide, however, your text may run off the right side of your screen, so you may have to compromise. In Figure 12-22, for example, the Normal Indent style name is cut off by the vertical line between the style area and the text area, and the body text still runs off the screen on the right side. If you can recognize the style name even when it's cut off, there's no reason why you shouldn't make the style area narrower than your longest style name.

How to resize the style area

You can resize the style area at any time by choosing Tools Options View and changing the setting in the Style Area Width box. You can also use the mouse to move the vertical line that separates the style area from the text area. If you move the mouse pointer over the style area split bar (the vertical line at the right edge of the style area), the pointer will change to a vertical split pointer, as shown in Figure 12-23. When the pointer changes shape, press the left mouse button, drag the split bar to its new location, and release the button.

FIGURE 12-23

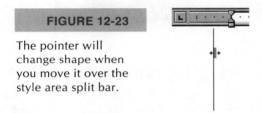

The pointer will change shape when you move it over the style area split bar.

How to close the style area

After you open the style area in a document, Word will show you a style area in each new document until you close the style area. To close it, choose Tools Options View, change the setting in the Style Area Width box to 0, and choose OK. Alternatively, you can use the mouse to drag the style area split bar to the left edge of the document window.

Printing Lists of Styles and Shortcut Keys

You'll find it easier to maintain consistency among style names in different documents if you have a printed list of the styles and a list of all the shortcut keys. That way, you can refer to the lists as you work on each document. You can easily print either list by choosing File Print, opening the Print What drop-down list, and choosing Styles or Key Assignments from the list, as appropriate. Figure 12-24 on the next page shows the drop-down list. You simply need to specify the item you want and choose OK to print it.

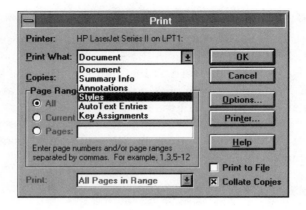

FIGURE 12-24

Among its print options, Word offers choices for printing a list of styles and a list of key assignments.

Using Styles and Direct Formatting Together

As you format a document, you can combine direct formatting changes with style formatting. In most cases, Word will simply add your direct formatting changes to the formatting features specified by the styles.

For example, suppose your document includes a paragraph style named Style1 that specifies 12-point bold Courier type. If you select some text that is formatted with this style and then use direct formatting to add italic, the paragraph will display italic formatting in addition to the bold and other features specified by Style1. Similarly, you can change the paragraph, tabs, border, and language format. In each case, the direct formatting changes will override the style formats, but Word will continue to display the style name in the style area and in the Style box on the Formatting toolbar, and it will continue to highlight the name in the Styles list in the Style dialog box.

This ability to override styles with direct formatting is essential in Word. Without it, you wouldn't be able to use direct formatting at all, given that every paragraph is assigned a style. Note that you can override both paragraph and character styles.

As a general rule, we strongly recommend that you use styles whenever possible. The reason is simple: If you format large amounts of text directly, you lose much of the benefit of styles because you can no longer make wholesale changes in your document simply by redefining a style.

Consider this: Direct formatting overrides style formats. That's why it works. So when you change the underlying style, the new style format will still be overridden by any direct formatting commands you've added. For example, if the Normal style is defined as Times New Roman, and if you've used direct formatting to change several paragraphs to Arial, those paragraphs will stay in Arial even if you change the Normal style definition to, say, Bookman Old Style.

Consider what would happen if you made your changes with a mix of styles and direct formatting. For example, suppose that after you directly format several paragraphs as Arial, you then change the definition of the Normal style to Arial. Later you decide to change the Normal style's font to Bookman Old Style. Before you redefine the Normal style, all the paragraphs with that style will look the same, since all will be set in Arial. But after you redefine it, any paragraphs that were originally formatted as Arial with direct formatting commands will still be Arial, whereas any that were formatted with styles only will change to Bookman Old Style. And there is no easy way to tell beforehand which paragraphs will change and which won't.

Some formatting commands act as toggles, which can add still more potential confusion. For example, suppose you've formatted one sentence within a paragraph as italic for emphasis. If you then redefine the style for that paragraph as italic, Word will automatically toggle the emphasized sentence to nonitalic (roman). This makes good sense, for it automatically maintains the emphasis. However, if you've directly formatted an entire paragraph in italic—to indicate a long quote, for example—and you then redefine the style as italic, you'll find that the italic text changes to roman in that situation too. Once again, the best way to avoid confusion is to use styles whenever possible.

This same effect, in which a formatting command acts as a toggle, can also crop up when you use character styles. But you are not likely to format an entire paragraph with a character style because the handiest tool in that case would be a paragraph style.

When you're first learning about styles, it's hard to use them as consistently as you might, if only because you have to define a new style every time you need a new format. This can create problems when you return to work on a document after learning more about styles or when you work on a document created by someone who hasn't taken advantage of styles. Fortunately, Word provides some shortcuts to make it easier to work with documents that are already formatted with a mix of styles and direct formatting. These shortcuts help to remove the direct formatting and reset the text to the format defined in the underlying style.

Resetting paragraph-level and character-level formatting

To understand how the reset commands work, you must first understand how Microsoft Word uses its two levels of formatting: character and paragraph. Character-level formatting is similar to (but not exactly the same as) the set of formatting choices that are available when you choose Format Font or the equivalent formatting shortcuts. Paragraph-level formatting is similar to the set of formatting choices available when you choose Format Paragraph or the equivalent shortcuts.

Character-level formatting includes any formatting that applies to individual characters—font, font size, bold, or italic, for example. It also includes the Language setting, which is available through the Tools Language command. Paragraph-level formatting applies to entire paragraphs and includes such formatting as indents, line spacing, space before and after, borders, and tabs. Word provides a simple reset command for each of these two levels.

The shortcut for removing paragraph-level formatting is ResetPara, a built-in command that by default isn't on any menu but is assigned to the shortcut keys Ctrl-Q. To use the command, simply place the cursor or selection in the paragraph or paragraphs you want to reset, and press Ctrl-Q.

Removing character-level direct formatting with the ResetChar command is similarly straightforward. Select the text you want to reset and press Ctrl-Spacebar or Ctrl-Shift-Z. Word will remove all character-level direct formatting.

You can reset a selection of any size, from one character to your entire document. If you want to reset the text for your whole document, press Ctrl-NumPad5 (5 on the numeric keypad) to highlight the entire document, and then press Ctrl-Q, followed by Ctrl-Spacebar.

Merging Styles from Another Document

Early in this chapter, we explained how to use Word's Style Gallery feature to copy all the styles from any template to the document you're working with. But Word lets you copy styles from other documents as well as from templates, and it also lets you copy styles one or a few at a time. The ability to copy styles can save you from having to redefine styles in more than one document.

How to copy one style

The most straightforward way to copy a style from one document to another is to copy a paragraph or some text formatted in that style. More precisely, to copy a paragraph style, you can copy a paragraph mark from a paragraph formatted in that style. To copy a character style, you can copy a character formatted in that style. Although the technique works for either kind of style, we'll use paragraph styles for this example.

Suppose you've created the style Long Quote in a document called CHAPTER1.DOC and you want to copy the style to the document CHAPTER2.DOC. Start by formatting a paragraph in CHAPTER1.DOC with the Long Quote style. Next select the paragraph mark at the end of that paragraph, by itself or with text, and choose the Edit Cut or Edit Copy command to place the formatted paragraph mark on the Clipboard. If you have not set Word to display paragraph marks, you can still select and copy to the Clipboard the equivalent of a paragraph mark. Move the cursor to the immediate right of the last character in the paragraph and then select from that position as far to the right as possible, to the end of the line, using the mouse or the keyboard. If you then choose the Edit Cut or Edit Copy command, Word will place what amounts to an invisible paragraph mark on the Clipboard. For the rest of this discussion, we'll simply refer to a "paragraph," by which we mean a paragraph mark or the equivalent, with or without text.

When the paragraph is on the Clipboard, you can open CHAPTER2.DOC (or move to that document window if it is already open) and paste the paragraph into the document. When you paste it, Word will automatically add the style name and the style definition to that document's list of styles.

When you copy a style this way, watch out for duplicate style names. If you try to copy a style into a document that contains a style with the same name, Word will not redefine the style in the destination document to match the formatting of the style in the source document. Instead, the paragraph will take on the formatting of the style that is already defined in the current document.

If the style definition you're copying includes a based-on style, Word may modify the formatting instructions when you paste the paragraph into the destination document—but only if the modification is needed to maintain the formatting. For example, suppose you are working in a document that contains styles named Sub1 and Sub2. The formatting instructions for Sub1 specify 14-point Arial type. Sub2, based on Sub1, specifies 12-point Arial type, so its definition reads *Sub1 + Font: 12 pt*. If you copy a paragraph formatted as Sub2 into a document that doesn't have a Sub1 style and whose Normal style is defined as Times New Roman, Word will add the Sub2 style using these formatting instructions: *Normal + Font: Arial 12 pt*.

Similarly, if the destination document has a Sub1 style that's formatted with 10-point Times New Roman, bold, and double spacing, Word will retain Sub1 as the based-on style but will change the Sub2 definition to read *Sub1 + Font: Arial 12 pt, Not Bold, Line Spacing Single*. In both cases, Word maintains the format of Sub2 in the destination document to match the format it had in the source document.

The best way to avoid uncertainty about the effect of copying a style from one document to another is to make sure you don't have duplicate style names, which may mean deleting a style of the same name in the destination document before copying. Of course, you can't avoid having a Normal style or other built-in style in each document, which prevents you from copying and pasting built-in styles between documents. One of your first steps in setting up a new document should be to set the Normal style to suit that particular document. Then, if you copy any styles based on Normal from one document to another, you'll need to watch carefully for unwanted format changes and make adjustments as necessary.

How to import styles with Word's Organizer

In addition to letting you copy individual styles by copying text and letting you copy sets of styles using the Style Gallery feature, Word also offers a far more elegant tool that will let you copy a single style, a designated subset of styles, or an entire set of styles between documents, between templates, or between a document and a template. This feature is Word's Organizer. For now, we'll take only a brief look at the Organizer. We'll cover it fully in Chapter 27, "Templates," starting on page 928, after we've discussed templates further.

To open the Organizer dialog box, shown in Figure 12-25, choose Format Style, and then choose the Organizer button.

FIGURE 12-25

To manage Word's styles, choose Format Style and then the Organizer button to open the Organizer dialog box.

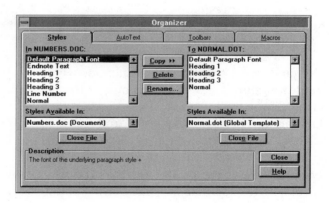

Although the Organizer offers several cards, we're interested only in the Styles card at the moment. The left and right sides of the card, each with two boxes and one button, are essentially identical. If you choose the Close File button on either side of the card, Word will erase all information from the two boxes above the button and will change the button to Open File. If you then choose Open File, you'll see the Open dialog box, which is the same dialog box you see when you choose the File Open command.

You can use the Open dialog box to choose a file—meaning any Word-format document or template file—for either the left or right side of the card. As you can see in Figure 12-25, Word lists the styles available in that file in the top box on that side and enters the filename in the Styles Available In box. You can then highlight one or more styles on either side of the card and copy them to the file on the other side of the card by choosing the Copy button. You can also highlight styles to delete them or rename them, using the Delete and Rename buttons. For more details on using the Organizer, see "The Organizer dialog box" on page 945.

Changing Defaults

If you create certain styles that you plan to use in virtually any document, you'll want to add them to the Normal template so that they'll be available to each new document. Similarly, if you prefer different default formats than those Word provides for Normal or other built-in styles, you'll want to change the definition of those styles in the Normal template. Otherwise, you'll have to change them in every new document you create. Fortunately, changing styles in the Normal template is no more complicated than changing styles in a document.

The effect of changing a style in a template

It's important to understand the effect of making a change in a template. Some changes to a template apply to all documents that have the modified template attached, no matter when those files were created. Other changes apply only to files that you create after making the changes.

Style changes fall into the second category. That means that if you want to make style changes to existing documents, you must import the modified styles, using any of the techniques we've discussed. It also means that you're free to change styles in a template without worrying about making inadvertent changes to existing documents.

How to modify styles in the Normal template from a document

One way to add styles to the Normal template—or any other template, for that matter—is to open the template and define the styles the same way you would in a document file. In fact, you can open, edit, and change a template just as you can any other Word document. But you have other choices as well, starting with the Organizer feature we discussed earlier.

Suppose you have a document that has only the Normal template attached and that already contains style definitions that you want to add to the Normal template. Start by opening the document and choosing Format Style. Then choose the Organizer button to open the Organizer dialog box. One side of the Styles card will be labeled with the document name; the other side will be labeled NORMAL.DOT. To copy styles to the Normal template, highlight them in the list box on the document side of the card, and choose Copy. When you're done, choose Close to close the dialog box. That's all there is to it.

You can also create or modify document styles and Normal template styles at the same time. In the lower left corner of the New Style and Modify Style dialog boxes is the Add To Template check box. If you check this box, Word will add the style you're currently modifying or creating to the template that's attached to the document as well as to the document itself. Note that whenever you open either dialog box, the check box is initially cleared to prevent you from modifying a style in the template by accident.

These techniques work exactly the same way for copying styles to any other template. Simply start by opening a document that contains the styles you want and that is attached to the supplementary template you want to copy the styles to. For details on templates, see Chapter 27, "Templates," starting on page 928.

How to save changes to styles in a template

Depending upon the current settings on the Tools Options Save card, Word may or may not prompt you for permission to save changes to NORMAL.DOT. If Prompt To Save Normal.dot is cleared (the default), Word will save changes to NORMAL.DOT when you save the document. When you make changes to styles in other templates, Word does not save those changes on disk immediately. When you save a document attached to the changed template, Word will prompt you separately for permission to save the changes to the template. If Prompt To Save Normal.dot is checked on the Tools Options Save card, Word will also prompt you for permission before saving changes to NORMAL.DOT. Simply answer Yes to save the changes. Alternatively, select File Save All to ensure that the changes to all attached templates are saved.

How to return to Word's original default settings

If you've changed the default styles in the Normal template and you later decide you want to restore the styles to their original form, you can simply delete the Normal template file, NORMAL.DOT, from your hard disk. The next time you start Word, the program will revert to its default settings for the Normal template. You can use any deletion technique you feel comfortable with to delete the file, including the File Delete command in the Windows File Manager, the DELETE command in MS-DOS, or your favorite MS-DOS or Windows-based utility program.

If you delete NORMAL.DOT, however, you'll also lose any other changes you've made to the Normal template, including AutoText entries, macros, and other advanced customizations that we'll discuss in Part Five. A more selective approach is to open the NORMAL.DOT file and modify the list of styles only, using the techniques discussed in this chapter. We'll look at editing templates in Chapter 27; for now, in the next two chapters, we'll move on to other advanced formatting issues.

TOPIC FINDER

Numbering Lines   470

- How to view line numbers
- How to remove line numbers

Numbering Paragraphs and Creating Lists   475

- How to number paragraphs in sequence
- Bullets
- NEW! Multilevel numbered paragraphs: Classic outlines

NEW! **Numbering Headings   483**

Multisection Documents   485

- How to divide a document into sections
- The Page Setup dialog box
- How to change page numbering from one section to another
- Section headers and footers
- How to combine two document sections

13

Bullets, Numbering, & Sections

n Chapter 7, we explained the basics of formatting Word documents. In Chapter 12, we covered styles. In this chapter and the two that follow, we'll cover some of Word's more complex formatting features (that is, features for complex formatting, not features that are hard to use). We'll cover automatic numbering, and we'll also explore sections, a topic that we've mentioned in earlier chapters but that we've not looked at in detail.

Word's numbering features can be broken down into two categories: by line and by paragraph. Numbering by paragraph can be further broken down into numbering that affects all paragraphs regardless of style (a category that includes bullets as one aspect) and numbering that affects only paragraphs formatted with certain styles. We'll start with the most detailed level of numbering—lines—and work our way through the other categories.

For most of the examples in this chapter, we'll use the text in Figure 13-1 on the next page. What makes it appropriate for illustrating the concepts we'll discuss is that it's representative of many real-world documents, with several levels of headings separating paragraphs of body text.

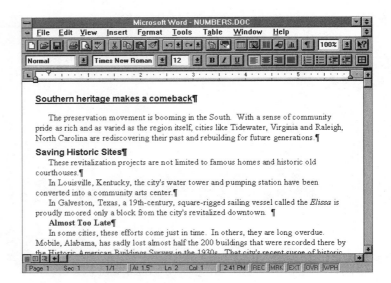

FIGURE 13-1

We will use this sample text in our examples of the different numbering options.

Numbering Lines

Some people need to create documents with numbered lines. The numbers may appear next to each line of text, next to every fifth line or tenth line, or at some other interval. Word not only makes it easy to create numbering, it automatically updates the line numbers to reflect changes as you revise the document.

To create line numbers in your documents, choose File Page Setup and then choose Layout to open the Layout card, shown in Figure 13-2. We'll discuss this card in detail later in this chapter. For now, we're interested only in the Line Numbers button at the bottom of the card and the Apply To box next to it.

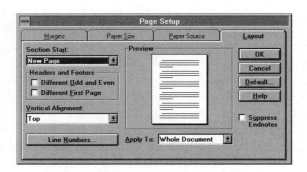

FIGURE 13-2

The Page Setup Layout card lets you choose line numbering for your document.

The choices in the Apply To drop-down list vary depending on your document, but the Whole Document choice always appears. Another choice always is either This Point Forward (if you haven't selected any text in the document) or Selected Text (if you have). If the document includes more than one section, you'll see a third choice as well: either This Section (if you haven't selected any text in the document) or Selected Sections (if you have). To add line numbers, select the appropriate Apply To option, and then choose the Line Numbers button to open the Line Numbers dialog box, shown in Figure 13-3.

FIGURE 13-3

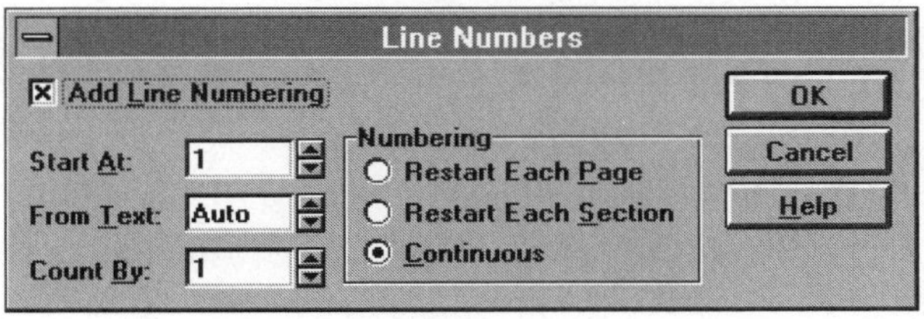

The Line Numbers dialog box provides options for numbering lines of text.

Line Numbers
X Add Line Numbering
Start At: 1
From Text: Auto
Count By: 1
Numbering: ○ Restart Each Page ○ Restart Each Section ● Continuous
OK Cancel Help

When you first open the Line Numbers dialog box, most of the choices will be grayed. To make them available and to turn on line numbering, check the Add Line Numbering check box.

The Start At text box tells Word what number to use as the starting number for the first line. This is a useful feature if you've broken a long document into several files and want to maintain continuous numbering. The default is 1, but you can enter any number from 1 through 32,767.

Even with 60 lines per page, the maximum starting number of 32,767 allows nearly 550 pages before you run out of acceptable starting numbers. But note that although you can't enter a larger *starting* number, Word is quite willing to continue numbering lines past this point.

The From Text box lets you specify the distance between the right edge of the line numbers and the left edge of your text. The default setting is Auto, which will serve most needs. However, you can set this to as high as 22 inches, although this is farther from your text than you'll ever need since 22 inches is also Word's maximum page width. Note that if you click the arrows to the right of the box, Word will change the setting in increments of 0.1 inch, but you can use the keyboard to enter other increments, such as 0.25 or 0.27 inch.

The Count By option specifies how often the line numbers appear. The default is every line, but you can set any number of lines that you like. For example, if you set Count By to 5, every fifth line will be numbered, and the numbers will appear as 5, 10, 15, and so on.

The Numbering options tell Word whether and when to restart counting, starting with the setting you've entered as the Start At number. You can tell Word to restart the numbering at the beginning of every new page or every new section, or you can choose Continuous for continuous numbering. The default setting is Restart Each Page.

How to view line numbers

For now, we'll accept all the default values, choose OK, and then choose OK again on the Layout card. If Word is in Normal or Outline view, you may be surprised to see that the document is unchanged.

To see the line numbers, Word must be in either Page Layout view or Print Preview, or you must print the document. Figure 13-4 shows our sample document in Page Layout view, complete with line numbers. Note that the numbers appear in the margin of the document. If we reformat the document in two columns, the line numbers will appear to the left of each column of text, as shown in Figure 13-5. (We'll discuss multicolumn formatting in Chapter 14.)

FIGURE 13-4

Line numbers appear to the left of your text.

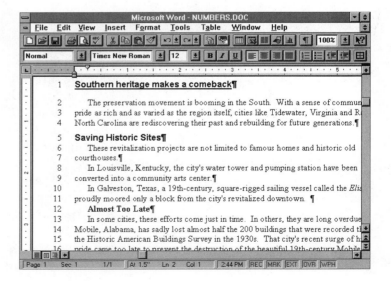

FIGURE 13-5

If your document is formatted with multiple columns, line numbers will appear to the left of each column. In this example, the Count By option is set to 5.

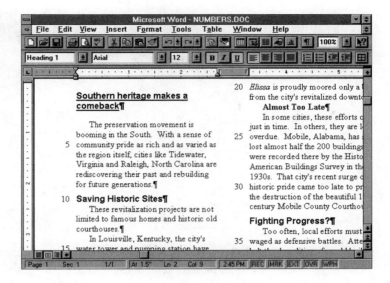

As you can see in these examples, Word counts every line. In fact, if your document contains a blank line that you created by pressing Enter, Word will count that line as well. However, if you've formatted a paragraph to have extra space between lines or between paragraphs, Word will not number that space, as you can see by the space between lines 1 and 2 in Figure 13-4. Figure 13-5 shows how a Count By setting of 5 affects the line numbering.

How to remove line numbers

If you want to get rid of all the line numbers, choose File Page Setup, choose Layout, choose the Line Numbers button, and remove the X from the Add Line Numbering check box.

There might be times, however, when you want to selectively remove line numbers from your document. For example, you might want to number only the body text and leave the headings out of the count. To remove numbering from selected paragraphs, first place the cursor or selection in the paragraph or paragraphs you don't want numbered, choose Format Paragraph, and then choose Text Flow to see the Text Flow card, shown in Figure 13-6 on the next page. To exclude the paragraph or paragraphs from line numbering, check the Suppress Line Numbers check box on the left side of the card.

FIGURE 13-6

The Paragraph Text Flow card includes the Suppress Line Numbers check box, which lets you exclude a paragraph from line numbering.

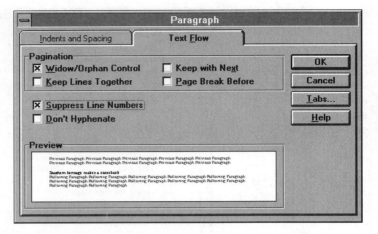

Figure 13-7 shows our sample document with the Suppress Line Numbers option active for the headings, leaving line numbers beside body text only. As you can see, the Suppress Line Numbers option not only suppresses the display of numbers for these paragraphs, it leaves the headings out of the count altogether.

FIGURE 13-7

In this sample, the Suppress Line Numbers option is active for all the headings, so only the body text lines are numbered.

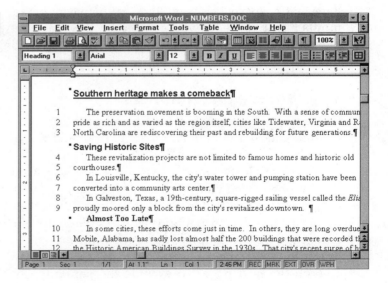

You can automatically skip line numbering for headings by formatting your heading paragraphs with styles, defining the heading styles with the Suppress Line Numbers option. For more details on paragraph formats in styles, see "Working with Styles" on page 432.

Numbering Paragraphs and Creating Lists

If you need to number paragraphs rather than lines, you can use Word's paragraph-numbering feature. More precisely, Word will let you use numbers, letters, or typographical bullets to mark paragraphs. It even provides outline formats that mix letters and numbers. For this discussion, we'll use *numbering* as a generic term for adding Arabic or Roman numerals, letters in alphabetical order, or any combination of these.

One difference between line-numbering and paragraph-numbering features is that paragraph numbering is not an all-or-nothing proposition that you turn on for the entire document and then have to make specific exceptions for. Rather, you select only those paragraphs that you want numbered and then give the command to number them. Another difference is that you can see the results of paragraph numbering in all views, not merely in Page Layout view, in Print Preview, and on the printed page.

There is one important similarity between the Bullets and Numbering feature and line numbering: The numbers are not inserted as text. In Word 2.0, when you numbered a list, the numbers were inserted as part of the text and could be edited like any other part of your document. In Word 6.0, the numbers (or bullets) are not part of the text but are instead anchored to the paragraph. If you move the paragraph, the line number changes. If you delete the paragraph, you also delete the line number.

There are two ways to number paragraphs in a document. You can number each one in sequence, as you do in a list, or you can number them according to different levels, as you do in an outline. Word can automatically update numbers as you add, move, or delete paragraphs. We'll start with numbering in sequence.

How to number paragraphs in sequence

Certain kinds of documents—particularly certain kinds of legal documents—use numbers for individual paragraphs. But most people use Word's paragraph-numbering feature for lists. In either case, you can add the numbering before or after you've created the text. If you're just starting the first paragraph you want numbered, simply press Enter to create the paragraph, and with the cursor in the new paragraph, choose the Format Bullets And Numbering command. Then choose the Numbered tab to display the Numbered card, shown in Figure 13-8 on the next page. If you've already created the text (in one or more paragraphs), highlight it first and then choose the command.

FIGURE 13-8

The Numbered card in the Bullets And Numbering dialog box offers settings for numbering paragraphs.

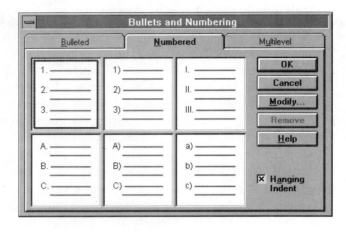

The Numbered card contains six thumbnail sketches of predefined numbering formats. To use one, simply select the one you want and choose OK. The Hanging Indent check box in the lower right corner lets you format the paragraphs so that the subsequent lines of text in each paragraph are indented, with the numbers in a column to the left of the text.

To create your own format for numbering, first select the predefined format that's closest to what you want, and then choose the Modify button to open the Modify Numbered List dialog box, shown in Figure 13-9.

FIGURE 13-9

The Modify Numbered List dialog box lets you define the format for numbering.

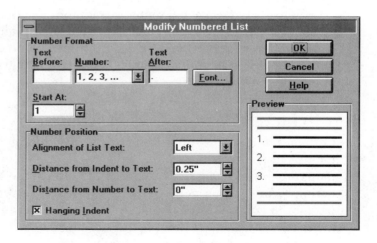

The Modify Numbered List dialog box contains two group boxes and a Preview box, which shows the effects of your choices. The Number Format group box has four text boxes and a button. The Text Before and Text After boxes let you specify text and punctuation to use with every number. (You are limited to a total of 32 characters in the Text Before and Text After boxes combined.)

The Number box has a drop-down list that shows the available choices for format. You can number your paragraphs using any of these (or none if you prefer):

1, 2, 3, 4

I, II, III, IV

i, ii, iii, iv

A, B, C, D

a, b, c, d

1st, 2nd, 3rd, 4th

One, Two, Three, Four

First, Second, Third, Fourth

The Start At box tells Word the starting number to use in its count. As with line numbering, the maximum value for a number format you can start with is 32,767, but Word will continue numbering paragraphs with values higher than that if you are using Arabic numerals or a numbering format based on spelled-out numbers. If you are using Roman numerals, the highest number you can start with is MMMCMXCIX (3999), but the numbering will stop there and the next paragraph will be numbered I. For letters, the highest starting number is 780 (30 Zs in a row), and the next item will be marked with an *A*.

Note that the Preview box does not always match the final result. In particular, the 1,2,3... number format is displayed as *32766, 32767, 0, 1,...* in the Preview box, but the numbering comes out correctly in the final document. Something similar happens with the 1st, 2nd, 3rd... format.

Choosing the Font button opens the Font dialog box, in which you can specify font formatting for the numbers. We covered the Font dialog box in "The Font dialog box" starting on page 246.

The Number Position group box controls the placement of the numbers and text. The first choice, Alignment Of List Text, lets you align the numbering as Left, Right, or Centered in the space between the first-line indent and the value specified in Distance From Indent To Text. The position of the first-line indent is based on the indention of the starting paragraph. If you've checked the Hanging Indent check box, Word will use the Distance From Indent To Text value for the left indent of the paragraph, putting the numbers to the left of the text, with all text starting at the same indent. If you haven't checked Hanging Indent, the left indent will be equal to the position of the first-line indent. The Distance From Number To Text choice lets you control the position of the text on the first line.

Figure 13-10 shows our sample document after we created a numbered list using default settings. Notice how the hanging indents place the numbers to the left of the text.

FIGURE 13-10

This document was numbered using the Format Bullets And Numbering command.

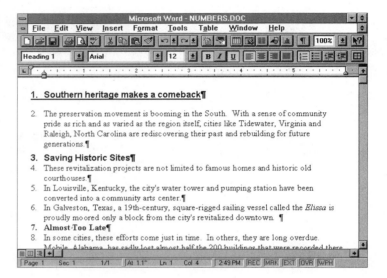

You can also number paragraphs by placing the cursor or selection in the paragraph or paragraphs you want to number and then clicking on the Numbering button on the Formatting toolbar—the fifth button from the right. Word generally uses the default numbering format. However, if the paragraph immediately before or after is already formatted as numbered, Word will use the same formatting as the already numbered paragraph.

Note too that if you select a single blank paragraph and choose the Numbering command, Word will add a number. However, if you select more than one paragraph, Word will indent, but not add numbers to, any blank paragraphs. Rather, Word will assume that you want a single, continuous numbering system throughout the selection and that you also want to skip the blank lines.

How to remove numbering

Word automatically adds numbering to paragraphs that you create by pressing Enter while the cursor is already in a numbered paragraph. When you finish entering the last paragraph in a list and you press Enter to start a new paragraph that you don't want numbered, you need to remove the numbering from the new paragraph. To remove numbering from one or more paragraphs at the beginning or end of a sequence, place the cursor or selection in the appropriate paragraph or paragraphs, and then either choose Format Bullets And Numbering and choose the Remove button from any of the cards in the dialog box or click on the Numbering button on the Formatting toolbar. Be aware, however, that the Numbering button will sometimes produce unexpected results if you have selected more than one blank paragraph.

There may also be times when you want to remove numbering from paragraphs that are in the middle of a group of numbered paragraphs. To remove numbering, select the appropriate paragraph or paragraphs, and either choose Format Bullets And Numbering and then choose the Remove button or click on the Numbering button on the Formatting toolbar.

However, there is an important difference between these two choices. If you use the Format Bullets And Numbering command, Word will revert to the paragraph format of the Normal style and break the list in two, and the numbering will start at the beginning number for the paragraph after the newly un-numbered paragraphs. If you want to maintain a single sequence and the indent, use the Numbering button on the Formatting toolbar; Word will change the remaining numbers to maintain a single sequence and will indent the unnumbered paragraph to match the rest of the paragraphs.

Another way to skip a paragraph but keep the numbering sequence intact is to place the cursor or selection in the paragraph or paragraphs you want to skip, and with the mouse pointer in any of the paragraphs in the sequence, click the right mouse button to bring up a context-sensitive pop-up menu. Choose Skip Numbering to remove the numbering from the selected paragraph or paragraphs. The numbering sequence will continue with the next paragraph. (This is the same as clicking on the Numbering button.) This menu has two other commands. Stop Numbering removes numbering, reverts to the Normal paragraph format, and restarts the numbering sequence for any subsequent paragraphs. (This is the same as using the Remove button.) Bullets And Numbering opens the Bullets And Numbering dialog box. These three choices are not available if you've selected a paragraph that's formatted with a Heading style.

Bullets

In addition to the Numbered card in the Bullets And Numbering dialog box, there is also a Bulleted card, which works much the same way. A bullet is a symbol—typically a dot—that marks each item in a list. Almost any symbol can be a bullet, including a square, a diamond, or a box. A list that uses bullets is called a bulleted list. The Bulleted card is shown in Figure 13-11.

FIGURE 13-11

The Bulleted card in the Bullets And Numbering dialog box lets you add bullets to a list of paragraphs.

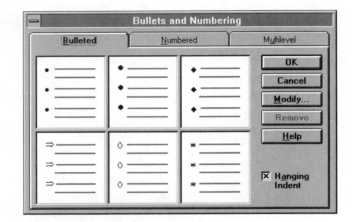

You can either choose from six thumbnail sketches or define your own format. To define a format, choose the Modify button to open the Modify Bulleted List dialog box, shown in Figure 13-12.

FIGURE 13-12

The Modify Bulleted List dialog box lets you define a format for bulleted lists.

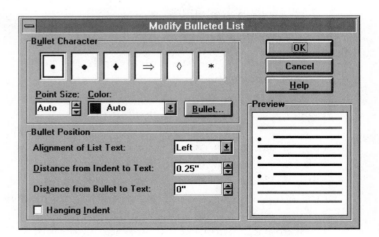

The dialog box offers six predefined bullet characters, as well as Point Size and Color boxes that let you modify the character you choose. In addition, you can choose another character by clicking on the Bullet button to open the Symbol dialog box, which is also used by the Insert Symbol command. For details on the Symbol dialog box, see "The Insert Symbol command" on page 157.

The options in the Bullet Position group box are essentially identical to the equivalent options for numbers in the Modify Numbered List dialog box, and they work the same way.

> In fact, almost all of the bullet-related features work much the same as the equivalent features for numbering paragraphs. You can, for example, use the Bullets button on the Formatting toolbar to add or remove bullets from paragraphs. As with the Numbering button, the feature will generally indent, but not add bullets to, blank paragraphs when you select more than one paragraph. You can use the right mouse button to bring up a context-sensitive menu for bulleted paragraphs that is the same as the menu for numbered paragraphs. The bullet and number features are so closely related, in fact, that the choices on the menu still say Skip Numbering and Stop Numbering. Choose Skip Numbering to remove a bullet but keep the indent. Choose Stop Numbering to remove both a bullet and the indent.

Figure 13-13 shows our sample text with bullets added to the second and third paragraphs after the second heading. To get this result, we selected both paragraphs and used the default bullet settings in the Format Bullets And Numbering dialog box.

FIGURE 13-13

Word's bullet feature helps you set off lists from the rest of your text, making them easier to read.

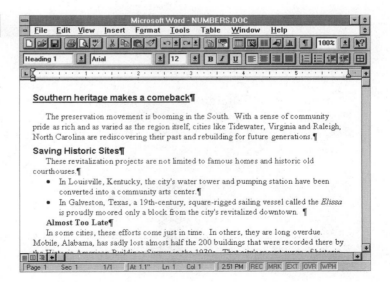

Multilevel numbered paragraphs: Classic outlines

You can think of Word's multilevel numbered paragraphs as a tool for producing classic outlines—the kind you probably learned in high school—with each paragraph numbered appropriately, depending on how it's indented. Don't confuse this feature with Word's View Outline feature, which is a collapsible outliner for working with documents in outline form. (We'll cover View Outline in Chapter 19.) The multilevel-numbering feature is a tool for producing an outline format in which the outline itself is the final product. For purposes of this discussion, we'll call this an outline list or a multilevel list, to distinguish it from Word's collapsible outliner.

To create an outline, or multilevel, list, start by placing the cursor or selection in the paragraph where you want numbering to start or in the paragraphs you want to add numbering to. Then choose Format Bullets And Numbering and choose the Multilevel card, as shown in Figure 13-14.

FIGURE 13-14

The Multilevel card in the Bullets And Numbering dialog box gives you control over paragraph numbering in outlines.

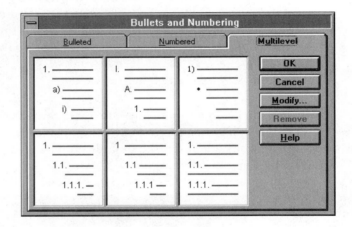

Like the other two cards in this dialog box, the Multilevel card offers six thumbnail sketches of predefined formats. Because all the predefined formats rely on hanging indents, there is no check box for hanging indents on the card. The Modify button takes you to the Modify Multilevel List dialog box, which is nearly identical to the Modify Numbered List dialog box, with three notable exceptions.

First, because multilevel numbering offers nine levels and because you can format each level separately, you'll find a scrollable Level box that lets you choose which level to format. Second, instead of a Number box, you'll find a Bullet Or Number box, which lets you choose a predefined number format *or* a predefined bullet, *or* you can choose New Bullet from the list to open the Symbol dialog box, in which you can select any available symbol.

The Include From Previous Level option lets you define the current level to include the numbers, the numbers and position, or nothing from the previous (next highest) level. Choose the Numbers option if you want the number format to include the full numbering scheme, as in *1.2.2.* Choose Numbers And Position if you want each item in the numbering scheme to be in a line directly below the numbers in the higher level. The Preview box shows the current settings for all nine levels. Figure 13-15 shows a document with three short outline lists, demonstrating the effect of each choice available in the Previous Level box.

FIGURE 13-15

The same short outline list is shown here with three different numbering formats.

1.   Southern heritage makes a comeback¶
       1.   Saving Historic Sites¶
              1.   Almost Too Late¶
2.   Fighting Progress?¶

1.   Southern heritage makes a comeback¶
1.1.   Saving Historic Sites¶
            1.1.1.   Almost Too Late¶
2.   Fighting Progress?¶

1.   Southern heritage makes a comeback¶
1.   1.   Saving Historic Sites¶
1.   1.   1.   Almost Too Late¶
2.   Fighting Progress?¶

When you're satisfied with the numbering format definition, choose OK to close the Modify Multilevel List box. As with the other numbered paragraph options, Word doesn't number any paragraphs that lack text.

> You can use the Increase Indent and Decrease Indent buttons on the Formatting toolbar to promote or demote paragraphs to different levels, or you can use the Alt-Shift-Right arrow and Alt-Shift-Left arrow shortcut keys, or the Promote and Demote commands on the pop-up menu. In all cases, Word automatically renumbers the paragraphs and changes the indents appropriately. To produce the outline list shown in Figure 13-15, for example, we entered some paragraphs, applied multilevel numbering, added more paragraphs, and either demoted or promoted each paragraph to its appropriate level as we worked with the text.

You can use the right mouse button to call up a pop-up menu to either skip or stop numbering.

Numbering Headings

Word provides an alternative for producing outlines that's related to the collapsible outline feature. You'll generally find it the more efficient approach when you want an outline of the entire document and you want to include unnumbered text paragraphs within the outline. This second approach takes advantage of heading styles.

As we discussed in Chapter 12, Word comes with a variety of built-in style definitions, including nine levels of heading styles, named Heading 1, Heading 2, Heading 3, and so on. If you've defined paragraphs with these styles, you can tell Word to number them automatically. If you use this feature, Word will number only those paragraphs that use heading styles 1 through 9, in contrast to multilevel numbering, which creates an outline list that numbers all paragraphs that include text.

The feature is called heading numbering, and it's an all-or-nothing proposition—you turn it on or off for the entire document. Figure 13-16 shows our sample document with heading numbering turned on. The style area in the figure shows the style for each paragraph.

FIGURE 13-16

This sample document shows the effect of the Format Heading Numbering command. Note that Word numbers only those paragraphs that are formatted with a heading style.

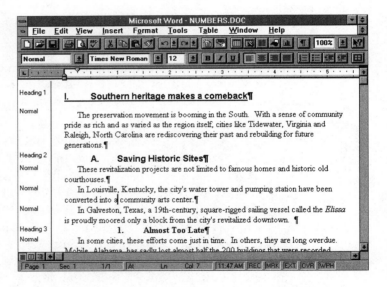

To turn on heading numbering and define the format to use, choose Format Heading Numbering to open the Heading Numbering dialog box, shown in Figure 13-17.

This dialog box is similar to the Multilevel card, described in the preceding section, and it works the same way. You can choose one of the six thumbnail sketches of predefined formats, or you can choose the Modify button to define your own. The Modify Heading Numbering dialog box is nearly identical to the corresponding dialog box for multilevel numbering, except that it has a check box labeled Restart Numbering At Each New Section. This check box lets you start each chapter in a document as a separate section and have Word automatically number the chapter for you.

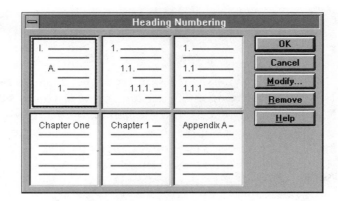

FIGURE 13-17

The Heading Numbering dialog box is similar to the Multilevel card in the Bullets And Numbering dialog box.

Multisection Documents

So far in our discussions of formatting, we've treated each document as a single large chunk of text consisting only of paragraphs, words, and characters. As we've mentioned several times, however, there is another level of organization: the section, which presents a whole new range of formatting options.

For example, we mentioned section headers and footers when we discussed headers and footers. You might use these when you have a long document broken into separate chapters that you want to keep in one file. If you define each chapter as a section, you can create a different header and footer for each.

Sections have a place in shorter documents as well. For example, if you want to vary the number of columns, you'll need to create sections. We'll discuss how to use columns in "Multicolumn Formatting" starting on page 497.

In fact, you will need to use multiple sections whenever you want to change any of the following in your document:

- Margins
- Paper size or orientation
- Paper source
- Line numbering
- Contents and position of headers or footers
- Number of text columns
- Page numbering
- Numbering and formatting of footnotes or endnotes

When you create a new section, it inherits the formatting from the previously existing section. This means that if you split up a document into sections, all will start out with the same settings. You can then make formatting changes to the individual sections without affecting the whole document. If you want to change a format for only one section—to switch the page orientation for a single page, for example—you can save some steps by creating two new sections (for a total of three) and moving to the first new section to make your changes. When you go to the second new section, it will still have the original format.

How to divide a document into sections

Every new Word document initially consists of one section. If you want to create a new section, place the cursor where you want the section to begin, and choose Insert Break to open the Break dialog box, as shown in Figure 13-18. As you can see, the dialog box includes option buttons for Page Break and Column Break, plus four options in the Section Break box labeled Next Page, Continuous, Even Page, and Odd Page. For the moment, we're concerned only with the four section break options.

FIGURE 13-18

The Break dialog box lets you insert four kinds of section breaks into your document.

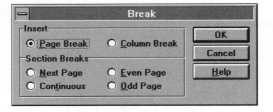

Any of the options in the Section Break box will insert a section break, but they differ in how Word will treat the resulting section break.

If you choose the Continuous option, Word will start the new section without starting a new page. This is especially useful when you want to mix different column layouts on a single page.

If you choose the Next Page option, Word will immediately begin a new page and a new section. The first paragraph in the new section will be printed at the top of a new page, meaning that part of the previous page might be left blank.

If you choose the Even Page or Odd Page option, Word will not only start the new section at the top of a new page, but it will make sure that the page is even numbered (left) or odd numbered (right), as appropriate. If necessary, Word will insert a blank page to force the new section to start on the even-numbered or odd-numbered page.

You might want to use the Even Page or Odd Page choice in a long report that you plan to hand out in a binder. In books, for example, it's a common practice to begin each chapter on an odd-numbered page. Similarly, if your report contains charts and descriptions, you might want to ensure that all the charts appear on even pages and their descriptions appear on odd pages.

After you select the kind of section break you want, choose OK to close the dialog box. If you are in Normal view or Outline view, Word will mark the section break on your screen with a horizontal line and the label *End of Section*, as shown in Figure 13-19. The markers will not appear in Print Preview or on a printed document. They will appear in Page Layout view, but not as individual lines and only if Word is set to show all nonprinting characters (with the Tools Options View card or with the Show/Hide Toolbar button).

FIGURE 13-19

Word marks section breaks on your screen with a horizontal line.

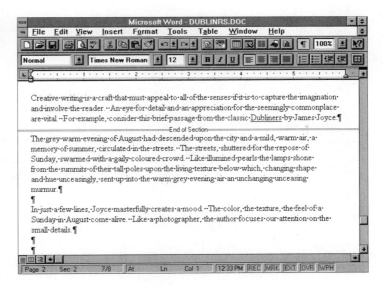

After you divide a document into two or more sections, Word uses the Sec indicator in the status bar to indicate the section the cursor is currently in. For example, notice that the status bar in Figure 13-19 displays *Page 2 Sec 2*. This tells you that the cursor is on page number 2 in the second section of the document.

Note that this page is not necessarily the second page in the document. If you are using continuous numbering, it is, but if you've used the Format option of the Insert Page Numbers command to number each section separately starting with page 1, the second page in section 2 will be page number 2, no matter how many pages are in section 1. To see the difference, look to the right of the Sec indicator. In Figure 13-19, you'll see *7/8,* which means you're on the seventh page of an 8-page document, with 5 pages in section 1.

The Page Setup dialog box

Many of the options for section-level formatting are available in the Page Setup dialog box, which we touched on briefly at the start of this chapter and which is shown again in Figure 13-20. To open this dialog box, choose File Page Setup.

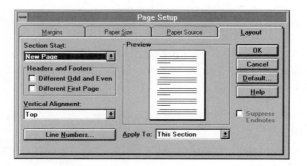

FIGURE 13-20

The Page Setup dialog box lets you vary certain characteristics from section to section.

The cards in this dialog box let you specify settings for margins, paper size, paper source, and layout. We have already covered most of these settings elsewhere in this book.

At the bottom of each card in the Page Setup dialog box, you'll see an Apply To box with a drop-down list. The choices in this list always include This Point Forward and Whole Document. If the document includes at least two sections, you'll also see This Section (or Selected Sections if you have selected text). Whole Document and This Section are self-explanatory. Less obvious is that if you choose This Point Forward, Word will insert a section break and apply whatever format change you've just defined to the new section only.

Also note that if you selected some text before opening the Page Setup dialog box, Word adds the choice Selected Sections if the selection includes more than one section and adds both Selected Sections and Selected Text if the selection is limited to part of one section. Here again, Selected Sections is self-explanatory. If you choose Selected Text, Word will insert section breaks before and after that text, to make it a separate section.

How to change the type of section break

A few additional options on the Layout card deserve mention here.

The Section Start list box lets you change the type of section break without deleting the current section break and insert another. Figure 13-21 shows the options available in the list box. Four of these match the options available in the Break dialog box when you insert a section break. New Column tells Word to start the new section at the start of a new column and applies only to multicolumn formats.

Section Start:

New Page	▼
Continuous	
New Column	
New Page	
Even Page	
Odd Page	

> If you need to change the type of section break (the Section Start setting), keep in mind that the change will apply to the section the cursor or selection is currently in. For example, if you originally inserted a section break that starts section 2 on a new page and you want to change the break to Continuous, position the cursor in section 2 before choosing Format Section Layout.

How to set vertical alignment

The Vertical Alignment option on the Layout card lets you tell Word how to position text between the page's top and bottom margins. Figure 13-22 on the next page shows how each of the Vertical Alignment options affects a sample printed page.

By default, Word selects the Top option, which tells Word to place the first line on each page just below the top margin. If there are not enough lines of text to fill the entire text area between the top and bottom margins, Word leaves all the blank space at the bottom of the page.

The Center option spaces the text evenly between the top and bottom margins. If there are not enough lines to fill a page—either because it is the last page of a section or because of a manual page break—Word will center the text vertically on the page. This option is handy for creating a title page.

The Justified option tells Word to insert an equal amount of space between the paragraphs on each page. (This option does not affect the spacing between the lines within each paragraph.) As with the Center option, this only makes a difference when there are not enough lines to fill the page. The amount of space inserted between paragraphs depends on how much extra space there is on the page. If two pages have 20 lines of text, but one page has only two paragraphs of 10 lines each and the other has five paragraphs of 4 lines each, the spacing between paragraphs on the two pages will be very different.

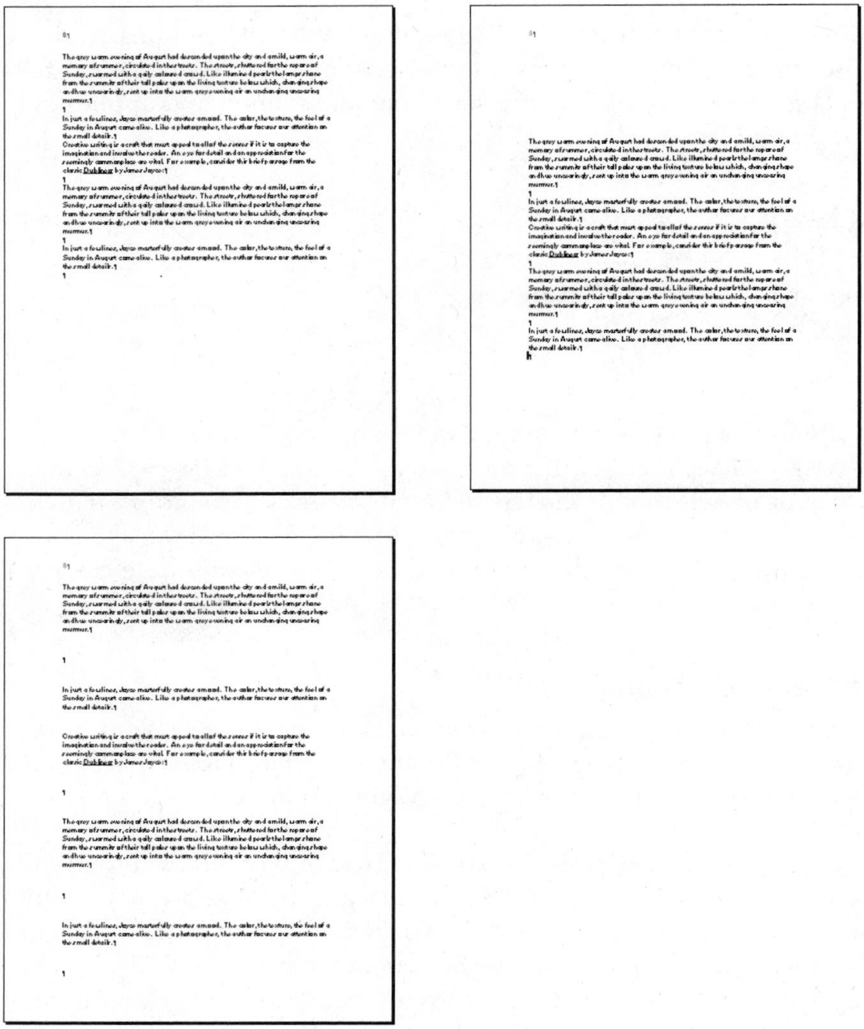

FIGURE 13-22

The Vertical Alignment options (Top, Center and Justified) in the Page Setup dialog
box let you control the vertical position of the text on a page.

Be aware that the effects of the Vertical Alignment options are not visible
except in Page Layout view, in Print Preview, or on a printed page. Also, the
Preview box on the Layout card looks the same no matter which setting you
have chosen because the preview assumes an entire page of text.

How to change page numbering from one section to another

In Chapter 5, we explained how to number pages by inserting a page number in a header or footer or by using the Insert Page Numbers command. We also introduced the five numbering formats for pages and explained how to position page numbers in the header. As we mentioned, you can optionally restart numbering with each new section. You can also use different numbering schemes and entirely different headers and footers in each section.

For this discussion, we'll assume that you already have a header or footer in your document and that you need to change the page numbering for one or more sections. Because the commands for headers and footers are essentially identical, we'll follow the same convention we used in Chapter 5 and talk primarily about headers, except where explicitly stated otherwise, although these comments apply to both headers and footers.

 Changing the numbering of pages is straightforward. First be certain that the cursor or selection is in the section that you want to change. (It may be in some other part of the document than is currently displayed on your screen, so use the position information in the status bar to check the current section.) If the selection crosses section boundaries, the status bar will show the position for the end of the selection, and the changes you make will affect only the section that shows in the status bar.

Regardless of whether you have numbered your pages by using Insert Page Numbers or by inserting a field in a header or footer, you can change the numbering by choosing Insert Page Numbers and then choosing the Format button to open the Page Number Format dialog box, shown in Figure 13-23.

FIGURE 13-23

Word's Page Number Format dialog box lets you control page numbering section by section.

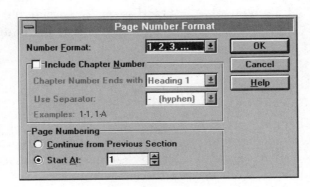

How to number sections separately

The Number Format box in the Page Number Format dialog box lists five numbering systems.

The Page Numbering box has two option buttons that let you determine the starting value for the section's page numbering. The Continue From Previous Section option takes whatever number was used by the previous section and uses the next consecutive number as its starting point. This is Word's default setting.

If you choose the Start At option, you can specify what to use as the section's first number or letter. Word uses the existing number format unless you tell it otherwise. If you enter 1 here, Word will use *A*, *a*, *I*, or *i*, depending on the format. However, you can also enter the starting number in the appropriate format—letters or Roman numerals. You can specify any number from 0 through 32,767 as the Start At value for the *1, 2, 3...* format, 1 through 780 for the letter formats, or 1 through 3999 for the Roman numeral formats. But you will typically use 1 to restart numbering for a new section.

After you make your changes, choose OK to close the Page Number Format dialog box, and OK again to close the Page Numbers dialog box and return to your document. Word will show the numbering change (but not the number format change) in the status bar, and both the numbering and number format will change in the header or footer page numbers.

> The ability to use different number formats and to restart the numbering is particularly useful for long documents with, for example, a preface or an introduction that you want to number differently from the main portion of the text. One common numbering scheme is to make the front matter one section and to number it using the lowercase Roman numerals: i, ii, iii, iv, and so on. The rest of the text would be a second section, using Arabic numerals: 1, 2, 3, 4, and so on. You assign the format separately to each section and start the numbering over at page 1 for the first page of the first chapter.

Section headers and footers

In Chapter 5, we showed how to create, position, and format headers and footers and how to create a special header or footer for the first page of a document. As we've already suggested, these settings are also tied to sections, so you can vary the headers and footers from one section to another. This feature is useful when your section breaks correspond to major document divisions, such as chapters. For example, you can take advantage of the feature to include the chapter number or title for each section. However, you can change headers and footers at any location by adding a section break.

> It's important to understand how Word handles headers (or footers) for a multisection document. If you simply create a header anywhere in a document, the header will show up in all sections of the document. This holds true whether you created the header before or after you inserted the section breaks and regardless of which section you were in when you created the header. If you then change the header while in any section in the document, the change will carry over to all the other headers unless you specifically break the link between headers in different sections. For example, if you change the header in section 2 of a three-section document, you'll see the change in sections 1 and 3 as well, unless you break the link first, as we'll describe in the next section.

To vary the text or format of the header or footer for a particular section, first make certain that the cursor or selection is in the section that you want to change. Then choose View Header And Footer, or, if you're in Page Layout view or Print Preview, double-click on the header or footer you want to change. Word will show you the header, which will look much like the sample in Figure 13-24.

FIGURE 13-24

The top of the header area displays the section number for that header.

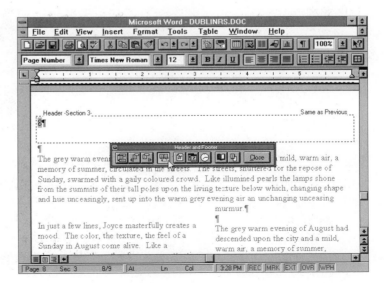

How to break or reestablish a link between section headers or footers

> As you can see in Figure 13-24, Word adds two pieces of identification at the top of the header. One, on the left side, identifies the particular header you're working with, in this case labeled Header Section 3. The other, Same As Previous, on the right side, identifies this header as being the same as the header in the previous section. As long as the headers from two or more sections are linked so that each one after the first shows this *Same As Previous* message, any changes you make to any header in the linked group will apply to all the headers in that group.

The fourth button on the Header toolbar, which is also shown in Figure 13-24, is named Same As Previous. You can choose this button to break the link between the header in the current section and the previous one or to reestablish it later. When the header of the current section is already linked to the previous section, this button will appear to be depressed. (Because the first section of a document has no previous section, the button will never appear depressed for section 1.)

When you choose the Same As Previous button to reestablish a link, Word asks for confirmation. If you choose Yes, not only will Word change the header or footer to match the previous section, but the change will cascade forward to any headers in later sections that are linked to the current section.

> Word does not come with a shortcut key defined to let you break or reestablish links from the keyboard. However, you can easily add one, using the techniques we'll describe in Chapter 28, "Custom Menus, Keys, and Templates." The command to attach the shortcut key to is ToggleHeaderFooterLink.

The Different First Page option

In Chapter 5, we explained how to use the Different First Page option on the Page Setup Layout card. By choosing the Different First Page option, you can create a separate header (or footer) for the first page of a document or effectively eliminate the header from the first page by creating a blank header. This same option lets you create separate headers and footers for the first page of each section.

If you want the first-page header of a later section to be different from the first-page header of an earlier section, place your cursor in the appropriate section, choose File Page Setup, choose Layout, and be sure the Different First Page check box is checked. Return to the document, choose View Header And Footer or double-click on the header if you're in Page Layout view, and choose the Same As Previous toolbar button to break the link to the previous header. Finally, make whatever changes you want to the header

How to combine two document sections

If you want to combine two adjacent document sections, simply delete the section-break marker between them by selecting the marker, or moving the cursor to it, and pressing Delete. If the two sections have different settings, the new, merged section will retain the settings from the second section. (This is similar to what happens when you merge two paragraphs by deleting the paragraph mark at the end of the first one. The merged paragraph will retain the format of the second paragraph, whose paragraph mark was not deleted.)

If you want to merge two sections but use the settings for the first section, cut the section marker to the Clipboard. Then move the cursor to the end of the second section, insert the first marker before the second one, and delete the second marker.

We're not quite finished with sections, but to discuss them further, we need to look at them in the context of other features. Until now, we have dealt mostly with text that flows smoothly from the top of a page to the bottom and then to the top of the next page. In many cases, you'll want to create more complex documents, with multiple columns, pictures, graphs, or other items that make the final product more visually interesting. Some of these items work with sections—occasionally, at least. In the next chapter, we will look at how to add these other elements to your document and how to use them with sections when appropriate.

Topic Finder

Multicolumn Formatting   497

- Why use multiple columns?
- How to add column formatting with the Columns button
- How to remove column formatting with the Columns button
- How to control column formatting with the Format Columns command
- How to add columns only to selected text
- How to control column breaks
- How to format with both single and multiple columns
- How to create columns of equal length

Frames: Positioning Text and Graphics on the Page   509

- Frames in different views
- How to add a frame
- How to add a frame to existing text
- How to move the cursor to a frame
- How to adjust frame settings
- The Frame dialog box
- How to align frames
- How to remove a frame

NEW! Text Boxes and Callouts   525

- How to insert a text box
- How to adjust text box settings
- The Drawing Object dialog box
- Callouts
- When to use frames, and when to use text boxes or callouts

Some Formatting Tricks with Frames and Text Boxes   531

- How to create scholar's margins
- How to repeat a frame or a text box on every page
- How to create a watermark

Pictures   535

- How to insert a picture
- How to size a picture
- How to add a frame to a picture
- NEW! How to add a caption or other text to a picture
- How to place a border around a picture
- How to position a picture in a table

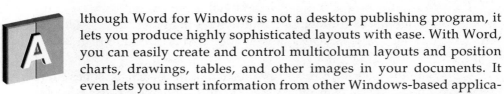

Columns, Frames, & Pictures

lthough Word for Windows is not a desktop publishing program, it lets you produce highly sophisticated layouts with ease. With Word, you can easily create and control multicolumn layouts and position charts, drawings, tables, and other images in your documents. It even lets you insert information from other Windows-based applications easily. In this chapter and the next, we'll look at all of these features, starting with multicolumn formats.

Multicolumn Formatting

Almost every one of our sample documents to this point has been formatted as a single stream of text, flowing from the top of one page to the bottom and then continuing at the top of the next page. The only notable exceptions were in Chapter 11, where we covered tables. Tables format text in columns, but even tables are based on the concept that the text area goes from the left margin of the page all the way across to the right margin, and from top to bottom.

There are times when you'll want to format a page into narrower columns that flow from the bottom of one column to the top of the next, as in a newspaper. This layout is often called snaking columns, newspaper-style columns, or simply columns. All these terms are interchangeable. For our purposes, we will usually refer to some variation of columns, text columns, or multiple columns. The Standard toolbar button that goes with the feature is called the Columns button.

Why use multiple columns?

Before microcomputers and laser printers, the vast majority of American business documents were produced on typewriters, using monospaced fonts. (Monospaced fonts use the same amount of horizontal space for each character, as opposed to proportional fonts, which use more horizontal space for wide characters such as *m* and *w* than for narrow characters such as *i* and *l*.) Most often the font was Courier at 10 characters to the inch, also called 10-pitch, or pica, spacing. To squeeze more information on a page, some people used a Prestige font at 12-pitch (elite) spacing.

Most people prefer 10-pitch over 12-pitch for letter-size documents. In general, the most readable formats contain one and a half to two alphabets' worth of characters—39 to 52 characters per line. One-inch margins on a letter-size page yield 65 characters per line for pica spacing or 78 characters for elite spacing. A line that contains 65 characters is a bit longer than ideal but is still acceptable. A 78-character line is so long that it is hard to read.

When the laser printer and proportional fonts such as Times Roman arrived on the scene, computer users began to move away from typewriter-style monospaced fonts. Proportional fonts allow more characters on a line. This is both good news and bad. The good news is that you get more text on a page; the bad news is that more characters per line makes the pages more difficult to read.

This is where multiple columns come in. If you take the text within the 1-inch margins, carve it into thinner vertical strips, and put some space between the strips, you end up with almost the same amount of text per page but with shorter lines, which are much easier to read. This isn't enough reason to format a business letter with an unconventional two or three columns, but it's a strong argument for formatting other kinds of documents that way—a newsletter for clients, for example.

How to add column formatting with the Columns button

You can quickly transform any document into a multiple-column format. Word allows one column definition per section, which is another way of saying that columns are a section-level formatting feature. If you want to apply the format to just the current section or selected sections, the easiest way is with the Columns button on the Standard toolbar.

When you click on this button, Word shows you a thumbnail sketch of a multiple-column format, with four columns, as in Figure 14-1. If you click and drag the mouse pointer across these columns, left to right, Word will highlight them and use the area below the columns to report the number of columns it will create. If you need more than four, continue dragging the mouse to the right, and the thumbnail sketch will expand, to a maximum of six columns. If you highlight two of the four columns, as in Figure 14-1, and then release the mouse button, Word will reformat the document as in Figure 14-2 on the next page (which is set to Normal view). Alternatively, you can click on a column to indicate how many you want to use. In this case, you would click on the second column. Whichever approach you take, Word will use its current settings for the amount of space between the columns and for whether it will add a line between the columns. (We will cover both of these shortly.)

FIGURE 14-1

The Columns button on the Standard toolbar lets you quickly create columns.

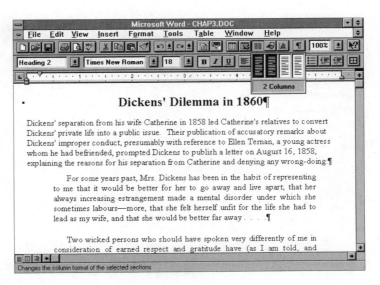

FIGURE 14-2

In Normal view, multiple columns appear as a single column on screen. The ruler displays the column width and tab settings.

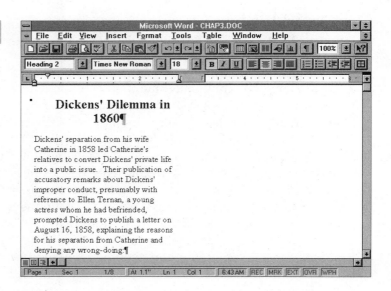

Since Figure 14-2 shows the document in Normal view, it shows only one column on the screen. Note that the ruler displays the new column width and tab settings and also indicates a second column on the right side, even though it doesn't show any text there. To see the columns on screen as they will print, choose View Page Layout to switch to Page Layout view, shown in Figure 14-3.

FIGURE 14-3

In Page Layout view, multiple columns display side by side, as they will look on the printed page.

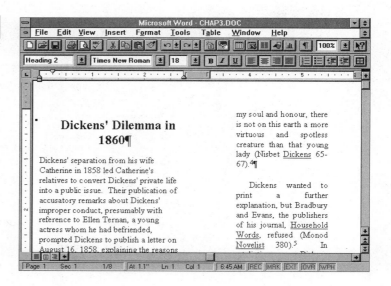

In Page Layout view, you can see how Word automatically formats the document so that a predefined amount of space appears between the two text columns. Note that the headline on the page in Figure 14-3 is formatted to fit into one column rather than spread across the entire width of the page. Word will let you change both the amount of space between columns and the format for the headline, subjects we'll cover shortly.

To use the Columns button to add columns to only a portion of your text, select the text before clicking the button. When you do, Word adds section breaks before and after the selection and applies the column formatting only to the selection.

How to remove column formatting with the Columns button

If you want to remove column formatting immediately after adding it, you can use the Edit Undo command or simply click on the Columns button and then drag it or click on the leftmost column in the thumbnail sketch.

How to control column formatting with the Format Columns command

You can achieve a similar formatting effect, but with more control over the format, by using the Format Columns menu command instead of the toolbar button. Choose Format Columns to open the Columns dialog box, shown in Figure 14-4.

FIGURE 14-4

The Columns dialog box lets you control the formatting of text columns.

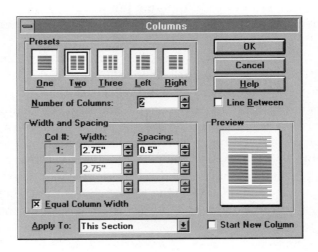

The Columns box includes a Preview box with a thumbnail sketch of how the page will look. As you make changes to the settings, the page in this box will change to reflect your choices.

Word provides five predefined column formats in the Presets group box. You can choose a one-column, two-column, or three-column format with equal column widths, or two columns of unequal widths with the thinner column to the left or to the right.

The Number Of Columns text box accepts whole numbers starting with 1, but the upper limit depends on the paper size, orientation, and margin settings defined in the File Page Setup dialog box. Word insists on a minimum 0.5 inch per column, so on an 8.5-by-11-inch page in portrait orientation, with 1.25-inch margins, you can have up to 12 columns. The maximum number of columns is 44, which requires a 22-inch-wide page with no margins. In any case, the number of columns available is greater than you're likely to need.

If you check the Line Between check box, Word will print a vertical line, centered between the columns. The line will be as long as the longest column to either side. You won't see these lines on the screen unless you choose Page Layout view or Print Preview mode.

The Width And Spacing group box lets you define the width of each column and the space between them. As you can see in the figure, the group box has three sets of text boxes for width and spacing. If you've set the number of columns to more than three, Word will add a scroll bar at the left of the group box so that you can scroll to see settings for the other columns. If you want all the columns the same width, check the Equal Column Width check box. Word will then gray everything in the Col #, Width, and Spacing columns except the first row. The logic is that all columns will have the same settings, so you need to define the width and spacing only once. If you do not check the Equal Column Width box, you can define different widths and different spacing for each column.

When you change almost any setting in the Columns dialog box, Word will automatically adjust other settings to match. If you choose Two in the Presets box, for example, Word will check the Equal Column Width box and, assuming default page size and margins, set Width to 2.75 inches. If you change the settings in the Number Of Columns box to 3, Word will change the Presets setting to Three and set the column widths to 1.67 inches. In short, Word tries hard to make sure that everything will fit properly on the page, but its automatic changes may not match what you want—particularly if you accidentally made the wrong choice somewhere along the line. So be sure to double-check the settings when you've finished.

To minimize the number of iterations you have to go through when adjusting settings for unequal columns, start with the first column width, adjust spacing, go on to the second column width, and so on. Word makes its automatic changes to the subsequent column width settings in each case—unless you change the last column's width setting, at which point Word makes equal changes to all previous Spacing settings.

Columns and sections

The Apply To list box determines what part of your document Word will apply the column specification to. If you didn't have any text selected when you chose Format Columns, this list would offer a minimum of two choices: Whole Document and This Point Forward. In addition, if the document includes more than one section, you'll find the choice This Section. (We'll discuss the choices you'll see when text is selected in a moment.) We covered sections in Chapter 13, so this discussion assumes that you're at least vaguely familiar with sections. If you're not, take a look at "Multisection Documents" starting on page 485.

If you choose This Section in the Apply To box, the settings you select will apply only to the current section (the section where the cursor was located when you opened the dialog box). If you choose Whole Document, the settings will apply to all sections (whether your document consists of one or more sections). If you select This Point Forward, Word will insert a new section break at the cursor location and will apply the formatting to that new section and all later sections.

In some cases, you will want to restrict the new column format more than these three options easily allow. For example, you might want to create a three-column section for part of a page that is otherwise formatted as a single column. You can do that by highlighting the text you want to apply the format to before choosing Format Columns.

How to add columns only to selected text

If you select some text before opening the Columns dialog box, you'll find a slightly different set of options in the Apply To box. You'll still find the Whole Document option. But if the selection is confined to a single section (whether you have one section in the document or more), the second option will be Selected Text. And if the document already has more than one section, the third choice will be Selected Sections, whether the selection extends into multiple sections or not.

As the name implies, the Selected Sections option applies the new settings to any sections the selection was in when you opened the dialog box. (If the selection was in only one section, this option is equivalent to choosing This Section.)

More interesting is the Selected Text option, since it will do several things at once. If you apply a column format to selected text, Word will insert a section break both at the beginning and at the end of the selection, and it will format only the newly defined section. This is how we created the three-column section in Figure 14-5, with single-column text before and after. This choice lets you create the new sections and apply the format to the selected text in a single step.

FIGURE 14-5

If you highlight text before choosing Format Columns to open the Columns dialog box and then you choose the Apply To Selected Text option, you can insert section breaks and format the text as a new section at the same time.

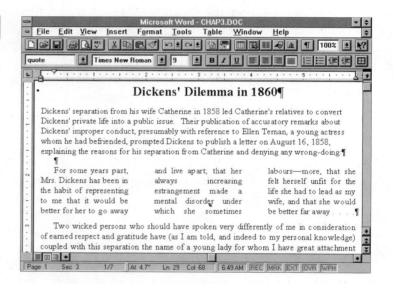

When you choose the Apply To Selected Text option, Word applies the column format only to the selected text even if the selection starts or ends in the middle of a paragraph or even a word, so be careful to select all the text you want to format.

Choosing the Start New Column check box will have a different effect depending on the setting in the Apply To box. Figure 14-6 summarizes the effect of the option with the different choices.

When You Apply It To...	Start New Column Has This Effect...
Whole Document	No effect
This Section	Forces a new column to start with the current section
This Point Forward	Inserts a section break at the current cursor location and forces a new column at the start of the new section and all later sections
Selected Text	Inserts section breaks before and after the selected text and forces a new column at the beginning of each of the new sections
Selected Sections	Generally forces a new column at the beginning of all selected sections

FIGURE 14-6

The choices and their effects for the Start New Column option.

How to control column breaks

Word provides several ways to control column breaks. For example, you can use the Keep Lines Together option in the Paragraph dialog box to prevent Word from splitting a paragraph between two columns. Similarly, you can use the Keep With Next option to ensure that a given paragraph, such as a section heading, is in the same column as the next paragraph.

Word also lets you force the start of a new column by inserting a column break. Simply place the cursor where you want the column break, choose Insert Break, and then choose the Column Break option. Alternatively, place the cursor where you want the column break, and press the shortcut key combination Ctrl-Shift-Enter.

In Normal view, Word shows a column break as a dotted line labeled *Column Break*. In Page Layout view, it simply moves the text to the top of the next column. If you want to see the dotted line indicating a column break even in Page Layout view, set Word to show all nonprinting characters on the Tools Options View card, or click on the Show/Hide ¶ button on the Standard toolbar.

How to format with both single and multiple columns

Each section in a document can have only one setting for columns. To change the column format for some of your text but not all, you must create a new section. We mentioned earlier that you can combine different column formats. Here's a closer look at the process.

Consider the sample document we've been using in this chapter. When we formatted it as two columns, the title text wrapped to two lines, as shown in Figure 14-7. Since the title's paragraph is formatted as centered, the title remains centered in the one column, not centered on the page.

FIGURE 14-7

The title in this document has wrapped to a second line in this two-column format.

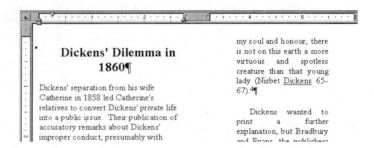

You can easily change this document so that the headline remains on one line, centered across the entire width of the page. The trick is to put the headline in a section of its own and define that section as one column.

To create a new section, simply place the cursor before the first character of the first paragraph after the title, and insert a section break with the Insert Break command; use the Continuous option here since you want the title on the same page as the rest of the text.

After you insert this new section break, the status bar will indicate that the first paragraph of body text is in section 2 rather than section 1. If you move the cursor to the title, the status bar will show that the current section is 1.

With the cursor in the section that contains the title, reformat that section as a single column using the Format Columns command or the Columns button on the Standard toolbar. Figure 14-8 shows the result, as seen in Page Layout view, with the title centered above two columns of text.

You can enter the section break and reformat the first section in a single step. Start by selecting the title paragraph. Then choose Format Columns to open the Columns dialog box, set Number Of Columns to 1, choose Selected Text in the Apply To box, and choose OK. Alternatively, after selecting the text, click on the Columns toolbar button and drag to define the number of columns as one.

FIGURE 14-8

Page Layout view shows the title centered over two columns.

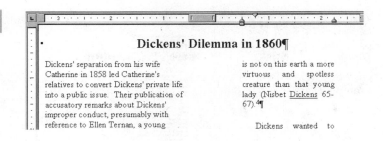

Dickens' Dilemma in 1860¶

Dickens' separation from his wife Catherine in 1858 led Catherine's relatives to convert Dickens' private life into a public issue. Their publication of accusatory remarks about Dickens' improper conduct, presumably with reference to Ellen Ternan, a young

is not on this earth a more virtuous and spotless creature than that young lady (Nisbet <u>Dickens</u> 65-67).⁴¶

Dickens　wanted　to

You can use this technique to position two tables side by side on a page that is otherwise using a one-column format. Simply add a two-column section to the page, with the section starting immediately before the first table and ending immediately after the second.

How to create columns of equal length

You can also use section breaks to create columns of equal length. For example, suppose you're writing a newsletter and you have two stories on the same page, each of which takes half a page. If you format the page as a single section with three text columns, the first story will run from the top of the first column to the middle of the second column, and the second will run from the middle of the second column to the end of the third. A more sophisticated layout would place the first story in three columns on the top half of the page and the second in three columns on the bottom half. You can create this layout by entering a section break at the end of the first story.

Whenever a page contains one or more sections with multicolumn formatting, Word will break the columns at the section boundaries and wrap the columnar text within the sections. In other words, inserting a continuous section break tells Word to wrap the columns within each section separately from the other sections. That means you can use section breaks to determine the depth of the columns within each section.

You can also use this technique to balance columns at the end of a section. For example, in Figure 14-9 on the next page, the last page of our sample document in Print Preview mode shows that there is not enough text to fill the page. Instead of having most of the text on one side of the page, you might prefer to have two equal-length columns at the top of the page.

FIGURE 14-9

Print Preview mode shows that there is not enough text in this example to fill the page.

To create two equal-length columns, simply insert a section break with the Continuous option at the end of the text. Word will automatically reformat the two columns to equal length, as shown in Figure 14-10.

FIGURE 14-10

If you insert a new section break at the end of the text, Word will reformat the text from Figure 14-9 into two balanced columns.

The combination of section breaks and column formatting gives you a great deal of control over mixing column formats within a document and even within a page. However, there are times when you need even more control over the placement of elements on the page. For that, you need to use frames.

Frames: Positioning Text and Graphics on the Page

Most of our discussion of formatting so far has treated a Word document as a linear sequence of text, with each line following the one before it. (Headers, footers, and footnotes are the exceptions, but they are set off in their own reserved text areas.) But there are times when you may not want a linear sequence. For example, you may want to place a box filled with text or a graphic at a specific position on a page and have other text flow around the box as you enter or edit the text.

That, in part, is what frames are for. Frames let you place whatever you want wherever you want it. We'll start with examples that use text, but keep in mind that you can also insert pictures, tables, graphs, and even objects from other Windows applications into frames. We'll cover these other items in the next chapter. For now, we'll concentrate on the concept of frames.

 Frames are close relatives, in both behavior and capabilities, of two other Word features—text boxes and callouts, both of which are among Word's drawing capabilities. We will save the discussion of text boxes and callouts for later in this chapter, but be aware that much of this discussion—including virtually all of the concepts and many of the details—applies to text boxes and callouts as well.

Frames in different views

Frames and their contents look different in the different Word views. Figure 14-11 on the next page shows a sample document, complete with a frame, as it appears in Page Layout view.

Figure 14-11 shows a two-column format and a headline (in its own section) that spans both columns. It also shows a box in the middle of the page that includes a quote. (In publishing circles, this is referred to as a readout, or a pull quote.) Notice how the text in the columns flows around the box, and notice that the text in the box can't readily be described as coming either before or after any particular paragraph of text in the columns.

FIGURE 14-11

This document has a frame that contains some text; you can see its position in Page Layout view.

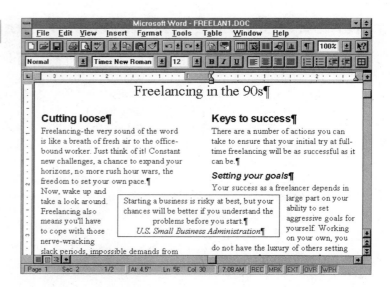

Frames in Normal view

Figure 14-12 shows the same document in Normal view. As you can see, it looks very different from Figure 14-11: The body text appears as a single column, the section break appears below the headline, and the readout box and text have a specific linear placement relative to the column of text—namely, between the first and second paragraphs.

FIGURE 14-12

The same document as in Figure 14-11 in Normal view shows the frame's linear position in relation to the text in the document, not its position on the page.

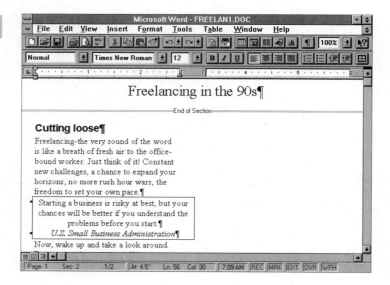

Word adds small squares to the left of the first line of each paragraph in the box. These squares (visible only if you have Word set to show paragraph marks) are markers indicating that these paragraphs are contained within a frame. The box around the text is simply a border around the paragraphs in the frame. You can get rid of the box if you want, as we'll discuss a little later. If you choose to get rid of the border, the squares become important as a way to identify text that's within the frame.

Frames in Outline view

As shown in Figure 14-13, Word does not mark a frame at all in Outline view. In fact, Word will not show a frame's border in Outline view, even if the frame is defined to have a border.

FIGURE 14-13

In Outline view, Word does not mark frames at all.

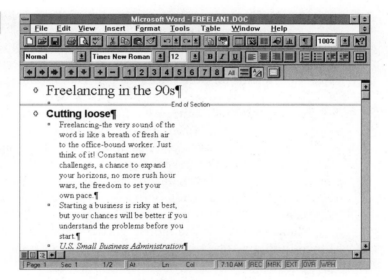

The importance of using Page Layout view

In general, you will want to set Word to Page Layout view when you are working with frames. Not only will you be able to see the actual layout, but you'll be able to easily edit, resize, and move the frame on the page, and you'll see the results immediately.

Page Layout view is so central to working with frames that Word even offers to switch to Page Layout view if you try to add a frame while in Normal view. All of this brings us to the mechanics of adding a frame.

How to add a frame

Word lets you add an empty frame or add one around an existing part of your document. The only difference between the two choices is whether you highlight some text (or other items) before choosing the Insert Frame command. If you start by selecting some text, Word will place the selection inside the frame and automatically set the frame size to match the existing text. You can then move and resize the frame. If you don't select the text first, Word waits for you to define a position and size for the frame. You can then enter text in the frame by typing it in or by copying already existing text using Word's Cut, Copy, and Paste commands. As an example, we'll start with an empty frame and create the sample document we've been using for the frames discussion.

As we just pointed out, you'll usually want to be in Page Layout view to work with frames. In fact, if you choose Insert Frame while in Normal view, Word will display a message box asking whether you want to switch to Page Layout view. If you choose No, Word will return you to your document without inserting a frame (unless you selected some text first). If you choose Yes, Word will switch to Page Layout view, where you can insert the frame. For purposes of this example, we'll assume you're in Page Layout view.

When you choose Insert Frame, the mouse pointer changes to a crosshair, and Word displays a prompt on the status line that says *Click and drag to insert a frame.* Use the mouse to position the pointer where you want one corner of the frame, and then anchor that corner by pressing and holding down the left mouse button. Drag with the mouse to enlarge the frame to the size you want.

When you release the mouse button, Word creates an empty frame, as shown in Figure 14-14. (The figure uses Word's default settings for frames. We will discuss the settings in detail shortly.) Note that the frame includes a paragraph symbol inside a border (because Word is set to show paragraph marks). Note too the blank space between the border and the surrounding columns of text.

If you're familiar with Word 2.0, you may know that with Word 2.0 you could position the crosshair pointer and define the frame from the keyboard, using the arrow keys and the Enter key. Unfortunately, Word 6.0 doesn't allow this more precise approach to creating frames. You can create a frame using the keyboard, but only if you have already entered part of the frame's contents in your document. We'll discuss how to create a frame around existing text (or objects) in a moment.

FIGURE 14-14

Word's default settings for frames include wrapping surrounding text and adding a thin border. The pattern of diagonal lines surrounding the frame indicates that the cursor is inside the frame.

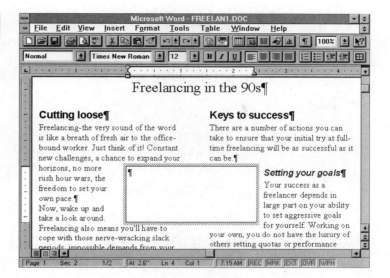

Figure 14-14

 Notice the pattern of diagonal lines around the frame. The pattern indicates the actual borders of the frame. The fact that you can see it indicates that the cursor is inside the frame. It's important to be able to tell when you're working inside the frame.

At this point, you can add text. With the cursor inside the frame, simply type the text and format it if you like. When you've finished, the result should look something like Figure 14-15. In the figure, we've also formatted the last line in italics and formatted the paragraphs as centered.

FIGURE 14-15

You can format the text within a frame.

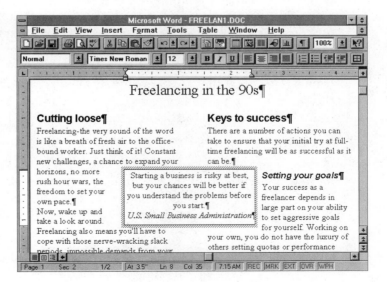

Figure 14-15

How to add a frame to existing text

You can also add a frame to existing text—from a word to a group of paragraphs. Select the text you want to put in a frame, and choose the Insert Frame command. Word will add the frame around the text.

> Because you don't need to define a frame with the crosshair pointer when you use the Insert Frame command, you can create a frame by using the keyboard as easily as by using the mouse with this technique. Note too that this technique lets you define a frame without switching to Page Layout view.

How to move the cursor to a frame

Although Word's default settings for frames will often serve your needs, there may be times when you'll want to change those settings. The first step in making any changes to a frame—including editing or formatting the text in the frame—is to move the cursor inside the frame.

In most cases, it's easier to move to a frame with the mouse than with the keyboard. If the cursor isn't already in the frame, simply position the mouse pointer anywhere within the frame and click. Word will move the cursor to the frame and show you the frame's border.

You can use the keyboard to move the cursor to a frame in either of two ways. First you can move the cursor to the point in the document where the frame is located linearly (as Word will show it in Normal view). In Normal view, this is easy enough, but in Page Layout view, this position does not necessarily bear any relation to where the frame appears on the page. Word treats the start of the frame as the start of a paragraph, but it can show another paragraph (or several paragraphs if the frame spans more than one column) wrapping around the frame.

If you are in Page Layout view, you can also move to a frame by starting from a line of text that appears directly above or below the frame, and using the Down or Up arrow key to move into the frame. You cannot move into a frame from text that is adjacent horizontally.

Anchors

If you are in Page Layout view and you want to find out where the frame is located linearly within the document, you can move the cursor inside the frame using any of the above methods and then press the Right arrow key repeatedly until the cursor leaves the frame. When the cursor leaves the frame, it will go to the position immediately after the point where the frame is located within the text. However, there's another, more elegant, way to find out where the frame is located.

Word keeps track of frames by anchoring each to the paragraph that follows it in linear sequence—the paragraph displayed immediately after the frame in Normal view. While you are in Page Layout view, you can see which paragraph your frame is anchored to. From Page Layout view, choose Tools Options View, and you'll find an Object Anchors check box in the Show box. If you check Object Anchors, whenever you highlight a frame Word will indicate the anchor paragraph with a small anchor to the left of the first line of the paragraph, as shown in Figure 14-16. If you drag the frame to a new position, and the new position changes the frame's linear position in the document, Word will move the anchor on the screen. (You can also toggle the anchor symbols on and off with the other nonprinting characters by clicking on the Show/Hide button on the Standard toolbar.)

FIGURE 14-16

Word can display an anchor symbol to indicate the paragraph a frame is anchored to.

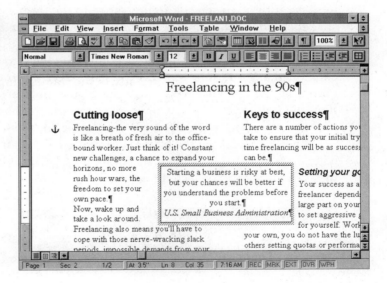

Word may align the left edge of the text on the left edge of your display so that you can't see the anchor symbols, which Word generally places in the margin. To be sure you can see the anchors, either scroll the display to the left or adjust the Zoom setting so that you can see the left margin.

The anchor symbol can help prevent accidental deletion of a frame when you're working in Page Layout view. If you should delete a selection that includes the paragraph before the anchor, plus any part of the anchor paragraph, you will delete the frame and its contents as well. Since the frame may be positioned where you can't see it when editing the anchor paragraph, you might not notice that it is selected along with the text you want to delete. If you select the frame before working in the area around the frame, you can locate the anchor symbol, and you'll know where the frame is. In general, however, if you're about to do substantial editing anywhere near a frame, it's safest to switch to Normal view.

How to select a frame to change its shape, size, or position

To change the shape or size of a frame by dragging with the mouse, you need to select it first. To select a frame, move to the frame so that you can see the shaded border. Then move the mouse pointer over the border. When the pointer is at the proper position, it changes to a left-pointing arrow with a four-headed arrow below it. At this point, drag the frame to move it, or simply click on the frame to select it. (You can select the frame even without the border showing. When you move the mouse pointer over the proper position, the pointer changes, whether you can see the border or not. However, it's easier to point to the border if you can see it, so move to the frame first.)

When you click on the frame, Word adds eight square boxes around the edge of the frame, as shown in Figure 14-17. These boxes, called handles, indicate that you've selected the frame.

FIGURE 14-17

When you click on a frame, Word shows the frame with eight handles around its edge.

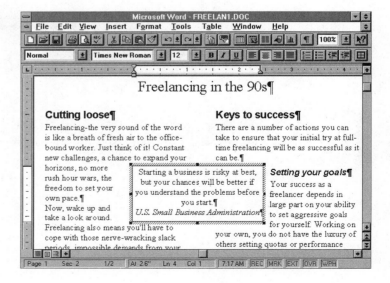

As we'll discuss shortly, you can use the mouse to grab the handles and resize the frame by dragging. Unfortunately, there is no way to select the frame or use the handles with the keyboard; you must use the mouse. Be aware, however, that with the frame selected and the Typing Replaces Selection option on, Word deletes all text in the frame if you type anything.

How to adjust frame settings

Frame settings fall into two categories. One category consists of settings specific to frames, such as size or position. The other consists of paragraph-level formatting. Most of the settings in the second category are straightforward applications of formatting techniques you can use on any text. For example, you can center text within a frame by formatting the paragraphs as centered. One setting in the second category—for borders and shading—is worth special mention, since you'll often apply it to the frame as a whole.

Borders and shading

The default setting for a new frame includes a single-line border. To change the border, either select the frame or place the cursor inside the frame and then choose Format Borders And Shading to open the Frame Borders And Shading dialog box.

 Be careful not to highlight any text or objects within the frame before you choose Format Borders And Shading, or else the settings you choose will affect only the selected paragraph or object, rather than the whole frame. One way to be certain your choices will apply to the frame and not just to some of its contents is to click on the frame to select it.

We discussed this dialog box in detail in Chapter 7. All the options we discussed there apply here as well, including all the shading options. For this discussion, we'll simply stay with the default settings. Keep in mind, however, that you can use this dialog box to define lines for some sides of the frame but not others. You can also choose the Shading card to create effects that will make readouts and other framed items stand out visually from the rest of your text. For details on using these features, see "Paragraph borders and shading" starting on page 236.

How to move and size the frame with the mouse

Among the features specific to frames are the commands for moving and resizing them. Word lets you move and resize either by dragging with the mouse or by entering settings in a dialog box. Each approach has its advantages.

Dragging with the mouse is more natural because you're working with a visual representation of the page. When you click and drag, you can see the results of the changes almost immediately (depending on the speed of your system). The dialog box offers more precision, but it loses the immediate visual feedback. We recommend that you use dragging techniques for broad changes—moving a frame to the approximate position, for example—and then shift to the dialog box to make fine adjustments.

As we already mentioned, when you click on a frame, eight handles appear around the edge of the frame. If you then move the mouse pointer over the frame, you'll find that it changes shape depending on where it is in respect to the frame and the handles. If you place it directly over one of the handles, it will turn into a two-headed arrow—pointing left and right if it's on one of the two side handles, pointing up and down if it's on the top or bottom handle, or pointing diagonally if it's on a corner handle. When the pointer changes to any of these shapes, you can click and drag to resize the frame in the directions indicated by the arrows. (The diagonal arrows let you change height and width simultaneously.)

If you hold down the Ctrl key as you click and drag to resize a frame, Word will change the position for the current and the opposite side of the frame simultaneously—meaning top and bottom, left and right, or opposing corners. This lets you change the size and shape of a frame while keeping it centered on its current position. If you hold down the Shift key while dragging a corner handle, Word will keep the proportions the same as it resizes the frame. And if you hold down both the Shift and the Ctrl key while dragging a corner handle, Word will keep the proportions the same while also keeping the center of the frame at the same position.

We used this click-and-drag technique to modify our frame to the one shown in Figure 14-18, making the frame wider than it was originally and not as tall. Word reformats the text to fit the frame. In our sample document, the text is now on four lines instead of five.

The mouse pointer in Figure 14-18 is near the upper left corner of the frame, between two of the handles. The outline arrow with a four-headed arrow pointer indicates that you can use it to drag the frame to a new location.

Register Today!

Return the
Word 6 for Windows™ Companion
registration card for:

✔ a Microsoft Press® catalog

✔ exclusive offers on specially priced books

U.S. and Canada addresses only. Fill in information below and mail postage-free. Please mail only the bottom half of this page.

Word 6 for Windows Companion—Owner Registration Card

_____

NAME

_____

INSTITUTION OR COMPANY NAME

_____

ADDRESS

_____

_____

CITY   STATE   ZIP

Your feedback is important to us.

Include your daytime telephone number, and we may call to find out how you use *Word 6 for Windows Companion* and what we can do to make future editions even more useful. If we call you, we'll send you a **FREE GIFT** for your time!

(_____)_____

DAYTIME TELEPHONE NUMBER

1-55615-575-1A

Get Quick Answers About Microsoft Word 6 Commands

FIGURE 14-18

We used the frame's handles to change its size.

FIGURE 14-18

We used the frame's handles to change its size.

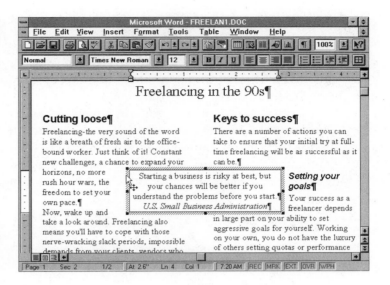

In this case, it's a good idea to move the frame down a bit since it's forcing the heading *Setting your goals* into two lines. By clicking on the frame and dragging it down, we can get the heading to appear on its own line, as shown in Figure 14-19.

FIGURE 14-19

Word will reformat the document around the frame when you move the frame to a new location.

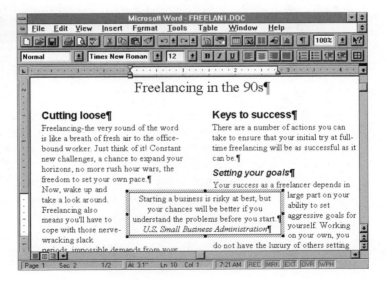

The Frame dialog box

The next step in this example is to center the frame between the two columns. You could use the mouse to drag the frame and wind up reasonably close to the right position. But this is the sort of fine adjustment that's better handled through the Frame dialog box.

To open the dialog box, you can move to or select the frame you want to adjust and double-click on the edge of the frame, choose Format Frame, or use the right mouse button to open a context-sensitive menu and choose Format Frame there. Word will respond with a dialog box like the one in Figure 14-20. All of the settings will match the current settings for the frame.

FIGURE 14-20

The Frame dialog box gives you precise control over frame settings.

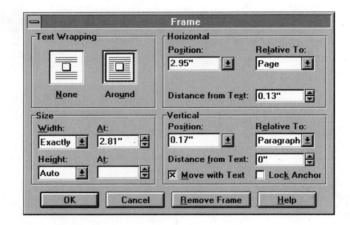

How to flow text around a frame

The upper left box in the Frame dialog box is labeled Text Wrapping. This defaults to the Around setting, as shown. As indicated in the thumbnail sketch, the setting tells Word to wrap text around the frame, as we've shown in our sample document up to now. If you change Text Wrapping to None, Word will not print any text on the lines level with the frame. Figure 14-21 shows the result for our sample document. Regardless of the setting for Text Wrapping, Word will not flow text into an area that is 1 inch wide or less.

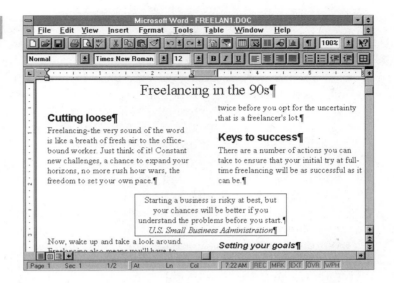

FIGURE 14-21

If you set Text Wrapping to None, Word will format the document so that no text prints on the lines level with the frame.

Frame size

The Size box lets you specify width and height for the frame. As you can see in Figure 14-20, there are list boxes for both Width and Height, and each is paired with its own At text box, in which you can enter a dimension. The Width list box offers two choices: Auto and Exactly (the default). The Height list box offers the same two options, plus a third: At Least. This is the default setting. The Auto setting in each case tells Word to enlarge or shrink the frame's size based on its contents. The Exactly settings let you specify a precise size that Word won't change, regardless of contents. The At Least setting in Height lets you specify a minimum height for the frame, but it still tells Word to automatically enlarge the height beyond that minimum, based on the frame's contents.

How to align frames

The two group boxes on the right side of the Frame dialog box are Horizontal and Vertical. The settings in these boxes let you precisely position the frame on the page, and they let you specify a distance from other text. They also let you tell Word to determine the frame's position relative to some other element on the page. These positioning features are worth examining in detail.

Horizontal alignment

The Horizontal box offers three items to set: Position, Relative To, and Distance From Text.

When you first create a frame or drag it with the mouse, Word determines the horizontal position as a specific location, and it shows the location for the left edge of the frame as a specific measurement in the Position box, as shown in Figure 14-20 on page 520. (The number matches the edge's position as measured by Word's ruler.) Since we want to center the frame horizontally on the page, we could calculate the correct position based on page width and frame width and enter the result in the Position box. But it is much easier to let Word do the work.

If you open the drop-down list attached to the Position box, you will see five choices: Left, Right, Center, Inside, and Outside. If you choose Center, Word will automatically center the frame, as in the centered frame in Figure 14-22. As long as the frame is defined as centered, Word will keep it centered, even if you change the width of the frame. (The precise effect of choosing Center for horizontal position depends on the setting in the Relative To box. In Figure 14-22, the frame is defined as centered relative to the page. We'll come back to this issue in a moment.)

FIGURE 14-22

Word automatically positions a frame if you choose the Left, Center, or Right option for the horizontal position setting.

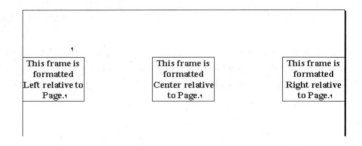

The other four settings for horizontal position also let you automatically place a frame in a specified location. The Left and Right options move the frame to the left or right edge of the page, placing it in the margin, as also shown in Figure 14-22. (Again, this assumes the position is defined as relative to the page. In Figure 14-22, we've set the View Zoom setting to show both edges of the page.)

The Inside and Outside settings are similar to the Left and Right settings except that they let you choose the correct position when you've defined Mirror Margins on the File Page Setup Margins card. Mirror Margins, which we discussed in Chapter 7, is useful when you'll be printing a document on both sides of each page, with a center binding. The Inside setting places the frame all the way to the right on even-numbered pages and all the way to the left on odd-numbered pages so that the frame is always to the inside of the page, next to the binding. The Outside setting is just the opposite, placing the frame on the outside of the page.

The Relative To list box offers two choices in addition to the Page choice: Margin and Column. The default setting is Page, which is why we've used it until now. The other two choices produce slightly different results.

As shown in Figure 14-22, setting the horizontal position to the left or to the right relative to the page moves the frame to the extreme edge of the page. This may not print correctly, since many printers cannot print to the edge of the page. Also, although there are times when you might want to place a frame in the margin (as we'll discuss a little later in this chapter), more often you'll want to place a frame within the text area. By positioning the frame left or right relative to the margins, you can automatically line up the edge of the frame with the edge of the text area. Similarly, if you're using a multiple-column format, and you position a frame relative to the column, Word will place the frame at the left or the right edge or in the center of the column.

The Distance From Text text box lets you enter the amount of blank space for Word to put between the outside of the frame and any adjacent text to the left or right. The default setting of 0.13 inch will usually provide an attractive layout, but you can change it if you prefer.

Vertical alignment

The settings in the Vertical box are similar to those in the Horizontal box. In particular, the vertical alignment Position box settings, in addition to a measured position on the page, are Top, Bottom, and Center. The choices in the Relative To box are Page, Margin, and Paragraph (the default setting). The Distance From Text text box works the same way as the Distance From Text box for horizontal placement, but it determines the distance for text above and below the frame. The default setting is 0, or no space.

In our sample document, the frame is positioned a specific distance relative to the upper left corner of the closest paragraph. The Relative To Paragraph setting is not relative to the paragraph closest to the frame's linear position as seen in Normal view; rather, it is based on the frame's visual proximity to the nearest paragraph in Page Layout view.

Figure 14-23 on the next page shows how Word positions frames set for Top, Center, and Bottom relative to the page.

 The warning we gave about placing a frame in the nonprintable region for any given printer applies to vertical as well as horizontal placement.

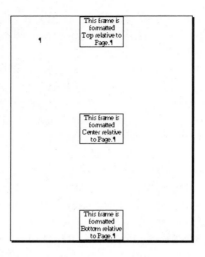

FIGURE 14-23

Word has settings that let you automatically position a frame at the top, center, or bottom of a page.

How to position with text

There are two more items in the Vertical box: Move With Text and Lock Anchor. We discussed anchors earlier in this chapter when we pointed out that Word keeps track of frames by anchoring them to the paragraph that comes immediately after them in the linear sequence you see in Normal view.

Move With Text tells Word to move the frame with the paragraph it's anchored to when you edit or format that paragraph. If you define a frame to move with the text, however, Word may change the anchor paragraph automatically if you move the frame on the page. The Lock Anchor option ensures that the frame will remain anchored to the same paragraph it is currently anchored to, which means it will always be on the same page as that paragraph. You'll still be able to move the frame, but the anchor will not move. We discussed anchors, and how to see which paragraph a frame is anchored to, in "Anchors" starting on page 514.

How to remove a frame

There are several ways to remove a frame from your document. For example, you can move to or select the frame, open the Frame dialog box by choosing Format Frame, and then choose the Remove Frame button. This will remove the frame itself (and any border that may have been assigned to the frame) without deleting the contents of the frame.

To remove a frame along with its contents, highlight the frame so that its eight handles appear, and choose the Edit Cut command to copy the frame to the Clipboard; choose Edit Clear or press the Del key to discard the frame and contents altogether.

Text Boxes and Callouts

As we pointed out earlier, frames are close relatives of text boxes and callouts, two features that are among Word's drawing tools. In fact, you can think of text boxes as a variation on frames.

The key difference between frames and text boxes is that frames force text either to wrap around them or to break the text so that there is no text on a horizontal line with the frame, but text boxes let body text print over the text box. With text boxes, in fact, there's no way to prevent the overprinting. Note too that unlike frames, text boxes will not automatically grow in size vertically as you add more text. Callouts are a special kind of text box that includes an attached line you can use to point to a particular item. Callouts are most often used within graphics as a way to label parts of the graphic.

 Be aware that the term *text box* is a bit of a misnomer since you can add pictures and other graphic objects inside a text box just as you can add them inside a frame. *Text box*, however, is the term Word uses for the appropriate toolbar button. Be aware too that unlike with frames, which Word shows in Normal view if set appropriately, you cannot see text boxes at all in Normal view—or in Outline or Master Document view, for that matter.

Because text boxes are so much like frames, we'll take a look at them here, independent of the rest of Word's drawing tools. We'll continually refer to many text box features as working the same way as the same features for frames. The rest of this discussion assumes that you're already familiar with frames.

How to insert a text box

To insert a text box, click on the Drawing button in the Standard toolbar—three buttons to the left of the zoom percentage text box—or choose View Toolbars and check the Drawing check box. Word adds the Drawing toolbar, shown in Figure 14-24. By default, Word places the Toolbar at the bottom of the Word window.

FIGURE 14-24

By default, Word adds the Drawing toolbar at the bottom of the Word window when you click on the Drawing button.

The Text Box button is sixth from the left on the Drawing toolbar. To insert a text box, click on the button, and then define the box with the mouse pointer, just as you would define a frame. As Figure 14-25 shows, the text box, unlike a frame, does not force text to wrap around it or break. Instead, the text simply prints over the same area as the text box does. (Unlike with a frame, you cannot add a text box around existing text. More precisely, you can add a text box to the same area as existing text, but the text will not be part of the text box's contents.)

FIGURE 14-25

When you add a text box, such as the top rectangle here, Word does not alter the layout of the body text in any way. With a frame, Word does alter the layout, as you can see by the middle and bottom rectangles.

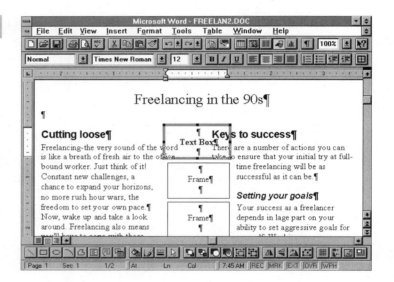

How to adjust text box settings

Among the more important features that text boxes share with frames are the ways you enter and format both text and graphics objects within the frame or text box. Text boxes also let you use the mouse the same way you use it with frames. You can move the text box or select the text box and then drag a handle to resize the box. As with a frame, you can delete a text box and its contents by highlighting the text box so that its eight handles appear and then choosing Edit Cut or Edit Clear. Unlike with frames, you can't remove the text box and leave its contents.

Text boxes have some advantages over frames. You can move text boxes with more precision from the keyboard than you can with the mouse. Simply select the text box, and then use the arrow keys to move the box up, down, left, or right. To move in even more precise increments, hold the Ctrl key down as you press the arrow keys. If you have more than one text box or other drawing object (such as a line created with Word's other drawing tools) on the current page, and one of the objects is already selected, you can use the Tab key to cycle through the objects, selecting another object each time you press Tab.

> Another, more critical, difference between text boxes and frames is the way you move to a text box to work with the contents of the text box, rather than with the body text that shares the same area on the page. Although you can use the same mouse technique as with a frame—clicking on the text box—there is no way to move into the text box from adjacent text. As with frames, however, when you move into a text box, Word outlines the border of the box with a shaded border to give visual confirmation that you're working in the box.

The Drawing Object dialog box

You can control size and positioning of a text box, like a frame, through a dialog box. To size or position a text box, you use the Drawing Object dialog box, shown in Figure 14-26. To open the dialog box, move to or select a text box and then choose Format Drawing Object. You can also double-click on the border or use the right button menu to access the dialog box.

FIGURE 14-26

The Drawing Object dialog box lets you control the size and position of text boxes, as well as other drawing-related objects.

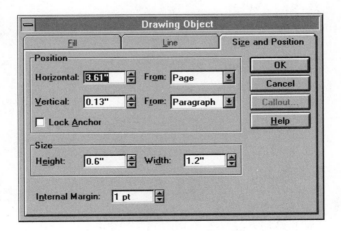

The Drawing Object dialog box offers three cards: Fill, Line, and Size And Position. The Size And Position card, shown in Figure 14-26, is analogous to the Format Frame card we've already discussed, and it even offers many of the same settings.

Most of the available settings are self-descriptive. In the Position group box, for example, the Horizontal and Vertical settings let you specify where to place the box. Unlike with the equivalent choices for frames, you're limited to entering an actual measurement, but like the choices for frames, the From boxes let you specify Margin, Page, or Column for the horizontal position or Margin, Page, or Paragraph for the vertical position.

The Lock Anchor check box has the same function here as in the dialog box for frames. If you check Lock Anchor, the text box will stay anchored to the paragraph it's currently anchored to, and it will be on the same page as that paragraph.

The Height and Width boxes in the Size group box simply control the height and width of the text box, as their names imply. The Internal Margin setting determines how much space you'll have between the border of the box and the text inside the box. Think of it as a margin setting. The Callout button is grayed unless you've selected a text box you created as a callout—a subject we'll come back to later.

The Line and Fill cards: Borders and shading

You can use the Format Borders And Shading command with text boxes much as you can with frames, but text boxes offer an alternative, and in some ways more flexible, approach to borders and shading in the Fill card, shown in Figure 14-27, and the Line card, shown in Figure 14-28.

FIGURE 14-27

The Fill card in the Drawing Object dialog box lets you control the color and pattern of the background for a text box.

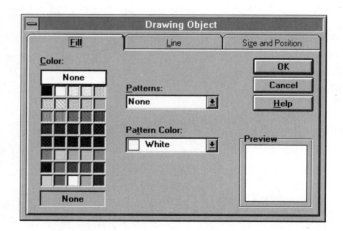

The Fill card lets you choose a background color for the text box, a pattern to overlay the color, and a color for the pattern overlay.

FIGURE 14-28

The Line card in the Drawing Object dialog box lets you control the format for a line border to a text box.

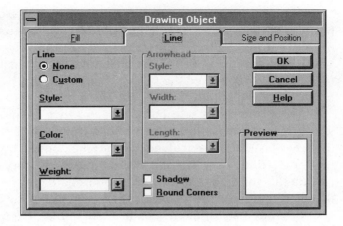

The Line card lets you add a border to the text box and specify the kind of line, using any of several patterns (solid line, dashes, or dots) and your choice of colors and line weight. You can also add a shadow effect or rounded corners, with the two check boxes on the card. The Arrowhead group box is grayed in Figure 14-28, since the feature doesn't apply to a standard text box. However, it would apply for a callout box, which has a line you can use to point to a particular item. The Preview box on both cards lets you see the effect of your choices.

Callouts

As we've already said, a callout is a variation on a text box that includes an attached line you can use to point to or from a particular item. Figure 14-29 shows three sample callouts, one with an arrow pointing from the item to the callout, one with an arrow pointing from the callout to the item, and one with a line that lacks an arrowhead.

FIGURE 14-29

Callouts are variations on text boxes, with lines attached to let you tie the callouts to other items.

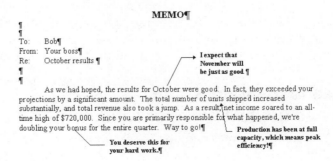

To insert a callout, you follow the same procedure as for inserting a text box except that you use the Callout button, which is immediately to the right of the Text Box button on the Drawing toolbar. When you select a callout, you'll find that the attached line includes its own handle or handles, which you can drag to change the position and length of the line. (The number of handles depends on the style of the line.)

If you move to or select a callout and then choose Format Drawing Object, you'll see the same set of cards as you do for standard text boxes. One difference is that the Arrowhead group box on the Line card is available, so you can define the width and length of the arrowhead and the style, which includes the direction the arrow is pointing: to the box, from the box, in both directions, or in no direction (a line without an arrowhead).

A callout also differs from a text box in that if you move to the Size And Position card, you'll find that the Callout button is available. Choose it to open the Format Callout box, shown in Figure 14-30.

FIGURE 14-30

The Format Callout dialog box lets you define the format for the line attached to the callout box.

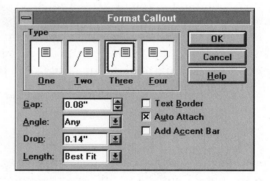

The Format Callout dialog box lets you define the format for the attached line, including how many handles are available within the line, the gap between the callout line and the text, whether the line is parallel to or pointing to the callout text, and so on. After specifying the settings, choose OK to close the dialog box and set the new format. You can also open this dialog box by moving to or selecting the callout and clicking on the Format Callout button, immediately to the right of the Callout button.

When to use frames, and when to use text boxes or callouts

You can use frames and text boxes more or less interchangeably in any situation in which there is no possibility of conflicting with body text in the same area. If you're adding a graphic or text in the margin, for example, you can generally use either choice.

If you want text to flow around an object, however, as you might with a graphic you're referring to within your text, you must use a frame. If you want text to print over an object, to produce a watermark effect, such as the word *DRAFT* written across a page of text, you will generally want to use a text box. (You can also use a frame for a watermark, as we'll discuss later, but the text box is the more straightforward choice.)

If you want an arrow pointing to or from some object, a callout is usually the preferred choice. But if you need text to wrap around the box, you can use a frame and then use Word's other drawing tools, which we'll cover in the next chapter, to create a line or an arrow between the box and the item you want to connect to. Callouts are usually the most useful way to label parts of graphics.

Some Formatting Tricks with Frames and Text Boxes

You can use frames or text boxes to create highly sophisticated formats for your documents. Before we move on to another subject, it may be helpful to look at some ways in which you can take advantage of frames and text boxes. Specifically, here's a look at how to create scholar's margins, repeat text or graphics on multiple pages, and create watermarks such as *DRAFT*, *CONFIDENTIAL*, or *TOP SECRET* to print across each page.

How to create scholar's margins

The sample document in Figure 14-31 on the next page shows a layout that has what is often called scholar's margins. The layout leaves ample white space beside the text so that readers can write notes. This layout also provides a convenient place to put section headings and subheads to help guide the reader through the material. We created the headings and subheads in the figure by using frames.

The page in Figure 14-31 is formatted with a 2.3-inch left margin. The subheads are in frames and are horizontally positioned with paragraph formatting to indent them by 0.3 inch from the left and the right; this indention ensures that the text does not fall outside the printer's printable region at the edge of the page. The vertical position is specified as 0 inches relative to the paragraph, which automatically aligns each subhead with its associated paragraph. The frames are formatted with a Distance From Text setting of 0 inches since the paragraph indenting will suffice to keep the frame away from the text.

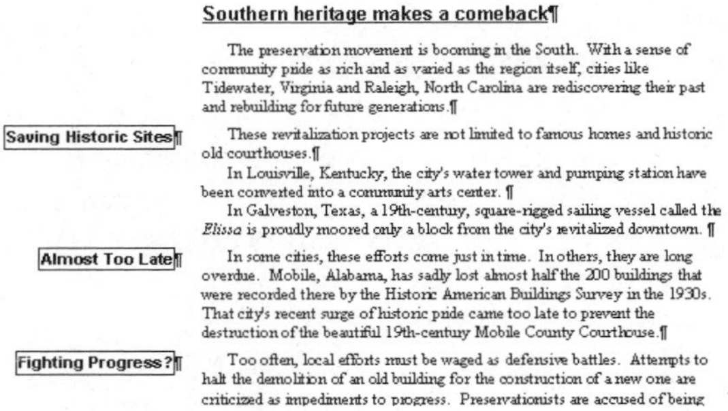

FIGURE 14-31

This document uses frames to put the text headings in the margin. Because the frames are defined to move with the text, their vertical positions will change as text is added to or deleted from the document.

Southern heritage makes a comeback

The preservation movement is booming in the South. With a sense of community pride as rich and as varied as the region itself, cities like Tidewater, Virginia and Raleigh, North Carolina are rediscovering their past and rebuilding for future generations.

Saving Historic Sites

These revitalization projects are not limited to famous homes and historic old courthouses.

In Louisville, Kentucky, the city's water tower and pumping station have been converted into a community arts center.

In Galveston, Texas, a 19th-century, square-rigged sailing vessel called the *Elissa* is proudly moored only a block from the city's revitalized downtown.

Almost Too Late

In some cities, these efforts come just in time. In others, they are long overdue. Mobile, Alabama, has sadly lost almost half the 200 buildings that were recorded there by the Historic American Buildings Survey in the 1930s. That city's recent surge of historic pride came too late to prevent the destruction of the beautiful 19th-century Mobile County Courthouse.

Fighting Progress?

Too often, local efforts must be waged as defensive battles. Attempts to halt the demolition of an old building for the construction of a new one are criticized as impediments to progress. Preservationists are accused of being

If you create this sort of layout, check the Move With Text and Lock Anchor check boxes to ensure that the headings stay with their paragraphs. In a finished design, you would probably want to remove the borders that Word automatically adds to frames, but we left them in our sample since borders make the frames easier to see.

If you're printing on both sides of each page, use the Mirror Margins choice in the File Page Setup Margins card so that the 2.3-inch margin in Figure 14-31 is defined as an outside margin rather than as a left margin. You then format the frames to have a horizontal position of Outside relative to the page so that the headings will always appear in the outside margins. Figure 14-32 shows how this page looks as a right-hand page. Notice that the wide margins and the headings both fall to the right of the text. (Notice also that you can't use text boxes for this since you cannot define text box position as inside or outside.)

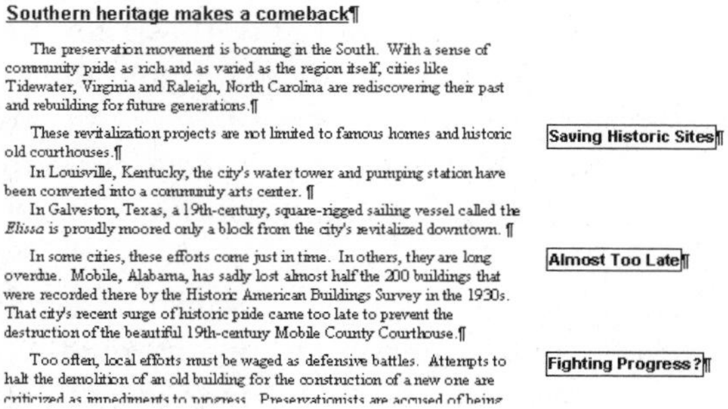

FIGURE 14-32

If you choose Mirror Margins and then use the Outside horizontal position setting for the headings in frames, the headings will automatically stay in the outside margin even if reformatting shifts them to another page.

Southern heritage makes a comeback

The preservation movement is booming in the South. With a sense of community pride as rich and as varied as the region itself, cities like Tidewater, Virginia and Raleigh, North Carolina are rediscovering their past and rebuilding for future generations.

These revitalization projects are not limited to famous homes and historic old courthouses.   **Saving Historic Sites**

In Louisville, Kentucky, the city's water tower and pumping station have been converted into a community arts center.

In Galveston, Texas, a 19th-century, square-rigged sailing vessel called the *Elissa* is proudly moored only a block from the city's revitalized downtown.

In some cities, these efforts come just in time. In others, they are long overdue. Mobile, Alabama, has sadly lost almost half the 200 buildings that were recorded there by the Historic American Buildings Survey in the 1930s. That city's recent surge of historic pride came too late to prevent the destruction of the beautiful 19th-century Mobile County Courthouse.   **Almost Too Late**

Too often, local efforts must be waged as defensive battles. Attempts to halt the demolition of an old building for the construction of a new one are criticized as impediments to progress. Preservationists are accused of being   **Fighting Progress?**

The beauty of all this is that once you create them, you do not need to manually place any of the headers—Word will place them for you. If you edit your text so that it changes, the headings will move freely with their adjacent paragraphs, falling to the left or the right automatically, depending only on whether they are on a left-hand or a right-hand page.

How to repeat a frame or a text box on every page

You can also use frames and text boxes in headers and footers. Any frame or text box that's part of a header or footer will automatically be printed on every page where that header or footer appears. Given the flexible positioning for frames and text boxes, you can place either one anywhere on the page, even outside the header or footer area. What's more, since frames and text boxes can hold pictures as well as text, you can use a frame in a header or footer to place a logo or other repeating illustration on every page of a document—in the top or bottom margin, in a corner, centered horizontally and vertically in the middle of the page, or printed as a watermark, such as *DRAFT* or *TOP SECRET*, across the text.

When you use the Insert Page Numbers command, Word puts the page number in a frame in the header or footer. The following, then, is an example of how to insert a frame in a header. The procedure is exactly the same for both frames and text boxes and for both headers and footers.

To add a frame to a header, first be sure you're in Page Layout view. Then choose View Header And Footer, and, if necessary, use the Switch Between Header And Footer button on the Header And Footer toolbar to move to the header. Next add the frame, placing it anywhere on the page; it does not need to be within the header or footer area. Figure 14-33 shows a page with both frames and text boxes inserted in the header, but appearing both in the margins of the page and in the body text area.

FIGURE 14-33

This page includes two text boxes and two frames. All four were added in the header, even though they show elsewhere on the page.

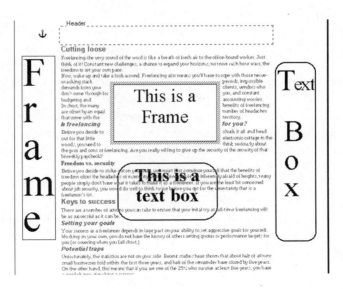

Regardless of where you put the frame, if you've set Word to show object anchors and then you move to or select the frame, you'll see that the anchor is attached to a paragraph in the header area, as shown in Figure 14-33.

Remember that you can change header and footer contents by dividing your document into sections, as we discussed in Chapter 13. You can use sections to turn the repeating frames on and off or change their contents at different points in your document. Remember too that you can use the Page Setup Layout card to specify different headers and footers for first pages, and for odd and even pages, so you can, for example, create different repeating headers for odd and even pages and leave the repeating header off the first page.

How to create a watermark

Although the heading for this section is "How to create a watermark," in truth we've already shown how. A watermark in Word is any text or object that is printed in the same place as other text. It can consist of a word, such as *DRAFT*, across a page, or a graphic image that you print text over. So whenever you create a text box in the area of the page where body text goes, you have, in fact, created a watermark. If you put the text box in the header, the watermark will be repeated on every page. The text box in Figure 14-33 that says *This is a text box* is also a watermark.

You can use any font available on your system formatted any way you like to produce a more interesting-looking text watermark. You can use color to have the watermark appear light gray rather than solid black so that you can read the text that the watermark overprints. In fact, one of the colors available for fonts on the Format Font Font card is light gray.

Remember that whether your printer will actually print the text in light gray depends on your printer. Print a test page using text of different colors to see how your particular printer reproduces them on the page.

You can insert a graphic in the frame in addition to or instead of text. That means you can use not only graphics but fancy text formats, such as those you can produce with the WordArt miniapplication, which we'll discuss in the next chapter.

If, for whatever reason, you would prefer to use a frame to create a watermark rather than a text box, you can. The trick is simply to define the top margin in the File Page Setup Margins card with a negative number. Briefly, if you use a positive measurement, such as 2", Word will start the text at that point—in this case, 2 inches down from the top of the page. If you add more lines to the header, Word will push the text farther down automatically. If you insert a frame when you are using a positive measurement, Word will wrap body text around the frame, as in Figure 14-33.

If you use a negative measurement, such as –2", Word will *always* start the body text at the designated point and will expand the header to fill the entire page. If you add more lines to the header than will fit in the 2 inches, the additional lines will overprint the body text. If you insert a frame when you are using a negative measurement, the frame will overprint the body text as well. This technique can be particularly handy when you want to take advantage of the additional positioning features available only with frames.

Pictures

The discussion of frames and text boxes so far has centered on text. However, both features work just as well for positioning pictures. One of Word's strongest features is that it will let you add pictures and other graphic objects. Word provides several tools for manipulating pictures within a document, letting you size, crop, and position a picture as needed. Word also offers ways to modify a picture or even create a new one from scratch, as we'll discuss in Chapter 15.

Although you can insert a picture into a document by itself, it's best to place your pictures in a frame or a text box—and preferably a frame, unless you are creating a watermark. Either a text box or a frame will let you position the pictures with a minimum of effort. In addition, a frame will let you easily format text to flow around the pictures. For the rest of this section, we'll concentrate on using pictures with frames, but you can apply much of this discussion to text boxes as well.

How to insert a picture

For now we will focus on using an existing picture that you've created in another program. Word offers support for many types of graphics files and offers many ways to bring them into your documents. For example, if you are working in another Windows-based application, you can cut or copy an image to the Clipboard and then paste it into your document. You can also insert picture files stored in a variety of file formats by importing them directly into a document. (We will cover the different formats that Word supports in Chapter 18, when we look at importing and exporting files.)

To simplify this discussion, we'll limit ourselves to the graphics files that come as part of the Word package. If you used the Setup program to install the complete version of Word, you should have a subdirectory named CLIPART in your Word program directory, and it should contain a number of images.

All of the clipart files have the filename extension WMF. This signifies that they are in the Windows Metafile format, which is an object-oriented graphics file format.

There are two major classes of graphics images—bitmapped and object-oriented. Bitmapped images define individual dots that make up the picture; object-oriented images are based on combinations of shapes such as lines, polygons, and circles. Some of the popular bitmapped image formats include files with the extensions PCX, BMP, and TIF; some of the popular object-oriented formats use the extensions WMF, CGM, and DRW. (We will discuss these formats and some of the programs that generate them in Chapter 18.) Bitmapped images offer the advantage of being able to handle mixed colors and subtle shadings more easily than object-oriented images can, but they have the disadvantage of often losing picture quality when resized. If you have a choice of which type to use, keep this difference in mind.

We will insert a picture into the sample document that we used for our discussion of frames. The original document is shown in Page Layout view in Figure 14-34.

Note that the cursor is at the start of the second paragraph of text in the document. This is the position where we'll insert the picture. You can either create an empty frame first and then place a picture in the frame or create the picture first and then add the frame. In this example, we'll import the picture first. We'll then add the frame and use the frame to position the picture between the two columns of text, as we did with the text example earlier in this chapter.

FIGURE 14-34

We will add a picture to this document using the clipart files that come with Word for Windows.

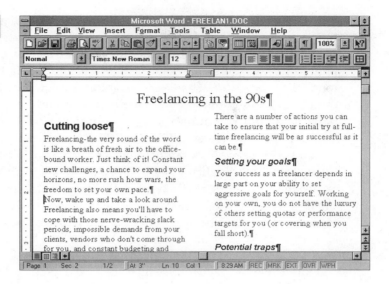

The Picture dialog box

Since this document is an article about free-lance work, and since this topic appeals to people's desire for fun and freedom, we want to add a picture that has something to do with these issues. Start by looking at the clip art Word has to offer. While in Page Layout view and with the cursor at the start of the second paragraph, choose Insert Picture to open the Insert Picture dialog box, shown in Figure 14-35. Note that the Directories box shows that we've already moved to the CLIPART directory in the Word program directory.

FIGURE 14-35

You can use the Insert Picture dialog box to select an image and insert it into your document.

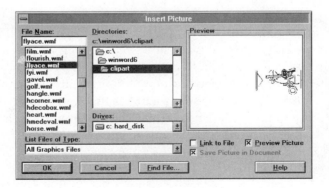

This Insert Picture dialog box should look familiar since it's similar to the Save As, Open, and other dialog boxes. The list of filenames and the Directories, Drives, and List Files Of Type boxes are essentially identical to the items with the same names in the Save As and Open dialog boxes, and they work the same way. The OK, Cancel, and Find File buttons also work the same way as in the Save As dialog box, although they are in different positions. The Find File button takes you to the same Find File dialog box that you can open by choosing File Find File.

One difference in detail between the Picture dialog box and similar dialog boxes is that the List Files Of Type list box lists picture-format file types rather than text-format file types. The list includes an entry for each image-file import filter you've installed for your copy of Word.

Four items are specific to the Insert Picture dialog box: the Preview box and the Preview Picture, Link To File, and Save Picture In Document check boxes.

The Preview Picture box lets you see a picture from a file before you bring it into your document. This makes it easy to browse through the clip art on your disk to look for the right file.

The Preview Picture check box lets you turn the preview feature on and off. For example, in Figure 14-35, FLYACE.WMF is highlighted in the list of filenames and the picture appears in the Preview box. If you remove the check from the check box, the picture will disappear from the preview box. But as long as there's a check in the check box, Word will preview each file as you highlight the name. If you have a relatively slow system, you may want to turn this feature off and then turn it back on again only when you reach the name of a file that sounds likely.

The Link To File check box tells Word to enter a field in your document that creates a link to the picture file on disk. You'll still be able to see the image in your document, however, as long as you set Word to show field results rather than field codes. Remember, you can toggle this setting with the Field Codes check box on the Tools Options View card.

One advantage of using a link is that if you change the image on the disk, you can update the image in the document without having to go through all the steps of importing the image again. If you don't use a link, the image is stored only as part of the document itself, as a duplicate of the original image, and completely divorced from it.

A second advantage of using a link is that you then have the option of clearing the Save Picture In Document check box. If this box is checked, as it always is if you aren't using the link feature, Word will store a copy of the image as part of your document. Obviously, this is required if you don't have a link to the original file. If you have a link, however, storing a copy in your document will let Word load the file faster. Choosing not to store a copy of the picture in your document means Word will take longer to load the file since it will have to update the image based on the link to the image, but it will also make the file substantially smaller.

For this example, we will simply place the image in the document without establishing a link. This leaves you free to modify the image on disk for other purposes, without having to worry about how it will affect any given document.

After you've made your choices in the Insert Picture dialog box and chosen OK, Word will return to the document and insert the picture, as shown in Figure 14-36.

FIGURE 14-36

Word inserts the picture so that you can see it in your document, shown here in Page Layout view.

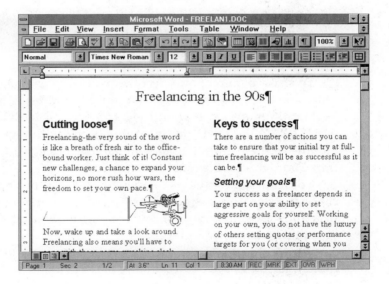

How to size a picture

Note how the picture in Figure 14-36 is aligned with the left margin. As our next step, we can either adjust the picture's size and then add a frame so that we can adjust the picture's position or add a frame and then adjust both size and position by adjusting the frame.

In this example, we'll adjust the size first and then add a frame, but note that most of the sizing techniques work the same way in either case. Note too that when you select a picture and then insert a frame, you'll find that you cannot resize the frame—or even select the frame—independently of the picture unless you choose Format Frame and change the frame size through the dialog box. You'll also find the same is true if you create the frame first and then take care to insert only a picture. However, if you create a frame that includes any additional elements besides the one picture, even a single-space character, you'll find that Word treats the frame and picture as separate elements. In general, working with pictures in frames is much easier if Word treats them as a single element, and the easiest way to ensure that will happen is to insert the picture in your document, select the picture, and choose Insert Frame (or Frame Picture from the right mouse button menu)—either before or after changing the picture size. Note too that these comments apply to text boxes as well.

To size a picture, first select the picture by clicking on it with the mouse or by moving to its immediate left or right and using the same keyboard selection techniques you would use to select an individual character. Word will indicate the selection by adding a box with eight handles around the picture, so the picture will look much like a selected frame, but without the frame border with diagonal lines.

You can use the mouse either to scale or to crop the picture. Scaling changes the picture's dimensions—along the horizontal dimension, the vertical dimension, or both at once. Cropping lets you cut pieces off the edges as you might with a photograph.

We want to make the picture of the airplane and banner a little larger rather than shrink or cut it, but any of these modifications are easy to make. Figure 14-37 shows three versions of the same picture. The version at the top was simply inserted into a Word document. The middle version was proportionally scaled to half its size. The bottom one is in the original proportions but is cropped to eliminate unwanted parts.

You can scale and crop by using the mouse to drag the handles located around the selected picture (or frame or text box), or you can enter a specification for the changes in a dialog box. As with frames, the mouse techniques provide interactive control with immediate visual feedback, which is useful for broad changes. The dialog box provides precise control for finer adjustments. You will likely use both methods, making broad changes with the mouse before making final changes with the keyboard. We'll start with the mouse in this example as well.

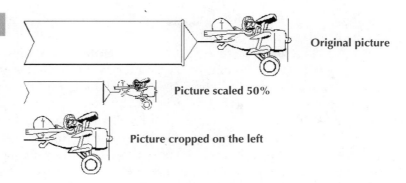

FIGURE 14-37

These three images show the difference between resizing a picture by scaling and by cropping.

Original picture

Picture scaled 50%

Picture cropped on the left

How to scale and crop by dragging with the mouse

You can scale a picture simply by moving the mouse pointer to one of the eight handles around a selected picture, clicking, and dragging the handle to a new position. However, the handle you grab makes a difference in the kind of change you can make.

If you use any of the four corner handles, the mouse pointer will turn into a two-headed diagonal arrow pointer. This pointer maintains the picture's current proportions as you change the size of the picture. In other words, you'll be able to make the picture half as tall only if you also make it half as wide. Note too that the operative phrase here is *current proportions*: If you've already changed the picture from its original proportions, Word will maintain that change when you scale the picture this way.

Note that this does not work the same way as when you are resizing frames. With frames, the diagonal double arrow does not force you to maintain the same proportions.

If you use the handles on the sides, top, or bottom of the picture, you will change the scale along only one dimension: vertical or horizontal. Be careful when making this sort of change; it can yield an image that looks stretched or squashed. Although this will not be a problem for some images and can even result in an interesting visual effect for others, the result can look strange if you distort a face or some other recognizable subject.

Fortunately, it's easy to restore a picture to its original proportions. Whenever you're dragging a handle, Word puts a message in the status bar showing the scaling proportions for whatever dimension or dimensions you're currently adjusting. If you're dragging a corner handle, Word will show the current scaling factors for both height and width. If you're dragging a top, bottom, or side handle, it will show the scaling factor for just height or width, as appropriate. Scaling factors are in terms of the original picture, so if both height and width show the same scaling factor, the picture has its original proportions.

To crop a picture, just hold down the Shift key before you click on a handle. When you move the pointer over the handle, the pointer shape will change to a square whose lines overshoot two of the corners with a thin diagonal line through the square. If you then drag the edge or corner handle to make the picture smaller, Word will cut off any part of the original image outside the edge or edges. However, the full image is still available to Word, so if you crop too much, you can drag the handle out again to restore some or all of the picture. (You can also drag the handle away from the original, complete, picture. This has the effect of adding blank space around the picture.) As with scaling, Word displays a message at the bottom of the screen showing how much you have cropped the picture—showing the measurement this time rather than the proportions. In general, you will probably want to crop just one side at a time, using the left, right, top, or bottom handle. If you use one of the corner handles, Word will maintain the overall picture's proportions and will crop two sides at once.

How to scale and crop with the Picture dialog box

Word provides a dialog box for formatting pictures. Like the Frame dialog box, the Picture dialog box lets you make changes with mouse or keyboard and has the advantage of greater precision than dragging with the mouse. Also like the Frame dialog box, the Picture dialog box has the disadvantage of not letting you see the effect of your changes until you close the dialog box. To open the Picture dialog box, select a picture and choose Format Picture. Word responds with the dialog box shown in Figure 14-38, with settings taken from the currently selected picture.

FIGURE 14-38

The Picture dialog box lets you scale and crop a picture with precision.

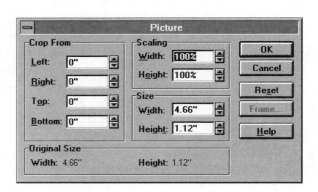

The entries in the Picture dialog box interact with each other. The Crop From box has four text boxes, one for each side of the picture. These text boxes have default settings of 0. To crop part of a picture, simply enter a positive number for the appropriate edge. To add white space around the image, enter a negative number. When you enter a setting for cropping the picture, it affects the height or width of the picture. That, in turn, changes the entry in the Height or Width text box in the Size box. If you start with a 4-inch-wide picture, for example, and crop 1 inch on the left side, Word will automatically change the width entry in the Size box to 3 inches.

In much the same way, the Width and Height text boxes in the Scaling and Size boxes are also related to each other. Change either width setting, and Word will automatically change the other. Similarly, if you change either height setting, Word will automatically change the other. For example, suppose the Crop From text boxes are all set at 0 for a 4-inch-wide picture, and you change the scaling width to 50 percent. Word will change the setting in the Size Width box to 2 inches.

If you want to maintain (or regain) the original proportions for the picture, simply be sure that the Width and Height scaling factors are set to the same value. If you want to return to the original values, choose the Reset button. Notice also that Word shows the picture's original dimensions in the Original Size box at the bottom of the dialog box.

How to add a frame to a picture

Notice that the Frame button is grayed in Figure 14-38. If the picture were already in a frame, the Frame button would be available. Choosing the button would then open the Frame dialog box and would be equivalent to selecting the frame with the picture and then choosing Format Frame.

One reason for putting a picture in a frame is so that you can change its position on the page. Another reason is to let text wrap around it, with text on the same horizontal lines as the picture. To add a frame, select the picture, and choose Insert Frame or Frame Picture from the right button menu. Word will add the frame, which you can tell by the shaded border around the picture while you have it selected. In contrast to empty frames or frames you add around text, a frame added around a picture will, by default, not include a border.

How to position a picture

With the frame in place around the picture, you can move the picture just as you can move a frame filled with text. Figure 14-39 on the next page shows our sample document after we resized the picture, inserted a frame, and moved the frame to its new position, centered horizontally relative to the page.

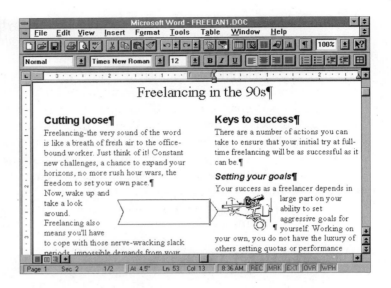

How to add a caption or other text to a picture

We might want to add a caption that will stay with the picture rather than
stay with the body text if we later move the picture again or edit or reformat
the document. We might also want to add some text, such as *Take Off on Your
Own!,* inside the banner in the picture to provide a tie-in to the document
content. You can easily add either or both of these items with a text box,
using a slight modification of the techniques we described earlier in this
chapter.

The easiest, most reliable way to add a text box and have it stay with the
picture is to add it as part of the picture itself. If you then double-click on the
picture, Word will open the Word Picture editing window, with the picture
loaded. The screen will still look much like the Word document-editing
screen, but all your text will disappear. In addition, you'll see the Drawing
toolbar, whether it was visible before or not, along with the Picture toolbar,
which includes the Close Picture button, and the Reset Picture Boundary
button, which looks like a tic-tac-toe grid.

Click on the Text Box button, define the text box inside the banner, and
then enter and format the text you want to use. Then you can repeat the procedure for the caption. The result should look much like Figure 14-40.

FIGURE 14-40

The picture-editing window looks much like a document-editing environment. Note that the caption's text box lies partly outside the picture boundary lines.

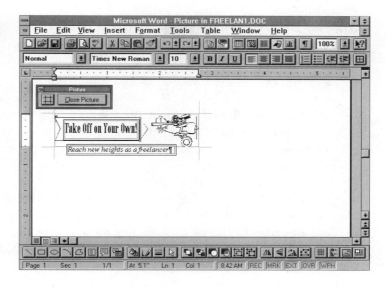

In Figure 14-40, the text box with the caption, immediately below the picture, lies partly outside the four lines that designate the picture boundaries. If you choose Close Picture at this point, the part of the text box that lies outside the boundaries will not show up in the picture when you return to the document. To include the entire text box in the picture, click on the Picture Boundary button. Word repositions the boundaries to include the entire picture. If you then choose Close Picture, you should see the entire picture, including the full caption, as in Figure 14-41.

FIGURE 14-41

If you add a caption as part of the picture, the picture and caption will always stay together.

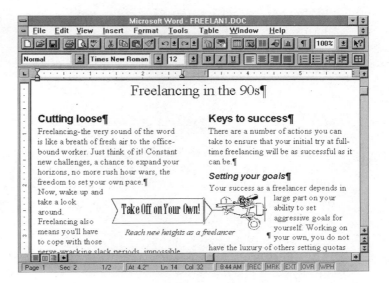

How to place a border around a picture

In many cases, you'll want to add a border around your picture. How you proceed depends on whether your picture is in a frame, and whether there is anything else in the frame. If the picture is not in a frame, simply select the picture and choose Format Borders And Shading to open the Picture Borders dialog box. If the picture is within a frame, and is the only item within the frame, select the frame and choose Format Borders And Shading to open the Frame Borders And Shading dialog box. In this case, the picture's border is not accessible. In either case, the options on the Border card will be the same and you can add a border using the techniques discussed earlier in this chapter and in Chapter 7. If the picture is in a frame that contains any other item (such as a caption), the picture and the frame are independent and you can add a border to the picture, to the frame, or to both using the techniques discussed here. Figure 14-42 shows a picture within a frame that has been formatted with a border.

FIGURE 14-42

If your picture is in a frame, you can create a border by adding a border to the frame.

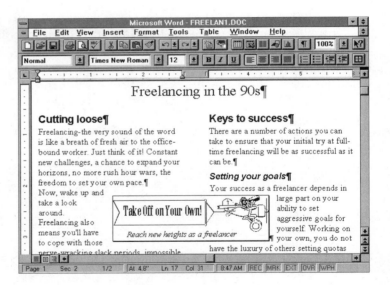

A final option is to edit the picture and add a border to the actual picture. You do this by double-clicking on the picture to open Microsoft Word Picture and drawing a rectangle around the picture—by choosing the rectangle button and dragging the rectangle's boundaries around the picture, much as you would define a text box.

How to position a picture in a table

Another way to control the positioning of a picture is by inserting a picture into a cell of a table rather than using a frame. This technique does not give you the positioning features and ability to wrap text around the graphic that you get with a frame, but it offers a quick and easy way to arrange pictures and text side by side. You might prefer using a table rather than a frame for a simple layout.

As much as we've covered in this chapter, we've barely begun to look at Word's capabilities for inserting and manipulating graphics. In fact, Word comes with a set of applications for drawing, graphing, creating fancy text for titles, and more. Word will also let you insert data created in other programs. We'll take a look at these features in the next chapter.

TOPIC FINDER

NEW! **Using Word's Drawing Tools**   550

- A closer look at the drawing tools
- How to use Word's picture editing window

Working with Word's Mini-Applications   559

NEW! How to use the Object dialog box

NEW! **Creating Font Effects with Microsoft WordArt**   561

- How to insert a WordArt object as an icon
- How to create a dropped capital letter

Creating Charts with Microsoft Graph   572

- How to use the Graph menus
- Where to go from here

Inserting Other Objects   577

15

Drawing, Graphics, & Other Objects

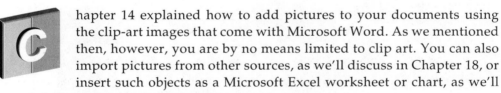

hapter 14 explained how to add pictures to your documents using the clip-art images that come with Microsoft Word. As we mentioned then, however, you are by no means limited to clip art. You can also import pictures from other sources, as we'll discuss in Chapter 18, or insert such objects as a Microsoft Excel worksheet or chart, as we'll briefly explain at the end of this chapter.

What's more, you can create your own images by using Word's built-in drawing features or any of three tools that come with Word: Microsoft WordArt, Microsoft Graph, and Microsoft Equation Editor. We'll cover Equation Editor in Chapter 23 because it serves as a mathematics editing tool rather than a graphics program. But all three of these programs are Windows mini-applications. Although we do not stress the point in Chapter 23, Equation Editor actually inserts an image of your equations, which is why you can scale the equations after you add them to your document, just as you can any other picture. The other two mini-applications work much the same way: You use them to create an image and then embed it in your document.

Unfortunately, the very sophistication of the Word drawing tools and the mini-applications leads to a problem: Trying to cover them in depth would demand many more pages than we can justify by their importance to most users. Our aim in this chapter, then, is to introduce and provide an overview of the drawing tools and two of the programs. But keep in mind that we are merely opening a door on the subject. It's as if we were writing a book about the United States and had to explain football, baseball, and basketball in one chapter. We can cover most of the rules, but we won't get anywhere near describing the nuances of each game.

Using Word's Drawing Tools

Word's drawing tools differ from its mini-applications in that the tools are part of Word itself. If you click on the Drawing button on the Standard toolbar (third to the left of the Zoom button), Word will add the Drawing toolbar, shown in Figure 15-1. By default, this toolbar is displayed at the bottom of the Word window, and Word switches to Page Layout view.

FIGURE 15-1

When you click on the Drawing button, Word positions the Drawing toolbar at the bottom of the Word window by default.

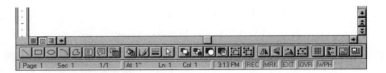

We introduced the Drawing toolbar in Chapter 14, where we showed you how to use its Text Box and Callout buttons to insert text boxes in your document. Text boxes are actually drawing objects. For this discussion, we'll assume that you're familiar with text boxes and the related features and concepts explained in Chapter 14. If you're not, we suggest that before you proceed here, you read "Frames: Positioning Text and Graphics on the Page" on page 509, with particular attention to "Text Boxes and Callouts" on page 525.

In addition to creating text boxes, you can use the Drawing toolbar to draw other objects directly in your document—including lines, arrows, rectangles, ellipses, and freeform shapes. Figures 15-2 and 15-3 list the toolbar buttons and their purposes. If you know how to work with text boxes, many, if not most, of these buttons should be self-explanatory; others will be familiar to users of nearly any object-based drawing program.

Button	Tool Name	Lets You Click and Drag to Insert This Kind of Drawing Object
Tools for inserting lines and shapes		
	Line	Straight lines
	Rectangle	Rectangles, including squares
	Ellipse	Ellipses, including circles
	Arc	Arcs
	Freeform	Freehand polygons and other shapes
Text box tools		
	Text Box	Text boxes
	Callout	Callout text boxes

FIGURE 15-2

The Drawing toolbar buttons for inserting objects.

Many of the buttons in Figure 15-3 on the next page are equivalent to choosing the Format Drawing Object command and setting options on the Fill, Line, or Size And Position card in the Drawing Object dialog box. Figure 15-3 mentions the equivalent dialog box options where appropriate, including the card in the Drawing Object dialog box on which the options can be found. We looked at these options, in Chapter 14, where we discussed text boxes.

Button	Tool Name	Purpose
Formatting tools		
	Format Callout	Opens the Format Callout dialog box for formatting all selected callouts; equivalent to choosing the Callout button on the Size And Position card
	Fill Color	Opens a grid of colors plus shades of gray to change the fill color of all selected objects; equivalent to the Color grid on the Fill card
	Line Color	Opens a grid of colors plus shades of gray to change the line color of all selected objects; equivalent to the Color list on the Line card
	Line Style	Opens a list of various line styles and weights, with and without arrowheads, to change the line style of all selected objects; equivalent to the Arrowhead group box and the Style and Weight options in the Line group box on the Line card
	Select Drawing Objects	Lets you click and drag to create a rectangle designating the objects that will be affected by formatting or other subsequent commands
	Bring To Front	Positions the selected objects in front of others so that the selected objects hide, or partially hide, the objects in back
	Send To Back	Positions the selected objects behind others so that the selected objects are hidden, or partially hidden, by the objects in front
	Bring In Front Of Text	Similar to Bring To Front, except that it positions the selected objects to hide text in the same area of the page
	Send Behind Text	Similar to Send To Back, except that it positions the selected objects to be overwritten by text in same area of the page
	Group	Groups all currently selected objects into one object

FIGURE 15-3

(continued)

The Drawing toolbar buttons for formatting and other tasks.

FIGURE 15-3. *continued*

Button	Tool Name	Purpose
	Ungroup	Breaks a set of grouped objects into individual objects so that you can format them individually
	Flip Horizontal	Flips all the selected items in a horizontal plane; if more than one item is selected, the items flip as a group
	Flip Vertical	Flips all the selected items in a vertical plane; if more than one item is selected, the items flip as a group
	Rotate Right	Rotates all the selected items 90 degrees clockwise; if more than one item is selected, the items rotate as a group
	Reshape	Shows all available handles on a freeform object so that you can click and drag to reshape the object
	Snap To Grid	Opens the Snap To Grid dialog box shown in Figure 15-4
	Align Drawing Objects	Opens the Align dialog box shown in Figure 15-5
Other tools		
	Create Picture	Opens a window for creating a picture if no objects are selected; converts any selected drawing objects to a single picture object
	Insert Frame	Equivalent to choosing the Insert Frame menu command

A closer look at the drawing tools

Word's drawing features are object-oriented—that is, all the images you create with the drawing tools are composed of either individual lines or filled objects. The objects are defined by straight and curved lines, which are themselves defined by a set of points.

To use the tools that create lines and shapes, you simply click on the appropriate button on the Drawing toolbar. Then click on a spot in your document to anchor one end of a line or one corner handle of a shape, hold down the mouse button, and drag to draw the line or shape. Release the button to finish creating the line or shape.

For shapes—such as rectangles and ellipses—Word will fill the inside of the shape using the current fill settings for drawing objects, and it will create a line defining the outside of the shape using the current line settings. If you've set the line format to include an arrowhead, the arrowhead will appear on any lines you draw but not on closed shapes, such as rectangles and ellipses.

After you create an object, you can move it. You can also reshape it, by moving the points that define its lines. To get a sense of how this works, think of the lines—whether curved or straight—as rubber bands that are tacked down in some places and attached to invisible wires in others. If you pull on the invisible wires or move the tack-down points, the rubber bands will change shape, size, or both. Word also lets you change the color of an object, as well as such details as the weight and color of the outside line, by changing the settings for the fill and the line.

It's important to note that although you can resize and reshape objects, you can work with them only as complete objects. You cannot, for example, erase part of a line; instead you must resize it. This approach differs from the one you'll find in bitmap-oriented programs, such as Windows Paintbrush, in which you create images with a group of dots, or bits. Bitmapped images are more like paintings on canvas, in which you define shapes by where you put the paint. To change shapes in bitmapped images, you must change the position of the bits. When you change color, you change the color of each individual dot. And, unlike the way you work with drawing objects, you can erase part of a bitmapped line by erasing only certain bits.

Another important feature of drawing objects allows you to group objects together or break a group of objects apart. You can also select one or more objects and move them either in front of or behind other objects. The objects in back will be partly or completely hidden by the objects in front.

If these concepts seem a bit difficult, we suggest that you experiment with the drawing tools a bit to see how they work on the screen and then come back and read these sections again. We'll also offer some notes on specific tools in the following section, covering important aspects of those tools that may not be immediately obvious.

If you click on one of the Drawing toolbar buttons to draw a line or a shape, Word will deactivate the button as soon as you finish drawing one object. If you initially double-click on the button, however, Word will keep it active until you click on it again or click on another button. As long as the button is active, you can create as many objects with that tool as you need. Like all toolbar buttons, when the button is active, it will look as if it has been pressed.

How to control movement of objects

In practice, you'll find that it's hard to move an object or a handle in an exact vertical, horizontal, or diagonal direction. To make the task easier, hold down the Shift key as you drag. When you do so, you will be able to move the object only in a precisely vertical or horizontal direction (or to move the handle in a precisely vertical, horizontal, or diagonal direction). If you are resizing an object (by moving the handles), each handle will move only in a specific direction—side handles move horizontally, top and bottom handles move vertically, and corner handles move diagonally. When you are moving an object, the object can move only horizontally or vertically. If you drag the object diagonally, it will move only in one or the other direction. If your diagonal dragging is uneven, the object may appear to jump from being moved horizontally to being moved vertically.

How to use the Shift and Ctrl keys

If you're creating an ellipse, holding down the Shift key as you drag will draw a circle (rather than an oval). Similarly, if you're creating a rectangle, you can hold down Shift to draw a square. If you're drawing a straight line and holding down Shift, Word will draw only a vertical line, a horizontal line, or a line at a 30-, 45-, or 60-degree angle to the vertical or horizontal. If you're extending an existing line, holding down the Shift key will maintain the current angle—that is, you can only extend the line, not rotate it.

To resize an object around its center point, hold down the Ctrl key. Word will then adjust all appropriate parts of the object as you drag. You can also hold down Ctrl-Shift to combine the keys' effects when resizing, so that the object retains its proportions. If you hold down Ctrl when you create an ellipse or a rectangle, the first click will anchor the center of the shape rather than a corner handle.

The Freeform button

The freeform tool has two modes of operation. If you click on the Freeform button, click in one position on the screen, and then click in another, you'll get a straight line between the two points. If you move the pointer and click a third time, you'll get a second line between the second click position and the third. You can create a closed freeform object consisting of straight lines by adding as many lines as you need and then positioning the end of one line at the starting point of the first line. (Note that you can zoom in on the image with Word's Zoom feature, for precise placement.)

To use the second freeform drawing mode, hold down the mouse button and drag. You'll get a line that follows the pointer's movement, as if you were using a pen or pencil. When you release the mouse button, the pointer will stop drawing this way and will return to the first mode.

If you create a closed polygon, the freeform tool will recognize when the object is finished and will turn off automatically. To turn off the tool manually at any point in drawing a line, press Esc or double-click.

The Reshape button

Freeform objects can display two sets of handles. The first set consists of eight handles arranged around the object along a rectangular outline. The second set consists of a variable number of handles, which lie on the line that defines the object, at places where the direction of the line changes. To go back to our rubber-band analogy, the first set of handles acts as the points to which the invisible wires are attached, allowing you to resize the object as a whole. The second set of handles, available only on freeform objects, represents the points where the rubber bands are tacked down. You can move these handles to alter the shape. To toggle between the first and second set of handles, select a freeform object and click on the Reshape button.

The Snap To Grid button

The Snap To Grid button opens the Snap To Grid dialog box, shown in Figure 15-4. If you're familiar with graphics programs, you probably already know that the concept *snap to grid* constrains movement to discrete increments. This makes it easier to control position, size, and shape, since you can drag objects only in increments defined by the grid.

FIGURE 15-4

By default, the Snap To
Grid increments are
0.1 inch.

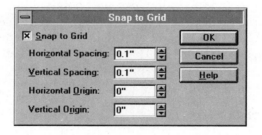

As you can see in Figure 15-4, the default Snap To Grid settings are 0.1 inch. You can use this dialog box to change the settings for horizontal and vertical movement—or to turn the feature on or off, by checking or clearing the Snap To Grid check box. The Horizontal Origin and Vertical Origin boxes let you specify where the grid should start in relation to the page.

> If you hold down the Alt key as you start to drag with the mouse, Word turns off the Snap To Grid feature. This can be useful if the grid increments are too large to let you position an object where you want it to appear, saving you the effort of turning the feature off and then on again.

The Align Drawing button

The Align Drawing button opens the Align dialog box, shown in Figure 15-5. The dialog box choices enable you to align the currently selected object or objects relative to the page or to one another, in both horizontal (Left, Center, Right, or None) and vertical (Top, Center, Bottom, or None) directions.

FIGURE 15-5

The Align dialog box lets you quickly align selected objects with one another or in relation to the page.

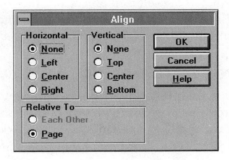

This alignment feature can be quite helpful. If you want to create several concentric circles, for example, you can create the circles quickly, without worrying about their positions. You can then use the Select Drawing Objects button to select them all, click on the Align Drawing button, set the dialog box options to center the circles horizontally and vertically relative to one another, and choose OK.

The Create Picture button

If you select at least one drawing object before clicking on the Create Picture button, Word will convert the object to a Word picture object, which we'll discuss in a moment. If you select more than one object first, Word will join them and convert them to a single picture object. Generally, you will want to convert a drawing object (or group of objects) to a single picture object so that you can place it as a picture within your document (rather than as separate drawing objects). You can then work with the new picture using the techniques described in the previous chapter. If you simply want to work with a group of objects as a single drawing object temporarily, use the Group button instead. You can use the Ungroup button to break a group of drawing objects back into individual objects. There is no way to convert a picture object to a drawing object.

Joining multiple objects into a single picture object makes it impossible to get at the individual parts. However, you can still modify parts of the picture if you open a Word picture editing window (which we touched on briefly in Chapter 14). To open a picture editing window to modify a picture object, simply double-click on the picture object. Alternatively, you can select the object, choose the Edit Picture Object command, and then choose Open. (The Object command on the Edit menu is usually grayed. When you select an appropriate object, however, such as a picture object, the command name changes to match the selected object and the command becomes available.) You can also open a blank picture editing window by clicking on the Create Picture button with no drawing object selected.

How to use Word's picture editing window

As we mentioned in Chapter 14, a picture editing window is a special kind of window Word provides for editing picture objects. Figure 15-6 shows a picture editing window that was opened by double-clicking on a set of concentric circles we created with Word's drawing tools and then converted to a picture object.

FIGURE 15-6

Word's picture editing window is similar to a document window in Page Layout view.

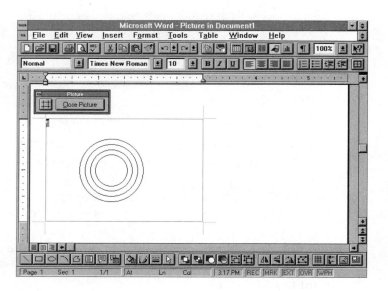

As you can see in Figure 15-6, the picture editing window is quite similar to a document window in Page Layout view. You can, for example, still use most of Word's menu commands and toolbar buttons. But the only item you can edit is the picture object itself. Notice that the title bar in Figure 15-6 is labeled *Microsoft Word - Picture in Document1*. That's precisely what you'll see: the single picture you are currently editing.

When you open a picture editing window, Word will add the Drawing toolbar (if it isn't already displayed) and the Picture toolbar. The Drawing toolbar and all the drawing tools work the same way in a picture editing window as they do in a document window. The Picture toolbar contains two buttons. The Reset Picture Boundary button expands or shrinks the boundary that defines which part of the picture Word will insert in your document. If you edit the picture so that it no longer matches the original boundary, click on Reset Picture Boundary to ensure that the entire picture is inserted in your document. (The current boundary is represented in the window by a rectangle that is formed by thin lines and delineated with crop marks—two short lines at right angles—at each corner.) The Close Picture button closes the picture editing window and returns you to the document window with the modified or newly created picture inserted.

 You can use Word's drawing tools either to annotate text (for example, with a callout) or to create an image. When you annotate text, obviously you'll want to enter the drawing objects directly in your document, where you can see the text. But if you want to create a complex illustration, and particularly if you want to ensure that you won't accidentally change its elements later while working in the document, you'll be better off working in a picture editing window.

You can also use a picture editing window to edit images imported from other sources. For most bitmapped images, such as those with PCX, BMP, or TIF filename extensions, Word can only resize or reproportion the image. With object-oriented images, such as those whose filenames end with a CGM or WMF extension, you can generally do more.

Working with Word's Mini-Applications

Unlike Word's drawing tools, which are integrated into the program, the mini-applications that come with Word stand somewhat apart from Word. To use them, you must first place the cursor in your document where you want to add the new element and then choose Insert Object. (Word provides an Insert Chart button on the Standard toolbar, but we'll ignore that for the moment.) Word will open an Object dialog box similar to the one shown in Figure 15-7.

FIGURE 15-7

The Object dialog box lists different object types that you can insert.

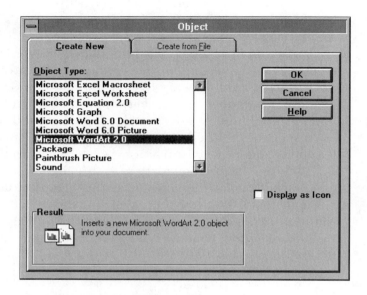

The list you see in the Object Type list box on your screen can differ from the one shown in Figure 15-7. What you'll see depends on how you installed Word and what other applications you have installed. For example, if you haven't installed Microsoft Excel, you won't see the Microsoft Excel Worksheet option. At the moment, however, we're concerned only with Microsoft WordArt 2.0, which comes with Word and should be available on your system. If it's not, you can install it from the original Word disks (or a backup copy) by running the Setup program again.

How to use the Object dialog box

As you can see in Figure 15-7, the Object dialog box includes two cards: Create New and Create From File. The Create From File card looks much like Word's Open dialog box. You can use it for files created in other programs, such as Microsoft Excel, to insert the contents from an existing file into Word. You can then edit the file later in the original application. We'll cover the Create From File card in Chapter 18, "Sharing Data with Other Programs" on page 618.

The Create New card lets you create an object and insert it at the same time. The Object Type list shows all available types of objects. You can use the Display As Icon check box, which you'll find on both cards, to insert the object into your document as an icon. To see the object's contents, you can then double-click on the icon in your document to call on the application in which the object was created.

If you check the Display As Icon check box, the Object dialog box will display the icon that Word will use and will also display a button labeled Change Icon. If you click on this button, you'll be able to choose a different icon if you know which file contains the icon you want.

When you create an object such as a spreadsheet, a graph, or another document whose contents need to be visible in your Word document both on screen and in printed form, be sure that you do not check the Display As Icon check box. When you want to create a hypertextlike link that will open another application so that you can see and edit an item in that application, you should check this check box.

Creating Font Effects with Microsoft WordArt

Of Word's three mini-applications, WordArt 2.0 is likely to be of most interest to most people.

If you're familiar with Word 2.0, you may also be familiar with the version of WordArt that came with Word 2.0. If you're one of the users who considered that program too wimpy for serious work, we suggest you take a look at the new WordArt, which offers far more flexibility than the old version did—so much so that we've marked this section as a new feature.

Simply put, WordArt now lets you create a rich variety of special font effects using a wide range of typestyles. As is the case for any fancy effect, you won't want to overdo it, but you'll find this program a fun and flexible way to add some visual pizzazz to your documents, from memos to newsletters. To give you a flavor of what WordArt can do, Figure 15-8 presents some sample WordArt images.

As you can do with any image, you can place a WordArt image in a frame so that you can control its placement on the printed page. See Chapter 14, "Columns, Frames, & Pictures" on page 496.

FIGURE 15-8

WordArt offers many
font effects that you
can use to dress up
your printed pages.

Suppose, for example, that you want to add a fancy title to the newsletter shown in Figure 15-9. Because you'll want the WordArt image to span all three columns, after you've created the image you'll want to place it in a frame and then resize the frame to fill the top of the page.

FIGURE 15-9

We will use WordArt to
add a title at the top of
this sample newsletter.

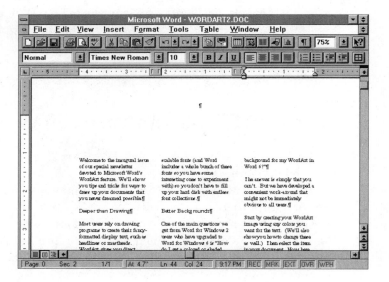

Be sure that the cursor is at the top of the document. To insert the WordArt object, choose Insert Object, highlight Microsoft WordArt 2.0 in the Object Type list box, and choose OK to start WordArt. As shown in Figure 15-10, WordArt will replace the usual Word menu bar with a modified menu bar, replace the Word toolbars with its own toolbar, display the phrase *Your Text Here* as the default text for the WordArt object, and open a dialog box labeled Enter Your Text Here. In short, WordArt lets you see your document, but it modifies your working environment.

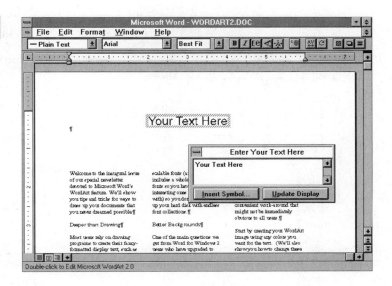

FIGURE 15-10

When WordArt starts, it leaves you in your Word document but modifies the screen.

While you're working with WordArt, the Edit menu consists of a single menu item: Edit WordArt Text. You can choose this command to return to the Enter Your Text Here dialog box after working with the Format menu or the WordArt toolbar. (You can also return to the dialog box by clicking on it.) The Format menu offers several formatting commands specific to WordArt, which we'll look at as part of this example. Each command is also available through a toolbar button. The File and Window menus are essentially unchanged.

The title for this newsletter is *Stone & Poor's WordArt Tips*. Start by typing this title in the dialog box. You can then choose the Update Display button to update the text displayed in the WordArt image, although WordArt will automatically update the text when you open a menu or drop-down list. (Choosing the Insert Symbol button in the dialog box opens the Insert Symbol dialog box, which is similar to but more limited than the Symbol dialog box you see when you choose Word's Insert Symbol command.)

After entering the text, you'll need to tell WordArt how to format it. You can add the formatting in any order. For most formatting, you can use the WordArt toolbar shown in Figure 15-10. The WordArt tools and their actions are listed in Figure 15-11 on the next page. In our discussion, we'll work our way from left to right across the toolbar.

Tool	Tool Name	Action
— Plain Text ▼	Line And Shape	Selects pattern for laying out text
Arial ▼	Font	Selects the font
Best Fit ▼	Font Size	Select the font size
B	Bold	Turns bold on and off
I	Italic	Turns italic on and off
Ee	Even Height	Makes all letters, regardless of case, the same height
◁	Flip	Rotates each letter 90 degrees counterclockwise (generally used in combination with text rotation)
⁺A⁺	Stretch	Stretches the text to fill the width of the frame
▤	Alignment	Aligns the text within the frame
AV↔	Spacing Between Characters	Controls the spacing between characters and word kerning
↻	Rotation	Rotates and scales the text
▨	Shading	Defines the fill pattern and color for the text
▣	Shadow	Defines the shadow position, style, and color
▤	Border	Defines the pattern and color for character borders

Figure 15-11

The WordArt Toolbar.

The first item on the left of the WordArt toolbar is the Line And Shape box. If you open the drop-down list, you'll see the grid shown in Figure 15-12. Each shape on this grid represents a different pattern for laying out the text. As you'll see in a moment, you can modify these further. Figure 15-12 shows some samples of how our newsletter title would look with some of the choices in this grid. For our example, we'll use Curve Up, which is the fourth item down in the left column of the grid.

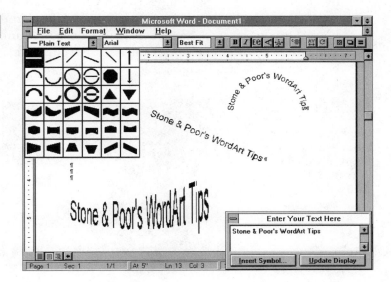

FIGURE 15-12

These sample WordArt images differ only in the Line And Shape box setting.

Next on the toolbar are the Font and the Font Size drop-down lists. The Font list is a list of all of the TrueType fonts installed on your system. For our example, we'll use Arial Rounded MT Bold. (This is the font's full name, although it may be only partially displayed in the list.) For Font Size, you can choose Best Fit or specify a size. We'll stay with Best Fit.

Fifth from the left is the Stretch button, the first one we'll use in this example. Choose this button to have WordArt set the text so that it will stretch to fill the frame around the object. Clicking on this button is equivalent to choosing the Format Stretch To Frame command and will even add a check mark next to Stretch To Frame on the menu.

The next button to the right is the Alignment button. Although we won't use this button, it requires a bit of explanation. Click on this button, and WordArt will open a menu that lets you specify how to align the text: Center, Left, Right, Stretch Justify, Letter Justify, or Word Justify. The best way to understand the differences among these settings is to try each one. Before you can see the differences, however, you'll have to turn off the Stretch To

Frame feature and make the frame larger than the text. We'll show you how to make the frame larger a little later as part of this example.

Next is a group of two buttons: the Spacing Between Characters button, with a short double-headed arrow underneath the letters *AV*, and the Rotation button, with a curved arrow pointing clockwise. If you click on the Spacing Between Characters button, you'll open the Spacing Between Characters dialog box, shown in Figure 15-13. (You can open this same dialog box by choosing Format Spacing Between Characters.) As you can see, you can set the spacing of the characters in preset levels from Very Tight to Very Loose, or you can set a custom spacing. Check the Automatically Kern Character Pairs check box if you want WordArt to automatically adjust spacing between pairs of characters.

FIGURE 15-13

You can control character spacing in WordArt with the Spacing Between Characters dialog box.

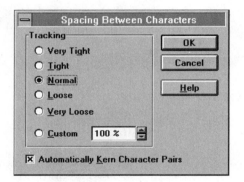

If you click on the Rotation button, you'll open the Special Effects dialog box, shown in Figure 15-14. (Again, you can open the same dialog box through the Format menu, by choosing Format Rotation And Effects.) The settings in the Special Effects dialog box will vary depending on the shape you selected in the Line And Shape box. For now, we'll look only at the options that go with the Curve Up choice.

FIGURE 15-14

You can rotate text and adjust the relative size of characters with the Special Effects dialog box.

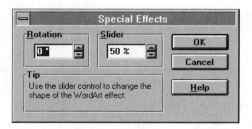

The Rotation setting in the Special Effects dialog box lets you control the rotation for the WordArt text as a whole. Rotate a straight horizontal line of text by 270 degrees, for example, and the text will be vertical but on its side. You can then use the Flip button to rotate each letter and wind up with text that reads from top to bottom. Again, the best way to see how these features interact is to experiment with them a bit. For purposes of this example, we'll leave the Rotation setting at 0 degrees.

The Slider setting determines whether the size of the text grows from left to right. If this setting is 0, the text will be the same height across. By default, the Curve Up shape uses a setting of 50 percent. To exaggerate this effect, we'll use a setting of 100 percent.

Next are the last three buttons on the toolbar: the Shading, Shadow, and Border buttons. Each one displays a dialog box, and each has an equivalent command on the Format menu that opens the same dialog box. The menu commands are Format Shading, Format Shadow, and Format Border.

The Shading dialog box, shown in Figure 15-15, lets you define the fill for the characters in the WordArt text. You can pick a pattern in the Style box and select foreground and background colors. The Sample box will show you the effect of your settings. For our example, we'll use a solid pattern, with a black foreground.

FIGURE 15-15

The Shading dialog box lets you adjust the fill pattern for the text characters.

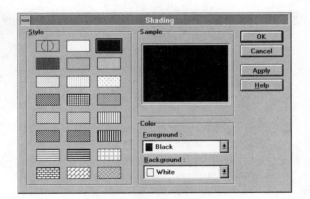

If you click on the Shadow toolbar button, WordArt will open the grid shown in Figure 15-16 on the next page. You can then choose a shadow to complement your text, or you can choose More to open the Shadow dialog box, also shown in Figure 15-16. To open this dialog box directly, choose Format Shadow. As you can see, the dialog box will let you pick not only a type of shadow but also a shadow color. For our example, we'll stay with silver for the color, pick the rightmost shadow type, and then choose OK to close the dialog box.

FIGURE 15-16

Choose the Shadow button to open a grid of shadow types. Choose More on the grid or choose the Format Shadow command to open the Shadow dialog box.

The last button on the WordArt toolbar is the Border button. If you click on it or choose Format Border, WordArt will open the Border dialog box, shown in Figure 15-17. You can pick both a line thickness and a line color in the Border dialog box. We won't use this effect in our example.

FIGURE 15-17

The Border dialog box lets you set the thick-ness and color for a line that appears around each WordArt character.

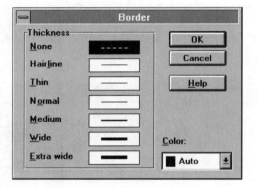

If you add a border, it appears around each individual character, not around the WordArt image as a whole. If you have a color printer, this feature can produce a striking outline effect. If you want to add a border around the entire object, you must return to Word, select the object, and use Word's Format Borders And Shading command to add the border.

Once you've defined the WordArt object the way you want it, you can re-turn to Word's editing window by clicking anywhere on your screen outside the WordArt image, the WordArt toolbar, or the Enter Your Text Here dialog box. If you then click on the object in your document, you'll see a rectangle that frames the object, along with the usual eight handles that you can drag to change size and proportions. Use these handles to stretch the rectangle to the right margin. If you've followed all the steps in our example precisely, the result should look much like the sample shown in Figure 15-18.

FIGURE 15-18

We now have an eye-catching title at the top of our newsletter.

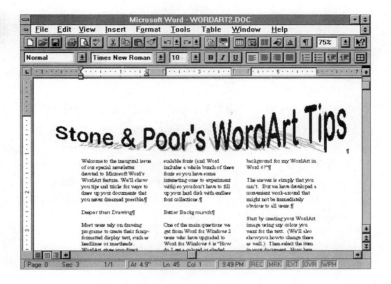

If you want to move a WordArt object on your page, add a frame by selecting the object and choosing Insert Frame. You'll then be able to move it around like any other object in a frame, using the techniques described in Chapter 14, "Columns, Frames, & Pictures" on page 496.

How to insert a WordArt object as an icon

If you choose to insert a WordArt object as an icon—by checking the Display As Icon check box when you first choose Insert Object—you'll find yourself working in the Word Art 2.0 dialog box, shown in Figure 15-19, rather than

FIGURE 15-19

If you choose to insert a WordArt object as an icon, you'll be working in this dialog box.

in the WordArt 2.0 window we've been describing. If you take a close look at the dialog box, however, you'll see that the differences are superficial. The dialog box includes all the features we've discussed; they're just arranged differently. You'll find that everything works the same way.

How to create a dropped capital letter

WordArt isn't limited to creating dramatic effects. Figure 15-20 shows a report that uses what is called a dropped capital letter, or "drop cap," in the opening paragraph. This popular typographic effect is easy to create using WordArt, even with a shadow, as shown in this example. Word also has a menu command for creating drop caps, but WordArt can create more visually interesting variations.

FIGURE 15-20

WordArt makes it easy to create fancy typographic effects such as this drop cap.

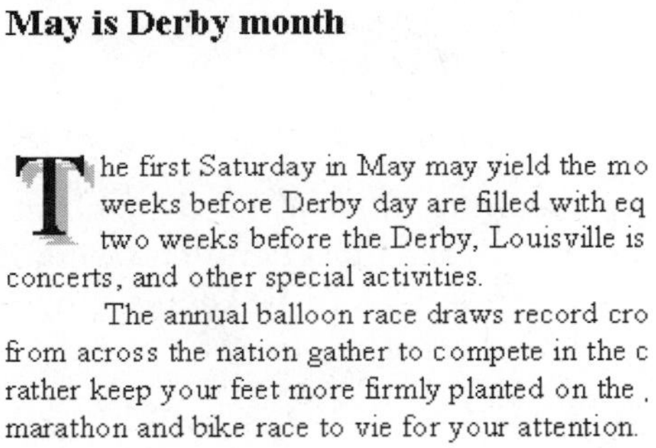

May is Derby month

The first Saturday in May may yield the mo weeks before Derby day are filled with eq two weeks before the Derby, Louisville is concerts, and other special activities.

The annual balloon race draws record cro from across the nation gather to compete in the c rather keep your feet more firmly planted on the . marathon and bike race to vie for your attention.

How to create a drop cap with Word's Format Drop Cap command

Certainly the quickest way to create a drop cap is with Word's built-in Format Drop Cap command. Start by placing the cursor in the paragraph where you want the drop cap. Then remove any first-line indent, and choose Format Drop Cap to open the Drop Cap dialog box, shown in Figure 15-21.

FIGURE 15-21

Word's Format Drop Cap command lets you define a drop cap using this dialog box.

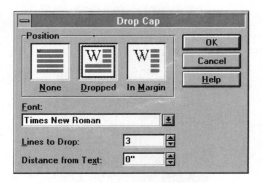

As you can see in Figure 15-21, the Drop Cap dialog box offers three choices for position: None, Dropped, and In Margin. You can also pick a font, define the number of lines for the drop cap, and set the distance from the text. We'll use the Dropped position and select Footlight MT Light as the font because it complements the Times New Roman font in the document but also adds a bit more visual flavor. And we'll accept the defaults of a 3-line drop and 0 distance from the text. You can see the result in Figure 15-22.

<table>
<tr><td>

FIGURE 15-22

This drop cap was produced by Word's built-in drop cap feature.

</td><td>

May is Derby month

The first Saturday in May may yield the mos weeks before Derby day are filled with equ two weeks before the Derby, Louisville is t concerts, and other special activities.

The annual balloon race draws record cro from across the nation gather to compete in the c rather keep your feet more firmly planted on the g marathon and bike race to vie for your attention.

</td></tr>
</table>

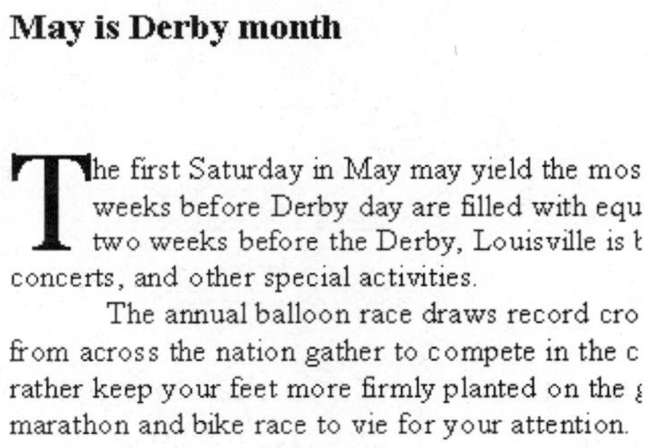

How to create a drop cap with WordArt

While there's nothing wrong with the drop cap shown in Figure 15-22, it just doesn't have the extra zip of the version you saw in Figure 15-20. To create the drop cap shown in Figure 15-20, start by deleting the first letter of the paragraph. Then, with the cursor at the leftmost position in the paragraph, choose the Insert Object command and start WordArt 2.0.

Figure 15-23 on the next page shows the finished WordArt image. The only text is a single capital *T* in the Footlight MT Light font. We also specified Best Fit in the Font Size box. We selected Plain Text in the Line And Shape box because of the simple horizontal orientation of the image. The image is also defined with solid black shading and with a shadow option that creates a drop shadow.

After you define the WordArt image, click on the document area to return to editing in Word, select the image, and choose Insert Frame to add a frame around it. You can then use the Word commands discussed in Chapter 14 to resize and reposition the character as needed. Also be sure that the frame is anchored to the paragraph that contains the drop cap. (You can use the mouse to drag the anchor to that paragraph.) We covered frames in detail in Chapter 14; for more details on anchoring in particular, see "Anchors" on page 514.

FIGURE 15-23

When inserted into a document and sized appropriately, this WordArt image will yield the drop cap shown in Figure 15-20.

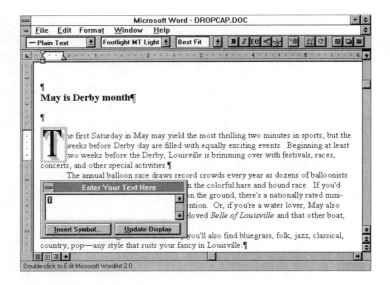

To finish the drop cap in the example, select the frame, choose Format Frame, set the Width and Height to Auto, set Distance From Text to 0.03 inch, and check the Move With Text and Lock Anchor check boxes so that the drop cap will move with the appropriate paragraph if you edit the page or change the page's formatting. Then choose OK.

It takes only a minute or so to create a drop cap with this method, and the extra visual appeal is well worth the effort. Note too that you can use WordArt (but not Word's built-in feature) to create a raised cap (a large first letter that reaches above the first line of text) as well as a raised cap and a drop cap (a large first letter that reaches both above and below the first line of text).

Creating Charts with Microsoft Graph

We're about to jump to a completely different subject: Microsoft Graph. Just about the only thing that Microsoft WordArt and Microsoft Graph have in common is that both are mini-applications that come with Word. Not only are they completely different kinds of applications, but they don't even work the same way: WordArt lets you work with a WordArt object in the context of the Word document that will contain the object, whereas Graph opens a separate window to work in and returns you to your document only when you finish working with the graph.

With that difference in mind, we'll also add a warning: Having taken a fairly complete look at WordArt, to give you a sense of the complexity of the mini-applications that come with Word, we'll take a much less detailed look at Microsoft Graph.

When you have a mass of numbers, it's usually far easier to make sense of them by looking at a chart rather than by looking at the numbers themselves. That's why spreadsheet programs such as Microsoft Excel, Quattro Pro, and Lotus 1-2-3 include graphing features. Word will let you import charts from any program that supports OLE—the Windows Object Linking and Embedding standard. But you might not own such a program. And even if you do, you may occasionally have a document with a set of numbers that needs to be converted to chart form.

Microsoft Graph lets you create attractive charts in short order. You start Graph in much the same way you start WordArt. Position your cursor where you want the graph to appear in your document. Then click on the Insert Chart button on the Standard toolbar or choose Insert Object, choose Microsoft Graph from the Object Type list box, and choose OK. Figure 15-24 shows the opening screen for Microsoft Graph (after it has been maximized).

FIGURE 15-24

Microsoft Graph will let you prepare attractive business graphs and charts quickly and easily.

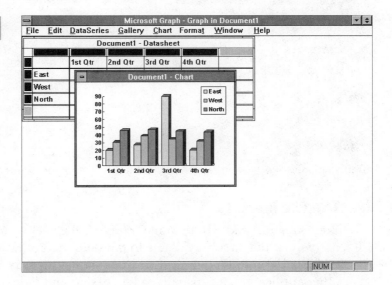

As you can see in Figure 15-24, Graph opens two windows in its workspace. The Datasheet window, in the upper left, looks like a spreadsheet made up of rows and columns. The Chart window, near the center, displays the image of the graph as defined by Graph's current settings. Figure 15-24 shows the default data and settings Graph uses when it first starts.

The fundamental concept of Graph is that you arrange your data in the datasheet and then select the rows and columns you want to use to create the chart. As you make changes in the Datasheet window, the Chart window will automatically reflect those changes. You can also change the settings that define the format of the chart itself.

How to use the Graph menus

Graph's menu commands include a number of sophisticated features. Figure 15-25 shows the menus; we'll take a quick look at each.

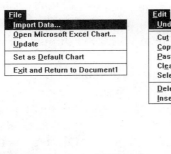

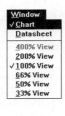

FIGURE 15-25

Graph's menus offer a wide range of commands that provide control over your charts.

The File menu

You can enter and edit data in Graph's Datasheet window manually. Alternatively, if the data is available in tab-delimited or table form, you can copy and paste it into the window. If the data has already been entered in some other application, it is usually faster, easier, and more accurate to import the data directly from that application with the File Import Data command. (This command will be grayed unless you select the Datasheet window before opening the File menu.) You can import up to 4000 rows and 256 columns of data this way. Note that labels and legend keys must be in the first row and column of the imported data, as they are in the sample datasheet displayed when you open Graph.

The remaining commands on the File menu will let you open a Microsoft Excel chart, update the embedded image in the destination Word document, set the current chart format as the new default, or exit Graph to return to your document.

The Edit menu

Most of the Edit menu commands apply only to the datasheet and are grayed unless the Datasheet window is active. In addition to the familiar Undo, Cut, Copy, Paste, and Clear commands, you'll find Select All (which selects all the cells in the datasheet), Delete Row/Col, and Insert Row/Col. When the Chart window is active, the Copy command becomes Copy Chart.

The DataSeries menu

The DataSeries menu lets you tell Graph how to treat the rows and columns that you've selected to use in the chart. Include Row/Col and Exclude Row/Col let you designate rows or columns in the datasheet that will or will not be included in the chart. Series In Rows and Series In Columns are mutually exclusive choices you can toggle between, telling Graph whether to treat each row or each column as a data series. Graph puts a check mark next to the choice that's currently active.

The first menu command, Plot On X Axis, is available only for XY charts (also known as scatter plots). You can use this to tell Graph which row or column to use for the tick-mark labels along the *x*-axis of your chart. You must first select the row or column and then the command.

In Graph, you can create a chart that is a combination of a basic chart and a separate overlay chart. The last two commands on the DataSeries menu, Move To Overlay and Move To Chart, let you specify that a given series of data (meaning a given row or column) be assigned to either the basic chart or the overlay.

The Gallery menu

The Gallery menu is the heart of the Graph program. As shown in Figure 15-25, it offers choices for different types of charts. The top section lists two-dimensional charts (area, bar, column, line, pie, XY, and combination). The bottom section lists three-dimensional charts (3-D area, 3-D bar, 3-D column, 3-D line, and 3-D pie). The two-dimensional Combination choice lets you create an overlay chart, in which you can have two charts of different types in a single image. There is no combination choice for any of the 3-D charts.

When you choose from the Gallery menu, Graph will show you a Chart Gallery dialog box like the one shown in Figure 15-26 on the next page. The choices in the dialog box will depend on the type of chart you've chosen. Figure 15-26 shows the eight predefined choices for 3-D column charts. If a given chart type has more predefined charts than the Chart Gallery dialog box can display at one time, the More button will be available. Choose it to see the additional chart types.

FIGURE 15-26

You can choose from a set of predefined chart types in the Chart Gallery dialog box.

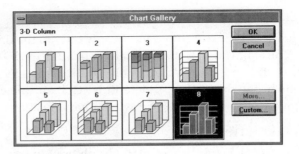

The Chart menu

The commands on the Chart menu affect the appearance of the chart in various ways, letting you define titles, labels, gridlines, and so on. All but two of these commands open dialog boxes that offer further choices.

Add Arrow lets you add arrows to point to important items. If your chart already contains an arrow, this command will change to Delete Arrow when you select the arrow. When you select a chart arrow, a handle appears at each end. You can use the handles to size and place the arrow, as you can with a drawing object.

The Delete Legend command works similarly, switching between Delete Legend and Add Legend. Since a chart can have only one legend, the command will be Delete Legend when your chart has a legend or Add Legend when it doesn't.

The Format menu

The Format menu offers a wide range of formatting controls. In general, the available commands will vary depending on what you have currently selected. If you want to choose Format Legend, for example, you must first select the legend. Any commands you choose will affect the selected item.

Most of these commands open dialog boxes, which will also vary depending on the current selection. For example, you can choose Format Patterns to create borders and patterns for almost any element, but the dialog box you'll get when you've selected an arrow in your chart differs from the dialog box you'll get when you've selected a column.

One choice on this menu is worth special comment: If you've chosen a 3-D design in the Chart Gallery, you'll be able to choose the Format 3-D View command. Like the other dialog boxes available through the Format menu, this one will vary somewhat depending on the type of chart, but the variations share key features. Figure 15-27 shows one example of what the Format 3-D View dialog box can look like.

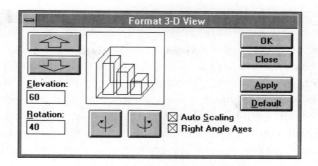

FIGURE 15-27

You can change the
3-D perspective of
your chart through
the Format 3-D View
dialog box.

You can create a dizzying range of alternatives with this dialog box, rotating charts about their axes. But keep in mind that although it's fun to spin the charts around, the effect is often more dramatic than it is useful. If your intention is to give a broad overall view, 3-D charts shown at dramatic angles may be appropriate. But if you expect the reader to make studied judgments based on the data in the chart, be aware that these perspective views can often clutter the message more than they clarify it.

The Window and Help menus

Graph also has Window and Help menus. Note that the Window menu includes commands that let you zoom in or out on a chart, in much the same way the Zoom Control box does on Word's Standard toolbar. The Help menu works much as it does in other Windows-based applications.

Where to go from here

We've just taken a quick romp through a complex program, but it should be enough to get you started. The best way to become familiar with the program is simply to experiment with it. Even if this is the first graphing program you've used, you should soon be creating sophisticated charts with minimal effort.

Inserting Other Objects

As we mentioned earlier in this chapter, you can insert other objects in your documents. The available choices will depend on the applications installed on your system. If you choose to insert one of these other objects, keep in mind that if you follow the techniques described in this chapter, the object will be available only through your document, not as a separate file that exists outside the document. If you want to make any changes to the object, you must open the document and either double-click on the object or select it and choose the Edit Object command.

For example, if Microsoft Excel is installed on your system, Word will let you insert Excel worksheets and charts in your Word documents. If you choose Insert Object and then choose Microsoft Excel Chart or Microsoft Excel Sheet, Word will load Excel so that you can create or edit the data. And when you leave Excel, Word will embed the object at the cursor location in your Word document, where it will be printed as if you had created it within Word. Choosing Edit Excel Chart Object or double-clicking on the object will load Microsoft Excel again, allowing you to edit the information further. For more about the various ways you can embed and link to objects, see Chapter 18, "Sharing Data with Other Programs," page 618.

TOPIC FINDER

Understanding Screen Fonts and Printer Fonts   **581**

- TrueType and ATM
- Bitmapped and scalable fonts
- Resident printer fonts

Setting Up Right and Left Pages   **586**

- How to add right and left headers and footers
- How to format facing pages using frames

Defining the Position of a Header or Footer   **588**

Working with Long Documents   **589**

- NEW How to use Master Document view

Using Special Fields for Formatting and Printing   **595**

- The BARCODE field
- The ADVANCE field
- The SECTION and SECTIONPAGES fields

16

Advanced Printing & Formatting

 n Chapter 7, we explained the basics of formatting in Word. We described how to determine the layout of pages, format individual paragraphs, and apply character formatting such as fonts and font size. In this chapter, we'll cover Word's more complex formatting features.

One of the tasks that many Word users find baffling is trying to get the screen to accurately predict the final printed page. To help minimize the confusion, we'll cover some of the fundamentals of screen and printer fonts. We'll also delve a bit further into how to set up different right and left page layouts. And we'll wrap up the chapter with a look at how to create long documents from two or more shorter documents.

Understanding Screen Fonts and Printer Fonts

One reason many people are drawn to Windows in general, and to Word in particular, is the WYSIWYG (What You See Is What You Get) display. But many users are disappointed to find that the reality falls a little short of the promise and that what they see on the screen is sometimes different from what they get at the printer—in some cases, very different.

To understand why this happens and how to minimize the differences, you have to understand the relationship between screen fonts and printer fonts. The most important point to understand is that these are two entirely different sets of fonts. If you've ever used an MS-DOS text-based program, with the monospace MS-DOS system font on the display, to print formatted text using, say, a Helvetica font, you already know how different screen and printer fonts can be. Windows, with its WYSIWYG display, hides the difference. But even in Windows, you have two different sets of fonts: one that the screen knows how to display, and one that the printer knows how to print. Problems arise when the two sets don't match.

Once you have that distinction firmly in mind, you also need to understand the difference between bitmapped fonts and scalable fonts. More important, your choice of a bitmapped or a scalable font affects how well the screen and the printer will match. We'll take a look at these issues and how they relate to each other.

TrueType and ATM

At the risk of jumping ahead of ourselves a bit, it's worth pointing out that the problems with matching the screen display and the printed result in Windows have been greatly simplified with Windows 3.1 and the introduction of TrueType fonts. These are scalable fonts that can both appear on screen and print on any printer that uses a Windows driver that supports graphics. (We'll explain what a scalable font is in a moment.) You can tell which fonts are TrueType by the double-T symbol in the font lists Word displays. Figure 16-1 shows an example. If you limit your font selections to TrueType fonts and set your printer driver to use TrueType fonts, your printed output will match your screen displays fairly closely.

FIGURE 16-1

In this Font list box, Word uses the double-T symbol to designate TrueType fonts.

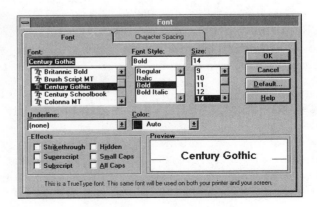

This advice to limit your font selections to TrueType need not constrain your creativity, since Windows comes with an assortment of TrueType fonts, as do other programs that you might have on your system. Also, any number of font packs are available from Microsoft and other sources.

Other kinds of fonts—notably Adobe Type 1 fonts—share some of the same benefits as TrueType fonts and, in some cases, offer other benefits as well. However, these other font types require additional utility programs, such as Adobe Type Manager (ATM). The real advantage of TrueType is that it comes as part of Windows 3.1. Unless you have a particular reason for using an additional font type, you're better off staying with TrueType. If you have a PostScript printer, with Adobe fonts built in, for example, and you want to produce desktop publishing output that will exactly match what a typesetter will produce with the same files, you will probably want to use ATM and Adobe fonts. But if you don't have this sort of specific need, there's little reason to bother with the additional utility.

Bitmapped and scalable fonts

You can think of bitmapped fonts as pictures of individual characters, with a different picture for every size of every character you want to use. Scalable fonts, in contrast, consist of a set of rules that describe characters. In theory, either kind of font can be either a screen font or a printer font. But given that Windows' TrueType fonts are scalable, you'll most often run into bitmapped fonts as printer fonts. And we'll base this discussion on the assumption that you're using scalable fonts for the screen.

The advantage of bitmapped fonts is that you get finely tailored images. The disadvantage is that all those individual pictures take up a lot of storage space. Also, if the computer tells the printer to print a 10-point Arial lowercase *a*, and the printer doesn't have the bitmapped character available, it will use a different size character or even a different typeface.

With scalable fonts, when the computer calls for a 10-point Arial lowercase *a*, all the printer needs to have on hand are the rules for Arial characters so that it can create the letter in the size the computer requests. And if the printer lacks the rules for the particular font, Windows can create the character instead and send it to the printer.

Although scalable fonts take less storage space than bitmapped fonts, they make greater demands on the processor—either in the printer's controller or in the computer, depending on which is generating the fonts. That, in turn, can slow printing speed.

Resident printer fonts

Nearly all printers come with at least some built-in fonts, if only a single draft-mode font of some kind. But many printers also come with more sophisticated fonts—either TrueType fonts or other kinds of fonts that may or may not offer the same benefits as TrueType. Hewlett-Packard LaserJet Series II printers, for example, are among the most common printers that use bitmapped fonts. The most common printers that use scalable fonts are compatible with either Adobe PostScript or Hewlett-Packard's PCL5 printer language (the version of HP's printer language that's found in the LaserJet III and LaserJet 4).

Resident, cartridge, and downloadable fonts

In general, unless your printer depends entirely on fonts that are created in Windows as graphics and sent to the printer from Windows, you must store printer fonts in one or more of three locations: in the printer's controller, in a font cartridge, or on a disk in your computer. (Some high-end printers also provide disks in the printer itself.)

Most commonly, the printer will store fonts in permanent memory in the printer controller. These are often referred to as the printer's resident fonts. The key advantage of resident fonts is that they are always available so that the printer can get at them quickly. The disadvantage is that they're limited to the fonts that come with the printer.

One way to add more fonts is with font cartridges, which store additional fonts in permanent memory of their own. Plugging one of these cartridges into your printer has the same effect as adding its fonts to the resident fonts. Font cartridges offer the same advantages as resident fonts, plus the benefit of letting you add and remove cartridges as needed. The drawback is that font cartridges are a relatively expensive way to buy fonts.

Yet another possibility is to store fonts on your computer's hard disk and copy them to the printer's memory as needed (a process known as downloading). This is often the least expensive way to add fonts, but downloading fonts can be time-consuming. What's more, the font files can eat up large amounts of disk space, especially if you are using bitmapped fonts. Some printers—typically, high-end PostScript printers—use a variation of this approach, by offering optional hard disks of their own. You download the fonts only once. The printer then stores them on the hard disk, where it can retrieve them just as if they were loaded in the printer's memory.

Which printer fonts do you have?

If you want to use any printer fonts, you must have a Windows printer driver that knows how to take advantage of the particular fonts in the printer—a fairly obvious requirement, once you think of it. Most Windows printer drivers support the fonts available for that printer. And in many cases, you'll find that you can designate which cartridges or downloadable fonts you have installed. These vary so much among printers that we can't cover specifics here. But you may find it helpful to go to the Windows Control Panel, choose Printers, and explore the setup options for your printer.

It also helps to know the fonts available to your printer. Most printers have a self-test feature that will print a list of all fonts; check the printer manual for details. In its font lists, Word will also indicate printer fonts with a small printer icon next to the font name, as shown in Figure 16-2.

FIGURE 16-2

In this Font list box, Word uses the printer icon to indicate printer fonts.

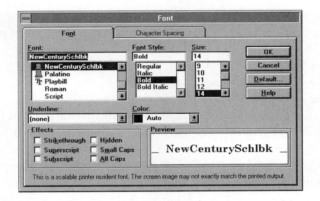

How to match screen fonts to printer fonts

In brief, if you want to see the fonts on screen as they will appear on the printed page, and if you want to use printer fonts that aren't TrueType fonts, you must install screen fonts that match the printer fonts. In many cases, the screen fonts will come with your printer or add-on font package when you buy it. If you do not have Windows screen fonts for your printer fonts, contact the printer vendor or font vendor. In most cases, screen fonts are available free or for a modest handling charge.

Many printer drivers will let you control which fonts your printer uses. PostScript drivers, for example, offer advanced options that let you map each TrueType font to a specific printer font. If you like, you can tell the driver to use Helvetica at the printer whenever you use the highly similar Arial font on screen. Or, if you prefer, you can specify that Windows download a specific font, such as Arial, to the printer as needed. Here again, we recommend that you go to the Windows Control Panel, choose Printers, and explore the setup options for your printer.

Setting Up Right and Left Pages

If you plan to print a document on both sides of each sheet of paper, you will probably want to take advantage of Word's ability to create different odd and even (or right and left) page layouts. This type of page layout is sometimes called facing pages, or mirror margins (because the left and right margins of facing pages mirror each other). This layout is especially useful for bound documents, making it easier to read pages that are bound along one edge. We've already covered many of these issues in earlier chapters, but here's a quick recap and a few additional pointers.

There are a couple of ways to create different formats on right and left pages. For example, instead of specifying left and right margins, you can specify inside and outside margins, with the inside margin on the binding edge of your paper. Standard practice is to start numbering with the page that faces you as you open a book, which means a page on the right-hand side. Odd-numbered pages will then fall on the right half of a two-page spread, and even-numbered pages on the left.

Generally, you'll want to make the inside margin wider than the outside to allow room for binding. Word lets you do this either by defining different sizes for inside and outside margins or by using equal margins and then adding a page gutter on the binding edge of a page. On odd-numbered pages, the page gutter is on the left; on even-numbered pages, it's on the right. If you use this second method, the space on the binding edge of each page will consist of the inside margin plus the gutter. Note that with either approach you'll need to check the Mirror Margins check box on the Margins card of the Page Setup dialog box.

To specify a setting for page gutter, inside and outside margins, or both, choose File Page Setup to open the Page Setup dialog box, and select the Margins card. For details on using this card and the other cards in the Page Setup dialog box, see "Margins" on page 211.

How to add right and left headers and footers

If you're using a mirror margin layout, you may also want headers and footers to be different on opposite pages.

As we mentioned briefly in Chapter 5, the Layout card in the Page Setup dialog box contains a Different Odd And Even check box for headers and footers, which lets you create different headers and footers for right and left pages. You may have noticed that books often use this type of layout, placing the book title at the top of even-numbered pages and the chapter title at the top of odd-numbered pages. Even when the text is the same on both right and left pages, it may vary in position. For example, in some magazines you might see page numbers on the outside edge, the name of the magazine in the center, and the date on the inside edge of each page.

The Different Odd And Even option on the Page Setup Layout card is independent of the Mirror Margins and the Gutter settings on the Page Setup Margins card. This means that you can vary your headers and footers for right and left pages even if you're not using a page gutter or inside and outside margins.

When you check the Different Odd And Even check box, Word will add Even or Odd to the label on the header and footer areas displayed in Page Layout view. Figure 16-3, for example, shows even and odd headers and footers. Notice that Word also displays the Header And Footer toolbar.

FIGURE 16-3

By zooming to two pages in Page Layout view, you can see the headers and footers for both even-numbered and odd-numbered pages of a book.

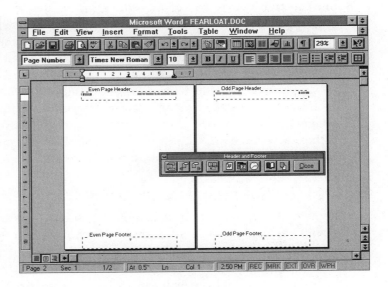

How to link right and left headers and footers

In our discussion of multisection documents in Chapter 13, we described how headers and footers for each section are linked to later sections. When you are using even and odd headers or footers in a multisection document, the situation remains essentially the same except that each kind of header or footer maintains a separate link to other sections.

For example, if you're working with a single-section document with different odd and even headers and with a different first-page header, you'll see one header on all odd pages, another on all even pages, and another on the first page only.

Now suppose you split your document into three sections. Initially, the even, odd, and first-page headers in the second and third sections will have the same text as the equivalent headers in the first section. If you change one of the headers in the second section—for instance, changing the even header to *Chapter 2*—the equivalent headers in the other two sections will also change unless you break the link to the previous section first.

When a header is linked to the corresponding header (even, odd, or first-page) in the section before it, the Same As Previous button on the Header And Footer toolbar will look as if it has been pressed. To break the link, simply click on the button. If you then change the even header in the second section, the even header in the first section will remain unchanged, but the change will cascade forward to headers in later sections. If you want to prevent this, move to the third section and break its link with the previous (second) section before you change the even header in the second section. To reestablish the link between the even headers for the second and first sections, you need only go to the even header in the second section and click on the Same As Previous button again. The current header will be replaced by the one from the previous section.

In short, when you have different even, odd, and first-page headers or footers, the rules for linking between sections are the same as those used when you have a single header or footer for each section. The only difference is that each of the three kinds of headers and footers maintains a separate set of links, allowing you to link or unlink each one independently of the others.

How to format facing pages using frames

Remember that you can use frames to place objects inside or outside paragraphs, as you saw in the example of scholar's margins in "How to create scholar's margins" on page 531. You can also use this feature to place other items, such as pictures, on the inside or outside of each page. The key to this technique is to position the frame inside or outside relative to the page or the margin. You can also use Word's drawing tools to set off areas with lines or boxes. See the section "Frames: Positioning Text and Graphics on the Page" on page 509 for more information on frames.

Defining the Position of a Header or Footer

We haven't yet covered two items on the Page Setup Margins card: the Header and Footer settings in the From Edge group box. To see the card, choose File Page Setup, and then select the Margins card.

The From Edge settings work much as you would expect. Enter *0.75"* in the Header box, for example, and Word will start the first line of the header

0.75 inch from the top edge of the paper. Enter *0.75"* in the Footer box, and Word will position the last line of the footer 0.75 inch from the bottom edge of the paper.

There is a little more to these settings, however. Both interact with—and can override—the top and bottom margin settings. If you set the top margin to 1 inch and set the header to appear 3 inches from the edge, the header will push down the top margin (and of course the text) so that the margin will be 3 inches deep instead of 1 inch. Similarly, if you set the footer's distance from the edge to be larger than the bottom margin, the footer will push up into the body text area, leaving less room for body text. Note, however, that the header or footer will intrude into the body text area only when you add text to the header or footer.

Word will automatically adjust the margins by pushing the text up or down whenever you create a header or footer that's too large to fit into the space Word allots by default. You can, however, override this feature. As we mentioned in Chapter 15, if you enter the margin settings as minus numbers, Word will always follow the margin setting exactly for defining the body text area on the page. If your headers or footers in this case are larger than their allotted space, Word will simply print both body text and header or footer at the same place on the page—usually an undesirable result, for obvious reasons. Occasionally, however, you might actually want to overlay a header on a page; see the discussion of watermarks in "How to create a watermark" on page 534.

Working with Long Documents

Although the length of Word documents is limited only by disk space, you'll find that it often makes sense to break long documents into shorter pieces. The longer the document, the longer it will take to move through the document, save it, and load it. The loss of performance depends on many factors, including the speed of your computer's processor and disk drive and the complexity of the document. But even if speed is not an issue, you may sometimes find it more convenient to work with different sections separately—when working with the chapters of a book, for example.

Unfortunately, breaking a long document into several files also presents problems. For example, you'll probably want to maintain continuous page numbering across files. And if you want to generate a table of contents or an index, you'll want a single table of contents or index for all files. In Word 6.0, you can handle these tasks quite easily by creating a Master Document to link the files.

There are actually two ways to create a Master Document with Word. One involves cobbling files together with fields, which can be a bit tedious. Easier by far is using Word's Master Document feature, which provides a simple tool for assembling a long document from separate files.

How to use Master Document view

Word's Master Document feature builds on Word's Master Document view, which is similar to Outline view. In fact, both views use the same Outlining toolbar. The difference is that Outline view works with a single document file, whereas Master Document view lets you assemble the parts of a long document to view them in outline form. The outline features make it easier to organize and change the sequence of the pieces. Because Master Document view is so similar to Outline view, we'll ignore the outline features here. For a thorough discussion of outline features, take a look at Chapter 19, "Outlining," starting on page 650.

How to create a Master Document

You can create a Master Document by converting a normal text document, by adding existing documents to your Master Document as subdocuments, or by some combination of the two methods, as we'll show here. Assume, for example, that you want to combine a few files that you already have on disk but that you also want to put them in the context of a larger outline. You can start by opening a new file and entering the outline.

If you're writing a book, for example, and you've already written the first three chapters, you might enter an outline that starts with Chapter 4. If you want Microsoft Word to recognize different sections as subdocuments, choose a heading style to mark the starting points. Assuming you've reserved Heading 1 for the book title, you might mark each chapter title with the Heading 2 style.

Once you've entered the outline, choose View Master Document. Word will switch to an outline format and will add the Outlining toolbar and Master Document toolbar on the same line at the top of the Word window, by default.

For purposes of this discussion, we'll ignore the Outlining toolbar here. Be aware, however, that the Outlining toolbar is useful for organizing your document and for controlling how much detail you can see—Word lets you collapse the outline to display only specified levels of headings. We'll cover the Outlining toolbar in depth in Chapter 19, "Outlining," page 650.

Figure 16-4 lists the buttons on the Master Document toolbar. This toolbar provides not only easy access to Word's Master Document functions but also a handy reference for what those functions are.

Button	Button Name	Action
	Create Subdocument	Converts selected portions of an existing Master Document to subdocuments based on a heading style
	Remove Subdocument	Coverts a subdocument to text in the Master Document
	Insert Subdocument	Inserts the contents of an existing file as a subdocument
	Merge Subdocument	Converts selected subdocuments to a single subdocument
	Split Subdocument	Splits an existing subdocument into two separate subdocuments
	Lock Document	Locks or unlocks a subdocument; no changes can be made to a locked subdocument

FIGURE 16-4

The Master Document toolbar buttons.

The first toolbar button on the left is Create Subdocument. You can use this button to convert selected text in the Master Document to a subdocument file. For instance, after entering text and assigning heading levels in your outline, you can select the parts of the outline containing the sections to be subdocuments, starting with the first heading level that marks the first section of text you want to place in its own subdocument. If you then click on the Create Subdocument button, Word will add an end-of-section marker just before each heading level that it recognizes as the start of a new subdocument. It will also surround each section of text with a box to delineate each subdocument and will add an icon in the upper left corner, as shown in Figure 16-5 on the next page. The next time you choose File Save, Word will create new files using names based on the first eight characters of each section of text. If a file with that name already exists, Word will change one or more of the last characters to digits in order to create a unique name.

Once you've divided your text into subdocuments, you can work on each individual subdocument directly, opening it from the Master Document. Simply double-click on the icon in the upper left corner of the subdocument,

FIGURE 16-5

In Master Document view, Word surrounds subdocuments with a box and adds an icon in the upper left corner, which will let you open the subdocument file.

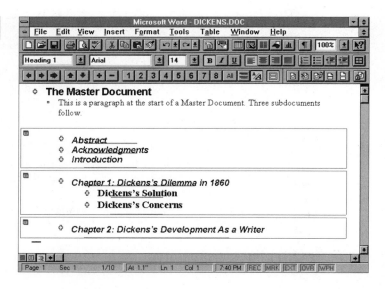

and Word will open the subdocument file in its own window. By opening individual subdocument files this way, you can work with more manageable portions of your text. (Note that you can also edit directly in Master Document view if you prefer.) You can use the Window menu to move between open subdocuments and the Master Document.

You can display a Master Document in Word's other views. Normal view is convenient for overall editing. You can use Page Layout view to see how your pages will look when they are printed. You can also use Print Preview to see the formatted pages.

How to add existing files to a Master Document

If you want to add existing files as subdocuments in a Master Document, choose the Insert Subdocument button (third from the left on the Master Document toolbar). Word will open the Insert Subdocument dialog box, which looks and works like the Open dialog box. Find the file you want to add, and choose OK. Word will insert the file as a subdocument, in its own section, starting at the cursor's current position.

You can insert a subdocument inside another subdocument if you position the cursor inside a subdocument before clicking on the Insert Subdocument button, but we recommend against it. Once you insert a second-level subdocument, it will show up as part of the higher-level subdocument whenever you edit that higher-level document. This defeats the main purpose of using a Master Document, which is to keep long documents broken into smaller, more manageable pieces. It's much better to use only one level of subdocuments.

How to lock subdocuments

You can control a subdocument's locked status using the button on the right end of the Master Document toolbar: Lock Document. If the cursor or selection is in a subdocument that's locked, this button will look as if it has been pressed. Click on the Lock Document button to toggle the status between locked and unlocked.

When you open a locked subdocument by double-clicking on its icon in Master Document view, Word will open it as read-only. Word indicates the locked status with a small padlock icon below the subdocument's icon in Master Document view. When you open a subdocument, that section will be locked in the Master Document.

The Master Document locking feature differs from the other protection features covered elsewhere in this book, but it also interacts with those features. If you protect a document for revisions using Tools Protect Document, for example, you may not be able to unlock that protection using the Master Document's locking feature. More precisely, if you try to remove the lock, you'll see a message telling you that the operation cannot be completed because the subdocument has a higher protection rating than the Master Document. If you add the same protection to the Master Document, however, you'll be able to remove the lock and edit the subdocument.

How to use other Master Document toolbar buttons

Let's look at the other three buttons on the Master Document toolbar. Second from the left is the Remove Subdocument button. The name is a little misleading, since clicking on this button doesn't remove the subdocument's text from the Master Document. Instead, it keeps the subdocument's contents in the Master Document but breaks the link to the file that contained the subdocument. To actually delete a subdocument and its contents, first unlock the subdocument if it is locked. Then click on the subdocument's icon to highlight the entire subdocument contents, and press the Del key.

The fourth button from the left is Merge Subdocument, which will let you join two adjacent subdocuments. To merge the two subdocuments, first highlight them both. (The easy way is to hold down the Shift key and click on each subdocument icon.) Then click on the Merge Subdocument button.

The next time you choose File Save, Word will save both merged subdocuments in the file that previously held the first subdocument. The file that previously held the second subdocument remains on your disk, but you can erase it if you don't need it.

The fifth button—Split Subdocument—does just what it says. Click on the button, and Word will split a subdocument into two subdocuments, starting at the current cursor position.

Format considerations for Master Documents

Word relies on paragraph styles to determine the structure of a Master Document. If you want to view your document as an outline, you must use Word's built-in heading styles: Heading 1, Heading 2, Heading 3, and so on.

When you look at a subdocument while in a Master Document, Word will use the style definitions stored in the Master Document. If you open the subdocument in its own window, however, Word will use the style definitions stored in the subdocument. If the two sets of styles differ, you'll find that the subdocument formats differently. For information about how to copy style definitions from one document to another to ensure consistency, see "Merging Styles from Another Document" on page 462.

Since Word places each subdocument of a Master Document in its own section, you can also control the contents of headers and footers and other section-dependent formatting. If you want a setting to apply to all parts of the Master Document, set it in the Master Document itself rather than repeating it in each subdocument. On the other hand, if you want a different setting for each subdocument, you can define the setting in each one. See "Multisection Documents" on page 485 for more about section-dependent formatting.

When Word creates a section break between subdocuments, it may not create the kind of break you want. If you want a subdocument to start on a new page (as a new chapter in a book would do), you would not want a Continuous section break. You can change the type of break by choosing File Page Setup and selecting the Layout card. See "How to divide a document into sections" on page 486 for more information about section breaks.

How to create table of contents or an index in a Master Document

Using a Master Document makes it easy to create a table of contents or an index for a long document. You add these features as part of the Master Document itself rather than making them part of any subdocument. This means you don't have to do anything special to have continuous numbering—or a continuous table of contents or index. You can simply create the index or the table of contents while in the Master Document file, just as you would in a single document file. For details on tables of contents and indexes, see Chapter 22, "Tables of Contents & Indexes" starting on page 760.

Using Special Fields for Formatting and Printing

Word has a number of special fields that you can use in formatting and printing your documents. We will cover the topic of fields in depth in Chapter 20, and you can look there for more information on how to insert fields. For now, you can simply choose the Insert Field command and insert a field from the Field Names list in the dialog box.

The BARCODE field

The BARCODE field lets you insert a postal bar code in your document. This is the same field used to put bar codes on envelopes with Word's envelope printing feature. See "How to create an envelope" on page 283.

This field uses the format

```
{BARCODE "text" [switches]}
```

where *text* is used to create the content of the barcode. It may be a ZIP code, or it may be the name of a bookmark that contains a ZIP code. If *text* is a bookmark, you must use the \b switch with the field. You can also use the switch

```
\f "letter"
```

where *letter* is either A or C. A produces a courtesy reply mark, and C produces a business reply mark.

Another switch that you can use with the BARCODE field is the \u switch, which signifies that you are using a United States postal address.

The ADVANCE field

The ADVANCE field offsets your document up or down or to the right or left. Any text that is moved beyond the margins or to a subsequent page will not be printed.

You can control the position of the text by using switches, each of which is followed by a number that represents a distance, measured in points. The \d switch moves the text down the specified number of points; the \u switch moves the text up. Similarly, the \l switch moves the text to the left, and the \r switch moves it to the right. The \x switch starts the text at a specified number of points from the left margin, and the \y switch starts the text at a specified distance from the top of the page.

The SECTION and SECTIONPAGES fields

These two fields do not use extra text or switches. Their results are numbers, based on your document. The SECTION field will return the number of the current section. The SECTIONPAGES field returns the total number of pages in the section. You may find it convenient to use these fields in conjunction with the PAGE field in a document header or footer—for example, *Page {PAGE} of Section {SECTION}* or *Page {PAGE} of {SECTIONPAGES}*.

Topic Finder

Managing Files   600

- Directories

Retrieving Documents   603

- How to define a basic file search
- How to define an advanced file search
- How to search for any text
- How to cast a wider or narrower net using the Options box
- How to search by date using the Timestamp card
- How to search by the last person who saved the file
- NEW! How to store a search definition for future use
- How to search for a file
- The Find File dialog box
- How to change summary information
- How to open one or more documents
- How to print, delete, or copy one or more documents

17

Advanced File Handling

f you've worked your way through all or most of the preceding chapters, by now you should be familiar with the basic techniques for opening, closing, and saving files. You are certainly aware that you can manage most of your file-handling needs through choices on the File menu. The one clear exception is file deletion. As we discussed in Chapter 2, "File Handling," to delete a file from within Word, you can open the Find File dialog box—by choosing File Find File or by choosing File Open and then Find File—locate the file, choose the Commands button, and then choose Delete.

In this chapter, we'll look at Word's most sophisticated file-handling features, all of which are available through the Find File dialog box. Among these are the ability to search for files in more than one directory, preview files, and sort lists of files in various ways. Before we look at the mechanics of advanced file handling, however, we'll discuss some strategies that will make it easier for you to keep track of your files.

Managing Files

After you've worked with Word for a while, your hard disk will likely contain dozens (possibly hundreds) of document files, including old memos, letters, reports, and so on. Of course, the more document files on your disk, the more of a challenge it is to find a particular file. You can make the process considerably easier by taking a little time to organize your files into logical groupings.

A common oversight among computer users is to pay little attention to the filing system for data files. Many users create a single data directory for each program—for example, dumping all their Word documents into one directory. Worse yet, some users save files with no regard to where the files are located.

An even more common mistake is to store all Word document files in the Word program directory. Unfortunately, Word makes this an easy trap to fall into. By default, every time you load Word, the directory for opening and saving files is the Word program directory.

The problem with any of these strategies—or lack of strategy—is that you'll find it increasingly difficult to find any particular file. Consider: You probably wouldn't take all your paper files and store them in a file cabinet without any divisions, logical groupings, or order. Dumping all your document files into a single directory on your hard disk amounts to the same approach.

Computer files are similar to paper files in some very important respects. Each contains information that you'll want to be able to find again. Being able to find the information requires some sort of filing system. If you're not following a clearly defined system, the odds are good that you'll lose your files with appalling regularity.

There is nothing mysterious about creating a filing system on your disk. The same principles apply to a computer filing system as apply to a paper filing system. Only the mechanics are different. With a filing cabinet, you use file folders, file drawers, and file drawer separators to group information. With a disk drive, you use directories and subdirectories.

We'll discuss the mechanics of creating directories in a moment, but first let's look at the far more important issue of deciding *how* to group your files. There are no hard-and-fast rules. The trick is to create divisions that make sense to you and make sense for the way you work. For example, you might create one directory for letters, one for memos, one for reports, and so on.

Or you might create a different directory for each client or each project. Or you might mix these concepts, using a directory for each client, for example, and subdirectories for each project within each client directory.

Some filing systems will meet your needs better than others, and it's worth putting some thought and effort into devising a system that's right for you. The main point is to devise a system and use it. If you come up with a better idea later, you can change the way your files are organized, just as you can reorganize a file cabinet.

In an earlier chapter, we suggested a simple approach to organizing data files, and we explained the mechanics of changing the default Documents directory on the File Locations card. Briefly, we suggested setting the default Documents directory to a main data directory that contains nothing but subdirectories with the actual data. You'll then start from the main data directory the first time you choose the File Open command in any given session, and you can easily move to the subdirectory you actually want. You can put the main data directory anywhere—even on another hard disk, if you have more than one on your system. For more details on both our suggestion and on setting default directories, see "The File Locations card" starting on page 314.

As files accumulate within any given data directory, you can create new directories and move files appropriately. For example, you might start with a single directory for a given project and later create subdirectories within the project directory for letters, memos, and reports. As a rule of thumb, you should consider creating a new level of subdirectories when the number of files in any given directory grows too large to scroll through quickly in various dialog box file lists.

Another strategy is to use subdirectories for files you've finished working with. For example, if you're still working on both a letter and a report for a given project, leave both in the active project directory. But when you've finished with them, move each to an appropriate subdirectory. Alternatively, you might perform such housekeeping functions only when you notice that a directory is becoming cluttered.

Unfortunately, Word does not offer a simple command for moving files. But, as we mentioned in Chapter 2, you can get the same effect by saving a file in the new directory and deleting the original. Even better, you can copy a file to a new directory without opening it first. We'll show you how at the end of this chapter.

Directories

If you're already familiar with MS-DOS directories and how to create them, you can skip this section and go to the discussion of retrieving documents. If you're not familiar with directories, however, here's a quick overview.

All files are stored in directories, even if you haven't created any directories on your disk, as is common with floppy disks. The one directory that a disk must have is called the root directory, or simply the root. (The root gets its name because the directory structure can look like an upside-down tree. The directory structure itself is known as the directory tree.)

All directories besides the root are located in other directories. Any that are located in a directory other than the root are called subdirectories. For example, if you installed Windows using the default settings, the installation process created a WINDOWS directory in the root and a SYSTEM directory, or subdirectory, in the WINDOWS directory. If you installed Word fully and used the default settings, Word created several directories, including a WINWORD directory in the root, an MSAPPS subdirectory in the WINDOWS directory, and separate EQUATION, GRPHFLT, MSGRAPH, MSINFO, PROOF, TEXTCONV, and WORDART subdirectories in the WINDOWS\MSAPPS subdirectory.

How to create directories

The most basic way to create a directory is from the MS-DOS command line. Suppose, for example, that you want to create the subdirectory DATA in the WINWORD directory—which in turn is in the root directory of drive C. One choice requires moving to the Word directory first: Log on to drive C by typing *C:* and pressing Enter. Then type *cd \winword*, and press Enter to move to the WINWORD directory (*cd* is an abbreviation for the Change Directory command). Next you would create the DATA directory by typing *md data* and pressing Enter (*md* is an abbreviation for the Make Directory command).

Alternatively, you can create a directory from anywhere within MS-DOS by giving the complete pathname as part of the command. You could, for example, be logged on to drive A, but you could still create the DATA directory on drive C by typing *md c:\winword\data* at the MS-DOS prompt and pressing Enter. You could also create the directory from either Program Manager or File Manager in Windows by choosing File Run and entering *command /c md c:\winword\data*. (This command runs another copy of COMMAND.COM. The */c* tells the new COMMAND.COM to read the rest of the line and run it as a command.)

If you use any of these choices to create a directory when File Manager is open and logged on to the same disk as the new directory, File Manager won't show the new directory until you log on to that disk again, or choose Window Refresh, or press F5, the Window Refresh shortcut key. You can avoid this extra step by creating the directory with File Manager's File Create Directory command. Choose File Create Directory, enter the name of the new directory in the Create Directory dialog box, and choose OK. The window will show you the name of the current directory. Here again, you can enter the new directory name by itself to create it in the current directory, or you can enter the entire pathname to create the directory anywhere on your system.

Finally, many MS-DOS shell programs and Windows utility programs have their own commands for creating directories. You can use any utility you're comfortable with.

Retrieving Documents

Storing your document files in multiple directories divided into logical groups makes it easier to find a given file. As a first step, you can go to the directory and limit your search to just that directory. Unfortunately, no matter how organized you are, you will occasionally store a file in the wrong directory. Even if the file is stored in the right place, you still need to be able to find the right file.

Word provides document-retrieval tools to help you find the right file. To take full advantage of these tools, you need to fill out the Summary Info dialog box for each file. As we discussed in Chapter 2, the Summary Info dialog box contains information such as title, subject, and author, as well as keywords and any comments you care to add. If you take the time to enter this information the first time you save each file, you can later use Word's retrieval tools to find files using any of these criteria. But even if you don't fill in the information, you can still search for files by author, creation date, and last date saved, among other choices.

To find one or more specific files on your disk, choose File Find File or choose File Open and then choose the Find File button. The first time you choose File Find File, and any time you choose File Open and then Find File, you'll see the Search dialog box, shown in Figure 17-1 on the next page.

FIGURE 17-1

The Search dialog box lets you specify the files to search for.

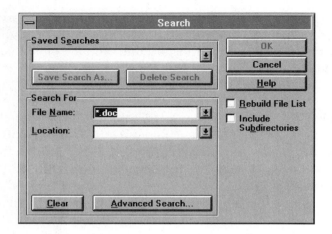

How to define a basic file search

The Search dialog box lets you give Word some basic search information or choose a more complicated search that you've previously defined and saved. We'll start with the basics: filename, location, and whether to include subdirectories.

If you can remember any part of the filename, you can enter it along with wildcard characters in the File Name text box. If you are looking for a letter and you always use the extension LET for letters, for example, you can enter the filename as *.let. Similarly, if you always use the recipient's initials to begin a filename and you're looking for a letter you sent to George Baker, you can enter the filename as gb*.let.

> You can also enter multiple items in the File Name text box, as long as you separate them with a semicolon: Entering *.mem;*.let tells Word to find files with either extension.

If you want, you can choose one of several extensions from the File Name drop-down list, including *.* for all files. If you choose an extension from the list box, however, Word will delete anything you've already entered in the text box, and it will set the first part of the filename to the * wildcard character. So if you use the list, use it *first*, before changing the first part of the filename or adding other items to the text box.

Below the File Name text box is the Location text box, which includes an attached drop-down list showing the drives available to search. In addition to entering a drive here, you can also enter a path, if you know the path you want.

If you enter a single dot, or period, in the Location text box, Word will search for files in the current directory. If you enter two periods, it will search the parent directory—the directory immediately above the current directory (toward the root). You can also enter multiple drives or paths by separating the locations with a comma or a semicolon. For example, entering *C:,D:;F:* tells Word to search drives C, D, and F.

The Include Subdirectories check box to the right of the Search For box lets you tell Word whether to confine the search to the directories you enter in the Location box or to search all subdirectories. For example, if you don't check this box and you enter simply *D:* as the location, Word will look for files only in the root directory of D. If you check the Include Subdirectories check box, however, Word will search the entire disk.

If you want to define a search from scratch, use the Clear button at the bottom of the dialog box to delete all current search criteria.

Use the Rebuild File List check box when you want to be sure that Word will create a new list of files when you choose OK. Otherwise, if you opened the Search dialog box from the Find File dialog box (which we'll describe a little later in this chapter) and haven't made any changes in the search criteria, Word will simply use the previously compiled, and possibly incomplete, list of files.

How to define an advanced file search

A basic search might be all you'll need in many cases, but sometimes you'll need Word's more sophisticated search capabilities. To use those features, choose the Advanced Search button at the bottom of the Search dialog box. Word will open the Advanced Search dialog box, shown in Figure 17-2 on the next page.

The Advanced Search dialog box lets you narrow or widen your search based on almost anything you can remember about the file you're looking for. As you can see in Figure 17-2, it offers three cards: Location, Summary, and Timestamp. We'll start with the Location card.

How to specify drives and directories to search using the Location card

The Location card lets you specify locations to search without typing them in the Location text box in the Search dialog box. Unless you want to search in only one or two directories and you know the full paths well enough to type them without stopping to think about them, we recommend that you use the Location card.

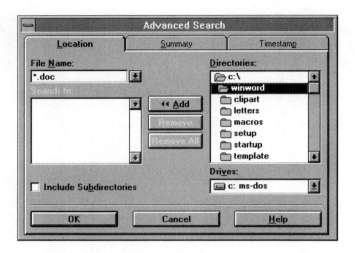

FIGURE 17-2

The Advanced Search
dialog box lets you set
advanced criteria for
finding files.

The File Name text box and Include Subdirectories check box are identical to the items with the same names in the Search dialog box. Any entries you make in these boxes are carried over to the Search dialog box.

The Include Subdirectories check box is an all-or-nothing choice. For example, you cannot define two paths to search on the Locations card and tell Word to include subdirectories for one path but not for the other.

To define a directory to search, use the Drives drop-down list to designate a drive, the Directories list box to designate a directory, and the Add button to add the selected directory to the Search In list box. To define multiple directories to search, simply repeat the process for each one.

If your computer is attached to a network, Word will also provide the Network button to open the Connect Network Drive dialog box.

How to delete directories from the search

After you add at least one directory to search, the Remove and Remove All buttons become available. To remove a single directory from the Search In list, select that directory and choose the Remove button. To remove the entire list so that you can create a new definition from scratch, choose the Remove All button.

How to search by title, author, keywords, or subject using the Summary card

The middle tab in the Advanced Search dialog box is for the Summary card, shown in Figure 17-3.

FIGURE 17-3

The Summary card lets
you set search criteria
based on a document's
Summary Info.

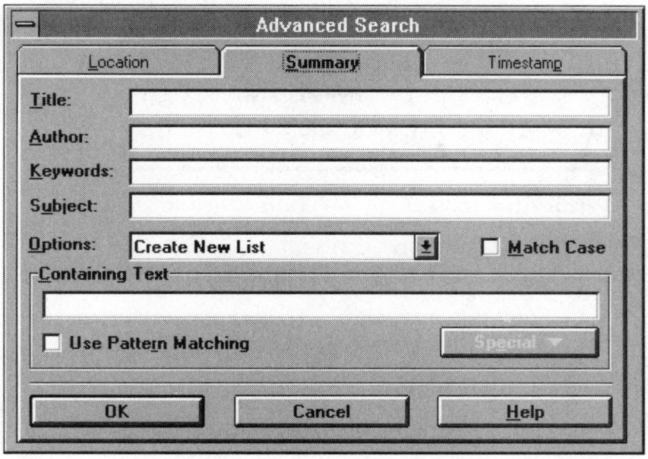

FIGURE 17-3

Advanced Search

| Location | Summary | Timestamp |

Title:

Author:

Keywords:

Subject:

Options: Create New List ☐ Match Case

Containing Text

☐ Use Pattern Matching Special ▼

OK   Cancel   Help

As we mentioned earlier, to take full advantage of the Find File feature, you should fill in the Summary Info dialog box for each file you create. This card is why. As you can see in Figure 17-3, the first four text boxes on the Summary card match entries for the Summary Info dialog box: Title, Author, Keywords, and Subject. If you can remember any of these entries for the file or files you're searching for, simply enter them in the appropriate box or boxes, and Word will look for matches in the Summary Info entries.

Keep in mind that even if you don't normally fill in the Summary Info box, Word will fill in the Author entry for you (although you can override the entry if you want). This automatic entry can help you find files in any case.

When Word searches for Summary Info entries, it also finds files that contain a superset of the search text. In other words, entering *M* in a text box is similar to entering *M**. You can use this to your advantage when you're not sure what you're looking for. If you're looking for files by M. David Stone, for example, and you don't know how the name is entered in User Info, you can enter *Dav* in the Author field. This will find any files with the author name stored as *M. David Stone, David Stone,* or *Dave Stone.* Of course, it will also find files by authors *David Poor* and *Alfred Davies,* so you need to use this trick with care.

Note too that filling in more than one text box tells Word to find matches for all the filled-in boxes, so the more text boxes you fill in, the narrower the search. Try to make your search criteria as specific as possible without excluding any of the documents you want to find.

Special characters for searching by Summary Info fields

Word provides six special search characters that let you further fine-tune your search. Figure 17-4 lists all six characters and their functions. All of these work for any Summary Info field.

This Character...	Tells Word to Do This...
? (question mark)	Match any single character.
* (asterisk)	Match a group of characters.
" "(quotation marks)	Treat the special character in quotes as a regular character.
, (comma)	Accept a file as a match if its summary information matches any or all items in the text box that are separated by commas. (This is a logical OR.)
& (ampersand)	Accept a file as a match if its summary information matches all of the items in the text box. (This is a logical AND.)
~ (tilde)	Select a file if its summary information does not match the item in the text box. (This is a logical NOT.)

FIGURE 17-4

Special characters you can use in searches using the Summary Info fields.

The question mark (?) and asterisk (*) are called wildcard characters, as they are in MS-DOS. Use the question mark to take the place of any single character within a word. At the end of a word, the number of question marks indicates the minimum number of characters that must match. For example, *B??* matches any words that start with B and that have three or more characters. Use the asterisk to take the place of multiple characters. For example, to find all files that have either an LET or an MEM extension, you could specify **.?e?* in the File Name text box.

The quote marks (" ") let you use any of the special characters as a literal character. You'll most often use this feature with commas, question marks, or ampersands. For example, if you rarely use a question mark in your titles and you want to search for the title *Are You Ready?*, you can simply enter *"?"* as the title in the Title text box.

The comma (,) lets you search for more than one possible match for an item. To search for all documents that include the phrase *Artificial Intelligence* or the phrase *Expert Systems* as keywords, enter *Artificial Intelligence,Expert Systems* in the Keywords text box.

The ampersand (&) lets you search for files that match more than one criterion for a particular text box. To search for documents that include both the phrase *Artificial Intelligence* and the phrase *Expert Systems* as keywords, enter *Artificial Intelligence&Expert Systems* in the Keywords text box.

Finally, the tilde (~) lets you search for files that don't match the stated criterion. For example, if you want to search for all files that do not have the word *Chapter* as part of the title, you could enter *~Chapter* in the Title text box.

How to search for any text

In many ways, the Containing Text text box is the most useful option for defining a search. It lets you enter any word, phrase, or other text to tell Word to search the full text of each document to look for matches. (For obvious reasons, this works only with documents Word can open and read.) This comes in handy when the document you're looking for contains a key word or phrase that you didn't enter as a keyword, or when you're looking for all documents relating to a specific project. For example, suppose you're writing a book, with each chapter in its own file, and you want to find every mention of a given topic throughout the book. If all the chapters are in one directory, you can search the full text of every file in the directory and list all files that contain mention of the topic.

The drawback to a full text search, as you might expect, is that it takes Word a relatively long time. As a result, you'll want to use this feature sparingly or as a last resort. You'll also want to include as many other search criteria as possible to keep the list of files to a minimum. In addition, you'll want to use the other search criteria *first* and then run the full text search on only those files, using the choices in the Options box, which we'll describe a little later in this chapter. But it's certainly the best choice for ensuring that you find all documents relating to a specific subject.

Special characters for searching for any text

In addition to the special characters for use with the Summary Info fields, Word provides a set of nine characters specifically for full text searches. To use them, you must first check the Use Pattern Matching check box.

Figure 17-5 on the next page shows the list of special pattern-matching characters that you'll see if you choose the Special button. These are the same pattern-matching characters that you can use for searching or replacing in Word. You can use the Special button to add these characters to the

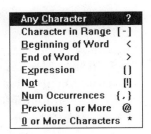

FIGURE 17-5

If you choose the Special button, Word will show you this list of pattern-matching characters.

Containing Text text box, or if you know the special characters you want to use, you can type them in directly. For details on how these pattern-matching characters work, see "How to use pattern matching" on page 113.

Matching case

Another way to narrow the search is to check the Match Case check box near the bottom of the dialog box. As the name implies, this option tells Word to search on uppercase or lowercase letters exactly as you've entered them. However, the option applies only to text in the Containing Text text box, despite the fact that the check box is not located in the Containing Text group box. Entering *Artificial Intelligence* as the search criterion in the Containing Text text box and checking the Match Case check box ensures that you'll match only files that include the phrase *Artificial Intelligence* with both words capitalized. However, checking the check box has no effect on the author criterion, for example. Entering *Fred* will still match *FRED, fReD, fred,* and so forth.

How to cast a wider or narrower net using the Options box

There's one other item on the Summary card: the Options box. The choices in the drop-down list let you widen or narrow a search, as appropriate.

If you have hundreds of document files on your disk, you may find that the list Word comes up with is overwhelming. At other times, if you're searching for several related files, you may find that Word hasn't found all the files you need. In both cases, the Options setting lets you modify the list of filenames, either by adding to it to cast a wider net or by trimming it to narrow the net.

To modify a list of filenames after running a search, you would first need to return to the Summary card in the Advanced Search dialog box by choosing Search from the Find File dialog box and then choosing Advanced Search. After you make the appropriate changes to the search criteria for the next search (including changes on the Timestamp card, which we haven't covered yet), you can open the Options drop-down list. The default choice for the Options box is Create New List, which creates a new list from scratch.

If you want to add matches from the second search to the files you've already found, choose the Add Matches To List option. If you want to trim the list, choose Search Only In List. This choice speeds the process since Word will look at only the files already in the list. You can then restart the search, using the techniques we'll discuss shortly, to modify the original list.

How to search by date using the Timestamp card

The rightmost tab in the Advanced Search dialog box is for the Timestamp card, shown in Figure 17-6.

FIGURE 17-6

The Timestamp card lets you set search criteria based on who created and last saved the file and when.

Advanced Search
Location	Summary	Timestamp

Last Saved
From:
To:
By:

Created
From:
To:
By:

OK   Cancel   Help

The Last Saved and Created group boxes on the Timestamp card each include From, To, and By text boxes. The first two boxes in each group box let you specify a date or range of dates to look for.

Suppose, for example, that you created a document yesterday, but you couldn't find it on your disk. One way to search for it is to look for files created after the day before yesterday and before today by entering the appropriate From and To dates in the Created box. This search will find only those documents that were created yesterday. Similarly, if you created the file some weeks ago, but you worked on it yesterday, you could enter the same dates in the From and To text boxes in the Last Saved box.

The By text box in the Created group box is equivalent to the Author box on the Summary card. In fact, if you enter or change information in either of these two text boxes, the change will show up in the equivalent text box on the other card.

How to search by the last person who saved the file

Word not only keeps track of the author and the creation date of each file, it also keeps track of the last person who saved the file. To search for files last saved by a particular person, enter that person's name in the Saved By box. If you're not sure how Word has recorded the person's name, you can open his or her installation of the program, choose Tools Options, and then choose User Info to see the name. This feature is useful when you're searching on a network for a document that someone else has edited.

How to store a search definition for future use

After you define the advanced search criteria, choose OK to return to the Search dialog box. At this point, you'll see the search criteria detailed in the Search For group box. As before, you'll only be able to edit the File Name and Location boxes, but each of the other criteria are also displayed, so you can easily see the search you've defined.

Having defined a search, you can save the definition by choosing the Save Search As button so that you can use it again. Word opens the Save Search As dialog box, where you can enter a name and choose OK to save it. The search name is now available in the drop-down list above the Save Search As button. To tell Word to use it, simply open the list and choose the name. You can delete a search definition at any time by selecting the name in the list and choosing the Delete Search button.

How to search for a file

Of course, the whole point of entering search criteria is to get the list of files. After defining a search, choose OK in the Search dialog box to start the search. Then sit back while Word does all the hard work. Word closes the Search dialog box and displays a message box. If you've chosen to include subdirectories, the box title will be Searching Directories. When Word finishes building the list of directories to search, it replaces this message box with the Building File List message box. If you didn't include subdirectories, the search will start immediately with the second message box.

Both message boxes report current status. The Searching Directories box displays the name of each directory as it works through the directory tree. The Building File List box reports the number of matches found. Both boxes include a Cancel button, so you can stop the search at any time. When Word finishes the search, it opens (or returns you to) the Find File dialog box, shown in Figure 17-7.

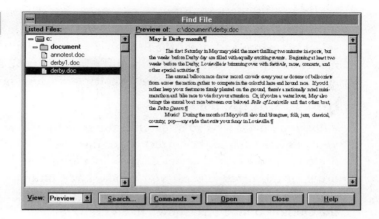

FIGURE 17-7

The Find File dialog box offers a variety of document-retrieval functions.

The Find File dialog box

The Find File dialog box provides features for opening, managing, and printing one or more documents. The dialog box consists of three areas. The Listed Files box on the left shows a list of all files that meet the current search criteria. On the right is an area that changes depending on which option you've chosen in the View box for the information to show along with the files. In Figure 17-7, the View box is set to Preview, this area is labeled *Preview Of*, and it shows the contents of the file currently selected in the Listed Files box. We'll discuss this area and the other choices for filling it a little later.

At the bottom of the screen are a drop-down list that lets you change the View setting and five buttons that let you open the Search dialog box, give commands for managing and printing files, open one or more files, close the dialog box, and ask for help.

How to select files

In Chapter 2, we discussed how to select files in the File Name list box so that you could delete them. The same techniques apply when selecting files to open, print, or copy. To select a file with the mouse, simply click on its name. To select more than one adjacent file, either hold down the mouse button as you extend the selection or click on the first filename you want to include and then hold down the Shift key as you click on the last one. Word will automatically highlight all the filenames between the two extremes. To select nonadjacent filenames with the mouse, hold down the Ctrl key while you click on filenames.

To select one file with the keyboard, use the arrow keys to highlight the filename you want to select. To select several adjacent files, hold down the Shift key as you extend the selection with the arrow keys. To select nonadjacent filenames, select any one and then press Shift-F8. To add more names, move the highlight outline to the appropriate filename and press the Spacebar to highlight the filename. To remove the highlight from any name, select the name and press the Spacebar again. If you've highlighted several names and want to remove the multiple highlights all at once, press Shift-F8 again and then press an arrow key to collapse the highlight to a single filename.

How to sort the list of files

After you've used Word's search features to find an appropriate list of files, you still have to find the correct file or files in the list. Word provides several options to help ease this task as well, including the ability to change the sort order of the listed files. If you choose the Commands button to open the Commands menu and then choose Sorting from the menu, Word will open the Options dialog box, shown in Figure 17-8.

FIGURE 17-8

The Options dialog box lets you choose the order in which Word will sort filenames.

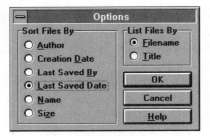

You can tell Word to sort the filenames by author, by filename, by size, by the date the file was created or last saved, or by the name of the person who last saved the document. Word will remember the most recent setting and continue to use it until you change it again.

To sort the filenames by any of these sort keys, choose the appropriate option in the Sort Files By box. When you close the Options dialog box by choosing OK, Word sorts the files in the specified order.

The second group box in the Options dialog box is List Files By, with Filename and Title as the only choices. If you choose Title, Word will list the titles if it finds them. For those files that lack titles, however, Word will list the filename set off with hyphens, so you don't have to worry about overlooking a file that doesn't happen to have a title.

How to choose the information to display for each file

As already mentioned, Word lets you specify the information to show on the right side of the Find File dialog box as you highlight each filename. The three choices are Preview, which shows you the actual contents of any file that Word can read; Summary, which shows you the Summary Info and statistical information stored with any Word file; and File Info, which shows you information such as filename, title, size, and author in columnar format, with one file per row. All three choices are available on the drop-down list in the View box at the bottom left of the Find File dialog box.

The precise information you'll see when View is set to File Info will vary somewhat, depending on the sort order of the listed files. If you sort by the person who last saved the file, for example, you'll see columns labeled *File Name, Title, Size, Last Saved By*, and *Last Saved*. If you sort by author, the last two columns will be labeled *Author* and *Last Saved*. If you sort by creation date, the last column will be labeled *Created*.

The order of the first two columns will depend on the setting for List Files By. If it's set to File Name, the first column will be File Name and the second will be Title. If it's set to Title, the two will be reversed.

When set to Preview, Word will show the contents of all documents it can read, changing the Preview image each time you highlight a different filename in the Listed Files list. If you have a relatively slow machine, moving through a list of files that include graphics will likely be tedious. If you need to use the preview feature on a slow machine, you might try using the File Info or Summary setting to find what seems like the likely file that you're looking for and then move to that file in the list before setting View to Preview. If it's not the right file, reset the View to one of the other choices before moving on.

How to change summary information

Another choice on the menu that opens when you choose the Commands button is Summary. If you choose Summary while you have a file highlighted that Word can read, you'll open the same Summary Info dialog box that you can reach from a document window by choosing File Summary Info.

The Summary command provides a convenient way to change summary information without opening a file. You may find this particularly useful if you haven't been filling in the summary information and decide to fill it in for all your older files at once. Word will let you add summary information to any document stored in a format that Word can read. In the case of files in other formats, however, when you finish filling in the Summary Info box and choose OK, Word will ask for permission before it resaves the file in Word format. For details on the Summary Info dialog box, see "Summary information" on page 56.

How to open one or more documents

You can open any one file in the Listed Files list by double-clicking on the filename or by selecting the filename and choosing the Open button. To open more than one file with a single command, simply select the files you want open using the techniques we described earlier in this chapter, and choose the Open button.

 You can also open one or more files as read-only by selecting them, choosing the Commands button, and then choosing Open Read Only from the menu.

How to print, delete, or copy one or more documents

Three other choices on the menu that opens when you choose the Command button are Print, Delete, and Copy. In each case, the command applies to all files you've selected before choosing the Command button. Here are some points to remember for each of the three commands.

The Print command

Choosing Print opens the same dialog box you reach by choosing File Print from a document window. The only difference is that when you open the dialog box from the Find File dialog box, you can print all the files you currently have highlighted. We covered the Print dialog box in "Using the File Print command" on page 263.

The Delete command

We covered file deletion in Chapter 2. Briefly, when you choose Delete, Word responds with a message box asking you to confirm the deletion of all the files. Choose Yes or No, as appropriate. As we pointed out in Chapter 2, you need to be careful when deleting multiple files: It's easy to highlight and delete an extra name. Pay careful attention to your selections, and be sure to read the filenames in the message box when Word asks you to confirm a deletion. Note also that you can delete any file with the Delete button, not just Word document files.

The Copy command

The Copy command lets you copy one or more files to another directory. Somewhat surprisingly, you can't copy to a file with a different name. Rather, the feature will copy a file only to another directory and only using the same name as the original file. This can be bothersome if a file with the same name already exists in the directory you want to copy to. But at least Word stops and asks whether you want to replace the file before overwriting it.

To copy one or more files to another directory, select the file or files, choose Commands, and then choose Copy. Word responds with the Copy dialog box, shown in Figure 17-9. You can then type the destination directory name in the Path text box, or you can select the appropriate drive in the Drives drop-down list and the appropriate directory in the Directories list box. You can also choose the New button to create a new directory to copy the file or files to. Word opens a dialog box to let you enter the new directory name. When you finish entering the target path in the Copy dialog box, choose OK to tell Word to copy the file or files.

FIGURE 17-9

Word's Copy dialog box lets you specify the drive and directory to copy files to, but it won't let you specify a new filename.

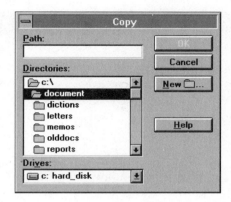

If Word finds one or more files in the target directory with the same name as one you are copying, it will stop and ask for permission to replace the destination files with files of the same names. Choose Yes, No, or Cancel, as appropriate. Note, however, that Word will not show you a separate message for each duplicate filename. Choosing Yes tells Word to overwrite all of the duplicate names it finds. Also note that copying files does not update the file list in the File Name list box. If the files you're copying would show up in the list, as determined by the current search criteria, you'll have to rerun the search before they'll appear.

How to rename and move files

Missing from Word's built-in file-management features are commands for renaming files and for moving files to another directory. The only way to rename files from within Word is to open each file, save each one under the new name with the Save As command, and then delete the old file. However, you can move files easily by copying them to the new directory and then deleting them from the old directory. First select the file or files you want to move, and then choose the command to copy them. When Word finishes copying, it will leave the files selected so that you can delete them simply by choosing the Delete command.

TOPIC FINDER

Some Thoughts on Exchanging Data   620

Opening Documents Stored in Other Formats   621
- How to import document files into Word
- Text file formatting issues

Importing Data   625
- How to import data using the Clipboard
- How to import data using the Insert File command
- NEW! How to import data using the Insert Database command

Moving Word Documents to Other Programs   632
- How to save Word documents in other formats
- How to use the Windows Clipboard

Customizing the Conversion Process   634
- How to use the Tools Options Compatibility card
- How to use the CONVERT.DOT template

Linking and Embedding   637
- Different kinds of links
- Linking vs. embedding
- How to embed data with the Insert Object command
- How to link data with the Insert Object command
- How to use the Edit Paste Special command to embed or link data
- How to update and maintain linked data
- A quick look at fields for embedding and linking
- How to create links in other Windows-based programs

Sharing Data with Other Programs

ord can share information with other programs in a variety of ways. The most straightforward is to convert a file from one format to another—either importing the file into Word format when you open the file or exporting it to some other format by specifying that format when you save the file.

Word can also share data in more sophisticated ways. Topping the list is that you can insert information from another program into a Word document in a way that lets you use the other program to edit the information. We've already covered some of these capabilities, since several of the tools that come with Word depend on them—including, for example, WordArt, which we discussed in Chapter 15. The variations on these more sophisticated data-sharing features are called *linking* and *embedding*. You can make use of Word's linking and embedding features to share data with any other Windows-based program that supports these features, including, for example, Microsoft Excel.

In this chapter, we'll look at both Word's file conversion features and its linking and embedding features.

Some Thoughts on Exchanging Data

Before we look at the mechanics of exchanging files with other word processing programs, it's important to understand some limitations of the process. First, and most important, although Word makes it reasonably painless to import files from and export them to a wide range of other word processor formats, the translation is not perfect. In fact, it's impossible for any program to convert documents to and from all major word processing formats with complete accuracy.

One of the key limitations for conversions involves character formatting, particularly the choice of fonts. Different programs use different techniques to define fonts. In particular, some character-based word processors maintain a list of available fonts as part of the program's configuration file rather than as part of the document itself. If you move a document to a computer that has different fonts available, the printed output may vary even if you use the same program. This approach to fonts gives Word no way to know which fonts to use when importing a file created in that program.

Other conversion problems relate to differences in capabilities. For example, if a word processor is limited to one-line headers, a Word document with multiple-line headers cannot possibly translate correctly to that format. And Word contains any number of other features—including hidden text, frames, embedded objects, and fields—that are handled differently in other programs or are not supported at all.

The moral of all this is simple: Keep your expectations low. If you convert a document to another format, don't be surprised if you lose some of the formatting in the process. In fact, complex formatting may well create problems, leaving you with a difficult clean-up job at the other end. Often your best bet is to simplify the source file as much as you can and then put back the formatting after you move the text to the other program. If you can afford the luxury of making a dry run, you can try a test conversion first to see which formatting features convert well and which create problems.

For detailed information about limitations on converting files between Word and other specific programs, use the Search feature in the Word help system to search for the word *readme*, and choose the File Conversion topic.

With these warnings in mind, we can take a look at how to exchange documents with other programs, starting with the process of importing files stored in other formats.

Opening Documents Stored in Other Formats

Word makes it easy to open or save a document that isn't saved in Word for Windows format, although the list of recognized formats will depend on how you installed Word. The Setup program can install file converters for a variety of word processing and graphics file formats. If you don't see as many options on your system as we'll discuss here (or if you don't see any at all), you may want to rerun Setup to add the file converters.

How to import document files into Word

To import a foreign-format document file (by which we mean a file in any format other than Word for Windows version 6.0 format), start by choosing File Open. Then use the options in the Open dialog box to specify the drive, directory, and file to open, just as if you were opening a document that had been created in Word.

By default, the entry in the File Name text box tells Word to list only those documents with the DOC filename extension (Word's default extension for documents). As we discussed in Chapter 2, however, you can easily list files with other extensions or with any arbitrary pattern, for that matter: Simply choose a different option from the List Files Of Type drop-down list at the bottom of the dialog box or type the pattern you want to match in the File Name text box. To see all files in the current directory, for example, type *.* in the text box and choose OK. Similarly, to see all files that start with the letter *L* and end with the TXT filename extension, type *l*.txt* and choose OK. Since many word processors don't automatically use a specific extension (and even when they do, you can usually override it), you will most often want to see names for all files in the directory. Figure 18-1 shows the Open dialog box, displaying a list of all the files in the current directory.

FIGURE 18-1

Enter *.* in the File Name text box to see all the files in a directory.

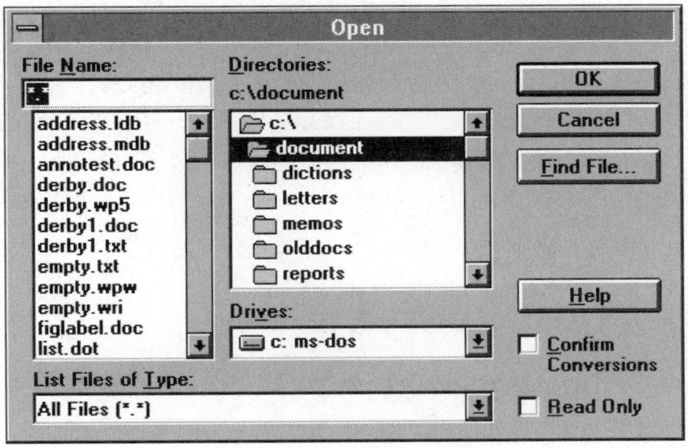

After you specify the pattern to match, you can open a file by highlighting the filename and choosing OK. Notice the Confirm Conversions check box in the lower right corner of the Open dialog box. If this box isn't checked and Word recognizes the format of the file you have selected, it will simply convert the file and load it. If the box is checked or if Word can't recognize the format, the program will display the Convert File dialog box, shown in Figure 18-2, and will wait for you to specify the format of the file. Simply highlight the appropriate format and choose OK.

FIGURE 18-2

Word can open documents stored in various formats.

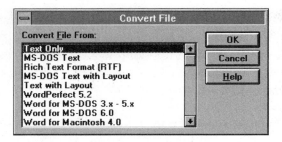

You can monitor the progress of the conversion by watching the status bar, which displays a visual gauge in the form of a line of blocks to indicate the proportion of the file that has been converted. When Word finishes the conversion, it will put the document in a new document window, using the original filename.

If you set Word to show hidden text in a document that you've converted from another format, you may see Word's PRIVATE field, which is displayed as the word *PRIVATE* surrounded by curly brackets. (To see hidden text, click on the Show/Hide ¶ button on the Standard toolbar to toggle all nonprinting characters on.) The PRIVATE field has no effect on the document while you're working with the document in Word. Rather, this field stores information that Word needs for converting the document back to its original form as closely as possible. If you plan to return the document to its original format, make sure you know where the PRIVATE field is so that you don't accidentally delete it.

Text file formatting issues

Most word processing programs, including Word, can save documents on disk as pure text files, with all formatting instructions stripped out. In addition, nearly every word processing program (and many spreadsheet and database programs) can read pure text files. This text file format is often called *ASCII format* or *ASCII text format* because all MS-DOS–based computers (and most others) use the ASCII (American Standard Code for Information Interchange) system to represent characters, including numbers, letters, punctuation, and other symbols.

As we mentioned at the start of this chapter, many of the problems you'll run into when converting files from one word processing format to another grow from differences in formatting features. Because files in ASCII format consist only of text, with no formatting, ASCII serves as a basic, and the simplest, format for all word processing documents. And ASCII text format is certainly the safest choice when you want to move text and don't care about formatting. Even ASCII files, however, allow some variation.

ASCII uses values from 0 through 127 to represent characters. For example, your computer knows the letter *e* as ASCII value 101. However, because of the way microcomputers store their information, it is more convenient to use a system that has 256 choices. ASCII defines characters only for the values 0 through 127, leaving 128 unused values. To take advantage of these values, many computer and software manufacturers, as well as the American National Standards Institute (ANSI), define their own sets of characters for the values 128 through 255. These characters are referred to as the *extended character set* or the *high-order characters*. When this set is combined with the ASCII set, the two together are often referred to as *extended ASCII*. Unfortunately, various manufacturers use different characters for these values, which means that many printers and programs interpret these characters differently.

Word offers four options for importing documents in text file format, with two variations for each of two categories: Text and MS-DOS Text. If your text consists of numbers, standard punctuation such as periods and commas, and the English alphabet (with no foreign-language characters), it doesn't matter whether you use the Text options or the MS-DOS Text options. They are identical for all characters with ASCII values of 127 and below. If you're using foreign-language characters or unusual symbols, however, the difference is important.

The Text options—Text Only and Text With Layout—are meant for exchanging files with Windows-based applications. The MS-DOS Text options—MS-DOS Text and MS-DOS Text With Layout—are meant for exchanging files with MS-DOS–based applications. The two categories differ in how they deal with high-order characters. The Text options follow the ANSI high-order character set. The MS-DOS Text options follow the character set used by MS-DOS (sometimes called the *OEM character set* or the *IBM extended character set*). If you want to compare the two character sets, take a look at Appendix B, "ANSI & OEM Codes," starting on page 995.

For each of the two categories of text file formats, Word offers two import options: without layout and with layout. Both the Text Only and the MS-DOS Text options—the two without layout—are absolutely literal about converting the source text file. If Word encounters a carriage return, it puts an end-of-paragraph mark at that point in the document. Unfortunately, some programs produce text files that have a carriage return than at the end of each line rather than at the end of each paragraph. This can cause problems when you use one of the Text options because Word will then treat each line of the file as a separate paragraph, and it won't wrap the text properly if you edit or reformat it.

If the file you're importing has a carriage return at the end of each line, you will probably want to use the Text With Layout or the MS-DOS Text With Layout option. With these choices, Word will try to identify each paragraph in the source file and format it as a paragraph. For example, it will recognize two carriage returns (indicating a blank line between paragraphs), a carriage return followed by a tab (indicating an indent at the beginning of a paragraph), or a carriage return followed by spaces (also indicating an indent) as indicating the start of a new paragraph, and it will format the text accordingly.

When you are importing files that do not include a carriage return at the end of each line, both of the With Layout options will often guess wrong—and will create extra work, since you'll need to clean up the incorrect guesses. It's best to avoid these options with files that don't have extra carriage returns.

For files that do include a carriage return at the end of each line, both With Layout options generally work well, especially if the document contains nothing but paragraphs of body text. But if the source file includes tables or lists, you may be better off importing the file twice, once without layout and once with layout. You can then use Edit Cut and Edit Paste to combine the properly formatted parts of each document.

Figure 18-3 offers a summary of the four options and the kinds of files each is best suited for.

For This Kind of File	Use This Option
Text files with a carriage return at the end of each paragraph only, or files that contain tables or lists	Text Only (for files produced by Windows-based applications)
	MS-DOS Text (for files produced by MS-DOS–based applications)
Text files with a carriage return at the end of each line	Text With Layout (for files produced by Windows-based applications)
	MS-DOS Text With Layout (for files produced by MS-DOS–based applications)

FIGURE 18-3

The four options for importing documents in text file format.

Importing Data

In addition to importing information by opening a file and converting it, Word offers three other methods for importing information: the Windows Clipboard, the Insert File command, and the Insert Database command.

How to import data using the Clipboard

In many cases, the simplest way to move information to Word will be to copy and paste, or cut and paste, by way of the Clipboard (which we discussed in Chapter 4). Of course, it's easier to use the Clipboard if you have both Word and the other program running simultaneously. But even if your system doesn't have enough memory to load more than one program at a time, you can still transfer data using the Clipboard.

First open the file containing the graphic, worksheet, or other information you want to copy into Word. Select the information you want to transfer, and choose Edit Copy or Edit Cut to have the application put a copy of the selection on the Clipboard. Next load Word or switch to the Word window, open the document that you want to paste the information into, and place the cursor where you want to insert the information. Then choose either the Edit Paste or the Edit Paste Special command to insert the contents of the Clipboard into your document.

If you choose Edit Paste, Word will insert the data either as text or as a graphics image, depending on what you originally cut or copied. If you're pasting information that started out in a Microsoft Excel worksheet, for example, the Edit Paste command will paste the text into your document as a table. The Edit Paste Special command lets you insert the item as a linked object, as we will discuss later in this chapter.

How to import data using the Insert File command

If you want to insert information from another program or another Word file directly into your document, you can use the Insert File command, which can read and convert all the same file formats as the File Open command. When you choose Insert File, Word will display the File dialog box, which is nearly identical to the Open dialog box, right down to the Confirm Conversions check box. However, it has two important additions: the Range text box and the Link To File check box. There is one missing element: the Read Only check box.

If you enter a filename in the File dialog box and choose OK, Word will insert the contents of the entire file into your document, just as if you had typed or pasted it. If you prefer, however, you can specify a portion of the file in the Range text box. The type of range you can specify depends on the type of file you're inserting. For example, if you've defined a section of text with a bookmark in a Word document, you can insert only that section of text by specifying the bookmark. Similarly, you can specify a named range of cells when inserting from a Microsoft Excel worksheet file.

If you check the Link To File check box before choosing OK, Word will insert the contents of the file as a linked field, which we'll cover later in this chapter.

How to import data using the Insert Database command

Database files create special challenges for importing data. Instead of simply translating the data into Word format, you may want to import only some of the information from the database, and you may need it sorted in a particular order.

A quick lesson in database jargon will help here: Databases store information as *records,* with each record consisting of related information such as a name and an address. They also divide records into *fields,* with each field consisting of a specific kind of information, such as first name, state, or zip code. Each field has a *field name* (such as FIRST, STATE, or ZIP), used to refer to the contents of that field across records. When you import database files into Word, you may want to import, or select (to use the proper jargon), only certain records. And you may want to import information from some of the fields but not from others. Word's Insert Database command provides tools for importing, selecting, and sorting all at one time, as well as for specifying which fields to include from each record. When Word imports the data, it will place it in a table, creating one row for each record and one column for each field.

> You might need to import data from a database file for any number of reasons, ranging from creating a simple table in your document to using Word as a sophisticated report generator for your database program. But one of the most important reasons for importing data is to use it for mail merges. The Insert Database command, with its ability to sort and select as it imports data, makes it easy to maintain a database in Microsoft Excel or in most database programs and then import the data into a Word table only when you need it for mail merging form letters, labels, and the like. For details on mail merging with Word, see Chapter 21 starting on page 714.

To import data from a database file, start by positioning the cursor where you want to insert the data in your Word document. Then choose Insert Database to open the Database dialog box, shown in Figure 18-4.

FIGURE 18-4

Use the Database dialog box to import, select, and sort data from a database file.

Database
Data Source:
[Get Data...]   [Cancel]
Data: C:\DOCUMENT\MAILLIST.DBF   [Help]
Data Options:
[Query Options...]   [Table AutoFormat...]
Insert the Data into the Document:
[Insert Data...]

From the Database dialog box, choose the Get Data button in the section labeled Data Source. Word will display the Open Data Source dialog box, which is identical to the Open dialog box except that the List Files Of Type drop-down list includes choices for database format files such as MS Excel Worksheets (*.xls), MS Access Databases (*.mdb), MS FoxPro Files (*.dbf), dBASE Files (*.dbf), and Paradox Files (*.db). There is also no Read Only option. You can use the same techniques you use in the Open dialog box to move to the appropriate directory and designate the file that contains the data you want to insert. Choose OK, and Word will start the application (if it is available) and prompt you to select the desired database. Once you've opened the database, Word will return to the Database dialog box, which now displays the path and name of the chosen file below the Get Data button, as shown in Figure 18-4.

How to define the database import options

Once you've specified the file to use, the two buttons in the Data Options section of the Database dialog box and the Insert Data button at the bottom of the dialog box will become available. Since you'll generally want to retrieve a subset of information from the database file, your next step will usually be choosing the Query Options button to open the Query Options dialog box, shown in Figure 18-5.

If your system has Microsoft Query installed—which might be the case if you also have Microsoft Excel 5.0—Word will offer to run that program instead of opening its own built-in query feature. Microsoft Query is more powerful, and you may prefer to use it; but because it is not part of the Word program, we will focus here on the built-in query feature instead.

FIGURE 18-5

The Filter Records card in the Query Options dialog box lets you specify which records to import.

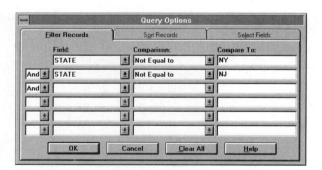

Figure 18-5 shows the Filter Records card, which lets you set the criteria for the records to select. Suppose, for example, that the database includes the names and addresses of your clients and that you want to include the records for all clients except those in New York and New Jersey.

As you can see in Figure 18-5, the dialog box contains four columns of text boxes, with only three boxes in the first row. The three columns labeled Field, Comparison, and Compare To let you define the filter, or selection criteria. Each row lets you define a criterion based on the information in one field of each record. The additional text boxes in the unlabeled column let you specify how to link the criteria: with *And* (the record must meet the earlier criteria *and* the criterion in this row), or with *Or* (the record must meet the earlier criteria *or* this one). When Word inserts the data, it will filter out the records that don't meet the criteria—to use the common database jargon, it will select those records that meet the criteria.

In Figure 18-5, the filter is defined to include all records in which the STATE field is not equal to NY and is not equal to NJ. To set the criteria, start by opening the Field drop-down list in the first row. The list will include all the fields in the database file. Click on the field name STATE or highlight the word and press Enter to enter it in the text box. Next use the same techniques to enter Not Equal To in the Comparison box in the first row. Then move to the Compare To box and type *NY*. (This example assumes that the database uses two-character abbreviations for states.)

Use the same techniques to fill in the text boxes in the second row. If you decide you want to start over at any point, you can choose the Clear All button at the bottom of the card.

You can also tell Word how to sort the records, using the Sort Records card, shown in Figure 18-6.

FIGURE 18-6

The Sort Records card in the Query Options dialog box lets you specify a sort order for the imported records.

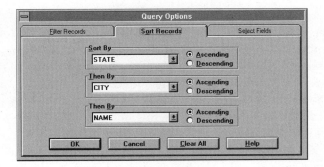

The Sort Records card will let you specify up to three levels of sorting. You might, for example, want a list of clients grouped together by state, by city within each state, and alphabetically by name within each city. To generate the list, you would sort first by state, then by city, and then by last name. To designate the field for each level of the sort, open the drop-down list for the appropriate text box and use the mouse or keyboard to choose from the list. The Ascending and Descending option buttons for each text box let you specify the direction for that level of the sort (ascending or descending order for numbers, and alphabetic or reverse alphabetic order for text). If necessary, you can choose the Clear All button to remove all entries.

The third and last card in the Query Options dialog box is the Select Fields card, shown in Figure 18-7. This card lets you tell Word to import only those fields that you want in your document. It also lets you specify the order for the fields.

FIGURE 18-7

The Select Fields card lets you specify which fields to import and in what order.

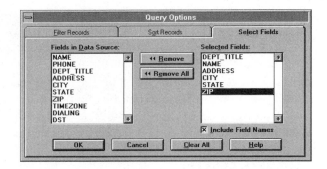

The Select Fields card includes two lists of fields. The Fields In Data Source list, on the left, includes all fields in the data file. The Selected Fields list, on the right, shows the fields Word will import, in the order in which it will import them.

When the highlight is in the Fields In Data Source list, the two buttons between the lists are labeled Select and Select All. When the highlight is in the Selected Fields list, the buttons will change to Remove and Remove All. Choosing the Select button will add the currently highlighted field name or names to the Selected Fields list, while choosing the Remove button will delete the currently highlighted field name or names from the list. Similarly, choosing the Select All button will add all the field names in the database file to the Selected Fields list, while choosing the Remove All button will delete all the field names.

When you first open the Select Fields card while defining query options for a database file, the list of selected fields will include all fields in the database file, in the same order as they appear in the database file. To change the list, highlight the field names and choose the Remove button as appropriate to take out those fields that you don't want to include or that are in the wrong order. To change the order of the fields, simply add the field names back in the new order.

To create the list shown in Figure 18-7, for example, we first chose Remove All to clear the Selected Fields list. Next we highlighted DEPT_TITLE and chose Select and then highlighted all the fields from NAME through ZIP and chose Select again. At that point, we had added two unwanted entries: PHONE and a second entry for DEPT_TITLE. To get rid of them, we simply highlighted them in the Selected Fields list and chose Remove.

The last item on the Select Fields card, just below the Selected Fields list, is the Include Field Names check box. If you want to include the field names in the table Word creates from the database, make sure this box is checked. If you don't want the field names included, make sure the box isn't checked.

When you're finished with the Query Options choices, choose OK to return to the Database dialog box.

How to define a format for the imported database data

In the Data Options section of the Database dialog box, you'll find the Table AutoFormat button. You can choose this button to open Word's Table AutoFormat dialog box and define a format for the table that Word will insert. This is the same dialog box you'll see if you choose the Table AutoFormat command. For details about this dialog box, see "How to use Table AutoFormat—with or without the Table Wizard" on page 367.

How to insert the database data

Once you've specified a data source and have (optionally) defined a query, you can choose the Insert Data button in the Database dialog box to open the Insert Data dialog box, shown in Figure 18-8.

FIGURE 18-8

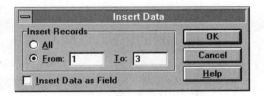

The Insert Data dialog box lets you specify whether to insert all records that meet your criteria or only certain records.

The Insert Data dialog box lets you specify whether to import all records that meet the criteria you've defined or whether to import a range of records. Enter *1* in the From text box and *3* in the To text box, for example, and you'll import only the first three records that meet your criteria.

Limiting the import to a range of records can be useful if you want to test a query definition. A quick test run will let you see whether the query does in fact retrieve the appropriate set of records in the format you want. To make a test run even faster, be sure not to include a sort definition.

If you check the Insert Data As Field check box in the Insert Data dialog box before choosing OK, Word will insert the contents of the file as a

DATABASE field, which maintains a link to the database. We'll explain links later in this chapter; see "Linking and Embedding" starting on page 637.

Moving Word Documents to Other Programs

So far in this chapter, we've concentrated on moving data into Word files. But you will probably need to move data in the other direction as well: from Word format to other applications. Word provides plenty of options for that too.

How to save Word documents in other formats

You can save a Word document in a foreign file format just as easily as you can load a document that's in a foreign format. Start by loading the document in Word. Then choose File Save As to display the Save As dialog box. We covered this dialog box in Chapter 2, and you should be familiar with most of its options. Here we're interested in the Save File As Type drop-down list. When you open this list, you'll see a list like the one shown in Figure 18-9.

FIGURE 18-9

The Save File As Type list offers a range of file formats for your document.

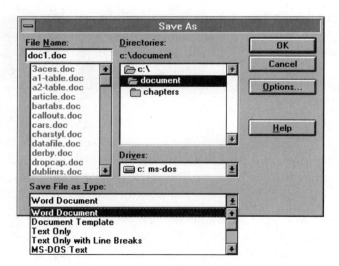

This list is similar to the one Word offers for confirming the format when you open a file that's already in a foreign format. Recall that if you have checked the Confirm Conversions check box in the Open dialog box, Word will pause and let you confirm the format before opening the file. In that case, Word shows you the list of file formats in a separate dialog box

(Convert File) after you choose OK in the Open dialog box. In contrast, when you save a file, you must designate the format before you choose OK.

There is another difference as well. In addition to the four types of text file formats discussed earlier, you'll find two more in the Save As dialog box: Text Only With Line Breaks and MS-DOS Text With Line Breaks. If you choose either of these line-break formats, Word will save the file as ASCII text without trying to preserve the layout, but it will end each line with a carriage return. This contrasts with the Text Only and MS-DOS Text options, which put a carriage return at the end of each paragraph only (wherever Word has an end-of-paragraph mark). The two With Layout options add spaces for tabs, indents, and other blank space.

If you're saving a document in text format to be edited in another program, you will probably want to use either the Text Only or the MS-DOS Text option so that you will not have to remove all the extra carriage returns when you import the file into the other program. If you intend to send the file as a message over an electronic mail system, however, you will probably want to use one of the With Line Breaks options to add a carriage return at the end of each line. Since most electronic mail systems can't handle lines of text longer than 80 characters, this will make the file more palatable to the system. If you need to maintain as much of the layout as possible—because you plan to print the file by copying it directly to a printer with the MS-DOS COPY command or the equivalent, for example—you will want to use one of the With Layout options.

> Remember that, aside from the text options, your list of available file formats may not match the lists that appear in our illustrations. The list you see will depend on the conversion filters you have installed.

How to use the Windows Clipboard

You can also move data from Word documents to other applications with the Windows Clipboard. Simply copy or cut the portion of the document that you want to move, and then switch to the other application. If that application is Windows-based, you can use its Paste command to insert the data.

If you are running Windows in 386 Enhanced mode, you can also paste text into most MS-DOS–based applications that run in a character display mode (as opposed to a graphics mode). Open the MS-DOS application in a window (rather than full screen) or, if it is currently set as a full-screen program, press Alt-Enter to convert it to a window. Next place the program's cursor where you want the information to go. Then open the window's Control menu, and choose Edit Paste. Windows will enter the text from the Windows Clipboard as if you had typed it into the application. Note that text copied from Word will lose all formatting when pasted into another application, whether the application is based on MS-DOS or on Windows.

Customizing the Conversion Process

As we've discussed, word processing files can contain complex formatting information, and it can be difficult to reliably convert the formatting from one file format to another. While we recommend that you put as little formatting as possible into any document that you intend to convert, we also recognize that you can't always get away with minimal formatting. You may, for example, need to exchange files with a client or co-worker who uses a different word processor. For those occasions when you must import or export heavily formatted files, Word provides an impressive array of features to let you fine-tune the way it converts and displays files.

How to use the Tools Options Compatibility card

One of the more sophisticated and easier-to-use features for working with heavily formatted imported files is the set of options on the Tools Options Compatibility card, shown in Figure 18-10.

FIGURE 18-10

The Tools Options Compatibility card controls how Word displays documents on screen.

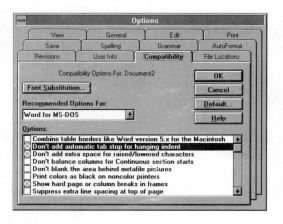

The settings on this card do not affect in any way the information stored in the file. Rather, they affect how Word interprets that information to format the document on screen and on paper. You can use these settings to tell Word to treat certain kinds of formatting information the same way as another specific program treats it, to have Word more closely match the way the other program displays the file.

For example, the second item in the Options list is Don't Add Automatic Tab Stop For Hanging Indent. Ordinarily, when you create a paragraph with a hanging indent (also known as an outdent in earlier versions of Word), Word will automatically define a tab stop so that the first tab on the first line of the paragraph is lined up vertically with the first character of the second and later lines. Other programs don't provide that convenience. As a result, if you have a 1-inch hanging indent in a paragraph in Word for Windows and one tab at the beginning of the first line, the text will start 1 inch from the left of the beginning of the first line. In Word for MS-DOS, in contrast, the same tab character will indent the first line by only 0.5 inch, since Word for MS-DOS leaves its default tab stops untouched. To tell Word for Windows to display the paragraph with the same indents and tab stops that you would see in Word for MS-DOS, you need to turn off the automatic tab stop by making sure you've checked the Don't Add Automatic Tab Stop For Hanging Indent check box.

Word has several predefined sets of options for the Compatibility card, each designed to make Word mimic the behavior of some other specific program. The predefined choices, which will set all the Compatibility options at one time, turning them on or off as appropriate, are available in the Recommended Options For drop-down list, along with a choice for a custom definition. You can use these predefined sets or create a custom definition to set the options as needed. More important, Word stores the settings separately for each file, so you can save a different set of options for each file.

Word will normally use the recommended option settings for Word for Windows 6.0 as its default (with none of the check boxes in the Options list checked). Most users will want this as the default. If you work with a lot of files from another program, however, and you want your default settings to match the other program's formatting, you can set the options in the Options list the way you want them and then choose the Default button to make that set of options the new default for all documents based on the Normal template.

Font conversions

One potentially troublesome issue in converting file formats is finding the right fonts to use. Word provides help for that aspect of file conversion as well. Choose the Font Substitution button on the Compatibility card, and Word will open the Font Substitution dialog box, shown in Figure 18-11.

FIGURE 18-11

The Font Substitution dialog box lets you substitute fonts in a converted document, on either a temporary or a permanent basis.

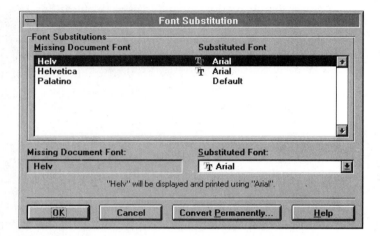

NOTE If all the fonts specified in the converted document are available to Word, you will not be able to open the Font Substitution dialog box. Instead, when you choose the Font Substitution button, you will see a message box stating that no font substitution is necessary.

The Font Substitutions list box, which takes up the top half of the dialog box, consists of two columns. The Missing Document Font column lists any fonts specified in the converted document that are not available within Word. The Substituted Font column shows what Word is using instead—which either will be a specific font, if you've defined one to use, or will simply be listed as Default.

If you highlight an entry in the Font Substitutions list, Word will display the appropriate parts of that entry in the Missing Document Font and Substituted Font text boxes. It will also display a message below the text boxes indicating the font it's using as a substitute. If you've chosen a specific font, the message will simply repeat the information that appears in the Font Substitutions list and in the two text boxes. If the substituted font is set to Default, the message will state what the default font is. If you want to change the setting, open the Substituted Font drop-down list to choose a different font from the list of fonts available on your system.

The substitutions listed in the Font Substitution dialog box affect only the way Word works with the file. The original font information is still stored in the file, and if you convert the file back to its original format, the original fonts remain. If you want to change the original fonts to the substituted fonts permanently, choose the Convert Permanently button.

How to use the CONVERT.DOT template

Word also provides a template you can use to automate and customize file conversions. The template's filename is CONVERT.DOT. Assuming that you chose the appropriate options when you installed Word, you'll find the template (along with several other templates containing macros) in the MACRO subdirectory of your Word program directory. If it's not there, you can use the Setup program to add the files to your disk.

Because these macros are designed to be self-explanatory, we won't discuss them here except to say that if you regularly convert files, you should take time to explore the macros in CONVERT.DOT. In particular, take a look at the macros named BatchConversion and EditConversionOptions. BatchConversion lets you convert an entire batch of files at one time—a significant convenience when you are converting more than one file, since you can avoid opening and saving each file individually. EditConversionOptions lets you change the default settings for the predefined sets of options on the Tools Options Compatibility card.

The easiest way to make the macros in this template available is to choose File Templates to open the Templates And Add-Ins dialog box. Then choose the Add button to add the template to the Global Templates And Add-Ins list. When you want to use the macros, choose File Templates, and make sure that the check box for the CONVERT.DOT template is checked. You can then run any of the macros by giving the Tools Macro command, highlighting the macro, and choosing the Run button. For more information on using macros, see Chapter 24, "Recording Macros," starting on page 842. For more on using the Templates And Add-Ins dialog box, see "Normal, Supplementary, and Global Templates" starting on page 938.

Linking and Embedding

All the features we've covered in this chapter so far deal with importing data into Word or exporting data from Word on an essentially permanent basis. What you wind up with in either case is a snapshot of the file's original contents. If you import data into a Word document with File Insert (and without checking Link To File), for example, later changes to the original file will not appear in the copy that's in the Word document. And if you want to change some imported data, you have to make the changes with Word.

At times, these limitations will be precisely what you want, either because you don't want changes in the source data to affect your Word document or because you want to make changes within the Word document without affecting the source. But there will also be times when you'll want the two applications to share information. If you've inserted a section of a worksheet into a Word document, for example, you might want the convenience of being able to make changes once, in the worksheet, and have them appear in the Word document as well.

In addition, you'll find that it's more convenient to edit certain kinds of data—such as spreadsheet data, for example—using the application that created it in the first place. This can be important whether you want to share the data between Word and another program or simply want the convenience of using the more appropriate tool for the task. For these needs, Word provides linking and embedding features.

Linking and embedding can be confusing topics. Part of the problem is that Word handles both features through fields, a subject we'll discuss in Chapter 20. Trying to learn all the different fields, along with the variations for each, can be overwhelming. However, Word will insert the fields for you automatically if you choose the appropriate menu commands, which means that you can take advantage of linking and embedding without knowing anything about fields.

For purposes of this discussion, we'll largely ignore fields, although we'll mention which commands create which fields, and we'll talk about moving the cursor or selection to a given field—by which we mean placing the cursor or selection in the imported text, graphic, or other data. (As we'll discuss in Chapter 20, Word can also display codes for the fields rather than the data itself.) We'll focus here on using the menu commands, which include Insert Object, Edit Paste Special, Insert Picture, Insert File, and Insert Database.

Different kinds of links

Any time you establish a connection between two data files in a way that lets them share data, you've established a link. But how that link behaves can vary a great deal—depending on what kind of field the link is based on and what settings, or switches, the field is using.

Some kinds of links will automatically update the data in Word if you change the original, or source, file. Other links require that you give a command to update the data. Similarly, some kinds of links will let you import text into Word and edit the text in Word just as if it were normal text—although you'll lose your edits if you update the field. Other kinds of links will let you edit the text only by calling the program the text was created in and using that program to edit. All links, in short, are not created equal. It's important to keep that in mind.

Earlier we discussed the Insert File command and pointed out the Link To File check box. If you check this box before choosing OK in the File dialog box, Word will create an INCLUDETEXT field. This inserts the text in a way that lets you either edit the text within Word or edit it by opening the source program and loading the source file.

When you create a link with the Insert File command, however, Word will not automatically update the text in one place when you edit in the other. Rather, once you've edited the source file, you can give a manual command to update the inserted text in the Word document. To update, place the cursor or selection in the field and press F9. Alternatively, you can move the mouse pointer to the field, click the right mouse button, and choose Update Field from the context-sensitive menu. In either case, Word will reimport the text from the linked file, and you'll lose any changes you've made to the text you previously imported into Word.

You can establish a similar kind of link with the Insert Database command, which we also discussed earlier in this chapter. In this case, the equivalent check box is labeled Insert Data As Field. If you check it before choosing OK in the Insert Data dialog box, Word will create a DATABASE field. The DATABASE field differs from the INCLUDETEXT field in detail, but it behaves much the same way. Here again, you can edit the text within Word or in the original file. You can use F9 or Update Field to update the field in Word; and if you update it, you'll lose any changes you made to the imported version of the data.

The Insert Picture dialog box includes a Link To File check box that serves much the same purpose for pictures. If you insert a picture without checking this check box, Word will insert the picture itself. If you check the box, Word will use an INCLUDEPICTURE field; you can edit the picture by using the source application, as you can edit text added with the INCLUDETEXT field or the DATABASE field, and you can then update it in Word with F9 or the Update Field command. For details on using the Insert Picture command, see "How to insert a picture" starting on page 535.

A more sophisticated kind of link is one that takes advantage of a Windows feature called Object Linking and Embedding (OLE) and uses Word's LINK field. OLE links are generally preferable to other kinds of links, although you can't always use them because not all programs support OLE.

If you choose Insert Object and then select the Create New card, you will see an Object Types list that lists all the programs that have been installed on your system that support OLE. In some cases, you'll see more than one entry for a program; for Microsoft Excel, for example, the list includes both Microsoft Excel Worksheet and Microsoft Excel Chart. We'll talk about how to use this card later in the chapter.

There are actually two levels of OLE: OLE 1 and OLE 2. These differ only in the way you edit the images, as we'll discuss in a moment. With either version of OLE, Word inserts an image of the text, graphic, or other item in your document. Windows calls this an object because you can't work with the data directly using Word commands, regardless of the kind of data. You can work only with the object as a whole, moving it, resizing it, or otherwise modifying it as a complete object.

To edit the data in a linked object, you can edit the original file by loading the source application and then loading the data file. More interesting is that you can also open the source application and automatically load the data file from within your Word document simply by double-clicking on the object in the Word document or by selecting the object and choosing the Edit Object command. (The precise name for the Object command on the Edit menu will vary depending on the kind of object you've selected.)

When you choose Edit Object, Word will use the Windows OLE feature to open the appropriate program, load the appropriate file, and let you edit the data. With OLE 1, Windows will open the source program and display the data in an editing window much as if you had opened the program directly. With OLE 2, Windows will replace the Word menu and toolbars with the equivalents from the source program but will continue to display the Word document so that you can see the object in context. (If you've used WordArt 2.0 with Word 6.0—as we described in Chapter 15—you've seen an example of OLE 2.) Word will automatically use OLE 2 with programs that support it and will use OLE 1 only with programs that support OLE 1 but not OLE 2.

Linking vs. embedding

The difference between linking and embedding is subtle but straightforward. In both cases, if you're working in Word, you can double-click on the object (or choose Edit Object) to edit the object in the source application. With a linked object, the data exists in a file outside your Word document: You can open it directly by loading the source application and then opening the file. With an embedded object, however, the data exists only in the Word document: There is no way to work with the data without first loading Word and the appropriate Word document. Some programs—WordArt 2.0, for example—will let you create embedded objects only.

Use embedding when you don't need to share the data with another file (not even with another Word document). Embedding is often more convenient than linking because all the data is stored in the Word document file. This means that you don't have to keep track of extra files, and you still have quick access to the source application when you want to edit the data.

If you need to share information among files, however, linking will let you update the information in one place and make the update easily available to all linked files. It will also let you edit the linked data by loading the source application and opening the data file directly. When linking files, you'll generally be better off using OLE links rather than the less sophisticated kinds of links we discussed earlier (such as using the Insert File command) unless, of course, you're linking to data created by programs that don't support OLE. In that case, you can use the less sophisticated kinds of links as a fallback.

How to embed data with the Insert Object command

The easiest way to embed an object in Word is with the Insert Object command, which opens the Object dialog box. As we explained in Chapter 15 when discussing WordArt 2.0, you can create new objects and embed them at the same time by using the Create New card in the Object dialog box. For details on using this card, see "How to use the Object dialog box," page 560.

You can also embed the contents of existing files using the Create From File card, shown in Figure 18-12.

FIGURE 18-12

Use the Create From File card in the Object dialog box to embed the contents of an existing file.

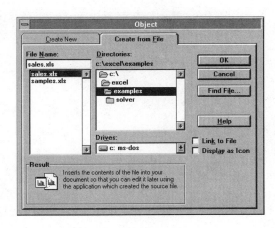

The Create From File card is similar to Word's Open dialog box and lets you specify a file the same way. The Display As Icon check box lets you tell Word to display an icon instead of the object's contents. The Link To File check box lets you create an OLE link to a file rather than inserting its contents as an embedded object. (We'll cover this possibility in a moment.) To embed the contents of an existing file, leave this check box cleared.

When you specify a file on the Create From File card and choose OK, Word creates an EMBED field, which, in essence, creates a copy of the file as an embedded object. Because an embedded object is associated with a particular application, you can edit the object by double-clicking on it or by selecting the object and choosing the Edit Object command. Word will automatically open the associated application. If that application supports OLE 2—as Microsoft Excel 5.0 does, for example—you can edit the object while still seeing it in the context of your Word document.

Figure 18-13 shows a Word document that contains an embedded Microsoft Excel 5.0 worksheet. This figure lets you see how the worksheet normally appears in the document. Figure 18-14 shows how a Microsoft Excel 5.0 worksheet looks when it's open for editing. Notice that the menus and toolbars shown in Figure 18-14 are Excel menus and toolbars.

FIGURE 18-13

This is how an embedded Microsoft Excel 5.0 worksheet normally looks in a Word document.

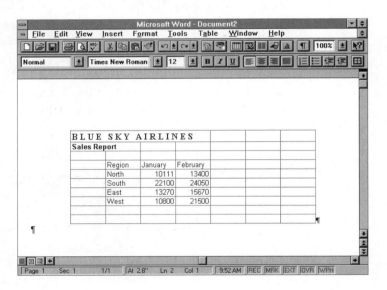

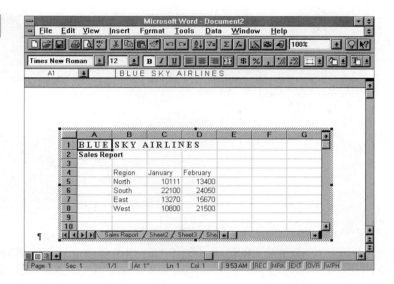

FIGURE 18-14

Here you can see the visual effect of editing a Microsoft Excel 5.0 worksheet embedded in a Word document.

How to link data with the Insert Object command

The easiest way to create a linked object is to use the Insert Object command to link to an already existing file. However, make sure you've checked the Link To File check box on the Create From File card before choosing OK. Word will then create a LINK field rather than an EMBED field and will set it to automatically update the data in the Word document if you change the data in the source file.

How to use the Edit Paste Special command to embed or link data

You can also embed or link data using Word's Edit Paste Special command. Start by loading the source application, opening the appropriate file, and using that program's Edit Copy (or equivalent) command to copy the data to the Windows Clipboard. Then open your document file in Word, and choose the Edit Paste Special command to open the Paste Special dialog box, shown in Figure 18-15 on the next page.

FIGURE 18-15

You can embed or link data from other applications using the Windows Clipboard and the Edit Paste Special command.

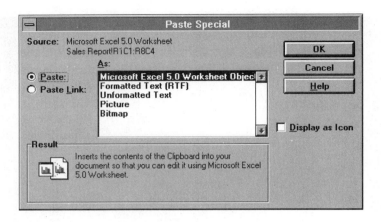

The Paste Special dialog box shows the source of the data that is currently on the Clipboard. It also provides option buttons that let you choose whether to paste or "paste link" the data. If you choose the Paste option button, choosing an item from the As list that is described as an object—such as Microsoft Excel 5.0 Worksheet Object—will result in an embedded object. Other choices from the As list, such as Formatted Text (RTF), Unformatted Text, Picture, and Bitmap, will add data you can edit directly, either as text or as a picture.

If you choose the Paste Link option button, choosing any item in the As list will result in a linked object, although the behavior and appearance of the object will vary because Word will insert the LINK field with different settings depending on the choice. Using Paste Link with an object results in an OLE link.

If you are unsure about how a given choice from the list will be inserted, you can choose the Paste or Paste Link button and then highlight the item in the list. In the Result section of the dialog box, Word will display a short explanation of how the choice will be inserted.

How to update and maintain linked data

If your document includes links to other files using any of several fields—including LINK, INCLUDETEXT, and INCLUDEPICTURE—you can easily change the link settings with the Links dialog box, shown in Figure 18-16. To open the dialog box, choose the Edit Links command, with the cursor or selection located anywhere in the document. (If you haven't defined any links, the Links command on the Edit menu will be grayed.)

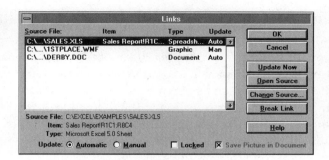

FIGURE 18-16

You can use the Links dialog box to maintain the links between objects in a Word document and their source applications.

The Links dialog box lists all the links currently defined for your document. For each link, it shows the source file, the item (an identification such as a cell range), the type of link (indicating the name or the type of the source application the item was created in), and whether the link is set for manual or automatic update or is locked, which prevents any update.

You can modify the links by highlighting one or more entries in the list and then setting the appropriate options in the dialog box. To highlight a link, simply click on it or move the highlight to it with the arrow keys. You can highlight multiple links by using the standard Windows keyboard or mouse techniques.

After you highlight the links you want to change, you can set the Update option. To keep Word from updating the linked information under any conditions, be sure to check the Locked check box at the bottom of the dialog box. When this check box is checked, Word will gray the Automatic and Manual option buttons. If the box isn't checked, these two option buttons will be available, and you can set the link for either automatic or manual updates, as appropriate.

The Update Now button will update all highlighted links, based on the current version of the source file or files. (There is no reason to choose this button for links that are set for automatic update.) The Open Source button will be available only if you have highlighted a single link. Choose this button to activate or load the source application and to either load the source file or activate the window the source file is already loaded in.

The Break Link button will break the highlighted link. (When you break a link, Word will convert linked text to text and a linked picture to a picture.) If you choose the Change Source button, Word will open the Change Source dialog box, which is similar to Word's Open dialog box. You can use this dialog box to specify a different source file for a link. You can also use the Item text box at the bottom of the dialog box to specify which portion of the linked file to use, such as a range of cells in a Microsoft Excel worksheet.

A quick look at fields for embedding and linking

Although we purposely haven't discussed fields much here, since we'll cover the subject in Chapter 20, one or two additional details demand mention. In particular, you should be aware that you can toggle between seeing field results—such as an embedded object—and seeing field codes by placing your cursor or selection in the field code or field result and either pressing Shift-F9 or checking the Field Codes check box on the Tools Options View card. Figure 18-17, for example, shows both an embedded object and the field code that produces it.

FIGURE 18-17

This figure shows an embedded object—the result of a field—and the field code that produces the field result.

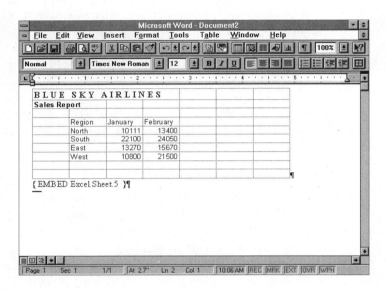

You can create or modify LINK and EMBED fields directly if you like. As we mentioned earlier, you can use a number of optional settings, or switches, with the LINK and EMBED fields. Word's default settings, which it adds when you create these fields with the menu commands, will serve in most cases, but you may want to explore the available choices more closely. To see the list of switches and other information about the field type, use one of the techniques just described to set Word to show the field code, place the cursor in the field, and press F1 to see the Word Help screen for that field.

Many Windows-based programs that don't support OLE do support a feature called dynamic data exchange, or DDE, which is an older, less sophisticated technique for sharing data among programs. Word supplies two fields that take advantage of DDE: DDE and DDEAUTO. Because more and more programs support OLE, odds are that you'll never need to know anything about the DDE fields. But if you do need to use them, you should be aware that these fields are not available on the Insert Field list that we'll discuss in Chapter 20. However, you can still insert them manually by pressing Ctrl-F9 to create Word's field characters and then typing the field code directly into your document. (We'll cover this procedure fully in Chapter 20.)

Both fields use the same format:

{FieldName AppName FileName PlaceReference}

FieldName is either DDE or DDEAUTO, depending on which one you want to use. The DDE field must be updated manually with the F9 key or the Update Field command, while the DDEAUTO field automatically updates the field based on changes in the source file. *AppName* is the name of the source application, such as Excel. *FileName* is the name of the source file. *PlaceReference* is optional, but you can use it to specify a portion of the source file, such as a range of cells in a Microsoft Excel worksheet.

How to create links in other Windows-based programs

Keep in mind that other Windows-based applications can embed and link objects created in Word, just as Word can embed and link objects created in other programs. Look for commands named Paste Special or Paste Link on the Edit menus of other programs; these are the most common choices for implementing these features. You might also want to check the programs' manuals.

PART FOUR

POWER TOOLS

TOPIC FINDER

Headings and Body Text   654

Building an Outline   654
- How to view an outline in Normal view
- How to add body text
- New! How to simplify Outline view
- If you don't like writing from outlines

Selection Techniques   660

Collapsing and Expanding an Outline   662
- A navigation tip

Editing in Outline View   664
- How to change a heading level
- How to insert a new heading
- How to delete a heading
- How to move text and headings

Outline View and Styles   671

Printing an Outline   672

Outline Numbering   673

Master Documents   673

19

Outlining

O utlining is one of those subjects that often seem like religious issues. Some people swear by outlines as a way to help them organize their thoughts, and they wouldn't write anything without one. Others swear at outlines as a constraint to creativity and have no idea what the outline for a given piece of writing should look like until after they've finished writing.

If you fall into the first group, you'll find Word's outlining feature a tremendous help, and you'll probably use it whenever you can.

If you fall into the second group, you may find that the outlining feature can help the way you work as well. Even if you never create an outline to organize your thoughts before writing, you can use the feature after the fact. If your documents include headings of any sort, you can format those headings with Word's heading styles and then use the outline feature to quickly move sections around when you want to change the organization. You can also use the outlining feature to move quickly through a document. Or you can simply use it to look at the current organization while you decide what to write about next.

The basis of Word's outlining feature is Outline view. Outline view works with many of Word's other features to provide a sophisticated, yet easy to use, fully integrated outlining feature.

Outline view provides a collapsible document outline. By *collapsible*, we mean that you can collapse the outline to show just the headings or just certain levels of headings. And because you can easily move from Normal or Page Layout view to Outline view and back, you can use the outline as an aid to organization even while you write.

> Do not confuse Word's outline feature with Word's ability to produce outline-style lists. The collapsible outline feature lets you work with large text documents, collapsing them to show only headings so that you can better grasp the organization of the full document. It also gives you a convenient way to reorganize your document: Move a heading, and all of the collapsed text under that heading moves with it.
>
> In contrast, an outline-style list is simply that: a list that follows an outline format like the one you probably learned in high school. Outline-style lists, which Word calls *multilevel lists*, serve a purpose different from that of a collapsible outline. Because a multilevel list is, in essence, a numbered list rather than an outline in the sense of Word's outline feature, we'll cover it with other numbered lists. For details on creating and using multilevel lists, see "Multilevel numbered paragraphs: Classic outlines" starting on page 482.

To switch to Outline view, choose View Outline. Word will add the Outlining toolbar below the Standard and Formatting toolbars if they are displayed, replacing the ruler if it is displayed. Figure 19-1 shows the buttons on the Outlining toolbar. To leave Outline view, choose View Normal or View Page Layout.

The Outlining toolbar contains a set of buttons you can use to assign heading levels to paragraphs in your document, to expand and collapse your view of the document, to move text, and also to adjust what parts of the document Word displays. We'll look at each of these buttons as we discuss how to use Outline view.

Button	Button Name	Action
	Promote	Changes the selected heading styles (or text) to the next higher level
	Demote	Changes the selected heading styles (or text) to the next lower level
	Demote To Body Text	Changes the selected headings to text under the previous heading
	Move Up	Moves the selected text up one paragraph
	Move Down	Moves the selected text down one paragraph
	Expand	Reveals the next level of headings (or text) below the selected heading or within the selected headings
	Collapse	Hides the lowest level of headings (or text) currently displayed below the selected heading or within the selected headings
 	Show Heading 1 through Show Heading 8	Selects the lowest level of headings to display. All higher-level headings are also displayed
	Show All	Displays all levels of headings and text paragraphs
	Show First Line Only	Displays only a partial first line for all text paragraphs
	Show Formatting	Toggles between displaying the headings and text as formatted and without character formatting
	Master Document View	Displays the Master Document toolbar

FIGURE 19-1

The Outlining toolbar buttons.

Headings and Body Text

Outline view recognizes two categories of text: headings and body text. Each heading is assigned a level, labeled Heading 1 through Heading 9. Everything that's not a heading is body text. You enter headings as you would any other text, usually as single-line paragraphs. You then identify these paragraphs as headings and assign a heading level at the same time, either by directly applying the appropriate heading style or by switching to Outline view and using the appropriate buttons on the Outlining toolbar to apply the style.

The nine heading levels represent categories and subcategories in an outline. For example, in writing this book we've used Heading 1 for section titles; Heading 2 for chapter titles; and Heading 3, Heading 4, and Heading 5 for three levels of headings within each chapter. You can use all of these entries as headings in your finished document, as we have, or you can hide them from view after you finish writing and editing by formatting the heading paragraphs as hidden.

Word helps you visualize the relationships between different parts of your outline by indenting the different levels when you're in Outline view. The headings for main topics—those labeled Heading 1—start at the left margin. Heading 2 entries are indented $1/2$ inch, Heading 3 entries are indented 1 inch, and so on, with each new level indented an additional $1/2$ inch. Body text for any level is indented an additional $1/4$ inch from the heading itself. (More precisely, the amount of indention for each level matches the default tab setting for the document. To see the current default setting for any given document, choose Format Tabs. If you change this setting, Word will change the amount of indention for each level in the outline.)

Building an Outline

The easiest way to become familiar with Outline view is to create a sample document. To illustrate, we'll create the article about free-lancing that we used in Chapter 14 to illustrate multiple text columns. We'll assume the approach of someone who likes to use an outline to help organize ideas and then build on the outline to create a finished document. If you'd like to follow the example, open a new document and choose View Outline to switch to Outline view.

Figure 19-2 shows a portion of our sample article's outline. To create this outline, start by typing the first heading, *Cutting loose*, and then press Enter to start a new paragraph. Whenever you begin a new outline, Word assumes that your first paragraph will be a Heading 1 entry. It also assumes that each subsequent paragraph will be the same level as the previous entry unless you indicate otherwise.

FIGURE 19-2

We'll start by entering headings in Outline view and assigning levels to them.

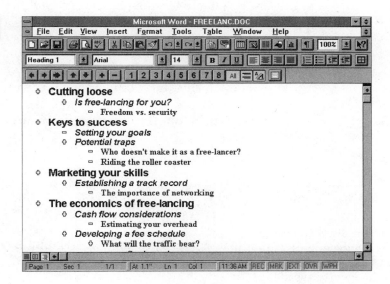

To create the subordinate heading on the second line of the sample outline, you can click on the Demote button on the Outlining toolbar or press Alt-Shift-Right arrow, or you can apply the Heading 2 style by choosing the Format Style command or using the Style drop-down list on the formatting toolbar. Any of these choices will assign both the Heading 2 style and the Heading 2 level to the paragraph.

You can type the text for the paragraph before or after assigning the heading level. Type the phrase *Is free-lancing for you?* Notice that Word has demoted the second paragraph to the Heading 2 level and indented the paragraph $1/2$ inch. You can also see the heading levels by specifying a non-zero setting in the Style Area Width box on the Tools Options View card and using the mouse to adjust the width of the style area as needed. (We covered styles and setting the Style Area Width in Chapter 12.)

Press Enter again to begin the third paragraph; set the heading to level 3 by clicking on the Demote button, pressing Alt-Shift-Right arrow, or applying the Heading 3 style. Then type the text for this heading as well: *Freedom vs. security.*

In addition to the various levels of indention, notice in Figure 19-2 that Word has assigned different character formats to the heading levels. The formats for each heading are defined in the document or its template. If you prefer not to see these formats, you can click on the Show Formatting button or press the slash key on the numeric keypad. (These are toggles, so you can easily switch back and forth between seeing the character formatting and not.) Seeing the text without the formatting, as in Figure 19-3, may make it easier to interpret the structure of your document.

Note also that if you have numbered your outline headings with Format Heading Numbering, the font formatting for the numbers will not change when you use the Show Formatting button to turn off the character formatting of the headings themselves.

FIGURE 19-3

You can click on the Show Formatting button or press the slash key on the numeric keypad to suppress the display of character formatting in Outline view.

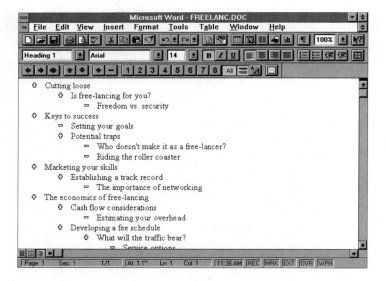

After you type the text for the third heading, you're ready for the next major topic: *Keys to success*. You'll want this paragraph to use the same heading level as the first heading in Figure 19-2. When you press Enter at the end of the third paragraph, however, Word assumes that you want this new paragraph to be at Heading 3 level as well. You'll need to promote the paragraph to Heading 1 level by clicking on the Promote button twice, pressing Alt-Shift-Left arrow twice, or applying the Heading 1 style.

To complete the outline, continue typing the sample text shown in Figures 19-2 and 19-3. Adjust the heading levels as appropriate by clicking on the Promote and Demote buttons, pressing Alt-Shift-Left arrow and Alt-Shift-Right arrow, or assigning the styles directly. Although our sample outline uses only four heading levels, you can create as many as nine. Note that if you're using Word's default styles, there won't be a Heading 4 style in your Formatting toolbar's drop-down Style list until you've created a Heading 4 level by using either of the first two techniques for assigning headings or by typing the style name in the Style text box.

We'll discuss this issue in more detail in a moment. But before we go any further, you should be sure you're familiar with the icons Word uses for headings and body text. You'll see these icons to the left of the paragraphs in Outline view. A small square icon indicates a paragraph of body text. A plus sign indicates a heading with subordinate text or subordinate headings, and a minus sign indicates a heading without subordinate text or subordinate headings. (By *subordinate text and subordinate headings*, we mean all the headings and body text between the current heading and the next heading of an equal or higher level.)

How to view an outline in Normal view

As you enter the outline text, keep in mind that Outline view is really just another type of document view. Any actions you take in Outline view will also affect what you see in other views. For example, if you return to Normal view after typing the sample outline shown in Figure 19-2, your screen will look like the one in Figure 19-4. As you can see, Word's default style formats still make it easy to identify the relationships among the headings.

FIGURE 19-4

If you switch back to Normal view, the document's text will look like this.

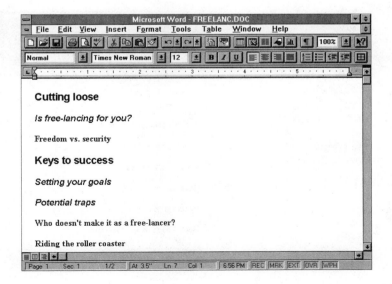

When you return to Normal view, you'll see that each heading level carries different character and paragraph formats. If you observe the Style box on the Formatting toolbar as you move the cursor through your text (or if you set the style area to a non-zero value, as we've already suggested), you'll see the heading style assigned to each paragraph.

When you create an outline, Word assigns styles behind the scenes, even if you don't explicitly assign styles yourself. As we discussed in Chapter 12, Word's default is to offer the styles Heading 1, Heading 2, and Heading 3 in every document's drop-down Style list. If you need more, you can access additional styles, as we've indicated by demoting a paragraph in Outline view to create a heading at one of the additional levels (through Heading 9). And, of course, you can modify the style definitions to change the format for different heading levels. We'll come back to this idea later in this chapter. First, however, we'll add some body text and explore techniques for editing a document in Outline view.

How to add body text

You can add body text to a document while in Outline view, but you'll generally want to use Normal view instead. In Normal view, you can see more text on screen at once, without the indents on each line to indicate outline level. If you're following our example and you're ready to add some body text, switch to Normal view (if you're not there already) by choosing View Normal. Next place the cursor immediately before the paragraph mark at the end of the first paragraph, and press Enter to create a new paragraph. Word will automatically format the paragraph as Normal, applying the Normal style as defined in your document, as shown in Figure 19-5.

FIGURE 19-5

In Normal or Page Layout view, when you position the cursor after the last character in a heading paragraph and press Enter, Word automatically assigns the Normal style to the next paragraph.

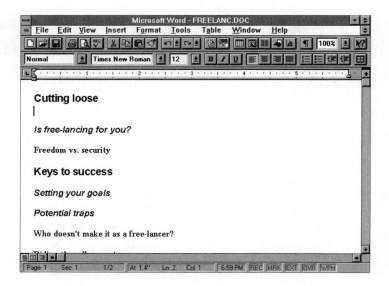

After typing some body text, toggle back to Outline view and notice what happens to the outline. As Figure 19-6 shows, Word redisplays the indentions to show the relationships between headings. Also notice that each body-text paragraph is indented ¼ inch more than the heading it falls under, providing another visual clue to the document's organization.

FIGURE 19-6

When you return to Outline view, you'll see that each body-text paragraph is indented ¼ inch to the right of the heading it falls under.

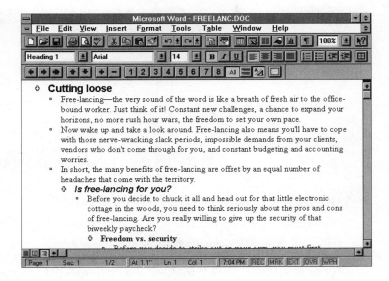

How to simplify Outline view

To help reduce clutter in Outline view and see the structure of your document better, you can toggle between seeing all of the body text and seeing just the first line of each paragraph by clicking on the Show First Line Only button on the Outlining toolbar—the third button from the right—or by pressing the equivalent shortcut keys. By default, the shortcut key is Alt-Shift-L. Press Alt-Shift-L or click on the button once and, as shown in Figure 19-7 on the next page, you'll see just enough text for each paragraph to help remind you of the topic. When you condense the body text this way, Word will place ellipses at the end of each line to indicate that there's more in the paragraph. If you want to view the full text again, press Alt-Shift-L or click on the Show First Line Only button a second time.

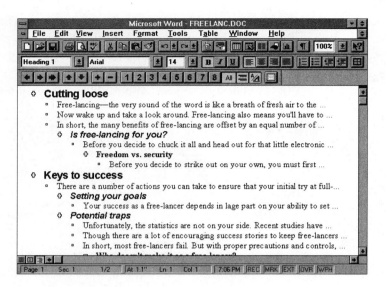

FIGURE 19-7

To simplify your view of the document, press Alt-Shift-L to show only the first line of each text paragraph.

If you don't like writing from outlines

So far we've assumed that you'll start by creating an outline before filling in the text. But even if you don't, you can get to this same point by a different route. If you prefer writing without an outline (or keeping the outline in your head), simply write the text as you usually would, but be sure to assign the appropriate heading and body styles to each paragraph, as we described in Chapter 12. Even if you never switch to Outline view, you'll want to assign the heading styles to the heading levels just for their formatting capabilities. As we'll discuss shortly, however, you can make good use of Outline view for other purposes.

Selection Techniques

After you've entered some or all of the headings and body text for your first draft, you'll probably need to make some changes in your text and reorganize it a bit. At this point, it doesn't matter whether you started with an outline or not, provided you've used the heading styles for your headings.

Word offers several shortcuts for editing a document in Outline view. As in Normal view, you must select the text before you can edit it. More important, Word provides selection techniques that work only in Outline view.

When you're working within a single paragraph of an outline, you can use Word's standard selection techniques (described in Chapter 3) to select the text to work with. For example, to select an entire word, you can double-click on that word, or place the cursor anywhere in the word and press F8 twice. To select an entire sentence, press the Ctrl key and click on that sentence, or place the cursor anywhere in the sentence and press F8 three times.

In Normal view, you can select an entire paragraph by double-clicking in the selection bar next to that paragraph or by placing the cursor in the paragraph and pressing F8 four times. In Outline view, F8 works the same way; however, selection with the mouse works a little differently. You need to click only once in the selection bar to select an entire paragraph, whether it is a heading or body text. You can also select an entire heading by placing the cursor anywhere in the heading and then holding down the Shift key while clicking on the heading's icon. (The pointer will change to the four-headed arrow shape when it is on the icon.)

If you double-click in the selection bar next to a heading or click on a heading's icon without pressing the Shift key, you will highlight not only the heading next to the pointer, but also all the subordinate text and headings below that heading.

For example, if you click once in the selection bar next to the Heading 1 entry *Cutting loose* at the top of the outline in Figure 19-7, you will highlight that entire paragraph. If you double-click in the selection bar next to this heading, however, or if you click on the heading icon next to this heading once, your screen will look like the one shown in Figure 19-8. As you can see, Word highlights the paragraph containing the text *Cutting loose* as well as the subordinate text up to the next Heading 1 paragraph.

FIGURE 19-8

To highlight a heading and all its subordinate text and headings, double-click in the selection bar next to the heading or click on the heading icon once.

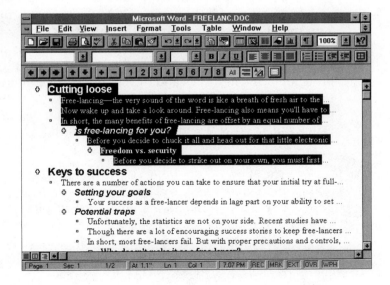

Collapsing and Expanding an Outline

Even if you're displaying only the first line of each paragraph of body text, the outline can get pretty lengthy after you've created several levels of headings and inserted body text under each. If you lose the sense of the document's organization, you can eliminate some of the clutter by collapsing the outline to hide the body text and selected levels of headings.

For example, suppose you want to see only the Heading 1 entries in your outline. To collapse the outline, click on the Show Heading 1 button (labeled *1*) on the Outlining toolbar, or press Alt-Shift-1. As shown in Figure 19-9, Word will hide all body text and subheadings below the level 1 headings. In addition, Word will place a faint underline under any headings that have subordinate text or headings hidden from view.

FIGURE 19-9

When you click on the Show Heading 1 button, Word will collapse your outline to show only Heading 1 entries.

To expand the outline again, click on another Show button to indicate the highest-numbered level you want shown, or press the equivalent Alt-Shift key combination. For example, if you click on the Show Heading 3 button or press Alt-Shift-3, Word will expand the outline to display all Heading 1, Heading 2, and Heading 3 entries, with body text still hidden from view. To bring all of the headings and the body text back into view, click the All button, press Alt-Shift-A, or press the asterisk key (*) on the numeric keypad. (Note that there is no Show button for level 9 headings. You must use the keyboard shortcut, Alt-Shift-9, to show heading level 9.)

The Show buttons affect the display of the entire outline; however, the Expand and Collapse buttons—indicated with a plus for the Expand button and a minus for the Collapse button—affect only the currently selected portions of an outline. You can also use the plus and minus keys on your numeric keypad as Expand and Collapse keys by themselves, or use the plus and hyphen keys in the top row of your keyboard in combination with Alt-Shift.

For example, suppose you want to collapse only the headings and body text below the second Heading 1 entry (*Keys to success*) in the document shown in Figure 19-8. Position the cursor in the heading and then click on the Collapse button, press the minus key on your numeric keypad, or press Alt-Shift-Hyphen. As shown in Figure 19-10, Word will collapse all of the body text that originally appeared under that heading. If you use the collapse feature again, Word will collapse all Heading 3 entries below that heading; if you use it a third time, Word will collapse all Heading 2 entries. To reverse this process, place the cursor in the heading and then click on the Expand button, press the plus key on the numeric keypad, or press Alt-Shift-Plus.

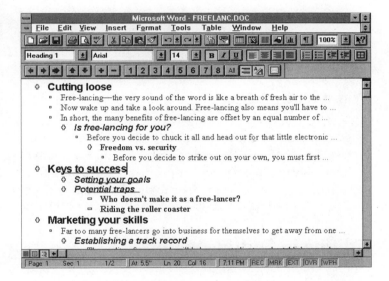

FIGURE 19-10

You can use the Collapse button, the minus key on your numeric keypad, or Alt-Shift-Hyphen to collapse selected portions of the outline.

As you can see in Figure 19-10, when you use these expand and collapse techniques, Word will act on only the text that falls between the current heading and the next heading of an equal or higher level. In our example, Word collapsed only the text between the second and third Heading 1 entries. You could also move the cursor to a Heading 2 entry to collapse all text between that heading and the next heading of the same or a higher level.

To collapse or expand all subordinate text and headings below a particular heading in one step, first click on the plus symbol next to the heading to select all text under that heading. Alternatively, you can select the entire heading and then use the collapse feature by clicking on the Collapse button or pressing the equivalent shortcut keys.

Selecting the heading with the keyboard can be a little tricky because the part you really need to select is the paragraph mark. If paragraph marks are showing, simply select the paragraph mark and Word will automatically highlight the rest of the heading. However, if the paragraph marks are not showing, you can start with the cursor near the end of the heading and extend the selection. As you extend the selection toward the end of the paragraph, you will eventually select the invisible paragraph mark, and Word will automatically select the rest of the heading paragraph. You can then use the collapse or expand feature. When collapsing text, you can extend the selection into the next paragraph without changing the way the collapse feature will work. When expanding text, however, be sure to select only those headings you want to expand.

A navigation tip

When you are working with a long document that contains headings and you want to move to a particular area, you can use Outline view to quickly move to the section you want to go to. Switch to Outline view, and collapse the outline to the level appropriate for seeing the heading you want to look for. Next, move the cursor to that heading, and switch back to Normal view. At this point, Word will display the part of the document you want to see.

Editing in Outline View

In Outline view, you can use any of Word's usual editing techniques to edit text. However, be aware that if you use the Edit Find or Edit Replace command, Word will not search collapsed text or headings.

If you want to search or replace throughout the text in your document, you'll usually find it easier to do so in Normal or Page Layout view. However, if you want to search only through text that appears in headings, you may be able to streamline the search or search-and-replace procedure by working in Outline view, set to see the appropriate level of headings.

In addition to the standard editing techniques, Word offers a number of special editing features for use in Outline view only. These include commands for changing heading levels and for adding, deleting, and moving headings.

How to change a heading level

You can change the level of a heading at any time, using the commands we discussed in the context of creating the outline. Place the cursor or selection in the paragraph or paragraphs you want to change. Then you can click on the Promote button or the Demote button, or you can press Alt-Shift-Left arrow to promote the heading one level or Alt-Shift-Right arrow to demote the heading one level, or you can apply the appropriate style to the paragraph.

When you use the promote or demote feature to change a heading level, Word will immediately assign the new heading level to the paragraph, change the indention of the paragraph to reflect its new level, and adjust the indention of any body text immediately below the heading. Unless you tell it to, however, Word will not change the levels of subordinate headings in the outline or body text under those headings.

If you want to promote or demote a heading and all of its subordinate text and headings, you must first select the subordinate text and headings along with the heading. You can then click on the Promote or Demote button or use the appropriate keyboard commands to change all the heading levels at the same time.

After you've selected a heading and all of its subordinate text and headings, you can press Alt-Shift-Left arrow or Alt-Shift-Right arrow to promote or demote the entire block at once. (Don't apply styles, because a style would apply to all of the selected text.) Alternatively, you can drag the heading icon for the highest-level heading to the left or right. The mouse pointer will take the shape of a double-headed arrow as you drag, and Word will display a dotted vertical line to indicate where the heading will appear when you release the mouse button. The line will move in $\frac{1}{2}$-inch increments, snapping to each possible level.

For example, let's say that you click on the heading icon next to *Keys to success* in Figure 19-7 on page 660 (or double-click in the selection bar), to select the heading and its subordinate text, and then click on the Demote button. Your outline will look like the one shown in Figure 19-11 on the next page. It will also look like Figure 19-11 if you drag the heading icon one level to the right. If you're using the keyboard, place the cursor before the word

Keys in the Heading 1 entry and use the Shift-arrow key combinations to select all subordinate headings and body text down to the next Heading 1 entry. Then, to demote the highlighted text, press Alt-Shift-Right arrow.

FIGURE 19-11

To demote a heading
and its subordinate
text and headings, first
select everything you
want to demote, and
then use the demote
feature.

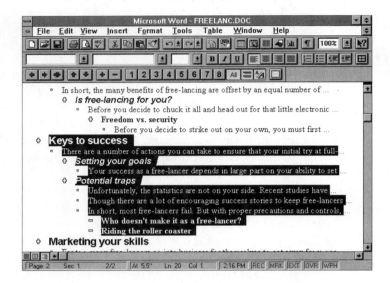

Whichever route you choose, Figure 19-11 shows how Word will demote
all subordinate headings and body text between the *Keys to success* heading
and the next Heading 1 entry. The *Keys to success* heading and its subordinate
text now fall under the first Heading 1 entry, *Cutting loose*.

How to convert body text to a heading

You can convert body text to a heading with the same commands you use for
changing heading levels. If you place the cursor in a body-text paragraph
while in Outline view and then click on the Promote button, press Alt-Shift-
Left arrow, or drag the body-text icon to the left, Word will convert that
body text to the same level as its immediately superior heading. For example, if you move the cursor to the body-text paragraph that begins *Free-
lancing—the very sound* in the second line of our sample outline and then click
on the Promote button, Word will promote the entire paragraph to a level 1
heading. If you click on the Demote button instead, Word will convert the
body text to a heading one level below its immediately superior heading. As

Figure 19-12 shows, when you convert the paragraph to a heading, Word will display the entire contents of that heading rather than only the first line.

When you convert body text to a heading, Word also shows the full paragraph.

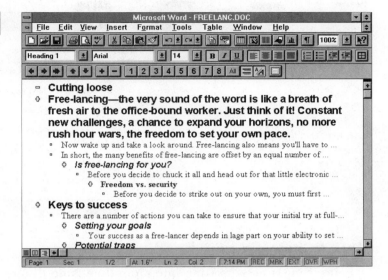

How to convert a heading to body text

To convert a heading to body text, place the cursor in the heading and then click on the Demote To Body Text button or press Alt-Shift-NumPad5 (5 on the numeric keypad). Note that NumLock must be *off* for the Alt-Shift-NumPad5 keystroke to work.

When you convert a heading to body text, Word will change the indention of that paragraph and any subordinate body text immediately below it so that it is $^1/_4$ inch to the right of the heading immediately preceding it. In short, the paragraph and any body text between it and the next heading become part of the subordinate body text for the preceding heading.

For example, if you start with our sample document as it appears in Figure 19-10 on page 663, move the cursor to the Heading 2 entry *Is free-lancing for you?* and click on the Demote To Body Text button, your screen will look like the one shown in Figure 19-13 on the next page. Notice that the body text formerly attached to the Heading 2 level now shows the same indention as the rest of the body text for the Heading 1 entry *Cutting loose*. As you can see, however, Word did not change the Heading 3 entry *Freedom vs. security* below the converted Heading 2 entry.

FIGURE 19-13

You can use the Demote To Body Text button or Alt-Shift-NumPad5 (5 on the numeric keypad) to convert a heading to body text.

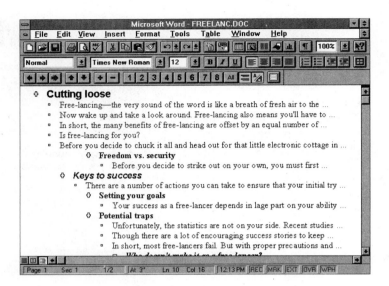

How to insert a new heading

Inserting a new heading into an outline is no different from inserting any other kind of text. Place the cursor where you want the heading, press Enter, and then use any of the techniques we've discussed to set the appropriate heading level.

How to delete a heading

Just as you can insert a heading like any other text, so too can you delete a heading. Be careful, though. Before you delete a heading, be sure to expand the outline or switch to Normal or Page Layout view. Otherwise, you may inadvertently delete all subordinate text for the heading as well.

It's important to realize that when you select a heading in a collapsed outline, you also select the subordinate text for that heading. For example, if you select the Heading 1 entry *Cutting loose* as shown in Figure 19-9 on page 662 and then expand the outline, you'll see that Word has selected all of the subordinate text between the first level 1 heading and the second one. In short, any changes you make to a heading while the outline is collapsed will affect all subordinate text and headings below that heading.

How to move text and headings

There are four ways to move blocks of text while in Outline view. The first is the standard cut-and-paste procedure. Select the heading and any subordinate text you want to move, choose Edit Cut, select the spot where you want to place the text, and choose Edit Paste. Similarly, you can use Word's drag-and-drop technique (assuming the option is active) to drag any text selection from one place to another in the document. Word also provides several methods of moving text that are meant primarily for Outline view: the Move Up and Move Down buttons, the equivalent keyboard commands Alt-Shift-Up arrow and Alt-Shift-Down arrow, and a click-and-drag technique in which you click on a heading or body-text icon and drag the text.

When you use the Edit Cut command to delete or move text while in Outline view, your changes may affect more than the text that is currently visible. Keep in mind that selecting a heading that includes collapsed subordinate text and headings automatically selects the collapsed text and headings as well.

If you do not want Word to move the subordinate text along with the selected heading, you'll need to expand the outline before you select the heading and choose the Edit Cut command. However, if you want Word to include the subordinate text in your selection, you may find it easier to collapse the outline before you begin the cut-and-paste procedure. (The same comments apply to copying text.) Similarly, when you select your paste area, you may want to expand any collapsed text in that area to ensure that you're inserting the text exactly where you mean to.

Note that these comments about moving selected text, including collapsed subordinate text and headings, apply to all techniques for moving text or headings in Outline view. In fact, this is one of the strengths of Outline view—it gives you the ability to reorganize a document, including all the text in each section, simply by collapsing the document and moving the headings. You can then rewrite as necessary to maintain logical transitions between the sections.

You can use the Move Up and Move Down buttons to move selected text without cutting it first. To use the buttons, place the cursor or selection in the paragraph you want to move, or extend the selection into the paragraphs you want to move. Then click on the Move Up button to move the text up one paragraph, or click on the Move Down button to move the text down one paragraph. If you've selected only part of a paragraph, Word will extend the selection to include the entire paragraph and any collapsed subordinate text and headings before it moves the text. The shortcut keys for this function are Alt-Shift-Up arrow (move up) and Alt-Shift-Down arrow (move down).

 When you move text up or down by one paragraph, you'll move the text by paragraphs that currently show on screen, skipping any collapsed text. If you need to move the text a long distance, you can save time by collapsing some or all of the outline text before you begin.

One of the most convenient ways to move text is by clicking and dragging. Just as you can drag text to the left and right to promote and demote paragraphs, you can point to a heading icon or a body-text icon, hold down the mouse button, and drag the icon—and the text it represents, including any subordinate text—up or down to reposition it in your document. If you click on a heading icon, you'll automatically select all subordinate body text and headings and move those too, even if that section of the outline isn't collapsed. If you click on a body-text icon, you'll select only the one paragraph. When you drag an icon, Word displays a line across the Word window to indicate where the text will be inserted.

You can use Alt-Shift-Up arrow and Alt-Shift-Down arrow to move text in Normal or Page Layout view also. Place the cursor in the paragraph you want to move, or extend the selection to include any other paragraphs you want to move, and then press Alt-Shift-Up arrow or Alt-Shift-Down arrow, as appropriate. Word will select the entire paragraph or paragraphs and move them up or down by one paragraph for each keystroke.

This can be a handy trick for moving text around. But if you use it in Outline view, be careful. The selection that Word automatically makes in the text to decide how much text to move up or down depends on the setting for the Show buttons. If the setting in Outline view is Show All, then Word will highlight and move just the paragraph or paragraphs that the cursor or selection is in. If Show is set to any other level, however, Word may highlight more text than you intend. If it's set to Show Heading 1, for example, and you press Alt-Shift-Up arrow in Normal view, Word will highlight all text between the cursor and the next paragraph formatted as Heading level 1. It will then proceed to move the entire selection.

Note, too, that several other outline shortcut keys will work in Normal mode as well. Alt-Shift-Right arrow and Alt-Shift-Left arrow will promote and demote selected paragraphs, and Alt-Shift-NumPad5 (provided that NumLock is off) will convert a selected paragraph to Normal style. This last shortcut, in particular, can be handy when you're reformatting your documents.

Outline View and Styles

As we've mentioned, Outline view works in conjunction with styles. When you edit a document in Outline view, Word assumes you will want to use each topic in the outline as a heading in your document, and it assigns each level of heading an automatic style named for that level—Heading 1, Heading 2, and so on.

In Chapter 12, we pointed out that Word has nine automatic heading styles corresponding to nine heading levels. By default, Word supplies three of these in the Formatting toolbar's Style drop-down list. It automatically adds the others as needed, when you create the first heading in any document at level 4, level 5, or beyond.

In addition to giving you a head start by providing automatic styles, Word provides some clear differences in the formatting for these styles. Figure 19-14 shows the default definitions for each.

Style Name	Default Definition
Heading 1	Normal + Font: Arial, 14 Point, Bold, Space Before 12 pt After 3 pt, Keep With Next
Heading 2	Normal + Font: Arial, 12 Point, Bold, Italic, Space Before 12 pt After 3 pt, Keep With Next
Heading 3	Normal + Font: 12 Point, Bold, Space Before 12 pt After 3 pt, Keep With Next
Heading 4	Normal + Font: 12 Point, Bold, Italic, Space Before 12 pt After 3 pt, Keep With Next
Heading 5	Normal + Font: Arial, 11 Point, Space Before 12 pt After 3 pt
Heading 6	Normal + Font: Arial, 11 Point, Italic, Space Before 12 pt After 3 pt
Heading 7	Normal + Font: Arial, Space Before 12 pt After 3 pt
Heading 8	Normal + Font: Arial, Italic, Space Before 12 pt After 3 pt
Heading 9	Normal + Font: Arial, 9 Point, Italic, Space Before 12 pt After 3 pt

FIGURE 19-14

Heading styles and their default definitions.

You can easily change these style definitions. First, because they are all based on the Normal style, start by modifying the Normal style to suit the document, using the techniques we described in Chapter 12. You can then make additional changes to the definitions for each heading style.

To modify each style, follow the procedures we described in Chapter 12. Choose Format Style to open the Style dialog box, choose the name of the style you want to modify, and then choose Modify to open the Modify Style dialog box. Next specify the character and paragraph formats for that heading level. When you're satisfied with your changes, choose OK to return to the Style dialog box, and repeat the process for the next style you want to change. When you're done, choose Close to close the dialog box, and Word will apply the specified formats to the headings in your document.

If you don't want a particular heading level to appear in your finished document, simply format the style for that heading level as Hidden. Then choose Tools Options and choose the Print card to verify that the check box for printing hidden text is cleared. Finally, to make sure that the page breaks on your screen will match the page breaks when the document is printed, choose Tools Options, choose the View card, and make sure the Hidden Text check box is cleared there too so that Word won't show the hidden text on screen either.

If you change the definitions for the heading styles, you may want to change the Based On styles as well. You can base each heading style on the next-highest heading style instead of Normal. You might want to leave Heading 1 based on Normal but base Heading 2 on Heading 1 and base Heading 3 on Heading 2. That way, if you make format changes to the Heading 1 style—new indention settings, for example—those changes will affect all heading levels for the document automatically.

Printing an Outline

To print an outline, simply switch to Outline view, if you're not there already, and choose File Print. You can control which levels will be printed by expanding or collapsing the outline. In general, what you see on the screen is what will be printed, with one exception: Even if only the first lines of any body-text paragraphs are displayed, Word prints all paragraphs in their entirety.

In the printed outline, Word will ignore paragraph formatting for the text, using the indentions you see on the screen in Outline view instead;

however, it will apply the character formatting, as well as any headers, footers, section breaks, or manual page breaks you've added to the document. Figure 19-15 shows the printed version of the outline for our sample document, collapsed to show heading levels 1, 2, and 3.

FIGURE 19-15

You can use the File Print command to print a copy of your outline.

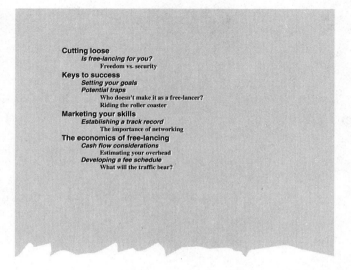

Outline Numbering

After you have created an outline, you can use Word's automatic numbering feature to number some or all of the outline's headings and body text. Choose Format Heading Numbering, and then choose the numbering system you want to use. We covered automatic numbering in detail in Chapter 13, "Bullets, Numbering, & Sections," page 468.

Master Documents

There is one button on the Outlining toolbar that we have not discussed: the far right button, Master Document View, which switches between Outline and Master Document views. Master Document view is similar to Outline view in that both use the Outlining toolbar. And knowing how to work in Outline view is important for working with a master document. Because Master Document view is intended for working with long documents, however, it's more appropriate to discuss it along with other features for working with long documents. We'll cover master documents in "How to use Master Document view" starting on page 590.

TOPIC FINDER

What Is a Field?   675
- Result fields   • Marker fields   • Action fields

The Format for Fields   676
- Field types   • Field characters   • Arguments

Inserting Fields   679
- NEW! How to insert fields with the Insert Field command   • How to insert fields with the Insert Field key (Ctrl-F9)   • How to insert fields with other menu commands

Field Results vs. Field Codes   683
- How to change the Tools Options View Field Codes setting   • How to toggle between codes and results for selected fields or for the whole document   NEW! How to set field shading to indicate fields   • How to update a field's result (F9)   • How to update a source for an INCLUDETEXT field (Ctrl-Shift-F7)   • How to lock a field (Ctrl-F11 or Ctrl-3)   • How to lock a field that's part of a BOOKMARK, an INCLUDETEXT, or a REF field result   • How to unlock a field (Ctrl-Shift-F11 or Ctrl-4)   • How to unlink a field (Ctrl-Shift-F9)   • How to move to a field (F11, Alt-F1, Shift-F11, Alt-Shift-F1)

Editing Fields   689
- How to delete or copy a field

Formatting Field Results   690
- How to set character formatting for a field result   • How to control case   • How to control numeric formats   • How to use the numeric picture switch   • The Date-Time Picture switch

Nesting Fields   696

DATE and TIME Fields   696
- How to insert a date or a time

Summary Information Fields   700
- The TITLE field   • The SUBJECT, AUTHOR, KEYWORDS, and COMMENTS fields   • The INFO field

Statistical Fields   703
- The CREATEDATE field   • The EDITTIME field   • The FILENAME field   • NEW! The FILESIZE field   • The LASTSAVEDBY field   • The NUMCHARS field   • The NUMPAGES field   • The NUMWORDS field   • The PRINTDATE field   • The REVNUM field   • The SAVEDATE field   • The TEMPLATE field   • Using the INFO field instead of statistical fields

User Information Fields   707

Action Fields   707
- The MACROBUTTON field   • The GOTOBUTTON field

Other Fields and Where to Find Them in This Book   713

20

Fields

n this chapter, we'll look at one of Word's most notable strengths: fields. We've mentioned fields elsewhere, including Chapters 5, 16, and 18. In this chapter, we'll look at how to display and recalculate a field's result, how to edit a field, and how to change the format of a field result. We'll also look at some specific fields in depth—including Word's DATE and TIME fields—and we'll look at several categories of fields, including document information, user information, and document automation fields.

What Is a Field?

A field is a special code that you can enter in a document. You can use fields for something as straightforward as adding a date to a header or as complex as building an index. Fields give Word tremendous flexibility and broaden the range of what you can do with a word processor. Word offers approximately 70 fields that can be divided into three categories: result fields, marker fields, and action fields.

675

Result fields

Most of the fields you'll use frequently are result fields. Result fields retrieve a particular piece of information and place it in the document. When you enter the DATE field, for example, it retrieves the current date from your computer's system clock and enters that date at the field position. Similarly, the AUTHOR field retrieves the name of the document's author and places that information at the field position.

Marker fields

A marker field does not return a result. Rather, it supplies information to Word. For example, you can use the XE (Index Entry) field to mark entries for an index. The Index Entry field does not return a result; it merely provides the information that Word uses to compile the index.

Action fields

Unlike result and marker fields, action fields tell Word to perform an action. For example, the FILLIN field tells Word to prompt the user for information and to store that information in the document. Some action fields tell Word to perform the action only when you update the fields; others tell Word to perform the action automatically.

The Format for Fields

All fields share a similar format. All have names, and all are enclosed in field characters. In addition, many fields have one or more arguments, or instructions. The arguments may tell the field what to act on, or they may control the way the field displays its result. For example, in the field {DATE \@ "MMM-yy"}, the field name is DATE, the field characters are { and }, and the arguments are \@ and MMM-yy. This field tells Word to retrieve the current date from your computer's system clock and display it in the MMM-yy format, as in Jan-95.

Field types

A *field type* is a short, descriptive word or phrase that helps identify what the field does. For example, the DATE field returns the current date, the TIME field returns the current time, and the FILLIN field prompts the user to fill in a blank in the document. In most cases, the field type and the field name are the same; in some, however, the field name is an abbreviation for the field type. For example, the field name for the Index Entry field is XE. That is,

Index Entry is the field type; however, you must use the field name, XE, when inserting the field into a document.

Field characters

Field names are always enclosed in the field characters { and }. Word will treat the enclosed text as a field. You cannot generate these characters by typing curly brackets from your keyboard. You enter them by either pressing Ctrl-F9 or choosing the Insert Field command. We'll show you how shortly.

Arguments

Most of Word's fields allow *arguments*; some require them. An argument tells Word either what to operate on or how to display the field's result.

The argument in the field {INCLUDETEXT "budget.doc"} is the document name BUDGET.DOC. The INCLUDETEXT field tells Word to insert the contents of another document into the current document. The *budget.doc* argument tells Word which document file to insert.

Notice that we've enclosed this argument in quotation marks. Word requires quotation marks only around multiple-word arguments, to indicate that all the words are part of a single argument. However, it generally does no harm to add the quotation marks, and you may prefer adding them in every case to make sure that they're there when needed.

When a field requires more than one argument, you must either enclose each argument in quotation marks or separate the arguments by a space. As we discussed in Chapter 15, you can mark part of a document file with a bookmark and then use the INCLUDETEXT field to include just the bookmark. The field would have two arguments and would take the form {INCLUDETEXT budget.doc FirstQuarter} or {INCLUDETEXT "budget.doc" "FirstQuarter"}. You could also add a space between the two arguments in quotation marks.

If you need to use a literal quotation mark within an argument, you must precede it with a backslash (\). To include a backslash as part of an argument—as in the case of a pathname—you must type two backslashes (\\).

Field arguments can include literal text, formulas, bookmarks, identifiers, switches, or other fields. Here's a brief look at each type of argument.

Literal text

Some field arguments consist of literal text, as with the INCLUDETEXT field. To place the contents of the document BUDGET.DOC in the current document, you type the actual name of the document file so that the field reads {INCLUDETEXT "budget.doc"}.

Formulas

Other field arguments consist of a mathematical formula, or expression. The = (Formula) field takes a mathematical formula and calculates the result. For example, the field {= 2+2} would return the result 4. Note that the = (Formula) field does not accept quotation marks around its argument.

 If you're familiar with Word 2.0, you may recognize the = (Formula) field as a new name for the Expression field in Word 2.0. The = (Formula) field, however, offers new functions not available in Word 2.0. We'll discuss this field in detail in Chapter 23.

Bookmarks

As we discussed in Chapter 10, a bookmark is a name you assign to selected text in a document. You saw the FirstQuarter bookmark in our earlier example of using multiple arguments with the INCLUDETEXT field. You can use a bookmark as an argument in several different kinds of fields. The field {INCLUDETEXT "budget.doc" "FirstQuarter"} will return the text defined by the bookmark FirstQuarter in the BUDGET.DOC document. The field {PAGEREF "FirstQuarter"} will return the page number where you'll find the FirstQuarter bookmark in the current document. We'll discuss the PAGEREF field in "Creating Cross-References" on page 832.

Identifiers

Some fields require an *identifier* argument. This is simply a name that identifies a series of terms in a group. For example, you can use the SEQ (Sequence) field to label a specific series of items—such as figures, tables, or illustrations—for automatic numbering. Because you'll sometimes need to label two separately numbered series—such as tables and figures—in a document, you can optionally supply an identifier in the field to tell Word which sequence the field is part of.

For example, you could number each figure as Figure {SEQ "figure"} and each table as Table {SEQ "table"}. Word will maintain separate numeric sequences for the two sets of items. We recommend using identifiers that describe the items you are numbering, since they will be easier to remember.

Switches

Fields can also use *switches* as arguments. A switch consists of a backslash (\) followed by a single character. Some switches are followed by an additional argument. A switch changes the way a field works or the way it formats its result. Without a switch, the field {TIME} returns the current time in h:m AM/PM format. If you want a field that uses 24-hour format with a leading zero, add the switch \@HH:mm so that the field becomes {TIME \@ "HH:mm"}. We'll discuss this and other switches for the TIME field later in this chapter.

Inserting Fields

As we've already mentioned, you cannot type the curly brackets that serve as the beginning and end markers for a field definition. However, Word provides more than one way to enter the curly brackets: by themselves, in combination with field names, or as part of a complete field definition.

How to insert fields with the Insert Field command

It may take you a while to learn each of the fields that you'll use regularly, and you may never learn the format for fields that you use only occasionally. The Insert Field command is usually the easiest method for inserting those fields you're not familiar with.

Place the cursor where you want to insert a field, and then choose Insert Field to open the Field dialog box, shown in Figure 20-1. You can define the field completely from within this dialog box.

FIGURE 20-1

The Field dialog box is usually the simplest way to enter fields when you don't already know the field names and arguments.

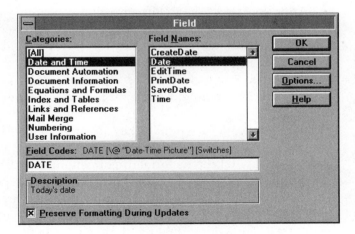

Word gives you two ways to find and choose a field. You can accept the default [All] choice in the Categories list box, and Word will list all fields in the Field Names list box. Alternatively, you can choose any specific category in the Categories list box, and Word will list only those fields from the chosen category.

As a rule of thumb, if you know the exact name of the field you want, you can usually find it most quickly by choosing [All] in the Categories list box, and then, in the Field Names list box, pressing the key corresponding to the first character of the field name as many times as necessary to highlight the name. If you don't know the exact field name, you can usually find it by choosing the appropriate category and then browsing through the shorter list in the Field Names list box. If necessary, you can move through the Field Names list box with the Up and Down arrow keys. As you highlight each name, Word will show you a description of that field in the Description box near the bottom of the dialog box.

To insert a field, select it in the Field Names list box. If you scroll through the list, you'll notice that Word automatically places the selected field name in the Field Codes text box below the Categories list box, and a short description of the field in the Description box just below that. The syntax for the field appears to the right of the title for the Field Codes text box. You can use the syntax sample as a guide for your own entry.

In Figure 20-1, we've selected the Date And Time category and the field name Date. Word has entered DATE in the Field Codes text box and displays the syntax, *DATE [\@ "Date-Time Picture"][Switches]*, above the text box. The comment *Today's date* appears in the Description box.

After you select the field name, you can simply choose OK, and Word will insert the field name in your document, enclosed in field characters. If you want to add any arguments, you can type them in. Alternatively, you can type an argument directly in the Field Codes text box, using the syntax above the text box as your model. When the entry is complete, choose OK. Word will insert the field name, argument, and field characters into your document.

By default, Word will add the format switch with the MergeFormat argument to fields you define with the Field dialog box so that, once formatted, the field will keep its formatting if you update it later. If you don't want this switch, clear the Preserve Formatting During Updates check box at the bottom of the Field dialog box. Alternatively, you can delete the switch from the field after Word inserts it into your document. For more about the format switch, see "Formatting Field Results" on page 690.

If you need more details for filling in the arguments—such as detailed information about the Date-Time Picture or Switches argument in Figure 20-1—choose the Options button. Word will open the Field Options dialog box, which contains cards similar to the ones shown in Figure 20-2.

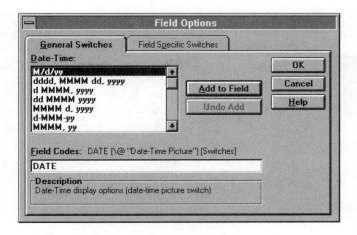

FIGURE 20-2

The Field Options dialog box will help you fill in specific arguments for fields.

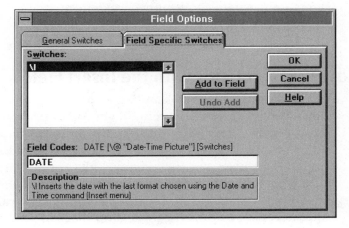

The specifics of the Field Options dialog box will vary, depending on the field you've selected in the Field dialog box. In some cases, the Options button will be grayed and the dialog box unavailable. Specifically, if the field allows arguments, you'll generally be able to choose the Options button and use the Field Options dialog box.

In Figure 20-2, the list box on the left side of the General Switches card, labeled Date-Time, contains format choices for Date-Time Picture. We'll discuss these later in this chapter. For the moment, simply note that you can highlight the format you want and then choose the Add To Field button; Word will add the argument to the Field Codes text box. (Notice that the text box still appears at the bottom of the Field Options dialog box.) Once you've added an argument, the Undo Add button will be active, and you can re-move the argument by choosing the button.

As you can see in Figure 20-2, the Field Options dialog box for the DATE field includes two cards. In this example, the tabs are la-beled General Switches and Field Specific Switches. These repre-sent the two bracketed sets of arguments, [Date-Time Picture] and [Switches], as they appear in the syntax example. The number of tabbed cards, if any, and the labels on the tabs will vary with the field. Choose the AUTHOR field, for example, and you'll find only one card in the dialog box.

As you can see in the Field Codes text box in Figures 20-1 and 20-2, Word enters field names in all uppercase letters. If you type them, you needn't worry about whether they're uppercase or lowercase. We'll continue refer-ring to field names in all uppercase letters to make them easier to recognize.

How to insert fields with the Insert Field key (Ctrl-F9)

For fields you're already familiar with, it may be faster to insert the field name and arguments by typing them. Word provides a function-key com-mand for this. Move the cursor to the appropriate place in the document, and then press Ctrl-F9. Word will insert a paired set of field characters around the cursor. You can then type the appropriate field name and argu-ments. For example, suppose you want to insert the field {AUTHOR}. Simply press Ctrl-F9 and type *AUTHOR*. Then press F9 to calculate the field result. Alternatively, you can type the text for the field first, select it, and then press Ctrl-F9. Word will add the field characters around the selected text.

Word must be set to Insert mode when you insert a field by typing text within the field markers. If Word is set for Overtype mode, it will not expand the space between the field characters { and } to let you add text.

How to insert fields with other menu commands

Be aware that some menu commands automatically insert fields for you. For example, if you select some text and then choose Insert Index And Tables, Mark Entry, and then Mark, Word will insert an Index Entry field for you. If you want, you can insert these fields with the Insert Field command or by typing them manually. However, for fields that Word provides specialized menu commands for, it's usually easier to use the menu commands and let Word insert the fields automatically. One menu choice worth special note is the Insert Date And Time command, which we'll discuss later in this chapter. It's limited to inserting fields that will produce the date, the time, or both.

Field Results vs. Field Codes

After you insert one or more fields into a document, you'll generally want to see the field results. At times, however, you'll want to see the fields themselves—to delete them, change them, or simply check that you've entered a particular item as a field rather than as regular text. You can toggle between seeing the field codes and seeing the field results.

How to change the Tools Options View Field Codes setting

If you're not sure how Word is currently set, you can find out by choosing Tools Options and then selecting the View tab. If the Field Codes check box is checked, Word is set to show field codes. If the check box is cleared, Word is set to show field results. You can change to the other setting by simply checking or clearing the check box.

You can display your text in both views at once, as shown in Figure 20-3. Open the file in two windows, or split a single window into two panes. Then set one to show field codes and the other to show field results. Figure 20-3 shows a single document split into two panes, with the top pane showing the field results and the bottom pane showing the field codes.

FIGURE 20-3

The Field Codes check box on the Tools Options View card toggles between showing field results, as in the top pane, and showing field codes, as in the bottom pane.

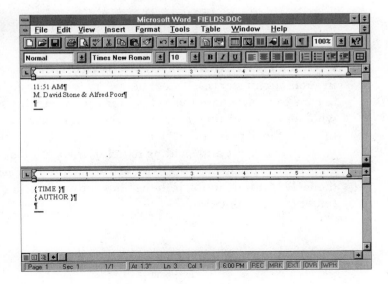

How to toggle between codes and results for selected fields or for the whole document

In addition to toggling the Field Codes setting by using the Tools Options View card, you can toggle it on and off with the shortcut keys Alt-F9. If you prefer, you can also toggle a single field or selected fields, rather than all fields in the document. Place the cursor in the field you want to toggle, or select more than one field, and then press Shift-F9. Word will toggle the display of just the selected field or fields, as shown in Figure 20-4. If you toggle the view for a field that appears in multiple panes or windows, Word will toggle the setting in all open panes, as shown in the figure.

FIGURE 20-4

You can use Shift-F9 to toggle selected fields between showing field codes and showing results. If the field is displayed in more than one pane or window, the field will toggle in all open panes.

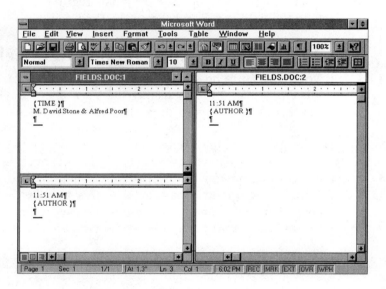

How to set field shading to indicate fields

In some circumstances, it's not necessary to see the actual field codes, as long as you can tell where the fields are. For example, you may want to know whether a date or time is entered as a field code or as text, without needing to know the details of the code itself.

You can easily add shading to fields; then you'll be able to spot fields at a glance. To set field shading, choose Tools Options. As shown in Figure 20-5, the Field Shading option is in the Show group box on the View card, near the center of the dialog box.

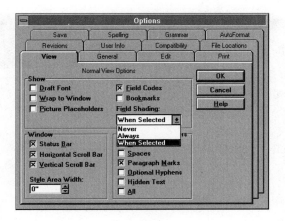

FIGURE 20-5

You can use the Field Shading option on the Tools Options View card to identify fields by adding shading.

The Field Shading drop-down list contains three choices: Never, Always, and When Selected. If you choose Never, Word won't add shading to fields under any conditions. Choose Always, and Word will always add shading. Choose When Selected, and Word will add shading only when you move your cursor or selection into a field.

Both Always and When Selected apply whether you are showing field codes or field results. We recommend that you choose one of the shading options because it can serve to warn you if you are about to delete or edit a field code, mistaking it for normal text. The choice between the two settings is largely a matter of personal preference.

How to update a field's result (F9)

In some situations, you'll see field codes even when Word is set to show field results and you haven't changed individual fields. In particular, if you insert a field by pressing Ctrl-F9 and then typing the field name, Word will initially display the field code even if it is set to display field results, as shown in Figure 20-6 on the next page. If you move your cursor or selection to the field and press Shift-F9 to show field codes, Word will show nothing for the date, as shown in Figure 20-7, also on the next page.

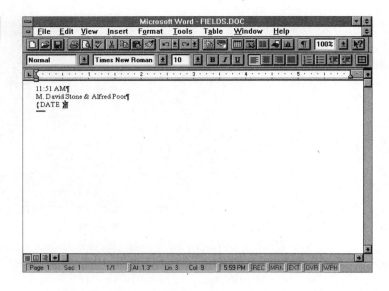

FIGURE 20-6

If you insert a field by pressing Ctrl-F9 and typing the field name, Word will initially show the field code as it was inserted, even if the program is set to show field results.

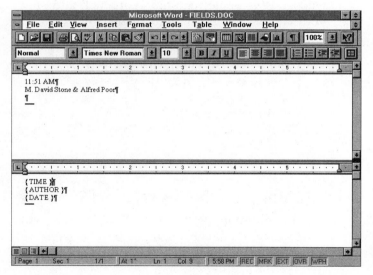

FIGURE 20-7

If you insert the field as shown in Figure 20-6 and then press Shift-F9, Word will show nothing for the result of the DATE field. (We created a second pane so that you can see the field codes.)

The reason Word doesn't show a date in this situation is simply that you haven't yet told it to calculate the field result by updating the field. To do so, you need to place the cursor or selection in the field and press F9. Word will immediately calculate the field and show the result. In contrast, when you insert a field with the Insert Field command, Word will handle this step automatically.

You also need to update most result fields whenever the results would change. For example, if you're inserting another document by using the INCLUDETEXT field and you make changes to the source file of the included document, you'll need to update the field if you want to include the revised document.

Word provides an option that will automatically recalculate result fields whenever you choose the Tools Mail Merge or File Print command. To set the option, choose Tools Options and then select the Print tab; then check the Update Fields check box in the Printing Options box. Regardless of how this option is set, however, you can use the F9 key at any time to update one or more fields. Simply place the cursor in the field you want to update, or extend the selection to include the fields you want to update, and press F9.

Note that if you have fields nested within fields (a situation we will discuss later in this chapter), updating a field automatically updates all of its nested fields. However, pressing F9 will not update marker and action fields. Also note that if you update a field accidentally, you can choose Edit Undo to restore the field's previous result.

How to update a source for an INCLUDETEXT field (Ctrl-Shift-F7)

As we've just mentioned, if you make a change in another document that has been included in the current document with an INCLUDETEXT field, you have to update the field to update the change. Word also provides a command with which you can copy changes you make in the INCLUDETEXT field result to the source document. (Note that this update source feature works for INCLUDETEXT fields only and only if the included document is a Word file.) To update the source, press Ctrl-Shift-F7.

How to lock a field (Ctrl-F11 or Ctrl-3)

If you need to, you can lock one or more fields to keep Word from updating the field results. Simply place the cursor in the field you want to lock, or extend the selection to include all fields you want to lock, and press Ctrl-F11 or Ctrl-3. Unfortunately, locked fields don't look any different from unlocked fields; the only way to tell whether a field is locked is to select it and press F9 to update the field. If the field is locked, Word won't update the field; your computer will beep to alert you.

How to lock a field that's part of a BOOKMARK, an INCLUDETEXT, or a REF field result

You should also be aware of how field locking applies to BOOKMARK, INCLUDETEXT, and REF fields or, more precisely, how it applies to any fields that are part of the result of a BOOKMARK, an INCLUDETEXT, or a REF field.

Suppose you're using an INCLUDETEXT field to insert several paragraphs from another document. In the source document, you have the NUMPAGES field (which returns the number of pages in a document). Unless you tell Word otherwise, updating the INCLUDETEXT field will also update the result for the NUMPAGES field *for the current document*. If you want the result to show the number of pages in the included document instead, you need to lock the fields inserted with the included text so that Word won't update them.

To lock the fields in the result, you add the lock result switch \! at the end of the field code. The INCLUDETEXT field, then, would take the following form: {INCLUDETEXT "filename" \!}.

How to unlock a field (Ctrl-Shift-F11 or Ctrl-4)

To unlock one or more fields locked with Ctrl-F11 or Ctrl-3, place the cursor in the field or extend the selection to include all of the fields, and then press Ctrl-Shift-F11 or Ctrl-4. You can't tell that the field is unlocked unless you try to update it.

Note that these shortcut keys have no effect on the results of fields locked with the lock result switch added. To change a BOOKMARK, an INCLUDETEXT, or a REF field so that the results of included fields are no longer locked, you have to remove the the lock result switch, as we'll describe in a moment.

How to unlink a field (Ctrl-Shift-F9)

Although you can lock a field to prevent Word from changing a field's result, you'll sometimes want to unlink the field for the same effect. When you place the cursor or selection in a field or fields and press Ctrl-Shift-F9, Word will replace the selected fields with their most recent results. If the selected fields have no result, pressing Ctrl-Shift-F9 will delete them. When you want to guarantee that you'll never accidentally unlock a field, unlink the field rather than locking it. Note that if you do unlink a field accidentally, you can restore the field with the Edit Undo command.

How to move to a field (F11, Alt-F1, Shift-F11, Alt-Shift-F1)

Word also provides keyboard commands for moving to the next or previous field in a document. To move to and select the next field, press F11 or Alt-F1. To move to and select the previous field, press Shift-F11 or Alt-Shift-F1.

Bear in mind two caveats if you've formatted any fields in your document as hidden text—other than fields, such as the Index Entry field, that Word normally inserts as hidden—and Word is set not to display hidden text. First, if you press F11 or Alt-F1 and the next field is hidden, Word will move the cursor onto the field, even though you can't see it. If you press F11 or Alt-F1 again, Word will remain at the hidden field position so that you don't miss it. To move to the next field with the shortcut key, simply move the cursor past the hidden field first. If you're moving backward, to previous fields, Word will stop at the hidden field but will continue to the next field the next time you press Shift-F11 or Alt-Shift-F1. Note too that Word will skip over any marker fields that are automatically assigned the hidden format (such as the Index Entry field)—even if Word is currently set to show hidden text. To move to a marker field, set Word to show hidden text, and use the Edit Find command to search for the field name.

Editing Fields

After you insert a field in your document, you can edit the text as you edit any other text. The only requirement is that you must be in Insert mode to add text between the field characters { and }. If you are in Overtype mode, you can type over characters that are already in the field, but you can't type additional characters. In Insert mode, however, you can edit any part of a field except the field characters, and you can add text as needed. For example, if you have the field {DATE \@ "d-MMM-yy"} and you want to change the argument to "MMMM, yy", you can simply change the text using any of Word's standard editing techniques.

If you're viewing field results rather than field codes, you can edit the text returned by result fields just like any other text. If you make changes to a field result and then update that field, however, Word will replace the changes with the new field result. In general, therefore, you won't want to modify a field result unless you also lock or unlink the field.

How to delete or copy a field

All of Word's standard cutting, copying, and pasting features work on fields themselves as well as the text within a field. To delete a field, for example, you can select the entire field and press the Del key. If field codes are displayed, you can select the entire field by selecting either the { or } character. If field results are displayed, you can select an entire field result by selecting its first or last character. (Note that if the field result ends with a paragraph mark, that is what you select.)

To cut or copy a field, select the field or result and choose the Edit Cut or Edit Copy command. Then move the cursor to where you want to insert the field, and choose the Edit Paste command.

Formatting Field Results

You can format a field result just like any other text. You can also assign character formatting—by which we mean some combination of font, paragraph, and style formatting—to an entire field result. And you can easily control case and numeric formatting in field results.

How to set character formatting for a field result

For some fields—such as the DATE field, which can specify the field result without additional arguments—you can define character formatting for the result by applying a format to the first character in the field name. The next time you update the field, Word will show the result in the new format.

For example, suppose you want the result of a DATE field to appear in boldface. You can format the result as boldface, or you can format the letter D in the field name, using Word's direct font-formatting commands, and then press F9 to update the field. You can format other characters in the field name too, but only the format of the first character will determine the format of the field.

How to set character formatting with CharFormat and the format switch

The character-formatting technique just described won't work with fields, such as the INCLUDETEXT field, that import data specified in arguments rather than by the field name itself. Rather, you have to add arguments to the fields by using the format switch.

You can use the format switch * to define character formatting, case, and numeric formatting for a field result. The syntax for the format switch is * *FormatName*, where *FormatName* is replaced with the argument that defines the special formatting you want to apply. The argument for applying character formatting to an entire field result is CharFormat.

When you add the format switch and the CharFormat argument to a field that uses an argument to specify the result, you can then proceed to format the entire field by formatting only the first letter of the field name. For example, suppose you're using the field

{INCLUDETEXT "c:\\data\\short.doc"}

to import the document file SHORT.DOC, all of whose data is formatted as italic. Word will import the data as italic unless you tell it otherwise.

To import the data and display it without italic formatting, you would enter the field as follows:

{INCLUDETEXT "c:\\data\\short.doc" * CharFormat}

To import the data and display it in boldface instead of italic, you would enter the field in exactly the same way. Then you would apply bold formatting to the *I* in INCLUDETEXT and press F9 to update the field. Word would display the entire field in boldface, nonitalic letters.

Finally, if you want to import the italicized data and display it in both italic and boldface, start with the field code; use the CharFormat argument, format the first character in both italic and boldface, select it, and press F9. If the source document has mixed character formatting, all formatting will be replaced with the formatting specified by the CharFormat argument.

How to set character formatting for part of a field result

You may want to format only part of a field result. You can format the text in the result directly, but unless you tell Word otherwise, it will reset that format the next time it updates the field.

If you use the MergeFormat argument, however, Word will retain any added formatting on a word-for-word basis when it updates the field. For example, assume that you're using the INCLUDETEXT field to import a few paragraphs from another document file and you've formatted the second sentence in the result as italic. Assume that the first sentence is five words long and the second, eight. Later you make changes to the source document and then update the field. If you've defined the INCLUDETEXT field as

{INCLUDETEXT "c:\\data\\any.doc" * MergeFormat}

Word will reimport the text and format the sixth through the thirteenth words as italic.

You have to be careful with this approach. If you've made changes to text that follows the formatted text, the updated field will maintain the formatting you want. But if you've made changes to the first and second sentences, the formatting won't necessarily appear where you want it. For example, if you delete the first sentence, the italics will start with the sixth word of the sentence you want italicized and will spill over into the next sentence. In short, you'll want to use this feature only when the position of the formatted text won't change.

How to set character formatting in a field result using AutoFormat

You can also set a field to use Word's AutoFormat feature. For example, if you use the INCLUDETEXT field to insert the file ANY.DOC, you can have Word automatically run AutoFormat on the inserted text. Simply enter the field as

{INCLUDETEXT "c:\\data\\any.doc" * Auto}

When Word inserts the text, it will run AutoFormat—but without letting you review the changes. For more information about using AutoFormat, see "The AutoFormat Feature" on page 420.

How to control case

Word offers four arguments to control the case for a field result: Upper, Lower, FirstCap, and Caps. The Upper argument formats all characters in uppercase; Lower formats them in lowercase. The FirstCap argument formats the first character of the first word in the result in uppercase and all remaining characters in lowercase. Caps formats the first character of each word in uppercase and the remaining characters in lowercase. Figure 20-8 shows the effect of each argument on the same text in the field result, using the AUTHOR field. The authors, as entered in the Summary Info dialog box for the document, are M. David Stone & Alfred Poor.

Field Code	Sample Result
{AUTHOR}	M. David Stone & Alfred Poor
{AUTHOR * Upper}	M. DAVID STONE & ALFRED POOR
{AUTHOR * Lower}	m. david stone & alfred poor
{AUTHOR * FirstCap}	M. david stone & alfred poor
{AUTHOR * Caps}	M. David Stone & Alfred Poor

FIGURE 20-8

Field codes and sample results, using the AUTHOR field with different arguments.

How to control numeric formats

The format switch recognizes eight arguments for numeric formats, or what Word calls its *number conversion category*. Figure 20-9 shows the complete field code and sample results for each, using the NUMPAGES field, which returns the number of pages in the current document.

The arguments are self-explanatory, except perhaps CardText, OrdText, and Hex. The CardText argument spells out the cardinal number, the OrdText argument the ordinal number. Hex is short for hexadecimal, a numbering system often used to translate between the decimal system that people use and the binary system that computers are based on; the hexadecimal system uses a base of 16, rather than 10 as in the decimal system. The first 16 numbers in the hexadecimal system (not including 0) are 1, 2, 3, 4, 5, 6, 7, 8, 9, A, B, C, D, E, F, 10.

Format Code, Including Argument	Sample Result
{NUMPAGES}	11
{NUMPAGES*Arabic}	11
{NUMPAGES*Ordinal}	11th
{NUMPAGES*Roman}	XI
{NUMPAGES*Alphabetic}	K
{NUMPAGES*CardText}	Eleven
{NUMPAGES*OrdText}	Eleventh
{NUMPAGES*Hex}	B
{NUMPAGES*DollarText}	Eleven and 00/100

FIGURE 20-9

Field codes and sample results, using the NUMPAGES field, for numeric formats recognized by the format switch.

For two of the arguments (Roman and Alphabetic), the case of the result is determined by the case of the first letter of the argument. For example, *Roman* or *ROMAN* would produce *XI*, but *roman* would produce *xi*. You can control the case of arguments that produce a text result (CardText, OrdText, and DollarText) by using the case arguments discussed previously (Upper, Lower, FirstCap, and Caps). In fact, you can control the case of both Roman and Alphabetic by either method.

How to use the numeric picture switch

As you will discover, many fields return a numeric result. For example, the NUMCHARS field returns the number of characters in the current document, and EDITTIME returns the number of minutes the current document has been open.

Unless you specify otherwise, Word will always display numeric results in a general numeric format, without special characters such as commas or percent signs, and it will display as many digits as necessary after the decimal point. If you prefer, you can use the numeric picture switch \# to define a format. For example, if a field returns the value 1234.1, you can tell Word to show the result as 1,234.10 or as $1234.10.

Figure 20-10 beginning on the next page shows the characters available for creating a model, or *numeric picture*. You can redefine the decimal separator character and the thousands separator character by opening the Windows Control Panel, choosing International, and then choosing the Change button for Number Format. For this discussion, we'll assume you've accepted the default decimal separator character (a period) and the default thousands separator character (a comma). Note that if you include the numeric picture switch in a field that does not return a numeric value, the switch will not affect the field's result.

Argument	Name and Function
0	**Zero (digit placeholder).** If the result has fewer digits than there are zeros in the numeric picture, Word adds zeros. If there are more digits to the right of the decimal point than in the numeric picture, Word rounds the number. (The format \# "$000.00" applied to 12.4 yields $012.40. The same format applied to 0.4 yields $000.40.)
#	**Number sign (digit placeholder).** If the result has fewer digits than there are number signs in the numeric picture, Word adds spaces rather than zeros to the left or right of the decimal point. If there are more digits to the right of the decimal point than are included in the numeric picture, Word rounds the number. (The format \# "$###.##" applied to 12.456 yields $ 12.46. The same format applied to 0.4 yields $ 0.4 .)
x	**x (truncating digit placeholder).** If x is the leftmost character in the numeric picture and the result has more digits to the left, those digits are truncated. If x is the rightmost character after the decimal point, Word rounds the number. (The format \# "x##.#x" applied to 123456.348 yields 456.35.)
.	**Period (decimal separator character).** Defines the position of the decimal point, as the examples in this table illustrate. (The decimal separator character and the thousands separator character match those defined in your system settings.)
,	**Comma (thousands separator character).** If the result includes more than three digits to the left of the decimal point and you've included the separator character in the numeric picture, Word will add a comma separator character. (The format \# "#,###.#" applied to 123456.3 yields 123,456.3. Applied to 1123456.3, it yields 1,123,456.3.)
−	**Minus (negative) sign.** If the result is negative, Word will display a minus sign before the number, which is the default in any case. If the result is positive, Word will add a space before the number. (The format \# "−###.##" applied to −123.23 yields −123.23. Applied to 123.23, it yields 123.23, with an extra space in front of the number.)

FIGURE 20-10

(continued)

Characters available for creating a numeric picture.

FIGURE 20-10. *continued*

Argument	Name and Function
+	**Plus (positive) sign.** If the result is negative, Word will display a minus sign before the number. If the result is positive, Word will display a plus sign. (For example, the format \# "+###.##" applied to –123.23 yields –123.23. Applied to 123.23, it yields +123.23.)
;	**Semicolon.** Lets you define two or three variants, to provide different formats for positive, negative, and zero results. If you have two numeric pictures separated by a semicolon, the first will apply to positive results and zero, the second to negative results. If you have three numeric pictures separated by semicolons, the first will apply to positive results, the second to negative results, and the third to results of zero. (The format \# "$0.00;($0.00);0" applied to 123.23 yields $123.23. Applied to –123.23, it yields ($123.23). Applied to 0, it yields 0. Do not add spaces before the semicolons since Word will add the space to the result. If you add quotation marks, use a single set of quotation marks around the entire numeric picture.)
'text'	**Any text (literal text).** Adds text to the result, using exactly the same characters as defined in the numeric picture. (The format "###.## 'tax'" applied to 123.23 yields 123.23 tax. Note the quotation marks around the full argument and the single quotation marks around the literal text.)
Other	**All other characters.** To include other characters, such as a dollar sign, or parentheses to indicate a negative number, simply type the character(s) in the appropriate place, as in the examples earlier in this table.

The Date-Time Picture switch

Word offers several fields that will return dates or times: DATE, TIME, CREATEDATE, PRINTDATE, SAVEDATE, and EDITTIME. By default, Word will use the date format you've specified for Windows. (To change the date or time format, open the Windows Control Panel, choose International, and change the format.)

You can specify a different format by using the Date-Time Picture switch \@. As with the numeric picture switch, you create a picture, or model, for Word to follow. For example, if a field returns the date 3/31/98, you can use the Date-Time Picture switch to display the resulting date as March 31, 1998, or Mar-31, 1998, or in another form.

If you include the Date-Time Picture switch in a field that does not return a date or time, the switch will not affect the field's result. We'll take a closer look at this switch shortly, in the section "DATE and TIME Fields."

Nesting Fields

Occasionally, you'll want to use a field as an argument in another field. For example, you might use FILLIN fields as arguments in an INFO field:

{INFO {FILLIN "Which item?"}{FILLIN "New entry"}}

As we've mentioned, a FILLIN field prompts the user to enter information. An INFO field returns information taken from a document's Summary Info dialog box and lets you change it. By combining the two, you can create a field that prompts the user to type some information and then changes the entries in the Summary Info dialog box.

The FILLIN fields in the preceding example collect input from the user and return that input as arguments in the INFO field. Note that Word always evaluates the innermost field first and the outermost field last.

DATE and TIME Fields

For the rest of this chapter, we'll look at specific fields and how to use them. We'll start with the two fields you're likely to use most often, the DATE and TIME fields.

How to insert a date or a time

The DATE field returns the current date, as given by your computer's system clock, and it displays the result in the format defined in the Windows Control Panel. The form of this field is simply {DATE}. You can, however, display the date in another format by adding the Date-Time Picture switch. The field will then take the form

{DATE \@ "Date-Time Picture"}

The TIME field returns the current time, from your computer's system clock. By default, it uses the format defined in the Windows Control Panel. The form for this field is simply {TIME}. You can display the time in another format by adding the Date-Time Picture switch. The field will then take the form

{TIME \@ "Date-Time Picture"}

Although the default results for the DATE and TIME fields differ, you can use either field to display the date, the time, or both. Add the Date-Time Picture switch with any format to either field, and you'll get the same result.

One of the most common places to display a date or time is in a header or footer. As explained in Chapter 5, you can click on buttons on the Header

And Footer toolbar to insert the DATE or TIME field. However, if you want to display either the date or the time in some format other than the default, you'll have to modify the field or insert it some other way—by pressing Ctrl-F9 and typing in the field code, by choosing Insert Field, or by choosing Insert Date And Time.

For most purposes, choosing Insert Date And Time is the fastest way to insert the date or time and specify a format simultaneously. Figure 20-11 shows the Date And Time dialog box.

FIGURE 20-11

The Date And Time dialog box offers a total of 13 formats for a date, a time, or both.

The dialog box offers 13 formats for a date, a time, or both. Each choice shows the current date, time, or both, in a specific format. To insert the field with this dialog box, place the cursor where you want the date or time to appear, choose Insert Date And Time, and highlight the format you prefer. Be sure the Insert As Field check box is checked, and choose OK.

> The Insert As Field check box is easy to miss, but important. If the box is not checked, Word will insert the date or time as text rather than as a field. Inserting as text is preferred if you don't want the date or time to change—as with a date and time stamp on a note, for example, where the whole point of adding a date and time is to document when you wrote the note.

If you insert any of these variations of the date or time and then view the field code, you'll see a representation of the formats. Figure 20-12 on the next page shows the samples from Figure 20-11, with the Date-Time Picture switch forms that define the formats. If you look at the field codes, you'll find that Word uses the TIME field in each case.

This Form of the Date-Time Picture Switch...	Yields This Format...
\@ "M/d/yy"	8/3/98
\@ "dddd, MMMM dd, yyyy"	Monday, August 03, 1998
\@ "d MMMM, yyyy"	3 August, 1998
\@ "MMMM d, yyyy"	August 3, 1998
\@ "d-MMM-yy"	3-Aug-98
\@ "MMMM, yy"	August, 98
\@ "MMM-yy"	Aug-98
\@ "MM/dd/yy h:mm AM/PM"	08/03/98 5:52 PM
\@ "MM/dd/yy h:mm:ss AM/PM"	08/03/98 5:52:02 PM
\@ "h:mm AM/PM"	5:52 PM
\@ "h:mm:ss AM/PM"	5:52:02 PM
\@ "H:mm"	17:52
\@ "H:mm:ss"	17:52:02

FIGURE 20-12

Date-Time Picture switches and sample results.

You can also insert the TIME or DATE field by choosing Insert Field. Highlight either [All] or Date And Time in the Categories list box, and select TIME or DATE in the Field Names list box. If you then choose the Options button, you'll find that Word offers the same format choices as in Figure 20-12, plus one more: \@ "dd MMMM yyyy" (which gives the date in the form 03 August 1998). To insert the DATE or TIME field after choosing the Insert Field command, highlight either field in the Field Names list box. Then optionally add a Date-Time Picture, and choose OK. Alternatively, after selecting the field, choose Options, highlight a Date-Time Picture in the Date-Time list box, and choose the Add To Field button. Then choose OK to close the Field Options dialog box, and choose OK again to insert the field into your document.

How to define custom date and time formats

In addition to the built-in formats Word supplies, you can define a custom format for any DATE or TIME field. That way, you can create fields that return the day of the week as well as the date, month, and year. You can also create combinations of dates and times in the same field.

To create a custom format, you type the Date-Time Picture switch along with the abbreviations and literal text that define the format you want. You can create the field from scratch by using Ctrl-F9 to insert the field characters and then typing the field name, the \@ Date-Time Picture switch, and the format in the form

{DATE \@ "Date-Time Picture"}

Alternatively, you can insert the field with any technique we've already described and then modify the format as needed. Figure 20-13 lists all date and time abbreviations that Word recognizes. If you add any literal text in the Date-Time Picture switch, including commas or spaces, Word will include it in the field result.

Abbreviation	Description	Sample Result
M	Number of month	1 through 12
MM	Number of month with leading zeros	01 through 12
MMM	Three-letter month abbreviation	Oct
MMMM	Full month name	October
yy	Year as two digits	98
yyyy	Year as four digits	1998
d	Date as one or two digits	1 through 31
dd	Two-digit date with leading zeros	01 through 31
ddd	Three-letter day of the week	Wed
dddd	Full day of the week	Wednesday
h	Hours on a 12-hour clock	1 through 12
hh	Hours on a 12-hour clock with leading zeros	01 through 12
H	Hours on a 24-hour clock	1 through 24
HH	Hours on a 24-hour clock with leading zeros	01 through 24
m	Minutes	1 through 59
mm	Minutes with leading zeros	01 through 59
AM/PM	Uppercase AM or PM	9 AM, 5 PM
am/pm	Lowercase am or pm	9 am, 5 pm
A/P	Uppercase A or P	9A, 5P
a/p	Lowercase a or p	9a, 5p

FIGURE 20-13

Date-time abbreviations accepted by Word, with descriptions and sample results.

How to combine date and time

As we've said, the DATE and TIME fields will return the same result when you include a Date-Time Picture switch. This means you can use any combination of the abbreviations listed in Figure 20-13 to create a field that displays both date and time. For example, to insert a field that returns date and time in the format

Oct-15, 1995 at 5:30 PM

you can create either of the following two fields:

{DATE \@ "MMM-d, yyyy 'at' h:mm AM/PM"}

{TIME \@ "MMM-d, yyyy 'at' h:mm AM/PM"}

Summary Information Fields

Word offers six fields that return information stored in the Summary Info dialog box: TITLE, SUBJECT, AUTHOR, KEYWORDS, COMMENTS, and INFO. These are listed in the Field dialog box under the Document Information category. Figure 20-14 uses a split screen to show how the first five fields appear in a document. The top pane shows the field codes; the bottom pane, the field results.

FIGURE 20-14

Summary information fields retrieve information from the Summary Info dialog box.

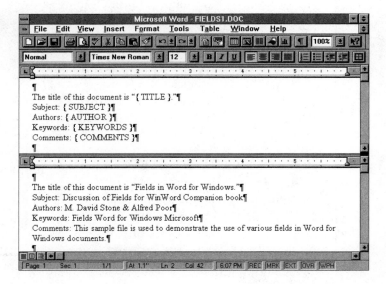

All summary information fields work essentially the same way. In each case, the field can take one of two forms: {FIELDNAME} or {FIELDNAME "NewEntry"}. If you use the first form, as in Figure 20-14, the field will simply return the current information stored in the Summary Info dialog box: The TITLE field will return the current title, the SUBJECT field the current subject, and so on. If you use the second form, Word will replace the information in the dialog box with the new entry you've added as an argument. It will then return that new entry as the result for the field. The following section gives an example, using the TITLE field.

The TITLE field

The TITLE field returns the title stored in the current document's Summary Info dialog box. The two forms for this field are

{TITLE}

{TITLE "NewTitle"}

The first form returns the entry stored in the Title text box in the Summary Info dialog box. For example, line 1 of the example document shown in Figure 20-14 contains the text

The title of this document is "{TITLE}."

If the current file is titled *Fields in Word for Windows*, Word will return this title as the result when it updates the field, as shown in the lower pane of Figure 20-14.

The second form of the TITLE field changes the entry in the Summary Info dialog box to whatever new title you've entered as the *NewTitle* argument. If the title consists of more than one word, it must be enclosed in quotation marks. For example, if you insert and update the field

{TITLE "Chapter 20: Field of Fields"}

Word will change the Title entry in the Summary Info dialog box to *Chapter 20: Field of Fields* and return that entry as the field result.

The SUBJECT, AUTHOR, KEYWORDS, and COMMENTS fields

The other summary information fields work similarly to the TITLE field.

The SUBJECT field returns the entry stored in the Subject text box in the Summary Info dialog box. The forms of this field are

{SUBJECT}

{SUBJECT "NewSubject"}

The AUTHOR field returns the name stored in the Author text box in the Summary Info dialog box. The forms of this field are

{AUTHOR}

{AUTHOR "NewAuthorName"}

The KEYWORDS field returns the entry stored in the Keywords text box in the Summary Info dialog box. The forms of this field are

{KEYWORDS}

{KEYWORDS "NewKeywords"}

The COMMENTS field returns the comments stored in the Comments text box in the Summary Info dialog box. The forms of this field are

{COMMENTS}

{COMMENTS "NewComments"}

In each of these cases, the first form of the field retrieves the appropriate entry from the Summary Info dialog box. The second form lets you change the entry to whatever new text you've entered as the argument.

The INFO field

The last summary information field is the INFO field. This field lets you define which entry to retrieve from or update in the Summary Info dialog box. Otherwise, INFO works the same way as the other fields. The forms are

{INFO InfoType}

{INFO InfoType "NewEntry"}

InfoType can be any of the other five fields we've just discussed. For example, if you insert the field {INFO TITLE}, you will get the same result as if you insert the field {TITLE}. If you insert the field {INFO TITLE "NewTitle"}, you will get the same result as for {TITLE "NewTitle"}.

At first glance, the INFO field appears redundant; however, it can be handy under some conditions. For example, you can use it in combination with the FILLIN field to prompt for information and then change any of the summary information fields. You can create the nested field

{INFO {FILLIN "Change which info item?"}{FILLIN "Change to what?"}}

When you update this field, Word will open a dialog box asking, "Change which info item?" You respond with one of the summary information field names and choose OK. Word will ask, "Change to what?" When you type a new entry and choose OK, the INFO field will then change the appropriate item.

Statistical Fields

Word also offers 12 fields that will return statistical information about the current document: CREATEDATE, EDITTIME, FILENAME, FILESIZE, LASTSAVEDBY, NUMCHARS, NUMPAGES, NUMWORDS, PRINTDATE, REVNUM, SAVEDATE, and TEMPLATE. All of these fields return information that you can otherwise see by choosing File Summary Info and then the Statistics button. Word lists some of these in the Field dialog box as part of the Document Information category and others as part of the Date And Time category. (REVNUM is under Numbering.) Figure 20-15 shows Word's statistical fields in two panes, with Word set to show field codes in one pane and field results in the other.

FIGURE 20-15

Word's statistical fields retrieve the same information you can see by choosing File Summary Info and then choosing the Statistics button.

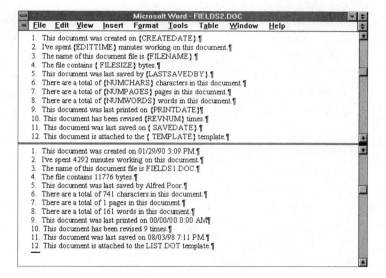

Many of these fields recognize one or more field-specific switches for modifying the field results; we'll cover these switches along with each field. But note too that you can control the format for many of these fields with the format, numeric picture, and date-time switches discussed earlier in this chapter. For details on using these switches, see the section "Formatting Field Results" starting on page 690.

Here's a look at each of the fields, in the same order as they appear in Figure 20-15.

The CREATEDATE field

The CREATEDATE field returns the date and time the document was created. The form of this field is simply

{CREATEDATE}

By default, Word will display the date in the format defined in the Windows Control Panel. However, you can change the format with the Date-Time Picture switch.

The EDITTIME field

The EDITTIME field returns the total number of minutes the document has been open since it was created, as of the moment you update the field. The form of this field is

{EDITTIME}

The EDITTIME field recognizes the numeric picture switch and the format switch options for controlling numeric format and case.

The FILENAME field

The FILENAME field returns the filename of the current document. The form of this field is

{FILENAME}

The FILENAME field recognizes the \p switch, which will add the drive and full path to the filename. In addition, it recognizes the format switch options for controlling case.

The FILESIZE field

The FILESIZE field returns the size of the current document file. The form of this field is

{FILESIZE}

The FILESIZE field recognizes the \k switch, for displaying the result in kilobytes, and the \m switch, for displaying the result in megabytes. In addition, the FILESIZE field recognizes the numeric picture switch and the format switch options for controlling numeric format and case. By default, the FILESIZE field returns file size in bytes.

The LASTSAVEDBY field

The LASTSAVEDBY field returns the name of the person who last saved the document, as of the moment you update the field. The form of this field is

{LASTSAVEDBY}

The LASTSAVEDBY field recognizes the format switch options for controlling case.

The NUMCHARS field

The NUMCHARS field returns the number of characters in the document, as of the moment you update the field. The form of this field is

{NUMCHARS}

The NUMCHARS field recognizes the numeric picture switch and the format switch options for controlling numeric format and case.

The NUMPAGES field

The NUMPAGES field returns the total number of pages in the document, as of the moment you update the field. If you've divided the document into sections, Word totals the number of pages in all sections. The form of this field is

{NUMPAGES}

The NUMPAGES field recognizes the numeric picture switch and the format switch options for controlling numeric format and case.

The NUMWORDS field

The NUMWORDS field returns the number of words in the document as stored in the Statistics dialog box, as of the moment you update the field. The form of this field is

{NUMWORDS}

The NUMWORDS field recognizes the numeric picture switch and the format switch options for controlling numeric format and case.

To get a precise count of the words in a Word 2.0 document, you had to go through two steps, first updating the Statistics dialog box and then updating the NUMWORDS field. Word 6.0, however, automatically updates the information in the Statistics dialog box.

The PRINTDATE field

The PRINTDATE field returns the date and time the document was last printed. The form of this field is

{PRINTDATE}

If you've never printed the document, the date and time will be 0/00/00 0:00 AM, as shown in Figure 20-15. By default, Word displays the date in the format defined in the Windows Control Panel. You can use a Date-Time Picture switch to change the format.

The REVNUM field

Each time you create a new document, Word assigns it revision number 1. Each time you save the document, Word increments the revision number by one. The REVNUM field returns the revision number of the current document, as of the moment the field is updated. The form of the field is

{REVNUM}

The REVNUM field recognizes the numeric picture switch and the format switch options for controlling numeric format and case.

The SAVEDATE field

The SAVEDATE field returns the date and time the document was last saved, as of the moment you update the field. The form of this field is

{SAVEDATE}

By default, Word will display the date in the format defined in the Windows Control Panel. However, you can use a Date-Time Picture switch to change the format.

The TEMPLATE field

The TEMPLATE field returns the name of the document's template file, as of the moment you update the field. The form of this field is

{TEMPLATE}

By default, the result takes the form NORMAL.DOT. However, you can add a drive and path to the filename by using the \p switch. The TEMPLATE field also recognizes the format switch options for controlling case.

If you've used Word 2.0, you may know that the TEMPLATE field in Word 2.0 would not return a result if the current document used the NORMAL.DOT template. Word 6.0, however, can return NORMAL.DOT as a result.

Using the INFO field instead of statistical fields

Just as the INFO field can use any of the summary information field names as its *InfoType* argument, it can also use any of the statistical field names. With the statistical fields, however, you can only get information with the INFO field; you cannot change it. The only form of the INFO field for statistical information is

{INFO InfoType}

where *InfoType* is the field name for the particular statistical field. There is really no good reason for using the INFO field this way, since the field merely duplicates the result for the equivalent statistical field.

User Information Fields

Word offers three user information fields. These normally return information stored on the Tools Options User Info card, although you can also override the information. The three fields are USERADDRESS, USERINITIALS, and USERNAME. The first field returns the user's mailing address; the second, the user's initials; and the third, the user's name. The forms for the three fields are

{USERADDRESS ["OverrideAddress"]}

{USERINITIALS ["OverrideInitials"]}

{USERNAME ["OverrideName"]}

OverrideAddress, *OverrideInitials*, and *OverrideName* are optional arguments you can add to override the information stored on the User Info card. Unlike the *NewEntry* arguments for the INFO field, these arguments do not replace the information on the User Info card; they only override it when inserting the information into the document for the particular field.

Action Fields

We said early in this chapter that, to some extent, fields redefine what a word processor can do. Action fields provide the basis for that statement. So let's take a look at some action fields now to get a sense of what they are. Here, then, is a look at the MACROBUTTON and GOTOBUTTON fields.

The MACROBUTTON field

A macro is a set of command instructions you've written or recorded for the purpose of customizing your Word program. For example, if you often print just the page you're working on, you could have Word record a macro as you give the commands to print the current page. You can then assign the macro to a shortcut key, to a toolbar button, or—as we're about to discuss—to a MACROBUTTON field. Thereafter, you can print the current page by simply pressing the shortcut key, clicking on the toolbar button, or double-clicking on the MACROBUTTON field. We'll cover macros in Part Five of this book, "Customizing Word." For the moment, simply note that macros give you the ability to create essentially new commands that can be customized for particular tasks.

You use the MACROBUTTON field to create a button in your document that's similar in concept to the buttons on Word's toolbars. After you create the button, you can double-click on it to run a macro or a command. The MACROBUTTON field takes the form

{MACROBUTTON "MacroOrCommandName" DisplayLabel}

where *MacroOrCommandName* is the name of the macro or command you want the button to run, and *DisplayLabel* is the text or graphic that will serve as the button in the document.

If you use text for *DisplayLabel,* do not enclose it within quotation marks, or they will appear as part of the button text. Note also that Word's online Help calls the first argument *MacroName.* This is slightly misleading because a MACROBUTTON field can also run built-in commands. If you create the macro using the Insert Field dialog box, you can choose one of Word's built-in commands or a macro by choosing Options and then choosing the command or macro in the (misnamed) Macro Name list box.

When you display the result of the MACROBUTTON field, you'll see the button, meaning either the text or the graphic you've specified as the *DisplayLabel* argument. Word will automatically update the field result any time you edit the argument. Note that if you create the field code by pressing Ctrl-F9 and then typing the field code, you'll have to toggle the field (with the cursor in the field, press Shift-F9) to display the result. Simply pressing F9 won't do anything, even if Word is currently set to show results.

You use a MACROBUTTON by double-clicking on the text or graphic returned by the field. If you prefer using the keyboard, select the button with the usual keyboard commands and press Alt-Shift-F9.

The ability to run macros or commands with a button you've placed in a document expands what you can do with a word processor. For example, suppose you have a monthly report that rarely changes except for some changes in the numbers and names it contains. You've automated the updating process with a macro that imports information from other files, asks the user to enter other details, reformats the report, and prints five copies.

If you assign a shortcut key to this macro, you may have trouble remembering it because you use it only once a month. Similarly, there is little point in taking up space on a toolbar for a button you'll use only once a month.

If you add a MACROBUTTON field to the top of the document, however, and you use UPDATE as the display text, you will have the benefit of automating the task without any risk of forgetting how to run the macro. Figure 20-16 shows a simple example, using a macro named UpdateMacro and the text *UPDATE* for the *DisplayLabel* argument.

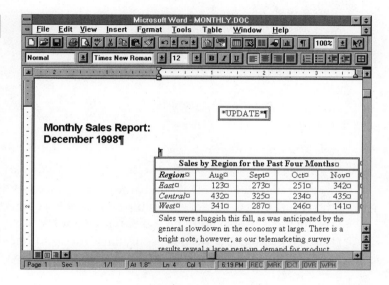

FIGURE 20-16

By adding a MACROBUTTON field, as with the button labeled *UPDATE* in this document, you can run a macro or command simply by double-clicking on the field or placing the cursor on it and pressing Alt-Shift-F9.

To produce a button like the one shown in Figure 20-16, you create the field as

    {MACROBUTTON "UpdateMacro" *UPDATE*}

Make sure the field is in a paragraph of its own. Then place the cursor or selection in that paragraph, choose Format Borders And Shading, and define a border. (Defining a border is not necessary, but it helps set off the button.) Finally, adjust the paragraph indents so that the border is no wider than the word it's surrounding.

You can also create a fancier button. Figure 20-17 on the next page shows a MACROBUTTON field that uses a WordArt graphic for the *DisplayLabel* argument. For information about using WordArt, see "Creating Font Effects with Microsoft WordArt" on page 561.

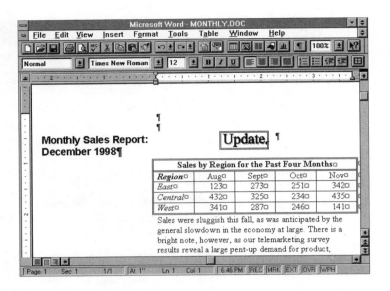

FIGURE 20-17

The MACROBUTTON field shown here is identical to the one shown in Figure 20-16, except that it uses a WordArt graphic as the *DisplayLabel* argument.

The field code for the MACROBUTTON field shown in Figure 20-17 is

{MACROBUTTON "UpdateMacro" {EMBED WordArt \s * MergeFormat}}

The nested EMBED field is automatically added by Word when you use the Insert Object command, choose Microsoft WordArt 2.0, and then define the image. We also added a frame with a border to the WordArt object. Note that by putting the border around the frame rather than around the paragraph, we've avoided having to adjust the paragraph indents.

The GOTOBUTTON field

As you can with the MACROBUTTON field, you can use the GOTOBUTTON field to create a button in your document. In this case, however, choosing the button takes you to a specified destination in the document. The field takes the form

{GOTOBUTTON "GoToInstruction" DisplayLabel}

where *GoToInstruction* is any destination you can type or select in the Go To dialog box, and *DisplayLabel* is the text or picture you want to display as the button. Do not enclose the *DisplayLabel* argument in quotation marks.

GOTOBUTTON is similar to MACROBUTTON in several ways. When you display the result of a GOTOBUTTON field, you'll see the text or picture you've specified in the *DisplayLabel* argument. If you like, you can apply some character formatting to the *DisplayLabel* argument to distinguish the button text from the surrounding text. Word will update the result of the GOTOBUTTON field whenever you edit the field code. As you do with

MACROBUTTON, you use a GOTOBUTTON field by double-clicking on it with the mouse or by moving the cursor to the button and pressing Alt-Shift-F9.

GOTOBUTTON gives you the ability to create something like hypertext. Hypertext is extensively cross-referenced text that takes advantage of a computer's capabilities to jump quickly and easily among referenced areas. Word's Help system is an example of hypertext, with its ability to jump to related subjects or display a definition of selected terms that are referenced on any given screen. The GOTOBUTTON field enables you to create hypertext buttons in your document, which you can use to jump to other locations in the document.

For example, suppose you've created the document shown in Figure 20-18. The text discusses technology in the automotive industry. Elsewhere in the document, you've included some definitions for many of the specialized terms you've used, including the term *Multivalve Engine*, which we've high-lighted in the figure. If your readers will be reading this file on a computer while running Word, you could provide a way to jump to the term's defini-tion. You need only mark the definition with a bookmark and replace the term with a GOTOBUTTON field. The reader can then choose the button to see the definition.

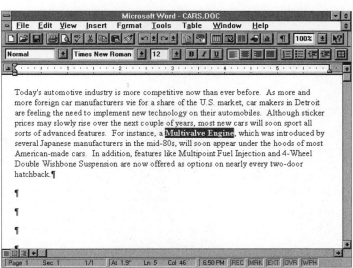

FIGURE 20-18

We'll use a GOTOBUTTON field in place of the term *Multivalve Engine* to enable the reader to jump to that term's definition.

To set up the button, first define a bookmark named Multivalve at the be-ginning of the definition for *Multivalve Engine*. Next return to the text shown in Figure 20-18, and replace the phrase *Multivalve Engine* with the field

{GOTOBUTTON "Multivalve" Multivalve Engine}

as we have done in Figure 20-19. When you view the result of this field, you'll see the text *Multivalve Engine,* as shown in Figure 20-20. Notice that we've formatted this text in boldface to give a visual clue that it is a GOTOBUTTON field. (We could also format the font in a different color.) To view the definition, the reader can simply double-click on the term or move the cursor to the term and then press Alt-Shift-F9. Word will immediately move the cursor to the Multivalve bookmark.

FIGURE 20-19

Word will show the formatting you've applied to the *DisplayLabel* argument when it displays the field result.

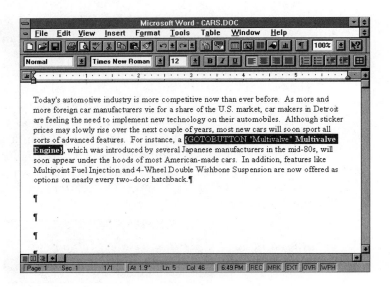

FIGURE 20-20

With the GOTOBUTTON field defined, a reader can jump to the definition of *Multivalve Engine.*

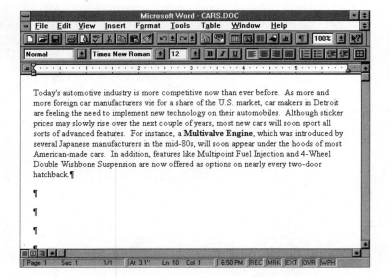

Other Fields and Where to Find Them in This Book

We've covered about 30 fields in this chapter, out of approximately 70 that Word provides. Some of the remaining fields are automatically inserted by Word so that you'll rarely, if ever, need to know about them. Other fields are covered elsewhere in this book. For example, the TC and TOC fields are both related to creating tables of contents; you'll find them discussed in Chapter 22 as part of the process of building a table of contents.

TOPIC FINDER

Benefits of Using Mail Merge   716

Preliminaries: Database Definitions   716

Using the Tools Mail Merge Command   717

- NEW! How to designate the main document
- NEW! How to create a data file with Word's help
- Other choices for creating a data file
- How to edit the main document
- Merge options
- Header files

Using Special Fields for Mail Merging   737

- Ask
- Fill-In
- If...Then and If...Then...Else
- Merge Record #
- Next Record and Next Record If
- Quote
- Set Bookmark
- Skip Record If
- NEW! Merge Sequence #
- The INCLUDETEXT field

Mail Merging Envelopes, Mailing Labels, and Catalogs   747

- Envelopes and labels
- Catalogs
- How to change to a different data file and main document type
- How to change a main document back to a normal Word document

NEW! **Creating Forms**   752

- How to enter a drop-down form field
- How to enter a text form field
- How to enter a check box form field
- Finishing touches
- How to fill in a form on your computer

21

Form Letters, Labels, & Forms

f you're like most Word users, you often need to say the same thing—though perhaps in slightly different ways—to a large group of recipients such as clients or customers. One of the benefits of word processing in general is that it can automate such tasks. The good news is that Word 6.0 goes further than most word processing programs, offering a feature that even helps automate the process of producing the files you need.

Word calls this feature *mail merge.* (Longtime Word users may know it as *print merge,* the term Word used before version 6.0.) Briefly, mail merge lets you combine two files to create customized documents. One file stores standard text, such as a form letter. The other stores information that will vary, such as names and addresses. When you merge these two files, Word creates merge documents, using the standard text from the first file and customizing each document with the variable information from the second file.

The mail merge feature depends heavily on fields. To best understand this chapter, you should first make sure you're familiar with the concepts of fields, discussed in Chapter 20.

Benefits of Using Mail Merge

If you've ever dealt with a cantankerous word processor that makes your form letters look like glued-together bomb threats from an illiterate terrorist, you may have doubts about the usefulness of mail merging. Even if you haven't used the feature, you've probably received computer-generated form letters with your name either truncated because it's too long or floating in the middle of white space because it's too short for the allotted space. For example, the name Catherine Hammerschmidt can come out as *Catherine Hammers*.

In truth, such awkward mail merge results are all too common. But Word's mail merge feature is among the best, with sophisticated capabilities that avoid these problems. Word will automatically adjust the text to format each document properly, with no gaping holes.

Of course, Word's mail merge also provides all the advantages of any mail merge feature. Because you create only one copy of the form letter (or other standard text), and one data file for the variable information, you save disk space and time when creating the files. And you save more time when printing because one command prints all the documents.

Still another advantage is that you need to create any given main document (the standard text) or any data file only once. You can, for example, send monthly mailings to your entire client list using the same data file each time. Similarly, you can use one main document with any number of data files; for instance, you can create a letter introducing your services and mail it to different groups of people at different times. This ability to reuse information not only saves time but also minimizes errors. Get the information right once, and you don't have to worry about getting it right again.

Preliminaries: Database Definitions

As you'll see shortly, Word's automation features will let you use mail merge without having to know much about the details. However, it will be easier to talk about mail merging if you understand some core terms.

A *record* consists of all the specific information that's meant for a single merge document. For example, if you're including a name, address, and salutation in each merge document, a single record will include one specific name, address, and salutation.

A *field* in the data file consists of the information that fills in one blank, or field, in the main document. These two uses for *field* are obviously different from one another, but having two meanings for one term isn't a problem. The type of field we're talking about at any time will usually be obvious from the context, but we'll sometimes talk about *merge fields* in a document to distinguish them from fields in a data file.

Note also that these two kinds of fields are related. If you have one field in the main document for an entire name and a second field for an entire address, for example, you need to divide each record in the data file into two fields—one for the name and one for the address. On the other hand, if you have fields in the main document for first name, last name, street address, city, state, and zip code, you'll need six fields in each record in the data file to match the six in the main document.

> For maximum flexibility in using the data in a data file, you should divide each record into the maximum number of fields you're ever likely to need. For example, even if you're creating a form letter that will use full names only, you should create separate fields for first and last names. That way, if you ever need to use the same data in a letter that will use either the first or last name by itself, you won't have to retype all the names. Before you create the data file, invest some time considering how you might use that data, and decide how many fields to include.

A *field name* refers to a given field in every record. For example, if you create a field for first names, you might identify it with the field name FirstName. When you create merge fields in the main document, the field names indicate which information goes in which merge field.

A *variable* is the data that varies from one record to the next, such as names and addresses in a data file.

A *value* is the actual data for a given field within a record. If the state for a specific record is California, for example, then CA is the value of the State field for that record.

A *variable name* is the name for the variable that goes in a given field. The field name and the variable name are always the same; for example, the State field holds the State variable.

Using the Tools Mail Merge Command

As we've already mentioned, mail merging needs at least two files: a main document, or main file; and a data file. (You can also use additional files, as we'll discuss later.) The main file contains the text to print in each document. The data file contains text that will vary from one document to the next. Word combines the information from both files to create customized merge documents. (For purposes of this discussion, the terms *main document* and *main file* are interchangeable, as are *data file, data document*, and *data source*.)

You can create the main file and the data file manually. However, the easiest way to use (or learn) mail merge is to take advantage of Word's ability to partially automate the task of creating the files. For most of this discussion, we'll assume that's what you're doing.

The starting point for mail merging is the Tools Mail Merge command, which opens the Mail Merge Helper dialog box, shown in Figure 21-1. The choices in the dialog box function as a checklist for the most important steps in creating the files you need. We'll start with an example of using the Mail Merge Helper to create a form letter.

FIGURE 21-1

The Mail Merge Helper dialog box is the starting point for automating many of the tasks involved in creating and using files for mail merging.

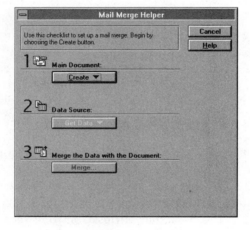

How to designate the main document

The first step in setting up a mail merge, as you can see in the dialog box, is designating which main document to use. Choose the Create button in the Mail Merge Helper dialog box to open the menu shown in Figure 21-2.

FIGURE 21-2

Choose the Create button in the Mail Merge Helper dialog box to see this menu, which lets you designate the kind of main document to use.

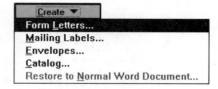

The Create menu offers several choices for the type of main document. For this example, choose Form Letters to see the message box shown in Figure 21-3.

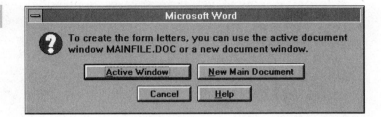

The message box lets you choose whether to use the document in the active window to create the form letters or open a new document window. When you choose the appropriate button, Word will return to the Mail Merge Helper, as shown in Figure 21-4.

In Figure 21-4, notice that Word has now added several items in the Main Document section of the dialog box. Two new lines under the Create button show the merge type (Form Letters, in this case) and the name of the main document (MAINFILE.DOC, in this case). An Edit button is added to the right of the Create button. Also notice that the Get Data button is no longer grayed.

How to create a data file with Word's help

Once you've designated the main document, you can choose the Edit button, but you'll be limited in what you can do since you haven't specified a data file, or data source, yet. In most cases, you should instead choose Get Data next, which will open a drop-down menu with three choices: Create Data Source, Open Data Source, and Header Options. We'll discuss each in turn. For the moment, however, we're concerned only with the Create Data Source item. When you choose it, Word will open the Create Data Source dialog box, shown in Figure 21-5.

FIGURE 21-5

The Create Data Source dialog box prompts you for the field names that will be used in the data file.

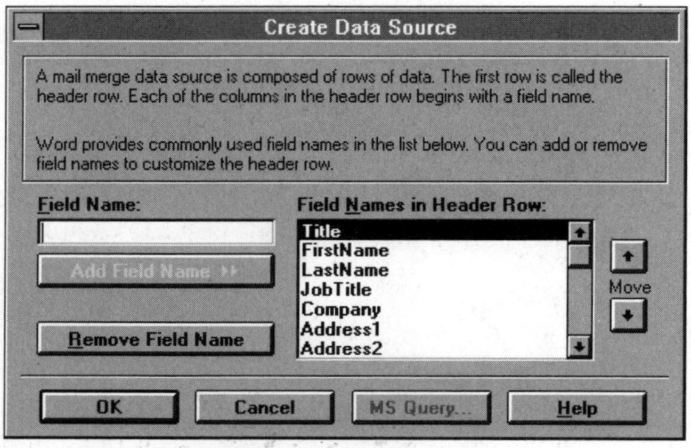

> **Create Data Source**
>
> A mail merge data source is composed of rows of data. The first row is called the header row. Each of the columns in the header row begins with a field name.
>
> Word provides commonly used field names in the list below. You can add or remove field names to customize the header row.
>
> **Field Name:**   **Field Names in Header Row:**
>
> [   ]   Title
>
> [Add Field Name »]   FirstName
>
> LastName
>
> JobTitle
>
> [Remove Field Name]   Company
>
> Address1
>
> Address2
>
> **Move** ▲ ▼
>
> [OK]   [Cancel]   [MS Query...]   [Help]

The Create Data Source dialog box makes it easy to name the fields in the data file you're about to create. When you first open the dialog box, you'll find a number of field names in the Field Names In Header Row list box. (The *header row* is the first row in the data file; it contains the names of the fields.) You can browse through the list and delete any fields you don't want by highlighting the field name and choosing Remove Field Name.

To add a field name, type it in the Field Name text box, and choose Add Field Name. Word will always add a field name at the end of the list. To change a name's position, highlight the name in the list, and choose the up or down arrow button to the right of the list box.

If you have Microsoft Query installed on your system, the MS Query button at the bottom of the Create Data Source dialog box will be available. You can choose this button to run Microsoft Query and search an existing database file for records that match any criteria you set. Because Microsoft Query does not come with Word, however, we'll ignore that choice here.

Once you've defined the field names, choose OK. Word will open the Save Data Source dialog box, which looks and works just like the Save As dialog box. Designate a drive, a directory, and a filename, and choose OK to create the file.

A Word message box will then point out that the new data file contains no records and that you can either add new records at this point or add merge fields to your main document. The message box offers three buttons in addition to Help: Edit Data Source, Edit Main Document, and Cancel. The first two are self-explanatory. Choosing the Cancel button will return you to the Mail Merge Helper dialog box. As you can see in Figure 21-6, after you've defined a data file, Word will add an Edit button to the dialog box just to the right of the Get Data button.

FIGURE 21-6

After you create a data file, Word will give you the choice of editing the main document, editing the data file, or closing the Mail Merge Helper dialog box.

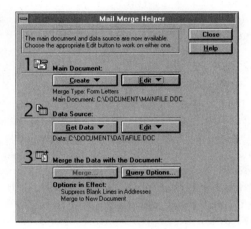

If you choose the Edit button in the Main Document section of the Mail Merge Helper dialog box, Word will open a one-item menu showing the filename of the main document. You can then press Enter or click on the menu choice to edit the main document. Similarly, if you choose the Edit button in the Data Source section of the dialog box, Word will open a one-item menu showing the name of the data file. You can press Enter or click on the menu choice to edit the data file.

How to enter and search records with the Data Form dialog box

For this example, we'll assume you want to add some records to the data file at this point. Choose Edit in the Data Source section of the Mail Merge Helper dialog box, and choose the data file from the one-item menu. Word will open a Data Form dialog box like the one shown in Figure 21-7 on the next page.

FIGURE 21-7

The Data Form
dialog box lets you
add, delete, and find
records in a data file.

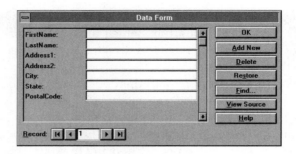

The Data Form dialog box includes a list of the field names in the data file, with a text box for each field. Word provides a scroll bar to the right of the fields so that you can scroll through the list if necessary. You can enter the data for each record by typing it in the appropriate text boxes. Then choose the Add New button (or press Enter while in the bottom text box) to save the current record and start a new one.

Just below the list of field names is the Record text box, with arrow buttons on either side. The text box shows the number of the record you're currently viewing. If you know the number of a record you want to move to, you can type that number in the text box and press Tab or Enter to move to that record. Alternatively, you can choose the arrow button to the right of the text box to move to the next record in the data file or the button farther to the right to move to the last record in the file. Similarly, you can choose the equivalent buttons to the left of the text box to move back one record or to the first record in the file. (You can choose these buttons by clicking on them or by tabbing to the button and pressing the Spacebar or the Enter key.) Each time you move to another record, you'll save any changes you made in the previous record.

You can also use the Data Form dialog box to manage data. When a record is displayed in the dialog box, you can delete the record by choosing Delete, or you can modify it by editing the entry. When you move to another record, Word will automatically save the changes. If you make a mistake and need to return to the original text for a record before saving the changes, choose the Restore button.

You can also find records by searching for specific entries. If you choose the Find button in the Data Form dialog box, Word will open the Find In Field dialog box, shown in Figure 21-8.

FIGURE 21-8

Use the Find In Field
dialog box to search for
a record in a data file.

To search for a record, open the In Field drop-down list and select the field to search through. Then, in the Find What text box, enter the value to search for. If you're searching for a New York address, for example, you would choose the State field and type the value *NY* in the Find What box. Then choose Find First to find the first record with an NY entry. The Find First button will change to Find Next so that you can use it to find the next record with an NY entry. Once you find the record you're looking for, you can modify it or delete it as appropriate.

How to view the data file

By using the Data Form dialog box, you can enter and modify the records for mail merging without ever seeing the data file itself. If you choose the View Source button, however, Word will close the dialog box and show you the data file.

As you can see in Figure 21-9, Word stores the data in a table, using one row for each record and one column for each field.

FIGURE 21-9

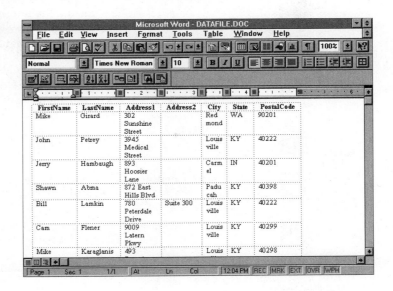

The data file that Word
creates uses a table to
store the data, with one
row for each record
and one column for
each field.

The top row in the table—the header record—consists of the field names. Unless you tell Word otherwise, it will always treat the first record in a data file as the header record and will use those entries to define the field names for the data file and the main file. This approach will always be the most convenient choice when you create the data file with Word's help. In some cases, however, it's more convenient to keep the header record in a separate file. For example, if you maintain the data with a database program and routinely import the data into Word format for monthly mailings, you can create the header record once and keep it in a separate file. We'll discuss this option later in this chapter.

How to work in the data file

You can edit the table in the data file directly, using the table features we discussed in Chapter 11. More interesting is that you can manipulate the data in various ways using the Database toolbar, which Word automatically provides when you're working in the data file. You can see the Database toolbar just above the ruler in Figure 21-9. Although we'll discuss the use of some of these buttons elsewhere, Figure 21-10 lists the 10 buttons on the Database toolbar and the actions they represent.

Button	Button Name	Action
	Data Form	Opens the Data Form dialog box, using the information in the first row of the table as the field names
	Manage Fields	Opens the Manage Fields dialog box, in which you can add, delete, or rename fields
	Add New Record	Adds a new record to the end of the database or table
	Delete Record	Deletes any records containing the selection
	Sort Ascending	Sorts the records in ascending order using the selected column
	Sort Descending	Sorts the records in descending order using the selected column

FIGURE 21-10

The Database toolbar buttons.

(continued)

FIGURE 21-10. *continued*

Button	Button Name	Action
	Insert Database	Selects the current database for updating from an external source
	Update Fields	Updates the contents of the current field or selected fields in the document, including DATABASE field links to an external data source
	Find Record	Opens the Find In Field dialog box and lets you search for a match within a specific field
	Mail Merge Main Document	Switches from a mail merge data source to the main document

The leftmost toolbar button is the Data Form button, which opens the Data Form dialog box. Next on the toolbar is the Manage Fields button, which opens the Manage Fields dialog box, shown in Figure 21-11. If you enter a name in the Field Name text box and choose the Add button in this dialog box, Word will add a field, in the form of a column, at the end of the table. You can also delete a field from the table by highlighting a name in the dialog box list and choosing Remove. If you highlight a name and choose Rename, Word will open another dialog box that will let you enter the new field name. Word will automatically apply any of these changes to the table in the data file.

FIGURE 21-11

The Manage Fields dialog box lets you add, remove, or rename fields in your data file.

The next two buttons on the Database toolbar are the Add New Record button and the Delete Record button. Choose Add New Record, and Word will add a record, as a blank row, at the end of the table. Choose Delete Record, and Word will delete the row (or rows) where the cursor or selection is currently located.

Next come the Sort Ascending and Sort Descending buttons. To use either of these, place the cursor or selection in one column of the table and click on the button. Word will select the entire column and sort the table based on that column, in either ascending or descending order, depending on which button you choose.

Next is the Insert Database button. Choosing this button is equivalent to choosing the Insert Database menu command, which we covered in Chapter 18. We'll explain why you might want to use this command shortly. For details on the Insert Database command, see "How to import data using the Insert Database command" starting on page 626.

To the right of the Insert Database button is the Update Fields button, which will update any fields that the cursor or selection is in. This is equivalent to pressing the F9 shortcut key for updating fields.

The next button on the toolbar is the Find Record button. It will open the Find In Field dialog box described earlier. The rightmost button is the Mail Merge Main Document button, which will return you to the main document.

Other choices for creating a data file

In addition to creating a data file with Word's help, you can also create a data file manually, by building the table from scratch; or you can import data from another file format, such as a Microsoft Excel spreadsheet or a dBASE or Microsoft Access data file. (We discussed importing data in Chapter 18.) Word will also let you organize the data without using a table. In fact, if you have more than 31 fields in each record, you must use a different organization, since 31 columns is the maximum a table allows. Figure 21-12 shows a data file, complete with a header record, that we created manually.

FIGURE 21-12

Word also recognizes this alternative data file format, with each record in a single paragraph and fields separated by tabs.

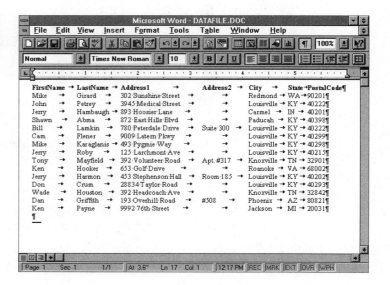

In Figure 21-12, each record is in its own paragraph, with fields separated by tabs. It's not important that each record fit on a single line, although that makes the data easier to read. The important detail is that you must use a paragraph mark after each record.

You can separate the fields with commas rather than with tabs. This third format, called *comma-delimited variable format* or *comma-separated variable format,* is a popular choice for exporting data from database programs. However, data is somewhat difficult to read in this format.

If you choose to create your data files manually, remember that you can put the field names in a separate header file. See "Header files" on page 737.

How to use a data file created without Word's Help

To use a data file created without help from Word, start by creating the file and saving it on a disk. You can then open a file for the main document, choose Tools Mail Merge, and designate the open file as the main document. Next, in the Mail Merge Helper dialog box, choose Get Data, and then choose Open Data Source.

Word will respond with the Open Data Source dialog box, which looks like the Open dialog box and works the same way. Specify the data file you want to use, and choose OK. A message box will tell you that Word found no merge fields in your main document. You can then choose Edit Main Document or choose Cancel to return to the Mail Merge Helper dialog box, where you can choose any of the options we've described.

How to enter tabs, commas, paragraph marks, and quotes as data

Because Word interprets tabs and commas as field delimiters and recognizes paragraph marks as indicating the end of a record, you may be wondering how to enter literal tabs, commas, and paragraph marks in your data. If the data file uses the table format, this isn't a problem, since Word recognizes each cell (the intersection of a column and a row) as a field, regardless of what's in it. If the data is in tabular (fields separated by tabs) or comma-delimited (fields separated by commas) format, however, you must enclose the entire field in quotation marks if it includes a tab, comma, or paragraph mark.

For example, you would enter the company name MegaCorp, Inc., as *"MegaCorp, Inc."* The quotation marks around the entry tell Word to interpret the contents—including the comma—literally.

To include quotation marks as part of the data, enter two sets of quotation marks. For example, suppose you have a client who insists on calling himself Jim "Pop" Stallone. You would enter the name in the data file as *Jim ""Pop"" Stallone*. Word will interpret this as one set of literal quotation marks around the word *Pop*.

If you're using a tabular or comma-delimited format and you enter data with the Data Form dialog box, Word will add the quotation marks automatically for all these cases.

How to edit the main document

So far in this chapter, we've largely ignored the main document—and for good reason. Although you can create a main document and even add text to it at any time, it's difficult to add merge fields until after you've defined the field names in the data file. Once you've defined the field names, however, creating the main document is straightforward.

To move to the main document from the Mail Merge Helper, choose Edit in the Main Document section of the dialog box. To move to the main document from the data file, click on the Mail Merge Main Document button on the Database toolbar or use one of Word's usual methods of moving among document windows: Press Ctrl-F6, or choose the document name from the Window menu.

How to insert a merge field

When you move to or open the main document, Word will add a new toolbar, called the Mail Merge toolbar. In Figure 21-13, you can see the

FIGURE 21-13

Word adds the Mail Merge toolbar, shown here just above the ruler, to the main document.

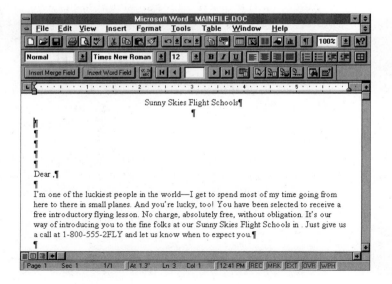

toolbar just above the ruler. You can also see that we've added the standard text (the text we want to include in every merged document). However, the document does not yet include the merge fields.

Among its other useful features, the Mail Merge toolbar can help automate the process of adding merge fields. The first button on the left is labeled Insert Merge Field. To use it, place the cursor where you want to add a field, and click on the button. In Figure 21-13, for example, the cursor is immediately to the left of the first left-justified paragraph mark in the letter, which is where we want the address to start.

Figure 21-14 shows the menu that opens when you choose the Insert Merge Field button. This menu lists all the field names as they appear in the header record. To insert a merge field from the menu, you can simply click on the field name, or highlight it and press Enter. Word will insert the field at the cursor location.

FIGURE 21-14

The Insert Merge Field menu makes it easy to insert mail merge fields into a main document.

If you prefer using the keyboard rather than the mouse, you can ignore the Insert Merge Field button and press Alt-Shift-F instead. Word will open the Insert Merge Field dialog box, shown in Figure 21-15.

FIGURE 21-15

You can use the Insert Merge Field dialog box to insert mail merge fields into a main document.

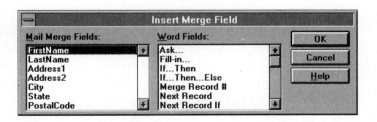

The Insert Merge Field dialog box contains two list boxes: the Mail Merge Fields list box and the Word Fields list box. The Mail Merge Fields list contains the same field names the Insert Merge Field menu does. To insert a merge field, highlight a field name in this list, and choose OK.

The Word Fields list box offers essentially the same list of fields you'll see if you choose the Insert Word Field button on the Mail Merge toolbar. In either form, this list offers advanced control over merging. We'll discuss these fields later in this chapter; see "Using Special Fields for Mail Merging" on page 737.

Figure 21-16 shows the main document after we've inserted the FirstName field. We've opened two panes, one showing the field code and one showing the field result. (You can toggle between seeing field codes and field results by placing the cursor or selection in the field and pressing Shift-F9.)

FIGURE 21-16

These two views of the mail merge field show that the field name FirstName (in the top pane) is the result of a Word MERGEFIELD using the field name FirstName (in the bottom pane).

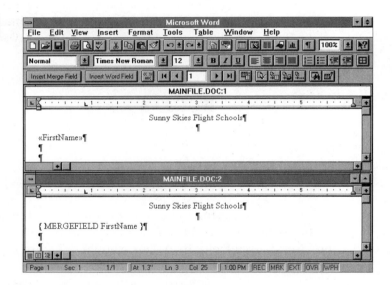

As Figure 21-16 shows, if Word is set to show field results, you will normally see the field result as the field name, or variable name, surrounded by what are sometimes called chevrons (« and »). If Word is set to show field codes, however, you can see that the field code consists of the MERGEFIELD field plus the variable name.

Figure 21-17 shows the sample main document with all the mail merge fields inserted and Word set to show field results. We have used the FirstName field twice—once in the address and once in the salutation. You can use a field name as many times as you like in a main document. You can also choose not to use some fields from the data file. Note that if you apply direct character formatting to merge fields, the merged result will retain the formatting.

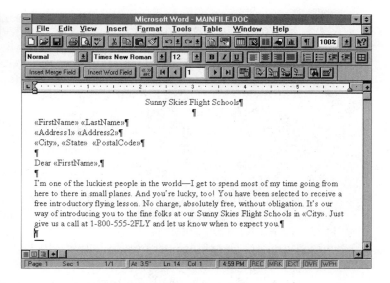

FIGURE 21-17

The finished sample form letter includes the merge fields inserted at the appropriate locations.

How to view data from the main document

When you run the mail merge, Word will replace each merge field in the main document with data from the data file, using successive records for each copy of the main document.

If you like, however, you can have Word show actual data in the main document on screen before you run the mail merge: Simply click on the View Merged Data button, the third from the left on the Mail Merge toolbar. By default, Word will display the data from the first record in your data file. However, you can specify another record or browse through the data one record at a time using the set of four buttons and a text box to the right of the View Merged Data button.

These toolbar items are identical to the text box and arrow buttons in the Data Form dialog box, and they work the same way. To move through the data records, choose the First Record, Previous Record, Next Record, or Last Record button, as appropriate, or enter a number in the Go To Record text box to move directly to a specific record.

Being able to see the data on screen before you run the merge can save a lot of wasted effort, since it will give you a preview of how your merged documents will look. You'll often find that your data file includes variations you hadn't thought of: names with *Esq.* at the end instead of a title such as *Mr.* or *Ms.* at the beginning, for instance. By browsing through the records, you may spot complications in spacing or punctuation that you can easily fix, before you print the merged documents.

If you prefer the keyboard to the mouse, you will be disappointed to find that Word has no built-in keystrokes that let you see the data or change the current record. However, you can use the techniques we'll cover in Chapter 28 to add most of the relevant commands to menus or to attach them to your choice of shortcut keys. The Word commands that you'll need in order to define the menu items or shortcut keys are MailMergeViewData, MailMergeFirst-Record, MailMergePrevRecord, MailMergeNextRecord, and Mail-MergeLastRecord.

The two buttons at the far right end of the Mail Merge toolbar are also concerned with viewing or working with data. Second from the right is the Find Record button, which will open the Find In Field dialog box we discussed earlier. The rightmost button is the Edit Data Source button, which will open the Data Form dialog box.

Figure 21-18 lists the Mail Merge toolbar buttons we've discussed so far, as well as other buttons that are discussed in the following section.

Button	Button Name	Action
Insert Merge Field	Insert Merge Field	Inserts a mail merge field into the main document
Insert Word Field	Insert Word Field	Inserts one of Word's special merge-related fields into the main document
« » ABC	View Merged Data	On screen, replaces the merge fields in the main document with the matching information from the current data record in the data file
⏮	First Record	Moves to the first record in the data file
◀	Previous Record	Moves to the previous record in the data file
▶	Next Record	Moves to the next record in the data file
⏭	Last Record	Moves to the last record in the data file

FIGURE 21-18

The Mail Merge toolbar buttons.

(continued)

FIGURE 21-18. *continued*

Button	Button Name	Action
	Mail Merge Helper	Opens the Mail Merge Helper dialog box
	Check For Errors	Opens the Checking And Reporting Errors dialog box, in which you can choose to simulate or perform the mail merge and have Word either report errors as they occur or produce a list of error messages
	Merge To New Document	Performs the mail merge and sends the result to a new document
	Merge To Printer	Performs the mail merge and immediately prints the result
	Mail Merge	Opens the Merge dialog box, which lets you control the record selection and the output for a mail merge
	Find Record	Opens the Find In Field dialog box and lets you search the data file for a match within a specific field
	Edit Data Source	Opens the Data Form dialog box using the fields defined for the current data file

How to use toolbar buttons to start a merge

As you move to the right of the Last Record button on the Mail Merge toolbar, you'll see the Mail Merge Helper button. Choosing this button is equivalent to choosing the Tools Mail Merge menu command; both open the Mail Merge Helper dialog box.

Next comes a group of four buttons that are all concerned with giving the command to run a merge. We'll start with the rightmost of these, the Mail Merge button, and work our way back to the left. When you click on the Mail Merge button, Word opens the Merge dialog box, which we'll discuss shortly. Choosing this button is equivalent to choosing Tools Mail Merge and then choosing the Merge button in the Mail Merge Helper dialog box.

The two buttons to the left of the Mail Merge button are shortcuts for starting a merge without going through the dialog box. The Merge To New

Document button gives the command to perform the mail merge and place the results in a single new document, with each individual merge document in its own section. The Merge To Printer button sends the merge documents directly to the active printer.

The leftmost button in this group is the Check For Errors button. Click on it, or press Alt-Shift-K, to open the Checking And Reporting Errors dialog box, shown in Figure 21-19.

FIGURE 21-19

The Checking And Reporting Errors dialog box lets you check your data files for errors in form.

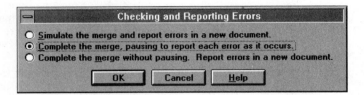

In this dialog box, Word gives you three choices for checking for errors in form—errors such as an extra comma in a comma-delimited file, which Word will see as indicating one too many fields in the record. You can choose to simulate the merge and have Word report errors in a new document, to actually run the merge and have Word pause to report each error it finds, or to run the merge without stopping but have Word report errors in a new document.

If you have any doubts about your data having exactly the right format—as you might, for example, if you entered a great deal of data—you should use one of these options. Which one you choose is a matter of taste and of how much confidence you have in your data. Note that if you use either of the options that actually run the merge, Word will not stop to ask whether to merge to a new file or directly to a printer. Rather, it will use whichever choice is currently set in the Merge dialog box (to a new document, by default).

Merge options

Once you've designated a data file to use and created the main document, complete with mail merge fields, you can start the mail merge by choosing any of the four toolbar buttons we've just mentioned or by choosing Tools Mail Merge and then choosing the Merge button in the Mail Merge Helper dialog box. If you choose the Merge button (or the Mail Merge button on the toolbar), you'll open the Merge dialog box, shown in Figure 21-20.

FIGURE 21-20

The Merge dialog box provides control over the mail merge output.

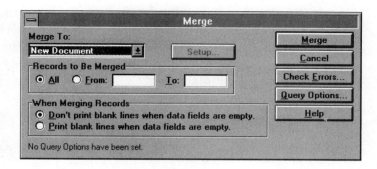

The Merge To drop-down list in the dialog box offers a minimum of two options: New Document and Printer. The New Document option creates a new document file with each individual merged document in its own section. This can be useful if you want to review the merged data before printing. If your system is set up for electronic mail or fax—subjects beyond the scope of this book—the Merge To list will also contain either or both of those options. If you specify either option in the Merge To box, Word will make the Setup button available so that you can enter the e-mail address or fax number.

The Records To Be Merged section lets you merge all records in the data file or merge a range of records based on their positions in the data file (such as records 1 through 10). You can specify the range in the From and To boxes.

Keep in mind that you can use the sorting feature on the Database toolbar to arrange a data file so that all the records you want to merge are together in a group. You can then specify the group as a range of records.

The two option buttons in the When Merging Records section let you specify how to treat blank lines that result from empty fields. Consider a mailing list with some addresses that need only three lines and others that need a fourth line—for a company name, for example. You'll need to include a field for the company name in your main document. But when the address doesn't include a company name, you want to avoid printing a blank line between the name and the street address. The option button labeled Don't Print Blank Lines When Data Fields Are Empty tells Word not to print these blank lines, which is the default setting. The Print Blank Lines When Data Fields Are Empty button tells Word to print them.

If you like, you can also define a query for a mail merge, to select a subset of records from the data file and sort them in a particular order. To define a query, choose the Query Options button to open the Query Options dialog box, shown in Figure 21-21. (You'll also find a Query Options button in the Mail Merge Helper dialog box.)

FIGURE 21-21

The Query Options dialog box lets you tell Word to select only those records that match a filter you define and to sort them in a specified order.

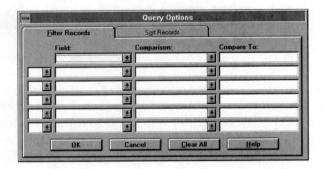

This is the same Query Options dialog box that we discussed in Chapter 18 in the context of importing data with the Insert Database command. Briefly, you use the Field and Comparison drop-down lists on the Filter Records card to specify the fields to base the selection on and the comparison to use. You then enter the field value for that comparison in the Compare To box for the appropriate row. The first box in all rows but the first lets you tie the criteria together with AND or OR. The other card in the dialog box, Sort Records, lets you choose up to three fields to sort by and allows you to specify whether to use ascending or descending order for each. For more details on how to use the Query Options dialog box, see "How to define the database import options" on page 628.

After you finish defining a query, choose OK to close the Query Options dialog box and return to the Merge dialog box. At this point you may want to choose the Check Errors button. This will open the Checking And Reporting Errors dialog box, which we discussed in the preceding section, and will give you a chance to check the effect of your settings.

The ability to define a query to select records is highly useful, but it can also be confusing at first. We strongly recommend that you test a new query definition by merging a relatively few records and sending the results to a new document, rather than risk wasting time and paper merging an entire data file and sending the results to the printer.

When you're satisfied with all your settings, choose Merge, and Word will run the merge, sending the output to your printer or to a new file. If you've chosen to merge to your printer, Word will open the Print dialog box to let you set print options before printing.

Header files

The only time you'll need a header file is when your data file does not include the field names as headings in the first row. In those cases, you'll need to create a separate file that contains only the field headings. (Note that if you attach a header file, the first row in your data file will be treated as data even if it actually contains headings.) Header files are useful if you routinely use data files in which the structure of the data files remains the same from one mail merge to the next, with data imported from other programs that cannot conveniently add headings as the first row.

Since the sample data file we used earlier included headings in the first row, we didn't need a header file. If you need one, the easiest way to create it is with the Mail Merge Helper dialog box. Choose Get Data, and then choose Header Options from the Get Data menu. In the Header Options dialog box, choose Create. Word will open the Create Header Source dialog box, which works the same way as the Create Data Source dialog box. You can use the same procedures we described for creating a data file to create the header file.

Using Special Fields for Mail Merging

Word offers a number of special merge-related fields, including fields that insert text from other Word documents, fields that let you update specific information manually each time you merge a given main document, and fields that let you create logical criteria for printing selected parts of the main document.

You can enter these fields in your main document using any of the techniques described in Chapter 20. When you're working in a main document that's already attached to a data file or a header file, however, Word provides easy access to many of these fields. You can click on the Insert Word Field button on the Mail Merge toolbar to open a drop-down menu of these fields. Alternatively, you can press Alt-Shift-F to open the Insert Merge Field dialog box, shown in Figure 21-22 on the next page, which also offers a list of these fields.

FIGURE 21-22

The Insert Merge Field dialog box has a list of merge-related Word fields that you can use in a main document.

The Insert Word Field drop-down menu is slightly different from the Word Fields list in the Insert Merge Field dialog box. In particular, the Merge Sequence # choice (for the MERGESEQ field) is available only on the drop-down menu, and the Quote choice (for the QUOTE field) is available only from the Word Fields list.

There's another difference between using the Insert Word Field drop-down menu and the Insert Merge Field dialog box. Some fields require more than just a field name. The FILLIN field, for example, requires a prompt that asks the user for information to fill in. When you insert one of these fields from the drop-down menu, Word provides a dialog box with appropriately labeled text boxes in which you fill in the information. After you enter the required information and choose OK, Word creates the field for you and inserts it into the text.

In contrast, when you insert the same field from the list in the Insert Merge Field dialog box, Word will not open a dialog box for the field. Instead, it will immediately insert the field, complete with reminders that show the form each field takes. To complete the field, you'll need to substitute the actual information for the reminders and then delete the reminders. You get the same reminders for what to add, but in a less elegant form.

For purposes of this discussion, we'll ignore the Insert Word Field drop-down menu and assume that you're using the Insert Merge Field dialog box. If you understand the fields well enough to replace the reminders with the appropriate text, however, you should have no trouble with the dialog boxes you'll see if you use the drop-down menu. Here, then, is a look at each choice in the Word Fields list box.

Because some of Word's terminology is a bit arcane, we'll occasionally use different terms than those Word uses, to aid understanding. When we use different terminology, however, we'll also mention the terms that Word uses.

Ask

The first choice in the Word Fields list box is Ask, which will enter an ASK field in the main document. Most commonly, you use the ASK field to allow you to enter information in the main document by typing that information from the keyboard during the merge.

For example, suppose you want to create personalized letters, using the recipient's first name in some cases and a more formal form of address in others. You could enter the information as a field in the data file. But if several people in your office generate letters using the same file, the appropriate salutation may change depending on whose signature goes on the letter. In this case, you may want to enter the salutation with the ASK field.

As we discussed in Chapter 20, you can enter a field by pressing Ctrl-F9 to enter the field characters (curly brackets, {}) and then typing the text for the field inside the field characters. If you enter a bookmark name between the field characters, the result for the field will be the text defined by the bookmark. In this particular case, you'll define the bookmark text with the ASK field.

Start by creating a field using the bookmark name Salutation so that the appropriate line of your main document reads

Dear {Salutation}:

Now that you've designated where you want the information to go, you can enter the ASK field. We recommend placing all ASK fields at the beginning of the main document to make them easier to find if you need to modify them. The basic form of the ASK field is

{ASK Bookmark "Prompt"}

In this example, the bookmark is Salutation, and the prompt is the text that Word will use to prompt users so that they will know what data to enter.

When Word encounters an ASK field during a mail merge, it will display the prompt as part of a dialog box and will wait for the user to type a response in the dialog box's text box. The response will define the bookmark text to use in the appropriate bookmark field or fields. For example, in this case you might define the ASK field as

{ASK Salutation "What greeting do you want for {MERGEFIELD FirstName} {MERGEFIELD LastName}?"}

This field will produce the dialog box shown in Figure 21-23 on the next page. The prompt includes the results of the FirstName and LastName fields so that you can see the full name of the addressee. Without those fields, it would be difficult to know who the addressee was for each letter or what the salutation should be.

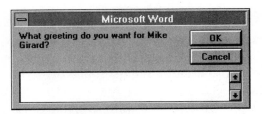

FIGURE 21-23

You can embed mail merge fields in your ASK fields to keep track of which record is being processed.

After you enter a response in the text box and choose OK, Word will treat your response much as it treats any other data, assigning it to the appropriate bookmark name. As with merge fields, you can use the same bookmark name in more than one place in the main document.

How to create a default response to an ASK field

The ASK field has two option switches. You can create a default response with the \d switch, using the form

{ASK Bookmark "Prompt" \d "Default"}

\d is the default switch. The text you enter as the default, following the switch, will appear automatically in the text box of the dialog box Word displays when it encounters the ASK field (for example, the dialog box shown in Figure 21-23).

How to enter a response for all merged documents at one time

The other switch is \o, which tells Word to prompt for a response to an ASK field once at the beginning of a mail merge and then to use that response for all the merged documents, rather than to prompt for each individual document. This is handy when you create many batches of documents from the same main document but want to be able to change one item for all the documents in each batch—such as the sender's name.

Fill-In

The Fill-In choice in the Word Fields list box inserts a FILLIN field, which resembles an ASK field in that it tells Word to prompt for a response that Word then uses in the merged document. The main difference is that the FILLIN field does not define a bookmark that you can then enter in any number of places within the document. Instead, the field itself marks the location for the data you're entering. The field takes the form

{FILLIN "Prompt"}

As with the ASK field, you can include merge fields as part of the prompt. You can also use the same switches you use for the ASK field: \d for a default response and \o to prompt one time at the start of a mail merge for a response to be used in all the merged documents.

If...Then and If...Then...Else

The next two choices in the list box both insert an IF field. In either variation, the IF field provides great flexibility for personalizing merged documents. You can use it to have Word make decisions about what to include in each document, based on information in each data record.

The If...Then choice inserts a field in the form

{IF ConditionalTest "TrueResult"}

The If...Then...Else choice inserts a field in the form

{IF ConditionalTest "TrueResult" "FalseResult"}

(Note that Word uses different terminology when it inserts this field, as we'll discuss in a moment.)

The first item, *ConditionalTest*, is an expression that Word can evaluate as either true or false. If *ConditionalTest* is true, the field will return *TrueResult*. If *ConditionalTest* is false, the field will return *FalseResult* for the If...Then...Else choice or nothing for the If...Then choice.

When Word inserts an IF field, it uses the term *Exp Op Exp* rather than *ConditionalTest*. *Exp Op Exp* is an abbreviation for *Expression1 Operator Expression2*, which is a literal representation of the format, as opposed to the descriptive *ConditionalTest*. Briefly, *ConditionalTest* compares two expressions using one of the conditional operators shown in Figure 21-24.

Operator	Definition
>	Greater than
<	Less than
=	Equal to
>=	Greater than or equal to
<=	Less than or equal to
<>	Not equal to

FIGURE 21-24

The operators available to an IF field.

You can use any of these operators with both text and numeric entries. With text entries, Word will use the ANSI value of the text to perform the test. For example, all of the following expressions are conditional tests:

{MStatus}="Single"

{NumItems}>100

{Spouse}<>""

Any expression that uses one of the conditional operators must be either true or false. Consider the conditional test *{NumItems}>100*. If the value of the *NumItems* variable in the current record is 100 or less, the result is false. If the value is greater than 100, the result is true.

Note also that Word uses the terms *TextIfTrue* and *TextIfFalse* when inserting the fields rather than the terms *TrueResult* and *FalseResult*. (However, the Help screen for the IF field refers to *TrueText* and *FalseText*.) But *TextIfTrue* and *TextIfFalse* are somewhat misleading since these results need not be limited to text. They can, in fact, be fields, including ASK fields or nested IF fields. (The SET and INCLUDE fields, which we'll discuss later in this chapter, can be particularly useful as a result of an IF field.)

The actual text for the *TrueResult* or *FalseResult* returned by an IF field can be any length and can contain page-break markers and section-break markers. If the item consists of either a single word or a single merge field, you don't need to enclose it in quotation marks. In most situations, however, you'll probably use more than one word, so we recommend that you get in the habit of always using quotation marks. You can use the IF field anywhere in the main document.

One common use of the IF field is to determine whether a particular field in the current record contains an entry. For example, suppose your data file stores names in three fields: F, MI, and L (for first name, middle initial, and last name). If you want to include a person's full name in your main document, you might use the merge fields

{MERGEFIELD F} {IF {MI}<>"" "{MERGEFIELD MI} "}{MERGEFIELD L}

Notice that the conditional test *{MI}<>""* tests for the presence of an entry in the MI field of the data file. If there's an entry for the field, the result of the conditional test is true (the MI field is not empty), and the IF field will use whatever you've defined as *TrueResult*—in this case, the MI field plus a space. If the MI field is empty, the result of the test is false, and the IF field will use whatever you've defined as *FalseResult*. Since we didn't specify *FalseResult*, Word will print nothing, and you won't wind up with an extra space between the first and last names.

You can also use the IF field to print text that isn't part of your data file. For example, assume your data file has a field named Spouse that contains the name of each customer's spouse—if he or she has one. You can use this information to personalize a message, using a field like this:

{IF {Spouse}<>"" "Of course, we'd also be thrilled if {Spouse} could accompany you! The more, the merrier!" "Please feel free to invite a guest to help us celebrate!"}

If any given record includes a spouse's name, Word will print the first sentence in the merged letter, including the spouse's name. If the Spouse field is empty, the test condition will be false, and Word will print the second sentence, inviting the customer to bring a guest.

You can also combine IF fields to create more sophisticated conditional tests. For example, to create an And condition, nest IF fields so that the second field is the *TrueResult* of the first. Consider the following IF field:

{IF State="CA" {IF Married="Y" "We have a special rate in our California office for married couples."}}

In this case, both conditions must be true for Word to include the sentence in the merge document. If the state is California, the first IF condition is satisfied, but its *TrueResult* is another IF field. If the Married field is Y, the second IF field is also true, and Word will print the sentence. But because neither IF statement includes a *FalseResult*, Word will print nothing if either condition is false.

The easiest way to create an OR condition is to use two separate IF fields with the same *TrueResult*, such as

{IF State="CA" "We have special rates for California and Washington residents."} {IF State ="WA" "We have special rates for California and Washington residents."}

Word will test each field separately and will print the message if either condition is true.

You can also use nested IF fields to take full advantage of If...Then...Else logic. For example, suppose you have two discount rates—one for California residents and one for married couples—and suppose you want to mention the California discount only to California residents and the married-couple discount only to married couples outside California. In that case, you would enter the fields as follows:

{IF State="CA" "We have special rates for California residents." {IF Married="Y" "We have special rates for married couples."}}

Merge Record

The Merge Record # choice inserts a MERGEREC field. The form of the field is simply *{MERGEREC}*. When Word comes across a MERGEREC field during a merge, it places the number of the current mail merge record in the merge document, using 1 for the first record in the data file, 2 for the second record, and so on. The most common use for the MERGEREC field is as a debugging tool when you are creating and testing main documents, especially those that use the Next Record, Next Record If, and Skip Record If fields.

Next Record and Next Record If

When you set mail merge to send output directly to the printer, Word will start each merged document on a new page. Similarly, when you set it to send output to a new document, Word will put each merge document in its own section, with the section break defined to start a new page.

In most cases, this approach will be exactly what you want—starting a new page for each copy of a form letter, for example. However, in some situations you'll want data from more than one record on the same page. In those cases, you can choose Next Record or Next Record If from the Word Fields list box to enter the NEXT field or the NEXTIF field in your main document. Either field will prevent Word from automatically starting a new page for each record.

The NEXT field

The NEXT field tells Word to move to the next record in the data file and fill the remaining MERGEFIELD fields in the main document, without starting a new page. The form of the field is simply {NEXT}.

For example, suppose you want to create a list of client names, with 10 names on each page. If you simply create a main document with the fields

{MERGEFIELD FirstName} {MERGEFIELD LastName}

Word will print one client name on each page. If you repeat the line 10 times, Word will print the same name 10 times.

To print 10 different names on each page, use the NEXT field in front of each line except the first. Lines 2 through 10 will read as follows:

{NEXT}{MERGEFIELD FirstName} {MERGEFIELD LastName}

Each time Word reaches a NEXT field, it will move to the next record in the data file and use the entries for that record until it reaches another NEXT field or reaches the end of the main document.

The NEXTIF field

The NEXTIF field is equivalent to a NEXT field placed inside an IF field, using the form

{IF ConditionalTest "{NEXT}"}

You can instead use the simpler form

{NEXTIF ConditionalTest}

to get exactly the same effect.

The NEXTIF field produces either of two effects, depending on the result of the conditional test. If the result is true, the field will act like a NEXT field, telling Word to read the next record of the data document and to use the entries for that record until it reaches another NEXT or NEXTIF field or the end of the main document. If the result is false, Word will use the entries for the current record until it reaches another NEXT or NEXTIF field or the end of the main document. Note that Word uses the term *Expression* rather than *ConditionalTest* when it inserts the NEXTIF field into your document. This is inconsistent with the terminology the program uses for the IF field, however, since the actual format for *ConditionalTest* is *Expression1 Operator Expression2* (which, oddly enough, is the format Word uses in the NEXTIF Help screen).

Quote

The Quote choice in the Word Fields list box inserts the QUOTE field into a main document. The QUOTE field, which inserts literal text, takes the form

{QUOTE "LiteralText"}

where *LiteralText* is the text (enclosed in quotation marks) that you want to insert into the document. Word will update the QUOTE field as soon as you modify its field code. The most likely reason for using the QUOTE field is to specify an ANSI character as an ANSI code. Simply put the code outside the quotation marks that enclose *LiteralText*.

For example, if you enter the field

{QUOTE "Word for Windows Companion, c 1995"}

in a document, the field result will be *Word for Windows Companion, c 1995.* If you enter the field

{QUOTE "Word for Windows Companion," 169 "1995"}

the field result will be *Word for Windows Companion, © 1995.* The code 169 in fact appears outside two separate sets of quotation marks, not inside quotation marks. And because 169 appears outside the quotation marks, Word substitutes ANSI character 169 (the copyright symbol). Appendix B offers a complete list of ANSI characters and their associated codes.

Set Bookmark

The Set Bookmark choice inserts a SET field, which takes the form

{SET Bookmark "text"}

(Word uses the term *data* rather than *text*, but to avoid confusion, we prefer reserving the term *data* for information stored in the data file.)

The SET field serves much the same function as an ASK field using the \o switch. By entering the bookmark name in one or more fields in the main document (using Ctrl-F9 to enter the field characters around the bookmark name) and then defining the text for the bookmark with the SET field, you can enter the text for that bookmark one time, and Word will use the same text for every copy of the merged document.

The main difference between defining the bookmark text with an ASK field and defining it with a SET field is that with an ASK field Word prompts you for the text when you start the mail merge. With a SET field you enter the text directly in the main document. Another difference is that with the ASK field you must enter the text each time you run a merge. With the SET field the text remains stored in the document until you change it.

Because the SET field and the ASK field with the \o switch are so similar in function, they are almost interchangeable. However, the SET field is the preferred choice when you want to use the same text repeatedly and change it only occasionally. The ASK field with the \o switch is the preferred choice when the text rarely remains the same from one merge run to the next or when you want to ensure that you enter the correct text each time.

> We recommend placing SET fields at the beginning of the main document so that you can find them easily if you need to change them.

Skip Record If

The Skip Record If choice enters a SKIPIF field in your main document. Like the NEXTIF field, SKIPIF is a variation on the IF field. The form of the field is

{SKIPIF ConditionalTest}

The effect of the field depends on the result of the conditional test. If the result is false, the field has no effect. If the result is true, however, SKIPIF tells Word to skip the current record, move to the next record in the data file, and start a new page, starting at the beginning of the main document. The actual format for *ConditionalTest* is *Expression1 Operator Expression2*, as it is for the IF field, although Word enters the SKIPIF field as *{SKIPIF Expression}*.

Merge Sequence

As we mentioned earlier, the menu attached to the Insert Word Field button on the Mail Merge toolbar offers one choice that isn't in the Insert Merge Field dialog box: Merge Sequence #. When you choose this from the Insert Word Field menu, Word will insert a MERGESEQ field at the cursor position. The form of the field is simply *{MERGESEQ}*.

MERGESEQ is similar to the MERGEREC field in that when Word comes across a MERGESEQ field during a merge, it places a number in the merge document to represent the current record. However, the number for the MERGESEQ field is based on the order of the mail merge, not on the position of the record in the data file. If you're merging record numbers 50 through 100, for example, the MERGEREC field will return the numbers from 50 through 100, whereas the MERGESEQ field will return numbers from 1 through 50. This can come in handy when you want to create a sequential set of numbers, such as invoice numbers or serial numbers.

The INCLUDETEXT field

Although it is not available through the Insert Merge Field dialog box, one other field can be especially useful for mail merging and is generally considered a merge-related field: the INCLUDETEXT field. Since it is not in the Word Fields list box, you'll need to insert it using one of the techniques we discussed in Chapter 20, such as the Insert Field command.

The INCLUDETEXT field lets you extract large sections of text from another Word document file and insert them into your merge documents. The field takes one of the two forms

{INCLUDETEXT "Filename"}

{INCLUDETEXT "Filename" Bookmark}

where *Filename* is the path and name of the file containing the text you want to insert and *Bookmark* is a selection of text that you've defined as a bookmark in that file. Keep in mind that you must put two backslash characters in the pathname to distinguish it from a switch.

There are at least two situations in which you might want to use the INCLUDETEXT field to place text in your merge documents rather than simply entering that text in the main document. First, you can use the field to include text from the same file in any number of main documents, saving the time, effort, and disk space required to enter the text in each of several files. Second, you can use the conditional fields discussed in this chapter to insert different INCLUDETEXT fields in different merged documents. That makes it easy to provide different versions of the merged document with large sections of text that vary, yet still have the variations automatically controlled by some aspect of the merged record.

Mail Merging Envelopes, Mailing Labels, and Catalogs

Word automatically recognizes four types of main documents. If you choose Tools Mail Merge and then choose the Create button in the Mail Merge Helper dialog box, you'll see Envelopes, Mailing Labels, and Catalog listed on the Create menu in addition to Form Letters. You can choose any of these when you first specify a main document. You can also change the document type at any time by reopening the dialog box, choosing the Create button, and choosing a different type of main document from the menu. If you started from an existing main document, Word will ask you whether you want to change the document type or create a new main document. Simply choose the appropriate answer to continue.

Envelopes and labels

If you designate a main document as a Mailing Label or Envelope type, Word will add a Setup button rather than an Edit button to the Main Document section of the Mail Merge Helper dialog box. After designating your data source, choose Setup. Word will open either the Label Options dialog box, shown in Figure 21-25, or the Envelope Options dialog box, shown in Figure 21-26, as appropriate.

FIGURE 21-25

If you designate the main document as a Mailing Label type, Word will provide a Setup button that opens the Label Options dialog box.

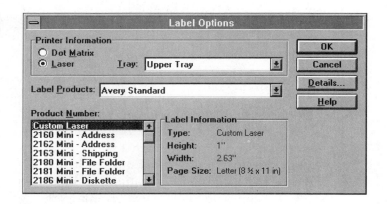

FIGURE 21-26

If you designate the main document as an Envelope type, Word will provide a Setup button that opens the Envelope Options dialog box.

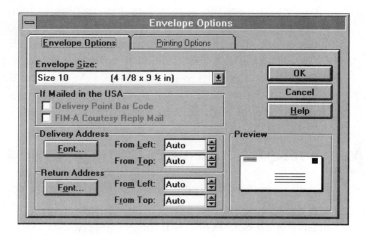

You can use the dialog box options to set the envelope or label format. We explored both of these dialog boxes in Chapter 8; for details on how to use them, see "Envelopes and Labels" starting on page 282.

When you finish with the Label Options or the Envelope Options dialog box, choose OK. Word will close the dialog box and open either the Create Labels dialog box or the Envelope Address dialog box. The options in both dialog boxes will be essentially the same, with a text box, an Insert Merge Field button, and an Insert Postal Bar Code button, as shown in Figure 21-27.

FIGURE 21-27

When you finish with the Label Options or the Envelope Options dialog box, Word will open a dialog box like this one.

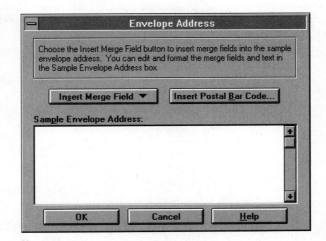

You can use the buttons to create an address format in the text box. To insert a field in the address, place the cursor where you want the field to appear, choose the Insert Merge Field button to see a menu of all the fields in the attached data file, and then choose a field from the menu.

To insert a postal bar code, choose the Insert Postal Bar Code button. Word will open a dialog box that will let you specify which merge field represents the zip code and which represents the street address. You'll also find a check box to add a FIM code to an envelope if you need to. (If you don't know what a FIM code is, you almost certainly don't need it.)

When you first return to your document, you may get a text message about invalid zip codes. Don't worry. This message will be replaced with the proper symbols when you view your data or merge the document.

When you choose OK to close the Create Labels or Create Envelope Address dialog box, Word will format the main document either as an envelope or as mailing label stock. Word will also add the merge fields to the document, return you to the Mail Merge Helper dialog box, and change the Setup button to an Edit button. Figures 21-28 and 21-29 show sample main documents for labels and envelopes.

FIGURE 21-28

The Mail Merge Helper automated much of the work in creating this main document for merging labels.

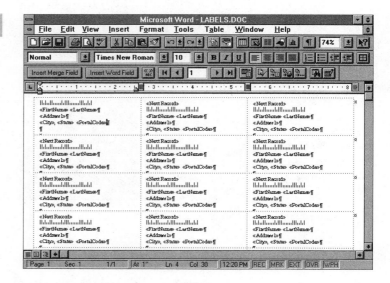

FIGURE 21-29

Although formatting a main document for envelopes takes less work than formatting one for labels, the Mail Merge Helper automates the job to make it even easier.

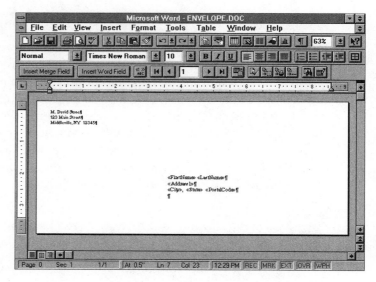

Once you've created the main document, mail merging envelopes or labels is much the same as mail merging form letters. However, we recommend that you take a look at Chapter 8 for details about Word's envelope and label features.

Catalogs

The fourth, and last, type of main document Word recognizes is the Catalog type. This choice is meant for producing repetitive information such as you'd find in a catalog, a directory, or even a simple list.

When you define a main document as a Catalog type, Word does not start a new page for the merge documents each time it comes to the end of the main document. Rather, it continues on the same page, using the next record. The result is equivalent to defining a main document that repeats itself as many times as there are records in the data file and starts each repetition with a NEXT field, to prevent starting a new page. Use the Catalog choice when you want to print a continuous list of data, fitting as many repetitions of the merged information on each page as possible.

How to change to a different data file and main document type

As we've indicated, you can change the main document type at any time by opening the Mail Merge Helper dialog box, choosing the Create button, and choosing any of the main document types from the Create menu. You can also choose a different data file for a main document at any time. In the Mail Merge Helper dialog box, choose Get Data, and then choose either Create Data Source or Open Data Source. You can then specify or create a different data file, using any of the techniques we've already discussed.

How to change a main document back to a normal Word document

The Create menu in the Mail Merge Helper dialog box also offers the choice Restore To Normal Word Document. If you decide, for whatever reason, that you don't want to use a given file as a main document anymore, you can change it back to a normal document file simply by opening the Mail Merge Helper dialog box and choosing Restore To Normal Word Document from the Create menu. Then choose Yes when Word asks for confirmation. When you return to the document, you'll find that Word will no longer display the Mail Merge toolbar in the document window.

Creating Forms

Although forms are not a mail merge feature, they provide a similar capability, making it easy to create documents combining information that remains the same on all copies of the form with information that varies from one document to the next. They are also similar in that you fill in fields to add the variable information. Instead of using a main document, however, you store the form as a template and use the template to create a new document when you want to fill in a form.

We'll cover templates in detail in Chapters 27 and 28. For the moment, you need to know only that creating a template is just like creating any other document except that you save it as a template instead of as a document. After you save a template, however, you can open new documents based on the template. Word will automatically insert text, fields, and other items it finds in the template into the new document. You can then edit the new document without disturbing the template.

The basic building blocks of a Word form are the FORMCHECKBOX, FORMDROPDOWN, and FORMTEXT fields. However, these form fields are not ordinary fields. If you try to enter them with the techniques described in Chapter 20, you'll find that Word doesn't recognize them. Instead, you must enter them from a menu, as we'll explain here.

As a simple example, we'll create a standard phone message form. To create the form, start by choosing File New. Choose the Template option in the New section of the dialog box, accept Normal as the template to base the new template on, and then choose OK to open a new, untitled template.

Next fill in the text, lines, and other non-varying features that you want in the form, including a heading, labels for fields, and so on. If you like, you can create a table to define a grid for entering text and fields and use the Format Borders And Shading command to build lines or boxes with the techniques discussed in Chapter 11.

If you prefer, you can use Word's drawing tools to add lines and boxes. To make the drawing tools available, choose View Toolbars, check the Drawing check box, and choose OK to return to the document, where the Drawing toolbar will be displayed. For details, see "Using Word's Drawing Tools" starting on page 550.

Once you've entered the background text, your screen should look something like the one shown in Figure 21-30. At this point, you can enter the form fields.

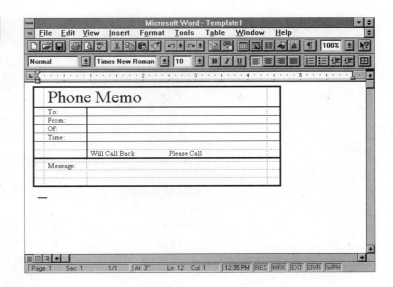

FIGURE 21-30

Starting with this phone message format, we'll create a phone message form.

How to enter a drop-down form field

To enter the first form field, move the cursor to where you want the field to appear—in this case, just after the To: label on the first line below the heading. Then choose Insert Form Field to open the Form Field dialog box, shown in Figure 21-31.

FIGURE 21-31

To insert a form field, start with the Form Field dialog box.

In the dialog box, you can choose one of three types of form fields: text, check box, and drop-down. An Options button lets you set options for each individual form field. For our example, we'll assume you have a limited number of people in your office, which means that it makes sense to create a drop-down list for the To: field. Choose the Drop-Down type, and then choose the Options button to open the Drop-Down Form Field Options dialog box, shown in Figure 21-32 on the next page.

FIGURE 21-32

The Drop-Down Form Field Options dialog box lets you customize each drop-down form field.

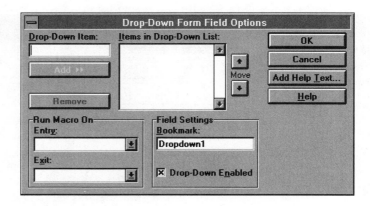

The dialog box shown in Figure 21-32 offers a number of features. For example, the two text boxes in the Run Macro On section give you the option of telling Word to automatically run a macro when you either move to or leave the field. In the Field Settings section, you can define a bookmark name so that a macro can refer to the field. You can also choose to enable the drop-down list so that users can open it when they're filling in the form. Also notice the Add Help Text button. This button opens a dialog box in which you can specify help messages that will be displayed in the status bar or in response to pressing F1 when the cursor is in the form field.

In the Drop-Down Form Field Options dialog box, you can create the drop-down list by entering each item for the list in the Drop-Down Item text box and then choosing the Add button. If you make a mistake, you can delete the item by highlighting it and choosing Remove. If you want to move an item to a different position in the list, highlight it and choose the up or down arrow button to the right of the list box. When you've finished, choose OK to return to the editing screen, where the form field will be entered at the cursor position.

How to enter a text form field

Most of the other fields in the Phone Memo form will be text form fields, which you will use to type some text when you fill in the form. To enter a text form field, position the cursor where you want the field to appear. Then choose Insert Form Field, select the Text type, and choose Options. Word will open the Text Form Field Options dialog box, shown in Figure 21-33.

Many of the options in this dialog box are the same as those for the drop-down form field. For this example, we're interested only in the options that are specific to the text form field.

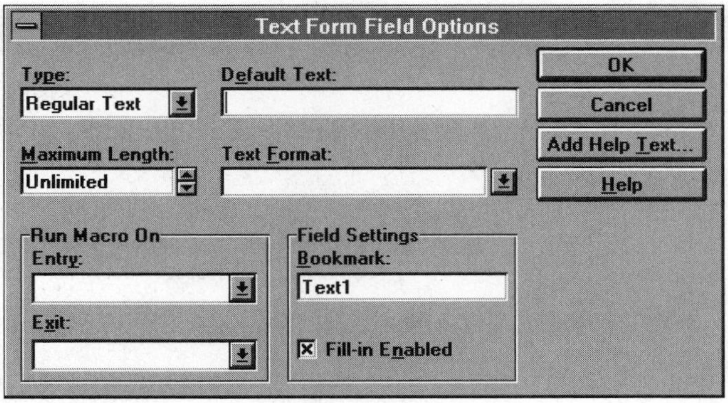

FIGURE 21-33

The Text Form Field Options dialog box lets you customize each text field.

Let's start with the Type drop-down list. The list of text form field types includes six choices: Regular Text, Number (the field will accept numbers only), Date (the field will accept dates only), Current Date (the field will automatically enter the current date), Current Time (the field will automatically enter the current time), and Calculation (lets you enter an = (Formula) field within the form field to calculate a result).

For the phone memo form we're creating, you would want to use Regular Text form fields for the fields that accompany the From:, Of:, and Message: labels. For the Time: label, you'd probably want to add both a Current Date and a Current Time form field after the label.

Other options that you can set for a text form field include a maximum length and a default entry. For regular text, you can also choose a capitalization format from the Text Format drop-down list: Uppercase, Lowercase, First Capital (the first character of the entry is capitalized), or Title Case (the first character of each word is capitalized). For dates, times, and numbers, you will be able to select from an appropriate set of formatting options. With the possible exception of setting a maximum length, however, these other options are irrelevant for our sample form. To finish entering each field after you set the options, choose OK.

How to enter a check box form field

All that remains in our sample form is to create two check boxes for the Will Call Back and Please Call items on the form. To enter a check box form field, position the cursor where you want the field to appear. Choose Insert Form Field, select Check Box, and then choose the Options button to open the Check Box Form Field Options dialog box, shown in Figure 21-34 on the next page.

FIGURE 21-34

The Check Box Form
Field Options dialog
box lets you customize
each check box form
field.

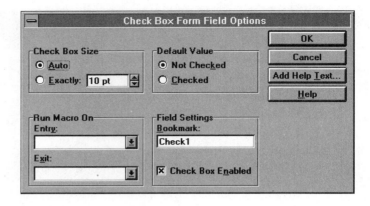

This dialog box is similar to the two we just discussed; only four items
are specific to the check box form field. In the Default Value section, you can
decide whether the check box should be checked as a default. For this form,
we'll select Not Checked for both boxes. In the Check Box Size section, you
can define a size for the check box, or you can let Word automatically determine the size. We'll choose Auto for both check boxes. When you've finished
with the dialog box, choose OK to close it and insert each check box
form field.

Finishing touches

Once you've finished entering the form fields, you can add any finishing
touches you like to the form: color, shading, lines, boxes, and so forth.

When the form is completed, you should choose Tools Protect Document, choose the Forms option in the Protect Document dialog box, and
choose OK. If you don't set this option, users will be able to move anywhere
within the document when they fill in the form and could accidentally
change the supposedly static text. If you set the protection feature, users will
be limited to moving among the fields and won't be able to change the form
itself. After you've set the protection feature, you can save the form and
close the file, remembering to save it as a template instead of as a document.

As you create forms, you may find it convenient to use the Form Field
toolbar, described in Figure 21-35. You can add the toolbar to the screen by
choosing Insert Form Field and then choosing the Show Toolbar button.
You'll see buttons on the toolbar for inserting each of the three kinds of form
fields and for opening the appropriate Options dialog box for a currently
selected field. You'll also find buttons for inserting a table, inserting a frame,
adding or removing shading, and turning on the form protection feature.

Button	Button Name	Action
 ab	Text Form Field	Inserts a default text form field
 ⊠	Check Box Form Field	Inserts a default check box form field
	Drop-Down Form Field	Inserts a default drop-down form field
	Form Field Options	Opens the appropriate Options dialog box for the current form field
	Insert Table	Inserts a table or lets you modify an existing one
	Insert Frame	Inserts a new empty frame or frames the current selection
 a	Form Field Shading	Turns form field shading on or off throughout the document (form fields are shaded by default)
 🔒	Protect Form	Protects the current document as a form so that changes can be made only to the contents of form fields

FIGURE 21-35

The Form Field toolbar.

How to fill in a form on your computer

Once you've created a form as a template, you can use it whenever you like. For example, choose File New and specify the form you just created as the template to use. The new file should look much like the one shown in Figure 21-36 on the next page.

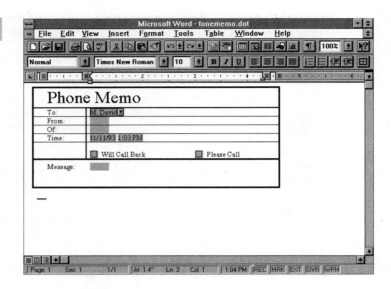

FIGURE 21-36

If you open a new
file using the form
template, you'll see
a finished phone
message form like
this one.

When you create the new file based on the form template, Word will automatically fill in the current date and time in the appropriate fields. You can
fill in the rest of the form in much the same way as you make choices in a
dialog box—tabbing or clicking to move from field to field, entering text,
checking a check box, and selecting from a drop-down list. In fact, if you
remembered to protect the form, you'll find that you can't move anywhere
but within the fields, so that filling in the form is almost identical to working
in a dialog box. You can even toggle the checks in the check boxes on and off
by moving to a check box and pressing the Spacebar.

There is one important difference, however: Although you can open a
drop-down list in a form by clicking on the adjacent down arrow with a
mouse, you can't open the list by pressing the Down arrow key. If you try,
you'll simply move to the next field. To open the list with the keyboard, tab
to the field and press F4.

TOPIC FINDER

A Note on Index-Related and Table-Related Fields   762

Creating a Table of Contents   762
- How to number pages in a table of contents
- How to build a table of contents from styles
- How to update a table of contents
- How to build a table of contents from fields
- How to restrict a table of contents to a portion of a document
- NEW! How to format a table of contents

Creating a Table of Figures   771
- How to build a table of figures using styles
- How to build a table of figures using fields
- How to build a table of figures using captions
- NEW! How to format a table of figures

Creating an Index   775
- A quick example
- How to define index entries
- How to choose a format for the index
- How to break up an index
- How to update an index

NEW! **Creating a Table of Authorities**   783
- How to define table of authorities entries
- How to format and create a table of authorities

NEW! **Working with Long Documents**   785
- How to create chapter-page numbers

22

Tables of Contents & Indexes

ne of the most time-consuming tasks involved in creating a document is developing a reference aid such as an index, a table of contents, a table of figures, or a table of authorities. With its index and table features, however, Word takes much of the tedium out of this chore.

The steps for creating an index and for creating these various kinds of tables are similar. To flag the entries you want to include, you enter markers in the body of your document. The markers can be fields for indexes or tables, or, for tables of contents and tables of figures, they can be your choice of paragraph styles. In all cases, you use the Insert Index And Tables command to enter a field that compiles the final result.

We'll first cover the basics of creating a table of contents, a table of figures, an index, and a table of authorities. Then we'll look at how to create these elements for large documents broken into several files. Because Word's indexing and table features are based on fields, to get the most from this material you should be familiar with the concepts presented in the first half of Chapter 20 before you read this chapter.

A Note on Index-Related and Table-Related Fields

If you're familiar with Word's fields, you can create all the index-related and table-related fields in Word using any of the techniques covered in Chapter 20. Most users, however, will find that the special tools Word provides for creating these particular fields are far easier to use than the tools for creating fields in general.

For instance, if you choose your options from a dialog box, you don't have to worry about learning the switches used to change settings for the various fields; Word will enter them for you, along with the rest of the field. Even if you're a longtime Word user who has memorized the switches for each index-related and table-related field, you'll find that many of these more specialized tools will save you work. For example, the Mark Index Entry dialog box includes an option that will mark all occurrences of a given word or phrase throughout your document with a single command.

Because you don't need to learn all the details of how each field operates, we won't look at the fields themselves in much depth in this chapter. But we will explain them well enough to show you how to change the text entry for each marker field, or otherwise modify the field, without having to delete the field and redefine it.

If you're the sort of person who wants to know what's going on under the hood, you can easily learn more about any field discussed in this chapter, including the details of the various switches for that field. Start by creating the field using the tools we'll discuss here. For those fields that show field results in the form of an index or a table, toggle the view to show the field code by placing the cursor or selection in the field result and pressing Shift-F9. Then highlight the field and press F1 to bring up the Help screen that explains the switches for that field.

Creating a Table of Contents

Word gives you a choice of how to mark entries for a table of contents. If you've used the outline feature (discussed in Chapter 19) or styles (discussed in Chapters 12 and 19) in your document, you can tell Word to compile a table of contents directly from the headings in your text. Alternatively, you can enter TC fields to indicate entries for the table of contents. We'll cover both techniques, starting with styles. But first there's one issue you need to consider before you create a table of contents—or any other table, for that matter: the effect of the table on page numbers.

How to number pages in a table of contents

Normally you'll want to put a table of contents at the beginning of your document. If you simply add it there, however, it will change the pagination for the rest of your text, pushing the text forward by as many lines as the table uses. Adding a page break after the table will also change pagination, forcing you to generate a new table of contents. Add more front matter, such as a table of figures, and you'll change the pagination once again.

The elegant solution to this problem is the one that most books use: Create a separate numbering scheme for your table of contents pages, along with any other front matter such as the title page and the acknowledgments page. A common scheme is to use lowercase Roman numerals (i, ii, iii, and so on) for this part of the document.

Word can manage this trick easily. To number the front matter pages separately from the rest of the document, first make sure the table of contents is in its own section, with other front matter if appropriate. You can insert a section break by choosing Insert Break, specifying any of the section-break options, and then choosing OK. In this case, you'll probably want to use the Next Page option. For information about multisection documents and the section-break options, refer to "Multisection Documents" on page 485.

Next place the cursor anywhere in the section containing the table of contents. If you want to use page numbers only, without additional text in the header or footer, you can choose Insert Page Numbers and then choose the Format button to open the Page Number Format dialog box. Open the Number Format drop-down list, highlight the format you want to use, and then choose OK to close the dialog box and return to the Page Numbers dialog box.

To finish, open the Position drop-down list, and choose either the Top Of Page (Header) or the Bottom Of Page (Footer) option. Then open the Alignment drop-down list, choose an alignment option, and choose OK. Repeat the process in the next section of the document, choosing an appropriate format in the Page Number Format dialog box and setting the numbering to start at 1 by entering the number *1* in the Start At text box.

> **N O T E** If you want to add text to the header or footer, you'll need to use the View Header And Footer command. For details on creating a header or footer, see "Creating Headers and Footers" starting on page 167 and "How to change page numbering from one section to another" starting on page 491.

If you created the table of contents before you put it in its own section, be sure to update it after you've adjusted all the page numbers: Simply place the cursor or selection anywhere in the table and press F9.

How to build a table of contents from styles

In Chapter 19, we discussed how to assign a special set of style names to a document's headings. Major headings use the Heading 1 style; subheadings use Heading 2, Heading 3, and so on, up to as many as nine levels of headings. For documents that use headings, these styles provide the easiest way to create a table of contents. If you haven't already assigned heading styles to the document, you can assign them using any of the techniques we covered in Chapters 12 and 19.

Word will also let you use any paragraph style or styles to flag paragraphs that you want to include as entries in the table of contents. In most cases, however, heading styles will be the preferred choice, since the paragraphs you'll want to include in a table of contents will almost always be section headings. For this discussion, then, we'll assume that you'll normally be using heading styles when creating a table of contents from styles.

How to compile a table of contents using heading styles

After you create a document that includes heading styles, you can compile the table of contents by moving the cursor to the position where you want the table to appear—usually the beginning of the document. Then choose the Insert Index And Tables command, and Word will open the Index And Tables dialog box, shown in Figure 22-1. The dialog box offers four tabbed cards, including the Table Of Contents card.

FIGURE 22-1

To compile a table of contents, first choose Insert Index And Tables to open the Index And Tables dialog box, and then choose the Table Of Contents card.

Most of the options on the Table Of Contents card are concerned with defining the format for the table—a subject we'll return to later. For this example, we want to choose the Options button to open the Table Of Contents Options dialog box, shown in Figure 22-2.

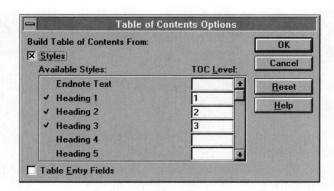

FIGURE 22-2

To tell Word how to compile a table of contents, choose Options from the Table Of Contents card to open this dialog box.

The Table Of Contents Options dialog box offers two check boxes that let you tell Word whether to use styles, table entry fields, or both. By default, Word checks the Styles check box. You can then specify which styles to use.

When you compile a table of contents from paragraphs formatted with specific styles, Word looks for the paragraphs with those styles and uses the text from those paragraphs in the table of contents. As you can see in Figure 22-2, the Available Styles section of the dialog box includes a list of the heading styles, plus a TOC Level text box for each. In the text boxes, you can specify whether to include each style and at what level.

By default, Word will include the first three levels of heading styles. Paragraphs formatted with the Heading 1 style will become first-level entries, paragraphs formatted with the Heading 2 style will become second-level entries, and paragraphs formatted with the Heading 3 style will become third-level entries. You can easily change this, however. For example, if you've used Heading 1 for a book title and Heading 2 for your chapter titles, you can tell Word not to include Heading 1 paragraphs in the table of contents and to treat Heading 2 paragraphs as first-level entries. Simply delete the number from the TOC Level text box for Heading 1, enter *1* in the text box for Heading 2, and adjust the TOC Level boxes for the other heading levels accordingly. You can also set the same level for two or more styles. If you've made changes but decide that you want to return to the default, choose the Reset button.

After you've specified the appropriate levels for the styles, choose OK to accept the settings and return to the Table Of Contents card. Then choose OK again to compile the table.

Word will start by looking to see whether a table of contents already exists in the document. If it finds one, it will highlight the table and ask whether you want to replace the existing table. Choose Yes, No (to add a second table of contents), or Cancel, as appropriate. If you are in an existing table of contents when you select the command, the No option will not be available.

Word can find a table of contents easily because the table is actually a TOC field, not ordinary text. To toggle between seeing the table of contents, which is the TOC field result, and seeing the field code, place your cursor or selection in the field, and press Shift-F9.

If your document does not already contain a table of contents or if you chose OK in response to Word's question, Word will repaginate the document, search for the heading styles, and compile the table of contents, complete with page numbers. (If you need to interrupt the compilation for any reason, you can press Esc.) Word will finish by inserting the table at the cursor position—or at the same position as the previous table of contents if you've chosen to replace an existing table.

Figure 22-3 shows a sample table of contents. Each entry contains the table of contents text, followed by a tab with dot leaders, the page number, and a paragraph mark to end the entry. Note that Word will ignore hidden text when compiling a table of contents.

When it creates a table of contents, Word adds a set of TOC styles to the document's list of styles. If you look at the Style drop-down list on the Formatting toolbar or choose Format Style and look at the list of styles in use, you'll see that the list now includes the style names TOC 1, TOC 2, and so on through TOC 9. Later in this chapter, we'll discuss how to change the table's format by modifying these styles.

FIGURE 22-3

When Word compiles a table of contents, it adds styles to the document's list of styles and applies those styles to the table of contents entries.

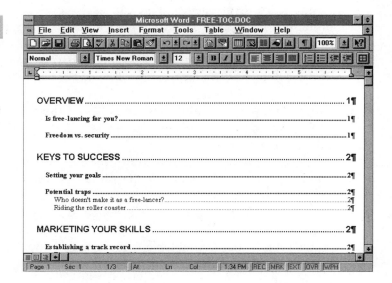

How to update a table of contents

To update a document's table of contents, use the Insert Index And Tables command and replace the existing one, or place the cursor or selection anywhere in the table and press F9 to update the field. If you use F9, Word will respond with a dialog box that lets you choose to update the entire table or to update the page numbers only. (The second choice is useful if you've applied direct formatting to the table and you want Word to leave the formatting alone.) Choose the appropriate setting, and then choose OK to update the table.

> The best time to compile or update a table of contents is immediately before you print the document. If you edit or reorganize the document after updating, the page numbers may change, and the table will no longer be accurate.

How to build a table of contents from fields

If you don't want to use headings as table of contents entries, or if you need more entries than you have headings, you can use TC fields to create the entries—either instead of or in addition to using paragraphs formatted with particular styles.

The TC field takes the form

{TC "text" [switches]}

where *text* is the text you want to appear in the table of contents. Figure 22-4 on the next page shows an example of a document where TC fields can come in handy. The first TC field in Figure 22-4 is at the beginning of the text. The second, {TC "Is free-lancing for you?"}, is near the bottom of the screen. The first field defines a table of contents entry for a section of text that doesn't have its own heading. The second field repeats text that's functioning as a heading but is part of the same paragraph as body text, so you can't format the heading with its own paragraph style. Note that when you use TC fields, you must specify the full entry for the table of contents, even if the text already appears in your document. The \f switch is followed by the table identifier (in this case, C), the default for a table of contents. The \l switch identifies the level of the entry.

A TC field's sole purpose is to mark table entries (including entries for other kinds of tables, as we'll discuss later in this chapter). There are no field results, so you won't see a difference if you toggle between viewing field codes and viewing field results. When you enter the field, however, Word

FIGURE 22-4

This sample document
includes two TC fields.

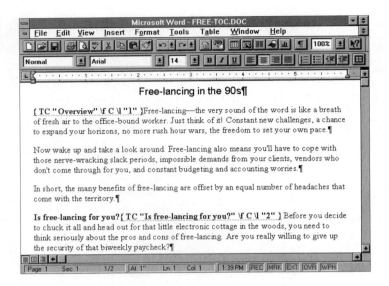

will format it as hidden. If you want to see it, either choose the Show/Hide ¶
button on the Standard toolbar or choose Tools Options, choose the View
card, and check the Hidden Text check box.

How to enter a TC field

By far the easiest way to enter a TC field is with the Mark Table Of Contents
Entry dialog box, shown in Figure 22-5.

FIGURE 22-5

This dialog box makes
it easy to enter a TC
field.

To use the dialog box, first position the cursor where you want to insert
the field. Alternatively, if all or part of the text you want to use for the table
of contents entry already appears in your document at the position where
you want to insert the field, select the text. Then press Alt-Shift-O to display
the Mark Table Of Contents Entry dialog box.

Next enter the text for the table of contents entry in the Entry text box. If
you didn't select any text before opening the dialog box, the text box will be
blank. If you selected text first, Word will have inserted the selection for you,
although you can modify it if you like. For now, we'll ignore the Table Identifier drop-down list except to say that the default entry C is the right choice
for a table of contents entry. The Level box lets you set a level for the entry,
from 1 through 9.

Choose the Mark button, and Word will insert the TC field into your document at the cursor position (or immediately after the selection if you have selected text). Word will not close the dialog box, however. In fact, once the dialog box is open, you can use it to create as many TC fields as you like. To move between the dialog box and your document, point and click with the mouse or press Ctrl-Tab. While in the document, you can position your cursor for the next TC field and even select text for automatic entry in the dialog box. You can then move back to the dialog box, add or change the entry and the level as appropriate, and choose Mark to enter the next TC field. When you've finished, choose Close to close the dialog box.

How to compile a table of contents using TC fields

Compiling a table of contents from TC fields is much like compiling one from headings. After you've entered all the fields, position the cursor where you want the table of contents to appear. Next choose Insert Index And Tables, and choose the Table Of Contents card. Choose the Options button to open the Table Of Contents Options dialog box, shown in Figure 22-2 on page 765. In this case, you'll want to make sure that the Table Entry Fields check box is checked. You can also check the Styles check box or not check it, as appropriate.

When you choose OK to close the Table Of Contents Options dialog box and then choose OK to create the table of contents, Word will follow the same procedure we described earlier. It will check to see whether a table of contents already exists, ask whether to replace the table if it finds one, repaginate the document, search for TC fields (and for styles if you checked the Styles check box), compile the table, and insert the TOC field at the cursor position or at the position of the TOC field it's replacing.

How to restrict a table of contents to a portion of a document

You can tell Word to compile a table of contents for only part of a document. This restriction can come in handy if your document is divided into sections or chapters and you want a separate table of contents for each section or chapter.

First define a bookmark indicating the part of the document you want to compile the table of contents for. Then move to where you want to insert the table of contents and create a TOC field of the form

{TOC \o \f \b "bookmark"}

where *bookmark* is the name of the bookmark you've defined. The \f switch tells Word to compile the table of contents using any TC fields. The \o switch tells Word to include entries formatted with the built-in heading styles. In our example, we've used both, but you need to specify only one or the other.

Alternatively, you can use Insert Index And Table to insert a table of contents for the entire document, use Shift-F9 to view the field code, and add the \b switch and the bookmark name. With either method, when you update the field (by using F9 and selecting to update the entire table), the new table of contents will include only those entries that fall within the bookmark.

How to format a table of contents

Until now, we've largely ignored the Table Of Contents card in the Index And Tables dialog box, rushing past it on the way to the Table Of Contents Options dialog box. But if you're concerned with how your table of contents looks, you'll want to take advantage of the formatting options on this card. To see the card, shown in Figure 22-6, choose Insert Index And Tables, and select the Table Of Contents card.

FIGURE 22-6

To format a table of contents, choose Insert Index And Tables, and choose the Table Of Contents card.

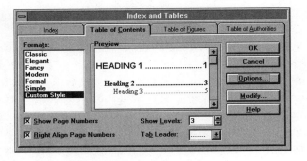

As you can see in Figure 22-6, the Formats list box offers six predefined formats, plus one custom style. The Preview box shows a sample of the high-lighted format with the current settings, so you can browse through the list of formats and see what each will look like.

Below the Formats list box is the Show Page Numbers check box. By default, this box is checked for each format choice, but you can eliminate page numbers by clearing the check box. When this box is checked, you can also check or clear the Right Align Page Numbers check box. And when the Right Align Page Numbers box is checked, you can define a tab leader. The choices in the Tab Leader drop-down list are no leaders, solid lines, dashed lines, and dotted lines. The default settings for right-aligned page numbers and for tab leaders vary depending on the predefined format.

If you choose the Custom Style format, you can choose the Modify button to open the Style dialog box. This is essentially the same dialog box you'll see if you choose Format Style. When you open it from the Index And Tables dialog box, however, the only choices available will be for the TOC styles. You can then modify any of the TOC styles to suit your custom table of contents, using the techniques discussed in Chapter 12. When you finish, choose OK in the Style dialog box. Word will apply the new settings to all paragraphs formatted with that style.

Before you change the formatting instructions for one or more TOC styles, you might want to change the based-on style. Instead of using Normal in each case, you may prefer to base each TOC style on the next-highest TOC style. For example, you can base TOC 3 on TOC 2, which would be based on TOC 1, which would be based on Normal. With this approach, you can change the TOC 1 style, and the change will affect all other TOC styles, which makes it easier to maintain consistency throughout the various levels in a table of contents.

Creating a Table of Figures

You can use the Index And Tables dialog box to compile other types of tables, such as a table of figures. As you can for a table of contents, you can use styles, fields, or both to build these tables. You can also use entries created with Insert Caption.

How to build a table of figures using styles

If you are not using captions in your document, creating a table of figures is similar to creating a table of contents in both concept and mechanics. You can, for example, use a paragraph style to mark text in your document simply by formatting the text with the appropriate style. You can even give the style a descriptive name, such as For Table of Figures.

Once you've formatted the text with the appropriate style, move the cursor to the point in your document where you want the table to appear. Then choose Insert Index And Tables, select the Table Of Figures Card, and choose Options to open the Table Of Figures Options dialog box, shown in Figure 22-7 on the next page.

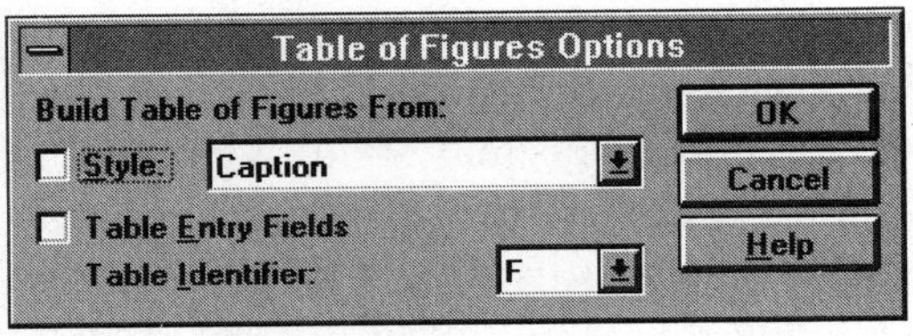

FIGURE 22-7

FIGURE 22-7

To create a table of figures, choose Insert Index And Tables, select the Table Of Figures card, and choose Options to open this dialog box.

Table of Figures Options

Build Table of Figures From:
- [ ] S_t_yle: Caption
- [ ] Table Entry Fields
  Table I_dentifier: F

OK
Cancel
Help

The Table Of Figures Options dialog box resembles the Table Of Contents Options dialog box, but it is simpler because you can use only one style to compile any given table of figures. Here, too, the dialog box offers two check boxes that let you tell Word whether to use a style, table entry fields, or both to compile the table.

If you want to use a style only, check the Style check box and clear the Table Entry Fields check box. Then open the Style drop-down list, and choose the style to use. Because a table of figures can have only one level of entry, Word lets you pick only one style from the list. When you've made your choice, choose OK to return to the Table Of Figures card, and then choose OK again to compile the table.

If the cursor is in a table of figures when you give the command to compile a table, Word will ask whether you want to replace the existing table of figures. Answer OK or Cancel, as appropriate. If you choose OK, Word will repaginate the document, search for the appropriate style, compile the table of figures, and insert the table at the cursor position. If you toggle the field to show the field code, you'll see that it's a TOC field.

How to build a table of figures using fields

If you prefer, you can use TC fields to define the entries in a table of figures. To use a TC field, you must add an identifier to distinguish these fields from entries that are meant for the table of contents or for other tables.

To insert a TC field with the appropriate identifier, first press Alt-Shift-O to open the Mark Table Of Contents Entry dialog box, shown earlier in Figure 22-5 on page 768. This is the same dialog box you use for creating TC fields for a table of contents. The only difference is that you'll need to take advantage of the Table Identifier drop-down list.

As we mentioned earlier, the C identifier is the correct choice for marking an entry to be used with the Table Of Contents card. Any other letter marks entries to be used to create tables with the Table Of Figures card. There is one important difference between the two. Only tables created using the Table Of Contents card have levels of entries. Tables created with the Tables Of Figures card have only one level.

It doesn't matter what letter you use, however, as long as you are careful to mark all related entries with the same letter. To make it easy to remember, you might want to use the first letter of the table name as the Table Identifier. For a table of maps, for example, you might use M, and for a table of illustrations, you might use I. If you are marking figures, equations, and tables with Insert Caption, there is no need to mark them separately with TC fields.

After you insert the TC fields in your document using the techniques described earlier in this chapter, you can compile the table of figures. Choose Insert Index And Tables, choose the Table Of Figures card, and choose Options. Check the Table Entry Fields check box, and set the Table Identifier box to match the identifier you used in the TC fields. And, unless you want to compile the table using both TC fields and a style, be sure to clear the Style check box. Then choose OK to return to the Table Of Figures card, and choose OK again to compile the table.

How to build a table of figures using captions

The easiest method for creating a table of figures depends on having identified all of your figures with inserted captions. Insert Caption can be used to maintain separate captions for figures, equations, or tables. Although each of these captions is formatted with the same style, Word uses a different type of field for each. This serves two purposes. Word numbers each type of caption independently, and the captions for each type of item can be gathered into separate tables using the Table Of Figures card. To specify the type of caption to gather for the table, use the Caption Label list on the Table Of Figures card, shown in Figure 22-8.

FIGURE 22-8

To create a table of figures based on captions, choose the type of caption from the Caption Label list.

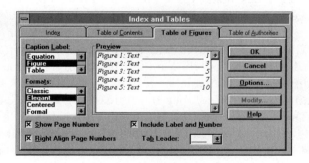

If you specify a type of caption, it is not necessary to use the Style or Table Entry Fields option on the Table Of Figures Options card. After choosing the type of caption to be gathered from the Caption Label list, select OK, and Word will follow the process described earlier for generating the table.

You can create a single table which includes entries that are collected from captions, marked with a separate style, marked with a TC field, or any combination. To do this, simply check the appropriate boxes on the Table Of Figures Options card and then select OK to return to the Table Of Figures card to select the type of caption to include. You cannot select the type of caption first because it is always set to None when you return from the Table Of Figures Options card. Because all captions are formatted with the Caption style no matter whether they are for figures, tables, or equations, it is possible to generate a single table containing all of these captions by specifying the Caption style on the Table Of Figures Options card and leaving the Caption Label set to None.

How to format a table of figures

You can format a table of figures with the options on the Table Of Figures card in the Index And Tables dialog box. To see the card, choose Insert Index And Tables, and choose the Table Of Figures card, shown in Figure 22-8.

The Tables Of Figures card is similar to the Table Of Contents card, with a list of predefined formats (including a Custom Style option) and a Preview box to show the effect of current settings. Other shared features include check boxes that let you choose whether to show page numbers and whether to right-align the page numbers. You'll also find the Tab Leader drop-down list. All of these features work the same way as they do on the Table Of Contents card. You can refer to our earlier discussion, "How to format a table of contents" on page 770, for details.

The Table Of Figures card includes two items that aren't on the Table Of Contents card: the Include Label And Number check box and the Caption Label list box discussed in the previous section. The Include Label And Number check box works only with tables based on captions. When it is checked, the caption identified (for example, Figure 1) is included in the table. When it is cleared, only the actual caption text is included.

The Table Of Figures card also includes a Custom Style choice in the Formats list box. If you choose the Custom Style format, Word will make the Modify button available, as it does on the Table Of Contents card. Choose Modify to have Word open the Style dialog box.

The only style you'll be able to modify in the Style dialog box is the Table of Figures style, which Word adds to your document when you first create a table of figures and which the program uses by default for formatting the table. As with TOC styles, you can modify the Table of Figures style however you like, using the techniques we discussed in Chapter 12. When you choose OK in the Style dialog box, Word will apply the new instructions to all the paragraphs that are formatted with that style.

Creating an Index

Creating an index is similar in many ways to creating a table of contents or a table of figures from TC fields. To define index entries, you use an XE (Index Entry) field. The compiled index is the field result of an INDEX field. You can enter the INDEX field with the Insert Index And Tables command, in the same way that you entered a TOC field for a table of contents or figures. You can also insert the XE field automatically.

We'll explore each of Word's indexing features, but it will be helpful to start with a simple example to put the more complex features in context.

A quick example

Suppose that you've created the document shown in Figure 22-9 and that you want to define the heading Division of Parts as an index entry. (In this example, and for most of this discussion, we'll assume that Word is set to show hidden text and to show field results rather than field codes.)

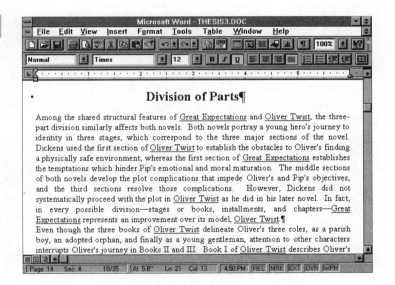

FIGURE 22-9

We'll use this document to demonstrate Word's indexing capabilities.

To define the entry, select it, and then press Alt-Shift-X to open the Mark Index Entry dialog box, shown in Figure 22-10 on the next page.

You can also open the Mark Index Entry dialog box by choosing Insert Index And Tables, choosing the Index card, and choosing the Mark Entry button. The Alt-Shift-X shortcut is much faster, however.

FIGURE 22-10

The easiest way to define index entries in your document is with the Mark Index Entry dialog box.

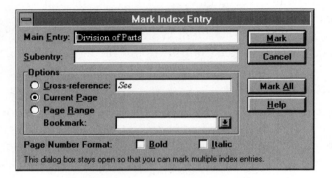

As you can see in Figure 22-10, Word will automatically place the text you've selected in the Main Entry text box. If you want, you can edit the entry in the text box. When you choose the Mark button, Word will insert an XE field after the text you selected, as shown in Figure 22-11. This field, which defines the index entry, is {XE "Division of Parts"}. Notice that the field appears with a dotted underline, indicating that it's formatted as hidden text.

FIGURE 22-11

The Mark Index Entry dialog box inserts an XE field immediately after the text you selected.

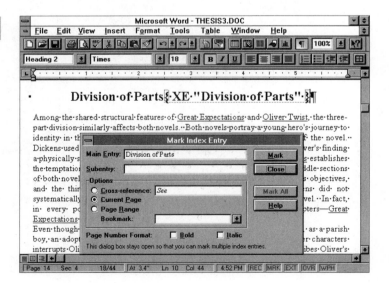

The Mark Index Entry dialog box will remain open so that you can make further entries. You can use this dialog box to define all the index entries for your document, moving between the document and the dialog box by pointing and clicking with the mouse or by pressing Ctrl-Tab. Close the dialog box when you're done. When you're ready to compile the index, move the cursor to where you want to locate the index—typically, at the end of the document. Then choose Insert Index And Tables, and select the Index card, shown in Figure 22-12.

FIGURE 22-12

To compile an index, choose Insert Index And Tables, select the Index card, and choose OK.

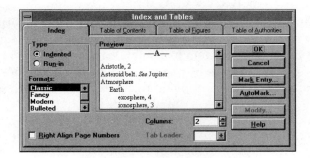

To keep this example as simple as possible, we'll ignore the options on the Index card for now. Choose OK to accept the default options, and Word will repaginate your document, search for index entries, and insert an index like the one shown in Figure 22-13.

FIGURE 22-13

This sample index, shown in Page Layout view, uses Word's default index settings.

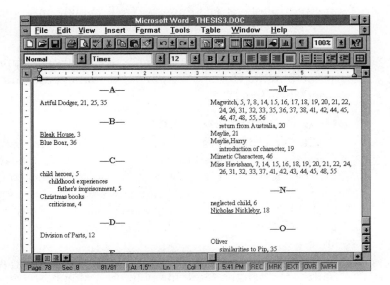

When you compile an index, the index is inserted into its own section and its pages are numbered separately, using the same techniques we discussed above for the table of contents. Refer to "How to number pages in a table of contents" on page 763.

That's all there is to it. Of course, this example illustrates only the basics of creating an index. Word offers other indexing features that you will likely want to take advantage of.

How to define index entries

For any but the simplest index, your first step before you define an index entry is to decide whether you want to create a term entry or a topic entry. A term entry always refers to a single page, such as 49 or 156, but a topic entry can refer to a range of pages, such as 49–51 or 156–62. After you decide which type of entry you want to create, you can define the entry.

How to define term entries

To create an index entry for a particular word or phrase in your document, start by highlighting that word or phrase. Then press Alt-Shift-X to open the Mark Index Entry dialog box, shown in Figure 22-10 on page 776. As we've already pointed out, Word will place the text you highlighted in the Main Entry text box. If you like, you can then edit the entry in the text box.

If you need to insert a colon, be sure to precede it with a backslash (\), or you won't get the results you expect. (Word uses the colon character to create multiple-level headings, as we'll explain in a moment.) If the original highlighted text included a colon, Word will automatically insert the backslash for you.

To create the index entry as a term entry, be sure that Current Page is selected in the Options section of the dialog box before you choose Mark to insert the XE field.

How to define topic entries

Creating a topic entry is somewhat different from creating a term entry. Before you can create a topic entry, you must first assign a bookmark to the block of text the entry will refer to. For example, to create the index entry *getting started* that refers to the first 12 paragraphs in your document, you'll first need to highlight those paragraphs, choose Edit Bookmark, type an appropriate name such as *GettingStarted* in the Bookmark Name text box, and choose Add.

After you've assigned a bookmark name to the block of text, press Alt-Shift-X to open the Mark Index Entry dialog box. Then enter the text for the index entry—*getting started*, in this case—in the Main Entry text box. Next open the Bookmark drop-down list in the Options section of the dialog box, and select the bookmark name for the entry—GettingStarted, in this example. Finally, choose the Page Range option button, and choose the Mark button to enter the XE field.

> Although you can enter the XE field for a topic entry anywhere in your document, we suggest you enter it immediately before or immediately after the bookmark it refers to so that you'll know where to find it later if you want to change or delete it.

How to define multilevel entries

Word also lets you create multilevel index entries, which are important when you need to break a topic into subtopics. For example, you might want to create a group of entries like this:

printing

envelopes, 326–29

graphics, 325

legal-size paper, 329–30

To create multilevel entries, simply use the first-level entry as the main entry for all the related entries. Enter the first-level entry in the Main Entry text box, and enter each second-level entry in the Subentry text box when you define the entry.

For example, to create the sample group of entries under *printing*, you would enter three fields at the appropriate places in your document, using *printing* as the main entry in each case, but using *envelopes*, *graphics*, and *legal-size paper* as the subentries. When Word inserts the XE field, the main entry and the subentry are separated by a colon.

How to refer to other entries

Sometimes you'll want to create an index entry that refers to another entry instead of a page number. For example, you might want to create this entry:

Word. *See* Microsoft Word

To create such entries, press Alt-Shift-X to open the Mark Index Entry dialog box, and enter text in the Main Entry text box (and optionally in the Subentry text box), as already described. Then select Cross-Reference in the Options section of the dialog box, and enter the cross-reference in the text box to the right of the option button. Word provides the word *See* in the text box, so you simply need to type the reference itself. Here again, choose the Mark button to enter the XE field.

Like fields that define topic entries, fields that refer to other entries can appear anywhere in a document. However, we recommend that you enter these fields at the end of the document, just before the INDEX field that compiles the entries, so that you can find them easily if you want to change or delete them.

How to format page numbers

Two check boxes at the bottom of the Mark Index Entry dialog box let you set the format for page numbers. The boxes are labeled Bold and Italic. If you want the page number reference for the index entry printed in bold, italic, or both, be sure to check the appropriate check box or boxes. This feature is available for all types of entries.

How to mark a word or phrase throughout a document with Mark All

Near the beginning of this chapter, we mentioned that Word will let you mark all occurrences of a given word or phrase throughout your document with a single command. That feature is found in the Mark Index Entry dialog box: the Mark All button.

The Mark All button is available only when you are defining term entries—that is, when you're using the Current Page option—and only when you've selected some text in your document. But it can be useful.

To take advantage of this feature, start by selecting some text. Then open or return to the Mark Index Entry dialog box. If you choose Mark All, Word will mark all occurrences of the selected text throughout your document. If you like, you can change the main entry text, add subentry text, or do both before choosing Mark All. Word will still find all occurrences of the selected text and mark them with the main entry text and subentry text that you've defined.

How to mark a word or phrase throughout a document with AutoMark

Word also offers another choice for marking a word or phrase throughout a document. To use this alternative, you must first create a second file, called a *concordance file*. Start by opening a new Word document file and inserting a two-column table. Enter a word or phrase that you want to index in the left column of each table row, and enter the index entry to use for that word or phrase in the right column. When you finish entering the information, save the file. If you need information on working with tables, see Chapter 11, "Building Tables," starting on page 360.

Once you've created the concordance file, open the file you want to index, and choose Insert Index And Tables. Choose the Index card, and choose the AutoMark button. Word will open the Open Index AutoMark File dialog box, which is similar to the Open dialog box and works the same way. Use it to designate the concordance file, just as you would designate a file to open, and choose OK. Word will then work its way through your file, finding all matches to the words and phrases in the first column of the concordance file and entering XE fields using the text in the second column.

How to choose a format for the index

Once you've defined the index entries in a document, you can create the index. As we've already discussed, you can compile the index by choosing Insert Index And Tables, selecting the Index card, and choosing OK. But before you do so, you might want to adjust some of the settings on the Index card to format the index.

Indented vs. run-in format

In the Type section of the Index card, you can choose between two kinds of indexes: indented and run-in. If you choose the Indented option (the default), Word will indent each subentry on a new line under the main entry, as shown in the Preview box in Figure 22-12. If you choose the Run-In option, Word will include each subentry in the same paragraph as the main entry, as shown in Figure 22-14. A colon after the main entry sets it off from the subentries, and semicolons separate the subentries from each other.

FIGURE 22-14

The Run-In option tells Word to include each subentry in the same paragraph as its main entry.

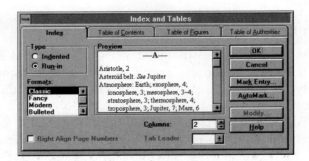

Other format choices for indexes

In addition to choosing an index type, you can specify how many columns the index should contain by setting the Columns box on the Index card. And if you've chosen to use an indented format, you can specify right-aligned page numbers, using the Right Align Page Numbers check box. You can also use the Tab Leader drop-down list to define the tab leader as a solid, dashed, or dotted line or to specify no leader.

The Index card has two other features in common with the Table Of Contents and Table Of Figures cards. Here, too, you can browse through a list of predefined formats and see the effect of each in the Preview box. You'll also find the Custom Style choice in the list of formats. If you highlight Custom Style, the Modify button will become available. You can choose this button to open the Style dialog box and modify the index styles that Word automatically adds to the document. In this case, the styles are for nine levels of index entries, from Index 1 through Index 9.

How to compile an index for a portion of a document

In this discussion, we've assumed that Word is set to display field results rather than field codes. If you place the cursor or selection in the index and press Shift-F9 to toggle the view, you'll find that the index, like a table of contents, is actually the result of a field—in this case, the INDEX field. The form of the field is simply {INDEX [*switches*]}.

You can compile an index for a portion of your document using essentially the same technique we described earlier for compiling a table of contents for only part of a document. First create a bookmark that defines the part you want to index. Then add the \b switch and the bookmark name in the INDEX field. For example, if you've created a 50-page document and you want to compile an index for pages 1 through 25, highlight the first 25 pages, choose Edit Bookmark, and assign a name to those pages. For this example, we'll use the bookmark name FirstHalf. To compile an index for those pages only, you would add this switch to the INDEX field:

\b "FirstHalf"

How to break up an index

If you create an index that contains a few thousand entries, your computer may run out of memory (or run slowly) when it compiles the index. Fortunately, Word offers a switch that lets you break the process into smaller pieces.

To compile part of an index, edit the INDEX field to include the \p switch followed by a starting letter and an ending letter. For example, if you want to divide an index into two parts, you can use these INDEX fields:

{INDEX \p a-m}

{INDEX \p n-z}

When you compile the index, simply update each INDEX field individually. You can also break the index into still smaller parts by adding more INDEX fields with a smaller range in each field.

How to update an index

To update a document's index, you can use the Insert Index And Tables command to replace the current index, or you can simply place the cursor or selection anywhere in the index and press F9. To avoid constant updating, it's best to compile an index just before you print the final version of a document. If you edit or reorganize the document after compiling the index, the page numbers may change, so the index will no longer be correct.

Creating a Table of Authorities

Tables of authorities are a reference aid that lawyers often need. If you don't know what they are, you don't need them. If you need them, however, Word's table of authorities feature can be invaluable.

Although the final result of this feature is called a table, the feature really has more in common with indexing. It lets you select some text, open a dialog box in which you can create the citation by editing a copy of the selected text, and then insert a TA field that takes this form:

{TA "LongCitation" "ShortCitation" [*switches*]}

After you finish entering the TA fields in your document, you can use the Insert Index And Tables command to compile the fields into a table. We'll take a closer look at each of these steps, starting with marking the entries in your document.

How to define table of authorities entries

To create a table of authorities entry, start by selecting the text you want the table to refer to. Then press Alt-Shift-I to open the Mark Citation dialog box, shown in Figure 22-15 on the next page.

 You can also open the Mark Citation dialog box by choosing Insert Index And Tables, choosing the Table Of Authorities card, and then choosing the Mark Citation button. The Alt-Shift-I keyboard shortcut is more direct, however.

When you open the dialog box, Word will insert two copies of the text you selected—one in the Selected Text text box and one in the Short Citation box. The entry in the Short Citation box is the one used by Word to identify the citation. Edit the text in the Short Citation box so that it is in the format you intend to use for the short citation. The first time you use a particular

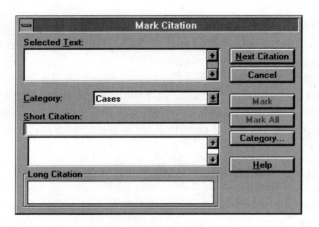

FIGURE 22-15

To enter the marker
fields for a table of
authorities, open
the Mark Citation
dialog box.

citation, edit the text in the Selected Text box so that it is in the proper format for the long citation. (When you first create a short citation, Word uses this text for the Long Citation information.)

To designate the proper category for the citation, open the drop-down Category list and select from the list of 16 choices. (You can rename any of the categories by choosing the Category button to open the Edit Category dialog box.) Select Mark to insert the TA field for the highlighted text only, or select Mark All to insert TA fields for all occurrences of the short citation.

After Word inserts the TA field or fields, the Mark Citation dialog box stays open so that you can mark additional citations. To individually mark other occurrences of existing citations, return to your document, highlight the appropriate text, move back to the Mark Citation dialog box, and select the appropriate entry from the Short Citation drop-down list (or type it if you prefer). Confirm that the Long Citation displays the correct information for the citation, and select Mark. To insert a new citation, highlight the first occurrence of the citation and follow the steps described previously.

The Next Citation button will take you to the next TA field in the document and show you the short and long citations as well as the category for that field. It will also help you find text that looks as if it should be marked as a citation, stopping at occurrences of the text *In Re*.

How to format and create a table of authorities

Once you've finished entering the TA fields, you can generate the table of authorities. Position your cursor where you want the table to be located. Then choose Insert Index And Tables, and select the Table Of Authorities card, shown in Figure 22-16.

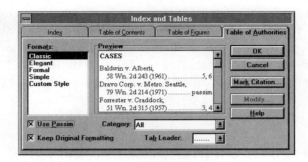

FIGURE 22-16

To format and generate a table of authorities, select the Table Of Authorities card in the Index And Tables dialog box.

The Table Of Authorities card resembles the other cards in the dialog box, with a Formats list containing a set of predefined formats, a Preview box that shows the effect of the current settings, and a Tab Leader drop-down list. Here, too, if you select Custom Style in the Formats list, the Modify button becomes available so that you can easily open the Style dialog box and modify the styles related to the table of authorities—in this case, the Table of Authorities and TOA Heading styles.

Three options on the card are specific to the table of authorities feature. If you check the Use Passim check box, the word *passim* will be substituted for individual page references if there are five or more references to the same authority. The Keep Original Formatting check box tells Word to maintain the character formatting that the original text had in your document. The Category box lets you tell Word to include all TA fields or only those for a specific category.

When you finish setting the options on the card, choose OK to have Word generate the table of authorities. Word will repaginate the document, compile the TA entries, and insert the table of authorities as the field result of a TOA field.

Working with Long Documents

Historically, the chore of creating a research aid such as an index or one of the tables we've discussed in this chapter was exceeded only by the major headache involved in creating the same research aids in a document shared among multiple files. The tricks involved in cobbling together the data from several files to produce a single, integrated index or table often seemed like more trouble than the task was worth. So it's no small matter to say that creating an index or a table in Word version 6.0 is no different for a document spread out over multiple files than for one that's fully contained in a single file.

To use any of the features we've discussed in this chapter on multiple files, first create a master document that includes all the separate files as subdocuments. Then open the master document, choose View Normal, and use the index, table of contents, table of figures, and table of authority features exactly as you would use them on any other document. It's that simple. For more information on using the master document feature, see "Working with Long Documents" starting on page 589.

How to create chapter-page numbers

If you use Word to create chapters for a book or manual, you might want to create a numbering scheme that reflects both the chapter number and the page number. For example, you might want to refer to page 1 of Chapter 8 as page 8–1. Of course, if you use this sort of page numbering, you'll probably want the same numbering scheme in the table of contents and the index.

The first step is to be sure that your chapter or section titles are all formatted with the Heading 1 style and that no other text in your document uses that style. The next step is to use Format Heading Numbering to add numbers to your chapter or section titles. In most situations, you will add the numbers only to the first level of heading rather than to all headings in your document. You can modify the numbering format to contain whatever text you want. The only thing that must be included is the automatic chapter number. For more information, see "Numbering Headings" on page 483.

If your first chapter is not your first section, you will need to format the title with a style other than Heading 1. To ensure consistency throughout your document, you might want to create a Title style based on Heading 1 with no additional formatting. For more information about working with styles, see "Taking a Closer Look at Styles" on page 427.

Once the chapter titles are numbered using this technique, Word will use whatever page numbering format is in effect for each section for entries drawn from that section. By default, this format is Roman numerals starting on the first page and numbered continuously. To take advantage of the chapter numbers, you need to change the page number format using Insert Page Number. You will want to use the Page Number Format dialog box (available in the Insert Page Numbers dialog box) to include the chapter number as part of each page number. You can highlight all of the sections that are to share the same format and change them with one command. For more information about page numbering, see "How to change page numbering from one section to another" on page 491.

You might want to use different page numbering formats for different sections. For example, if your first section uses Roman page numbering (as is common for an introduction) and the other sections use the chapter number and page number, the index and table of contents entries will reference each set of pages in the proper format.

TOPIC FINDER

Sorting   789

- Alphanumeric sorts
- Numeric sorts
- Date sorts
- How to sort in Outline view
- How to sort tabular lists
- How to sort comma-delimited lists
- How to sort a Word table

Performing Mathematical Calculations   800

- Word's = (Formula) field
- Operator precedence
- How to use bookmarks in an = (Formula) field
- Functions
- The Formula dialog box

Setting Up a Spreadsheet with a Table   812

- How to refer to cells

Equation Editor   813

- The Equation Editor menus
- How to use the template and symbol icons
- Keyboard shortcuts
- An example

Character Formulas: The EQ Field   824

Numbering Items in Sequence   824

- NEW! The Caption dialog box
- The SEQ field

Creating Cross-References   832

- NEW! The Insert Cross-Reference command

The STYLEREF Field   835

The PRINT Field   838

Creating Special Characters   839

- ASCII, ANSI, and OEM character sets
- How to enter ANSI and OEM characters
- How to use AutoText to store symbols

23

Assorted Goodies

ost of the features we've discussed in the last few chapters, such as mail merge and tables of contents, are potentially critical to those who need them. But Word offers an assortment of other features—small touches that are rarely critical but that can help you work more efficiently. In this chapter, we'll cover a number of these, including Word's ability to sort, perform mathematical calculations, create equations to use within body text, create references, and send commands directly to a printer. Here, then, is a potpourri of Word's more specialized features.

Sorting

Word's Table Sort command can rearrange paragraphs of body text, tabular lists (text separated by tabs), comma-delimited lists (text separated by commas), and Word tables. (Note that the exact wording of the Sort item on the Table menu and the name of the Sort dialog box will vary depending on the selection that you're sorting, but we'll use the names *Table Sort* and *the Sort dialog box* throughout this discussion.) When you choose Table Sort, Word opens the Sort dialog box, shown in Figure 23-1 on the next page. Choose the Options button to open the Sort Options dialog box, shown in Figure 23-2.

FIGURE 23-1

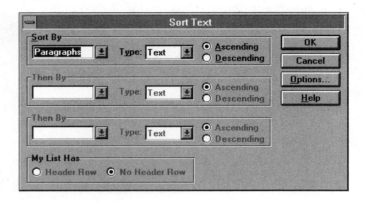

FIGURE 23-1

Word opens this dialog box when you choose the Table Sort command.

FIGURE 23-2

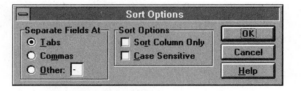

Choose the Options button from the Sort dialog box to open this dialog box.

If you're sorting paragraphs of standard text, the only choice in the Sort Options dialog box that matters is the Case Sensitive check box. If it's checked, words containing uppercase letters will come before the same words containing lowercase letters. If you're sorting a list that's in tabular, comma-delimited, or similar format, with each row broken into what are called *fields*, you can set the proper separator character in the Separate Fields At box. The Sort Column Only check box is available only if you are sorting text organized in a Word table or are selecting columns. Choose Sort Column Only when you want to sort only the currently selected column or columns.

> The Help file (in the original release of the program, at least) says the Sort Column Only check box is available for newspaper-style columns. What the Help file doesn't mention is that you must first select the text by using the Alt key.

After you finish with the Sort Options box, choose OK to close it and return to the Sort dialog box. As you can see in Figure 23-1, you can use this box to define up to three sort levels. For each one, you can set the type—text, number, or date—and choose whether to sort in ascending or descending order. The My List Has box lets you tell Word whether a table, tabular list, or comma-delimited list includes a header row. If you indicate that your list or table has a header row, Word will use each entry in the first row as the name for each field in the list or table, and it won't include that row in the sort.

If you don't select any text before choosing Table Sort, Word will automatically highlight the entire document—unless the cursor or selection is in a Word table, in which case it will highlight the table. (In this context, a Word table is a table created with Word's table feature, as distinguished from a list created with tabs.) By default, Word sorts all the paragraphs in your document by the first character in each paragraph. If two or more paragraphs begin with the same character, Word will compare the second characters, then the third, and so on, until it finds a variation to base the sort on or until it reaches the end of identical paragraphs.

As an example, suppose you've created the list of used cars shown in Figure 23-3, and you want to sort the list in alphabetic order based on the manufacturer's name and then the model name, the first two items in each row. Since you want to sort only the paragraphs that are part of the list, start by selecting those paragraphs. Next choose the Table Sort command, and choose OK to accept the default settings. Word will sort the selected paragraphs as shown in Figure 23-4 on the next page.

FIGURE 23-3

This is the list of used cars before sorting.

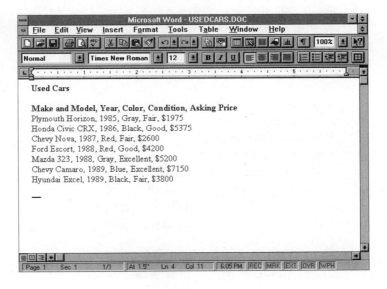

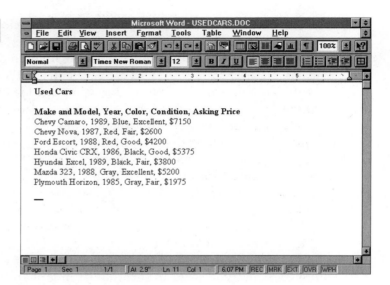

FIGURE 23-4

This is the same list as in Figure 23-3 after alphabetic sorting.

When sorting paragraphs, Word sorts the entire document as one unit, without regard to section boundaries. If you want to sort only part of a document, be sure to select the text to sort before you choose Table Sort. Also note that you can undo a sort with the Edit Undo command.

Alphanumeric sorts

Word usually recognizes the type of data in the selection and automatically sets Type in the Sort By section of the dialog box to Text, Number, or Date, as appropriate. If Sort By is set to Text, Word will sort in alphanumeric order, which specifies a sort order for letters of the alphabet, numbers, and all other printable characters. The ascending sort order starts with punctuation marks and other symbols, goes on to numbers, and ends with letters.

If a paragraph begins with an indent, a tab, or a space, Word will ignore the blank space and sort the paragraph according to the first character after the white space. Blank paragraphs—that is, paragraphs that consist of a paragraph mark with no text—precede non-blank paragraphs in an ascending sort.

By default, Word ignores case when sorting letters. For example, in an ascending sort, a paragraph that begins with *able* will come before a paragraph that begins with *Apple* because *b* comes before *p* in the alphabet. However, if you check the Case Sensitive check box in the Sort Options dialog box, a paragraph that begins with *Apple* will precede one that begins with *able* because *Apple* begins with an uppercase *A*.

The Case Sensitive option affects only those sorts that use Text for the Type setting.

Numeric sorts

If you set Type to Number, Word will look at the actual value of each number it's sorting, rather than comparing the numbers character by character, left to right. If you set Type to Text, for example, to sort 6 and 10, Word will compare the 6 to the 1 and decide that 10 should come first in an ascending sort. But if you set Type to Number, Word will compare the value 6 to the value 10 and decide that 6 should come first. The Number setting also recognizes negative numbers, so -6 is treated as less than 0, and -23 is treated as less than -6. Finally, you can format the numbers with commas or with a currency symbol.

If a paragraph contains more than one number, Word will evaluate that paragraph as an equation if Type is set to Number: A paragraph that reads *2 + 3* will be treated as *5*, and a paragraph that reads *3 – 2* will be treated as *1*. If the paragraph contains more than one number but doesn't include an actual equation, Word will add the numbers together. For example, it will treat a paragraph that reads *14 gibberish 6* as *20*. If Word finds any paragraphs that lack numbers during a numeric sort, it will treat them as less than the lowest number it finds in the sort, even if that number is negative. Note, however, that it will treat all such paragraphs the same way, without any attempt to sort them alphabetically.

Date sorts

In addition to alphanumeric and numeric sorts, Word can sort properly formatted data as date values. For Word to recognize text as a date, the text must follow one of the formats shown in Figure 23-5 on the next page.

Date Format	Example
MMM d	Jan 8
MMM-yy	Jan-95
MMM d, yyyy	Jan 8, 1995
MMMM d, yyyy	January 8, 1995
M/d/yy	1/8/95
M-d-yy	1-8-95
d-MMM-yy	1-Jan-95
M/d/yy h:mm AM/PM	1/8/95 3:30 PM

FIGURE 23-5

Acceptable date formats.

Word will use all the information included in your date values when it sorts. For example, if you sort *Dec-92, Nov-92,* and *Jan-93,* Word will arrange the paragraphs in the order *Nov-92, Dec-92,* and *Jan-93.* If you include the time, Word will sort by time for all entries on a given date. When you use numbers, you can include the zero for single-digit months or days (for example, *01/08/95*).

How to sort in Outline view

You can also sort while in Outline view, in which case Word will base the sort on the highest-level paragraphs in the selection. For example, Figure 23-6 and Figure 23-7 show the same file before and after sorting, based on the second-highest-level paragraphs shown in the figures. Notice that Word moved the third-level sections along with the second-level headings, without changing the order of the third-level sections. Whenever you sort in Outline view, Word sorts only the highest-level paragraphs selected.

How to sort tabular lists

Word's ability to sort tabular lists is similar to the sort features in many simple database programs. Assume, for example, that you've created a simple tab-delimited list, with information in columns that are aligned at tab stops and with each row consisting of one paragraph. To use database terminology, each column represents one field, with the fields separated by tabs. Each paragraph is a separate record. (You can replace the tabs with commas, and a paragraph can include as many lines as needed to hold all its fields. But, for the moment, we'll stay with the simplest possibility—a tabular list with one line in each paragraph—to make the examples easier to follow.)

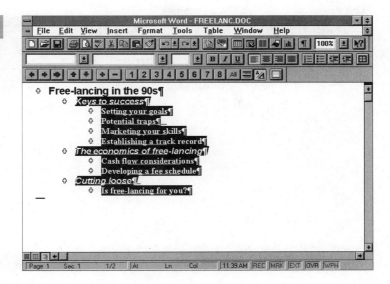

FIGURE 23-6

This figure shows a file in Outline view before sorting. Note that the selection does not include the highest-level paragraph in the figure, but it includes all others.

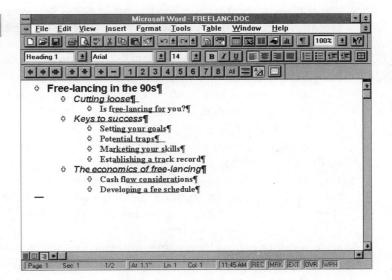

FIGURE 23-7

When you sort in Outline view, Word keeps subordinate paragraphs under the same headings without sorting them.

How to sort a tabular list by key column

By default, Word will sort a tabular list based on the first column (field) of each paragraph (record). However, you can sort the list based on any field. Suppose, for example, that you've created a document that includes the list shown in Figure 23-8 on the next page. You want the most recently hired employees to be at the top of the list, which means you need to sort this information in descending order by year hired.

FIGURE 23-8

You can use Word to sort a tabular list like this one.

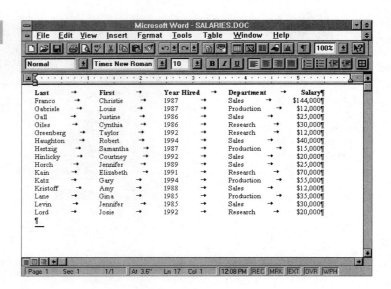

If there is anything in the file besides the list, you'll want to start by selecting the list so that you won't sort other paragraphs as well. For this example, however, we'll assume there's nothing else in the file. Start by choosing Table Sort to open the Sort dialog box and automatically select the entire file. Then choose the Header Row option to indicate that the selection contains a header row, and choose the Options button to open the Sort Options box. Be sure that Separate Fields At is set to Tabs. Then choose OK to return to the Sort Text box.

Because you want the sort to be based on the Year Hired column, move to the Sort By drop-down list, and choose Year Hired from the list. Next, in the Sort By section of the dialog box, choose the Descending sort order option, and set Type to Number. (When you are working with a year in this format, you can set Type to either Number or Text, but not to Date. Word does not recognize a year by itself as a date.) To also sort by department within each year (to help show patterns for each department), open the first Then By drop-down list, which is now available, choose Department from the list, and be sure that Type is set to Text and that the sort order is set to Ascending.

If you also want to sort by a third column, you can enter the appropriate settings in the second Then By section of the dialog box, which is now available. To sort by salary within department, for example, choose Salary from the second Then By drop-down list, and be sure that Type is set to Number and the sort order is set to Ascending. Finally, choose OK. Word sorts the list as shown in Figure 23-9.

FIGURE 23-9

When you sort the tabular list shown in Figure 23-8, you can sort it by any combination of up to three columns. In this case, we've specified sorting by year, then by department, and then by salary.

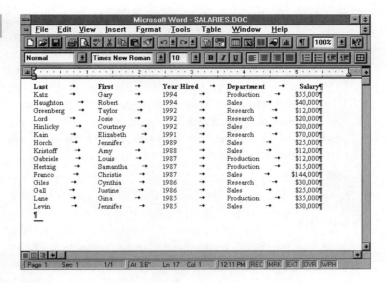

How to sort data in a single column

In addition to letting you sort rows based on the entries in a column, Word can also sort a single column without disturbing other columns. This type of sort can be useful when you're organizing a document that includes unrelated columns. For example, Figure 23-10 shows a list of contributors, with individual contributors in the left column and corporate contributors in the right column. You might want to sort each list independently of the other.

FIGURE 23-10

When you have unrelated columns of data, it's often useful to sort the columns independently.

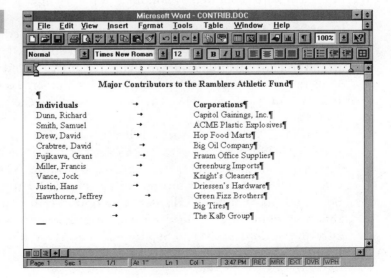

To sort a single column, first select the column to sort. To use the mouse, hold down the Alt key as you extend the selection. To use the keyboard, place the cursor at one corner of the area you want to select, press Ctrl-Shift-F8, and then use the cursor control keys (including the arrow keys, PgUp, PgDn, and so on) to define the selection. With the column selected, choose Table Sort, choose Options to open the Sort Options dialog box, check the Sort Column Only check box, and choose OK. Then make any other appropriate settings in the Sort Text box, and choose OK. Word will sort the entries in the selected column only.

When you set the options in the Sort Text box, be sure the Sort By entry is set either to Paragraphs or to the first field (either Field 1 or the name of the field as shown in the header row). This is essential, even if you are sorting a column other than the first. Although it would seem to make more sense to set the Sort By entry to match the field number or the name of the column you're sorting, Word will not sort the column if you set it that way.

How to sort comma-delimited lists

As we've already mentioned, Word can also sort paragraphs that contain entries separated by commas. The procedure for sorting comma-delimited lists is identical to the procedure for sorting tabular lists. However, because the entries are separated by commas, you must specify the Comma Separator option in the Sorting dialog box.

For example, Figure 23-11 shows the list of used cars that we started with at the beginning of this discussion on sorting. Notice that each paragraph (record) includes a set of fields for one car. And each paragraph contains the same number of fields arranged in the same order, starting with the manufacturer and model of the car, followed by the year, color, condition, and price.

Suppose you want to sort this list in ascending order based on the year of each car—which happens to be the second entry, or field, in each record. First select all the paragraphs in the list, excluding the title and blank line at the top of the document but including the header row. Then choose Table Sort, and make sure the Header Row option button is selected, indicating that you've included a header row. Next choose the Options button, make sure the options are set to Separate Fields At Commas, and choose OK to return to the Sort Text dialog box.

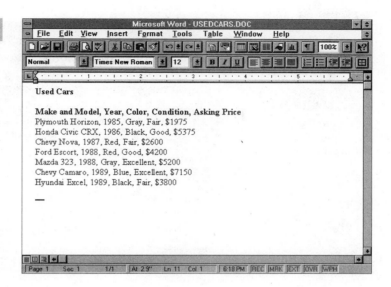

FIGURE 23-11

Word can also sort a comma-delimited list like this one.

To finish up, choose Year from the Sort By drop-down list, choose Number for Type, and choose Ascending for the sort order. (As we pointed out earlier, you need to use Number or Text rather than Date for Type because Word will not recognize a year by itself as a valid date format.) When you choose OK, Word sorts the list.

How to sort a Word table

Sorting a Word table (a table built with Word's table feature) is similar in many ways to sorting a tabular list or a comma-delimited list. With a Word table, however, the contents of each field is in its own cell (the intersection of a row and column), each column is a field, and each record is a separate row in the table. In determining how to sort a table, Word looks at the first character, or characters, in each cell. If a cell contains more than one paragraph, sorting the table will not affect the order of paragraphs within the cell.

As we've already mentioned, if you want to confine a sort to a table, you don't have to specifically select the table before choosing Table Sort. If the cursor is in the table when you choose the command, Word will automatically select only the table, rather than the entire document. In every other way, sorting a table is nearly the same as sorting a tabular list or a comma-delimited list, except that you don't have to specify either a comma or a tab separator. In fact, the Separator choice isn't available in this case.

Suppose, for example, that you've created the table shown in Figure 23-12. (The table has the same information we used in Figure 23-11.) Suppose also that you now want to sort the information alphabetically by condition.

FIGURE 23-12

This table has the same data as in Figure 23-11, but in table format.

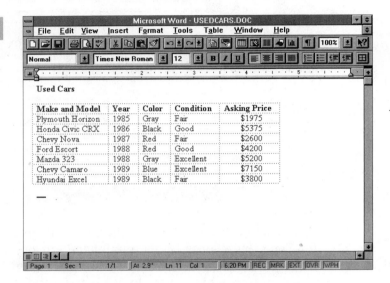

Used Cars

Make and Model	Year	Color	Condition	Asking Price
Plymouth Horizon	1985	Gray	Fair	$1975
Honda Civic CRX	1986	Black	Good	$5375
Chevy Nova	1987	Red	Fair	$2600
Ford Escort	1988	Red	Good	$4200
Mazda 323	1988	Gray	Excellent	$5200
Chevy Camaro	1989	Blue	Excellent	$7150
Hyundai Excel	1989	Black	Fair	$3800

To sort the table by condition, first place the cursor anywhere in the table. Choose Table Sort, set the options appropriately, and then choose OK to tell Word to sort.

Most of the sort options work the same way for tables as for tabular or comma-delimited fields. However, note that if you don't have a header row when sorting tables, the choices in the Sort By drop-down list will refer to columns rather than fields.

As with tabular lists, you can easily sort a single column without changing the order of other columns by highlighting the one column and selecting the Sort Column Only check box. One difference is that Word automatically puts the selected column number (or name from the header row) in the Sort By box and doesn't give you any other choices in the Sort By drop-down list.

Performing Mathematical Calculations

As we mentioned in the sorting discussion, Word automatically evaluates basic mathematical expressions while performing a numerical sort. But

Word's ability to perform mathematical calculations is a specialized feature by itself, independent of sorting. Word can add, subtract, divide, multiply, and more. It can also enter the results in your documents automatically.

For example, suppose you've created a table of cash receipts, as shown in Figure 23-13, and you want to compute the total receipts for the week. Simply move the cursor to the cell where you want the total, just to the right of the cell with the word *Totals*, and choose Table Formula to open the Formula dialog box, shown in Figure 23-14.

FIGURE 23-13

Word can add a column of numbers such as the cash receipts in this table.

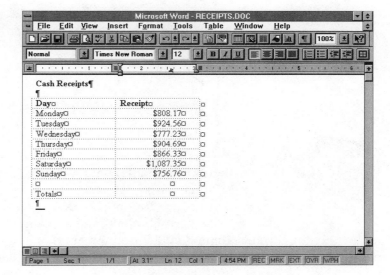

FIGURE 23-14

Choose Table Formula to open the Formula dialog box and add a formula to your tables.

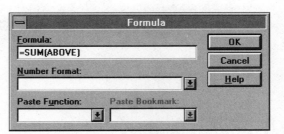

Word supplies the formula =SUM(ABOVE) as a default entry in this case. This formula returns the sum of all numbers in all cells above the current cell. Since this is exactly the formula you want to enter, choose OK to let Word enter it in the cell. Figure 23-15 on the next page shows the result in two panes, one showing the $6,125.09 total and the other showing the formula that produces the total.

FIGURE 23-15

After you enter the = (Formula) field (shown in the bottom pane), Word calculates the total (as shown in the top pane).

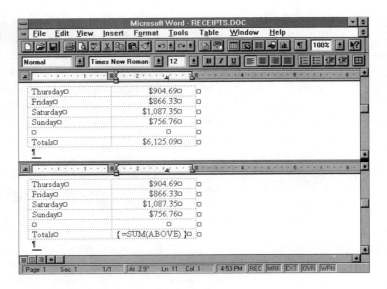

The field we just used to calculate a total in a Word table is one form of Word's = (Formula) field. We mentioned this field briefly in Chapter 20. You can use any of the techniques we discussed in Chapter 20 to insert formula fields in your document. Keep in mind that the Formula dialog box, available through the Table Formula command, helps automate the task and is generally the preferred choice unless you have all the variations for the field memorized. Most important, be clear that despite the location of the Formula choice on the Table menu, you can use the Table Formula command to enter the = (Formula) field anywhere in your document.

There's more to be said about using the = (Formula) field in tables, but we need to take a look at the field itself first.

Word's = (Formula) field

Word's = (Formula) field offers a straightforward approach for performing mathematical calculations in your document. The form of this field is

{= Formula}

where *Formula* is the mathematical formula you want to evaluate.

The simplest variation on the = (Formula) field uses numbers and common mathematical operators, such as a plus sign (+) and a minus sign (−) to specify the formula. For example, *{= 2+2}* would have a field result of *4*, while *{=10-8}* would have a field result of *2*.

In addition to recognizing the plus sign (+) for addition and the minus sign (−) for subtraction, the = (Formula) field recognizes the asterisk (*) for multiplication, the slash (/) for division, the percent sign (%) for calculating a percentage, and the caret (^) for calculating the power or root of a number. Figure 23-16 summarizes these six operators.

Character	Operation
+	Addition
−	Subtraction
*	Multiplication
/	Division
%	Percentage (divides the number by 100 and then uses the result)
^	Power (if the number following is greater than or equal to 1) or root (if the number following is between 0 and 1)

FIGURE 23-16

Word's mathematical operators.

Arithmetic expressions in Word follow much the same rules you would use to calculate results with pencil and paper. You enter the +, −, *, and / operators to the left of the number you want to add, subtract, multiply by, or divide by. You can also use the % sign directly after a number to indicate percentage (or division by 100). To calculate 18 percent of 70, for example, you could enter the = (Formula) field *{=18%*70}*, which gives you the same result as the field *{=0.18*70}*.

Operator precedence

When a formula includes more than one operator, Word follows the same rules of precedence that you may remember from school. This order is summarized in Figure 23-17. Unless you've entered parentheses to indicate otherwise, Word will first calculate any power or root in the formula. It will then go on to multiplication and division and finish with addition and subtraction. Given the field *{=5+10*4}*, for example, Word will first multiply 10 by 4 and then add 5, yielding a field result of *45*.

Operator	Precedence
^ and %	1
* and /	2
+ and −	3

FIGURE 23-17

The order of precedence for mathematical operations.

You can indicate a different order of precedence with parentheses. Here again, Word follows basic mathematical rules, evaluating anything inside the parentheses before evaluating anything outside the parentheses. Given the field {=(5+10)*4}, Word will first add 5 plus 10 (yielding *15*), and then it will multiply by 4, yielding a field result of *60* rather than the *45* it would return without the parentheses.

In addition to recognizing mathematical operators, the = (Formula) field recognizes several logical operators that you can use as part of logical expressions (as distinguished from mathematical formulas). You might want to use a logical expression as part of a formula that first tests a condition and then takes a particular action, depending on the result. We'll discuss this a bit more when we talk about the IF function later in this chapter. Figure 23-18 lists the logical operators.

Operator	Description	Operator	Description
=	Equal to	<=	Less than or equal to
<	Less than	>=	Greater than or equal to
>	Greater than	<>	Not equal to

FIGURE 23-18

Word's logical operators.

Keep in mind that the = (Formula) field behaves much like any other Word field. In particular, Word will update the field result only when you place the cursor within the field and press F9, or when you print the file. (This assumes that Word is set to update fields when it prints. To confirm that this option is set, choose Tools Options, then choose Print, and make sure the Update Fields check box is checked.) Before you take any results from the = (Formula) field too seriously, make sure you update the field—after updating any fields that the field depends on.

How to use bookmarks in an = (Formula) field

One way to automate calculations is to use bookmarks to define numbers and then use bookmark names in the formula as operands. For example, suppose you've assigned the bookmark name *SALES* to the number 1000 and the bookmark name *COGS* to the number 700. To calculate the value of SALES minus COGS, you can insert the field *{= SALES − COGS}* in the document, which will yield the field result *300*.

Defining an = (Formula) field this way has no advantage for a one-time-only calculation. But it can be extremely useful as part of a regular report. For example, suppose you have to calculate the total of SALES minus COGS at the end of each week to include in a letter to the home office. After you define the bookmarks and formula once, you need only change the numbers each week, highlight the = (Formula) field (or the whole document), and press F9 to update the result.

Functions

In addition to using operators and bookmark names in an = (Formula) field, you can use a set of built-in functions as well. Figure 23-19 on the next page lists all the functions. We'll briefly discuss each one.

The ABS function

The ABS function returns the absolute (positive) value of a number or formula. The form of this function is

ABS(Formula)

where *Formula* is the number or formula whose absolute value you want to determine. For example, both *{= ABS(-5)}* and *{= ABS(5)}* return the value *5*.

The AND function

You can use the AND function to join two logical expressions to form a single complex expression. The form of this function is

AND(Logical1,Logical2)

where *Logical1* and *Logical2* are the two logical expressions you want to test.

Function	Result
ABS	The absolute value of a number
AND	1 if both arguments are true; 0 if either argument is false
AVERAGE	The average of a list of values
COUNT	The number of values in a list
DEFINED	1 if the expression can be calculated without error; 0 if the expression cannot be calculated without error
FALSE	0 (see the discussion of the IF function)
IF	One of two user-specified values, depending on the outcome of a conditional test
INT	The integer portion of the number (the part to the left of the decimal)
MAX	The highest value in a list
MIN	The lowest value in a list
MOD	The remainder of a division operation
NOT	The inverse of a logical value
OR	1 if either argument is true; 0 if both arguments are false
PRODUCT	The product of a list of values
ROUND	The rounded value of a number
SIGN	The sign of a value (−1, 1, or 0)
SUM	The sum of a list of values
TRUE	1 (see the discussion of the IF function)

FIGURE 23-19

Word's built-in functions.

If both *Logical1* and *Logical2* are true, this function will return the value *1* (true); if either is false, it will return the value *0* (false). For example, the field *{= AND(1<2,3<4)}* returns the value *1*, and the field *{= AND(1<2,3>4)}* returns the value *0*.

The AVERAGE function

The AVERAGE function returns the average (arithmetic mean) of a list of values. The form of this function is

AVERAGE(Value1,Value2,...ValueN)

where *Value1, Value2,* and so forth are either the values you want to average or the formulas whose results you want to average. For example, the field *{= AVERAGE(2,4,6)}* returns the average of 2, 4, and 6, which is 4.

The COUNT function

The COUNT function counts the number of items in a list. The form of this function is

> COUNT(Value1,Value2,...ValueN)

where *Value1*, *Value2*, and so forth are the values or formulas you want to count. For example, the field *{= COUNT(3,49,10.8)}* returns the value 3.

The DEFINED function

The DEFINED function determines whether an expression can be calculated without error. The form of this function is

> DEFINED(Expression)

where *Expression* is the expression you want to check. If *Expression* can be calculated without error, the function will return the value *1* (true). If the expression cannot be calculated without an error, the function will return the value *0* (false). For example, the field *{= DEFINED(5/0)}* returns the value *0*; the field *{= DEFINED(5/1)}* returns the value *1*.

The IF function

The IF function returns either of two user-specified values based on the result of a conditional test. The form of this function is

> IF(ConditionalTest,TrueResult,FalseResult)

Word will evaluate *ConditionalTest* as either true or false. And if *ConditionalTest* is true, the function will return the value you entered as *TrueResult*. If *ConditionalTest* is false, the function will return the value you entered as *FalseResult*. For example, the field *{= IF(2<3,1,0)}* evaluates the conditional test 2<3. Because 2<3 is true, the function returns the value *1*— defined as the *TrueResult*.

Note that *TrueResult* and *FalseResult* normally are numeric values and that you'll most often want to use *1* for *TrueResult* and *0* for *FalseResult*, simply because Word, like most programs, uses the number *1* to represent the value *True* and the number *0* to represent the value *False* when it evaluates logical statements. If you like, however, you can define both *TrueResult* and *FalseResult* with any number, any formula that evaluates to a numeric value, or any bookmark that represents a numeric value. In each case, Word will return the specified value. Also note that Word recognizes the word *True* as equivalent to *1* and the word *False* as equivalent to *0* without your having to define the words as bookmarks.

The INT function

The INT function returns the integer portion of a specified value or formula (the numbers to the left of the decimal). The form of this function is

INT(Formula)

where *Formula* is the formula or value whose integer portion you want to calculate. For example, the field *{= INT(7/4)}* returns the value *1*, and the field *{= INT(–7/4)}* returns the value *–1*.

The MAX and MIN functions

The MAX and MIN functions let you find the highest or lowest values in a list. The forms of these functions are

MAX(Value1,Value2,...ValueN)

MIN(Value1,Value2,...ValueN)

where *Value1, Value2,* and so forth can be either values or formulas whose results you want to evaluate. For example, to find the highest value in the list 32, 19, 7, 2*40, 78, 34, you can use the field *{= MAX(32,19,7,2*40,78,34)}*, which returns the value *80*. To find the lowest value in the list, you can use the field *{= MIN(32,19,7,2*40,78,34)}*, which returns the value *7*.

The MOD function

The MOD function computes the modulus (remainder) that results from dividing one value by another a whole number of times. The form of this function is

MOD(Dividend,Divisor)

The result of this function is the remainder that results from dividing *Dividend* by *Divisor*. For example, the field *{= MOD(3+2,2)}* returns the value *1* because 5 divided by 2 equals 2 with a remainder of 1.

The NOT function

The NOT function inverts a logical value so that NOT applied to a true result evaluates to *0* (false) and NOT applied to a false result evaluates to *1* (true). The form of this function is

NOT(Logical)

where *Logical* is the logical value or expression you want to invert. For example, the field *{= NOT(2+2=5)}* returns the value *1* (true) because the formula 2 plus 2 equals 5 is false.

The OR function

You can use the OR function to join two logical expressions to form a single complex expression. The form of this function is

OR(Logical1,Logical2)

where *Logical1* and *Logical2* are the logical expressions you want to test. If either *Logical1* or *Logical2* is true or if both are true, this function will return the value *1* (true); if both *Logical1* and *Logical2* are false, the OR function will return the value *0* (false). For example, the field *{= OR(1<2,3>4)}* returns the value *1*; the field *{= OR(1>2,3>4)}* returns the value *0*.

The PRODUCT function

The PRODUCT function multiplies all of its arguments and returns their product. The form of this function is

PRODUCT(Value1,Value2,...ValueN)

where *Value1, Value2*, and so forth can be either values or formulas. For example, if you want to multiply the numbers 3, 4, 5, and 6 and the result of the formula 3+4, you can use the field *{= PRODUCT(3,4,5,6,3+4)}*, which returns the value *2520*.

The ROUND function

The ROUND function rounds the value of a number or the result of a formula to a specified number of decimal places. The form of this function is

ROUND(Value,NumPlaces)

where *NumPlaces* specifies the number of decimal places to use when rounding. For example, the field *{= ROUND(2*3.14159,3)}* will return the result *6.283*—the value that results from multiplying 3.14159 by 2 and then rounding to three decimal places.

The SIGN function

The SIGN function returns the sign of a specified value or result. The form of this function is

SIGN(Value)

If *Value* is positive, the function will return *1*; if *Value* is negative, the function will return *−1*; if *Value* is 0, the function will return *0*. For example, the field *{= SIGN(16/−32)}* returns the value *-1* because the formula results in a negative number.

The SUM function

The SUM function adds a list of values. The form of the SUM function is

SUM(Value1,Value2,...ValueN)

where *Value1, Value2*, and so forth can be either values or formulas. For example, to add the numbers 3, 4, 5, and 6 and the result of the formula 2*3+1, you can use the field *{= SUM(3,4,5,6,2*3+1)}*, which returns the value *25*.

The Formula dialog box

The Formula dialog box, which we've already touched on, is simply an aid to entering the = (Formula) field, using the functions and mathematical operators we've just described. To enter an = (Formula) field using the dialog box, choose Table Formula. Word opens the dialog box shown in Figure 23-20.

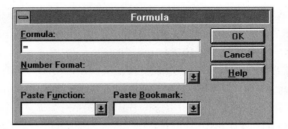

FIGURE 23-20

Choose Table Formula to open the Formula dialog box.

The Formula text box at the top of the dialog box is where you enter the formula for the field. Note in Figure 23-20 that Word has supplied only the equal sign to start the formula, since we're inserting the field outside of a table. When you choose the Table Formula command and the cursor is in a table, Word looks for clues in the table and makes its best guess as to the formula you want to enter, as in the example we gave earlier.

You can enter a formula by typing it in the Formula text box. This can be particularly handy when you simply want the equivalent of a pocket calculator to come up with an answer. If you need the total of 349.34 plus 282.98, for example, you can start with the equal sign that Word supplies, type *349.34+282.98*, and choose OK. Word will insert the field in your document and show you the total, *632.32*. Having Word calculate a result has an advantage over using a pocket calculator—you can look at the field (by moving the cursor to it and pressing Shift-F9) to check your entries.

You can type any formula, including functions and bookmarks, in the Formula text box, or you can have Word paste the functions and bookmark names for you by using the Paste Function and Paste Bookmark drop-down lists. Simply open either list, and choose an item from it. Figure 23-21, for example, shows the dialog box after we've pasted in the AVERAGE function and opened the Paste Function list to paste additional functions that we want the AVERAGE function to evaluate.

When you paste in a function, Word adds the parentheses, if the function needs them, and places the cursor between the parentheses. That makes it

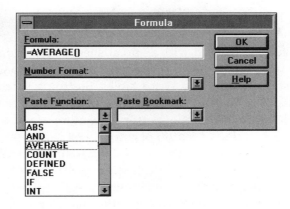

FIGURE 23-21

You can paste functions and bookmarks into the Formula text box by choosing them from the Paste Functions and Paste Bookmark drop-down lists.

easy to paste additional functions—or bookmarks—inside the parentheses. In this case, we want to calculate the average of the absolute value of two bookmarks, which we'll simply call One and Two. The finished formula will read *=AVERAGE(ABS(One),ABS(Two))*.

The other drop-down list in the Formula dialog box is the Number Format list. When you open the list, you can see a number of predefined formats to choose from, as shown in Figure 23-22. When you choose a format from this list, Word adds it to the end of the field, in the proper position for a number format—along with the required \# switch to indicate a number format. When you've finished entering the formula, choose OK to enter the field in your document. For information about using number formats, see "How to use the numeric picture switch" on page 693.

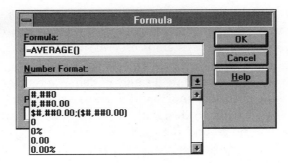

FIGURE 23-22

The Number Format drop-down list makes it easy to add a number format to an = (Formula) field.

You can also use the Formula dialog box to modify an existing = (Formula) field. Simply place your cursor in the field, and choose Table Formula. Word opens the Formula dialog box and places the field's formula in the Formula text box and the number format, if any, in the Number Format box.

Setting Up a Spreadsheet with a Table

If you've ever worked with a spreadsheet application such as Microsoft Excel or Lotus 1-2-3, you've probably noticed more than a few similarities between spreadsheets and Word tables. Sorting a Word table, for example, is much like sorting a spreadsheet. In truth, the similarities go even deeper.

Although Word cannot perform the more complex tasks that spreadsheet programs handle as a matter of course, you can use Word's tables along with Word's calculation features to set up a surprisingly capable spreadsheet within a document. In this discussion, we'll assume you're familiar with all the details about tables that we covered in Chapter 11. In particular, we'll assume you already know how to edit a table and how to make text and numeric entries. We'll also assume that you're familiar with the concepts of fields we discussed earlier in Chapter 20, with the = (Formula) field we have just looked at in detail, and with the concept of a cell as the intersection of a row and a column.

How to refer to cells

To set up a table as a spreadsheet, you need to enter formulas that refer to other cells in the table. First you must understand how to refer to those cells.

All cell references take the form

ColumnRow

where *Column* is given as a letter and *Row* as a number. The upper left corner of the table is A1. The cells to the right in the first row are B1, C1, D1, and so on. The cells down the first column are A1, A2, A3, and so on.

If you're familiar with almost any spreadsheet program, these labels will be familiar since this system is essentially identical to the way most spreadsheet programs designate cells.

You can also designate a range of cells—a rectangular group of adjacent cells—using the same shorthand as most spreadsheet programs use. For example, if you want to designate a range of cells that includes the first two columns (A and B) and the first three rows (1–3), you would enter *A1:B3*—specifying the upper left and lower right cells in the range, with a colon between them. You can use this in an = (Formula) field, along with a function, so the field result of *{=SUM(A1:B3)}* would be the sum of all values in all cells in the range. Note too that you can designate a complete column or row, so *{=SUM(B:B)}* will return the sum of all values in column B and *{=SUM(1:1)}* will return the sum of all values in row 1.

You can, in short, build formulas in tables, using cell references the same way you would in a spreadsheet program. There are six functions that can accept references to table cells: AVERAGE, COUNT, MIN, MAX, PRODUCT, and SUM. And, in addition to using cell references along with functions, you can use cell references by themselves in an = (Formula) field. For example, the field {=B2+B6} will return the sum of the value currently in cell B2 plus the value currently in B6.

 When you enter a formula in a table, the SUM function allows four variations that will often eliminate the need to enter specific cell references. The variations are ABOVE, BELOW, RIGHT, and LEFT. ABOVE, used earlier in this chapter in the field {=SUM(ABOVE)}, tells Word to calculate the total of all values in the cells above the current cell and below the first cell containing text (or the start of the table). As we've mentioned, when you enter an = (Formula) field in a table with the Table Formula command, Word often suggests one of these forms of the SUM function, if it seems appropriate for the data that's already in the table.

Equation Editor

In addition to Word's calculation feature, which lets you perform calculations, Word comes with an application called Equation Editor, which lets you insert virtually any equation into your document. Equations created with Equation Editor do not calculate results. Rather, they let you use equations as illustrations—for scientific and technical papers, for example.

Like WordArt (which we discussed in Chapter 15), Equation Editor is a separate program that you can call on to embed an object in your document. Word treats Equation Editor objects as graphics, so you can place, scale, and crop them as you can any other picture.

More than that, Equation Editor is a sophisticated program in its own right—so much so that we could easily spend several chapters exploring it. We'll cover it here only in enough depth to get you started.

What you see on screen when you start Equation Editor will vary. If you've set Word to show field codes, Equation Editor will open in its own window. If you can still see enough of the document, you may be able to see the EMBED field code that represents the Equation Editor object. If you've set Word to show field results, you'll be able to take advantage of the ability of OLE (Object Linking and Embedding) version 2 to show you the equation object in the context of the document itself. Unfortunately, you'll also find that many of Equation Editor's shortcut keys don't work because Word treats them as commands to Word instead of passing them on to Equation Editor. For this example, then, we'll assume that Word is set to show field codes. To set it, choose Tools Options, then choose View, and make sure the Field Codes check box is checked.

Be aware also that there are some slight differences in the menus available on the menu bar, depending on whether Equation Editor is running in its own window. The two most important differences are that Word will keep its own File menu and Window menu on its menu bar if you're editing the equation in the context of the document. If you're in a separate Equation Editor window, the File menu will be limited to two choices, as we'll discuss shortly, and you won't see a Window item on the menu.

The equations you build in Equation Editor are made up of separate characters and symbols. After you bring an equation into your Word document, however, you'll find it's been converted to a graphics image (an embedded object, to be precise). You can perform all the formatting and resizing tasks on it that you can on other images, but you will not be able to change any individual element in the equation while in Word. You can double-click on the equation, however, or select the object and choose Edit Equation Object and then Edit to return to Equation Editor. When you're back in Equation Editor, the equation is once again a collection of separate components that you can edit.

To open Equation Editor to create a new equation, choose Insert Object. Word opens a dialog box similar to the one in Figure 23-23. Highlight Microsoft Equation 2.0 in the Object Type list on the Create New card and choose OK to start the program. You will then see a screen similar to the one in Figure 23-24 or the one in Figure 23-25 on page 816.

FIGURE 23-23

The Object dialog box lists the programs on your system that support OLE (Object Linking and Embedding).

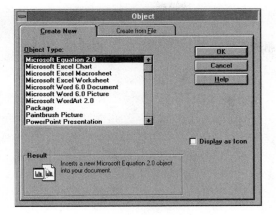

FIGURE 23-24

When Equation Editor starts, either it replaces the Word menu bar and toolbar, as shown here, or it runs in its own window, as in Figure 23-25, depending on the current settings in Word.

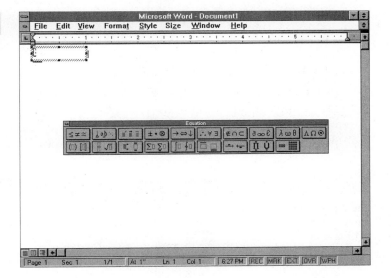

Note in Figure 23-24 that Equation Editor has replaced the Word menu bar with one that's similar to Word's but not identical, and it has replaced Word's toolbars with the Equation Editor's floating toolbar. Note too that the position where the cursor was located when you chose the Insert Object command is now surrounded by a crosshatched box. The box is the Equation Editor editing area. Inside the editing area is a dashed outline of a smaller box. The dashed outline indicates both the insertion point and the size of the next character you'll enter in the equation.

Before we look at an example of how to use Equation Editor, let's take a look at the program's menus, toolbars, and shortcut keys.

FIGURE 23-25

Equation Editor running
in its own window.

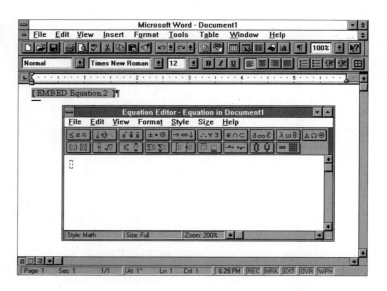

The Equation Editor menus

In many ways, the Equation Editor menus are similar to Word's menus. In fact, many of the commands and options are the same. But there are also notable differences, which are a direct result of Equation Editor's different purpose. Figure 23-26 shows the program menus.

FIGURE 23-26

The Equation Editor menus offer a full set of editing and formatting features.

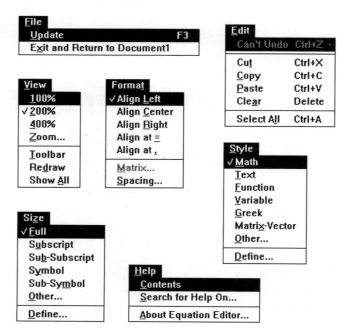

The File menu

As already mentioned, if you're working with Equation Editor in the context of the document, Word will keep its own File menu. The File menu in Figure 23-26 is the one you'll see if you're running Equation Editor in its own window. The menu has only two options, neither of which appears to have anything to do with saving your work. The commands are File Update and File Exit And Return To Document1. (The name of your document is displayed on the menu as part of the command.)

The File Update command places a copy of the equation, as it currently appears in Equation Editor, in your document without closing the Equation Editor window. The File Exit command exits the program and returns you to Word and your document. Before Equation Editor closes, it updates the equation in your document.

Neither of these commands is needed when you're working with the equation in the context of the document. After all, any changes you make are already in the document, so you don't need an Update command. When you leave the Equation Editor object to move to the portion of the document that Word controls, Windows automatically cleans up, removing the Equation Editor menus and toolbar from the screen and returning the Word menus and toolbars. To leave Equation Editor, you need only press Esc or click on any other part of the document.

The Edit menu

The Edit menu commands are Undo, Cut, Copy, Paste, Clear, and Select All. (Select All in this case selects all the items in Equation Editor's window or edit area.) Note that the Edit Cut and Edit Copy commands place the selected items on the Windows Clipboard, which makes the image available to most Windows programs.

The View menu

The View menu has commands for three magnifications—100%, 200%, and 400%—plus a Zoom command. However, these choices are not available when you're working with Equation Editor in the context of a Word document. Rather, the current Zoom settings for Word control the size of the image. If you want to change the Zoom setting, leave Equation Editor and change the setting in Word. All four choices are available when you're working in a separate Equation Editor window, and the Zoom command opens a dialog box that lets you specify a custom Zoom setting.

The Toolbar command toggles the display of the toolbar on and off. The Redraw command repaints the current window, which is useful if the display becomes cluttered. The Show All command will display all of the nonprinting characters.

The Format menu

The Format menu commands let you align multiple lines of equations in different formats, including left, center, and right options, similar to Word's paragraph alignment choices. There are also two other alignment options: Align At = (which aligns equations at their equal signs) and Align At . (which aligns at the rightmost decimal point).

The Format Matrix command lets you modify a previously created matrix and gives you the same options that were available when the matrix was first created. (If you don't know what a matrix is, don't worry about it; you probably won't need the feature.) The Format Spacing command opens a dialog box that lets you control automatic spacing options such as line spacing, superscript height, and subscript depth. Figure 23-27 shows the Spacing dialog box.

FIGURE 23-27

Equation Editor's Spacing dialog box lets you control the automatic spacing for your equations.

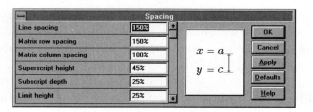

The Style menu

The Style menu commands let you apply several predefined font settings to the various elements of your equations. You can change these predefined settings with the Style Define command, and you can override any of the settings by using the Style Other command. By changing the current font, the Style menu commands also control such issues as whether you see Greek characters or the standard alphabetic characters when you type at the keyboard. (Choose Style Greek, for example, to type Greek characters.)

The Size menu

The Size menu commands let you apply text sizes to the various elements of an equation. You can change those settings with the Size Define command, or you can override them with the Size Other command. The Size Define command opens the Sizes dialog box, shown in Figure 23-28.

FIGURE 23-28

The Sizes dialog box lets you change the sizes of the various equation elements.

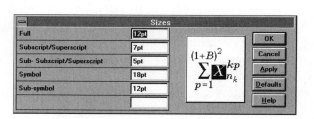

The Help menu

The Help menu is a valuable source of information while you learn to use Equation Editor.

The Window menu

As we mentioned earlier, Equation Editor has no Window menu of its own. If you're editing an equation in the context of a document, however, you'll see Word's usual Window menu as one of the choices in the menu bar.

How to use the template and symbol icons

In addition to the various menu commands, Equation Editor also offers 19 icons on the Equation toolbar, arranged in two rows. These icons are actually more like menus than they are like Word's toolbar buttons. If you move the mouse pointer to an icon and press the left mouse button, you'll open what amounts to a drop-down menu; Equation Editor calls these *palettes*. Using the Equation Editor terminology, the palettes come in two varieties: Symbol palettes on the top row and Template palettes on the bottom row. Each Symbol palette has a set of symbols. Each Template palette provides a set of templates—essentially a fill-in-the-blanks format that you can plug specific characters or symbols into. For example, the first icon from the left in the top row refers to various relational symbols. When you click on this icon, a palette of 11 symbols drops down from the icon. The palette attached to the second icon from the left in the second row, in contrast, offers 9 templates for representing division (or fractions) and root formulas.

The rest of the icons provide a wide range of symbols, embellishments, and formula templates. We encourage you to browse though the choices to see what's available. The name of the highlighted icon is displayed in the status bar.

To insert a symbol or a template into your equation, first open the appropriate palette by clicking on it, and then click on the specific item to insert it. Alternatively, if you're working with Equation Editor in its own window, press F2 to make the toolbar active, use the arrow keys to move to the palette you want, and press Enter to open it. Then use the arrow keys to highlight the specific item you want from the palette, and press Enter to insert it. This keyboard technique will not work if you're viewing the equation in the context of your document.

If you are working with Equation Editor in its own window, you can also enter a template or symbol by number. To enter a symbol, press Ctrl-Shift-K followed by the palette number (counting from left to right) and then by a number to represent the symbol (counting from left to right, from top to bottom). Press Enter to insert the symbol. Do not put a space between the numbers; use 0 to represent the tenth palette. To enter a template, follow the same procedure, but start with Ctrl-Shift-T instead.

Keyboard shortcuts

You can also insert the symbols and templates with keyboard shortcuts. Figure 23-29 lists the shortcuts available within Equation Editor as well as the keystrokes for inserting spaces, applying embellishments (such as a tilde over a character), and repositioning elements of an equation. Note, however, that most of the shortcuts for inserting symbols and templates will work reliably only if you're working with Equation Editor in its own window. They will not work if you're editing the equation in the context of your document, taking advantage of OLE 2. Most keystrokes for inserting spaces, applying embellishments, and repositioning will work in either case.

For inserting symbols

Symbol	Description	Press Ctrl-K Followed by This Key
∞	Infinity	I
→	Arrow	A
∂	Derivative (partial)	D
≤	Less than or equal to	< or .
≥	Greater than or equal to	> or ,
×	Times	T
∈	Element of	E
∉	Not an element of	Shift-E
⊂	Contained in	C
⊄	Not contained in	Shift-C

FIGURE 23-29

Equation Editor keyboard shortcuts.

(continued)

FIGURE 23-29. *continued*

For inserting common templates

Template	Description	Keystrokes
(☐)	Parentheses	Ctrl-9 or Ctrl-0
[☐]	Brackets	Ctrl-[or Ctrl-]
{☐}	Braces	Ctrl-{ or Ctrl-}
▯	Fraction	Ctrl-F
▱⁄▱	Slash fraction	Ctrl-/
▰˙	Superscript (high)	Ctrl-H
▰.	Subscript (low)	Ctrl-L
▰:	Joint sub/superscript	Ctrl-J
√☐	Square root	Ctrl-R
∫▯	Integral	Ctrl-I

For inserting other templates

Template	Description	Press Ctrl-T Followed by This Key
(☐)	Parentheses	(or)
[☐]	Brackets	[or]
{☐}	Braces	{ or }
|☐|	Absolute value	| (vertical bar)
▯	Fraction	F
▱⁄▱	Slash fraction	/
▰˙	Superscript (high)	H
▰.	Subscript (low)	L
▰:	Joint sub/superscript	J
√☐	Square root	R
ⁿ√☐	Nth root	N
Σ☐	Summation	S
Π☐	Product	P
∫▯	Integral	I
⊞	Matrix template (3x3)	M
▯	Underscript (limit)	U

(continued)

FIGURE 23-29. *continued*

For inserting spaces

Icon	Description	Keystrokes
a‍b	Zero space	Shift-Spacebar
a‍b	1-point space	Ctrl-Alt-Spacebar
a‍b	Thin space	Ctrl-Spacebar
a b	Thick space	Ctrl-Shift-Spacebar

For applying embellishments

Icon	Description	Keystrokes
ī	Over-bar	Ctrl-Shift-Hyphen
ĩ	Tilde	Ctrl-Tilde (~); Ctrl-Quote (") on some keyboards
ı⃗	Arrow (vector)	Ctrl-Alt-Hyphen
í	Single prime	Ctrl-Alt-Apostrophe (')
ı″	Double prime	Ctrl-Quote ("); Ctrl-Tilde (~) on some keyboards
i̇	Single dot	Ctrl-Alt-Period (.)

For repositioning the elements of an equation

Description	Select the Elements and Then Press This Key Combination
Left one pixel	Ctrl-Left arrow
Right one pixel	Ctrl-Right arrow
Down one pixel	Ctrl-Down arrow
Up one pixel	Ctrl-Up arrow

An example

To give you a feel for how to use Equation Editor, here's a simple example showing how to build two statements of the Pythagorean theorem. Figure 23-30 shows the final result.

FIGURE 23-30

You can use Equation Editor for relatively simple equations such as these or for far more complex statements.

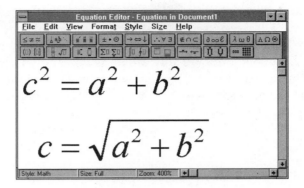

Starting with a blank screen in Equation Editor, type a lowercase letter c. The box outline disappears, and the c appears where the box outline was, while a blinking cursor similar to the Word cursor appears just to the right of the c. Next enter the superscripted 2. To use the mouse, click on the icon in the bottom row, third from the left of the toolbar; then click on the choice in the upper left corner. To use the keyboard, press Ctrl-H. (But note that this will work only if you are using Equation Editor in its own window.) Either method will produce a superscripted box, as shown in Figure 23-31, and will place the cursor there. You can then type a 2.

FIGURE 23-31

When you indicate that the next character should be super-scripted, Equation Editor uses the box out-line to show you the superscripted position.

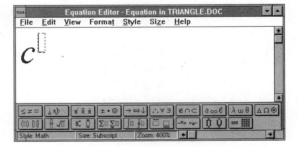

Next press the Right arrow key once to restore the full-size cursor, and then type an equal sign and a lowercase a. Add a superscript 2 to the a, as already described, and then add a plus sign and a lowercase b with a superscript 2. This completes the first formula.

Press the Right arrow key to restore the full-size cursor; then press Enter to move to the next line and start the second formula. Type $c=$ and then use the mouse or keyboard to enter the radical (square root) symbol. To use the mouse, click on the second icon on the bottom row of the toolbar, and then click on the fourth box down on the left side. To use the keyboard, press Ctrl-R. (Again, this will not work unless you are using Equation Editor in its own window.)

With the radical template in place, enter the remaining characters—a lowercase *a*, a superscript 2, a plus sign, a lowercase *b*, and a superscript 2—using the same techniques that you used for the first formula. Notice that the radical symbol automatically grows as you add characters below it.

The final step is to align the two statements. Simply select both equations (either by dragging with the mouse or by holding down the Shift key and using the arrow keys, as you would in Word). Then choose the command Format Align At =. Your screen should now look like the example shown in Figure 23-30.

Character Formulas: The EQ Field

Word offers another way to create formulas in your document—the EQ field, or equation field. The EQ field is actually a leftover from version 1 of the program, before Word included Equation Editor as part of the package. The EQ field lets you create an equation by describing it with codes.

If you've never used the EQ field in an earlier version of Word and you don't have any files that include EQ fields, there's no reason to use it. We strongly recommend using Equation Editor instead. If you have some files created in an earlier version of Word, however, and those files include EQ fields, Word will recognize those fields to display and print the formulas they define.

If you have an EQ field already in a file, you can convert it to an Equation Editor equation simply by double-clicking on the field. Word will convert it to an Equation object and will open Equation Editor.

Numbering Items in Sequence

Depending on the kind of documents you produce, you may need to number items in sequence—as with the figures in this book, for example. Depending on taste or house style, you may need a single numbering sequence for all kinds of items, or you may need a separate sequence for each kind—such as tables, equations, and illustrations.

One of the annoyances of numbering in sequence is the chore of figuring out the next number to use. Even more annoying is having to renumber when you add or delete one of the items—especially if you have more than one set of numbered items. Word's SEQ field turns both of these annoyances into non-issues by automatically supplying the numbers and renumbering as necessary if you add, delete, or move a numbered item.

Note that the renumbering is not fully automatic, in the sense of automatic updating of the numbers as you make each editing change. Rather, Word does not update anything until you manually update the fields (by selecting the fields and pressing F9) or until you print. The automated part of the update is the calculation that determines the correct number without any input from you.

You can enter the SEQ field manually, using any of the techniques we discussed in Chapter 20. But having to enter the field can be a bother, especially if you haven't memorized the various switches. To make this feature as painless as possible, Word provides a special tool for the field that doesn't require you to know anything about fields. The tool is the Caption dialog box, shown in Figure 23-33 on the next page, and you can get to it simply by choosing Insert Caption.

Because you don't need to know anything about the field codes to use the dialog box, we'll largely ignore the field code it produces for now (although we'll come back to the code itself at the end of this discussion). We'll assume, therefore, that you have Word set to show field results rather than field codes. To check the setting, choose Tools Options, then choose View, and make sure the Field Codes check box isn't checked.

The Caption dialog box

The easiest way to explain how to use the Caption dialog box is to give a simple example. Suppose you're creating a document that has three tables, such as the sample document in Figure 23-32. You can label these literally as Table 1, Table 2, and Table 3, or you can use the Caption dialog box to insert the label, or caption, for each.

FIGURE 23-32

We want to insert a label, or caption, for each of these tables.

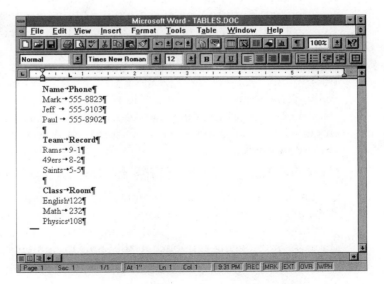

To insert the caption for the first table, start by selecting the entire table. Then choose Insert Caption to open the dialog box shown in Figure 23-33.

FIGURE 23-33

The Caption dialog box can insert fields for you that automatically keep numbered items—such as tables—numbered correctly.

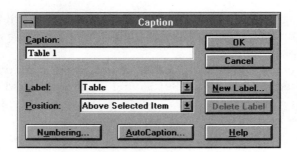

The Caption dialog box offers one text box, labeled Caption, and two drop-down lists, for label and position. The Label list offers three predefined names for captions—Equation, Figure, and Table. You can also add other names by choosing the New Label button, entering a name in the New Label dialog box, and choosing OK. Similarly, you can delete any label name that you've added to the list by highlighting it and choosing Delete. You can't delete the predefined choices.

The Position list offers two choices: Above Selected Item and Below Selected Item. If you didn't select anything before opening the dialog box, the Position choice will be grayed out, and Word will insert the caption at the cursor position.

In this example, we want to label all three tables as *Table* and put the caption above each table, so we'll choose Table for Label and Above Selected Item for Position. Since this is the first table in the file, Word will enter the text *Table 1* in the Caption text box, as shown in Figure 23-33. You can't delete this part of the entry, but you can add punctuation and a more descriptive caption after it, such as *Sample Phone List*. When you're satisfied with the entry, choose OK to enter the caption.

Next select the second table and repeat the process, this time adding the description *Sample Scores* to the Caption text box before choosing OK. Finally, repeat the process with the third table, adding the text *Sample Room List*. When you've finished, the result should look like the sample document in Figure 23-34. Note how Word automatically numbered the captions when it inserted them.

How to change the label for an item in a sequence

One of the Insert Caption command's most valuable features is its ability to renumber the items in a sequence automatically when you make a change that affects the numbering. Just as important is its ability to maintain more than one numbering sequence in the same document.

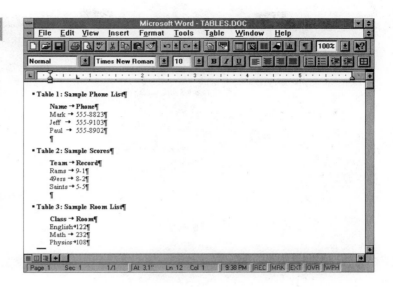

Suppose, for example, that you decide you want to make the second table part of a different sequence, which we'll call Illustrations. To change the caption, first select the part of the caption with the label and number—*Table 2* in this case—and choose Edit Clear. Then select the descriptive part of the caption (leaving the paragraph mark), and choose Edit Cut to place the text on the Clipboard. Next choose Insert Caption to open the Captions dialog box, and paste the Clipboard contents into the Caption text box by using the Ctrl-V or Shift-Ins keyboard shortcut.

At this point, you can choose Illustration from the Label list if it already exists. Otherwise, you'll have to create the label—by choosing the New Label button, entering the word *Illustration*, and choosing OK. Word displays Illustration in the Label box of the Caption dialog box and numbers the illustration appropriately, keeping the rest of the text for the descriptive caption. To enter the new caption, choose OK. Word inserts the new caption and renumbers the table captions, as shown in Figure 23-35 on the next page.

If you had selected the table before choosing Insert Caption, the captions would be, in order, *Table 1*, *Illustration 1*, and *Table 3*. To update the numbers automatically, select all the fields. (The easy way is to select the entire document by choosing Edit Select All, pressing Ctrl-A, or pressing Ctrl-NumPad 5.) Then press F9 to update the numbering. Word recalculates the numbers so that the captions are *Table 1*, *Illustration 1*, and *Table 2*. The advantage of highlighting the table before selecting Insert Caption is that Word uses the Keep With Next option on the Text Flow card of the Paragraph dialog box to ensure that the caption does not fall on a separate page from the table.

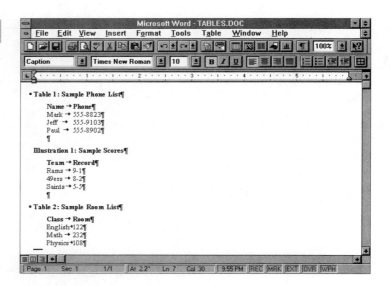

How to change the label for an entire sequence

You can also change the label for an entire sequence at once. Suppose, for
example, that you want to change all of the Table items to Illustration items.
Start by selecting the label and number for any of the Table items. Then
choose Insert Caption to open the Captions dialog box. Word automatically
inserts the Table choice in the Label and Caption boxes. Choose Illustration
from the label list. Word replaces Table with Illustration in the Caption text
box as well. When you choose OK, Word replaces all the Table items with
Illustration items. It also updates the numbering in the process, so the captions now read *Illustration 1, Illustration 2,* and *Illustration 3.*

How to define the number format

When you create or redefine a caption, you can specify number formats
other than the default Arabic numbers. To change the format, choose the
Numbering button at the bottom of the Caption dialog box to open the Caption Numbering dialog box, shown in Figure 23-36.

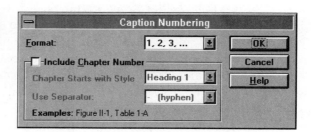

The Caption Numbering dialog box offers a drop-down list box containing several choices for the number format: Arabic numerals (1, 2, 3...), uppercase and lowercase letters (A, B, C... or a, b, c...), and uppercase and lowercase Roman numerals (I, II, III... or i, ii, iii).

The dialog box also offers an Include Chapter Numbering check box. If you want to restart the numbering sequence at 1 at the beginning of each chapter and you want to include the chapter number as part of the item number (as is the case with the figures in this book), make sure this box is checked. You can then specify the style that indicates the start of a new chapter by using the Chapter Starts With Style list, and you can indicate the separator between the chapter number and item number.

> To include the chapter number, you also have to number the chapters with the Format Heading Numbering command. Otherwise, Word will use a 0 (zero) for the chapter number in each caption. For details on how to number chapters, see "Numbering Headings" starting on page 483.

How to insert captions automatically

If some or all of the items that need sequential numbering are Word tables or objects that will be created in other programs and inserted in the document using OLE, you can use Word's AutoCaption feature to add the captions automatically. (We discussed OLE and importing data in Chapter 18.) To define the labels and numbering format for automatic captions, choose Insert Caption and then the AutoCaption button to open the AutoCaption dialog box, shown in Figure 23-37.

FIGURE 23-37

You can tell Word to add a caption to tables or to objects you import with OLE.

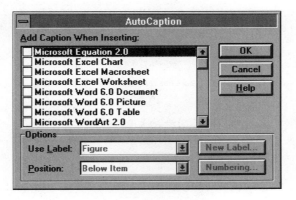

The choices you see in the Add Caption When Inserting list depend on which programs you've installed on your system that support OLE. The Microsoft Word 6.0 Table option is always available and refers to tables created within Word. To tell Word to add a caption for any of the items in the list, first check the item's check box and highlight the item, using the mouse or keyboard. Then choose a label in the Use Label drop-down list and a position from the Position drop-down list. Note that you can use different labels and other settings for each item in the list or use the same label for more than one type of item.

Note too the New Label button, which you can choose to open a dialog box that lets you define a new label, just as you can from the Caption dialog box. Similarly, you can choose the Numbering button to open the Caption Numbering dialog box and specify a numbering scheme. When you're finished with the AutoCaption dialog box, choose OK to close it and return to your document.

The SEQ field

We've been carefully ignoring the SEQ field so far. However, you can't do some things with the Caption dialog box—you need to use the SEQ field. So we can't completely avoid the SEQ field. To see the fields inserted by the dialog box commands, choose Tools Options, choose View, check the Field Codes check box, and choose OK. Your document should now look much like the one in Figure 23-38.

FIGURE 23-38

If you set Word to show field codes, you can see the SEQ fields Word uses to keep track of sequence numbers.

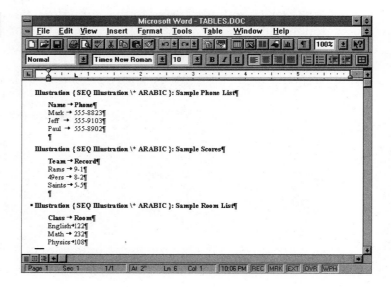

As you can see in Figure 23-38, when Word inserts a caption, it inserts part of it as text and part as a SEQ field. The format for the field is

{SEQ Identifier Switches}

where *Identifier* is the label you've chosen to identify the type of item, and *Switches* represents whatever additional options you've added. The only switch in Figure 23-38 is the format switch, * ARABIC, which tells Word to use Arabic numerals. The following are other switches you may want to add manually. If you choose to add them, you can insert the entire field manually, using any of the techniques we discussed in Chapter 20, or you can use the Insert Caption command, set Word to show the fields, and edit the field. Finish by resetting Word to show field results and updating the field you changed.

How to repeat the previous sequence number: \c

If you want a SEQ field to return the same number as the previous SEQ field, use the \c switch. For example, if you've used {SEQ Table * ARABIC} to generate a table number and you need to generate the same table number again—so that you can refer to that table by number in your text, for example—enter the second instance as {SEQ table *ARABIC \c}.

How to reset the sequence number: \r

If you want to reset the sequence number to a particular value, use the \r switch followed by the value you want to reset to. For example, to reset the sequence number to 1 for the first table in a new chapter, without having to include the chapter number, enter the field as {SEQ Table *ARABIC \r 1}.

How to create a placeholder SEQ field: \h

At times you'll want to set the sequence number without inserting the field result in your document. To create this kind of placeholder, enter the \h switch after any other switches in the field code. For example, if the current file contains the second half of a document that has 14 tables in the first half, you might want to enter the field {SEQ table \r 14 \h} at the beginning of the file. This ensures that Word will number the first table in the file as *15*, even if you later delete or move the table that you originally created as the first table in the file. Be aware that the \h switch will not hide a field that includes the * format switch.

How to use bookmarks in a SEQ field

If you've used earlier versions of Word, you may know that you can use bookmarks in SEQ fields to let you automatically update references to sequential items. We mention this here only to point out that although Word still recognizes cross-references created with this technique, it's no longer necessary. In fact, Word now provides a much simpler way to create cross-references of all kinds, as we'll discuss next.

Creating Cross-References

If you create documents that refer to an element—such as a chart, a detailed discussion, a chapter title, or a footnote—that appears pages away from the reference to that item, you probably feel that finding the right page, item number, or title to refer to is always a bother. Keeping references up to date after you edit your text or change formatting can be a time-consuming chore.

The good news is that Word can automatically *update* cross-references. (As with the caption numbers we've just discussed, *automatic* in this context refers to calculating the right number. You still have to choose the command manually to update the field.) The better news is that Word also makes it easy to *create* cross-references, and the feature works the same way for cross-referencing any type of item in your document.

The Insert Cross-Reference command

Word's Insert Cross-Reference command makes entering cross-references as easy as you could possibly hope for. Suppose, for example, that you're working with the file shown in Figure 23-39.

FIGURE 23-39

We want to add a cross-reference to the partial sentence at the bottom of this document.

The text in Figure 23-39 ends in the middle of a sentence that begins *As we discussed in*.

Suppose you want to add a reference to a section name and give a page number for that section as well (a format we use in this book, for example). To insert the reference, leave the cursor at the position where you want the reference, and choose the Insert Cross-Reference command. Word opens the Cross-Reference dialog box, shown in Figure 23-40.

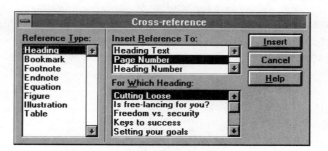

Word's Cross-Reference dialog box makes it easy to insert a cross-reference to any kind of item.

As you can see in Figure 23-40, Word lists all the available reference types in the document in the Reference Type list box. These include all the standard types, such as headings, bookmarks, footnotes, endnotes, equations, figures, and tables, plus any types that you've defined by defining labels for the Insert Caption command. The Illustration choice in Figure 23-40, for example, is one that we defined.

For whichever type you've highlighted in the Reference Type list, Word provides a complete list of those items in the For Which list and changes the name of the list as appropriate. In Figure 23-40, we've highlighted the Heading type, and Word has labeled the For Which box as *For Which Heading*. The choices include all the paragraphs marked as headings in the current document: *Cutting Loose, Is free-lancing for you?, Freedom vs. security*, and so on.

The Insert Reference To box lets you specify the kind of reference to insert. The kinds vary with your choice of reference type. For the Heading type, for example, the choices are Heading Text, Page Number, and Heading Number. For the Footnote type, in contrast, the choices are Footnote Number and Page Number. The important point is that the choice is always appropriate to the type of item.

In this example, we want to refer to the section *Cutting Loose*, followed by the page number. To insert the reference, highlight *Heading* in the Reference Type box, highlight *Cutting Loose* in the For Which Heading list, highlight *Heading Text* in the Insert Reference To list, and choose Insert. Then highlight *Page Number* in the Insert Reference To list, choose Insert again, and then choose Close to return to the document.

Assuming the heading was on page 1, Word enters the reference as *Cutting Loose1*. To finish, move the cursor to just before the *1* and then type a comma, a space, the text *starting on page,* and another space. You then need to add a period at the end of the sentence. The finished result, shown in Figure 23-41, is *As we discussed in Cutting Loose, starting on page 1.*

FIGURE 23-41

The finished cross-reference shown here inserts both the heading name and the page number.

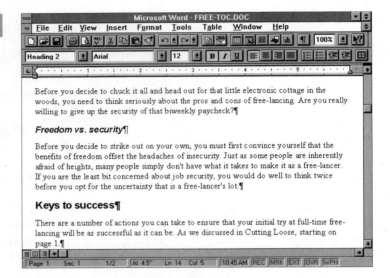

When you want to update the references after further editing, simply select the field, and choose the update command by pressing F9 or by clicking the right mouse button with the mouse pointer in the field and choosing Update Field from the context-sensitive menu.

Word updates changes to the heading text as well as to the page number. But if you change a heading, be careful to modify what's there rather than deleting all the text and starting again. If you delete the heading entirely, Word won't know that the new heading is a substitute for the old, and you'll get an error message when you try to update the field. Fortunately, if you make this mistake, you can define a new cross-reference easily enough.

A word about the reference fields

Although you can use Insert Cross-Reference for virtually all cross-reference needs, be aware that Word also lets you create cross-references manually, using bookmarks and several variations on reference fields. You may find this procedure handy if you're working with a file created in Word 2.0c or earlier, before Word added the Insert Cross-Reference command. The fields you use are REF, NOTEREF, and PAGEREF. You can find information about all of these in the Word help system by searching for them by name.

> The Insert Cross-Reference command also uses the reference fields, as you can see if you insert a reference and then set Word to show field codes. Instead of using names, however, the Insert Cross-Reference command uses numeric references that take the form RefXXXXXXXX, where the Xs represent a number that Word automatically assigns. Be aware that you should not edit these references. If you change them, Word will give you an error message if you then update the field.

The STYLEREF Field

The STYLEREF field is a specialized reference field designed to let you add information to a header or footer automatically. For example, if you're creating a glossary, you can use the STYLEREF field to show the first and last glossary words on each page automatically—the same format you'll find in a dictionary. You can also use the STYLEREF field to insert the current chapter name on each page automatically as part of a header or footer. The form of this field is

{STYLEREF "StyleName"}

{STYLEREF "StyleName" Switches}

where *StyleName* is the name of the style assigned to the text you want to return as the field result. To search for one of Word's built-in heading styles (such as Heading 1, Heading 2, and so on), you would enter the style name. (Note that the name must be enclosed in quotes.) Word searches for the nearest paragraph formatted with that style, such as the chapter title, and returns the text in that paragraph as the result for the field.

To use the STYLEREF field effectively, you need to understand how Word determines which paragraph is the nearest one. That determination depends on where the STYLEREF field is and on whether you've included the \l switch (the letter L). Note that the \l switch is available only in headers and footers. The switch tells Word to search from the bottom of the page, which means it lets you retrieve the style of the last paragraph on the page. Figure 23-42 on the next page summarizes all of the possibilities for the STYLEREF field.

If STYLEREF Is In	Word Will Search
Body text	From the field code to the beginning of the document and then from the field code to the end of the document
Footnotes or annotations	From the reference mark in the body text to the beginning of the document, and then from the reference mark to the end of the document
Headers or footers	From the beginning of the current page to the end of that page, then from the end of the previous page to the beginning of the document, and then from the beginning of the following page to the end of the document
With \l switch (available only in headers or footers)	From the end of the current page to the beginning of the document, and then from the beginning of the following page to the end of the document

FIGURE 23-42

How Word searches with STYLEREF.

Since the STYLEREF field is most often used in headers and footers, we'll confine this discussion to examples using headers and footers.

Figure 23-43 demonstrates the way you're most likely to use the STYLEREF field. In this document, we've assigned the Heading 1 style to all section headings and the Title style to the document title, and we've entered the header

{STYLEREF "Title"} - {STYLEREF "Heading 1"}

When Word updates the fields, as shown in Figure 23-43, and displays the field results, it inserts the document's title along with the nearest appropriate section heading that is formatted in the Heading 1 style, as shown in Figure 23-44.

Figure 23-45 on page 838 demonstrates how you can use the STYLEREF field to create dictionary-style headers. The document in this case is a glossary. Each glossary term is in its own paragraph, and each is assigned the Heading 2 style. In this case, the header fields take the form

{STYLEREF "Heading 2"} - {STYLEREF "Heading 2" \l}

This header is designed to show the first and last terms on each page so that a set of keywords appears at the top of the page.

FIGURE 23-43

The STYLEREF field in the header of this document retrieves the first section header on the current page or the nearest header before the current page.

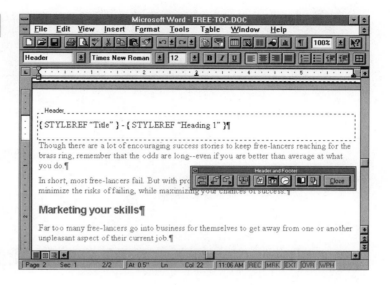

FIGURE 23-44

This is how the document shown in Figure 23-43 looks after you update the fields, assuming Word is set to show field results.

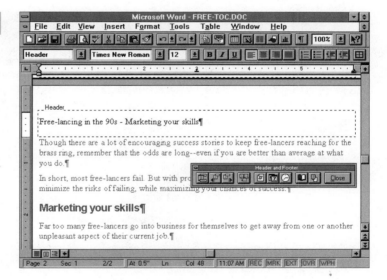

The first field in this header retrieves the glossary term that appears nearest the top of the page. The second field contains an \l switch, which retrieves the glossary term nearest the bottom of the page. Figure 23-46 on the next page shows how the document appears after you update and display the field results.

FIGURE 23-45

The STYLEREF fields in the header of this document yield dictionary-style headings.

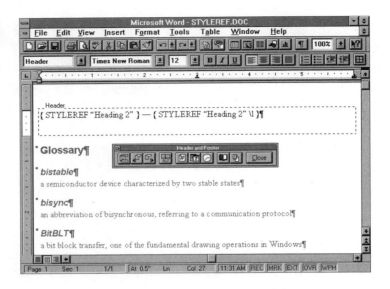

FIGURE 23-46

This is how the document shown in Figure 23-45 looks after you update the fields, assuming Word is set to show field results.

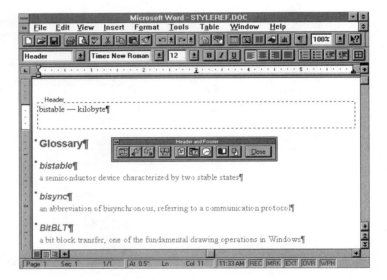

Note that the STYLEREF field also recognizes the \n switch, which inserts any paragraph numbering from the referenced paragraph.

The PRINT Field

We've covered most of Word's fields elsewhere in this book, either as part of our discussion of fields in Chapter 20 or in relation to the features they work with. But Word has one unusual field that's worth special mention: the PRINT field.

You can use the PRINT field to send printer control codes and PostScript programs to your printer. The field takes the form

{PRINT "PrinterInstructions"}

where *PrinterInstructions* are the control codes, or commands, you want to send to the printer. Because the PRINT field is an action field, it doesn't return a result. Instead, when you print a document, the PRINT field sends the printer control codes you've specified, exactly as you've entered them.

Because printers have different control codes and other commands, you need to consult your printer manual to determine the codes or commands to use. Since the whole point of the field is to let you send commands to the printer that Word can't send automatically, Word has no way to determine whether the instructions you specify are valid for your printer. If you specify an invalid set of control codes, your printer either will print those codes as literal text or will behave in unexpected ways.

If you're using a PostScript printer and you want to use a PostScript program as the *PrinterInstructions* argument, you'll need to precede the argument with the \p switch. This can become quite technical, however, and requires a knowledge of PostScript. You'll find some of the information you need on the Word Help screen for the PRINT field, along with references for books on PostScript.

Creating Special Characters

In Chapter 5, we discussed Word's Insert Symbol command and showed how you can use the command to insert special characters, such as math symbols, Greek letters, and copyright and trademark symbols. Although most users will find that the Insert Symbol command is the easiest way to enter these characters, you should be aware that there are other ways to enter special characters.

ASCII, ANSI, and OEM character sets

As we've explained elsewhere in this book, the lingua franca that Word and other programs use to define characters is ASCII, the American Standard Code for Information Interchange. Every letter, number, punctuation mark, and other symbol you can type on a standard American keyboard is defined by an ASCII code that ranges from 0 through 127. Even special instructions, such as carriage returns, paragraph breaks, page breaks, and tabs, are defined in ASCII code.

ANSI (American National Standards Institute) is a superset of ASCII. In addition to the 128 ASCII characters, ANSI contains foreign-language characters, such as å and ç. These 128 special characters are called *extended characters*. They do not appear on a standard American keyboard, but you can enter them in Word with the Insert Symbol command, as well as in other ways that we'll discuss in a moment.

In addition to the ANSI character set (and in addition to any special symbol sets you may have installed on your system), you can also use characters from what Microsoft calls the OEM (Original Equipment Manufacturer) character set, better known as the IBM character set or IBM extended ASCII character set. The first 128 characters of the IBM character set are identical to those in the ASCII and ANSI character sets. However, the extended characters (128–255) differ from extended ANSI characters.

How to enter ANSI and OEM characters

Despite the fact that the ANSI and OEM character sets use the same codes for different symbols, you can actually use both sets of codes in the same document. For example, in the ANSI character set, 163 is the British pound sign. In the OEM character set, 163 is a lowercase u with an acute accent.

To enter the ANSI character, first make sure Num Lock is on, and then hold down the Alt key while typing *0163* on the numeric keypad. After you type the number, release the Alt key; Word inserts the ANSI character at the cursor position.

To enter the OEM character, follow essentially the same procedure, but leave out the leading zero: Hold down the Alt key and type *163*. When you release the Alt key, Word inserts the OEM character at the cursor position.

How to use AutoText to store symbols

You can use Word's AutoText feature to store symbols. After you enter a character in your document, simply highlight the character, choose Edit AutoText, and enter an appropriate name. You can then use Word's AutoText commands to enter the character at any time. If you use a few symbols frequently, you may well find this approach faster and more convenient for those few symbols than using the Insert Symbol command.

PART FIVE

CUSTOMIZING
WORD

TOPIC FINDER

Recording a Macro   844

- How to record a macro
- Rules for macro names
- Macro descriptions, template assignments, and shortcuts
- How to create the macro
- How to correct mistakes
- How to end the recording of a macro

Running a Macro   857

- What happens when Word runs a recorded macro
- Running macros with macros
- A word of caution
- How to run a macro with the Tools Macro command
- How to run a macro with a shortcut key, a menu, or a toolbar button

Saving a Macro   860

- How to save a macro with the File Save All command

Modifying a Macro's Properties   861

- How to rename a macro
- How to change a macro's description
- How to delete a macro
- How to recover a deleted macro

Editing a Macro   863

24

Recording Macros

A s you use Word, you'll find yourself repeating some tasks far more often than others. For example, you may often want to delete or move a word, sentence, or line, enter a time stamp with the current date and time, and so on. Instead of handling these tasks manually, you can record them in macros. That way, you can give the command with one or several keystrokes using shortcut keys, with a two-keystroke or two–mouse click menu command, or with a toolbar button. We'll explain how to assign already existing macros to keystrokes and menus in Chapter 28, "Customizing Menus, Keys, & Templates," starting on page 950. You can find details on assigning already-existing macros to toolbars in "Customizing Toolbars" on page 316.

Computer programs in general often feature one or both of two kinds of macros: keyboard macros and programmed macros. A keyboard macro records keystrokes and then, when you run it, plays the keystrokes back just as if you had typed them yourself. A programmed macro may also include keystrokes or even be limited to replicating keystrokes, but the essence of a programmed-macro feature is that it offers you the tools to let you add programming logic. For example, a programmed macro might stop to ask a question by way of a dialog box and then perform one task or another, depending on your answer.

Macro features in most programs—particularly MS-DOS–based, as opposed to Windows-based, programs—offer either keyboard macros alone or keyboard macros plus a limited set of commands that add programming logic. The most sophisticated of these macro languages approach the flexibility of a true programming language, even though the underlying macro feature is built from the ability to record keystrokes.

Word goes much further. In fact, Word's macro feature is radically different from those you may be used to. First, there is no keyboard macro feature as such. And second, the macro language in Word does not simply approach the flexibility of a programming language. It *is* a programming language, called WordBasic.

Don't let the idea of macros as programs scare you. Word will still let you record macros, much as you can with a keyboard macro feature. However, because Word records commands rather than keystrokes, the results may sometimes surprise you—a point we'll come back to in Chapter 25.

In this chapter, we'll look at how to record macros, modify their properties—such as their names and descriptions—and edit them. In the two chapters after this, we'll look at how to write macros from scratch and how to use the Dialog Editor to help create dialog boxes for your macros.

Recording a Macro

Word's Record Macro feature, also called a learn mode, lets you create a macro by telling Word to record a procedure as you perform it manually. Suppose, for example, that you want the ability to quickly and easily delete a word at a time with the option to reinsert the word elsewhere—a useful editing capability that Word doesn't happen to supply as a built-in feature. You can already delete the word to the immediate right of the cursor by pressing Ctrl-Del, or the word to the left by pressing Ctrl-Backspace, but neither of these actions puts the deleted word on the Clipboard for pasting later. However, you can record the steps in a macro, assign the macro to a shortcut key, and add what amounts to a new feature to Word—one that lets you delete a word with the Edit Cut command so that it's placed on the Clipboard with a single keystroke.

How to record a macro

The first step in creating a macro is to decide exactly what you want the macro to do. This isn't to say that you can't change it later. As we'll describe in the final section of this chapter, you can edit the macro as needed after it has been created. However, you can eliminate lots of work, and lots of false starts, by giving some thought beforehand to what you want to accomplish.

Assume that you want the macro to cut from the current cursor position to the end of the current word, including any space that follows the word. The standard keystrokes in Word for manually performing this task are Ctrl-Shift-Right arrow followed by either Ctrl-X or Shift-Del. This puts the deleted text on the Clipboard so that you can paste it elsewhere with Ctrl-V or Shift-Ins.

To record the macro, you should first type a few words on the screen so that you'll be able to see the effect of your actions as you perform them. Place the cursor in a word, or just in front of one, and choose the Tools Macro command. Then choose Record to bring up the Record Macro dialog box, shown in Figure 24-1.

FIGURE 24-1

By default, the Record Macro dialog box suggests the name Macro1 for your first macro.

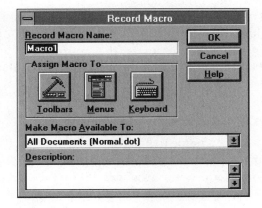

 You can start recording a macro either by choosing Tools Macro and then Record or by double-clicking on REC in the status bar at the bottom of the Word window. If you prefer, you can add a button to any of your toolbars that enables you to choose the Tools Macro Record command with a single mouse click; alternatively, you can define a keyboard shortcut that enables you to choose the command by pressing a shortcut key. For details on customizing toolbars, see "Customizing Toolbars" on page 316. For details on defining a keyboard shortcut, see "Keyboard Customization" on page 968.

After bringing up the Record Macro dialog box, you can type a name for the macro, such as *EraseWord*, in the Record Macro Name text box. Alternatively, you can accept Word's default macro name for now—Macro1, in this case. (The next time you record a macro, Word will suggest the name Macro2, and so forth.)

> If you use the default name (or any other name, for that matter), you can rename the macro at any time by choosing Tools Macro and then choosing Organizer to open the Organizer dialog box. You would then highlight the macro name you want to change and choose Rename. We'll cover this in a bit more detail in "How to rename a macro" on page 861.

To jump ahead of our example a bit, once you give the macro a name, you can choose OK and perform the task you want to record—in this case typing Ctrl-Shift-Right arrow and then Ctrl-X or Shift-Del. To stop recording, you can, among other choices, double-click on REC in the status bar, or choose Tools Macro and then Stop Recording. Once the macro is recorded, you'll be able to delete a word, or part of one, and put it on the Clipboard simply by moving the cursor to the appropriate word and running the macro. But before you actually record the macro, there are some issues you will want to consider.

Rules for macro names

First, as you assign a name to a macro, note that Word has a few simple rules for naming macros. The name must start with a letter of the alphabet, and it can contain only letters and numbers. If you type an invalid character, such as a space, in the Record Macro Name text box, Word will dim the OK button in the dialog box; you will not be able to close the dialog box to record the macro until you type an acceptable macro name.

Macro descriptions, template assignments, and shortcuts

In addition to typing a name, you can optionally add a description for the macro before you record it, using the Description text box at the bottom of the Record Macro dialog box. You can also assign the macro to a template, and you can specify a shortcut key, menu item, or toolbar button for running the macro.

As with the macro name, you can change descriptions, template assignments, shortcut keys, menu assignments, and toolbar button assignments at any time. We'll show you how to change a description in "How to change a macro's description" on page 862. We'll show you how to change a menu assignment or shortcut key in Chapter 28, "Customizing Menus, Keys, & Templates," on page 950, and how to change a template assignment in Chapter 27, "Templates," on page 928. Changing toolbar buttons works the same way for macros as for Word's built-in commands and is covered in "Customizing Toolbars" on page 316.

 You can define all three kinds of shortcuts—keystroke, menu assignment, and toolbar button—for any macro. But once you start defining them, you won't have the option of coming back to the Record Macro dialog box to change the macro name, description, or template assignment. So be sure you're satisfied with these before you complete the procedure of specifying a shortcut.

How to enter a macro description

As you can see in Figure 24-2, the Record Macro dialog box includes a Description text box in which you can type a description for the macro in addition to its name.

FIGURE 24-2

The Record Macro dialog box lets you give your macro a description as well as a name.

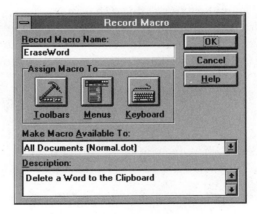

You don't have to give your macro a description. If you do, however, and you attach the macro to a menu, Word will display the description in the status bar when you highlight the menu choice. Similarly, if you attach the macro to a toolbar button, Word will display the description in the status bar when you move your mouse pointer over the toolbar button. (And it will show the macro name in the ToolTips box, assuming Word is set to show ToolTips. If not, you can turn the feature on by choosing View Toolbars, making sure the Show ToolTips check box is checked, and choosing OK.)

You can write a macro description of up to 255 characters—substantially longer than will fit in the Description text box without scrolling. However, you should try to limit the description so that it will fit. As you'll see when you run the macro, keeping the description short enough to see all of it at once will make it easier to find the right macro when you can't remember its name. And if you attach the macro to a menu or a toolbar button, keeping the description short will ensure that you can see the entire description on the status line. For our example, we'll use the description *Delete a Word to the Clipboard*, as also shown in Figure 24-2. As you type a description in the text box, you can start a new line by pressing Enter.

How to set a macro's template assignment

Immediately above the description box in Figure 24-2 is a text box labeled Make Macro Available To. The choices you'll see in the drop-down list depend on which templates you're using with the current document.

If you're even slightly familiar with the concept of templates—which we discussed briefly in Chapter 2 and also in Chapter 9—you probably already know that you can store macros in the Normal template so that they are available to all of your documents. Alternatively, you can store them in the current supplementary template so that they are available to only the documents that are based on that particular template. The Make Macro Available To box is where you specify which template to store the macro in. For a detailed discussion of templates, see Chapter 27, "Templates," on page 928.

Word will also let you load a template as a global template. When you create a macro, however, Word does not give you the option of storing the macro in any global templates that happen to be loaded. If you want to move the macro to one of your global templates, you have to use the Organizer. We'll describe the Organizer in Chapter 27.

If your current document is based on the Normal template, the only choice in the list for the Make Macro Available To box will be All Documents (Normal.dot), as in Figure 24-2. If you are using a supplementary template, however, you'll also see a choice for documents based on that supplementary template. If the template is LETTER.DOT, for example, you'll see the choice Documents Based On Letter.dot. If you have more than one choice available, simply select the template you want to store the macro in.

There are any number of reasons why you might want template-specific macros. For example, if you create a separate template for each of several users, you can write a different set of macros to match each individual's working habits and store each set in its own template. Until you're completely comfortable with templates, however, and unless you have a good reason for doing otherwise, we strongly recommend that you store your macros in NORMAL.DOT. For most of this discussion, we'll assume that you are using only the Normal template so that choosing where to store the macro is not an issue.

If you choose to assign a keystroke, menu, or toolbar shortcut to a macro, as we'll describe in the next three sections, you'll find that you can also store these shortcuts in either NORMAL.DOT or the current supplementary template. For example, the Keyboard card in the Customize dialog box, shown in Figure 24-3, provides an option for selecting the template: the Save Changes In box in the lower right corner. By default, Word will set the Save Changes In list box for the same template that you chose in the Record Macro dialog box, but you can change it.

Be aware that if you change the setting for storing the shortcuts, the change does not affect where Word stores the macros. You can, for example, assign a shortcut key to NORMAL.DOT that runs a macro stored in some other template—let's say LETTER.DOT. If you then attach LETTER.DOT to a document, the shortcut key will work. If you don't attach LETTER.DOT, nothing will happen when you use the shortcut key.

There are some situations in which this can come in handy. For example, suppose you have two templates, LETTER.DOT and MEMO.DOT. You might want macros in both that serve the same function but behave differently; for example, you might want to start the letter off with a letter format and the memo with a memo format. You can create two macros with the same name and store each in the appropriate template. You can then assign a shortcut key to a macro of the same name in NORMAL.DOT. That shortcut key will run the memo version of the macro when you attach MEMO.DOT, and the same shortcut key will run the letter version when you attach LETTER.DOT. This feature should be used with care because it can easily become confusing. For the rest of this discussion, we'll ignore the Save Changes In list box.

How to assign a macro to a shortcut key

As you can see in Figure 24-2, the Record Macro dialog box includes three items in the section below the Record Macro Name text box: Toolbars, Menus, and Keyboard. These are grouped together in the Assign Macro To box. You can choose any of these to open the Customize dialog box (shown in Figure 24-3 on the next page); when this dialog box is open, you can move back and forth among the Keyboard, Menus, and Toolbars option cards. However, the item you choose in the Record Macro dialog box determines which card is displayed when the Customize dialog box first opens. For purposes of this example, we'll start with the Keyboard card. If you choose it, Word will respond with the Customize dialog box as shown in Figure 24-3, displaying the options available on the Keyboard card.

FIGURE 24-3

To assign a shortcut key to a macro you are about to record, open the Customize dialog box by choosing Keyboard in the Record Macro dialog box.

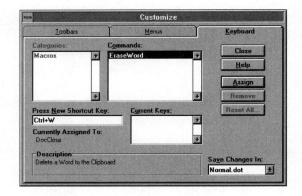

When you open the Customize dialog box from the Record Macro dialog box, the only item Word will let you customize is the macro you're about to record. That's why the only category in the Categories list box in Figure 24-3 is Macros, and the only command in the Commands list box is EraseWord, the name of the macro as we've typed it.

When Word opens the dialog box, it automatically positions the cursor in the Press New Shortcut Key text box. To assign a shortcut key, simply press the appropriate keys. If you choose a shortcut key that's already assigned, Word will let you know. In Figure 24-3, for example, we've used Ctrl-W as the shortcut key. Word responds below the text box with the message that the shortcut key is already assigned to DocClose. If you use a shortcut key that isn't already assigned, the message will read *Currently Assigned To: [unassigned]*.

If the shortcut key you used is already assigned and you don't want to change the assignment to the new macro, simply press Backspace and enter a different keystroke. For this example, we'll stay with Ctrl-W. When you're satisfied with the entry, choose Assign, and Word will list the key in the Current Keys list box. If you change your mind, you can then highlight the key in the list box and choose Remove to tell Word to remove the key from the list. When you close the Customize dialog box, Word will take you directly to the editing screen to record the macro, whether you've assigned a shortcut key or not. (If you want to specify a menu or toolbar assignment for this macro, choose the tab for that card in the Customize dialog box before you close it.)

You can assign as many shortcut keys as you like to the macro you're about to record. Each one will be displayed separately in the Current Keys list box. If you close the dialog box before choosing the Assign button, however, Word will not assign the shortcut key to the macro—even if a shortcut key name is displayed in the Press New Shortcut Key text box.

You can define shortcut keys by using Alt, Ctrl, Alt-Shift, Ctrl-Shift, or Alt-Ctrl-Shift in combination with any alphabetic character, any number, the function keys F2 through F12, or the Ins, Del, Home, End, PgUp, PgDn, or the arrow keys. (But keep in mind that Ctrl-Alt-Del, with or without Shift, is the command for rebooting your system.) If you're a Word 2.0 user, you may be aware that this greatly expands on the choices Word 2.0 allowed. Even better, Word 6.0 will let you define two-keystroke assignments—for example, Ctrl-P followed by P, which we'll indicate as Ctrl-P,P (with Ctrl-P counted as one keystroke). The second keystroke can be any of the keys listed above. For the second keystroke, you must use a key by itself or with Shift, but without Alt or Ctrl.

How to assign a macro to a menu

To assign the macro to a menu, you can choose Menus, rather than Keyboard, from the Record Macro dialog box shown in Figure 24-2. Alternatively, if you've just finished assigning a keystroke but haven't selected Close, you can select the Menus tab. Either way, you'll see the Customize dialog box with the Menus card, as shown in Figure 24-4.

FIGURE 24-4

To assign a macro you are about to record to a menu, choose Menus from the Assign Macro To box in the Record Macro dialog box, or select the Menus tab from within the Customize dialog box.

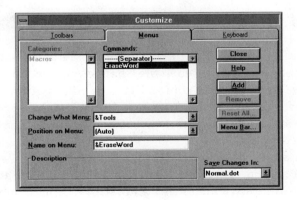

Because you opened the Customize dialog box from the Record Macro dialog box, Word will limit your choices on the Menus card primarily to customizing the macro you're about to record. (We say "primarily" because you can choose the Menu Bar button to customize the menu bar itself.) In addition, the only category in the Categories list box in Figure 24-4 is Macros, and the only macro available to work with is EraseWord, the macro we're about to record. For purposes of this discussion, we will ignore the Menu Bar button. But you can find details on customizing the menu bar in "Renaming, Adding, and Deleting Menus" on page 964.

The three items you need to be concerned with on the Menus card are the boxes labeled Change What Menu, Position On Menu, and Name On Menu.

As you can see from the partial list displayed in Figure 24-5, you can use the Change What Menu list box to pick from several menus. In addition to the menus on the menu bar, the list includes the File and Help menus that are displayed when no document is open, and a lengthy list of shortcut menus—the context-sensitive menus that Word displays in response to a click of the right mouse button. The first step in assigning a macro to the menu is to select the menu to use.

FIGURE 24-5

The Change What Menu list box lists all the menus on the menu bar plus all of Word's context-sensitive shortcut menus.

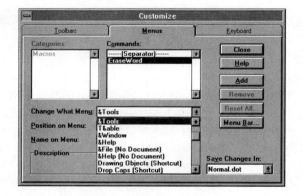

The list attached to the Position On Menu box changes to match whatever menu you've chosen in the Change What Menu box. The choices in this list give you complete control over where to put the new menu item in the menu; for the moment, let's accept the default choice of (Auto). For a detailed discussion of how to control the position of a menu item, see "Customizing the Menus" on page 952.

As a default, Word enters the macro name in the Name On Menu text box. You can accept this or change it. If you want the ability to select the item from a drop-down menu with a keystroke, be sure to type an ampersand (&) immediately before the character you want to use.

If two or more menu items on any given menu have the same trigger character—the character that tells Word to choose that menu command, called the *accelerator key* in the Word documentation—pressing the character will not tell Word to run the command. Instead, repeatedly typing the character will cycle through all of the menu commands that use that character. And to run the command from the keyboard, you'll have to select the command and then press Enter. If you want to designate the command and choose it in a single keystroke, you'll have to make sure that you choose a trigger character that isn't assigned to anything else on the same menu. A reasonable choice for the EraseWord macro, for example, would be to put the macro on the Edit menu, name it Delete Word, and put the ampersand in front of the W so that it reads *Delete &Word*.

After you've designated which menu to change, what position to put the menu item in, and what name to use, choose Add to assign the item to the menu. If you like, you can then repeat the process, adding the item to other menus; you can even use a different name on each.

How to assign a macro to a toolbar

Assigning a macro to a toolbar is a simple matter. If the Record Macro dialog box is still open (as shown in Figure 24-2), you can start by choosing Toolbars. Alternatively, if you've already opened the Customize dialog box, you can simply choose the Toolbars tab. In either case, you'll see the Customize dialog box with the Toolbars card, as shown in Figure 24-6.

FIGURE 24-6

To assign a macro you are about to record to a toolbar, choose Toolbars from the Assign Macro To box in the Record Macro dialog box, or choose the Toolbars card in the Customize dialog box.

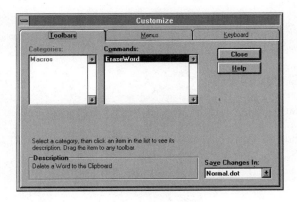

When you open the Customize box this way, Word will limit you to customizing the macro you're about to record. As you can see in Figure 24-6, the only category available in the Categories list is Macros, and the only macro available is EraseWord, the one we're working with. Note, too, that you're limited to putting the macro button either on a toolbar that's already displayed or on a new toolbar. To display one of Word's built-in toolbars, click on any visible toolbar and then use the right mouse button to select a toolbar from the pop-up menu. As you might expect, however, you can move the toolbar button later.

To create a button for the macro and place it on a toolbar, simply click on the macro name and hold the left mouse button down. Word will respond by showing the outline of a button at the mouse pointer. You can then drag the button to an appropriate position on any visible toolbar. If you want to place the button between two existing buttons, for example, point to the space or border between the two toolbar buttons and then release the mouse button. Word will rearrange the existing buttons to insert the new one. To create a new toolbar, drag the button to any spot outside the dialog box where there isn't already a toolbar.

After you define the position for the new button, Word will open the Custom Button dialog box, shown in Figure 24-7. Choose a button icon from the dialog box by clicking on the icon you prefer, and then choose Assign to assign the icon to the newly created button. Note, in passing, that you can also choose Edit from the Custom Button dialog box to change the way a button looks. For details on the button editor, see "How to add a button" on page 318.

FIGURE 24-7

After you indicate where you want a new toolbar button, Word opens this dialog box, and you can pick an icon for the button.

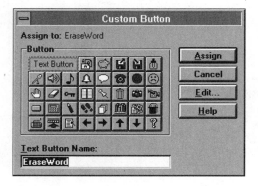

How to create the macro

After you choose OK in the Record Macro dialog box or finish selecting options in the Customize dialog box, Word will return you to the editing screen. Notice that the REC indicator in the status bar (as shown in Figure 24-8) is black, rather than grayed, indicating that you are recording a macro.

When you are recording a macro, Word changes the indicator REC in the status bar to black lettering.

The next step is to manually choose the commands that you want Word to record. In the example of our EraseWord macro, you would simply press Ctrl-Shift-Right arrow and then either Ctrl-X or Shift-Del. However, note that you can perform just about any task while recording a macro that you normally can perform in Word, using either the keyboard or the mouse. The only exceptions are that you can't use the mouse to move the cursor or to select text. Word indicates this by changing to the Macro Record mouse pointer, which consists of the left-pointing arrow with a small icon that looks like a tape cassette.

How to correct mistakes

If you make a mistake while recording a macro, you can easily make a correction. If you type the wrong text character, for example, you can press the Backspace key to back up, and you can then type the correct text. Instead of recording both the mistake and the correction (at least in this particular case), Word will record only the result—the final group of characters you type before choosing a command or moving the cursor. (We'll discuss what Word actually records in more detail in Chapter 25.)

If you accidentally change your document by choosing the wrong command—from a menu, the ruler, or a toolbar—you have two choices: You can stop the recording and start all over again, or you can correct the mistake with another command. For example, if you use the Formatting toolbar to change some 12-point text to 18-point and then realize you wanted to change it to 14-point instead, you can use the toolbar again to change the text to

14-point. Word will record the correction as well as the original mistake. You can then edit the macro at some later time to eliminate the mistake. We'll show you how in the final section of this chapter.

How to end the recording of a macro

After you finish performing the task you want to turn into a macro, you need to stop recording. Word offers three choices for stopping. Two of these were mentioned earlier in this chapter: choosing Tools Macro and then the Stop Recording button, and double-clicking on REC in the status bar. The third choice is to click on the Stop button on the Macro Record toolbar. As you may have noticed, when you start recording, Word adds a two-button toolbar to the screen, as shown in Figure 24-9. The left button in this pair is the Stop button. Click on it once to stop recording.

FIGURE 24-9

When you start recording a macro, Word displays the Macro Record toolbar.

The right button on the Macro Record toolbar is the Pause button. If you click on this while recording a macro, Word will suspend recording so that you can give commands or take other actions without recording them as part of the macro. This can be handy. For example, you may realize after starting the macro that the cursor is in a different position from where it should be. You can click on the Pause button and then move the cursor to the correct position. To resume recording, click on the Pause button again.

As shipped, Word offers only one convenient way to give the Pause Recorder command—the Pause button on the Macro Record toolbar. If you would like to have the command available from the keyboard, however, you can open the Customize dialog box and assign a shortcut key to the command. Choose Tools Customize, and then select the Keyboard card. In the Categories list box, select All Commands, and then in the Commands list box, select PauseRecorder. Next position the cursor in the Press New Shortcut Key text box, and press the shortcut keys you want to use—just as you would assign a shortcut key for a macro. To finish, choose Assign. For more details on using the Keyboard card for assigning keys to commands, see "Keyboard Customization" on page 968.

Running a Macro

After you've created a macro, you can run it in one of four ways: with the Tools Macro command or—if you've assigned one—by using a shortcut key, a menu command, or a toolbar button. We'll look at each of these in a moment, but before we do, a little background might be helpful.

What happens when Word runs a recorded macro

When Word runs a recorded macro, it repeats the actions you performed while recording that macro. If you chose menu commands or made dialog box entries while recording the macro, you won't see Word open the menu or the dialog box when you run the macro, but you will see the effects of those actions. For example, if the macro opens several files with the File Open command, you will not see the File Open dialog box at any time. The macro will simply open the files for you.

Running macros with macros

It's worth noting also that a macro can run another macro. If a given macro tells Word to run a second macro, Word will run the second one and then return to the first macro. As you might expect, Word will resume the main macro from the point where it left, rather than going back to the beginning.

A word of caution

Be aware that a macro that doesn't do what you intended can have disastrous effects. For example, it can erase a portion of a document you didn't want to erase. When you're creating macros that have the potential to do harm, save your active document and test the macro before going on. And with that warning, let's look at how to run a macro.

How to run a macro with the Tools Macro command

To run a macro with the Tools Macro command, first position your cursor where you want it to be when you run the macro. With the EraseWord macro, for example, you'll want to put the cursor at the appropriate position to delete everything from that position to the end of the word.

Now choose Tools Macro to open the Macro dialog box, shown in Figure 24-10 on the next page. Make sure that the Macros Available In option is set correctly. If the option is set to Word Commands, for example, the Macro Name list box will show Word's built-in commands rather than macro names.

FIGURE 24-10

You can use the Macro
dialog box to run a
macro or a built-in
command.

When you want to run a macro, you'll find at least three choices for the Macros Available In box. Set this option to Normal.dot (Global Template), and the Macro Names list box will show the macros in the Normal template. If you have a supplementary template attached to the current document, you'll also find a choice for the template, which will show the current supplementary template's name as part of the option name. Choose this one, and the Macro Name list box will show only those macros in the supplementary template. If you set the option to All Active Templates, you'll be able to see a list of all macros currently available in all current templates.

Unless there are so many macros that you want to limit the number you have to deal with at once, you'll most often want the Macros Available In option set to All Active Templates.

With the Macros Available In option set appropriately, type the name of the macro you want to run, or select it from the list box. If you entered a description for your macro when you recorded it, Word will display the description in the Description box at the bottom of the dialog box, as shown in Figure 24-11.

If you can't remember the name of the macro you want, you can browse through the descriptions by highlighting macros in the list box. Note also that if the descriptions are short enough to fit within the Description box, you can easily see the entire description for each macro as you browse through the list.

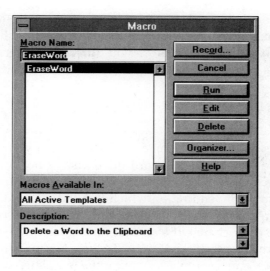

After you enter the appropriate macro in the Macro Name box, choose Run to run it. If you've chosen the EraseWord macro, Word will delete all text from the cursor to the end of the word the cursor is in and place the text on the Clipboard.

How to run a macro with a shortcut key, a menu, or a toolbar button

Running our sample macro with the Tools Macro command isn't worth the effort, since it takes more work than giving the commands manually. However, if you've assigned a shortcut key, you can get exactly the same effect by positioning the cursor and typing the shortcut key—Ctrl-W if you followed our example. Clearly, running the macro with a single key combination is an immediate improvement over Word's built-in commands on a simple macro like this, with which you are substituting one keystroke for two. For touch typists, the gain is even greater because the one keystroke doesn't force you to take your hands from the keys—as you must if you use the built-in commands. With more complex macros, even the Tools Macro command can save time, and the advantages of a shortcut key are multiplied further.

If you've assigned the macro to a menu item or a toolbar button, you can run it the same way you would run a built-in Word command: Simply choose the macro from the menu, or click on the button. Like using the Tools Macro command, this saves little or no work in our sample macro, compared with choosing the commands manually. With more complex macros, however, the advantages are obvious, particularly for those who prefer the mouse to the keyboard. Even for those who prefer the keyboard, however, using the menu or toolbar button may be the better choice for a macro if you don't use it often and therefore you don't remember the shortcut key. Ultimately, the best way to run a macro is a matter of individual taste.

Saving a Macro

Word does not save your macros to disk when you record them or change them. Unless you instruct Word otherwise, it holds the macros in memory while you continue working. It will eventually save the macros to disk in one of three ways, depending on which template you've assigned the macro to and on whether you've set Word to prompt before saving the Normal template. (To see or change the current setting for prompting, choose Tools Options and then Save. If the Prompt To Save Normal.dot check box is checked, Word will prompt you before saving the template.)

If you created or changed a macro assigned to the Normal template, Word won't save the macro on disk until you choose File Exit or File Save All. At that point, if Word is set to save the Normal template without prompting, it will simply save the template, macros and all.

If Word is set to prompt when saving the Normal template, however, it will respond with a message box asking whether to save the changed NORMAL.DOT.

If you've assigned the new or changed macros to a supplemental template, Word will ask whether you want to save them when you close the document attached to that template or when you choose File Save All. In this case, Word will always show you a message box asking whether you want to save the changed template. You can then choose Yes, No, or Cancel, as appropriate.

How to save a macro with the File Save All command

The problem with holding all macros in memory is that you can lose them if you have a system crash. As we just suggested, however, you can force Word to save all your current files on command—including any new or changed macros. Simply choose File Save All. As described above, for each file and template currently open that has any change since the last time you saved, Word will display a message box asking whether you want to save the changes. You can choose Yes or No for each, or you can return to your document without saving by choosing Cancel in any of the message boxes.

Modifying a Macro's Properties

After you create a macro, you can modify the macro's properties, including its name and description. You can also modify the macro itself by editing it. And you can delete a macro.

How to rename a macro

To rename a macro, first choose the Tools Macro command to open the Macro dialog box. Then choose the Organizer button to open the Organizer dialog box, shown in Figure 24-12; Word automatically selects the Macros card.

FIGURE 24-12

You can use the Macros card in the Organizer dialog box to rename macros, among other options.

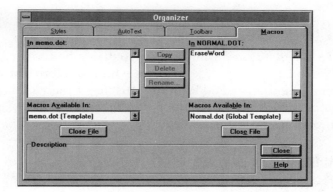

Next select a macro in the list of macros on either the left or the right side of the Organizer dialog box, as appropriate. Choose the Rename button, and Word will display the Rename dialog box, shown in Figure 24-13. You can then type the new name and choose OK. Word will replace the old name with the new one in the list of macros. Close the Organizer dialog box to return to the editing screen.

FIGURE 24-13

The Rename dialog box lets you change a macro's name.

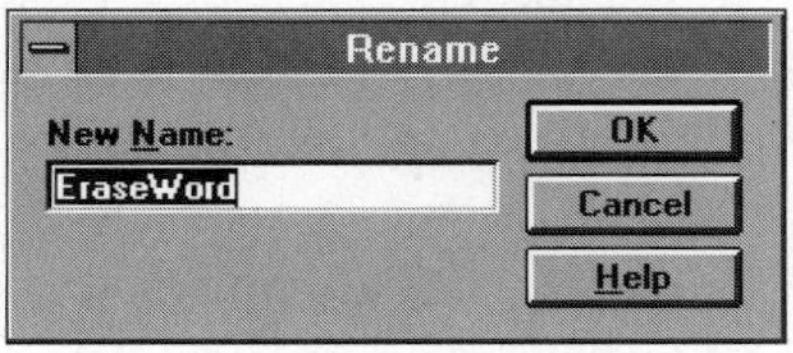

How to change a macro's description

To change a macro's description, choose Tools Macro to open the Macro dialog box, and then enter the name of the macro in the Macro Name box. You can then type the new description in the Description text box.

If you press the Esc key before you leave the Description text box, Word will ignore any changes in the description that you've typed. However, if you move out of the text box first—by pressing Tab or by clicking with the mouse—or if you choose any button (including Cancel), Word will accept the changed description.

How to delete a macro

To delete a macro from the Macro dialog box, enter the name in the Macro Name box, and choose the Delete button. Word will ask you for confirmation. Choose Yes, and Word will delete the macro. Once deleted, the macro is gone—at least in the sense that you cannot use the Edit Undo command to recover an accidental deletion.

How to recover a deleted macro

If you delete the wrong macro, you may still be able to recover it. Keep in mind that if the macro was ever saved to disk, it's still there, in the appropriate template file. That means there's a simple way to get it back. But use it only if you are absolutely sure that you haven't made any other changes to your macros or AutoText entries since you last saved the template to disk.

If the macro was stored in a supplemental template, close all files that are using that template, and choose No when Word asks whether to save the changes to the template. If the macro was stored in the Normal template, choose Tools Options and then Save, and make sure the Prompt To Save Normal.dot check box is checked. Then exit Word, and choose No when Word asks whether to save the changes that affect NORMAL.DOT. Either way, the next time you use the template, the macro will still be there.

This route to recovering accidentally erased macros offers a good argument for saving macros to disk with the File Save All command each time you create or change a macro. This may be a tedious chore if you have a slow computer, but it's a good habit to get into if your system is fast enough to save the changes in a reasonable length of time.

Editing a Macro

We've mentioned several times that you can edit macros as well as record them. This editing feature is essential for writing macros from scratch—a topic we'll cover in the next chapter. But the ability to edit macros can be helpful even if you're interested only in recording them. In particular, you can edit recorded macros to eliminate mistakes.

In truth, you don't have to fix mistakes. As long as the macro accomplishes the task, you can use it as is. Consider the example of accidentally changing some text to an 18-point font while recording a macro and then correcting it to 14-point. If you create such a macro, complete with the mistake and the correction, you will find that it works just fine for changing highlighted text to 14-point. However, the macro will change the text to 18-point first, just as you did when you recorded it. And the macro will run somewhat faster if you delete the extra step.

To practice fixing a macro, start by creating one that includes a mistake. Select some text, choose Tools Macro, and then choose the Record button. Give the macro an appropriate name, such as FourteenPt; type a description if you like, and assign the macro to a shortcut key, menu, or toolbar button. Then choose OK or close the Custom dialog box to start recording. Format the text with the Format toolbar, first as 18-point, and then reformat it as 14-point. (If you format it a different way, your screen won't match our sample in Figure 24-14.) Finally, stop recording—by choosing Tools Macro and then the Stop Recording button, or by double-clicking on REC in the status bar, or by clicking on the Stop button on the Macro Record toolbar.

To edit the macro, choose Tools Macro to open the Macro dialog box, enter the macro name in the box, and choose Edit. Word will open a macro editing window similar to the one shown in Figure 24-14 on the next page.

Word records your actions as a series of WordBasic instructions. The first line of the macro is Sub MAIN, and the last line is End Sub. These two lines mark the beginning and end of the macro and must be included as part of every macro. Between the beginning and ending lines are the macro instructions. In this case, the two instructions between Sub MAIN and End Sub are simply the two font commands. The first sets the font to 18 points; the second sets it to 14 points.

FIGURE 24-14

Word's macro editing window lets you review and edit your macros.

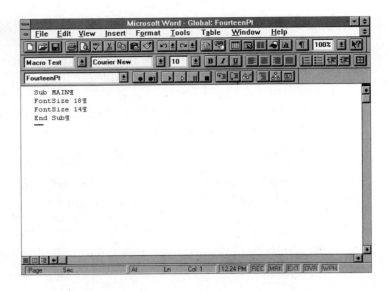

As you can see in Figure 24-14, the macro editing window is similar to a document window. The window name is Global: FourteenPt because the macro we're looking at is named FourteenPt and is stored in the Normal template. Notice that the Macro toolbar has changed in appearance from the one that was on the document screen during macro recording; it now contains 12 buttons and a drop-down list box, and it appears below the Standard and Formatting toolbars (or below the menu bar if you've set Word not to display toolbars). We'll discuss these buttons in the next chapter.

Word will dim most of the commands on the menus while you're in a macro editing window. For example, all commands on the Insert and Table menus will be grayed. However, you'll find that all of the commands you need for editing are still available.

The mechanics of editing a macro are the same as those used for editing a document. For example, you can use the Edit Cut, Edit Copy, and Edit Paste commands to move and copy text within a macro, between two macros, or between a macro and a document window. In fact, the macro editing window works much like a standard document window in most respects, including such capabilities as letting you activate another window with the Window menu. Similarly, you close a macro editing window by choosing the File Close command.

Far more difficult than the mechanics of editing a macro is knowing what changes to make. For complex macros, this means learning WordBasic and some elements of programming. For fixing mistakes in a simple macro such as FourteenPt, however, it's often easy enough to spot the offending command and delete it. In this case, you want to delete the command FontSize 18 and leave the command FontSize 14 unchanged.

To fix the FourteenPt macro, delete the command that sets the font to 18-point so that the screen looks like Figure 24-15. Then choose File Close. When Word asks whether you want to save the changes to Global: FourteenPt, choose Yes. (But remember that this doesn't save the changes to disk; it saves them only in memory.)

FIGURE 24-15

The corrected version of FourteenPt still starts with Sub MAIN and ends with End Sub. These starting and ending markers must be in every macro.

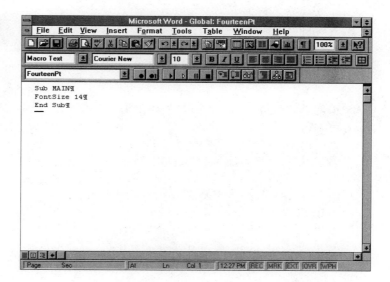

After you correct a macro, you should test it to verify that it still works. In this case, if you select some text and run the macro, it should go directly to 14-point size, without stepping through the 18-point size first.

This introduction to the mechanics of editing macros barely opens the door on the subject. Unfortunately, issues of programming are beyond the scope of this book. In the next two chapters, however, we'll open the door a bit wider and give you a look at some of the possibilities available with macros.

TOPIC FINDER

Limitations of the Record Macro Feature   **868**
- What Record Macro records

Writing a Macro from Scratch   **870**
- The SendKeys statement
- Macros that use Word's dialog boxes

Some General Considerations for Macros   **876**
- Choices for running a macro
- Auto macros

Testing, Modifying, and Debugging Macros   **879**
- New! The macro toolbar
- Word's macro editor tools
- How to change the macro toolbar buttons
- How to print a macro

A Dozen Quick 'n Dirty (but Useful) Macros   **890**
- Some navigation macros
- How to cut a word, line, sentence, or paragraph

25

An Introduction to Writing Macros

 f you've worked through the introduction to macros in Chapter 24, you should know enough about macros by now to be able to record and use your own. But as useful as you will find recorded macros to be, you will be limited in what you can do with them. To get beyond those limits, you'll need programmed macros.

A programmed macro may simply use features that Word's Record Macro feature has no way to record, as we'll show shortly. But the essence of a programmed macro is that it includes programming logic. Before choosing the File Open command, for example, a programmed macro might stop to ask whether to list all files or just those with a DOC extension. Depending on your answer, it would then list the appropriate files. The commands that let the macro ask questions and respond to the answers provide the programming logic.

All of Word's macros—whether recorded or written from scratch—are stored as WordBasic commands. WordBasic is a programming language that's drawn from Microsoft Basic but that also includes commands specifically designed for word processing—for example, setting font size.

Programming, of course, is a subject that's easily worth a book (or several books) of its own. We won't presume to try to teach even the fundamentals of programming in just one or two chapters. However, in this chapter, we will cover the mechanics of using Word's built-in tools for creating, testing, and fixing macros. In the process, we'll cover some aspects of programming, and we'll show you some simple but useful macros along the way.

Even if you're already familiar with programming concepts, you'll still need to learn the proper syntax for WordBasic's various instructions. Word's online Help contains a complete reference to WordBasic syntax. To use this reference, choose Help Contents, and then choose Programming With Microsoft Word. If you'd like detailed instructions on WordBasic programming, you might want to order the *Microsoft Word Developer's Kit*. The first part of the *Microsoft Word Developer's Kit* includes an instruction manual that will take you step by step from the beginner's level to advanced uses of this powerful programming language. To purchase a copy of the kit, refer to the supplemental offer card that came in your Microsoft Word package. For those who want to roll up their sleeves and delve into macros further, we'll recommend some additional books at the end of our introduction to macros, in the last part of Chapter 26.

In this chapter, we'll look primarily at the mechanics of writing, editing, and testing macros. We'll start with an example that the Record Macro feature simply can't create.

Limitations of the Record Macro Feature

If you've been working with Word for any length of time, you know that Word makes several assumptions about your filenames. In particular, when you choose File Open the first time, the program assumes that you want to see only those files with DOC extensions. If you prefer using varied extensions to indicate the type of file—LET for letters, MEM for memos, and so on—this can be a minor annoyance. Every time you start Word, you have to type *.* in the File Name text box, or select it in the List Files Of Type box, before Word will list all files.

The obvious solution to this problem is to create a macro that will run the File Open command and specify the *.* for you. It seems like a simple macro that you should be able to create by recording it. Unfortunately, you can't.

If you try recording the macro with the Tools Macro Record command, your first inclination will probably be to choose File Open, enter *.* in the

File Name box, choose OK so that Word will show you the list of files, and then either click on the Stop button or choose Tools Macro and the Stop Recording button. However, Word will not let you stop recording at that point. You first have to leave the Open dialog box, either by choosing Cancel or by loading a file. If you make either choice and then stop recording, you'll find you don't have the macro you want.

To see what these macros look like, choose Tools Macro to open the Macro dialog box; select the macro, and choose Edit. If you chose Cancel in the Open dialog box before you stopped recording, you'll see the macro shown in Figure 25-1. If you opened a file in the current directory first (such as EMPTY.TXT in our example), you'll see a macro similar to the one shown in Figure 25-2.

FIGURE 25-1

If you choose Cancel in a dialog box while recording a macro, the macro won't refer to the dialog box.

FIGURE 25-2

If you record a macro that gives a command through a dialog box, the macro will record only the result.

What Record Macro records

What both of these macros have in common is that they show the final result of what you did. In the first case, you chose Cancel in the dialog box. Because you didn't complete the command, Word didn't record one. The only statements in the macro are Sub MAIN and End Sub. As we discussed briefly in Chapter 24, these are beginning and end markers, and you must include them in all macros, so Word supplies them automatically.

In the second case, you actually opened a file, so Word recorded the command to open that specific file. Roughly translated, the FileOpen command in Figure 25-2 tells Word to open the file EMPTY.TXT in the current directory—without confirming the conversion format if Word detects a file format other than Word format, and without setting the file to read-only. The command also tells Word to add the filename to the File menu as a recently opened file, not to enter any passwords for the document or the template, and not to revert to the version of the file saved on disk if the file is already open.

In this example of recording a macro, you will get exactly the same result regardless of whether or not you specified *.*, whether you typed the file-name in the text box or selected it from the list, or even whether you first changed directories several times before returning to the directory you started from. The point is, Word records only the results of your commands.

Neither of these macros does what you set out to do, which is to open the Open dialog box and tell Word to list all files in the current directory. For that, you need to write a macro on your own.

Writing a Macro from Scratch

To write a macro from scratch, you open a macro editing window. Start by choosing the Tools Macro command, and then type the name for the new macro in the Macro Name text box. (You can also add a Description at this time if you want.) Next choose Create; Word will open a macro editing win-dow that looks much like Figure 25-3.

Except for the macro name and the blank line between the Sub MAIN and End Sub statements, Figure 25-3 is essentially identical to Figure 25-1. The window is initially empty except for these be-ginning and end markers, which Word automatically provides for you. You write the macro by inserting WordBasic instructions be-tween the markers.

FIGURE 25-3

When you open the macro editing window to write a new macro, Word provides the Sub MAIN and End Sub statements.

Note also that when you create a macro from scratch, Word does not give you the chance to assign a keyboard shortcut to it—which Word does allow when you record a macro. We'll explain how to assign a keyboard shortcut to the macro in Chapter 28, "Customizing Menus, Keys, & Templates," page 950. If you follow us through this discussion and create these macros as you go, you still can run the macros from the Tools Macro dialog box.

The SendKeys statement

Now that you know how to write the macro, the only issue is deciding what to write. What you need, in this case, is a way to tell Word to open a dialog box and then stop. The brute force method is to use the SendKeys statement. (This is not the best solution to the problem, but it's the easiest to understand. We'll cover a better alternative shortly.)

As the name implies, the SendKeys statement sends specific keystrokes to Word. Because Word won't record keystrokes, however, you have to write the macro manually.

Start by choosing the Tools Macro command, typing an appropriate macro name—such as FileOpenAny—and choosing Create. Word will respond with the screen shown in Figure 25-3. Next enter the line

```
SendKeys "^o*.*{Enter}"
```

between the Sub MAIN and End Sub statements. Your screen should look like Figure 25-4.

FIGURE 25-4

You type macro commands between the Sub MAIN and End Sub statements.

The caret character before the *o* is interpreted by Word as the Ctrl key, so *^o* is sent to the program as Ctrl-o (Word's keyboard shortcut for File Open). To designate Alt-o, you would type *%o*. For Shift-o, you would type *+o*. (You could also use a capital O, but you'll need to use the plus symbol when sending other shifted keys, such as *+{F12}* for Shift-F12.) Note that you can apply the ^ (caret), % (percent), or + (plus) to more than one key by using parentheses, and you can apply any of them to character keys as well. For example, "+ffff" would be sent to the program as *Ffff,* and "+(ffff)" would be sent as *FFFF.* Also note that you have to type the *{Enter}* as text, complete with curly brackets. The rest of the line is *∗.∗*—the characters you would type to choose the command manually.

Once you've created or modified a macro, you'll want to test it to verify that it works. In this case, you should still have the macro editing window open, and you can simply choose the Start button—the one with the small filled-in triangle pointing to the right—from the Macro toolbar. (Word will display the Macro toolbar when you open the macro editing window. The toolbar will stay visible unless you turn it off, by choosing View Toolbars and clearing the Macro check box.) If you've typed everything correctly, you'll be rewarded with the Open dialog box, as shown in Figure 25-5. The File Name list should contain all files in the current directory.

FIGURE 25-5

When you run the FileOpenAny macro, it should take you to the Open dialog box and display *∗.∗* in the File Name text box.

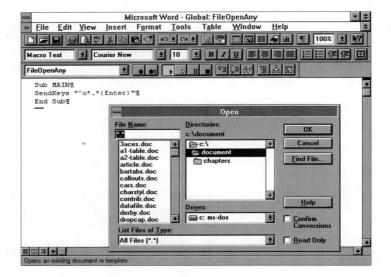

 Word will not check a macro for syntax errors (errors caused by mistakes in the statements you've written) until you run the macro, at which point you'll get an error message if you've made a mistake. If there is a syntax error, Word will highlight the line in the macro where it found the mistake.

When you're satisfied that the macro works, close the macro editing window. Word will ask whether you want to keep the changes. Choose Yes, but remember that choosing Yes does not save the changes on disk. If you want to save the macro immediately for future use, choose File Save Template.

Macros that use Word's dialog boxes

As already suggested, SendKeys is a less-than-ideal approach for opening dialog boxes. The problem with SendKeys is its inability to be as flexible as Word. For example, if you reassign the key combination that brings up the Open dialog box from Ctrl-o to Ctrl-Shift-o, the FileOpenAny macro we've just created will be useless. The only time it's completely safe to use this method is when you need a quick-and-dirty solution for a temporary macro.

Fortunately, there is little you can do with SendKeys that you can't also do with other WordBasic commands. In this case, the more elegant solution involves commands that enable you to create and control dialog boxes. Learning how to work with dialog boxes is an important technique in WordBasic because dialog boxes are central to Word and Windows.

To accomplish the same result without using SendKeys, choose Tools Macro, type an appropriate macro name (we'll stay with FileOpenAny), choose Create (or Edit if FileOpenAny already exists), and type the following statements between the Sub MAIN and End Sub markers:

```
Dim FileAll As FileOpen
FileAll.Name = "*.*"
Dialog FileAll
FileOpen FileAll
```

Remember to delete the SendKeys line between Sub MAIN and End Sub if you are editing FileOpenAny.

The first line in this macro uses the WordBasic Dim statement to create and open a dialog record named FileAll. (You can use the Dim statement for other purposes too, but we'll look only at its usefulness for creating a dialog record.) In effect, it creates FileAll as a carbon copy of Word's built-in File Open dialog box, complete with a set of empty fields that match the fields in the Open dialog box. Of particular interest for our purposes is the Name field, which we want to set to *.*.

The second line sets the Name field of the FileAll dialog record to *.*, after which the Dialog statement in the third line opens the dialog box, using the current values for FileAll. At this point in running the macro, you would select the file you want in the list box and then choose OK. Finally, the last line runs Word's built-in FileOpen command, using whatever choice you've entered in the dialog box.

Handling errors

The sample macro is not quite complete. If you choose Cancel to close the dialog box without loading a file, Word will respond with an error message when it tries to run the last line of the macro—the line that actually opens a file. You can get around the problem, literally, by adding a command to skip over the command instead of displaying the error message.

WordBasic provides an On Error control structure. On Error takes one of the following three forms:

```
On Error Resume Next
On Error Goto LABEL
On Error Goto 0
```

The first two choices turn off Word's error messages for the rest of the macro or until WordBasic sees the On Error Goto 0 statement—whichever comes first. The On Error Goto 0 statement sets Word back to its default state—showing error messages in response to errors. Use it in a macro only when you've used one of the other two formats earlier and you need to turn error messages back on.

The first of the three forms, On Error Resume Next, tells Word to ignore any errors and simply continue the macro. The second format lets you control program flow. Think of it as a trip wire. When you set it up, it tells Word to jump to a different part of the macro altogether if it trips over an error.

In this macro, you want Word to skip to the end of the macro if it encounters an error. Type the line

```
On Error Goto ForgetIt
```

In this example, you can enter the On Error statement anywhere before the Dialog FileAll statement. However, it's good practice to place the command just before you want it to come into play so that you don't inadvertently trigger the jump in response to some other error.

Remarks

Until you've tested a macro and verified that it works, it's not a good idea to turn off the error messages.

In this particular case, you'll want to enter On Error Goto ForgetIt but also mark the line so that Word will ignore the statement for now. You can do that by adding a single quotation mark (an apostrophe) or the REM statement at the beginning of the line with the On Error statement.

REM is short for Remark, and it is a valuable tool. You use it to add notes to a macro that can remind you of the purpose of each section should you need to revise the macro at some later date. Type *REM* or an apostrophe anywhere in a line, and Word will ignore everything that follows it on that line. If you put the REM statement after another statement on the same line, you have to precede the REM with a colon. If you use the apostrophe, you do not need a preceding colon.

When you use REM or an apostrophe, as in this example, to tell Word to temporarily ignore a line, the technique is usually called "REMming out the line" because you are telling Word to treat the line as a remark rather than as a statement. Once you know the macro works correctly, you can delete the REM or apostrophe and "turn on" the On Error statement.

Labels

In addition to using the On Error statement, you'll need to add the label ForgetIt so that Word knows where to jump. In this case, you want it to jump to the end of the macro, so you need to enter the label immediately before the End Sub statement. (There's no need to REM out the label because it simply marks the location.) When you finish writing the macro, it should look like the one in Figure 25-6.

FIGURE 25-6

The more elegant version of the FileOpenAny macro includes commands for handling dialog boxes.

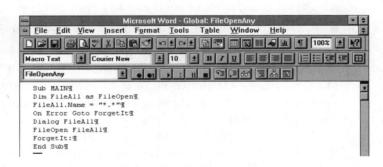

 WordBasic will recognize a label only if it's followed by a colon. Note also that WordBasic will recognize labels only if they start in the first position of the line. If you're writing a complicated macro, with some lines indented for readability, be sure not to indent the lines with labels.

When you run this second version of the FileOpenAny macro, you'll find that it works exactly like the version that used SendKeys. However, because it doesn't depend on sending particular keystrokes to the program, it leaves you free to reassign those keys. With this version of the macro, you can reassign the Ctrl-O keyboard shortcut without affecting the macro in any way. When you're satisfied that the macro works, you can edit out the REM or apostrophe at the beginning of the On Error statement. Then save the macro, and use it as needed.

Some General Considerations for Macros

The FileOpenAny macro is a bare-bones introduction to writing a macro. We'll go a little further into programming issues in the next chapter. First, however, we'll introduce some general considerations you ought to be aware of.

Choices for running a macro

As we've already mentioned in this chapter—and as we covered in some depth in Chapter 24—there are several ways to run a macro:

■ Clicking the Start button on the Macro toolbar (available only if you have a macro open for editing)

■ Choosing Tools Macro and then Run

■ Pressing a shortcut key (if one has been assigned to the macro)

■ Choosing a menu item (if one has been assigned)

■ Clicking on a toolbar button (if one has been assigned)

You'll find each of these possibilities discussed in Chapter 24, "Recording Macros," page 842; and you'll find the menu and shortcut key methods covered again, from a slightly different approach, in Chapter 28, "Customizing Menus, Keys, & Templates," page 950.

Still another option is to create a MACROBUTTON field as part of a document and then run the macro by choosing the button. We covered the MACROBUTTON field in Chapter 20, "Fields," page 674.

Auto macros

Even these choices for running macros don't exhaust all the possibilities. In fact, there are five other ways to run a macro, using Word's Auto macros.

Word recognizes five special names for macros—AutoNew, AutoOpen, AutoClose, AutoExec, and AutoExit. Use any of these names, and the macro will run automatically in response to a specific event. The AutoNew, AutoOpen, and AutoClose macros can go in any template, including NORMAL.DOT, and they apply to documents that use the particular template. The AutoExec and AutoExit macros go only in NORMAL.DOT, and they apply to all documents.

AutoNew

The AutoNew name tells Word to run the macro each time you create a new document. For example, suppose you have a memo template that uses FILLIN fields to prompt for the recipient and subject of a memo. See Chapter 20, "Fields," page 674, for a discussion of the FILLIN field.

You'll want Word to request the information to update these fields as soon as you open a new document based on that template. To handle this automatically, create a macro named AutoNew, with the two statements

```
EditSelectAll
UpdateFields
```

between the Sub MAIN and End Sub statements. As their names imply, EditSelectAll tells Word to select the entire document, and the UpdateFields statement tells Word to update all fields in the selection. Save this AutoNew macro in the appropriate template, and Word will automatically prompt you for the memo's recipient and subject every time you start a new memo based on that template.

AutoOpen

An AutoOpen macro will run every time you open a document. For example, suppose you share a computer with someone who prefers view options for the screen that are different from your preferences. You might like the ruler displayed, but he or she likes it hidden, for example. Each of you can create your own personalized templates with AutoOpen macros that set the screen the way you like it. Your AutoOpen macro would display the ruler every time you opened one of your documents; the other person's AutoOpen macro would hide the ruler. (We'll explain how to create separate templates in Chapter 27, "Templates," page 928.)

AutoClose

As you might expect from the name, an AutoClose macro runs every time you close a document. You can use an AutoClose macro in combination with AutoOpen. For example, suppose you want your view options set a particular way for one kind of document only. You could use the AutoOpen macro to set the options appropriately each time you open a document based on a particular template and then use the AutoClose macro to reset the options the way you normally prefer them.

AutoExec

AutoExec is similar in concept to the AutoOpen macro, except that it can go only in NORMAL.DOT, and it runs every time you start Word. You can, for example, use AutoExec to set Word to customized settings each time you start the program. Other possibilities include automatically opening the last file you loaded (with the instruction *File1*), automatically running a substitute for File Open (for example, you can use the FileOpenAny macro described in "Macros that use Word's dialog boxes," earlier in this chapter), or automatically loading a set of files that you are working with for a large project. (Use the Macro Recorder to record which files to load.)

Note that if you include the *File1* instruction in your AutoExec macro and you use any of the techniques we explained in Chapter 1 to start Word and open a specified document, Word will automatically open both the document you specify and your most recently opened document. For details on how to start Word and open a document at the same time, see "How to start Word and open a document simultaneously" on page 5.

Also note that you can start Word without running the AutoExec macro. One way to do this is to type *winword /m* in the File Run Command Line text box of Windows Program Manager.

If you create an AutoExec macro and you normally start Word from an icon in Program Manager, you might also like to create a second icon that will start Word with the /m switch. To create the new icon in Program Manager, highlight the Word icon, choose File Copy, designate the group to copy to, and choose OK. Then, with the new icon still highlighted, choose File Properties, and add /m at the end of the command in the Command Line text box. You may also want to change the description in the Description text box to indicate that this version of the icon will not run the AutoExec macro. When you're done, choose OK to save the changes.

AutoExit

AutoExit is similar to AutoExec in that it goes only in NORMAL.DOT, but it is exactly opposite in that it runs whenever you quit Word rather than when you start it. If you create an AutoExit macro, running the macro becomes the last thing Word does when you close the program. You can use the AutoExit macro to automate any task that you want to perform every time you leave Word.

For example, suppose you want to automatically back up your Word data files from drive C to drive D whenever you leave Word. Assuming your files are all in subdirectories in the DATA\WORD directory on both drives, you can create an AutoExit macro that reads

```
Sub MAIN
shell "command.com /c xcopy c:\data\word d:\data\word /s/m"
End Sub
```

The shell statement tells Word to go (or "shell out") to DOS to run another program, in this case loading the COMMAND.COM command processor to run XCOPY. The /c switch for COMMAND.COM tells the command processor to run the command on the same line—the XCOPY command in this case—and then return control to the primary command processor. As written, the XCOPY command copies all new or changed files from the C:\DATA\WORD directory to the D:\DATA\WORD directory. The /s tells XCOPY to copy from all subdirectories under the \DATA\WORD directory as well. The /m tells it to copy only those files that are set as having been modified since the last time they were copied with XCOPY or backed up. The result is that every time you leave Word, the AutoExit macro will back up your data files.

Testing, Modifying, and Debugging Macros

If you write or edit many macros, you'll find that they often don't perform the way you expect them to. This is such a truism that a programmer friend of ours insists that the first pass in writing a program should really be called *bugging*. The process of fixing the bugs, of course, is called *debugging*. Word provides several debugging tools for its macros.

The macro toolbar

Word displays the Macro toolbar whenever you open the macro editing window. Assuming Word's default settings—with the Standard toolbar just below the menu bar, and the Formatting toolbar just below that—the Macro toolbar is displayed just below the Formatting toolbar.

As you can see in Figure 25-7, the default version of the Macro toolbar includes 12 buttons and one text box with a drop-down list box. If you're familiar with the macro editor in Word 2.0, you'll notice immediately that this has changed considerably from the equivalent feature in Word 2.0. Not only are there more buttons, but they are identified on the toolbar by icons rather than text.

FIGURE 25-7

Whenever a macro editing window is open, Word displays the Macro toolbar at the top of the screen—even when the macro editing window is not active, as shown in the second figure.

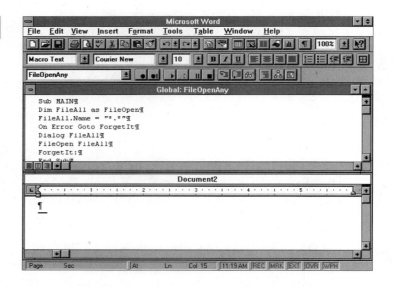

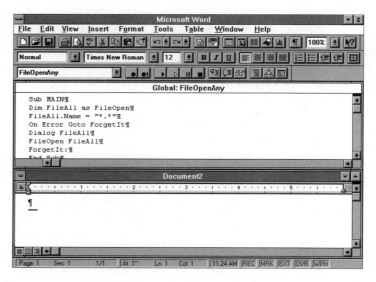

Taken together, the Macro toolbar buttons provide a complete tool kit for creating, modifying, and debugging macros. We'll look at each button shortly, but it will help to know a little about the Macro toolbar itself first.

As shown in Figure 25-7, Word displays the Macro toolbar whenever the macro editing window is open—whether it is the currently active window or not. In fact, this holds true even when the macro editing window isn't visible.

The ability to use the debugging tools regardless of which window is active and regardless of the window arrangement is a valuable feature. The FileOpenAny macro that we discussed earlier will work equally well from any window and with any arrangement. However, if a macro includes a search-and-replace command, for example, you cannot test it in the macro window itself. Word will not make the Replace command available to a macro within a macro editing window, as a safeguard to keep the macro from accidentally destroying itself.

For reasons that will become clear when we look at the buttons on the Macro toolbar, the preferred window arrangement for testing a macro is usually to make both the macro editing window and the document window visible at once, as in Figure 25-7. If you have only those two documents open, you can get this arrangement simply by choosing Window Arrange All.

There is one more issue to be aware of when you debug a macro. Make sure that the name of the macro you're debugging appears in the text box on the left side of the Macro toolbar. If you've opened only one macro editing window, that won't be a problem because there will be only one macro active. If you've opened more than one macro editing window, however, Word will display the name of the currently active macro in the text box. To activate a different macro, simply activate that macro's window and then return to the document editing window. Alternatively, you can display the drop-down list attached to the text box and choose the macro you want to activate.

Finally, before running the macro, go back to the document in which you want to test the macro and, if the starting position is important to the macro's function, be sure to move the cursor to an appropriate position. Then you can run the macro, using the appropriate debugging tool.

Word's macro editor tools

As already mentioned, Word's Macro toolbar offers a complete tool kit for creating, modifying, and debugging macros. First on the toolbar is a text box with a drop-down menu. This is followed by four groups of buttons. Unfortunately, the meanings of the icons on the buttons are less than immediately obvious. However, as with all toolbars, if you have the ToolTips feature turned on, you can point to each button with the mouse and see the name for the button you're pointing to. (You can turn the ToolTips feature on and off by choosing View Toolbars and then checking or clearing the Show ToolTips check box.) Figure 25-8 shows the Macro toolbar and its button names; we'll use those names throughout this discussion to identify each button.

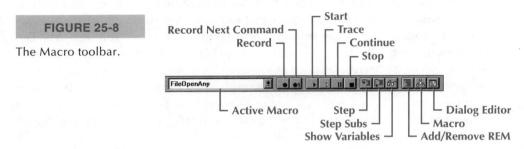

FIGURE 25-8

The Macro toolbar.

As we explained in the section before this, the text box, called the Active Macro text box, shows the name of the active macro, meaning the macro that will be affected by most of the toolbar commands. Click on the Macro toolbar Start button, for example, and it's the active macro that will start running.

Moving from left to right along the toolbar, the first group of two buttons are Record and Record Next Command; you can use these to create a macro, or part of one, by recording. The next two groups—of four and three buttons—consist of debugging tools: Start, Trace, Continue, and Stop in the first group, and Step, Step Subs, and Show Variables in the second. The last group consists of a miscellaneous assortment of tools: Add/Remove REM, Macro, and Dialog Editor. Here's a detailed look at each of these 12 buttons.

The Record button

The Record button is exactly equivalent to choosing Tools Macro and then Record; clicking it opens the Record Macro dialog box. You can then type a macro name and, if you want, a definition; optionally assign a shortcut key, menu, or toolbar button; and then record the macro. While you're editing a macro, you can use this feature to record a set of instructions that you'd like to incorporate into the macro you're editing.

When you've finished recording, you can open the new macro and copy the commands you've recorded into the macro you've been working with, using Word's standard Cut, Copy, and Paste commands. You can then delete the macro you've recorded. Alternatively, when you finish recording the macro, you can store the newly recorded macro if you want to keep it as a separate macro, and add a command to the macro you're working with to run the newly recorded macro. The command to run the macro takes the form

```
ToolsMacro .Name = "Macroname", .Run
```

where *Macroname* is the name of the macro.

The Record Next command button

As the name suggests, the Record Next Command button will record the next command you give, and only that command. Unlike the Record button, the Record Next Command button will insert the single command into the active macro editing screen at the current cursor location. Be sure your cursor is located at the beginning of a line—and the correct line, at that—when you choose the command. Otherwise, you'll have to move the new command after you record it. In general, you'll want to place the cursor in the correct position in the macro editing window, then switch to a document window to start recording and give the command. That way, the command will affect only the document in the document window, and not the macro itself. Use the Record Next Command button when you're writing or editing a macro and want to add a command without having to write the whole command yourself.

The Start button

The Start button tells Word to run the currently active macro. Choosing Start is equivalent to selecting the macro name in the Tools Macro dialog box and then choosing Run. Use this when you have a short macro, or when you think there are no bugs left and expect the macro to run problem-free.

The Trace button

The Trace button is similar to the Start button in that it tells Word to run the entire macro in a single step. However, when you use Trace, Word highlights each instruction in the macro before executing it. The best way to take advantage of the Trace button is with macros that stop every so often to ask a question. The stopping points will help bracket the source of the problem. Note also that if you're having trouble isolating a problem, you might even want to add a few stopping points in the macro strictly to help debug it. You can add these with the Input statement or with dialog boxes, both of which we'll discuss in Chapter 26, "Dialog Boxes & Other Macro Magic," page 896.

The Continue button

The Continue button works along with the two Step buttons—Step and Step Subs. Both Step buttons tell Word to run just the next step in the macro. (We'll discuss the differences between the two Step buttons in a moment.)

Choose the Continue button when you've stepped through part of the macro and want Word to execute the rest of the macro without pausing.

 If you're familiar with Word 2.0's Macro Edit Icon bar, you probably know that when you use the Step button in Word 2.0, the Start button changes to read *Continue*. The Continue button in Word 6.0 serves the same purpose as the Continue button in Word 2.0.

The Stop button

Like the Continue button, the Stop button works along with the two Step buttons—Step and Step Subs. As just pointed out, both Step buttons tell Word to run just the next step in the macro. Choose the Stop button when you've stepped through part of the macro and want Word to stop executing the macro. If you click on Stop and then click on one of the Step buttons, Word will start at the beginning of the macro again.

The Step button

The Step button tells Word to execute a single instruction and then pause. If you're running the macro from the macro editing window, or if you've set up your screen to display both the macro window and a document window, then Word's first step for running the macro will be to highlight, but not execute, the first instruction following the Sub MAIN statement. Choose Step again, and Word will execute the first instruction and highlight the second. You can then step through the macro one instruction at a time and see the effect in the document window of each highlighted step in the macro editing window. The Step feature is useful in finding out where a problem is.

Note that if you've set up your screen to show the document only, the Step command will still step you through the macro one instruction at a time, but you won't see the instruction highlighted at each step. This can still be useful. If you spot the point at which the macro goes awry, simply switch to the macro editing window. The culprit will (in most cases) be the instruction that Word executes just before the currently highlighted instruction. (However, be aware that the instruction that Word executes "just before" the current one may not be located just before it in the macro code; some macro commands tell Word to jump to different parts of the macro.)

The Step Subs button

The Step Subs button functions similarly to the Step button in that it tells Word to execute the macro one step at a time. You'll see the difference between the two only in macros that include *subroutines*.

Briefly, a subroutine is a section of a macro that performs a particular task and is separated out from the main body of the macro. In long macros, you'll often need to repeat a given set of instructions in several different places. A subroutine lets you enter those instructions once and then call on them as needed from different points in the macro.

The Sub MAIN and End Sub markers define the MAIN subroutine that Word requires in every macro. Additional subroutines take the same form. A subroutine called TRYTHIS, for example, would have the beginning marker

```
Sub TRYTHIS
```

and the end marker

```
End Sub
```

In general, a macro with multiple subroutines takes the following form:

```
Sub MAIN
        instruction 1
        instruction 2
        TRYTHIS
        instruction 3
        TRYTHIS
        instruction 4
End Sub

Sub TRYTHIS
        instruction a
        instruction b
End Sub
```

The TRYTHIS subroutine is run twice by the MAIN subroutine. When you run this macro, Word starts with the first instruction in the MAIN subroutine. When it reaches the instruction TRYTHIS, it jumps to the TRYTHIS subroutine, runs the instructions in that subroutine, and then goes back to MAIN, picking up at instruction 3. When it reaches the second TRYTHIS instruction, it runs the subroutine again and then, once again, goes back to MAIN. Then it picks up at instruction 4.

Step vs. Step Subs

The difference between the Step and Step Subs commands is in how they deal with subroutines. If you use the Step button, Word will branch to the subroutine and run through its instructions one at a time. It will then return to MAIN and continue where it left off. If you use the Step Subs button, Word will run the entire subroutine in a single step and then return to MAIN, to continue one step at a time. Use the Step Subs command when you already know that the subroutine is fully debugged—that it, in other words, is not the source of the problem.

Because you can run a macro from a macro, you can also treat the second macro as a subroutine when designing your macros. However, Word assumes that any other macro you call on is already debugged, and it will run the macro in a single step whether you are using Step or Step Subs.

The Show Variables button

The Show Variables button matters only when you're running macros that contain variables. (A *variable* is a name that references a piece of information that varies. The current item of information is the *value*. For example, any answer you give to a macro that asks a question is a value and is stored in the question's variable.) If a given macro uses variables, the Show Variables button will display the current value for the variables at any point while you're stepping through the macro, as the example in Figure 25-9 illustrates. You can also set a new value for the variables so that you can, for example, test unusual situations easily.

FIGURE 25-9

The Show Variables button will open the Macro Variables dialog box, in which you can view and set the current values of any variables in the macro.

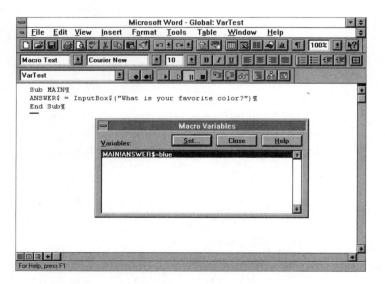

Choose the Show Variables button while stepping through a macro that includes variables, and Word will open the Macro Variables dialog box.

The Add/Remove REM button

The Add/Remove REM button will add or remove a REM, or remark, statement, at the beginning of all currently selected lines. As we discussed earlier in this chapter, REM is short for "remark." If you add a REM statement to any line in a macro, Word will ignore everything that follows on that line.

You can use the REM statement to write comments in the middle of a macro to help document what you're doing so that you can make sense of it later. You can also use the REM statement to temporarily turn off the effects of a line, which can be useful when you're trying to track down a problem. Such lines are generally referred to as being "REMmed out."

The Add/Remove REM button will add a REM statement to the beginning of a line if one isn't already there, and it will remove a REM statement at the beginning of a line if it finds one there. Note that, although you can type a REM statement into a line at any point, you can use the Add/Remove REM button only at the beginning of a line. To use the button, extend the selection to all lines that you want to add a REM statement to or remove a REM statement from. You don't have to select an entire line—the command will work as long as the selection extends into that line. Then click on the Add/Remove REM button to add or remove the REM statement.

Note that the Add/Remove REM button does not recognize apostrophes, even though Word otherwise treats an apostrophe as exactly equivalent to the REM statement. If you add an apostrophe to the beginning of a line and then move the cursor or selection to the line and click on the Add/Remove REM button, Word will add a REM statement to the beginning of the line. If you click on the button again, Word will remove the REM statement and leave the apostrophe, so the line will still be REMmed out.

The Macro button

Clicking on the Macro button is exactly equivalent to choosing Tools Macro: Word will open the Macro dialog box, and you can select any of the options contained in it. We covered many of the features of the Macro dialog box in Chapter 24, "Recording Macros," page 842.

The Dialog Editor button

The Dialog Editor button is exactly equivalent to opening the Word Dialog Editor from Program Manager. Click on this button, and Word will open the Dialog Editor program, a tool for helping you create dialog boxes. We'll cover the Dialog Editor in Chapter 26, "Dialog Boxes & Other Macro Magic," page 896.

How to change the macro toolbar buttons

Although the Word 6.0 Macro toolbar is an improvement on the Word 2.0 equivalent in that there are more commands available, it's also a step backward in that the Word 2.0 Macro Editor's Icon toolbar labeled the buttons with words and indicated keyboard shortcuts for those who preferred to run the commands from the keyboard.

If the icons on the Macro toolbar buttons are just so many hieroglyphics to you, you can change them to text buttons, as shown in Figure 25-10. Somewhat ironically, to change them to text buttons, you'll need to use the mouse.

FIGURE 25-10

If you like, you can change the Macro toolbar buttons to text so that you can easily see what each one is meant for.

First make sure the Macro toolbar is displayed by opening any macro to edit. (Choose Tools Macro, highlight a macro name, and choose Edit.) Then open the Customize dialog box by choosing View Toolbars and then the Customize button; or by pointing in the toolbar area of the screen, clicking the right mouse button, and choosing Customize. Next point to the Macro toolbar button that you want to change, and click with the right mouse button to bring up the context-sensitive menu shown in Figure 25-11. Now choose Choose Button Image to open the Custom Button dialog box.

FIGURE 25-11

If you open the Customize dialog box, choose the Toolbars card, point anywhere in the toolbar area, and then click the right mouse button, Word will display this context-sensitive menu.

In the Custom Button dialog box, shown in Figure 25-12, type the appropriate text in the Text Button Name text box, and choose Assign to change the button to text. Repeat the preceding steps for each button.

FIGURE 25-12

Use the Custom Button dialog box to define a text button.

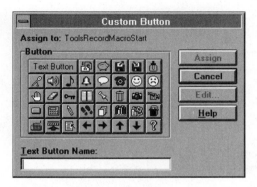

Depending on the display resolution you're using, you may then have to adjust button size to make all of the buttons fit on the screen legibly. To change button size, click on a button (with the Customize dialog box still open), and then point with the mouse to the edge of the button (the pointer will now change to the Vertical Split pointer); next click and hold down the left mouse button while you adjust the size of the toolbar button.

When you're done, close the Customize dialog box, and choose File Save All to save the changes to the toolbar. For more details on using the Customize dialog box to modify a toolbar, see "Customizing Toolbars" on page 316.

Changing to text buttons helps to identify each button, but it still doesn't let you run the commands from the keyboard. If using the mouse is too clumsy for your taste, you can assign a shortcut key to each command. From any editing window, choose Tools Customize and then the Keyboard card. Now you can assign a convenient shortcut key to each of the Macro toolbar button commands. The commands you need to match are shown in Figure 25-13 on the next page. For details on assigning keystrokes, see "How to assign a macro to a shortcut key" on page 849 and "Keyboard customization" on page 968.

To make the keystrokes easy to remember, you can show each one as a capital letter when you define the text buttons.

Word Command	Macro Toolbar Button Name
ToolsRecordMacroStart	Record
RecordNextCommand	Record Next Command
StartMacro	Start
TraceMacro	Trace
ContinueMacro	Continue
StopMacro	Stop
StepIn	Step
StepOver	Step Subs
ShowVars	Show Variables
MacroREM	Add/Remove REM
ToolsMacro	Macro
DialogEditor	Dialog Editor

FIGURE 25-13

Use this list of commands as a reference to help you assign shortcut keys to the buttons on the Macro toolbar.

How to print a macro

One last important debugging tool Word offers is the ability to print a macro. This can be particularly helpful for macros that are too long to fit on the screen at once. To print the instructions in a macro, first load the appropriate macro in a macro editing window by choosing Tools Macro and the Edit button. Then choose File Print to print the macro the same as you would any Word document.

A Dozen Quick 'n Dirty (but Useful) Macros

Ultimately, when it comes to working with macros, there is no substitute for jumping in and trying the real thing. Here are 12 macros that we find useful in our own day-to-day word processing. All of these were chosen so that you can create them either with the Record Macro feature (if you recognize the keystrokes that go with the commands) or by typing them in a macro editing window. Consider this a starter set for your own macro collection.

Some navigation macros

With all the choices Word gives you for navigating through a document, it still misses one feature that can be important for touch typists—the ability to move the cursor without taking your hands off the typing keys. Macros provide an easy way to add this missing feature.

The solution comes in two parts. First, you need macros that duplicate the navigation commands you need most often. At a minimum that includes up, down, left, left one word, right, and right one word. Second, you need some way to run the macros.

The first part is easy. The instructions for the six macros are in Figure 25-14. We've omitted the Sub MAIN and End Sub statements from each macro. However, note that, as with all macros, each of the six in the table must begin with a Sub MAIN and end with an End Sub statement; all you have to do is type the text listed in the Instruction column on a line between those two statements.

Macro Name	Purpose	Instruction
CursorDown	Move down one line	LineDown 1
CursorLeft	Move left one character	CharLeft 1
CursorRight	Move right one character	CharRight 1
CursorUp	Move up one line	LineUp 1
CursorWordLeft	Move left one word	WordLeft 1
CursorWordRight	Move right one word	WordRight 1

FIGURE 25-14

Six macros for moving the cursor.

To keep all similar macros together in the Tools Macro Name list box as shown in Figure 25-15 on the next page, we suggest giving them names that start with similar lettering, as do those in the Macro Name column of Figure 25-14: CursorDown, CursorLeft, CursorRight, CursorUp, CursorWordLeft, and CursorWordRight.

The more interesting problem is how to run these macros. One of the simplest ways is to assign the macros to Ctrl-key combinations, in a kind of "geographic" mnemonic. For example, if you look at the E, X, S, and D keys, you'll see that they sit at four points of the compass, as shown in Figure 25-16 on the next page.

To help you remember the keys, assign CursorUp to E, CursorDown to X, CursorLeft to S, and CursorRight to D. Carrying the logic one step further, you can assign CursorWordRight to F and CursorWordLeft to A.

Because Word lists macro names in alphabetic order, we suggest giving similar macros similar names, as shown with the navigation macros, all of which start with *Cursor*.

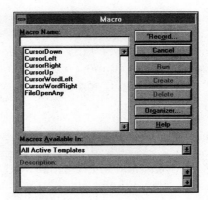

You can assign the navigation macros in a "geographic" mnemonic layout.

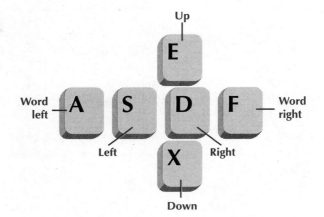

You may recognize this as the famous (or infamous, depending on your point of view) WordStar diamond. You may also notice that the combinations of these keys and Ctrl are already assigned to other purposes in Word as it is shipped. (Ctrl-S is assigned to FileSave, Ctrl-D is FormatFont, Ctrl-E is CenterPara, Ctrl-X is EditCut, Ctrl-A is EditSelectAll, and Ctrl-F is EditFind.) If you prefer the original assignments, you may find that you're more willing to reassign a different set of similarly positioned Ctrl keys—I, M, J, and K, for example. Alternatively, you may prefer to use these keys or another diamond of keys with Ctrl-Shift, even though that's a little clumsier to type.

In any case, if you choose to record these macros, you can assign them to keys while recording them, as we've discussed in "Recording a Macro" on page 844. If you choose to write the macros in a macro editing window, you can assign them to keys with the techniques we'll discuss in "Keyboard Customization" on page 968.

How to cut a word, line, sentence, or paragraph

Whether you're typing or editing text, it's often useful to cut a word, line, sentence, or paragraph—often with the intention of moving it elsewhere. Word has tools for most of these tasks, but here again, there's no easy way to use them without taking your hands from the typing keys. What's more, you generally need at least two keystrokes—one for selecting the text and one for cutting it. And in some cases, as with DeleteWord, the built-in command throws the text away rather than storing it on the Clipboard.

Figure 25-17 shows the macro instructions that will enable you to select and cut text in a single step. As before, we've given the macros similar names, all starting with *Cut*. This makes the names easier to remember and ensures that Word will group them together in the Macro Name list box so that they will be easier to find. As before, the table does not show the Sub MAIN and End Sub markers that each macro must include.

Macro Name	Purpose	Instructions
CutWord	Cut text from the current cursor position to the end of the current word and store the text on the Clipboard	WordRight 1, 1 EditCut
CutLineCut	the entire line the cursor is currently in and store the text on the Clipboard	StartOfLine EndOfLine 1 EditCut
CutSentence	Cut the entire sentence the cursor is currently in and store the text on the Clipboard	ExtendSelection ExtendSelection ExtendSelection EditCut
CutParagraph	Cut the entire paragraph the cursor is currently in and store the text on the Clipboard	ExtendSelection ExtendSelection ExtendSelection ExtendSelection EditCut

FIGURE 25-17

Four macros for cutting to the Clipboard.

As with the navigation macros, you'll want to assign these macros to keys that make sense to you so that you can easily remember them. We suggest trying to link macros in groups. For example, you might want to assign the Cut macros to Ctrl-C combinations, using Ctrl-C,P for CutParagraph, Ctrl-C,S for CutSentence, and so on. (This assumes, of course, that you don't mind losing Ctrl-C for copy.)

Notice, in passing, that all of these macros end with the EditCut command, which puts the deleted text on the Clipboard. If you'd rather throw the deleted text away, you could end the macros with EditClear—although this might be dangerous for anything longer than a line of text.

A more interesting variation would be to define the selected text as an AutoText entry called *Temp* and never use it for anything else. This way, you can cut text without disturbing whatever is currently on the Clipboard. You can record the procedure as part of creating the macro, or you can replace the EditCut statements with the following:

```
EditAutoText .Name = "temp",.Add
EditClear
```

This will define the AutoText entry Temp as the currently selected text and then delete the text from your document. If you take this route, you can paste the text elsewhere by typing *temp* and then pressing F3.

How to transpose a letter or a word

Finally, Figure 25-18 shows two macros for transposing text. The first will transpose two letters—when you've typed *intreesting*, for example, rather than *interesting*. The second will transpose two words—a useful feature if you want to unsplit an infinitive or move a misplaced modifier. Once again, the table does not show the Sub MAIN and End Sub statements; you should verify that they are in the actual macros.

To use the first macro, position the cursor immediately before the second letter in the pair you want to transpose. To use the second, position the cursor anywhere in the second word. When you run the TransposeChar macro, it will select the character to the right of the original position and then use the MoveText command to move the character to its proper location. The TransposeWord macro does essentially the same thing with an entire word. Note, however, that as it is written, the TransposeWord macro assumes that it will select and move a space after the word as well. That means it will not work properly if the second word is followed immediately by a period, comma, or other punctuation mark.

Macro Name	Purpose	Instruction
TransposeChar	Transpose two characters	CharRight 1, 1
		MoveText
		CharLeft 2
		OK
		CharRight 1
TransposeWord	Transpose two words	ExtendSelection
		ExtendSelection
		MoveText
		WordLeft 2
		OK
		WordRight 1

FIGURE 25-18

Two macros for transposing text.

To fix that shortcoming, you need more sophisticated macro commands than we have yet discussed. In particular, you need to know how to test the character after the word to see whether or not it is a space and then tell the macro to do one thing or another depending on what it finds. You may recognize this as a description of an If...Then...End If statement. And that's part of what we'll look at in the next chapter.

Topic Finder

Interacting with Macros   897

- The Input command
- If...End If
- Conditions
- Putting it all together
- How to run the macro
- Some variations
- The InputBox$() function
- Message boxes
- MsgBox results
- The GetCurValues command and branching execution
- How to use the quotation mark as part of a text string
- Loops: The While...Wend statement
- How to test for the end of the document
- Putting it all together

Designing Custom Dialog Boxes with the Dialog Editor   910

- How to run the Dialog Editor
- How to use the Dialog Editor
- How to create items
- Shortcuts for adding new items
- How to delete items
- How to position and resize items
- A special note about the dialog box
- How to edit the text for each item
- How to copy the definition to the Clipboard
- How to paste the definition into your macro
- What to do with a dialog box once you have one

Where to Go from Here   925

- Help for macros

26

Dialog Boxes & Other Macro Magic

 n Chapter 25, we looked at the mechanics of recording, writing, and debugging macros, but we made only passing mention of programming logic and WordBasic commands. In this chapter, we'll look at how to use the WordBasic programming language to build macros that you can interact with. We'll also discuss how to make the best use of dialog boxes, through both WordBasic programming and the Dialog Editor, which comes with Word.

Interacting with Macros

In Chapter 25, we showed you how to write a simple macro we called FileOpenAny. The macro was meant to substitute for Word's File Open command and display a list of all filenames in the current directory, rather than default to show only DOC files. It's worth taking this example one step further to see how a macro can ask questions, get answers, and then respond to the answers by following one set of commands or another.

Suppose, for example, that although you use varied extension names, there are times when you know the extension you're looking for and you don't want to see every possible choice. In such cases, you might want the FileOpenAny macro to stop and ask which files you want to see. To do this, your macro must ask for the extension, store the answer, and select the files to display based on the answer. As with most possibilities in programming, there is more than one way to get the same effect. We'll start with the simplest approach, and then we'll discuss some more elegant alternatives.

The Input command

One way to get the macro to ask a question is with the Input command. The command takes the form

```
Input "Any question you want to ask", VariableName$
```

where *VariableName$* is any name you want to use for this particular variable. A variable, as the name implies—and as we mentioned in the last chapter—references a piece of information that varies. In this case, it's your answer, since the variable's contents will depend on your response to the question. The $ at the end of the variable name indicates that this particular variable will consist of text rather than a numeric value. Such text variables are usually called *string variables*.

If you create a macro with this one line (between the Sub MAIN and End Sub statements, of course) and then run the macro, the question inside the quotation marks will be displayed at the bottom of the screen, complete with a question mark, as shown in Figure 26-1.

FIGURE 26-1

When a macro reaches an Input command, it reads the text included in quotation marks in the Input command and displays that text at the bottom of the screen.

Note that the question will appear on the bottom line of the screen, where the status bar is displayed, even if you've customized your screen to hide the status bar. If the horizontal scroll bar is displayed, the question will take its place. If both the status bar and the horizontal scroll bar are hidden, the question will appear in its own bar at the bottom of the Word window.

Suppose that with the FileOpenAny macro, you'll usually want to see all files, but on occasion you will want to see only a specific file extension. In this case, you'll want the macro to interpret a blank entry to mean that you want to see all files. You'll also want the macro to accept a text entry that specifies a file extension. The question should reflect that, and the command as you add the entry to the FileOpenAny macro might be the following:

```
Input "Which extension do you want to see in your list of files?
    (Blank entry shows all)", FileExt$
```

You can create a reasonably long question. However, be sure that it will fit on one line across the bottom of the screen. Note, too, that you will generally want to keep the command itself on one line in the macro editing screen. We've broken it into two lines here only because it won't fit on one line in this book.

When you run the macro and it reaches the Input command, it will display the question and pause until you answer. At that point, you'll either type the file extension you want to use and press Enter, or simply press Enter to indicate that you want to see a list of all files.

If...End If

Of course, asking a question—and even answering it—doesn't do much good unless the macro knows how to interpret the answer. And that brings us to the If...End If construction.

The If...End If statement offers you one way to tell a macro to branch to different commands, depending on a current condition. In its simplest version, the statement takes the form

```
If Condition Then Statement End If
```

This roughly translates to "If some particular condition holds true, then do some particular task; otherwise, ignore that task and move on."

If...End If constructions can also include ElseIf and Else clauses. These take the following form:

```
If Condition1 Then
    Statement1
ElseIf Condition2 Then
    Statement2
Else
    Statement3
End If
```

This version roughly translates to "If some particular condition (Condition1) holds true, then do whatever is in Statement1 and pick up the macro after the End If. If Condition1 does not hold true, check to see whether Condition2 holds true. If so, do whatever is in Statement2, and then continue the macro after the End If. If neither Condition1 nor Condition2 holds true, then do whatever is in Statement3, and continue the macro after the End If."

As you can see, you can build a wide variety of actions into the If...End If statement. There is no limit to the number of ElseIf conditions that you can include in a single statement.

Conditions

The conditions in the If...End If statement are built from a comparison of some sort—typically, a comparison of a variable to some fixed value. For example, the macro may test to see whether the variable *FileExt$* is blank. One appropriate comparison would be

```
If FileExt$ = "" Then Statement1...
```

which would tell Word to continue with Statement1 if the variable were blank. Another appropriate comparison would be

```
If FileExt$ <> "" Then Statement1...
```

which would tell Word to continue with Statement1 if the variable were not blank.

You can also define compound conditions with the logical operators And, Or, and Not. These operators mean the same here as they do in standard English. The compound Condition1 And Condition2 holds true if both Condition1 and Condition2 are true. ("If it's sunny and if I get an hour off from work, then I'll meet you on Friday.") Similarly, the compound Condition1 Or Condition2 holds true if either condition is true. ("I'll meet you on Friday if it's sunny or if you promise to pick up the check.") The compound Condition1 Not Condition2 is true if Condition1 holds true but Condition2 doesn't. ("I'll meet you on Friday if it's sunny but not if it's too hot.")

Figure 26-2 shows the available comparisons (called *relational operators*) for conditional commands.

Symbol	Meaning
=	Equal to
<>	Not equal to
>	Greater than
<	Less than
>=	Greater than or equal to
<=	Less than or equal to

FIGURE 26-2

Relational operators for conditional commands.

Putting it all together

We've now covered all the pieces we need for the macro we want to build. Choose Tools Macro, enter a new macro name or the FileOpenAny name in the Macro Name text box, and choose Create. Now start with the commands for defining, but not opening, the FileAll dialog box, as in the macro we built in Chapter 25. The first three lines will be the same as in the original macro we wrote in Chapter 25.

```
Dim FileAll as FileOpen
FileAll.Name = "*.*"
On Error Goto ForgetIt
```

As we discussed in Chapter 25, the first two lines create a dialog record called FileAll that matches FileOpen but sets the File Name field to *.*. The last line ensures that you won't see an error message if you cancel the macro. Instead, you'll jump to the label ForgetIt (which comes later in the macro). As we also discussed, it's not a good idea to turn off the error messages until you're sure the macro works, so you'll want to REM out the line until you've tested the macro. Simply add an apostrophe at the beginning of the On Error line, and Word will ignore it. (Alternatively, you can add the remark command, REM, at the beginning of the line, either by typing *REM* or by placing the cursor or selection in the line and clicking on the Add/Remove REM button—the third button from the right on the default version of the Macro toolbar.) For a more detailed look at each of these three lines, take a look at the section "Macros that use Word's dialog boxes" on page 873. For more information about remarks and about REMming out lines, see "Remarks" on page 874.

Next you need to add the Input command so that the macro will stop and ask which file extension to use:

```
Input "Which extension do you want to see in your list of files?
    (Blank entry shows all)", FileExt$
```

After the Input command, you'll use the If...End If statement to tell the macro to test the value of *FileExt$* and decide what to do next:

```
If FileExt$ <> "" Then
    FileAll.Name = "*." + FileExt$
End If
```

The first line of the If statement tests the value of *FileExt$*. If it is not blank, the macro goes to the next line and sets the File Name field so that the filename extension matches whatever you typed in response to the Input command. (When you respond to the question while running the macro, you will type only the extension because the If...Then command adds the wildcard asterisk and period. That's why the question is phrased "Which extension do you want to see....") If *FileExt$* is blank—meaning you pressed Enter—the macro will jump to the End If statement (leaving FileAll.Name set to *.*) and continue with the next line.

The rest of the macro includes the remaining three lines from the FileOpenAny macro in Chapter 25:

```
Dialog FileAll
FileOpen FileAll
ForgetIt:
```

As we discussed in Chapter 25, the first line opens the dialog box, and the second opens the file you designate in the dialog box. The third is the label you told the macro to jump to with the On Error command.

After you type all of these commands between the Sub MAIN and End Sub statements, the macro should look much like the one shown in Figure 26-3. Notice how indenting some lines makes the macro easier to read. In particular, notice that the line within the If...End If structure is indented, to indicate that the If...End If statement controls whether Word runs that command. You do not need to indent lines this way, but if you do, your macros will be easier to read and edit.

Keep in mind that you should not indent lines in a macro that contain labels. If you do, Word will not recognize the labels. So make certain that lines with labels are not indented.

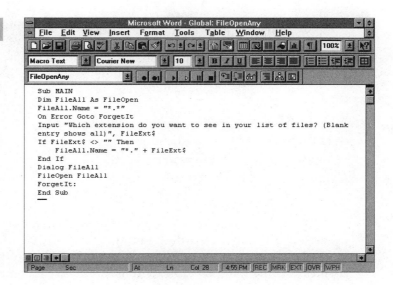

FIGURE 26-3

The Input and If...End If statements in the full version of the FileOpenAny macro tell the macro to ask you a question and act on your answer.

```
Sub MAIN
Dim FileAll As FileOpen
FileAll.Name = "*.*"
On Error Goto ForgetIt
Input "Which extension do you want to see in your list of files? (Blank
entry shows all)", FileExt$
If FileExt$ <> "" Then
    FileAll.Name = "*." + FileExt$
End If
Dialog FileAll
FileOpen FileAll
ForgetIt:
End Sub
```

How to run the macro

You can test this new version of the FileOpenAny macro by choosing the Start button on the Macro toolbar. (The Start button is the one with a right-pointing, filled-in triangle, the first button in the second group from the left.)

If you typed everything correctly, Word will ask you the question from the Input command by way of a prompt at the bottom of the screen. Press Enter, and Word will respond with the dialog box, showing a list of all files in the current directory. If you type in a filename extension instead, the dialog box will show only those files that use the extension, assuming any exist.

If you made any errors in writing the macro, Word will display an error message, and you'll get an opportunity to practice with Word's debugging features, which we've already described in Chapter 25. See "Testing, Modifying, and Debugging Macros" on page 879.

Remember that if the On Error statement is marked as a remark, you will get an error message if you choose Cancel. When you're sure the macro works, you can delete the apostrophe or the REM statement from the beginning of the On Error command to turn off error messages.

Some variations

Macros are nothing if not flexible. While you still have the FileOpenAny macro fresh in your mind, you should consider some variations that might better match the way you work. For example, you might never use any extension but DOC, but you may want the ability to specify the first part of the filename easily. In that case, you can change the line

```
FileAll.Name = "*.*"
```

to read

```
FileAll.Name = "*.DOC"
```

and then you can change the line

```
FileAll.Name = "*." + FileExt$
```

to read

```
FileAll.Name = FileExt$ + "*.DOC"
```

If you make these changes, just pressing Enter in response to the macro's question will display all files ending with the DOC extension; if you type some text and then press Enter, you can list files by the first part of their names. Typing *t*, for example, will list all files that begin with the letter *t* and end with the DOC extension. Note that you'll want to change the Input command to ask an appropriate question, and you may want to change the variable name to something more appropriate as well.

The InputBox$() function

Another possibility is to change the macro so that it asks its question within a dialog box. Word offers a simple way to create the dialog box with the InputBox$() function. To use a dialog box, modify the original Input line to read as follows:

```
FileExt$ = InputBox$("Which extension do you want to see in your list of
    files? (Blank entry shows all)", "File List")
```

If you replace the Input command with this InputBox$() expression and then run the macro, you'll see an input box similar to the one shown in Figure 26-4.

In the InputBox$() command within the macro itself, there are two sets of quotation marks inside the parentheses. As you can see in Figure 26-4, Word uses the text in the first set for the question it asks and the text in the second set as the title for the box. You can optionally add a comma and then a third text item within another set of quotation marks. Word will use the third item as the default entry for the InputBox$() text box.

FIGURE 26-4

The InputBox$() command offers much the same function as the Input command, but by way of a dialog box.

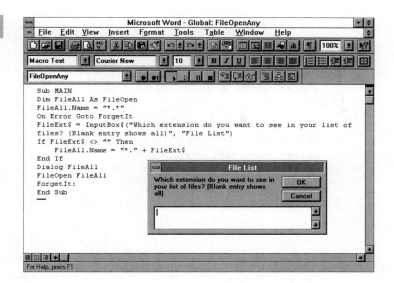

Message boxes

There are two commands in WordBasic that don't have direct relevance to the FileOpenAny macro but are similar enough to the Input and InputBox$() commands to be worth mentioning here: MsgBox and MsgBox().

Briefly, the MsgBox command takes the form

```
MsgBox "Any Message", "Any Title", Type
```

where *Type* is a number that represents button and icon choices, as we'll explain shortly. The MsgBox() command takes the form

```
SomeVariable = MsgBox("Any Message", "Any Title", Type)
```

As you can see, the structure of the two commands is similar. In fact, if you specify the same message, the same title, and the same type, they will produce identical dialog boxes. Figure 26-5 shows the dialog box you'll get with either command, with the message Any Message, the title Any Title, and Type set to 0.

FIGURE 26-5

MsgBox and MsgBox() display message boxes like this one.

The difference between the two is that the MsgBox() version returns a number to a variable that you can then test and use to control the macro behavior—in an If...End If statement, for example. We'll come back to that variable in a moment. To understand it, you first have to understand Type.

MsgBox and MsgBox() share a set of predefined features that you can designate by number. These include six sets of button types and four choices of icons (plus no icon as an additional choice). If you've chosen a set with more than one button, you can also designate which button is the default.

Figure 26-6 lists these predefined buttons and icons for MsgBox and MsgBox(). To designate your choices, select from the list and total their values. For example, if you want the OK button (0) and no icon (0), Type is 0, the default value. If you want Yes and No buttons (4), a question icon (32), and the second button as the default (256), Type is 4 + 32 + 256, or 292. You can display only one set of buttons and a single icon at one time.

To Designate...	Add This to the Type Value...
Buttons	
OK button	0
OK and Cancel buttons	1
Abort, Retry, and Ignore buttons	2
Yes, No, and Cancel buttons	3
Yes and No buttons	4
Retry and Cancel buttons	5
Icons	
No icon	0
Stop icon	16
Question icon	32
Attention icon	48
Information icon	64
Default button	
First button	0
Second button	256
Third button	512

FIGURE 26-6

Predefined buttons, icons, and default buttons for the MsgBox and MsgBox() commands.

MsgBox results

There is little point in defining a MsgBox to contain more than one button. The command does not return a number, and therefore you cannot tell the macro to test or act on the result. However, MsgBox() will return −1 for the leftmost button, 0 for the next button, and +1 for the next button. You can then use conditional comparisons to find out which button was pressed and a control statement such as If...End If to have the macro proceed accordingly.

For example, suppose you create a message box with this command:

```
PressedWhat = MsgBox("Continue?", "Paused", 4)
```

This will create a message box with the title Paused and the question Continue?; it is of Type 4, with a button for Yes on the left and No on the right. Choosing Yes, the leftmost button, will set PressedWhat to a value of −1. Choosing No, the next button to the right, will set PressedWhat to 0. Since there are only two buttons, these are the only two choices for PressedWhat.

After using the MsgBox() command, you can use an If...End If statement to test which button was pressed. The statement would take the form

```
If PressedWhat = -1 Then
    DoTheseInstructions
ElseIf PressedWhat = 0 Then
    DoTheseInstructionsInstead
End If
```

and the macro would then follow one set of instructions or the other, depending on which button was chosen.

The GetCurValues command and branching execution

One other technique that's worth passing mention is to use the current values in a dialog box to control what your macro does. If you've been working through this entire discussion on macros, you've already seen how to use the Dim...As statement to create a dialog record. For example,

```
Dim FmtChar As FormatCharacter
```

creates a dialog record named FmtChar, with a set of empty fields to match the fields in the FormatCharacter dialog box. The GetCurValues statement will let you set the values in the dialog record to match the current settings in the dialog box. The two lines

```
Dim FmtPara As FormatParagraph
GetCurValues FmtPara
```

create the record FmtPara, get the current values for the FormatParagraph dialog box, and store those values in the appropriate FmtPara fields. You can then use an If...End If statement to test the value of the FmtPara fields and control what the macro does.

Suppose, for example, that you want to put a border around paragraphs that you have previously indented ½ inch from the left. You could create a macro that moves forward one paragraph, gets the current values for that paragraph, and tests the values with a command similar to this:

```
If FmtPara.LeftIndent = .5 Then...
```

(Actually, this If statement won't work as shown. We'll explain why in a moment.) If the paragraph is indeed indented ½ inch, the macro can branch to commands that add a border. If it isn't indented, the macro can branch to commands that don't add a border.

How to use the quotation mark as part of a text string

As we just pointed out, the If statement we breezed past at the end of the preceding section will not work as shown. In fact, Word treats LeftIndent—and other paragraph indention settings—not as numeric values, but as text. Therefore, not only do you have to enclose the value in quotation marks to indicate that it's text, you have to give the entire value of the text string. Note too that for any given setting for a left indent, the actual text will vary, depending on whether you've set Measurement Units on the General card of the Tools Options dialog box for inches, centimeters, picas, or points. A ½-inch indent, for example, can show as *3 pi* for picas, *1.27 cm* for centimeters, or *36 pt* for points. Using inches creates an additional complication because Word uses the quotation mark as the symbol for inches. If you simply type *"0.5""*, Word will report a syntax error. Instead, you have to represent the 0.5" as

```
"0.5" + Chr$(34)
```

This translates to "0.5" followed by the ASCII character 34, which is the quotation mark, in parentheses. The entire line would read as follows:

```
If FmtPara.LeftIndent = "0.5" + Chr$(34) Then...
```

Loops: The While...Wend statement

The example of moving ahead one paragraph at a time and testing the current format for each paragraph assumes that the macro can loop back to the beginning of its own commands, move ahead to the next paragraph, test the new paragraph's format, and so on. One of the more common kinds of loops uses the While...Wend statement, which takes the following form:

```
While Condition
    Statements
Wend
```

This roughly translates to the following: "While the specified condition holds true, keep repeating all the instructions between the While and the Wend. When the condition no longer holds true, pick up the macro after the Wend."

In this particular case, the most reasonable condition for repeating the loop would be that you haven't yet reached the end of the document. Word provides a simple means of specifying this condition by way of two special bookmarks and the ability to compare bookmarks with the CmpBookmarks() command.

How to test for the end of the document

The two bookmarks are \Sel, which is the current selection, and \EndOfDoc, which is the end of the document. The CmpBookmarks() command can compare the two and determine whether they match. The appropriate command is the following:

```
CmpBookmarks ("\Sel", "\EndOfDoc")
```

More precisely, the CmpBookmarks() command compares the two bookmarks and returns a number. That number will be 0 if the two bookmarks are exactly equivalent, or some other number if they are not. (For example, 1 means the first bookmark is entirely below the second, and 2 means the first is entirely above the second.) The other numbers that CmpBookmarks() returns are of no importance for our purposes. What does matter is that Word uses the number to determine whether the condition is true or false. In particular, you can make the CmpBookmarks() command the condition in a While construction, in the following form:

```
While CmpBookmarks ("\Sel", "\EndOfDoc")
     Statements
Wend
```

In this example, until CmpBookmarks() returns the number 0 (meaning false), Word will consider the condition to be true and will keep repeating the loop. When the macro reaches the end of the file, CmpBookmarks() will return 0 and the macro will move past the While...Wend statement.

Putting it all together

Finally, taking all this into account, we wind up with the macro shown in Figure 26-7 on the next page for putting borders around already indented paragraphs. As written, the macro assumes you're using inches as your measurement units.

FIGURE 26-7

This macro contains a While...Wend statement that will keep repeating a set of commands until a given condition is no longer true.

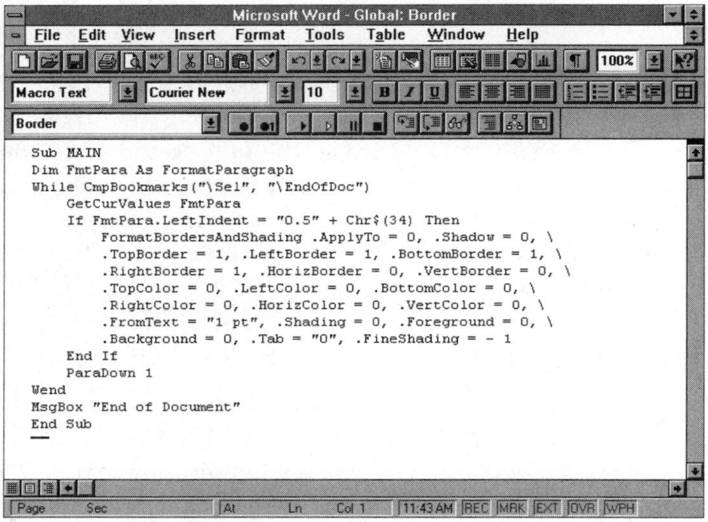
Microsoft Word - Global: Border
File Edit View Insert Format Tools Table Window Help
100%
Macro Text
Courier New
10
Border
Sub MAIN
Dim FmtPara As FormatParagraph
While CmpBookmarks("\Sel", "\EndOfDoc")
GetCurValues FmtPara
If FmtPara.LeftIndent = "0.5" + Chr$(34) Then
FormatBordersAndShading .ApplyTo = 0, .Shadow = 0, \
.TopBorder = 1, .LeftBorder = 1, .BottomBorder = 1, \
.RightBorder = 1, .HorizBorder = 0, .VertBorder = 0, \
.TopColor = 0, .LeftColor = 0, .BottomColor = 0, \
.RightColor = 0, .HorizColor = 0, .VertColor = 0, \
.FromText = "1 pt", .Shading = 0, .Foreground = 0, \
.Background = 0, .Tab = "0", .FineShading = - 1
End If
ParaDown 1
Wend
MsgBox "End of Document"
End Sub
Page Sec At Ln Col 1 11:43 AM REC MRK EXT OVR WPH

Note that most of the macro's action takes place within the While...Wend statement. First the macro creates a dialog record called FmtPara; then, on each pass through the loop, it gets the current values for that record and tests the record to see whether the left indent matches the criterion for adding a border. If so, it adds the border. If not, it skips to the End If statement, goes to the next paragraph, and starts again. When you reach the end of the document and the macro leaves the While...Wend loop, the MsgBox command notifies you that you're at the end of the document. This brings us back to the subject of dialog boxes.

Designing Custom Dialog Boxes with the Dialog Editor

Up to now in this chapter, we've been looking at message boxes and dialog boxes that are built in, in one way or another. You can clearly accomplish much with Word's standard dialog boxes and predefined message boxes, but you can accomplish even more by designing your own dialog boxes from scratch. Given that freedom, you can group options in any way that makes sense to you. For example, suppose you have two printers—one that uses PCL (the Hewlett-Packard printer command language) and one that uses PostScript. You might want to create a personalized Print With dialog box that would enable you to select a printer and give a print command in a single step. The finished dialog box might look like the example in Figure 26-8.

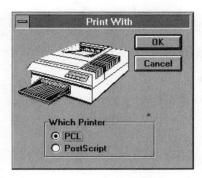

FIGURE 26-8

This dialog box offers
a possible design for a
Print With dialog box
that will enable you to
choose a printer and
to print in a single step.

WordBasic offers commands that enable you to design a dialog box any way you like, with option buttons, check boxes, push buttons, text boxes, and so on. You can then use the If...End If statement (or a similar WordBasic construction) to test the entries in the dialog box and act on them. Creating a dialog box by typing the appropriate commands in a macro editing window can be a chore. Word provides an easier alternative with the Dialog Editor. In the next few pages, we'll show you how to build a dialog box, using the Print With dialog box as an example.

How to run the Dialog Editor

The Dialog Editor is a separate program file named MACRODE.EXE. If you're familiar with Word 2.0, you may also be familiar with an earlier version of the program. The new version is similar to the old one. However, it offers several new choices for the items you can add to a dialog box, including drop-down list boxes and an entire new category of picture items. We'll cover these, along with all of the other available items, shortly.

If you specified the Custom/Complete installation when you installed Word, the Setup program automatically installed the Dialog Editor as well, in the same directory as WINWORD.EXE. The installation routine should have also created an icon for the Dialog Editor in Program Manager, in the same group as Word for Windows 6.0. Unless you've deleted the program file or the icon, you can run the Dialog Editor from Program Manager by double-clicking on the icon or by highlighting it and pressing Enter. If you specified the standard installation, you will need to run Setup again to add the Dialog Editor to your system. The Dialog Editor is included under the Tools option.

You can also run the Dialog Editor from within Word by clicking on the Dialog Editor button on the Macro toolbar. Remember that to see the Macro toolbar, you need to have a macro editing window open. You can edit an existing macro by choosing Tools Macro, entering the macro name in the Macro Name box, and choosing Edit. To edit a new macro, choose Tools Macro, type a name in the Macro Name text box, and choose Create. In either case, Word will display the Macro toolbar at the top of your screen when it opens the macro editing window. The Dialog Editor button is the rightmost button. When you click on it, Word will start the Dialog Editor, if it's not already running, and the Dialog Editor window will open.

How to use the Dialog Editor

When you start the Dialog Editor, the screen will look much like the one in Figure 26-9, with File, Edit, and Item menus and a blank dialog box in the center of the window.

FIGURE 26-9

The Dialog Editor window initially displays a blank dialog box in the center.

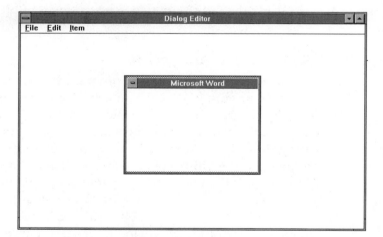

You can think of the Dialog Editor as almost a drafting program. Its various options provide images of option buttons, OK buttons, Cancel buttons, push buttons, check boxes, and other dialog box components. You can define a label for each item, resize the items, and move them around until the dialog box looks the way you want it to. When you're done, simply copy the dialog box to the Clipboard (it's copied as a set of text macro instructions) and then paste it into your macro editing window in Word.

There are essentially five steps in using the Dialog Editor: creating each item, positioning and resizing each, editing the text for each, copying the definition to the Clipboard, and pasting the definition into your macro. When you're actually creating a dialog box, these five steps won't separate out so neatly. You can easily move back and forth among the first three steps while in the Dialog Editor. Less obviously, you can further modify the definition after it's in your macro. You can even move it back to the Dialog Editor by way of the Clipboard and change it there. For purposes of this discussion, however, we'll assume you're doing everything from beginning to end in a straightforward, step-by-step manner.

How to create items

Whenever you start creating a new dialog box, either by starting the Dialog Editor or by choosing File New while in the Dialog Editor, the Dialog Editor starts you off with a blank dialog box in the center of the window. You can then add items with the Item menu. As shown in Figure 26-10, the choices on the Item menu include Text, Text Box, and Group Box, each of which inserts the appropriate item in a single step. In addition, you can choose Item Button to open the New Button dialog box, Item List Box to open the New List Box dialog box, or Item Picture to open the New Picture dialog box.

FIGURE 26-10

The Dialog Editor's Item menu includes commands for adding text, a text box, or a group box to your dialog box. Choose Item Button to open the New Button dialog box, Item List Box to open the New List Box dialog box, or Item Picture to open the New Picture dialog box.

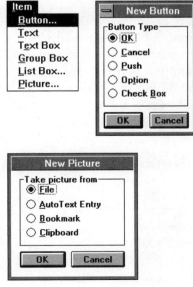

As you can see in Figure 26-10, the New Button dialog box contains options for adding an OK button, a Cancel button, a push button, an option button, or a check box to the dialog box you're building. The New List Box dialog box contains options for a standard (scrollable) list box, a combination text box and attached list box (Combo Box), or a drop-down list box—a new feature in Word 6.0.

The New Picture dialog box, also shown in Figure 26-10, offers four different picture types to choose from: File, AutoText Entry, Bookmark, and Clipboard. As the names imply, these four choices enable you to insert pictures into your dialog boxes from any of four sources; you can insert a picture that's stored in a file on disk, in an AutoText entry, in a document that's marked with a bookmark, or on the Clipboard. (The Clipboard option assumes that the macro has copied a picture to the Clipboard earlier in the macro.) If you create a dialog box with each of these picture items, you'll find that all four of them use variations on the WordBasic Picture command.

> All of these items will work in your dialog boxes just as they do in the built-in dialog boxes in Word and other Windows-based programs. To add any of them, simply choose the appropriate item. The Dialog Editor will insert the item in the dialog box that you're building. You can proceed, item by item, until you've added all the items you need.

For our example dialog box, we need to hold two option buttons—one for each printer—and a group box to hold them. We also need an OK button to tell Word when the option button is set properly, a Cancel button to give us a way to cancel the dialog box without printing, and a picture item to contain the picture of a printer. If you simply create these items in the order indicated, the Dialog Editor window will look like the one in Figure 26-11.

FIGURE 26-11

This is how the Dialog Editor window will look after you have added two option buttons, a group box, an OK button, a Cancel button, and a Picture item.

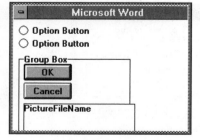

When you're grouping option buttons (or any other items, for that matter) in a group box, it helps to add the group box in the Dialog Editor first and then add the option buttons. If you add the option buttons first, you'll find that the group box will overlay the buttons on screen and hide them; what you want, of course, is a group box that *contains* the group of buttons. If you accidentally create the items in the wrong order, however, it's easy enough to fix the problem.

First select the option button (or other item) you want to move to the group box, and cut it using any of the Windows standard cut commands: Edit Cut, Ctrl-X, or Shift-Del. Then select the group box you want the item in, and paste the item back into the dialog box with any of the standard paste commands: Edit Paste, Ctrl-V, or Shift-Ins. The Dialog Editor will paste the item back in the same position from which you deleted it, but if you now move the item into the group box, it will appear inside the box rather than be hidden by it.

Shortcuts for adding new items

Although choosing items from a menu is a lot faster than typing each WordBasic command in a macro editing window as text, going through three levels of menus can also be a chore. The Dialog Editor provides shortcuts that make creating a dialog box easier.

In general, whenever you add an item to a dialog box, the Dialog Editor selects that item and indicates the selection with a dashed line around the item. You can also select any item at any time by pointing to it and clicking with the mouse or by using the Tab key to cycle through all items, including the dialog box. The Dialog Editor makes an educated guess as to what you might want to add next, basing its guess on the item currently selected. You can then add new items simply by pressing Enter.

In most cases, pressing Enter when an item is selected in the Dialog Editor yields another of whatever item is selected. For example, if an option button is selected when you press Enter, you'll get an additional option button. There are some exceptions, however. Knowing them will speed dialog box creation considerably. Figure 26-12 on the next page lists the exceptions.

Note also that, in some circumstances, the Dialog Editor will place a newly created item at the same position as an item that already exists. You'll then have to move the item to see the one that's hidden beneath it.

If This Item Is Selected...	Pressing Enter Will Add...
OK button	Cancel if none exists or a push button
Cancel button	OK if none exists or a push button
Push button	OK if none exists, then Cancel if none exists, and then a push button if both an OK and a Cancel button exist
Group box	Option button

FIGURE 26-12

Pressing Enter in the Dialog Editor will not create a duplicate of the selected item in these cases.

As you might figure out from Figure 26-12, you can create the items in the sample dialog box by starting with a group box and then pressing Enter twice to create two option buttons; then add either an OK button or a Cancel button, and then press Enter one more time to create the other button. Finish up by adding the Picture item.

How to delete items

As you're creating items for the dialog box, you may accidentally create more items than you want, or you may simply decide you want to get rid of one or more items. To delete an item, select it with the mouse or Tab key and then press Del or choose Edit Clear. In fact, all of the standard Windows editing keys for cutting and pasting that you're used to in Word will work in the Dialog Editor as well. You can also use commands from the Edit menu by selecting an item and then choosing Edit Cut, Edit Copy, Edit Paste, Edit Clear, or Edit Duplicate. Edit Duplicate is the equivalent of choosing Edit Copy followed by Edit Paste.

How to position and resize items

After you've added all the items that you want in the dialog box, the next step is to position and size each item. A good way to start is by changing the size of the dialog box itself, shrinking or enlarging it so that you can arrange the items inside the box in a visually attractive layout. In the case of our sample dialog box, you might want to make the group box smaller so that it surrounds only the option buttons, and you'll want to move the OK and

Cancel buttons away from the group box. When you're done, the window should look much like the one shown in Figure 26-13.

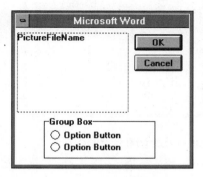

How to adjust size with the mouse

Since adjusting position and size is basically a graphical task, you will probably find that the mouse is the most natural way to approach it—although you may want to use the keyboard commands for fine-tuning. In most ways, adjusting size with the mouse is similar to adjusting a window size. Simply move the mouse pointer to the edge or the corner of the dialog box or item. When the pointer changes to a double-headed arrow, drag the edge or the corner to change the item's size. When the dotted outline is the size you want it to be, release the mouse button.

With OK, Cancel, a push button, or a text box, you can adjust only width—not height—unless you change the Auto default. Similarly, you cannot change the height or width of option buttons, check boxes, or text unless you change the Auto default. We'll cover the Auto default in "The Auto size selection and adjusting height and width" on page 921.

How to adjust position with the mouse

As you move the mouse pointer over items in the dialog box, you'll notice that it takes the shape of the four-headed arrow pointer, as shown in Figure 26-14 on the next page. When you see the four-headed arrow pointer, you can hold down the left mouse button and drag the item the pointer is on. Simply drag the item to the new position and release the mouse button.

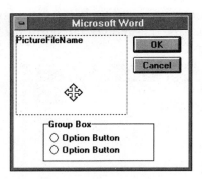

FIGURE 26-14

The four-headed arrow pointer indicates that you can hold down the mouse button and drag to move an object.

How to adjust size with the keyboard

If you prefer using the keyboard to adjust size, or if you want the finer control available keystroke by keystroke, press the Tab key until you've selected the item that you want to adjust. Then hold down the Shift key and press one of the arrow keys (Up, Down, Left, or Right) to activate resizing and to select the side to move. If you want to adjust from a corner, select a side and then use a second arrow key to move to the appropriate corner. For example, to move the upper left corner, you could hold down the Shift key and press the Left arrow and then the Up arrow. Once you have selected a side (or a corner), use the arrow keys to move that side. You can hold down the Ctrl key while pressing the arrow key to move in smaller increments.

As with the mouse, you'll find that with some items—OK, Cancel, and push buttons—you can adjust only the width; with other items—option buttons, check boxes, and text—you cannot adjust either width or height. Note that once you've begun adjusting size with the keyboard, the arrow key by itself will move the side in large increments, without the Shift key. You can switch between using the arrow keys alone and using them with the Ctrl key as needed for adjusting by large and small increments. When you're satisfied with the size of the dotted outline, press Enter to apply the new size.

How to adjust position with the keyboard

To move an item using the keyboard, once again select the item with the Tab key. Then use the arrow keys to adjust position. When you're happy with the position of the dotted outline, press Enter to complete the move. Note that you can move in small increments by holding down the Ctrl key as you use the arrow keys.

A special note about the dialog box

Be aware that whenever you start a new dialog box definition, the Dialog Editor assumes you will want the dialog box horizontally and vertically centered on the screen. And it anchors the box there unless you tell it otherwise. In general, there is no reason to move the dialog box. If you want to move it, however, either double-click on the box or select it and choose Edit Info. The Dialog Editor will display the Dialog Information dialog box, shown in Figure 26-15. If you clear the Auto check boxes under Position, you'll then be able to move the dialog box just as you would any other item.

FIGURE 26-15

The Dialog Information dialog box holds all of the information about the dialog box item.

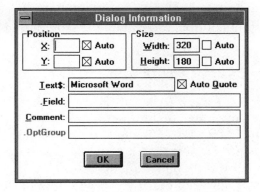

Note that as long as the dialog box is anchored at the center of the window, any time you change the size by dragging one edge, the opposite edge moves as well, as shown in Figure 26-16. After you clear the checks from the Auto check boxes, however, you can adjust each edge independently.

FIGURE 26-16

By default, the dialog box is anchored at the center of the window. As you drag one edge to resize the box, the opposite edge moves too—as shown here by the dotted line.

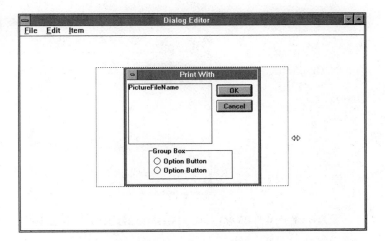

How to edit the text for each item

At this point, if you've been working along with our example, you have all the items you want arranged the way you want them. But they still have generic labels, such as Option Button. To edit the text for an item, either double-click on the item or select it and then choose Edit Info. The Dialog Editor will display a dialog box much like the one shown in Figure 26-15. The dialog box will vary slightly depending on the item. For example, an OK button must have *OK* and a Cancel button must have *Cancel* for the text, so the text choice for either of these buttons will be grayed. Similarly, the full name of the Information dialog box will change, depending on the type of item you're editing information for. The full name of the Information dialog box for an option button, for example, is Option Button Information.

The entries for each kind of item also have slightly different purposes, even though the Information dialog boxes are similar. For example, for the Dialog Information dialog box shown in Figure 26-15, anything you type in the Text$ text box will become the title for the dialog box. For a group box, the text becomes the label for the box. For an option button, the text becomes the label for the button. And for a picture, the text identifies the source of the picture. In this example, if you type *Print With* as the text for the dialog box, *Which Printer* as the text for the group box, *PCL* as the text for the upper option button, *PostScript* as the text for the lower option button, and the filename for the graphic as the text for the picture, your screen should look much like the one shown in Figure 26-17.

FIGURE 26-17

The finished dialog box as it appears in the Dialog Editor.

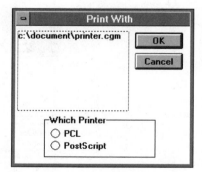

Other entries in the Information dialog box

Most of the other entries in the Information dialog box are beyond the scope of this discussion, but you should be aware of what they are in general. Briefly, each Information dialog box displays the information about the selected item that will become part of the macro statement for that item. For example, the X and Y text boxes under Position define the position of the upper left corner of the item. Similarly, Width and Height define the size of the item.

As with any macro command, the statement for each dialog box item must follow a precise syntax. Because command syntax is beyond the scope of this book, there is no point in explaining each item in the dialog box. However, it's worth noting that the Dialog Editor itself supplies most of the syntax for you.

When you adjust the position and size of each item, the Dialog Editor automatically supplies the correct syntax for defining that position and size. You'll note that if you've followed our example, the Dialog Editor entered *OptionGroup1* in the OptGroup text box for both option buttons. This identifies both options as being part of the same group, ensuring that you cannot select both at once.

Be aware, however, that the Dialog Editor is only an aid to creating dialog boxes, not the final arbiter. You may find that after you have created dialog boxes with the Dialog Editor, you'll occasionally have to clean up a few stray errors manually. And for this, you'll have to know some macro syntax. You might find enough information in Word's online Help. Choose Help Contents, and then choose Programming With Microsoft WordBasic. For more information about this and other reference sources, see "Where to Go from Here" on page 925.

The Auto size selection and adjusting height and width

Earlier in this chapter, we pointed out that you can't change the height of OK buttons, Cancel buttons, push buttons, and text boxes unless you change the Auto default. More specifically, if you look at the Information dialog box for any of these items, you'll see that the Auto option button next to the Height text box is checked. If you want to adjust the size of any of these items, simply clear the Height check box. Similarly, if you look at the Information dialog box for option buttons, check boxes, and text, you'll find the Auto check boxes for both Width and Height checked. Here again, if you want to adjust the size for these items, simply clear the appropriate check box.

How to copy the definition to the Clipboard

After you've created the dialog box with the Dialog Editor, you have to move it to the Clipboard. The procedure is similar to moving text or objects to the Clipboard while you're working in Word. Assuming you want to move the entire dialog box, simply choose File Exit. Word will prompt you to save changes to the Clipboard. Choose Yes.

> If you have already defined a dialog box in your macro editing window, you can copy just a part of the dialog box from the Dialog Editor by selecting only the portion you need to add to the macro. Most often, however, you'll want to move the entire dialog box. Also note that you can't save a dialog box as a separate Dialog Editor file.

How to paste the definition into your macro

When you copy the dialog box definition to the Clipboard, it's copied as text. In fact, if you look at the Clipboard at this point, it should look much like the one in Figure 26-18.

FIGURE 26-18

When you copy a dialog box definition from the Dialog Editor to the Clipboard, it is copied as text.

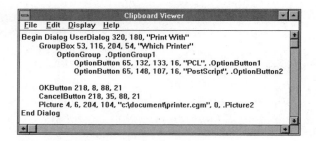

To paste the dialog box definition into a macro, you only have to go to your macro editing window, place the cursor where you want to insert the definition, and choose the Edit Paste command. At this point, you'll have a dialog box definition that starts with a Begin Dialog UserDialog statement and ends with an End Dialog statement. To actually use the dialog box as part of a macro, you'll have to add more commands. In particular, you need to add the following two lines after the End Dialog statement just to get the dialog box to appear on the screen:

```
Dim PrintDialog As UserDialog
Dialog PrintDialog
```

The first line creates a dialog record called PrintDialog to match the defined dialog box. The second puts the dialog box on the screen.

As we've already mentioned, you may still have to debug the definition itself. For example, the Dialog Editor will let you create a definition that consists of nothing but option buttons. However, if you try to use that definition, Word will respond with the WordBasic error message "Dialog needs End Dialog or a push button," which means that WordBasic couldn't find at least one of these items (in this case a push button, since the Dialog Editor automatically adds the End Dialog statement). The reason for the error message is that if you use only option buttons with no OK button, Cancel button, or other push button, there is no way to leave the dialog box once you open it.

What to do with a dialog box once you have one

Throughout this discussion of the Dialog Editor, we've concentrated on the mechanics of the process. But even though this is not a book about macros, it would be pointless to go through all of the foregoing steps without giving at least some idea of how to take advantage of a dialog box.

Figure 26-19 shows the full macro we've been discussing in our example, after we modified the lines created by the Dialog Editor and added other commands. If you look through it, you may find that you can apply many of these techniques to your own macros.

FIGURE 26-19

This personalized printing macro will ask you which of two printers to use. Then it will set Word for the appropriate printer and print.

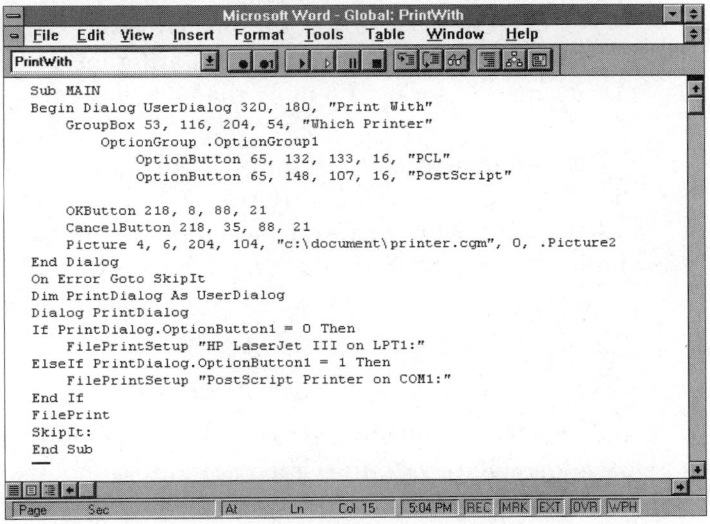

```
Sub MAIN
Begin Dialog UserDialog 320, 180, "Print With"
    GroupBox 53, 116, 204, 54, "Which Printer"
        OptionGroup .OptionGroup1
            OptionButton 65, 132, 133, 16, "PCL"
            OptionButton 65, 148, 107, 16, "PostScript"

    OKButton 218, 8, 88, 21
    CancelButton 218, 35, 88, 21
    Picture 4, 6, 204, 104, "c:\document\printer.cgm", 0, .Picture2
End Dialog
On Error Goto SkipIt
Dim PrintDialog As UserDialog
Dialog PrintDialog
If PrintDialog.OptionButton1 = 0 Then
    FilePrintSetup "HP LaserJet III on LPT1:"
ElseIf PrintDialog.OptionButton1 = 1 Then
    FilePrintSetup "PostScript Printer on COM1:"
End If
FilePrint
SkipIt:
End Sub
```

Note first that the macro consists of three main sections: the dialog box, the If...End If statement that tests which option button you've specified in the dialog box and then sets the printer accordingly, and the command to print.

The dialog box section was produced primarily by the Dialog Editor and then modified slightly. Note the syntax for each item in the dialog box. For example, the line

```
OKButton 218, 8, 88, 21
```

completely defines the OK button. The first two numbers (218 and 8) specify the upper left corner of the OK button, as measured from the upper left corner of the dialog box. The second two numbers (88 and 21) specify its size. More generally, the OKButton command takes the following form:

```
OKButton DistanceFromLeft, DistanceFromTop, Width, Height
```

You can also add an optional identifier at the end of the command, but we'll ignore that in this discussion.

> If you've used Word 2.0 macros, you probably know that Word 2.0 designates size and position using pixels. This often requires redesigning a dialog box, or at least some of its elements, if you change resolution. By contrast, Word 6.0 gives the size and position for a dialog box, as well as the elements in a dialog box, in increments of one-eighth of the system font for width and horizontal position; and it gives the size and position for height and vertical position in increments of one-twelfth of the system font. Because of this, a single definition for a dialog box will translate well to varying resolutions, which is a big help if you move to a new computer system with a different resolution or if you develop macros for use on more than one system.

The statement that produces the the Cancel button is nearly identical to the OKButton statement, differing only in that it starts with CancelButton rather than OKButton. And the other commands for dialog box items are similar. The OptionButton command takes the form

```
OptionButton DistanceFromLeft, DistanceFromTop, Width, Height, "Label"
```

and the group box statement takes the form

```
GroupBox DistanceFromLeft, DistanceFromTop, Width, Height, "Label"
```

The Picture statement has just a bit more information in it, taking the form

```
Picture DistanceFromLeft, DistanceFromTop,
    Width, Height, "PictureName", Type, .Identifier
```

Type here indicates whether this picture is stored as an AutoText entry (Type 1), identified by a bookmark in the current document (Type 2), taken from the Clipboard (Type 3), or, as shown in Figure 26-19, stored in a separate file (Type 0). PictureName is the name of the file, AutoText entry, or bookmark, depending on the picture type. If you were using Type 3, taking the picture from the Clipboard (as you might in a macro that had already copied a picture to the Clipboard), the PictureName would be given as a null value, with two double quotation marks and nothing inside them. The identifier gives you a way to refer to the picture in other commands.

The OptionButton and GroupBox button both allow an optional identifier at the end of the command, as does the OKButton. (But here again, we'll ignore the identifier in this discussion.) According to the Word Help file, the identifier is optional for the Picture command as well, but, in the first release of the program, at least, if you leave it out, you'll get an error message telling you the number of parameters is wrong.

The option buttons are both defined as being within OptionGroup1 simply because they immediately follow the line

```
OptionGroup .OptionGroup1
```

You could create a second group of mutually exclusive option buttons by adding the line

```
OptionGroup .OptionGroup2
```

before a second group of buttons.

Also part of the dialog box section are the following two lines:

```
Dim PrintDialog As UserDialog
Dialog PrintDialog
```

As we discussed earlier in this chapter, these lines create a dialog record called PrintDialog and put the dialog box on the screen. In addition, you'll note that we've added the line

```
On Error Goto SkipIt
```

before calling up the dialog box. As we've also discussed earlier, if you choose the Cancel option in the dialog box, this On Error statement tells the macro to jump to the label SkipIt rather than show you an error message.

The If...End If statement tests to see which button you chose. Note that by default, Word assigns the first button to 0, the second to 1, and so forth. Depending on which one you chose, the macro uses the FilePrintSetup command to set Word to the appropriate printer. (The variable for FilePrintSetup must exactly match what you see in the printer list box for each printer when you choose File Print Setup.) After setting Word to use either printer, the macro continues after the End If statement and gives the FilePrint command.

Where to Go from Here

At this point, you should have a pretty good idea of how to build some useful macros. However, even these three chapters on macros provide only an introduction to the subject. To learn more, you need a reference to all of the macro commands in Word and the syntax for each command.

Help for macros

You can find much of the information you need in the Word Help file. If you choose the Help Contents command, then Programming With Microsoft Word, and then Statements And Functions Index, you'll find an alphabetic list of WordBasic commands that you can then choose to see the proper syntax and examples for each. Alternatively, you can choose the Help Contents command; then choose Programming With Microsoft Word and then Statements And Functions By Category. Then you can choose the category of command you are looking for (such as Branching And Control) and browse through the choices to find the right command when you're not sure which one to use.

> Even better, if you know a macro command but you don't know the syntax, you can type the command in a macro editing window and press F1 to go directly to the Help window for that command.

You may find that having the commands in the Help file is not as convenient as having them in a reference book. As we mentioned at the beginning of Chapter 25, you should have received a return card for the *Microsoft Word Developer's Kit* in your Word for Windows package. This book includes both a complete reference to macro commands and a detailed set of instructions for macro programming. We firmly recommend that you send in the return card for the book.

If you decide to roll up your sleeves and get serious about learning WordBasic, there are three other books you should be aware of. *Windows 3.1 Programming for Mere Mortals,* by Woody Leonhard, and *Hacker's Guide to Word for Windows,* by Woody Leonhard and Vincent Chen—both published by Addison-Wesley—are required reading for any serious WordBasic programmer. They are filled with useful nuggets of information that you won't find elsewhere, documenting bugs and peculiarities in the way Word and WordBasic work. Even better, they are fun to read, which is quite an accomplishment for a book on programming. The *Hacker's Guide* also includes a complete reference to WordBasic commands. *Take Word for Windows to the Edge*, by Guy Gallo, published by Ziff-Davis Press, takes a more straightforward approach to the subject; it, too, is filled with useful information. Somewhat surprisingly, although all three books necessarily deal with overlapping subject matter, they are different enough to make all three worth having.

We've essentially completed our introduction to macros, but we're not quite finished with the topic of macros in general. In the last chapter of this book, we'll show you how to make macros even more useful by assigning them to key combinations and menus. (We'll also explain how to rearrange Word's default key assignments and menus.) Before we discuss these finishing touches about macros, we'll take a slight detour in the next chapter, to look more closely at Word's templates. Read on.

TOPIC FINDER

Creating a New Document Template: The Mechanics   929

- NEW! How to change the User Templates directory
- How to create a new template from scratch
- How to create a new template from an existing document
- How to base a new template on an existing template
- How to create a template by copying a document or template file
- NEW! How to create a template using a wizard

Editing a Document Template   937

- The effects of an edited template on an already existing document
- How to delete a template

Normal, Supplementary, and Global Templates   938

- Normal and supplementary templates vs. global templates

Why Use Supplementary and Global Templates?   943

- Word's templates

NEW! **Organizer: Moving Styles, AutoText, Toolbars, and Macros Among Templates   945**

- The Organizer dialog box

Templates

e've already worked with templates in Chapter 2 and Chapter 9. We've discussed how to create a new document based on any given template and how to attach a different template to any document. Templates are central to Word, and you need to know at least a little about them for everything from creating a new document to customizing Word's menus.

In this chapter, we'll discuss templates in more detail. We'll show you how to create and edit your own templates, and we'll discuss some of the possibilities for using templates.

Creating a New Document Template: The Mechanics

Word offers several choices for creating a new template. You can create one from scratch, or you can base it on an existing document or an existing template. Or you can use a wizard to generate a template.

The point of using templates is that you can create what amounts to different default settings for different kinds of documents. For example, you may want a default of single spacing for letters but double spacing for reports. If you don't have preprinted letterhead, you may want to create a heading in a letter template so that Word will automatically add it to the first page of each new letter. Word's templates are also capable of far more sophisticated automation than these examples suggest.

How to change the User Templates directory

With Word 6.0, you can define the directory you want to use for your templates. To see the current setting for the User Templates directory, choose Tools Options, and then select the File Locations card, shown in Figure 27-1. To change the setting, select User Templates in the File Types list box, and choose Modify to open the Modify Location dialog box, shown in Figure 27-2. You can then use the Directories and Drives boxes to select a different drive and directory on your system, or simply type a different drive and directory in the Location Of User Templates text box. Then choose OK to accept the new setting and return to the File Locations card, or choose Cancel to return to the File Locations card and keep the original setting.

FIGURE 27-1

The File Locations card in the Options dialog box will display a list of Word's current settings for file locations.

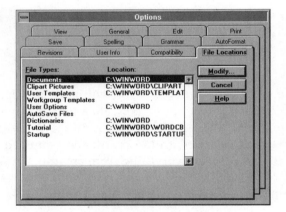

FIGURE 27-2

You use the Modify Location dialog box to change the locations where Word searches for particular kinds of files.

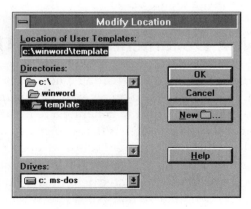

With the Modify Location dialog box open, you can also create a new directory for your templates if you like by choosing the New button. Word will open the Create Directory dialog box, shown in Figure 27-3. Type the new name in the Name text box, and choose OK to create the directory and return to the Modify Location dialog box. To close the Create Directory dialog box without creating a directory first, choose Cancel.

FIGURE 27-3

The Create Directory dialog box will let you create a directory and then return you to the Modify Location dialog box.

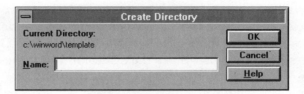

You can create more than one level of directory at a time. For example, suppose you want to change the User Templates directory to the \New\Template directory on the D drive. Even if there isn't a New directory on the drive, you can type *D:\New\Template* in the Name text box. When you choose OK, Word will create both the New directory and the \New\Template directory at the same time.

How to create a new template from scratch

To create a new template from scratch, choose File New, select the Template option in the New group box, and choose OK. Word will open a new document window with the title Template1. If you open additional new templates during the same session, Word will number them sequentially—Template2, Template3, and so on.

With the template showing on screen, you can modify it just as you would modify any other document. You can add, edit, and format text; define styles, AutoText entries, and macros; change format settings; change the View menu options; and more. In Chapter 28, "Customizing Menus, Keys, & Templates," page 950, we'll show you how to redefine the menu and shortcut key assignments as well.

Note that any formatting you add to text that's part of the template carries over to documents based on the template. The same is true of any formatting you define with the Page Setup or Columns dialog box. To set template-specific defaults for font, paragraph, tabs, borders and shading, and language, you can redefine the Normal style and other styles. You can override any of these formatting instructions within any given document based on the template by redefining the format while working in that document.

How to save a template file

You save a template by choosing File Save or File Save As, just as you would save any standard document. If you choose File Save As, Word will display the usual dialog box, but the Directories, Drives, and Save File As Type options will be grayed. When saving templates, Word automatically sets the directory and drive to whatever directory you've defined as the User Templates directory. Word also sets the file type to a DOT extension because, unless told otherwise, that's the extension Word uses for template files.

If you like, you can override any or all of these settings by typing the drive, path, or extension that you want, along with a filename in the File Name text box. However, if you change any of these settings, Word will not be able to find the file automatically for you later. As a general rule, unless you have a good reason for doing otherwise, you should accept these defaults and simply type in a filename. Word will automatically add the DOT extension.

After you type a name for the template, choose OK to save it. If Word is set to prompt you for summary information, the Summary Info dialog box will open. (To use this feature, choose Tools Options, select the Save card, and check the Prompt For Summary Info check box.) You can then type the summary information and choose OK to complete the save. Word will return you to the editing screen, where you can make further changes if you like. After you finish with the template, choose File Close to exit from the template file and save your changes.

If you try to save a template under the same name as an existing template, Word will ask whether you want to replace the existing template. Choose Yes, No, or Cancel.

After you save the template in the User Templates directory, Word will add it to the Template list box whenever you choose the File New command to start a new document. Similarly, Word will add the template name to the File Name list box when you choose the File Templates command and then choose Attach to open the Attach Template dialog box, shown in Figure 27-4.

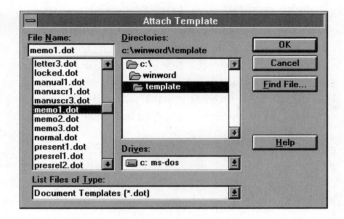

The Attach Template dialog box, which is similar to the File Open dialog box, will help you find a template to attach to the file you're currently working on.

Template security and passwords

You can bypass Word's default settings for template location and name. Doing so can serve as a mild security measure if you want to hide the template from other users. If you put the template in some other directory or give it an extension other than DOT, Word will not add it to any list of template files; you also won't be able to choose it from the list of templates when creating a new document, and it won't appear in the list of files in the Attach Template dialog box shown in Figure 27-4.

If you know the filename, however, you will still be able to designate the template when creating a new file; you simply type the name in the Template text box, complete with the drive, directory, and file extension if these differ from the Word defaults. In addition, when you use the File Templates command to change the attached template for a file you're working on, you can browse through your disk to find the template file, using the Drives and Directories boxes in the Attach Template dialog box. The dialog box looks and works just like the Open dialog box for opening a file.

You don't have to hide a template to keep others from using it, however. Word's file-level password security, which we discussed in Chapter 2, applies to templates as well, and it offers stronger security than simply changing the template's location or extension. You can add a password to a template at any time. With the template open, simply choose File Save As and then Options, and then type a password in the Protection Password text box. Word shows your keystrokes as asterisks and asks you to type the password a second time to confirm it. You can remove the password by first opening the file and then choosing File Save As; then choose Options and delete the asterisks in the Password Protection text box.

If you add a *protection* password, you'll have to enter the password whenever you open the template to edit it, whenever you try to attach the template to a document file, and whenever you open a document file that has the template already attached. Note that a template password is case sensitive; Word will not accept Hello, for example, as a match for HELLO.

You can also create a *write reservation* password for template files—either instead of or in addition to a protection password. Write reservation passwords work much the same way with templates as with documents; users who don't know the password can open the file, but they can't modify it. With templates, though, using only a write reservation password will also let you attach the template to a file, so you can use it without being able to modify it.

A write reservation password can be useful on templates that you create for others, particularly those templates that are meant to establish a companywide or groupwide standard—for AutoText entries or style formats, for example. You may want to give users access to a particular set of macros, AutoText entries, and so on, without letting them modify any of the template's customizations. You can add a write reservation password much as you add a protection password: With the template open, choose File Save As and then Options; then type a password in the Write Reservation Password text box. For more information on both kinds of passwords, see "File Save As options" on page 53.

How to create a new template from an existing document

At times you'll want to create a template from an existing document. For example, you may create a memo, a letter, or a fax cover sheet for one-time use and then decide later that you want to reuse the format. To convert a document to a template, start by opening the document and choosing File Save As. Next select Document Template in the Save File As Type list box. Word will automatically change the settings in the Drives and Directories list boxes to the currently defined User Templates directory, no matter what directory the original file came from, and those choices will be grayed. Word will also automatically add the file extension DOT to the file.

There are some circumstances in which Word does not automatically save a template file in the User Templates directory. For example, if you use the numbered list at the bottom of the File menu to open your template file, and if that file is listed together with an MS-DOS path, Word will keep that path in the File Name text box in the Save As dialog box, as shown in Figure 27-5, even though it shows the User Templates directory as the current directory in the Directories box. If you save the file at this point, Word will save it in the directory shown in the File Name text box.

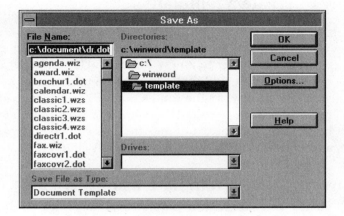

FIGURE 27-5

When you tell Word to save a file as a template, it sets the drive and directory to the User Templates directory, but it does not change any directory showing in the File Name text box.

To save the file as a new template in the User Templates directory, simply delete the path from the File Name text box, or delete the entire entry and retype only the template filename. Then choose OK to save the file. If you are prompted to do so, fill in the summary information, and choose OK to complete the save. Word will return you to the editing screen. After you finish editing the template, choose File Close to close it and save your changes.

How to base a new template on an existing template

As you develop a collection of templates, there will be times when you will want to base a new template on one that already exists. For example, after you develop a letter template, you may want a memo template that shares many of the same features but uses a different format for date and address. Rather than create an entirely new template, you can start with the first template and change just those items that you need to change.

One method for doing this is to choose File New and choose Template in the New option box; then, in the Template list box, select the template you want to start with. Choose OK, and Word will create a new template that includes all the customizations of the template you're basing it on. Make any changes you want, and choose File Save As, giving the template an appropriate name.

Alternatively, you can choose File Open to open the existing template and then use the Save As command to save it under a new name. If you choose this route, we recommend that you save the template under the new name immediately, before making any changes. This will ensure that you don't inadvertently save the changed file under its original name.

How to create a template by copying a document or template file

You can also create a new template by copying an existing template or an existing document to a new filename. Use any choice for copying that you feel comfortable with: the Windows File Manager, your favorite MS-DOS or Windows utility, or the MS-DOS COPY command. Be sure to give the new file a DOT extension, and store it in the User Templates directory unless you have a specific reason not to. After you copy the file, you can open it in Word and edit it, as we'll discuss later in this chapter.

How to create a template using a wizard

Finally you can create a template by using one of the wizards that come with Word. In Chapter 9, we described how to use wizards to create individual documents as you need them.

If you use the same format repeatedly, however, working through the wizard's questions each time can become tiresome. Instead, you can create a given format once and then save it immediately as a template by choosing File Save, typing an appropriate name, and specifying Document Template in the Save File As Type box. Word will add the DOT file extension and set the directory to the currently defined User Templates directory.

Once you've created a template, you can use the format whenever you like without having to answer all the wizard questions again. Simply open a new file and specify the appropriate template.

One advantage to creating templates from wizards is that you can customize the template file further if you like; for example, you can format some part of a letter differently from how the wizard formats it—and you need to make the changes only once. If you use the wizard to produce a new document each time, you have to add the same customizations repeatedly.

Editing a Document Template

After you create a template, you can open it and modify it just as you would any standard Word document, using either the File Open or the File Find File command. Be sure Word is set to look in the User Templates directory (as we discussed earlier in this chapter) and that it is set to list files with the DOT extension. If you use the Open dialog box, for example, first use the Drives and Directories boxes to move to the appropriate directory; then either type *.dot* in the File Name text box and choose OK, or select Document Templates (*.dot) in the List Files Of Type list box. Word will display a list of template files, as shown in Figure 27-6. Select the template file you want, choose OK, and Word will open the file. You can then make whatever changes you'd like, saving the file as you go.

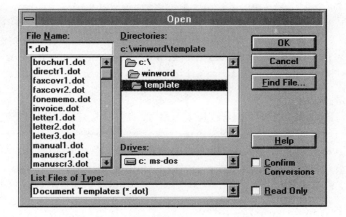

The effects of an edited template on an already existing document

After you modify a template, any new documents based on that template will include all the modifications you've made—whether to text, format settings, styles, AutoText entries, macros, toolbars, menu assignments, or key assignments. However, when you open an already existing document that was based on the original template, that document will not include all changes.

This makes sense because there are some features—notably, boilerplate text and format settings—that you'll usually want to have frozen after they're in a document. And indeed, Word will not apply the changes you make to a template's text, format, or style definitions to already existing documents. However, any changes you make to the template's AutoText entries, macros, toolbars, menus, or key assignments will show up in any file that uses the template, whether the document was created before or after those changes were made.

> If you've changed or added style definitions in a template, and you want to include those changes and additions in already existing documents, you can, using the Organizer feature. We'll cover the Organizer feature on page 945.

How to delete a template

As we've mentioned, by default Word stores document templates in the directory defined for User Templates in Tools Options on the File Locations card. To delete a template, simply delete the appropriate file from the directory. (We discussed deleting files in "Deleting a File" on page 62.)

Because Word lists the available templates based on the files it finds in the User Templates directory, deleting the template file will eliminate the template name from all list boxes that offer a choice of templates.

Normal, Supplementary, and Global Templates

As you may have noticed, we haven't yet drawn any distinctions in this discussion between the Normal template, supplementary templates, and global templates. Briefly, as we've discussed elsewhere, Word attaches the Normal template to all documents, and you can use the Normal template—the NORMAL.DOT file—to store any customizations that you want available to all documents. Any template other than NORMAL.DOT can function as either a supplementary template or a global template.

Unfortunately, the way Word 6.0 uses the term *global* can be confusing. In earlier versions of Word, *global* was essentially synonymous with the Normal template. And even Word 6.0 refers to NORMAL.DOT as a global template in some lists and message boxes. However, the only global behavior that the Normal template shares with templates you designate as global is that its customizations are available to all files. Among the differences:

■ When you designate a template as global, you can load or unload the template at any time. The Normal template is always loaded.

- When you designate a template as global, you cannot add or modify any customizations unless you edit the template file directly, attach it as the supplementary template, or use Word's Organizer. The Normal template lets you add or modify customizations while working on any document.

- When you designate a template as global, Word adds it to a list of check box items in the Templates And Add-Ins dialog box, which we'll discuss shortly. And if you try adding it to the list a second time, Word will merely ensure that the check box is checked. The Normal template is not on that list. If you try adding it you'll see a message stating that NORMAL.DOT is already open as an add-in program.

Given all these differences between NORMAL.DOT on the one hand and templates that you designate as global on the other, it's important to be clear on the distinction between them.

You may choose to think of NORMAL.DOT as a special kind of global template with its own set of features. But given that the two kinds of templates are so different, we think it's less confusing to put them in separate categories, with NORMAL.DOT the only representative of its category. For purposes of this discussion, we'll use *global template* to mean those templates that you designate as global. When we want to talk about the Normal template, we'll call it the Normal template, or NORMAL.DOT.

> The difference between a supplementary template and a global template lies not in the template file itself but in how you make it available to your document.

Figure 27-7 on the next page shows the Templates And Add-Ins dialog box, which you can open with the File Templates command. In the figure, we've designated LETTER1.DOT as a supplementary template by entering the name in the Document Template text box. (You can either type the drive, path, and filename in the text box or choose Attach to open the Attach Template dialog box to find and designate the file to use.) This is called *attaching the template,* a term that can apply either to NORMAL.DOT or to any supplementary template.

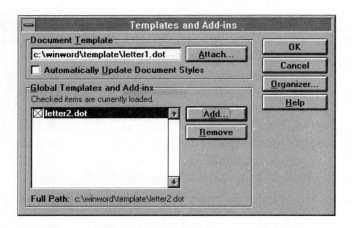

FIGURE 27-7

You use the Templates And Add-Ins dialog box to change the currently attached template and designate which global templates to load.

Notice that we've also added LETTER2.DOT to the Global Templates And Add-Ins box, with a check box next to its name. If you attach some other template to the file, using the Document Template text box, you can still make some of the customizations in LETTER2.DOT available in the current editing session by checking the check box—that is, by loading it as a global template. We'll discuss the differences between using the template as a supplementary template and using it as a global template in a moment.

Also notice the Add and Remove buttons. You can use these to add or remove filenames from the list of global templates. To add a file to the list, choose the Add button; Word will open the Add Template dialog box, which you use to designate a file. To remove a name from the list, simply highlight the name you want to remove and choose Remove. (You can also add a name to the list automatically by storing a template in Word's Startup directory, as we'll discuss in a moment.)

Normal and supplementary templates vs. global templates

For any given file, you can designate either the Normal template or any supplementary template as the attached template, although Word will attach the Normal template in any case, even when you attach a supplementary template. The key point, for the moment, is that when you *attach* a template, you attach it on a file-by-file basis. And the attached template is always loaded when you open the file it's attached to.

Global templates are not linked in any way to individual files. They are, rather, available or not available to all files you have open during the current editing session. For example, suppose you've created a template file called NAMES.DOT, with names and addresses included as AutoText entries. If you add the file to the list of global templates in the Templates And Add-Ins dialog box, as we described in the previous section, and check the template's check box, you'll find that the AutoText entries are available to any file you have open at the moment. Clear the check box, and the AutoText entries will disappear, no matter what file you move to or load. If you save a file when you have the check box checked, Word will not save the information about which global templates you had loaded. When you open the file again later, you'll find that the template is available only if the template's check box in the Templates And Add-Ins dialog box is checked.

How to load global templates automatically

As we mentioned earlier, you can have Word load a template as a global template whenever you start Word. You do this by placing the template file—be sure it has the DOT extension—in Word's Startup directory (by default, the directory called STARTUP, located in the Word program directory). Word will add the template name to the list of global templates in the Templates And Add-Ins dialog box and will automatically load it as a global template when you start Word.

You can find out which directory is defined as the Startup directory and change it if you like, using the same techniques as with the User Templates directory. For details, see "How to change the User Templates directory" on page 930.

How to customize the three kinds of templates

One of the most important differences between the Normal and supplementary templates on the one hand, and global templates on the other, shows up when you create customizations—such as an AutoText entry or a macro. When you customize any element of a document you're working on, you have the choice of saving the customization in NORMAL.DOT or in the document's supplementary template if there is one. You don't have the option of saving the customizations to a global template.

Most relevant dialog boxes, such as AutoText and Record Macro, include a text box with an attached list box to let you designate where to store each item as you create it. The text box is labeled with some variation of Make

This Available In, and the list of choices includes some variation on All Documents (Normal.dot). When you choose this option, Word will store the customization in NORMAL.DOT and make it available to all documents. (Note, however, that you can override the NORMAL.DOT customization with supplementary template customizations, as we'll explain shortly.) Any supplementary template attached to the currently active file will also be on the list as a choice for storing each customization. If one or more global templates are loaded, however, you won't find them on the list.

Your choice of where to store customizations determines when you can use them. For example, if you want a given macro available whenever you're using Word, store it in NORMAL.DOT. If you want it available only when working with letters, say, and out of the way otherwise, put it in a supplementary template for letters, along with other, related, customizations.

If you're not sure where to store a given customization, it's generally best to store it in the Normal template. If you decide you want it elsewhere, you can always move it by using the Organizer, which we will describe later in this chapter. And in the meantime, it will always be available.

Sometimes you may want to store a customization in a global template. Alas, Word doesn't offer global templates as an option; however, you can store the customization in the Normal template and then use the Organizer to move it to the template you really want it in.

Priorities among templates

The interaction of Normal, supplementary, and global templates can become complicated—particularly if you have conflicting customizations, such as a macro in a supplementary template with the same name as one in the Normal template. If there are any differences among templates, the supplementary template takes precedence over the global templates, and, in general, the global templates take precedence over the Normal template.

Special considerations for the Normal template

Creating or modifying the Normal template is just like creating or modifying a supplementary template—with one important difference. Even if you have no NORMAL.DOT file in your Word program directory, Word still attaches the Normal template to every file. In essence, a predefined Normal template is built into Word. And if Word doesn't find a NORMAL.DOT file on disk, it provides the built-in Normal template automatically and saves it on disk when you exit Word.

You can load the NORMAL.DOT file and modify it just like any other template. You can also take any template you've created and save it as NORMAL.DOT in the template directory. Word will recognize the name and use the file as its Normal template. In short, there is a subtle but real difference between working with Normal and working with a supplementary template. But the mechanics of modifying the Normal template differ hardly at all from the mechanics of modifying other templates.

Why Use Supplementary and Global Templates?

We've already suggested some reasons for using supplementary and global templates—creating one template for letters and one for memos, for example. Remember also that you can customize more than just text and default formats; you can create customized menus, special-purpose macros, specialized AutoText entries, and even field-based forms for each template.

Consider, for example, some menu commands you might add to a letter template: a Signature Block choice on the Insert menu; choices on the Format menu for block format, double-spaced format, and one-and-one-half-spaced format paragraphs. These formatting choices might use macros to set margins, paragraph spacing, and first-line indents with a single menu command. The possibilities are limited only by your imagination.

Global templates, in contrast, let you create a set of customizations that you can use along with the Normal template and any number of supplementary templates. For example, you could create a template with a set of names and addresses stored as AutoText and designate it as a global template. That would make the names and addresses available to you when you're writing memos or letters, but you could avoid loading the names and addresses—and cluttering up the AutoText choices—when you're working on a report.

If more than one person uses your copy of Word, you may each prefer different customizations. Each of you can store your own set of customizations in a personal template and load those customizations as global templates. That way, all of you can have your customizations available for the files you work on, and everyone can still use other templates as supplemental templates for particular kinds of files.

Word's flexibility is one of the program's great strengths, but when it comes to templates the flexibility can also be confusing. Here are some simple rules of thumb for using the three kinds of templates. We recommend that you follow them until you understand templates well enough to devise your own approach:

- Use the Normal template to store customizations (macros, styles, AutoText entries, and so on) that you want available to all documents.

- Use supplementary templates to store customizations that you need only for specific kinds of documents—for example, one supplementary template for letters and another for memos.

- Use global templates for customizations that you want available to a wider range of documents than you would use a supplementary template for but that you don't want to store in the Normal template.

Word's templates

A good way to get a feel for the possibilities of templates is to work with the set of supplementary templates and wizards included with Word. If you installed Word by using the Complete/Custom Installation choice, you would find both the templates and the wizards in the TEMPLATE directory located in your Word program directory. If the files aren't on your disk, use Word's Setup program to install them. (Note that you'll also find files with the DOT extension in the LETTERS directory, which is also located in the Word program directory. These files are prewritten letters that the Letters Wizard uses.)

Try using any of the templates (*.DOT) or wizards (*.WIZ) to see how it works. Then use the File Open command to open the template or wizard file, and explore it. If you open a wizard, for example, and then choose Tools Macro, you'll see that the magic in each wizard comes from a macro, called StartWizard, and that each WIZ file uses an AutoNew macro to run StartWizard. We discussed the AutoNew macro—and other macros to automate your work—in "Auto macros" starting on page 876.

You will probably find that some of the templates will serve a useful purpose exactly as they are. You should also look at each one—and at each wizard—for what it can teach you about designing your own templates. Most include sophisticated programming in their macros—far more sophisticated than you'll be ready for right away. But you can mine them for information and ideas. Take a look at what they do, and pick them apart to see how they do it.

Organizer: Moving Styles, AutoText, Toolbars, and Macros Among Templates

As you create more and more templates, you'll occasionally find that you've stored a style, macro, AutoText entry, or toolbar in the wrong template and that you need to move it. The Organizer dialog box, shown in Figure 27-8, makes it easy to move and manage any of these customizations.

The Organizer dialog box will help you manage your styles, macros, toolbars, and AutoText entries.

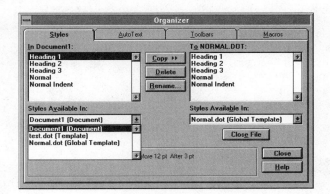

The Organizer dialog box

Word offers several ways of opening the Organizer dialog box. You can choose File Templates, or Format Style, or Tools Macros, and then, in each case, choose the Organizer button. Whatever route you take, you can choose any of the four cards—for Styles, AutoText, Toolbars, or Macros. We'll start with the Styles card.

How to manage styles with the Organizer dialog box

The Styles card, shown in Figure 27-8, consists of four areas. The left side includes a list box containing the names of all styles in a particular file—in this case, the file Document1 (the file that was active when we opened the dialog box).

Just below the list box is a text box labeled Styles Available In. In the drop-down list box attached to the Styles Available In box, you see a list consisting of Document1, TEST.DOT, and NORMAL.DOT. The list always includes the active document, the Normal template, and the supplementary template (if any) attached to the active document. If you change the selection in the Styles Available In box, the label on the list box above it changes to match the newly selected filename, and the list of styles changes to show the styles stored in that file.

Just below the Styles Available In box (but not showing in Figure 27-8) is the Close File button. If you choose this button, Word will remove all the choices for the Styles Available In box, so the box and the list above it will be blank; the Close File button will change to read Open File, as in Figure 27-9. If you choose the Open File button, Word will respond with the Open dialog box, and you can choose another file.

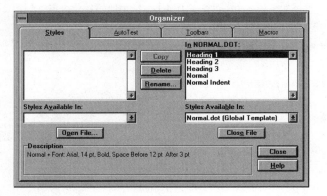

FIGURE 27-9

If you choose the Close File button in the Organizer dialog box, it will clear the box and the list above it. The button will change to an Open File button, and you can choose another file.

If you open a document file with the Organizer, Word will always list that file, as well as any attached templates, in the Styles Available In box. If you open a template file, Word will list the template file itself, as well as NORMAL.DOT.

The second area on the Styles card is on the right side; it is essentially identical to the first, even down to the labels on the Styles Available In box and the Close File button. Again, the list box lists the styles stored in the file whose name is showing in the Styles Available In box. Below that is the Close File button. The list, text box, and buttons all work exactly like the equivalent elements on the left side.

The third area is in the center of the Styles card, and it consists of three buttons: Copy, Delete, and Rename. These buttons perform the functions you would expect from their names; we'll discuss them in a moment.

The fourth area, at the bottom of the card, consists of a box labeled Description, a Close button (to close the dialog box), and a Help button. As long as only one style is selected on either the left or the right side, this box will contain a description of the selected style. This can be helpful as a reminder of what each style does, particularly if you have two styles with the same name in two different files; by selecting each in turn, you can see the differences between them.

How to delete a style. To delete one or more styles from a template or a document, first load the file you want to delete the style from. You can load the file on either the left or the right side of the Organizer dialog box. Then select the style or styles you want to delete, and choose the Delete button. Word will respond with a dialog box asking whether you want to delete the style. Answer Yes, No, Cancel, or Yes To All, as appropriate. (The Yes To All choice applies only if you have selected multiple styles. If you choose it, Word will delete all selected styles at once. Choose Yes, and Word will delete only the specific style named in the dialog box question, and it will then ask the same question again for the next selected style.)

How to rename a style. To rename a style in a template or a document, start by once again loading the appropriate file on either the left or the right side of the Organizer dialog box. Then select the style you want to rename, and choose the Rename button. Word will respond with a Rename dialog box. You can then type the new name and choose OK, or you can choose Cancel to return to the Organizer dialog box without changing the name.

How to copy a style. To copy a style from one template or document to another, first load both the source file (containing the style to be copied) and the destination file, using the left and right sides of the Organizer dialog box. Then select the style or styles you want to copy, and choose the Copy button. Unless there is a style in the destination file with the same name as a style you've told Word to copy, Word will simply copy the styles, adding them to the style list for the destination file. If there is a duplicate name, however, Word will respond with a dialog box asking whether you want to overwrite the existing style. Answer Yes, No, Cancel, or Yes To All, as appropriate. (As when deleting styles, the Yes To All choice applies only if you have selected multiple styles. Choose it, and Word will copy all styles with duplicate names at once. Choose Yes, and Word will copy only the specific style mentioned in the dialog box question and then ask the same question again for the next selected style with a duplicate name.)

How to move a style. To move a style, first copy the style, and then delete it in the source file list, using the steps previously described for copying and deleting.

Notice that the Copy button in Figure 27-8 includes two arrowheads that point to the right. Their direction indicates the direction in which the styles will be copied. You can use the arrows to help avoid confusion. If you select style names on the left side of the dialog box, the arrows will point to the right. If you select names on the right, the arrows will point to the left.

How to manage AutoText, toolbars, and macros with the Organizer dialog box

The Organizer dialog box works essentially the same way with all four cards. In fact, as you can see by comparing Figure 27-8 on page 945 to Figures 27-10, 27-11, and 27-12, the only differences among the cards are a few minor changes in labels; the Styles Available In label, for example, becomes AutoText Available In, Toolbars Available In, or Macros Available In, as appropriate. Deleting, renaming, copying, and moving AutoText, toolbars, and macros follow exactly the same procedures we've described for managing styles.

FIGURE 27-10

The AutoText card is almost identical to the Styles card shown in Figure 27-8, as are the Toolbars and Macros cards shown in Figures 27-11 and 27-12.

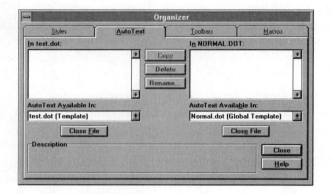

FIGURE 27-11

The Toolbars card is the third card in the Organizer dialog box.

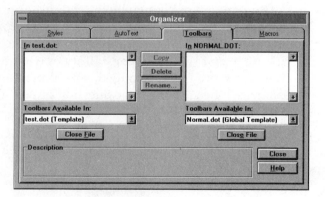

FIGURE 27-12

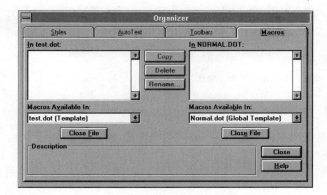

FIGURE 27-12

The Macros card is
the fourth card in the
Organizer dialog box.

We've now covered all the highlights of templates in this whirlwind
tour. But before you spend too much time working with multiple templates
on your own, take a look at the next chapter, where we'll show you how to
redefine menus and shortcut-key assignments, two important capabilities
for customizing Word and designing your own templates.

Topic Finder

Customizing the Menus   952

- How to create a practice template
- The Customize dialog box

NEW! ## Renaming, Adding, and Deleting Menus   964

- How to rename a menu or change the trigger key
- How to add a menu
- How to delete a menu
- How to move a menu
- Strategies for renaming menus

Keyboard Customization   968

- The Options Keyboard dialog box
- How to save menu and key assignments
- How to print key assignments

Another Macro Shortcut   975

- Push buttons
- The final flourish

28

Customizing Menus, Keys, & Templates

N o matter how comfortable you may be with Word's menu logic and default keyboard assignments, you may wish some features were arranged differently. For example, Word puts the Page Numbers command on the Insert menu and the Header And Footer command on the View menu. You might prefer to have both on the same menu, since page numbers are a type of header or footer.

Similarly, you might prefer to assign shortcut keys differently from their defaults. Perhaps you'd prefer to assign all your formatting keys to Ctrl-Shift combinations so that you could use J for justified paragraphs, L for flush left, R for flush right, and C for centered, rather than the default Ctrl plus J, L, R, and E (Ctrl plus C is assigned to Copy).

With Word, you can rearrange the menus and key assignments at will. You can also add your own macros to the Word menus and assign macros to your choice of shortcut keys. Better still, Word offers a feature that will let you assign easily remembered two-key mnemonics to your macros and the built-in commands. If you want both mnemonics and reminders, there is even a way to create two-key or three-key mnemonics that prompt you if you forget the keystrokes. We'll cover all of this, and more, in this chapter.

Customizing the Menus

You may find that Word's default menu structure seems intuitive and well organized—or you may feel that some menu items should be on different menus. Even if you like every default menu choice, you may want to add some of Word's built-in commands or your own macros as additional choices. You can make any such changes with the Menus card, which you can reach by choosing Tools Customize and then choosing the Menus card.

How to create a practice template

Before you change any menus, we recommend that you create a special template to practice with. If you make accidental changes to NORMAL.DOT or another template, you may have trouble getting back to the original menus without losing AutoText entries or macros that you've created.

As we discussed in Chapter 27, if you used the Custom/Complete Installation option when you installed Word, the program automatically created several template files (all with the DOT extension) and put them in a Template subdirectory within the Word program directory. Unless you've moved them or erased them, they should still be there.

As we discussed in Chapter 27, you can create a practice template easily by copying the NORMAL.DOT file to some other filename, such as PRACTICE.DOT or CUSTOM.DOT. You can copy NORMAL.DOT with any of the standard MS-DOS or Windows copying commands. Before you create the new file, however, be sure that you don't overwrite any file with the same name that you might have in the User Templates directory. We discussed the User Templates directory in "How to change the User Templates directory" on page 930. You can also create the new template file from within Word. Simply use the File Open command to load NORMAL.DOT, and then choose File Save As and save it as a template under the new name. For the rest of this discussion, we'll assume that you're using the name PRACTICE.DOT for your practice template.

After you create PRACTICE.DOT, open a new document by choosing File New and entering *Practice* in the Template box, as shown in Figure 28-1.

FIGURE 28-1

You can attach the PRACTICE.DOT template to a new file by entering *Practice* in the Template list box when you create the file.

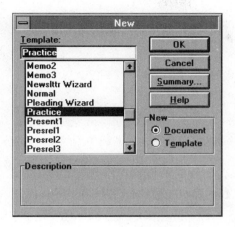

Alternatively, if you already have a new file open, you can attach the PRACTICE.DOT template to it by choosing File Template to open the Templates And Add-Ins dialog box, shown in Figure 28-2.

FIGURE 28-2

In the Templates And Add-Ins dialog box, you can designate a template to attach to your document.

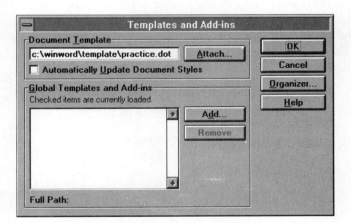

You can type a template name in the Document Template text box; alternatively, you can choose the Attach button to open the Attach Template dialog box, in which you can find and select the template. The Attach Template dialog box works just like the Open dialog box. When you select a file in the Attach Template dialog box, Word enters the filename in the Document Template text box. You then choose OK to attach the template.

Note that if you type *Normal* in the Document Template text box and then choose OK, Word will detach any currently attached supplementary template.

> If you're familiar with Word 2.0, you know that the equivalent dialog box will let you tell Word to store customizations in the Normal template or a supplementary template, or instruct Word to ask you where to store each one as you create it. Word 6.0 has no such option. Instead, you'll find list boxes in each of the various dialog boxes, in which you can specify where to store each customization. We'll discuss this later in the chapter.

The Customize dialog box

Starting with a new, blank document with the practice template attached, choose Tools Customize, and then choose the Menus card. Word will open a dialog box similar to the one shown in Figure 28-3. You can add, delete, or rename menus and menu items; move menu items to different menus; and assign built-in commands, macros, AutoText entries, and styles to menus. You can, in fact, completely redesign Word's menus and menu structure.

FIGURE 28-3

The Menus card in the Tools Customize dialog box will let you redesign Word's menus.

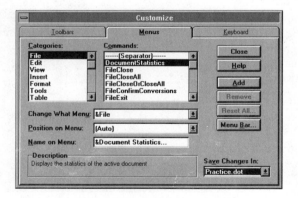

How to tell Word where to store your menu customizations

Notice first the Save Changes In box in the lower right corner of the Menus card. The possible settings for this choice are NORMAL.DOT and the document's supplementary template, if one is attached—in this case, PRACTICE.DOC. The setting for this option determines not only where Word will store changes you make, but also what you'll see in the list boxes.

> If you've added a menu or menu item to PRACTICE.DOT, for example, and you set the Save Changes In box to PRACTICE.DOT, Word will display the added entries in the appropriate list box. If you change the setting to NORMAL.DOT, Word will no longer show the entries. Choose NORMAL.DOT here both to store your changes in the Normal template and to display the current settings for NORMAL.DOT in the boxes labeled Change What Menu, Position On Menu, and Name On Menu. Choose the supplementary template name to store your changes in the supplementary template and to have the boxes display the current settings for the supplementary template.

If you created PRACTICE.DOT by copying the NORMAL.DOT file, as we suggested, you won't see any difference between the lists when you move between the two settings. But that's only because the two templates are still identical. Make sure that the Save Changes In box is set to PRACTICE.DOT, since that's where you want all your changes to go for now. Throughout the rest of this chapter, we will refer to PRACTICE.DOT, the practice template, and the supplementary template interchangeably.

How to assign an item to a menu

The Menus card contains two list boxes; the first is labeled Categories, and the second has different labels depending upon the category selected. It also contains two text boxes, labeled Change What Menu and Position On Menu, both of which include drop-down list boxes, plus another text box labeled Name On Menu.

In Chapter 24, we explained how to assign a macro to a menu when you record the macro. The techniques are exactly the same when you want to assign an existing macro, a command, or another item to a menu. You use the Change What Menu text box to specify the menu to assign an item to, the Position On Menu box to assign a position for the menu item, and the Name On Menu text box to specify the name of the menu item. For an introduction to using these three text boxes, see "How to assign a macro to a menu" on page 851.

The two elements we didn't deal with in Chapter 24 are the Categories list box and the second list box, labeled Commands in Figure 28-3. In the Categories list box, you specify the category of the item you are assigning to a menu. Category choices include all standard menus—File, Edit, View, and so on—plus Drawing, Borders, Mail Merge, All Commands, Macros, Fonts, AutoText, and Styles.

The category you choose determines the options available in the second list box. Choosing a name from the first section restricts the list to commands associated with that menu. The second section (Macros, Fonts, Autotext, and Styles) lists the contents of the current template. If you select Macros in the Categories box, for example, Word changes the label of the second box to Macros and lists all macros in the current template (the template specified in the Save Changes In box). If you choose Styles, Word changes the label for the second box to Styles and lists all styles in the current template.

After you select a category, you can scroll through the second list box, looking for a particular command, macro, style, AutoText entry, or font. If you don't know what a given item does, you can view a description in the Description box at the bottom of the dialog box, as shown in Figure 28-4.

FIGURE 28-4

If you select a category from the Categories list, and select an item from the second list box, Word will display an explanation for that item in the Description box at the bottom of the dialog box.

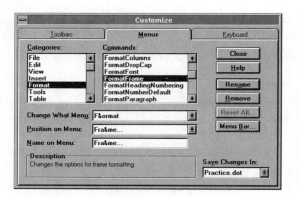

 Items listed as commands are also part of the WordBasic macro language. Note also that if you are looking for a specific command but you aren't sure which category to look under, you can see a list of all commands by choosing All Commands in the Categories box.

After you've chosen a category and an item from that category in the second list box, assigning the item to a menu is similar to assigning a macro to a menu when you record a macro. Select the menu in the Change What Menu box, a position for the menu item in the Position On Menu box, and a name for the item in the Name On Menu box. Then choose the Add button to add the item to the menu.

How to assign a position to a menu item

It is worth noting that the Position On Menu drop-down list box provides complete control over the placement of each item. The first three choices on the drop-down list, shown in Figure 28-5, are Auto, At Top, and At Bottom. At Top and At Bottom are self-explanatory; the Auto choice is less so.

FIGURE 28-5

The Position On Menu drop-down list provides complete control over the placement of each menu item.

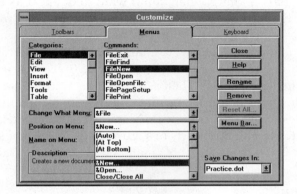

The Auto option tells Word to choose a menu position for an item you add to a menu. For example, if you add Document Statistics to the File menu, Word will add it by default just below the Templates command. You can then remove Document Statistics from the menu and add it back, for example, at the bottom of the menu. But if you select Auto when you add it back, Word will put it just below Templates again.

In general, the Auto choice maintains the logical categories of the menus as originally designed. If your menu customizations are minor, you're generally best off using the default (Auto) position. If you've made extensive changes in your menu structure, you probably won't want to use Auto.

Word does not restrict your choices to At Top, At Bottom, and Auto. Below these top three choices are listed all of the menu items in their current order. When you move the highlight into this part of the list, the Add button changes to Add Below. If you want to add a new menu item to a specific position, you simply select the item that you want just above the new item, and choose the Add Below button.

How to assign a name to a menu item

Word will enter a default name for you in the Name On Menu text box. This holds true for any kind of item, not just macros. You can accept the default name or not. And keep in mind that if you want to be able to choose a menu item with a trigger (also known as an accelerator key), you have to type an ampersand just before the character you want to use. For details, see "How to assign a macro to a menu" on page 851.

How to delete a menu item

There may be times when you'll want to delete a menu item that you never use or that just doesn't make sense to you. Suppose, for example, that you've added some macros to your Tools menu, and you want to cut down the size of the menu by deleting the Language command because you never use it.

To delete the Language command, first choose Tools Customize and then the Menus card. Then select &Tools in the Change What Menu box so that the items on the Tools menu will be displayed in the Position On Menu list. Next open the Position On Menu list and select &Language, the item you want to delete, as shown in Figure 28-6. Then choose the Remove button. Figure 28-7 shows the Tools menu before and after this change.

FIGURE 28-6

If you select a menu in the Change What Menu box, select an item in the Position On Menu box, and choose Remove, Word will delete the item from the Position On Menu list and from the menu as well.

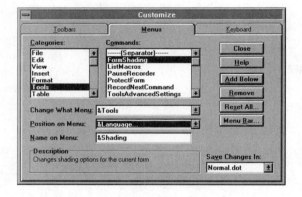

FIGURE 28-7

The before and after versions of the Tools menu. The default menu is on the left. The changed menu, with the Language menu item removed, is on the right.

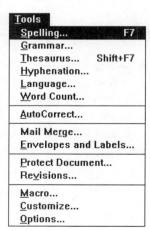

When you choose the Remove button, Word deletes the selected command from the menu without asking for confirmation. If you accidentally delete the wrong item, you can easily restore it. Use the Categories and Commands list boxes to specify the item, and make sure the correct menu name is showing in the Change What Menu box. Then select a position in the Position On Menu box (choose Auto to restore a standard command to its default position), and choose Add.

Word offers a shortcut for removing menu items that you need to know about—if only to avoid it. If you press Ctrl-Alt-Minus (using the minus on the typing keys rather than on the numeric keypad), the mouse pointer will change to a thick horizontal bar—a minus sign. If you then open a drop-down or context-sensitive menu, you can remove almost any item from that menu by clicking on it with the left mouse button. You can also remove a menu item by opening a drop-down menu with a keystroke, and then either typing the menu item's trigger key (also known as an accelerator key) or selecting the item and pressing Enter.

We find this shortcut to be more dangerous than helpful. If you generally give menu commands from the keyboard, you could accidentally press the shortcut key combination and end up removing a menu item the next time you try to choose a command. And even if you don't consider this a problem, the shortcut is a clumsy method for redesigning menus. As soon as you remove a menu item, Word returns to its usual behavior. So if you need to remove several menu items, you have to retype the shortcut key each time.

We firmly recommend that you remove this shortcut key assignment by using the technique we'll discuss in "How to delete shortcut keys" on page 972. The command to which the key is attached is ToolsCustomizeRemoveMenuShortcut in the All Commands category. Note too that there is a companion shortcut for adding menu commands. This second shortcut, Ctrl-Alt-Equal sign, isn't as dangerous, but it's clumsy to use. Type the key combination, and the mouse pointer will change to a plus sign. We recommend that you ignore this shortcut, but you may want to remove the shortcut key from this command. The relevant command is ToolsCustomizeAddMenuShortcut.

How to rename a menu item and change the trigger key

There may also be times when you simply want to rename a menu item or change the trigger key for selecting an item. For example, Word's Format menu by default uses C for Columns and E for Change Case. You might like to rename Change Case to Upper/Lower Case and assign U as the trigger key. Alternatively, if you rarely use columns but often need to change case, you might like to keep the names and change the accelerator keys, assigning C for Change Case and perhaps L for columns.

To change the name of an item, the trigger key, or both, first use the Categories and Commands list boxes to select the command you want to change. Word automatically fills in the appropriate entries in the Change What Menu, Position On Menu, and Name On Menu boxes. To change the name or the trigger key, type the new or changed name in the Name On Menu box. For example, if you want to change the Change Case command to Upper/Lower Case and use U as the trigger, select the FormatChangeCase command, and change the Name On Menu text to &Upper/Lower Case, as shown in Figure 28-8. Word will replace the Add button with a Rename button, which you choose to complete the change. Figure 28-9 shows the Format menu before and after the change. To change only the trigger key (to C), you change the text from its original Change Cas&e to &Change Case.

FIGURE 28-8

To change the name of a command, select the command, type the new name in the Name On Menu text box, and choose Rename.

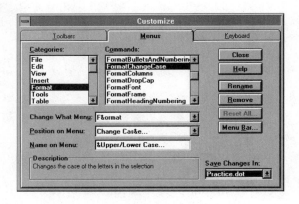

FIGURE 28-9

The before and after versions of the Format menu. The default menu is on the left. The changed menu, with Change Case renamed as Upper/Lower Case, is on the right.

Format		Format	
Font...		**Font...**	

Format
Font...
Paragraph...
Tabs...
Borders and Shading...
Columns...
Change Case...
Drop Cap...

Bullets and Numbering...
Heading Numbering...

AutoFormat...
Style Gallery...
Style...

Frame...
Picture...
Drawing Object...

Format
Font...
Paragraph...
Tabs...
Borders and Shading...
Columns...
Upper/Lower Case...
Drop Cap...

Bullets and Numbering...
Heading Numbering...

AutoFormat...
Style Gallery...
Style...

Frame...
Picture...
Drawing Object...

> **TIP**
>
> When you're looking for commands that are on the default menus, the command names will usually be a combination of the menu name and the menu-item name. The command for Change Case, for example, is FormatChangeCase; the command for Columns is FormatColumns. You can find these commands in the Commands list box by selecting the menu name in the Categories list box and then looking through the alphabetic list in the Commands list box.

How to move an item to or duplicate it on another menu

Suppose you'd like to move the Page Numbers command from the Insert menu to the View menu, where its close relative, Header And Footer, is located. Alternatively, you might like to create a duplicate command on the View menu and leave the original on the Insert menu so that you can choose it from either menu. This sort of multiple route to a given dialog box is already built into Word in many cases (with some of the Options cards, for example), and it helps minimize the number of times you'll search for a command because it's not where you expect it to be.

To duplicate a command, simply add it to another menu, using the standard procedure for adding menu items. You can add the same command to as many menus as you like, using the same name and trigger key or different names and trigger keys, as you prefer. To move a command, simply delete the item from one menu and add it to another.

How to change the position of a menu item

Although Word does not provide a specific command for changing the position of an item on a menu, you can still move any item however you like. Here again, you need only delete the menu item and then add it back—in this case, to the same menu but in a different position.

Macros, fonts, AutoText, and styles on menus

As we've already mentioned, the Categories list also includes choices for macros, fonts, AutoText, and styles. When adding, deleting, renaming, or otherwise working with items in any of these categories, follow the same procedure as when working with Word's built-in commands.

How to use separators

If you create or modify menus, you'll want to pay attention to separators—the horizontal lines that separate different sections of each menu and group related commands together. The default version of the File menu, for example, starts with all of the commands for opening and closing a file directly—New, Open, and Close—followed by a separator, followed by the commands for saving a file directly—Save, Save As, and Save All—followed by another separator.

You can add and delete separators much as you add and delete menu items. To add a separator, choose the (Separator) line in the Commands list box, as shown in Figure 28-10; use the Position On Menu box to select the

FIGURE 28-10

To add a separator, highlight the (Separator) line in the Commands list box, specify the position for the separator, and choose Add Below.

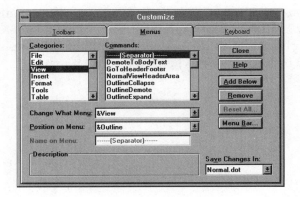

command below which you want the separator to go; and then choose Add Below. To delete a separator, select the separator you want to delete in the Position On Menu box, and choose Remove.

 Whatever choice you make in the Categories box, the (Separator) item will be the first choice in the second list box.

The Reset All button: Handle with care

The button second from bottom on the Customize Menus card is the Reset All button. You'll want to use this with care, if at all. As its name implies, this button resets every menu change you've made. If you choose it, Word will ask for confirmation before actually resetting the menus, but once you answer yes, you have no option for undoing the change.

The Reset All button does not reset menus back to where you started in the current session. It resets everything back to Word's defaults. In short, if you've customized your menus, choosing this button throws all of your customizations away. Note, however, that the reset applies only to changes stored in the template currently specified in the Save Changes In box.

How to recover from an accidental Reset All

As with macros and AutoText entries, Word doesn't try to save menu changes to disk until you choose the File Save All command, close the document that uses the supplementary template (if one is attached), or exit from Word and close the Normal template. To recover a supplementary template as it was last saved on disk, simply close all files that use that template, answer No when Word asks whether to save the changes, and reload the file or files you're working with. To recover the Normal template, first choose Tools Options, then choose the Save card, and make sure there's a check in the Prompt To Save Normal.dot check box. Then exit from Word and answer No when Word asks whether to save changes to NORMAL.DOT. The next time you start Word, it will reload the Normal template in its previous form.

As we pointed out in Chapter 24, this approach to recovering a template also loses any other changes you've made since the last time you saved the template to disk. And it provides a good argument for using the File Save All command whenever you've made changes you're satisfied with. Note also that it's a good idea to keep a backup of your template files, just as you should keep backups of your data files—whether on floppies, tape, removable cartridges, or another hard disk.

Renaming, Adding, and Deleting Menus

One of Word's most intriguing customization capabilities is that it will let you redefine even the menu names on the menu bar. In fact, you can add up to 30 additional menus to the menu bar, for a total of 39 menus. You can also delete and rename menus.

This feature is particularly useful if you're familiar with some other word processor and its menu logic. And if you've always thought you could do better than anything you've seen elsewhere, this feature, combined with the menu customization we've already discussed, gives you the ability to design your own menus from scratch.

With Word 2.0, the only way you could rename menus was with the RenameMenu macro command. Word 6.0 still accepts the RenameMenu command (though the syntax has changed), and it also provides a ToolsCustomizeMenuBar command (as well as other, related, WordBasic commands). More important, however, Word 6.0 provides a dialog box that makes it far easier to modify or add to the menu bar.

We won't cover either of these commands here because you can completely redefine the menu system without using them. Note, however, that it's useful to create a macro that will store your modifications so that, should you lose them, you can re-create them at any time. You can create that macro by recording your changes as you make them. Even if you don't make them all at once, you can record each one separately and then combine all of the commands into one macro, using Word's cut-and-paste features and other techniques we discussed in Chapter 25.

How to rename a menu or change the trigger key

Renaming a menu or changing the trigger key is much like renaming a menu item or changing its trigger key except that you make the changes in a menu through the Menu Bar dialog box, shown in Figure 28-11. To open the Menu Bar dialog box, first choose Tools Customize, and then go to the Menus card. Then choose the Menu Bar button.

FIGURE 28-11

You use the Menu Bar dialog box to add to or rename the menus on the menu bar.

To change a menu name or its trigger key, first select the menu in the Position On Menu Bar list box. Then type the new name for the item in the Name On Menu Bar text box, with an ampersand just before the letter you want to use as the trigger character. If you want to change the Format menu so that you can open it by typing Alt-F, for example, select Forma&t in the Position On Menu Bar box, and type *&Format* in the Name On Menu Bar box. Finish by choosing the Rename button. You can then make another change, or choose Close twice to close the Menu Bar dialog box and the Customize dialog box.

As with menu items, if you have more than one menu with the same trigger character, pressing that key will highlight one of the menus but not open it; pressing the key repeatedly will cycle through the choices. To open a menu, you have to press Enter when the menu name is highlighted. This would be the case with Alt-F, for example, if you assigned F to the Format menu without changing its assignment to the File menu.

How to add a menu

Adding a menu with the Menu Bar dialog box is similar to adding a menu item from the Menus card in the Customize dialog box. With the Menu Bar dialog box open, use the Position On Menu Bar button to define the position where you want the new menu. Choose First to put it in the leftmost position on the menu or Last to put it at the rightmost position (or wrap it around to another line). If you want to place the new menu between two existing menus, highlight the menu name that you want to have immediately before the menu you're adding.

After choosing the position, type the name for the menu in the Name On Menu Bar text box, along with an optional ampersand to indicate the trigger key. Finally, choose the Add button (which will change to Add After if you've highlighted one of the menu names in the Position On Menu Bar box). You can then close the Menu Bar dialog box to return to the Menus card and use the techniques we've already described to add menu items to the menu.

How to delete a menu

Deleting a menu with the Menu Bar dialog box is straightforward. Simply highlight the menu in the Position On Menu Bar list box, and choose Remove. Word will respond with a message box asking for confirmation. Answer Yes to confirm the deletion or No to return to the Menu Bar dialog box without deleting the menu. Note that removing the menu also removes all menu items assigned to it.

How to move a menu

Because deleting a menu removes all the menu items assigned to that menu, you can't easily move a menu by deleting it in one place and adding it in another. However, deleting and re-creating a menu is easier than you might expect. After deleting the menu and adding a replacement in another position, close the Menu Bar dialog box to return to the Menus card in the Customize dialog box. Then choose the appropriate category in the Categories list box, and work your way through the commands in the Commands list box, being careful to choose only those commands that you want on the menu.

If you are moving a standard Word menu, the names of most of the commands you want will closely match the combination of the original menu and menu item names. For example, ViewNormal is the command for the Normal choice on the View menu, and ViewOutline is the command for the Outline choice. There are some variations, however; the command for the Page Layout command, for example, is ViewPage.

Strategies for renaming menus

Word gives you the ability to completely redesign the menu system. But you should exercise some restraint and approach any changes with an overall design in mind. For example, you might want to keep the menus much as they are, but you'd like to press the first letter of each menu name to open the menu. Specifically, you may find it confusing to press O for Format and A for Table.

One possibility is to keep the default names but move the ampersand to the beginning of each word. If you do this, you'll have two menus that use F—File and Format—and two that use T—Tools and Table. As we pointed out earlier, if you then press Alt plus either of these letters, Word will highlight the first menu name with that letter. To get the second menu, you'll have to press the letter or Alt plus the letter again. And to open either menu from the keyboard, you'll have to highlight it first and then press Enter.

Although there is nothing wrong with this approach, you might consider renaming the menus altogether to avoid the conflict in trigger keys. For example, you could now rename the File menu &Document, change the Table menu to &Table, and rename the Tools menu &Utilities so that each menu starts with its own trigger key.

There is no reason to maintain Word's original menu logic. In fact, you can name the menus in any way that makes sense to you. Figure 28-12, for example, re-creates the Word for MS-DOS 5.0 menu choices. As you can see, the modified menu bar bears little relationship to the default Word for Windows menus.

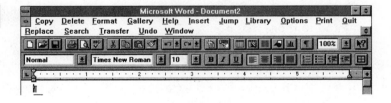

FIGURE 28-12

You can create just about any menu structure you like. The choices on this menu bar re-create the Word for MS-DOS 5.0 menus.

If you decide to redesign the menus from scratch, we recommend that you invest some time in designing a menu structure first. But don't be afraid to experiment—it's easy enough to go back to the default menus.

If you create a whole new set of menus for the menu bar, be careful not to close the Customize dialog box until you've added the ToolsCustomize command to one of your new menus or assigned it to a shortcut key. Otherwise, you won't be able to reopen the Customize dialog box to add commands to the menus.

Keyboard Customization

If you're like most people, you'll use the mouse a lot while you're learning Word because it's easier to point and click with the mouse than to remember arbitrary key combinations such as Ctrl-F2 for File Print Preview or Ctrl-K for Format AutoFormat. However, using the keyboard can be a faster way of choosing a command or performing other actions.

Word comes with a large number of shortcut keys already defined. (Appendix A includes a list of the default key assignments.) However, you can change any of them. Choose Tools Customize and then the Keyboard card to assign (or reassign) keys to built-in commands, macros, fonts, AutoText, and styles.

In addition, you can assign shortcut keys to a class of items that Word lists as Common Symbols. These symbols include foreign-language characters such as ç and é, typographical aids such as single and double curly quotes for better-looking output (' ' and " " instead of ' and "), and such common symbols as ™ for trademark and © for copyright. In all cases, you can assign the shortcut keys both to items that come with shortcut keys defined and to those that don't.

The Options Keyboard dialog box

The Keyboard card in the Customize dialog box is similar to the Menus card, which we discussed earlier in this chapter.

As we suggested earlier, if you want to practice with Word as you read through this discussion, start with a new, blank document and attach a practice template to it. Then choose Tools Customize and choose the Keyboard card to open the dialog box shown in Figure 28-13.

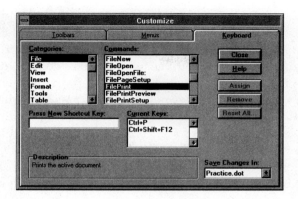

FIGURE 28-13

Use the Keyboard card in the Customize dialog box to assign shortcut keys.

How to tell Word where to store your keyboard customizations

The Save Changes In box in the lower right corner of the dialog box works the same way for key assignments as the equivalent box in the Menus card works for Menu assignments. Your choice of either NORMAL.DOT or the supplementary template determines both what you see in the Current Keys list box and where Word stores any changes you make. If you choose NORMAL.DOT, the Current Keys list box will display the current settings in the Normal template, and Word will store your changes there; if you select the supplementary template, the list will display the current settings in the current supplementary template, and Word will store your changes there instead.

Here again, if you created PRACTICE.DOT by copying NORMAL.DOT to the new filename, you'll start out with identical key assignments in the Normal and practice templates. If you switch back and forth between the two, you won't see any difference in the Current Keys list box. After you make changes, however, you will see differences.

The Categories, Commands, and Current Keys list boxes

The Categories box and the second list box, labeled Commands in Figure 28-13, are similar to their counterparts on the Menus card. The title on the second list box changes to match the category you've selected: Macros, Fonts, AutoText, Styles, or Common Symbols. We described these list boxes in detail in "How to assign an item to a menu" on page 955.

The one difference between these two boxes and the two on the Menus card is the extra category Common Symbols.

We've also covered most of what you need to know about the Press New Shortcut Key and Current Keys boxes in Chapter 24. Briefly, the Current Keys list box will display the shortcut keys currently assigned to whatever item you've selected with the two list boxes above. You assign a shortcut key in the Press New Shortcut Key box by pressing the keys you want to use. Word will display the key names in the Press New Shortcut Key box and add a message just below the box either identifying the command the key is currently assigned to, as in Figure 28-14, or stating that the key is currently unassigned, as in Figure 28-15. You can then either assign the keystrokes to the new command by choosing the Assign button or press Backspace to remove the entry and then press different keys instead. For a more detailed look at this part of the Keyboard card, see "How to assign a macro to a shortcut key" on page 849.

FIGURE 28-14

If the keystrokes you enter in the Press New Shortcut Key box are already assigned to a command, Word will tell you which one.

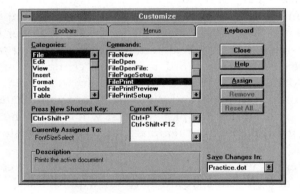

FIGURE 28-15

If the keystrokes you enter in the Press New Shortcut Key box are not already assigned to a command, Word will tell you so.

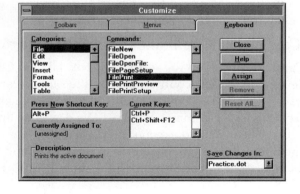

The Currently Assigned To line in the Keyboard card is all the warning you get when reassigning a key. Be sure to look at this line before choosing Assign to ensure that you're not reassigning a shortcut key that you may need later. In general, it's best not to reassign keys unless you're sure you'll never need the original assignments. In particular, we recommend leaving the default keys alone until you're ready to design your own fully customized interface.

You can define shortcut keys using Alt, Ctrl, Alt-Shift, Ctrl-Shift, or Alt-Ctrl-Shift in combination with most other keys, including any alphabetic character, any number, the function keys F1 through F12 (except Shift-F1), and most other keys on the keyboard (including Ins, Del, Home, End, PgUp, PgDn, and the arrow keys). In addition, you can use function keys F2 through F12 by themselves. You can also define multiple-keystroke assignments, such as Ctrl-P followed by P, which we'll indicate as Ctrl-P,P. For the last keystroke, you can use a key by itself or with the Shift key, but you cannot use the Ctrl or Alt key as part of the last keystroke.

In Word 2.0, you couldn't assign certain keys—notably, Alt-key combinations—except through the ToolsOptionsKeyboard command in WordBasic. Word 6.0 does not recognize ToolsOptions-Keyboard; instead, it uses the ToolsCustomizeKeyboard command.

We won't discuss this command because you can assign almost any keystroke through the menus. Note, however, that it can be useful to create a macro that will store your modifications so that, should you lose them, you can re-create them at any time. As with menu assignments, you can create that macro by recording your changes as you make them. Even if you don't make all of your keystroke customizations at the same time, you can record each one separately and then combine all of the commands into one macro, using Word's cut-and-paste features and other techniques we discussed in Chapter 25.

You can also create multiple shortcut keys for any command. This may seem superfluous, but it can come in handy. For example, suppose a colleague sometimes uses your computer. One of you likes using function keys and has all of Word's default shortcut keys memorized, including such arcane choices as Ctrl-F2 (Print Preview). The other prefers mnemonic shortcuts and wants to use, say, Ctrl-P,P for File Print Preview. The ability to define multiple shortcut keys for each command lets each of you use the shortcut keys you prefer. Note, however, that if two users have completely different ideas about how to customize Word, it would make more sense to create two separate templates—one for each user.

The ability to assign multiple-keystroke shortcut keys to a macro does more than simply increase the number of key combinations available. It also makes it easier to make mnemonic key assignments. With single-step shortcut keys, you will quickly run out of mnemonics and be forced into arbitrary choices that are hard to remember. With multiple-keystroke shortcut keys, you can use extensive mnemonics that make it much easier to remember your shortcut keys.

For example, suppose you have two printers—a black-and-white laser printer for text and a thermal wax transfer printer for color graphics. You might define Ctrl-P,L for the laser printer and Ctrl-P,C for the color printer. In fact, you could create a number of printing macros and have them all start with Ctrl-P: Ctrl-P,S to print the current selection, Ctrl-P,P for the current page, and so on.

The trick is to use the first keystroke to group macros into conceptual categories that are easy to remember—in this case, all printing macros. But, just as important, be sure to reserve the first keystroke for only those macros; don't assign it to macros used for other purposes.

How to delete shortcut keys

Deleting, or removing, key assignments is even easier than adding them. Suppose you decide, after you've added Ctrl-P,P as a shortcut key for FilePrintPreview, that you don't want to use it after all, since it means you can no longer use the default Ctrl-P for printing the active document. Simply select FilePrintPreview in the Commands list box, select the shortcut key you want to remove in the Current Keys list box, and choose Remove. Figure 28-16, for example, shows Ctrl-P,P highlighted prior to deletion. Note that you cannot select multiple shortcut keys to delete more than one at a time.

FIGURE 28-16

To delete a shortcut key, highlight it in the Current Keys list box, and then choose the Remove button.

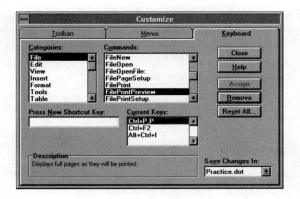

How to assign shortcut keys to macros, fonts, AutoText, styles, and common symbols

When you select any of the items in the Categories list, Word changes the label on the second list box to match your selection and displays a list of all the specified items. You can then assign shortcut keys to, or remove them from, any of these items.

For macros, if you choose NORMAL.DOT in the Save Changes In box, Word will display all of the specified items stored in the Normal template. If you choose the supplementary template, Word will display all of the specified items stored in both templates. This makes sense because if you have a macro stored in the Normal template, you can assign a shortcut key to it in the supplementary template, and you can assign different keystrokes in different templates. Thus, different users can use their own preferred shortcut keys for any item stored in the Normal template.

The Reset All button: Handle with care

The Reset All button on the Keyboard card works like its counterpart on the Menus card. Again, you'll want to use this button with care because it resets every key assignment you've made in the currently selected template. And again, the settings revert to Word's defaults, not to the settings you had when you started the current session.

As with the Reset All button for menu assignments, the reset applies only to changes stored in the template currently specified in the Save Changes In box.

Most important, as with the menu assignments, if you accidentally choose the Reset All button, you can go back to the last settings you saved on disk. The technique is identical to the one we described in the section "How to recover from an accidental Reset All" on page 963.

How to save menu and key assignments

The reason you can recover from accidentally choosing the Reset All button is that Word doesn't save your menu or key assignments to disk when you make those assignments. Rather, Word follows exactly the same strategy that it does with AutoText entries and macros.

Word holds the changes in memory; unless told otherwise, it will eventually save the changes on disk in one of two ways. If you made the changes in the Normal template, Word will wait until you exit from the program with the File Exit command. It will then simply save NORMAL.DOT or, if you've set the program to prompt before saving NORMAL.DOT, it will then announce that you've made changes in NORMAL.DOT and ask whether you want to save the changes. (To set Word to prompt before saving changes, select Tools Options, select the Save card, and add a check to the Prompt To Save Normal.dot checkbox.) If the changes are in a supplementary template, Word will ask whether to save them when you close the document attached to that template or when you exit Word, whichever comes first. In either case—for NORMAL.DOT or for the supplementary template—you can choose Yes or No, as appropriate, to tell Word to save or not.

It's generally much safer to save your changes as soon as you can. You can force Word to save all current files—including any changes to menu and key assignments—by choosing File Save All. For each currently open template that you've changed since the last save, Word will display a message box asking whether to save the changes. You can choose Yes or No for each one individually, or you can return to your document without saving by choosing Cancel.

How to print key assignments

After you define some custom key assignments, you may want to have a reference sheet listing them. To print such a list, choose File Print and open the Print What drop-down list. Choose Key Assignments, and then choose OK. Word will print a list of customized key assignments for the Normal template and for any currently attached supplementary template.

Another Macro Shortcut

As we've said, Word's ability to define shortcut keys with multiple keystrokes rather than with one keystroke opens the door to much more useful shortcut keys. However, even with Word's multiple-keystroke shortcuts, if you forget the mnemonics, you are forced to use the menu commands.

This can be a problem with macros that you run infrequently. You use shortcut keys for their speed. But if you forget the shortcuts, you need another convenient way to run the macro. Fortunately, Word can solve this problem, letting you have your shortcut keys and read them too. Here's how.

Figure 28-17 shows the macro we developed in Chapter 26 when discussing custom dialog boxes. We've made a slight change, however, so that the option button names now read HP PCL and Color Postscript, to match a scenario in which we have two printers—a Hewlett-Packard LaserJet and a color PostScript printer. We've adjusted the size of the two option buttons so that the full text for each will be displayed in the dialog box.

FIGURE 28-17

When you run this macro, it displays a dialog box with two option buttons.

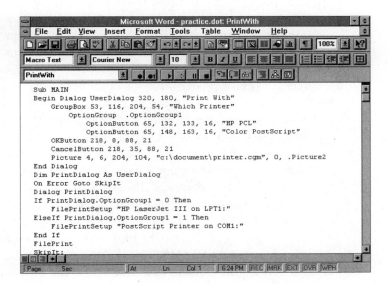

If you find it difficult to understand how this macro works, you might want to look back at "Designing custom dialog boxes with the Dialog Editor" on page 910 before you read the rest of this section. Briefly, this macro opens a dialog box like the one shown in Figure 28-18 on the next page. The dialog box has two option buttons, one each for the PCL and the color PostScript printer. When you select one and choose OK, the macro sets Word for the appropriate printer and gives the command to print the current file.

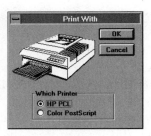

FIGURE 28-18

The macro in Figure 28-17 displays this Print With dialog box.

Push buttons

The part of this macro we're primarily concerned with here is the dialog box. We are going to replace the option buttons with push buttons, and then we'll change a few other items that relate to this primary change. The result will be fully equivalent to assigning two-key macros. In fact, it will have some advantages that two-key macros don't have.

A push button is similar in many ways to an OK button or a Cancel button in a dialog box: Choosing it closes the dialog box and initiates a specific action. You can build push buttons into dialog boxes by applying the same techniques we discussed in Chapter 26 for custom dialog boxes. In the present case, we'll simply replace the option buttons that are already there with push buttons of the same name.

The syntax for push buttons is nearly identical to that for option buttons, so we'll start by replacing the word *OptionButton* with the word *PushButton* in the two places where it occurs in the macro. We'll also delete the lines for OptionGroup and GroupBox, since push buttons aren't grouped together the way option buttons are. And we'll add an ampersand in front of the first character in each button name. This works just like the ampersands in menu names. When Word displays the dialog box, it will underline the character just after the ampersand in the macro. The user can choose the button from the keyboard by pressing the key for the underlined character.

You also need to change the part of the macro that determines which button you choose. Note that the original macro tests to see which option button you chose. As you would probably expect, the push buttons need a different command.

First you have to change the Dialog statement from

Dialog PrintDialog

to

Button = Dialog(PrintDialog)

Next you have to change the If...Else...End If statement to

If Button = 1 Then

    FilePrintSetup "HP LaserJet III on LPT1:"

ElseIf Button = 2 Then

    FilePrintSetup "PostScript Printer on COM1:"

Else

    Goto SkipIt:

EndIf

 Notice the addition of an Else statement at the end. This is needed with the PushButton commands to tell Word to skip over the printing step if you choose the Cancel button instead of either push button. (Notice also that push buttons, unlike option buttons, start numbering from 1, not 0.)

You should also delete the OK button in this example; it no longer serves any purpose because the macro will react immediately to either of the push buttons. Finally, you should delete the On Error statement, which also no longer serves any purpose. You should leave the Cancel button, however, so that you can close the dialog box without printing if you open it by accident. After you finish, the macro should look like the one shown in Figure 28-19.

FIGURE 28-19

This macro will create a dialog box that includes only push buttons and a Cancel button.

```
Microsoft Word - practice.dot: PrintWith
 File  Edit  View  Insert  Format  Tools  Table  Window  Help

Macro Text    Courier New      10    B I U

PrintWith

    Sub MAIN
    Begin Dialog UserDialog 412, 116, "Print With"
        PushButton 233, 25, 163, 16, "&HP PCL"
        PushButton 233, 47, 163, 16, "&Color PostScript"
        CancelButton 270, 78, 88, 21
        Picture 4, 6, 204, 104, "c:\document\printer.cgm", 0, .Picture2
    End Dialog
    Dim PrintDialog As UserDialog
    Button = Dialog(PrintDialog)
    If Button = 1 Then
        FilePrintSetup "HP LaserJet III on LPT1:"
    ElseIf Button = 2 Then
        FilePrintSetup "PostScript Printer on COM1:"
    Else
        Goto SkipIt
    End If
    FilePrint
    SkipIt:
    End Sub

Page      Sec          At      Ln      Col 1      6:34 PM  REC MRK EXT OVR WPH
```

We've moved the position of the buttons and changed the dialog box shape to create a neater appearance. The dialog box you see when you run the macro should look like the one in Figure 28-20.

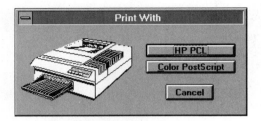

The final flourish

All that remains now, to realize the magic of multiple-keystroke macros combined with on-screen menus, is to assign a shortcut key to the macro that opens the dialog box, by using the techniques we described earlier in this chapter. Because this macro is meant for printing, you might use Alt-P. And that's it. You can now press Alt-P,H to call up the dialog box and print with the HP printer, or you can press Alt-P,C to print with the Color PostScript printer.

Nor is this all. Early on in discussing push buttons, we mentioned that building the equivalent of multiple-keystroke shortcut keys with push buttons had advantages over being able to assign two keys directly. In fact, there are two advantages.

First, there is no need to limit yourself to two-key mnemonics. You can build a macro that opens more than one dialog box so that you could, for example, press Alt-P,S,H to print the current selection on your HP printer or Alt-P,P,H to print the current page on the HP printer.

More interesting is that the dialog box provides what amounts to a Help screen for your shortcut keys. If you remember the full mnemonic and if you can type the keystrokes quickly enough, the dialog box will only briefly flash on your screen. But if you hesitate after Alt-P, Word will show you the dialog box complete with the push buttons for all macros and commands that are available through that dialog box. If you organize your macros with dialog boxes in ways that make sense to you, you don't have to remember each key sequence. You need remember only the first key; you can pick the rest from the dialog box.

You can even combine both advantages of push-button–based mnemonic shortcuts to create what amounts to a master dialog box that will function as a Help system for all of your shortcut keys. Simply define a dialog box that includes push buttons for all other shortcut-key dialog boxes and that will also call them up for you. Then assign to this master dialog box any shortcut key you can easily remember.

If you remember the shortcut key for any other dialog box, you can go to that box directly. If you forget the key, you can open the master dialog box, pick the dialog box to go to, and then pick the shortcut key in that box. This is particularly useful for shortcut keys that you don't use regularly but that you need to use repeatedly when you're using them at all—such as shortcut keys for building an index.

If you've followed the discussion through Part Five, by now you know enough to build what amounts to your own user interface for Word. Odds are you'll never need to customize the program so completely, but you'll be able to customize it as much as you need to. And as you'll discover, that's one of the real advantages of Word.

PART SIX

APPENDIXES

TOPIC FINDER

Mouse Fundamentals   983

Keyboard Fundamentals   984

Keyboard Shortcuts   985

- Cursor movement shortcuts   985
- Copy, cut, and paste shortcuts   986
- Deletion shortcuts for text and graphics   986
- Field-related shortcuts   987
- Formatting shortcuts   987
    Character (font) formatting   987
    Inserting special characters   988
    Paragraph formatting   989
    Style formatting   990
    Page formatting   990
- Mail merge shortcuts   990
- Outline editing shortcuts   991
- Selection shortcuts   991
- Table editing shortcuts   992
- Shortcut keys for moving among panes and windows and for moving windows   992
- Shortcut keys for menu commands   992

Mouse & Keyboard
Techniques

ike other Windows-based applications, Word makes good use of the mouse for many tasks. But if you prefer to keep your hands on the keyboard, you'll find that Word caters to your preferences as well, by offering at least one keyboard route to almost all features.

In this appendix, we'll quickly review the basic mouse and keyboard techniques for using menus and dialog boxes. We'll then list the keyboard shortcuts that let you bypass the menus. If you use Word a lot, you'll find that these shortcuts make the program faster and more efficient to use.

Also keep in mind that you can easily define your own keyboard shortcuts for both standard and custom tasks. (See Chapter 28 for more information on how to customize the program to suit your own needs and preferences.)

Mouse Fundamentals

There are four basic mouse operations: the click, the double-click, the drag, and the right button menus.

To click on an object or a region of the screen, position the mouse pointer and press the left mouse button once. (There are a few operations that use the right mouse button, but unless the right button is specified, you can safely assume that any instruction to click on something refers to using the left mouse button. Note also that you can use the mouse options in the Windows Control Panel to swap the left and right mouse button functions if you prefer.)

A double-click simply means pressing the left button twice in fairly rapid succession. The word "fairly" is imprecise, but then, so are the parameters for double-clicking. With the Windows default setting, a double-click will register if you make two clicks in less than about a half second. However, you can change this, using the mouse options in the Windows Control Panel, so that the two clicks either have to be closer together or can be farther apart. In general, you'll want to set this so that Windows will register a double-click every time you intend one, without having such a wide window that Windows will interpret two single clicks as a double-click.

The third technique is dragging. To drag, press and hold down the left mouse button while you move the mouse. When you reach the desired location, release the mouse button. Dragging is most often used for selecting text or graphics. The word *drag* is also used in a related, although somewhat different, operation called drag and drop. To drag and drop selected text or a graphics object from one location to another, select what you want to move, position the mouse pointer on the highlighted object, press the left mouse button, and move the mouse while still holding down the button. When the pointer reaches the desired location, release the button to drop the object into place.

Clicking the right mouse button in Word is worth a special mention because when you click on an object using the right button, Word offers a context-sensitive menu, with the context determined by the object you clicked on. All commands on the context-sensitive menus are also available through the pull-down menus, but because the right-button menus are context sensitive, they are limited to those commands that you are most likely to need.

Keyboard Fundamentals

There are a few standard keyboard functions that apply throughout Windows. Most important are the keyboard combinations for using menus. You can, for example, press the Alt key or F10 to activate the menu bar, and then press the letter key corresponding to the letter that's underlined in the menu's name, such as F for File or O for Format. (Remember also that you can change the menu names and their underlined letters, as discussed in Chapter 28.) After you open a menu, you can press the key for the underlined letter in the command you want, without using the Alt key.

When you are working with a dialog box, you can hold down the Alt key and press the key for the underlined letter in the option you want, or you can use the Tab key to move from one option to the next. When a dialog box has a command button with a heavy border around it, you can choose this button simply by pressing the Enter key.

Keyboard Shortcuts

Word's keyboard shortcuts can dramatically speed up your writing and editing. The following list of most-often-used shortcuts is organized by function, except for menu-command shortcuts, which are listed separately at the end.

Cursor movement shortcuts

To Move	Press
Left one character	Left arrow
Right one character	Right arrow
Left one word	Ctrl-Left arrow
Right one word	Ctrl-Right arrow
Up one line	Up arrow
Down one line	Down arrow
To the beginning of the current line	Home
To the end of the current line	End
Up one paragraph (or, in a table, one paragraph to the left)	Ctrl-Up arrow
Down one paragraph (or, in a table, one paragraph to the right)	Ctrl-Down arrow
To the top of the screen	Ctrl-PgUp
To the bottom of the screen	Ctrl-PgDn
Up one screen	PgUp
Down one screen	PgDn
Up one page	Alt-Ctrl-PgUp
Down one page	Alt-Ctrl-PgDn
To the start of the document	Ctrl-Home
To the end of the document	Ctrl-End
To a specified location	F5
To a previous location	Shift-F5
To the previous frame or object	Alt-Up arrow
To the next frame or object	Alt-Down arrow
To the next field	F11 or Alt-F1
To the previous field	Shift-F11 or Alt-Shift-F1

See also "Table editing shortcuts" later in this appendix.

Copy, cut, and paste shortcuts

To	Press
With the Clipboard	
Cut	Ctrl-X or Shift-Del
Copy	Ctrl-C or Ctrl-Ins
Paste	Ctrl-V or Shift-Ins or Ins (when the Use The INS Key For Paste option is turned on)
Without the Clipboard	
Copy	Shift-F2
Move	F2
With the Spike	
Place selection on the Spike	Ctrl-F3
Insert contents of the Spike and empty the Spike	Ctrl-Shift-F3
Insert contents of the Spike without emptying the Spike	Type *spike*, and then press F3 or Ctrl-Alt-V
Format Only	
Copy format	Ctrl-Shift-C
Paste format	Ctrl-Shift-V

Deletion shortcuts for text and graphics

To Delete	Press
One character to the left of the cursor, or the current selection	Backspace
From the cursor position (or the beginning of the selection) to the beginning of the word to the left	Ctrl-Backspace
One character to the right of the cursor, or the current selection	Del
From the cursor position (or the beginning of the selection) to the end of the first word to the right	Ctrl-Del

Field-related shortcuts

To	Press
Insert a DATE field	Alt-Shift-D
Insert a PAGE field	Alt-Shift-P
Insert a TIME field	Alt-Shift-T
Insert a blank field	Ctrl-F9
Update a field result	F9
Toggle between a field code and the field result for the field or fields the cursor or selection is in	Shift-F9
Toggle between field codes and field results for the entire document	Alt-F9
Update a source for an INCLUDETEXT field	Ctrl-Shift-F7
Unlink a field	Ctrl-Shift-F9
Lock a field	Ctrl-F11 or Ctrl-3
Unlock a field	Ctrl-Shift-F11 or Ctrl-4
Initiate the action defined in a GOTOBUTTON or MACRO-BUTTON field after positioning the cursor in the field (equivalent to double-clicking on the field)	Alt-Shift-F9
Go to the next field	F11 or Alt-F1
Go to the previous field	Shift-F11 or Alt-Shift-F1

Formatting shortcuts

Character (font) formatting

To Change the Font Format to or from	Press
Boldface	Ctrl-B
Italic	Ctrl-I
Double underline	Ctrl-Shift-D
Underline words and spaces	Ctrl-U

(continued)

Character (font) formatting *continued*

To Change the Font Format to or from	Press
Underline words only	Ctrl-Shift-W
All capital letters	Ctrl-Shift-A
Small capital letters	Ctrl-Shift-K
All uppercase, all lowercase, or first letter uppercase	Shift-F3
Subscript	Ctrl-Equal sign
Superscript	Ctrl-Shift-Equal sign
Hidden text	Ctrl-Shift-H

To	Press
Open Formatting toolbar font list	Ctrl-Shift-F
Open Formatting toolbar points list	Ctrl-Shift-P
Open Font dialog box	Ctrl-Shift-F twice or Ctrl-Shift-P twice (or either one once if Formatting toolbar is not visible)
Grow Font (increase to next available size)	Ctrl-Shift->
Shrink Font (decrease to next available size)	Ctrl-Shift-<
Grow font size by 1 point	Ctrl-]
Shrink font size by 1 point	Ctrl-[
Remove all direct font formatting	Ctrl-Spacebar or Ctrl-Shift-Z

Inserting special characters

To Insert	Press
Em dash	Alt-Ctrl-NumPad Minus
En dash	Ctrl-NumPad Minus
Nonbreaking hyphen	Ctrl-Shift-Hyphen
Optional hyphen	Ctrl-Hyphen
Nonbreaking space	Ctrl-Shift-Space
Copyright symbol	Alt-Ctrl-C
Registered symbol	Alt-Ctrl-R
Trademark symbol	Alt-Ctrl-T
Ellipsis	Alt-Ctrl-Period

(continued)

Inserting special characters *continued*

To Insert	Press
Single Opening Quote	Ctrl-Accent Grave, Accent Grave
Single Closing Quote	Ctrl-Apostrophe, Apostrophe
Double Opening Quote	Ctrl-Accent Grave, Double Quote
Double Closing Quote	Ctrl-Apostrophe, Double Quote
Any character using the Symbol font (for next character only)	Ctrl-Shift-Q

To View	Press
Nonprinting characters	Ctrl-Shift-Asterisk

Paragraph formatting

To Set the Paragraph to	Press
Left aligned	Ctrl-L
Center aligned	Ctrl-E
Right aligned	Ctrl-R
Justified	Ctrl-J
Single spacing	Ctrl-1
$1^1/_2$ spacing	Ctrl-5
Double spacing	Ctrl-2

To	Press
Move paragraph indent one tab stop to the right	Ctrl-M
Move paragraph indent one tab stop to the left	Ctrl-Shift- M
Move left indent, but not the first-line indent, one tab stop to the right to create a hanging indent	Ctrl-T
Move left indent, but not the first-line indent, one tab stop to the left	Ctrl-Shift-T
Toggle one line of space before paragraph on and off	Ctrl-0 (zero)
Remove all direct paragraph formatting	Ctrl-Q

Style formatting

To	Press
Open Formatting toolbar styles list	Ctrl-Shift-S
Open Style dialog box	Ctrl-Shift-S twice (or once if Formatting toolbar is not visible)
AutoFormat the document, without stopping at the AutoFormat dialog boxes	Ctrl-K
Format with the Normal style	Ctrl-Shift-N
Format with the Heading 1 style	Alt-Ctrl-1
Format with the Heading 2 style	Alt-Ctrl-2
Format with the Heading 3 style	Alt-Ctrl-3
Format with the List Bullet style	Ctrl-Shift-L

Page formatting

To Start a	Press
New paragraph	Enter
New line (but continue paragraph)	Shift-Enter
New page	Ctrl-Enter
New column (or split a table)	Ctrl-Shift-Enter

Mail merge shortcuts

To	Press
Check a mail merge for errors	Alt-Shift-K
Merge a document	Alt-Shift-N
Print the merged document	Alt-Shift-M
Edit a mail merge data document	Alt-Shift-E
Insert a merge field	Alt-Shift-F

Outline editing shortcuts

To	Press
Promote a paragraph or selection	Alt-Shift-Left arrow
Demote a paragraph or selection	Alt-Shift-Right arrow
Demote a paragraph or selection to body text	Ctrl-Shift-N
Move a paragraph or paragraphs up	Alt-Shift-Up arrow
Move a paragraph or paragraphs down	Alt-Shift-Down arrow
Expand text under a heading	Alt-Shift-Equal sign, or the plus on the numeric keypad
Collapse text under a heading	Alt-Shift-Hyphen, or the minus on the numeric keypad
Show all text and headings	Alt-Shift-A, or the asterisk on the numeric keypad
Display character formatting	The forward slash (/) on the numeric keypad
Toggle between showing all body text and showing the first line of body text	Alt-Shift-L
Show all headings up to and including level n	Alt-Shift-n (where n is any number from 1 through 9)

Selection shortcuts *

To	Press
Select the entire document	Ctrl-A
Select a block of text as you move the cursor	F8, and then arrow keys and other cursor movement keys
Select a block of text from the current cursor position to the next occurrence of the character	F8, and then any character
Collapse the size of the current selection	Shift-F8
Select a vertical block of text	Ctrl-Shift-F8, and then use arrow keys
Cancel selection mode	Esc

*You can also press Shift in combination with most cursor movement shortcuts to select text as you move the cursor.

Table editing shortcuts

To	Press
Move right one cell OR move to the first cell in the next row if currently in the last cell of a row, OR create a new row if currently in the last cell of the last row of the table. (Will highlight all the text in the cell you move to.)	Tab
Move left one cell OR move to the last cell in the previous row if currently in the first cell of a row. (Will highlight all the text in the cell you move to.)	Shift-Tab
Move to the first cell in the current row	Alt-Home
Move to the last cell in the current row	Alt-End
Move to the first cell in the current column	Alt-PgUp
Move to the last cell in the current column	Alt-PgDn
Insert a tab character in a cell	Ctrl-Tab
Select the entire table	Alt-NumPad5 (5 on the numeric keypad with NumLock off)
Split the table into two tables, inserting a paragraph mark above the row the cursor is currently in	Ctrl-Shift-Enter

Shortcut keys for moving among panes and windows and for moving windows

To	Press
Go to the next pane	F6
Go to the previous pane	Shift-F6
Go to the next document window	Ctrl-F6 or Alt-F6
Go to the previous document window	Ctrl-Shift-F6 or Alt-Shift-F6
Move a non-maximized document window	Ctrl-F7, followed by arrow keys, and then Enter

Shortcut keys for menu commands

For This Command	Press This Key or Combination
File Menu	
New	Ctrl-N
Open	Ctrl-O or Alt-Ctrl-F2 or Ctrl-F12

(continued)

Shortcut keys for menu commands *continued*

For This Command	Press This Key or Combination
File Menu *continued*	
Close	Ctrl-W or Ctrl-F4
Save	Ctrl-S or Shift-F12 or Alt-Shift-F2
Save As	F12
Print Preview	Ctrl-F2
Print	Ctrl-P or Ctrl-Shift-F12
Exit	Alt-F4
Edit menu	
Undo	Ctrl-Z
Repeat	Ctrl-Y or F4 or Alt-Enter
Cut	Ctrl-X
Copy	Ctrl-C
Paste	Ctrl-V
Clear	Delete
Select All	Ctrl-A
Find	Ctrl-F
Repeat Find	Shift-F4 or Alt-Ctrl-Y
Replace	Ctrl-H
Go To	Ctrl-G
Bookmark	Ctrl-Shift-F5
View Menu	
Normal	Alt-Ctrl-N
Outline	Alt-Ctrl-O
Page Layout	Alt-Ctrl-P
Insert Menu	
Page Numbers	Alt-Shift-P
Annotation	Alt-Ctrl-A
Date and Time	Alt-Shift-D
Footnote	Alt-Ctrl-F
Endnote	Alt-Ctrl-E
Mark Index Entry	Alt-Shift-X
Mark Citation Entry	Alt-Shift-I
Mark TOC Entry	Alt-Shift-O
Format Menu	
Font	Ctrl-D
Change Case	Shift-F3

(continued)

Shortcut keys for menu commands *continued*

For This Command	Press This Key or Combination
Format Menu *continued*	
AutoFormat	Ctrl-K
Style	Ctrl-Shift-S,Ctrl-Shift-S (press key combination twice)
Tools Menu	
Spelling	F7
Thesaurus	Shift-F7
Table Menu	
Select Table	Alt-NumPad 5 (on the numeric keypad with NumLock off)
Window Menu	
Split	Alt-Ctrl-S
Help Menu	
Contents	F1
Context-Sensitive Help	Shift-F1
Microsoft System Info	Alt-Ctrl-F1

ANSI & OEM Codes

very letter, number, punctuation mark, and other symbol you can enter in a Word document is defined by a code. This appendix lists all the characters in the two standard code sets—the ANSI character set and the OEM character set (also called the IBM Extended character set). The first 128 characters in each of these character sets are the same and are called the ASCII character set.

The characters in the ANSI and OEM character sets can be inserted using the Insert Symbol dialog box. To see the ANSI set most clearly, set the font on the Symbols card to (normal text). You'll notice that there are other characters, not part of the ANSI character set, that are part of the (normal text) font. To access the OEM character set, set the font on the Symbols card to MS LineDraw.

Both ANSI and OEM characters can also be inserted by typing codes with the numeric keypad. First make sure that NumLock is turned on. To insert an ANSI character, hold down the Alt key, type a zero, and then use the numeric keypad to type the character's code number as listed in the table beginning on the next page. Inserting an OEM character is a little more complicated. If the character in the OEM set has a code of 175 or below, hold down the Alt key and type the code number without a leading zero. If the character in the OEM set has a code above 175, you must first set the font in Word to MS LineDraw before typing the leading zero and the code.

Code	ANSI	OEM	Code	ANSI	OEM
0–31			71	G	G
32	(space)	(space)	72	H	H
33	!	!	73	I	I
34	"	"	74	J	J
35	#	#	75	K	K
36	$	$	76	L	L
37	%	%	77	M	M
38	&	&	78	N	N
39	'	'	79	O	O
40	(	(	80	P	P
41	)	)	81	Q	Q
42	*	*	82	R	R
43	+	+	83	S	S
44	,	,	84	T	T
45	-	-	85	U	U
46	.	.	86	V	V
47	/	/	87	W	W
48	0	0	88	X	X
49	1	1	89	Y	Y
50	2	2	90	Z	Z
51	3	3	91	[	[
52	4	4	92	\	\
53	5	5	93	]	]
54	6	6	94	^	^
55	7	7	95	_	_
56	8	8	96	`	`
57	9	9	97	a	a
58	:	:	98	b	b
59	;	;	99	c	c
60	<	<	100	d	d
61	=	=	101	e	e
62	>	>	102	f	f
63	?	?	103	g	g
64	@	@	104	h	h
65	A	A	105	i	i
66	B	B	106	j	j
67	C	C	107	k	k
68	D	D	108	l	l
69	E	E	109	m	m
70	F	F	110	n	n

Code	ANSI	OEM	Code	ANSI	OEM
111	o	o	151		ù
112	p	p	152		ÿ
113	q	q	153		Ö
114	r	r	154		Ü
115	s	s	155		¢
116	t	t	156		£
117	u	u	157		¥
118	v	v	158		₧
119	w	w	159		ƒ
120	x	x	160		á
121	y	y	161	¡	í
122	z	z	162	¢	ó
123	{	{	163	£	ú
124	|	|	164	¤	ñ
125	}	}	165	¥	Ñ
126	~	~	166	¦	ª
127			167	§	º
128		Ç	168	¨	¿
129		ü	169	©	⌐
130		é	170	ª	¬
131		â	171	«	½
132		ä	172	¬	¼
133		à	173	-	¡
134		å	174	®	«
135		ç	175	¯	»
136		ê	176	°	░
137		ë	177	±	▒
138		è	178	²	▓
139		ï	179	³	│
140		î	180	´	┤
141		ì	181	µ	╡
142		Ä	182	¶	╢
143		Å	183	·	╖
144		É	184	¸	╕
145	'	æ	185	¹	╣
146	'	Æ	186	º	║
147		ô	187	»	╗
148		ö	188	¼	╝
149		ò	189	½	╜
150		û	190	¾	╛

(continued)

continued

Code	ANSI	OEM	Code	ANSI	OEM
191	¿	┐	231	ç	τ
192	À	└	232	è	Φ
193	Á	┴	233	é	Θ
194	Â	┬	234	ê	Ω
195	Ã	├	235	ë	δ
196	Ä	─	236	ì	∞
197	Å	┼	237	í	ø
198	Æ	╞	238	î	ε
199	Ç	╟	239	ï	∩
200	È	╚	240	ð	≡
201	É	╔	241	ñ	±
202	Ê	╩	242	ò	≥
203	Ë	╦	243	ó	≤
204	Ì	╠	244	ô	⌠
205	Í	═	245	õ	⌡
206	Î	╬	246	ö	÷
207	Ï	╧	247	÷	≈
208	Ð	╨	248	ø	°
209	Ñ	╤	249	ù	•
210	Ò	╥	250	ú	·
211	Ó	╙	251	û	√
212	Ô	╘	252	ü	ⁿ
213	Õ	╒	253	ý	²
214	Ö	╓	254	þ	■
215	×	╫	255	ÿ	
216	Ø	╪			
217	Ù	┘			
218	Ú	┌			
219	Û	█			
220	Ü	▄			
221	Ý	▌			
222	Þ	▐			
223	ß	▀			
224	à	α			
225	á	ß			
226	â	Γ			
227	ã	π			
228	ä	Σ			
229	å	σ			
230	æ	µ			

INDEX

Special Characters

& (ampersand), 608, 609
^ (accent circumflex). *See* languages, foreign
´ (accent acute). *See* languages, foreign
` (accent grave). *See* languages, foreign
* (asterisk)
  in format switch (*), 690–92, 831
  as multiplication operator, 803
  "star-dot-star" (*.*), 47
  as wildcard character, 47, 113–14, 604, 608
@ (at sign)
  in date-time picture switch (\@), 695
  in pattern matching, 114
\ (backslash), 678, 778
• (bullet), 480–81
^ (caret)
  as exponent operator, 803
  in pattern matching, 115
: (colon), 778, 781
, (comma)
  as field delimiter, 727–28, 798–99
  as logical OR, 608
© (copyright symbol). *See* special characters
{} curly brackets, 114, 677
. (directory, current), 605
/ (division operator), 803
.. (directory, parent), 605
... (ellipses), 164
— (em dash), 161–62
– (en dash), 161–62
= (equal-to operator), 804, 901
= (Formula) field, 678, 802–3, 804, 805, 811
> (greater-than symbol)
  as operator, 804, 901
  in pattern matching, 114

>= (greater-than-or-equal-to operator), 804, 901
< (less-than symbol)
  as operator, 804, 901
  in pattern matching, 114
<= (less-than-or-equal-to operator), 804, 901
\! (lock result switch), 688
– (minus sign), 802, 803
<> (not-equal-to operator), 804, 901
\# (numeric picture switch), 693–95
() (parentheses), 115, 804
% (percent sign), 803
+ (plus sign), 802, 803
? (question mark), 113, 604, 608
" " (quotation marks)
  in file searches, 608
  in text strings, 727–28, 908
® (registered trademark symbol). *See* special characters
; (semicolon), 781
[] (square brackets), 114, 336
~ (tilde), 608, 609
™ (trademark symbol). *See* special characters

A

About Microsoft Word command (Help), 31–32
ABS function, 805
accelerator keys. *See* trigger keys, changing
accents (´ ^ `). *See* languages, foreign
action fields, 676, 707–12
addition operator (+), 802, 803
addresses. *See* envelopes; labels; mail merge

Adobe Type 1 fonts, 583
Adobe Type Manager (ATM), 583
Advanced Search dialog box
　　Location card, 605–6
　　Summary card, 606–11
　　Timestamp card, 611–12
ADVANCE field, 595
aliases, 444
Align Drawing Objects button, 553, 557
aligning frames, 521–24
aligning table rows, 399–400
aligning tables, 398
aligning text
　　centered, 223, 227, 232
　　flush left, 223, 227, 232
　　flush right, 223, 227, 232
　　with Formatting toolbar, 223
　　horizontally, 223, 227, 232
　　justified, 223, 227, 232
　　with Paragraph dialog box, 232
　　shortcut keys, 227–28
　　vertically, 489–90
Allow Fast Saves option, 38–39
Alphabetic argument, 693
Alt-Ctrl-F1 (Lock Field), 687
Alt-F1 (Next Field), 688–89
Alt-F9 (View Codes), 683
Alt-Shift-F1 (Previous Field), 688–89
Always Create Backup Copy option, 38
ampersand (&), 608, 609
anchors, 312, 515–16, 524, 534
AND function, 805–6
AND operator, 608
Annotation command (Insert menu), 336
annotations. *See also* hidden text
　　with author's initials, 336, 338–39, 707
　　deleting, 340
　　as go-to destination, 352
　　in Help system, 33
　　inserting, 336–39
　　locking documents for, 340–41
　　moving to/from document, 339–40
　　numbering, 338–39
　　overview, 336
　　printing, 271, 341
　　reference mark, 336, 337, 338–39

annotations, *continued*
　　sizing viewing pane, 339
　　sound, 338
　　viewing, 336–37, 339
Annotations command (View menu),
　　337–38
ANSI codes, 116, 118, 623, 839–40,
　　995–98
Apple LaserWriter II printers, 259
Application Control menu, 11
Arabic argument, 693
Arc button, 551
arguments
　　for numeric field formatting, 692–95
　　overview, 677–79
　　for text field formatting, 690–92
arithmetic operators, 802–4
arranging. *See* moving; outlines; sorting
arrow-and-question-mark pointer, 25, 27
arrow buttons, double, 301
arrow keys, 78–79, 301
art files. *See* drawing objects; graphics
ASCII codes, 839–40
ASCII text files, 623–25
ASK field, 739–40
asterisk (*)
　　in format switch (*), 690–92, 831
　　as multiplication operator, 803
　　"star-dot-star" (*.*), 47
　　as wildcard character, 47, 113–14,
　　　604, 608
ATM (Adobe Type Manager), 583
Attach Template dialog box, 932–33, 939
AUTHOR field, 692, 701–2
authorities. *See* tables of authorities
authors
　　changing default, 57
　　in document summaries, 57
　　searching for, 607
AutoCaption dialog box, 829–30
AutoClose macro, 878
AutoCorrect
　　adding entries, 137–38
　　vs. AutoText, 132–33, 142
　　and capitalization, 136–37
　　changing entries, 138–39
　　deleting entries, 139

AutoCorrect, *continued*
    formatting entries, 138, 139
    naming entries, 136
    overriding, 140
    overview, 132, 133
    renaming entries, 139
    Replace Text As You Type option,
      135–39
    and spelling checker, 182
    undoing usage, 140
AutoCorrect dialog box, 133–39
AutoExec macro, 878
AutoExit macro, 879
AutoFit, in tables, 371, 380–81
AutoFormat. *See also* Table AutoFormat
    default options, 420–23
    field use, 691–92
    reviewing changes, 424–26
    shortcuts, 427
    using, 423–27
AutoFormat button, 18, 427
AutoFormat dialog box, 423–24
automatic hyphenation, 199–201
automatic repagination, 219, 313, 351
Automatic Save option, 39, 54
automatic styles, 429
Automatic Word Selection option, 38
AutoNew macro, 877, 944
AutoOpen macro, 877
AutoText button, 142
AutoText dialog box, 140–46, 148–49
AutoText entries
    adding, 142–45
    vs. AutoCorrect, 132–33, 142
    deleting, 145–46
    formatting in, 144–45
    in global templates, 148
    inserting with AUTOTEXT field, 147
    inserting with Edit AutoText
      command, 140–41
    inserting with F3 key, 141
    naming, 142–44
    in Normal template, 146, 148–49
    overview, 140
    pictures as, 147–48
    printing, 150–51, 268–69
    renaming, 146

AutoText entries, *continued*
    revising, 145
    saving to disk, 149–50
    special characters as, 840
    Spike, 151–53
    storing in templates, 146, 148–49, 948
    symbols as, 840
    tables as, 367
AUTOTEXT field, 147
AutoText key (F3), 141, 153
AVERAGE function, 806, 810, 811, 813

B

background printing, 264, 270–71
background repagination, 219, 313, 351
backslash (\), 678
Backspace key, 71, 91
backup copies, 38
BARCODE field, 285, 595
bar codes, postal, 285, 288
bar tabs, 234
Based-On styles, 437, 438–40, 450–52
Beep On Error option, 313
best fit. *See* AutoFit, in tables
binding margin, 211–12, 586
bitmapped fonts, 583
bitmapped images, 536, 554, 559
blocks, text
    copying, 100–103
    defined, 74
    selecting (*see* selecting text)
blue background screen, 313
BMP files, 536
body text, outline. *See also* outlines
    adding to, 658–60
    demoting headings to, 667–68
    moving, 669–70
    overview, 654
boilerplate. *See* AutoText entries;
    templates; wizards
boldface text, 241–42
Bookmark dialog box, 334
bookmarks
    in ASK and SET fields, 740, 745–46
    in calculations, 805

bookmarks, *continued*
   defining, 333–35
   deleting, 335
   in fields, 678, 687
   in = (Formula) field, 805
   as go-to destination, 81, 335–36
   inserting in Help system, 33
   naming, 334–35
   overview, 333
   redefining, 335
   in SEQ field, 831–32
   viewing, 311
borders. *See also* lines, drawing
   adding to paragraphs, 236–39
   breaking between pages, 236–37
   custom, 238–39
   deleting, 412
   for frames, 517
   for pictures, 546
   in tables, 407–12
   and text spacing, 238
   for WordArt objects, 568
Borders And Shading dialog box, 517
Borders toolbar, 19, 240
bottom margin, 209, 210, 218–19
boundary lines, 299–301, 302, 310
boxes. *See* borders; text boxes
braces. *See* brackets
brackets
   curly ({ }), 114, 677
   square ([ ]), 114, 336
branching, 907–8
Break dialog box, 486–87
breaks
   column, 505
   line, 74, 219
   page, 219–21, 232–33
   section, 486–87, 488–89, 506, 507–8
Bring In Front Of Text button, 552
Bring To Front button, 552
built-in styles
   changing, 445
   how Normal style differs from, 448–49
   list of, 446–47
   overview, 428–29

bullets, 480–81
Bullets And Numbering dialog box
   Bulleted card, 480–81
   Multilevel card, 482–83
   Numbered card, 475–79
business forms. *See* forms
business reply mail, 285
Button Editor dialog box, 320
buttons, toolbar
   adding, 318–21
   deleting, 318
   editing, 320–21

C

calculations, 800–813
Callout button, 551
callouts, 525, 530–31
capitalization. *See* case; drop capitals
Caps argument, 692
Caption dialog box, 825–28
Caption Numbering dialog box, 828–29
captions
   in frames, 544–45, 546
   inserting, 825–30
   numbering in sequence, 825–30
   for pictures, 544–45
   in tables of figures, 773–74
cards. *See* Options dialog box
CardText argument, 692, 693
caret (^), 115, 803
carriage returns, 624. *See also* Enter key
cartridge fonts, 584
case
   in AutoCorrect, 136–37
   changing, 245
   in field results, 692
   matching, 112, 125–27, 610
   in spelling checker, 184, 187
catalogs, 751
Cell Borders And Shading dialog box, 407, 409–10
Cell Height And Width dialog box
   Column card, 379–83
   Row card, 384–86

cells. *See also* tables
    adding to tables, 394–95
    borders around, 407–12
    calculations in, 812–13
    deleting from tables, 394–95
    merging, 395, 396–97
    overview, 364–65
    shading, 408
centering text, 223, 227, 232
CGM files, 536
changes. *See* revision marks
chapter page numbering, 169–70
characters. *See also* fonts
    boldfacing, 241–42
    copying formatting, 108, 248, 250
    defined, 73
    deleting, 91
    formatting field results, 690–92
    formatting with Font dialog box,
        246–48
    formatting with Formatting toolbar,
        241–42
    formatting with shortcut keys, 243–46,
        987–88
    italic, 241–42
    lowercase, 245, 692
    nonprinting, 36, 72–73, 311
    point size of, 70
    spacing of, 246, 247–48
    special, 161–66, 839–40
    special, searching for, 115–18
    underlining, 241–42
    uppercase, 245, 692
    wildcard, 47, 113–14, 604, 608
CharFormat argument, 690–91
Chart Gallery dialog box, 575–76
Chart menu (Microsoft Graph), 574, 576
charts, creating in Microsoft Graph,
    572–77
Chart window, 573
Check Box Form Field Options dialog
    box, 755–56
check box form fields, 755–56
citations, 783–85
clearing. *See* deleting; hidden text
clicking, 983–84

CLIPART directory, 536, 537
Clipboard
    copying Help information to, 33
    copying text with, 100, 101–3
    copying text without, 103
    importing data with, 625–26
    moving data to other programs with,
        633–34
    moving text with, 103
    moving text without, 103–4
    naming AutoText entries with, 143
    overview, 94
    saving contents of, 102
    using with tables, 402–5
    viewing contents of, 101–2
Clipboard Viewer, 101–2
Close command, 61, 150
CLP files, 102
codes. *See* field codes
COL indicator, 22
Collapse button, 653, 662, 663
collapsing outlines, 662–63
column breaks, 505
columns, snaking
    equal-length, 507–8
    newspaper-style, 497–509
    in Normal view, 499–500
    in Page Layout view, 500–501
    in sections, 501, 503–5, 506–7
    when to use, 498
columns, table. *See also* tables
    adding, 391–93
    adjusting width with AutoFit, 371,
        380–81
    adjusting width with dialog box,
        379–81
    adjusting width with mouse, 378–79
    deleting, 394
    moving, 394
columns, tabular
    bar tabs between, 234
    selecting text in, 88–89
    sorting, 797–98, 800
Columns button, 18, 498, 499, 501
Columns dialog box, 501–5
combining documents. *See* linking; mail
    merge; master documents

combining paragraphs, 92, 93
comma (,)
  as field delimiter, 727–28, 798–99
  as logical OR, 608
comma-delimited format
  for data files, 727, 728
  sorting lists in, 798–99
COMMAND.COM file, 602
command prompt, MS-DOS, starting
    Word from, 8
commands
  changing key assignments, 968–73
  customizing menus, 952–64
  list of shortcut keys, 992–94
  using menus for, 12–15
  using toolbars for, 16–19
comments. *See* annotations
COMMENTS field, 701–2
common settings. *See* default settings
Compare Versions dialog box, 358–59
COM ports, 257, 258
concordance file, 780–81
connecting files. *See* linking; mail merge;
    master documents
contents. *See* tables of contents
Contents command (Help), 28, 29
context-sensitive help, 32
context-sensitive menus, 15–16
CONTROL.EXE file, 254
Control menu box, 11, 12. *See also*
    Document Control menu; Windows
    Application Control menu
Control Panel, 254, 262, 585
conversions, file
  with Clipboard, 625–26
  customizing, 634–35
  with File Open command, 621–22
  and font substitution, 636–37
  with Insert Database command,
    626–32
  with Insert Object command, 626
  overview, 620
  template for, 637
CONVERT.DOT file, 637
Convert File dialog box, 627–28, 631
Convert Table To Text dialog box, 401,
    416–17

Convert Text To Table dialog box, 413,
    415–16
Copy button, 17, 100
Copy command, 100, 101
Copy dialog box, 616–17
copying
  character formatting, 108, 248, 250
  with Clipboard, 100–103
  to designated location, 103
  between documents, 106–8
  fields, 689
  files, 616–17
  footnotes and endnotes, 347
  with Format Painter, 249–51
  formatting, 108, 248–51
  menu items, 961–62
  with mouse, 104–5
  paragraph formatting, 108, 248–49
  with shortcut keys, 101, 104, 986
  from Spike, 153
  styles, 462–64, 947
  templates, 936
  without Clipboard, 103
Copy key (Shift-F2), 103
copyright symbol, 164
Copy To feature, 103
COUNT function, 807, 813
counting words, 74
C:\> prompt, 8, 602
Create Data Source dialog box, 720
CREATEDATE field, 704
Create Directory dialog box, 931
Create Labels dialog box, 749
Create Picture button, 557–58
cropping pictures, 540, 542–43
cropping pointer, 25, 27, 542
cross-hair pointer, 24, 25
Cross-Reference dialog box, 833–34
cross-references
  in indexes, 779–80
  in text, 832–35
Ctrl-arrow key shortcuts, 78, 79
Ctrl-Del, 92
Ctrl-F3 (Spike), 152
Ctrl-F9 (Insert Field), 173, 682
Ctrl-F11 (Lock Field), 687

Ctrl-Home, 78, 80
Ctrl-hyphen, 198, 204
Ctrl-Ins, 101
Ctrl-Shift-F3 (Unspike), 152
Ctrl-Shift-F7 (Update INCLUDETEXT), 687
Ctrl-Shift-F9 (Unlink Field), 688
Ctrl-Shift-F11 (Unlock Field), 688
Ctrl-Shift-Spacebar, 73
Ctrl-Tab, 111, 407
curly brackets ({ }), 114, 677
curly quotation marks (" "), 134–35, 164
current directory, 46, 47
cursor. *See also* mouse pointer
    defined, 10
    in frames, 514
    list of shortcut keys, 985
    moving with keyboard, 78–82
    moving with mouse, 75
Custom Button dialog box, 319–20, 854–55
custom dictionaries
    adding to, 181, 186–87
    default options, 185
    editing, 187–88
Customize dialog box
    Keyboard card, 158–60, 454–56, 850–51, 968–73
    Menus card, 851–53, 954–63, 965
    Toolbars card, 317–19, 853–54
Customize Grammar Settings dialog box, 195–97
custom styles
    changing, 443–44
    creating, 449–53
    overview, 428–29
Cut button, 17, 94
Cut command, 94, 103
cutting and pasting
    within a document, 99–105
    between documents, 106–8
    with keyboard, 103, 104
    list of shortcut keys, 986
    "smart," 108
    in tables, 402–5

D

dashes, 161–62
data. *See* databases, importing; forms; mail merge; sorting; statistics; summary information
Database dialog box, 627–28, 631
DATABASE field, 639
databases, importing, 636–32
Database toolbar, 724–26
data documents. *See* data files
data files
    adding records to, 721–23
    creating, 720–21, 726–28
    editing, 724–26
    overview, 716, 717–18
    viewing, 723–24
Data Form dialog box, 721–23, 732
DataSeries menu, 574, 575
Datasheet window, 573
DATE field, 172, 173, 696–700
dates
    combining with times, 700
    formatting, 695, 698–99
    in headers and footers, 172, 173
    inserting, 696–700
    sorting by, 793–94
date-time picture switch (\@), 695
DDEAUTO field, 646–47.
        See also EMBED field
DDE (Dynamic Data Exchange), 646–47
DDE field, 646–47. *See also* EMBED field
debugging macros, 883–86
decimal tabs
    setting, 226
    in tables, 406–7
Decrease Indent button, 225
default settings. *See also* Options dialog box
    for keyboard configuration, 973–74
    for margins, 209–10
    for menu configuration, 963–64
    for Normal template, 467
    overview, 309–10
    for page layouts, 209–10
    for paragraph formatting, 221–22

DEFINED function, 807
Delete Cells dialog box, 390–91, 394
deleting
    annotations, 340
    AutoCorrect entries, 139
    bookmarks, 335
    borders, 412
    characters, 91
    fields, 689
    files, 62–63, 616
    footnotes and endnotes, 346
    macros, 862
    menus and menu items, 958–59, 966
    outline headings, 668
    paragraph marks, 92, 93
    shading, 412
    shortcut keys for, 986
    styles, 445, 947
    table columns, 394
    table rows, 389–91
    tables, 398
    tabs, 235
    templates, 938
    text, 91–92
    words, 92
Delivery Point Bar Code option, 288
Del key, 91
Demote button, 653, 655, 657, 665–66
Demote To Body Text button, 653,
    667–68
dialog boxes
    assigning shortcut keys to, 978–79
    creating, 913–23
    in macros, 873–76
    shaded, 313
Dialog Editor, 910–25
DIC files, 185
dictionaries
    adding to, 181, 186–87
    custom, 185, 186–88
    default options, 185
    editing, 187–88
    of exceptions, 188–89
    in WIN.INI file, 188
dictionary-style headers, 836–38
direct formatting, defined, 221

directional arrow keys, 78–79
directories
    changing, 46–47
    creating, 315, 602–3
    current, 605
    organizing, 314–15
    organizing files with, 600–601
    overview, 602
    parent, 47, 605
    root, 602
display. *See* previewing; screen display
Display As Icon option, 561
division operator (/), 803
DOC files, 7, 45, 48, 63, 621
Document1, 10
Document Control menu
    closing files with, 61
    defined, 13
    illustrated, 14
    location of menu box, 11, 12
documents. *See also* files
    backing up, 38
    comparing versions of, 358–59
    cutting and pasting between, 106–8
    elements of, 73–75
    finding, 48
    formatting, 209–19
    frames in, 509–25
    hidden text in, 119, 127, 245, 271, 311
    icons for, 6–8
    inserting pictures into, 535–39
    listing, 45–48, 313, 613–15
    locking for annotations, 340–41
    long, 590–95, 785–86
    master, 590–95, 785–86
    merging (*see* mail merge)
    multiple, deleting, 63
    multiple, opening, 615–16
    multiple, printing, 616
    multiple, saving, 60
    multisection, 485–95
    naming, 51, 53
    navigating, 75–84
    new, 44–45
    opening, 45–50
    opening at startup, 5–8

documents, *continued*
opening with File Find, 615–16
page numbers in, 167–75
previewing, 273–82
printing, 266–72
protecting, 53–56
read-only, 49–50, 55–56, 59
renaming, 56
reopening, 50
retrieving, 603–17
saving, 50–56, 59–60
saving as templates, 934–35
selecting, 90, 613–14
statistics on, 58
summary information, 56–59, 271, 615
templates for, 63–65
top-down design, 208
views of, 69, 293–309
Document Statistics dialog box, 58
document template, 326, 327, 328–29
document window, 10, 11, 12
DollarText argument, 693
DOS. *See* MS-DOS
DOT files, 48, 64, 326, 327, 328.
See also templates
dot-matrix printers, 287, 291
dots (space characters), 73, 74
double-arrow buttons
(Page Layout view), 301
double-clicking mouse, 85–86, 984
double spacing, 228–29, 231
downloadable fonts, 584
downward-pointing arrow, 24, 25
draft font
displaying, 295–96, 298, 312
printing, 270, 296
view option, 35, 69
drag-and-drop, 37, 104–5, 108
drag-and-drop pointers, 25, 27, 104
dragging mouse, 85, 104–5, 108, 984
Drawing button, 18, 525, 550
Drawing Object dialog box
Fill card, 528
Line card, 529
Size And Position card, 527–28
drawing objects. *See also* graphics
creating, 553–58

drawing objects, *continued*
editing, 558–59
grouping, 554
inserting, 560–61
moving, 555
printing, 272
Drawing toolbar
illustrated, 525, 550–53
list of buttons, 551–53
drawing tools, 550–58
Drop Cap dialog box, 570–71
drop capitals
creating in Drop Cap dialog box,
570–71
creating with WordArt, 571–72
Drop-Down Form Field Options dialog
box, 753–54
drop-down form fields, 753–54
DRW files, 536
duplex printing, 267–68
Dynamic Data Exchange (DDE), 646–47

E

Edit AutoText command, 140, 142
Edit Bookmark command, 334
Edit Copy command, 100, 101, 625
Edit Cut command, 94, 103, 625
Edit Find command, 82–83, 109–21
Edit Go To command, 80, 335, 350, 351
Edit menu (Equation Editor), 816, 817
Edit menu (Microsoft Graph), 574, 575
Edit menu (Word 6.0), 13, 14, 33
Edit Object command, 558, 577, 640
Edit (Options) card, 37–38
Edit Paste command, 94, 100, 101, 103,
625, 626, 634
Edit Paste Special command, 625, 626,
643–44, 647
Edit Picture dialog box, 558
Edit Redo command, 94, 95
Edit Repeat command, 95, 96, 160, 248
Edit Replace command, 121
EDITTIME field, 704
Edit Undo command, 94, 102
Edit WordArt Text command, 563

Ellipse/Circle button, 551
ellipses (...), 164
embedding
    with Edit Paste Special command,
        643–44
    fields for, 646–47
    with Insert Object command, 641–43
    vs. linking, 640–41, 644
    when to use, 641
EMBED field, 642, 646
em dashes, 161–62
em spaces, 163
en dashes, 161–62
en spaces, 163
End key, 78
endnotes. *See* footnotes and endnotes
end-of-cell mark, 363, 365
end-of-document marker, 10
end-of-row mark, 363, 365
en spaces, 163–64
Enter key, 67, 68
Enter Your Text Here dialog box, 563
Envelope Address dialog box, 749
Envelope button (Word 2.0), 282
Envelope Options dialog box
    Envelope Options card, 284–85
    in mail merge, 748–49
    Printing Options card, 285–86
envelopes
    adding to documents, 286–87
    bar codes on, 285
    and dot-matrix printers, 287
    feed options, 285–86
    and laser printers, 285, 286, 287
    in mail merge, 748–51
    printing, 286–87
    return address, 283–84
    setting up for printing, 283–86
    sizes of, 284
Envelopes And Labels dialog box
    Envelopes card, 283–84
    Labels card, 287–89
Epson MX-80 printer, 260
EPT ports, 258
EQ field, 824
equal-to operator (=), 804, 901

Equation Editor
    example, 822–24
    menus, 816–19
    overview, 813–14
    palettes, 819
    shortcut keys, 820–22
    starting, 814
    symbol icons, 819
    template icons, 819–20
Equation Editor toolbar, 815
equation (EQ) field, 824
equations
    as go-to destination, 352
    typesetting (*see* Equation Editor)
erasing. *See* deleting
Examples And Demos
    command (Help), 30
Excel. *See* Microsoft Excel,
    inserting data from
EXC files, 188–89
exclude dictionary, 188
Exit command, 149
exiting Word for Windows, 61, 149
Expand button, 653, 662, 663
expanding outlines, 662–63
exponent operator (^), 803
exporting files, 632–34
= (Expression) field. *See* = (Formula)
    field
expressions. *See* Equation Editor;
    formulas
Extend Selection key (F8), 89–90
extensions, filename, 47–48
EXT indicator, 22, 23, 89

F

F1 key (Help), 32
F2 key (Move), 104
F3 key (AutoText), 141, 153
F4 key (Repeat), 248
F5 key (Go To), 80, 335, 350
F6 key (Next Pane), 339, 346
F7 key (Spelling), 180, 185
F8 key (Extend Selection), 89–90
F9 key (Update), 685–87, 764, 767, 783

F11 key (Next Field), 688–89
facing pages, 168, 211–12, 586–87
Fax Wizard, 322–23
field characters, 677
field codes
    vs. field results, 683–89
    printing, 271
    viewing, 311, 683–84
    viewing in split screen, 683
Field Codes key (Shift-F9), 172, 173, 684
field delimiters, 727–28, 798–99
Field dialog box, 679–82
field names
    in databases, 626
    defined, 676–77
Field Options dialog box, 680–82
fields. *See also* merge fields
    action-type, 676, 707–12
    arguments in, 690–95
    bookmarks in, 678
    copying of, 689
    database, 626
    in data files, 716–17
    date, 172, 173, 696–700
    deleting of, 689
    editing of, 689
    for embedding, 646–47
    entering, 679–83
    format for, 676–79
    formatting results, 690–95
    on forms (*see* forms)
    formulas in, 678
    as go-to destination, 352
    in headers and footers, 172–73
    identifers in, 678
    index, 762, 776, 778, 779, 782
    inserting with Ctrl-F9 key, 682
    inserting with Insert Field command,
        679–82
    inserting with other menu commands,
        682–83
    for linking, 646–47
    list of shortcut keys, 987
    literals, 677–78
    locking of, 687–88
    for mail merge, 737–47
    marker-type, 676

fields, *continued*
    moving to, 688–89
    nesting of, 695
    numeric, 693–95
    overview, 675–76
    page number, 170–71, 172
    printing of codes, 271
    reference, 835–38
    results vs. codes, 683–89
    result-type, 676
    shading, 684–85
    statistical, 703–7
    summary information, 700–702
    switches in, 678–79, 690–95, 831
    table of contents, 762, 764, 766,
        767–69, 772
    time, 172, 173, 696–700
    types of, 676
    unlinking of, 688
    unlocking of, 688
    updating of, 270, 685–87
    user information, 707
    viewing of codes, 683–84
    viewing results, 311
field types, 676–77
figures. *See* tables of figures
File Close command, 61, 150
File Create Directory command, 603
File dialog box (Insert menu), 626
File Exit command, 61, 149
File Find File command, 603
File Manager, 5, 6, 603
File menu (Equation Editor), 816, 818
File menu (Microsoft Graph), 574, 575
File menu (Word 6.0), 13, 14
FILENAME field, 704
filenames. *See also* files, naming; files,
        renaming
    changing, 56, 617
    extensions, 47–48
    rules for, 53
File New command, 6, 44
FileOpenAny macro
    creating, 868–76
    making interactive, 897–910
File Open command, 45, 621
File Page Setup command, 210, 470

File Print command, 262, 263, 266
File Print Preview command, 273
File Run command (Windows), 5, 6
files. *See also* documents
    backing up, 38
    converting, 620–32
    copying, 616–17
    database, importing, 626–32
    deleting, 62–63, 616
    exporting, 632–34
    finding, 48, 603–17
    importing, 620–22
    listing, 45–48, 313, 613–15
    managing, 600–603
    moving, 617
    multiple, deleting, 63
    multiple, opening at startup, 6, 8
    multiple, saving, 60
    naming, 51, 53
    on network drives, 49, 52
    opening, 45–50
    opening at startup, 5–8
    opening other file formats, 621–25
    organizing, 314–15
    printing, 266–72
    protecting, 53–56
    read-only, 49–50, 55–56, 59
    recently used, 50
    renaming, 56, 617
    retrieving, 603–17
    saving, 50–56
    searching for, 603–17
    selecting, 613–14
    sorting list, 614
    text, 621, 623–25
    types of, 47–48
File Save All command, 60, 150, 860–61
File Save As command, 51, 53–56, 59, 632
File Save command, 51, 59
FILESIZE field, 704
File Summary Info command, 56
File Templates command, 326, 328, 953
Fill Color button, 552
FILLIN field, 738, 740
Find dialog box (Edit menu), 82–83,
    109–21
Find File dialog box, 613–15

Find In Field dialog box, 722–23
finding. *See* searching
finger-pointing hand, 25, 27
Firstcap argument, 692
first-line indent marker, 231
Flip Horizontal button, 553
Flip Vertical button, 553
floating toolbars, 316–17
flush-left aligning, 223, 227, 232
flush-right aligning, 223, 227, 232
Font dialog box
    Character Spacing card, 247–48
    Font card, 246–47, 582, 585
fonts. *See also* WordArt objects
    applying formats with Font dialog
      box, 246–48
    applying formats with mouse, 241–42
    applying formats with shortcut keys,
      243–46, 987–88
    bitmapped vs. scalable, 583
    cartridge, 584
    changing, 70
    changing default format, 248
    copying formats, 108, 248, 250
    defined, 242
    downloadable, 584
    draft output option, 270, 296
    listing, 582
    printer setup, 585
    resident, 584–85
    screen vs. printer, 582, 585
    selecting with Formatting toolbar, 243
    symbol, 246
    TrueType, 582–83
    types of, 242
    for watermarks, 534
    in WordArt, 565
Font Substitution dialog box, 636–37
footers. *See* headers and footers
Footnote And Endnote dialog box,
    342–43
footnotes and endnotes
    converting, 345
    copying, 347
    creating, 341–46
    deleting, 346
    editing, 346–47

footnotes and endnotes, *continued*
  formatting, 347–50
  as go-to destination, 352
  inserting, 346
  numbering, 342, 344–45
  overview, 341
  in Page Layout view, 304
  reference mark, 342–43, 347
  separators for, 348–50
  shortcut keys, 346
  swapping, 345
foreign-language characters, 165–66
Format AutoFormat command, 423
Format Borders And Shading command,
    236, 237, 407, 517, 528
Format Bullets And Numbering
    command, 475
Format Callout button, 552
Format Callout dialog box, 530
Format Columns command, 501
Format Drawing Object command, 551
Format Drop Cap command, 570
Format Font command, 246
Format Frame command, 524
Format Heading Numbering command,
    484, 656
Format menu (Equation Editor), 816, 818
Format menu (Microsoft Graph), 574,
    576–77
Format menu (Word 6.0), 13, 14
Format Painter, 17, 25, 27, 249–51
Format Paragraph command, 230, 473
Format Picture command, 542
Format Style command, 432, 433, 434,
    441
Format Style Gallery command, 429, 430
Format Tabs command, 233
formatting
  in AutoCorrect entries, 138, 139
  with AutoFormat, 420–27
  in AutoText entries, 144–45
  changing in Print Preview, 280–81
  of characters, 241–48
  copying, 108, 248–51
  of dates, 695, 698–99
  displaying information about, 27, 28
  of field results, 690–95

formatting, *continued*
  of footnotes, 347–50
  of headers and footers, 176
  of indexes, 781–82
  list of shortcut keys, 987–90
  of numbers, 692–93
  overriding of, 460–62
  of pages, 209–19
  of paragraphs, 221–41
  repeating, 248
  replacing, 127–28
  searching for, 119–21
  of sections, 488–90
  snaking columns, 497–509
  with styles, 419–67
  tables, manually, 405–7
  tables, with AutoFormat, 367–71
  of tables of contents, 770–71
  of text in fields, 690–92
  of times, 695, 698–99
  WordArt objects, 563–68
Formatting toolbar
  applying styles with, 457
  changing font size with, 70
  character formatting buttons, 241–42
  illustrated, 19, 222
  indent buttons, 225
  moving, 316–17
  overview, 19
  paragraph formatting with, 222–23
  selecting fonts with, 243
  text aligning buttons, 223
  turning on/off, 34
FORMCHECKBOX field, 752
FORMDROPDOWN field, 752
Form Field dialog box, 753
form fields. *See* forms
Form Field toolbar, 756–57
form letters. *See* mail merge
forms
  check box fields, 755–56
  creating, 752–57
  drop-down fields, 753–54
  filling in, 757–58
  printing, 272
  printing field information, 272
  text fields, 754–55

FORMTEXT field, 752
Formula dialog box, 810–11
= (Formula) field, 678, 802–3, 804,
    805, 811
formulas
    bookmarks in, 805
    creating, 810–11
    in fields, 678
    functions in, 805–10
    operators in, 802–5
    in tables, 812–13
Frame dialog box, 520–24
frame pointers, 25, 27
frames
    adding, 512–13
    adding text to, 513
    adding to pictures, 543–44
    adding to text, 514
    aligning, 521–24
    anchoring, 515–16, 524, 534
    borders for, 517
    captions in, 544–45, 546
    default options, 517
    deleting, 524
    flowing text around, 520–21
    in headers and footers, 533–34
    in margins, 531–32, 588
    moving, 517–19
    moving cursor to, 514
    in Normal view, 510–11
    in Outline view, 511
    overview, 509
    in Page Layout view, 511, 512, 514–16
    positioning, 524
    selecting, 516–17
    shading, 517
    sizing, 517–19, 520
    vs. text boxes, 525, 526, 527, 530–31,
        533
    views of, 509–11
    when to use, 530–31
    for WordArt objects, 569
Freeform button, 551, 555–56
FTNREF field. *See* NOTEREF field
Full Screen mode, 304–6
function keys. *See names of keys*
    (F1, F2, etc.)
functions, 805–10

G

Gallery menu, 574, 575–76
GetCurValues command, 907–8
global templates
    defined, 938
    vs. Normal template, 326, 938–39, 941,
        942, 943–44
    in versions of Word, 938–39
    when to use, 943–44
glossaries. *See* AutoText entries
GLOSSARY field. *See* AUTOTEXT field
glossary terms (Help), 30
Go Back key (Shift-F5), 80, 351
go-to
    annotations, 352
    bookmarks, 81, 335–36, 352
    endnotes, 352
    equations, 352
    fields, 352
    footnotes, 352
    graphics, 352
    line numbers, 352
    overview of, 350–51
    page numbers, 81, 351
    percentages, 353
    sections, 352
    tables, 352
GOTOBUTTON field, 710–12
Go To dialog box, 80–82, 335, 350–51
Go To key (F5), 80, 335, 350
grammar checker
    default options, 194–98
    how best to use, 197–98
    readability statistics, 192–94
    with/without spelling checker, 190,
        194
Grammar dialog box, 190–92
Graph button. *See* Insert Chart button
graphics. *See also* drawing objects;
        frames; pictures
    file formats, 536
    as go-to destination, 352
    repositioning pointer, 25, 27
greater-than-or-equal-to operator (>=),
        804, 901
greater-than symbol (>), 114, 804, 901

gridlines, 363, 364–65. *See also* Snap To Grid button
Group button, 552, 558
grouping objects, 554
gutter margin, 211–12, 586, 587

H

handles, 516, 541
hand pointer, 25, 27
hanging indentation, 231
hard page breaks. *See* manual page breaks
Header And Footer toolbar, 171–75, 493, 494, 587
header file, 737
headers and footers
    creating, 175–76
    date in, 172, 173
    default options, 175–76
    deleting, 176
    dictionary-style, 836–38
    displaying, 174
    editing, 174
    first-page, 174, 494–95
    formatting, 176
    frames in, 533–34
    linking, 588
    vs. margin dimensions, 588–89
    for odd/even pages, 173, 174, 586–87
    overview, 167
    in Page Layout view, 171–75, 303–4
    page numbers in, 167–71
    positioning, 176, 588–89
    previewing, 281
    in Print Preview, 281
    Same As Previous button, 494, 495
    in sections, 492–95, 587–88
    text boxes in, 533–34
    time in, 172, 173
    toolbar for, 171–75, 493, 494, 587
    viewing, 493
Heading Numbering dialog box, 484–85
headings, outline
    converting to body text, 667–68
    creating tables of contents from, 762, 764–66

headings, outline, *continued*
    deleting, 668
    expanding/collapsing, 662–63
    inserting, 668
    moving, 669–70
    numbering, 483–85
    overview, 654
    promoting/demoting, 655–56, 665–68
    styles for, 656, 671–72
heading styles, numbering, 483–85
Help button, 18, 32
Help menu (Equation Editor), 816, 819
Help menu (Microsoft Graph), 574, 577
Help menu (Word 6.0), 13, 14, 28–32
Help Options dialog box, 31
Help system
    annotating, 33
    context-sensitive, 32–33
    copying to Clipboard, 33
    inserting bookmarks in, 33
    menu commands, 28–32, 33
    printing from, 33
    for WordPerfect users, 30–31
Hewlett-Packard LaserJet printers, 259, 260, 584
Hex argument, 692, 693
hidden text. *See also* annotations
    finding, 119
    keyboard shortcut for, 245
    printing, 271
    replacing, 127
    viewing, 311
highlighting. *See* selecting text
Home key, 78
horizontal alignment, 223
horizontal ruler. *See* ruler, horizontal
horizontal scroll bar, 20, 35, 77
horizontal sizing arrow, 24, 25
horizontal split pointer, 24, 25
Hot Zone. *See* Hyphenation Zone option
hourglass, 24, 25
hyphenation
    automatic, 199–201
    manual, 199, 201–3
    when to use, 198, 203
    zone size, 200–201

Hyphenation dialog box, 199–201
Hyphenation Zone option, 200–201
hyphens
    deleting, 204
    non-breaking, 162
    optional, 163, 198, 204
    types of, 162–63

I

I-beam pointer, 23, 24, 25
IBM extended character set, 624
icon bars. *See* toolbars
icons. *See also* buttons, toolbar
    Equation Editor, 819–20
    inserting objects as, 561, 569–70
    selecting in Program Manager, 5
    for Word documents, 6–8
    Word for Windows, 4–5
identifiers, 678
IF field, 741–43
IF function, 807
If...End If statement, 899–900
images. *See* CLIPART directory; drawing
    objects; graphics
IMPORT field. *See* INCLUDEPICTURE
    field
importing
    with Clipboard, 625–26
    database files, 626–32
    with File Open command, 621–22
    with Insert Database command,
        626–32
    with Insert Object command, 626
    vs. linking, 638
    overview, 621–22
inches vs. centimeters, 212
INCLUDE field. *See* INCLUDETEXT
    field
INCLUDEPICTURE field, 644
INCLUDETEXT field
    and format switches, 690–92
    inserting files with, 639, 686–87
    locking results, 687–88
    in mail merge, 747
    updating, 687

Increase Indent button, 225
indentation, paragraph
    changing in Paragraph dialog box,
        231
    changing in Print Preview, 280
    changing on ruler, 224–25
    changing with Formatting toolbar,
        225
    changing with mouse, 224–25
    changing with shortcut keys, 227
    first-line, 231
    hanging, 231
    vs. margins, 216, 223
    negative, 231
    ruler markers for, 224–25
    in tables, 399–400, 406
Indent buttons, 225
Index And Tables dialog box
    Index card, 781–82
    Table Of Authorities card, 784–85
    Table Of Contents card, 764
    Table Of Figures card, 771
Index command (Help), 28, 29
index entry (XE) field, 776, 778, 779
indexes
    chapter page numbers in, 786–87
    compiling, 777–78, 781
    cross-reference entries in, 779–80
    example, 775–78
    fields, 762, 776, 778, 779, 782
    formatting, 781–82
    formatting page numbers in, 780
    inserting entries for, 778–80
    in long documents, 785–86
    marking all occurrences of a term,
        780–81
    for master documents, 594–95,
        785, 786
    multilevel, 779
    for multiple-file documents, 785–86
    overview, 775
    page ranges in, 778–79
    partial, 782
    splitting large, 782
    styles for, 782
    term vs. topic entries, 778–79
    updating, 783

INDEX field, 782
indicators, 22–23
INFO field, 702–7
initials, author, 336, 338–39, 707
InputBox$() function, 904–5
Input command, 898–99
Insert Annotation command, 336
Insert AutoText button, 18
Insert Break command, 486, 505, 506
Insert Caption command, 773, 826
Insert Cells dialog box, 388–89, 394
Insert Chart button, 18, 573
Insert Cross-Reference command, 832, 833
Insert Database command, 626, 639
Insert Data dialog box, 631–32
Insert Field command, 679–82
Insert Field key (Ctrl-F9), 173, 682
Insert File command, 639
Insert Footnote command, 342
Insert Form Field command, 756
Insert Frame button, 553
Insert Frame command, 512, 514, 543, 569
Insert Index And Tables command, 764, 767, 781
insertion point, 10. *See also* cursor
Insert menu, 13, 14
Insert Merge Field dialog box, 729–30, 738
Insert Microsoft Excel Worksheet button, 18
Insert mode, 91
Insert Object command, 559, 562, 573, 641–43
Insert Page Numbers command, 167–68
Insert Picture command, 537, 543, 639
Insert Picture dialog box, 537–39
Insert Rows button, 387
Insert Symbol command, 157, 840
Insert Table button, 18
Insert Table dialog box, 362–63
Ins key, 91
INT function, 808
invisible text. *See* hidden text
italic text, 241–42

J

joining paragraphs, 92, 93
jumping to. *See* Go To dialog box
jump terms, 29–30
justifying text, 223, 227, 232

K

Keep Lines Together option, 233, 505
Keep With Next option, 233, 505
kerning, 246, 247
keyboard. *See also* shortcut keys
    aligning text with, 227–28
    assigning keys to macros, 849–51
    changing fonts with, 245
    changing indentation with, 227
    changing line spacing with, 228–29
    changing margins with, 216, 218
    choosing menu options with, 13, 15
    copying formats with, 250
    copying text with, 101, 104
    cutting and pasting with, 101, 103, 104
    formatting characters with, 243–46, 987–88
    formatting paragraphs with, 226–30, 989
    getting context-sensitive Help with, 32
    list of shortcut keys, 985–94
    making key assignments, 970–74, 978
    moving cursor with, 78–82
    moving text boxes with, 526
    moving text with, 103, 104
    navigating tables with, 374–75
    overview, 984–85
    printing key assignments, 269, 459–60, 974
    resetting to default configuration, 973–74
    selecting text with, 89–90, 377
    using Find dialog box with, 111, 120–21
    using in Page Layout view, 301
    using in Print Preview, 280

key combinations. *See names of keys (Alt-F1, Ctrl-Home, etc.)*; keyboard; shortcut keys
KEYWORDS field, 701–2

L

Label Options dialog box
    in mail merge, 748–49
    for printing labels, 289–91
labels
    defining, 289–91
    and laser printers, 288, 291
    in mail merge, 748–51
    pages of, 288
    printing, 287–91
    for return addresses, 287–88
    saving document file, 289
    for shipping, 288
    single, 288
    types of, 289–90
landscape orientation, 213–14
Language dialog box, 436–37
languages, foreign, 165–66
laser printers
    and duplex printing, 267–68
    and envelope printing, 285, 286, 287
    and fonts, 584
    and label printing, 288, 291
    setup, 259, 260
LaserWriter printers, 259
LASTSAVEDBY field, 705
layout. *See* Page Layout view; Page Setup dialog box
leaders, tab, 234, 235
left-aligned tabs, 226
left-aligned text, 223, 227, 232
left-arrow pointer, 23, 24, 25
left indent marker, 224, 225
left margin, 209, 210, 216–17
less-than-or-equal-to operator (<=), 804, 901
less-than symbol (<), 114, 804, 901
letters, form. *See* mail merge
LEX files, 188
line breaks, 74, 219
Line button, 551

Line Color button, 552
line indicator, 22
line numbers
    creating, 470–72
    deleting, 473
    as go-to destination, 352
    intervals in, 472
    suppressing, 233, 473–74
    viewing, 472–73
Line Numbers dialog box, 471–72
lines, drawing, 551, 552, 553. *See also* borders
line spacing, 228–29, 231
Line Style button, 552
LINK field, 639, 643, 644, 646
linking
    with Edit Paste Special command, 643–44
    vs. embedding, 640–41, 644
    fields for, 646–47
    vs. importing, 638
    with Insert Object command, 643
    pictures, 538–39
    when to use, 641
links
    and data editing, 640
    OLE, 639–40, 829–30
    types of, 638–40
    updating, 644–45
    updating automatically, 313
    updating before printing, 270
Links dialog box, 644–45
listing
    files by type, 45–48
    files in File Find dialog box, 613–15
    last-used files, 313
    styles, 432–34, 443
lists
    bulleted, 480–81
    numbered, 475–79
    sorting, 794–98
literal text, 677–78
loading Word for Windows, 4–8
Lock Field key (Ctrl-F11), 687
locking
    documents, 53–56
    documents for annotations, 340–41
    fields, 687–88

locking, *continued*
  forms, 757
  revisions, 359
logical operators, 608, 804, 900
long documents, 589–95. *See also*
    master documents
loops, 908–9
Lower argument, 692
lowercase characters, 245, 692
LPT ports, 257

M

MACROBUTTON field, 707–10
MACRODE.EXE file, 911
Macro dialog box, 857–59
macro-recording pointer, 25, 27
macros, programmed
  Auto, 876–79
  debugging, 883–86
  examples, 890–95
  FileOpenAny example, 868–76
  Help file, 926
  interactive, 897–910
  multiple-key, 973–74, 978
  printing, 890
  vs. recorded macros, 867–70
  running, 876–79
  startup, 878
  when to use, 868–69
  writing, 870–76
macros, recorded
  assigning to menus, 851–53
  assigning to shortcut keys, 849–51
  assigning to toolbars, 853–54
  deleting, 862
  description, 846, 847–48
  editing, 863–65
  limitations of, 868–70
  multiple-key, 973–74, 978
  naming, 845–46
  pausing recording, 856
  printing, 890
  vs. programmed macros, 867–70
  recording, 844–56
  recovering, 862
  renaming, 861

macros, recorded, *continued*
  running, 857–60
  saving, 860–61
  storing in templates, 848–49, 860
Macro toolbar, 879–90
magnification indicator. *See* Zoom
    drop-down list box
magnifying pointer, 25, 27
Mail As Attach option, 313
mailing labels. *See* labels
mail merge
  adding merge fields, 728–34
  benefits of using, 716
  creating data file, 720–28
  designating main document, 718–19
  editing main document, 728–34
  fields for, 737–47
  list of shortcut keys, 990
  starting merge, 733–34
  viewing merged documents, 731–33
Mail Merge Helper dialog box, 718–20,
    721, 733, 751
Manage Fields dialog box, 725
manual hyphenation, 199, 201–3
manual page breaks, 219–20
margin release. *See* negative indentation
margins
  aligning text vertically, 489–90
  binding, 211–12, 586
  bottom, 209, 210, 218–19
  changing in Print Preview, 280–81
  changing with Page Setup dialog box,
    210, 211, 216, 217
  changing with ruler, 216, 217
  default, 209–10
  for facing pages, 211–12, 586–87
  frames in, 531–32, 588
  vs. header and footer position, 588–89
  vs. indentation, 216, 223
  left, 209, 210, 216–17
  mirrored, 211–12, 276, 586
  and negative indents, 231
  overview, 211
  previewing, 211
  right, 209, 210, 216–17
  scholar's, 531–33
  in sections, 281
  top, 209, 210, 218–19

Mark Citation dialog box, 783–84
marker fields, 676
marks. *See* paragraph marks; reference
    marks; revision marks
master documents
    adding files to, 592–93
    creating, 590–92
    indexes for, 594–95, 785–86
    sections in, 594
    subdocuments, 591–95
    tables of contents for, 594–95, 785–86
Master Document toolbar, 590–91
Master Document view, 69, 304, 590
mathematical calculations, 800–813
mathematical equations. *See* Equation
    Editor
mathematical functions, 805–10
mathematical operators, 802–4
mathematical typesetting. *See* Equation
    Editor
MAX function, 808, 813
Maximize button, 11
measurement units, 212, 313
menu bar, 12–15
Menu Bar dialog box, 965–66
menus
    adding, 965–66
    adding items, 955–58
    assigning macros to, 851–53
    choosing options with keyboard,
      13, 15
    choosing options with mouse, 13
    context-sensitive, 15–16
    copying items, 961–62
    customizing, 952–68
    deleting, 966
    deleting items, 958–59
    list of, 13, 14
    list of shortcut keys, 992–94
    moving, 966
    moving items, 961–62
    renaming, 965, 967–68
    renaming items, 960–61
    resetting to default configuration,
      963–64
    saving key assignments, 974
    separators, 962–63
    shortcut, 15–16

Merge dialog box, 733, 734–36
MERGEFIELD field, 730, 739, 742
merge fields
    adding to main document, 728–31
    defined, 717
MergeFormat argument, 691
MERGEREC field, 743
MERGESEQ field, 738, 746–47
merging. *See also* mail merge
    cells, 395, 396–97
    styles, 462–65
message boxes, 905–7
Metafile (WMF) format, 536
metric measurement, 212
Microsoft Draw. *See* drawing tools
Microsoft Excel, inserting data from, 560,
    578, 640
Microsoft Graph, 572–77
Microsoft Office, 4
Microsoft Query, 720
Microsoft Word 6.0 for Windows
    customizing, 33–40
    icon, 4–5
    new features (*see* new Word features)
    quitting, 61
    screen features of, 9–28
    starting from MS-DOS, 8
    starting from Windows, 4–8
    window, 11
Microsoft WordArt, 561–72. *See* WordArt
    objects
Microsoft Word Developer's Kit, 868
MIN function, 808, 813
mini-applications
    Microsoft Draw (*see* drawing tools)
    Microsoft Graph, 572–77
    WordArt, 561–72
Minimize command, 11
minus sign (–), 802, 803
mirror margins, 211–12, 276, 586
MOD function, 808
Modify Bulleted List dialog box, 480–81
Modify Location dialog box, 930–31
Modify Numbered List dialog box,
    476–78
Modify Style dialog box, 443–44
monospaced fonts, 242

mouse
  adjusting table column width with, 378–79
  aligning text with, 223
  changing indentation with, 224–25
  changing margins with, 216, 218
  choosing menu options with, 13
  copying formats with, 250
  cropping pictures with, 540, 542
  double-clicking, 85–86
  dragging, 85
  dragging and dropping text, 104–5
  and drawing objects, 554, 555
  formatting characters with, 241–42
  formatting paragraphs with, 222–26
  getting context-sensitive help with, 32
  indenting table rows with, 400
  moving cursor with, 75
  navigating with, 75–77
  overview, 983–84
  right mouse button, 984
  scaling pictures with, 540, 541–42
  scrolling with, 76–77
  selecting text with, 85–89, 376–77
  setting tabs with, 226
  sizing frames with, 517–19
  using in Page Layout view, 301–2
mouse pointer, 23–28
Move key (F2), 104
Move To feature, 104
moving
  to designated location, 104
  between documents, 106–8
  files, 617
  frames, 517–19
  menus and menu items, 961–62, 966
  in Outline view, 669–70
  with shortcut keys, 103, 104
  styles, 947
  table columns, 394
  table rows, 390
  text boxes, 526
  text with Clipboard, 103
  text with mouse, 104–5
  text without Clipboard, 103–4
  toolbars, 316–17
  WordArt objects, 569

MRK indicator, 22, 23, 353
MS-DOS
  command line, 8, 602
  printing from, 265–66
  starting Word for Windows from, 8
MsgBox command, 905–7
MsgBox() function, 905–7
MS Graph. *See* Microsoft Graph
MSINFO program, 32
multilevel paragraphs, numbering, 482–83. *See also* outlines
multiple documents
  deleting, 63
  opening, 615–16
  opening at startup, 6, 8
  printing, 616
  saving, 60
multiplication operator (∗), 803
multisection documents, 485–95

N

naming
  AutoCorrect entries, 136
  AutoText entries, 142–44
  bookmarks, 334–35
  documents, 51, 53
  styles, 435
navigating documents, 75–84
negative indentation, 231
nesting fields, 695
network drives
  accessing Word files on, 49
  saving Word files to, 52
New button, 17
New command (Windows), 6
New (File) dialog box, 44–45
newspaper-style columns. *See* columns, snaking
New Style dialog box, 434–40, 441–43, 449
new Word features
  AutoCorrect, 132–40
  AutoFormat, 18, 420–27
  context-sensitive menus, 15–16
  duplex printing, 267–68

new Word features, *continued*
   Format Painter, 17, 25, 27, 249–51
   Master Document view, 590–95
   multiple-level Undo, 94–95
   on-screen forms, 752–58
   shortcut menus, 15–16
   Style Gallery, 426, 429–32
   text boxes, 525–30
   vertical ruler, 218, 278–79, 280–81, 311
   wizards, 322–24
NEXT field, 744
NEXTIF field, 744–45
Next Style option, 437–38
non-breaking hyphens, 162
non-breaking spaces, 73, 163–64
   nonprinting characters, 36, 72–73, 245, 311
(no proofing) option, 189, 198, 436, 437
NORMAL.DOT file, 65, 327. *See also* Normal template
Normal style
   changing, 428, 445, 448
   defined, 447
   vs. other built-in styles, 448–49
Normal template
   adding styles to, 465–67
   AutoText entries in, 146, 148–49
   built-in styles in, 445–47
   changing, 942, 943
   deleting, 467
   vs. global templates, 326, 938–39, 941, 942, 943–44
   macros in, 849, 860
   overview, 65, 325–27
   restoring default configuration, 467
   saving style changes, 466–67
   specifying, 65
   storing shortcut keys in, 160
   using exclusively, 64
   when to use, 942, 944
Normal view
   changing to, 20
   columns in, 499–500
   with draft font, 295–96
   frames in, 510–11
   outlines in, 657–58
   overview, 294–95

Normal view, *continued*
   ruler in, 215–16
   zoom settings, 307
(no style) option, 453
Note Options dialog box
   All Endnotes card, 344–45
   All Footnotes card, 343–44, 345
not-equal-to operator (<>), 804, 901
NOTEREF field, 835
NOT function, 808
NOT operator, 608
numbering
   annotations, 338–39
   deleting, 473, 478–79
   footnotes, 342, 344–45
   lines, 470–74
   multilevel paragraphs, 482–83
   outline headings, 483–85
   outlines, 673
   pages, 167–75
   paragraphs, 475–79
   sequential, 824–32
numbers, formatting, 692–93
NUMCHARS field, 705
numeric picture switch (\#), 693–95
NUMPAGES field, 692–93, 705
NUMWORDS field, 705

O

Object Anchors option, 312
Object dialog box
   Create From File card, 560–61, 641–42
   Create New card, 560, 641
Object Linking and Embedding (OLE), 639–40, 829–30
object-oriented images, 536, 553–55, 559
objects. *See also* drawing objects
   embedding, 641–43, 644
   importing, 559
   inserting, 577–78
   inserting as icons, 561, 569–70
   linked (*see* linking)
   linked vs. embedded, 640–41
OEM codes, 116, 118, 624, 839–40, 995–98
Office. *See* Microsoft Office

OLE (Object Linking and Embedding), 639–40, 829–30
OLE objects. *See* objects
online forms. *See* forms
online Help. *See* Help system
Open button, 17, 45
Open dialog box, 45, 621–22
opening
    documents, 45–50
    multiple documents, 615–16
operators
    arithmetic, 802–4
    in formulas, 802–5
    lists of, 803, 804, 901
    precedence, 803–5
    relational, 901
optional hyphens, 163, 198, 204
Options dialog box
    AutoFormat card, 420–23
    Compatibility card, 634–35
    Edit card, 37–38, 314
    File Locations card, 314–15, 930–31
    General card, 36, 313
    Grammar card, 194–98
    overview, 35, 310
    Print card, 269–72
    Review card, 357–58
    Save card, 38–39, 53–56, 315
    Spelling card, 183–85
    Use Info card, 40
    View card, 35–36, 300, 310–12, 683, 684–85
Ordinal argument, 693
OrdText argument, 692, 693
OR function, 808–9
Organizer dialog box
    AutoText card, 146, 948
    Macros card, 861, 948, 949
    Styles card, 464–65, 466, 945–47
    Toolbars card, 321–22, 948
organizing files, 600–603
orientation, page, 213–14, 260
OR operator, 608
orphans. *See* widows and orphans
outdents, 231
outline pointers, 25, 26–27

outlines. *See also* multilevel paragraphs, numbering
    collapsing/expanding, 662–63
    creating, 654–60
    editing, 660–61
    list of shortcut keys, 991
    Normal vs. Outline view, 657–58
    numbering, 673
    overview, 651–53
    printing, 672–73
Outline view
    frames in, 511
    vs. Master Document view, 673
    navigating in, 83–84
    vs. Normal view, 673
    overview, 20, 297–98, 652
    sorting in, 794
Outlining toolbar, 652
overriding AutoCorrect, 140
overstriking. *See* Overtype mode
Overtype mode, 38, 91, 93
OVR indicator, 22, 23, 91, 93

P

Page Back button, 301
page breaks
    automatic, 219–20
    controlling in Paragraph dialog box, 232–33
    deleting, 220
    manual, 219–20
    and table rows, 386
    when not to insert, 220
    widow/orphan control, 220–21, 232
Page Down key, 78, 79
PAGE field, 170–71
page formatting, 209–19
Page Forward button, 301
page height, 209–10
Page Layout view
    boundary lines in, 299–301, 302, 310
    changing to, 20
    columns in, 500–501
    default options, 310, 311, 312
    double-arrow buttons, 301

Page Layout view, *continued*
    editing in, 303–4
    footnotes in, 304
    formatting in, 303–4
    frames in, 511, 512, 514–16
    headers and footers in, 171–75, 303–4
    and hyphenation, 201
    limitations of, 282
    navigating in, 301–2
    overview, 281–82, 298–99
    vs. Print Preview, 275, 281
    selecting text in, 303
    selection bar in, 303
    shortcut keys, 301
    text areas in, 299
    view options in, 300
    zoom settings, 306, 307, 308
page length, 209–10
page margins, 209–10, 215–18
Page Number Format dialog box, 169–70,
    491–92
page numbers
    chapter, 169–70
    entering with Header And Footer
        toolbar, 171–75
    entering with Insert Page Numbers
        command, 167–71
    as go-to destination, 81, 351
    in indexes, 778–79, 780, 786–87
    previewing, 168
    repagination, 219, 313, 351
    in sections, 487–88, 491–92
    status bar indicator, 22
    in tables of contents, 763
Page Numbers dialog box, 168–69
page orientation, 213–14, 260
PAGEREF field, 835
pages
    duplex printing, 267–68
    facing, 168, 211–12, 586–87
    formatting, 209–19, 990
    list of formatting shortcut keys, 990
    numbering, 167–71
    numbering by chapter, 169–75
    printing selected, 266, 267
    reversing print order, 270

Page Setup dialog box
    Layout card, 174, 215, 470–71, 473,
        488–90, 495, 587–88
    Margins card, 210, 211, 216, 218, 586,
        587, 588–89
    overview, 210
    Paper Size card, 212–13
    Paper Source card, 214–15
page size, 209–10, 212–14
Page Up key, 78, 79
page width, 209–10
panes
    for annotations, 336–37, 339
    for footnotes, 345–46
    for headers and footers, 177
    moving between (F6), 339, 346
    sizing, 339
    splitting windows into, 21
    for viewing field codes, 683
paper feed
    envelopes, 285–86
    label problems, 288
paper orientation, 213–14, 260
paper size, 209–10, 212–14
paper source
    default tray, 272
    envelopes, 285–86
    overview, 214–15
Paragraph Borders And
        Shading dialog box
    Borders card, 237–39
    Shading card, 239–40
Paragraph dialog box
    Indents And Spacing card, 230–32
    Text Flow card, 232–33, 473–74
paragraph marks
    copying, 108, 249
    in data files, 727–28
    deleting, 92, 93
    hiding, 71, 72
    overview, 71, 74
    viewing, 36, 71, 72
paragraphs
    adding borders to, 236–40
    combining, 92, 93
    copying formatting, 108, 248–49

paragraphs, *continued*
    default formatting options, 221–22
    defined, 74
    extra lines between, 229–30, 231
    formatting directly, 221–41
    formatting with styles, 419–67
    joining, 92, 93
    justified, 223, 227, 232
    keeping together, 233
    line spacing in, 228–29, 231
    multilevel, numbering, 482–83
    numbering, 475–79
    shading, 239–40
    shortcut keys for formatting, 226–30,
      989
    spacing between, 229–30, 231
    in tables, 401–7
parallel ports, 257
parent directory, 47, 605
parentheses (), 115, 804
passwords
    for files, 54–55
    to lock documents for annotation,
      340–41
    for templates, 933–34
paste area, 402–4
Paste button, 17, 100
Paste command, 94, 100, 101, 103
Paste Special dialog box, 643–44
pasting. *See* Clipboard;
    Smart Cut And Paste
pathnames, 46
PATH statement (MS-DOS), 5, 7
pattern matching, 609–10
PCX files, 536
percentage, as go-to destination, 353
percent sign (%), 803
Picture dialog box, 542–43
Picture Editor option, 314
pictures. *See also* drawing objects
    as AutoText entries, 147–48
    borders for, 546
    captions for, 544–45
    CLIPART directory, 536, 537
    cropping, 540, 542–43
    frames for, 535, 543–44
    importing, 536

pictures, *continued*
    inserting, 535–39
    linking, 538–39
    placeholders for, 296, 311
    positioning, 543–44, 547
    scaling, 540, 541–42
    sizing, 539–43
    in tables, 547
picture switches, 693–95
placeholders, 296, 311
plus sign (+), 802, 803
point size, 70
portrait orientation, 209–10, 213–14
ports, printer, 256–58
Postnet bar codes, 285, 288
PostScript printers, 585
PRACTICE.DOT file, 952–54
precedence, operator, 803–5
preferences. *See* Options dialog box
previewing
    Based-On styles, 451–52
    borders, 237
    document. *See* Print Preview
    margins, 211
    page numbers, 168
    pages. *See* Print Preview
    paragraph formatting, 230, 232
    pictures, 538–39
    styles, 430–31
Print button, 17, 263
PRINTDATE field, 706
Print dialog box, 262, 263, 266–72, 460
printer drivers, 256, 584, 585
printers
    adding, 255–56
    changing default, 262–63
    configuring, 256–62
    deleting after installation, 261–62
    designating default, 254–55
    installing, 253–56
    laser, 259, 260, 267–68, 287, 288,
      291, 584
    orientation option, 214
    ports, 256–58
    resident fonts, 582, 584–85
    setup options, 258–61
    timeout settings, 258

Printers dialog box, 254–56, 261
PRINT field, 838–39
printing
    of annotations, 271, 341
    of AutoText entries, 150–51, 268–69
    in background, 264, 270–71
    on both sides, 267–68
    of collated copies, 266
    default options, 269–72
    to disk, 257–58, 268
    draft output, 270, 296
    of drawing objects, 272
    of envelopes, 283–87
    of field codes, 271
    from File Find, 616
    of form field information, 272
    of forms, 272
    from Help system, 33
    of hidden text, 271
    of key assignments, 269, 459–60, 974
    of labels, 287–91
    of macros, 890
    merged, 737
    from MS-DOS, 265–66
    of multiple copies, 261, 266
    of multiple files, 616
    of odd/even pages, 267–68
    outlines, 672–73
    overview, 263, 264
    from Print dialog box, 262, 263,
      266–72
    from Print Preview, 274
    in reverse page order, 270
    of selected pages, 266, 267
    of selected text, 266, 267
    of styles, 459–60
    of summary information, 271
    troubleshooting, 265–66
    updating fields during, 270, 687
Print Manager
    and background printing, 264
    overview, 255
    using, 264–65
print merge. *See* mail merge
Print Preview
    editing in, 280–81

Print Preview, *continued*
    headers and footers in, 281
    mirror margins in, 276
    navigating, 280
    number of pages, 276–77
    overview, 273
    vs. Page Layout view, 275, 281
    toolbar, 274–80
Print Preview button, 17, 273
Print Setup dialog box, 262–63
print spoolers. *See* Print Manager
PRIVATE field, 622
PRN files, 258
PRODUCT function, 809, 813
Program Item Properties dialog box, 6–7
Program Manager
    selecting icons in, 5
    starting Word from, 4–8
programming. *See* macros, programmed
Promote button, 653, 656, 657, 665, 666
prompt, MS-DOS, starting Word from, 8
Prompt For Summary Info option, 39
proportional fonts, 242
Protect Document dialog box, 340, 756
protecting documents, 53–56
protection passwords, 54, 55

Q

Query Options dialog box
    Filter Records card, 628–29, 736
    Select Fields card, 630–31
    Sort Records card, 629
question-mark-and-arrow pointer,
    25, 27
question mark (?) as wildcard character,
    113, 604, 608
Quick Preview command (Help), 30
Quick Preview screen, 9, 30
quitting Word for Windows, 61
quotation marks
    changing to "smart," 134–35
    curly (" "), 134–35, 164
    in file searches, 608

quotation marks, *continued*
  replacing using Find and Replace, 134–35
  straight (" "), 134
  in text strings, 727–28, 908
QUOTE field, 738, 745

R

Readability Statistics dialog box, 192–94
read-only mode
  file sharing option, 55–56
  opening files in, 49–50
  saving files in, 60
Recently Used File List option, 50
REC indicator, 22, 23, 855, 856
recording macros, 844–56
Record Macro dialog box, 845–56
records, defined, 626, 716
Rectangle/Square button, 551
redlining. *See* revision marks
Redo button, 18
Redo command, 94, 95
reference fields, 835–38
reference marks
  annotation, 336, 337, 338–39
  footnote and endnote, 342–43, 347
REF field, 687, 835
relational operators, 901
removing. *See* deleting
renaming
  AutoCorrect entries, 139
  AutoText entries, 146
  files, 56, 617
  macros, 861
  menus and menu items, 960–61, 965, 967–68
  styles, 444, 947
reopening documents, 50
repagination, 219, 313, 351
Repeat command, 95, 96, 160, 248
Repeat key (F4), 248
Replace dialog box, 121–29
Replace Text As You Type option, 135–39

replacing
  case matching in, 125–27
  from Clipboard, 105–6
  of formatting, 127–28
  of hidden text, 127
  of special characters, 128–29
  of styles, 127–28
  of text, 91, 92–93, 105–6, 121–27
Reshape button, 553, 556
resizing. *See* sizing
restoring. *See* Undo command
result fields, 676
retrieving documents. *See* opening
return addresses
  on envelopes, 283–84
  labels for, 287–88
Review AutoFormat Changes dialog box, 424–26
Review Revisions dialog box, 357–58
revision marks
  accepting changes, 356–58
  adding, 353–54
  colored, 354
  overview, 353
  rejecting changes, 356–58
  reviewing, 356, 357
  undoing, 356
revision numbers, 706
Revisions dialog box, 353–54, 356, 357
REVNUM field, 706
right-aligned tabs, 226
right-aligned text, 223, 227, 232
right-arrow pointer, 24, 25
right margin, 209, 210, 216–17
right mouse button, 15, 984
Roman argument, 693
root directory, 602
Rotate Left button, 553
Rotate Right button, 553
ROUND function, 809
rows, table. *See also* tables
  adding, 386–88
  aligning, 399–400
  breaking across pages, 386
  deleting, 389–91

rows, table, *continued*
    height, 384–86, 406
    indenting, 399
    moving, 390
RTF files, 48
ruler, horizontal
    changing indentation with, 224–25
    changing margins with, 217, 218
    default, 215
    illustrated, 20
    in Normal view, 215–16
    overview, 19–20, 215–16
    in Print Preview, 278–79, 280–81
    setting tabs with, 226
    and text boundary lines, 302
    turning on/off, 34
    using with tables, 371–73
ruler, vertical, 218, 278–79, 280–81, 311
rules (lines). *See* borders
Run dialog box (Windows), 5, 6

S

sans serif fonts, 242
Save All command, 60, 150
Save As command, 51, 53–56, 59
Save As dialog box, 51–52, 632–33,
    934–35
Save button, 17, 51, 59
Save command, 51, 59
Save Data Source dialog box, 721
SAVEDATE field, 706
saving documents
    automatically, 39, 54
    with backup copies, 38
    default options, 38–39, 53–56
    fast vs. full saves, 39
    first time, 51
    multiple open, 60
    to network drives, 52
    in other file formats, 632–33
    read-only, 60
    as templates, 933–34
    as text files, 633
    troubleshooting, 59
saving macros, 860–61

scalable fonts, 583
scaling pictures, 540, 541–24.
    See also sizing
scholar's margins, 531–33
screen display
    blue with white characters, 313
    Full Screen mode, 304–6
    overview, 9–28
    3-D effects, 313
    views, 69, 293–309, 310–12
screen fonts, 582, 585
scroll arrows, 20, 76, 77
scroll bars, 20–21, 35, 76–77
scroll boxes, 20, 76–77
scrolling, 76–77
Search dialog box, 604–5
Search For Help On command (Help), 28
searching
    case matching in, 112, 610
    for files, 603–17
    for formatting, 119–21
    for hidden text, 119
    for marked revisions, 357–58
    pattern matching in, 113–15
    for special characters, 115–18
    for styles, 119–21
    for text, 109–15
    with wildcards, 113–14
SECTION field, 595
sections
    breaks between, 486–87
    changing margins in, 281
    changing page numbering, 491–92
    changing type of break, 488–89
    columns in, 501–8
    combining, 495
    creating, 486–88
    for envelopes, 286–87
    formatting, 488–90
    as go-to destination, 352
    headers and footers in, 492–95, 587–88
    in master documents, 594
    overview, 485
    page numbering in, 487–88, 491, 492
    status bar indicator, 22, 487
    for tables of contents, 763

Select Drawing Objects button, 552
selecting files, 613–14
selecting text
    all, 90
    blocks, 87–89
    in columns, 88–89
    with keyboard, 89–90
    list of shortcut keys, 991
    with mouse, 85–89
    in Page Layout view, 303
    with selection bar, 87–88, 376–77
    sentences, 87
    in tables, 375–77
    words, 86
selection bar, 87–88, 303, 376–77
Send Behind Text button, 552
SendKeys statement, 871–73
Send To Back button, 552
sentences
    defined, 74
    selecting, 87
SEQ field, 678, 824, 825, 830–32
sequence identifiers, 678
sequential numbering, 824–32
serial ports, 257
serif fonts, 242
SET field, 745–46
Setup HP LaserJet III dialog box, 259, 260
shading
    deleting, 412
    and frames, 517
    overview, 239–40
    in tables, 408
    in text boxes, 528
    WordArt objects, 567
Shift-Del, 94, 103
Shift-Enter, 74
Shift-F1 (Help), 32
Shift-F2 (Copy), 103
Shift-F3 (Case), 245
Shift-F4 (Repeat Search), 111
Shift-F5 (Go Back), 80, 351
Shift-F7 (Thesaurus), 154
Shift-F8 (Shrink Selection), 63
Shift-F9 (Field Codes), 172, 173, 684
Shift-F11 (Previous Field), 688–89
Shift-Ins (Paste), 103

Shift-Tab, 374, 375
shortcut keys
    for aligning text, 227–28
    for applying font formats, 243–46,
        987–88
    for applying styles, 456
    assigning macros to, 849–51
    assigning styles to, 454–56
    assigning to dialog boxes, 978–79
    for copying, 986
    for cursor movement, 985
    for cutting and pasting, 986
    for deleting, 986
    in Equation Editor, 820–22
    field-related, 987
    for footnotes and endnotes, 346
    for indenting, 227
    for inserting special characters,
        161–66
    for inserting symbols, 158–60
    for line spacing, 228–29
    for mail merge, 990
    making assignments, 970–74
    for outlines, 991
    overview, 15
    for paragraph formatting, 226–30, 989
    for paragraph spacing, 229–30
    for selection, 991
    for special characters, 988–89
    storing in Normal template, 160
    for style formatting, 990
    for tables, 992
    window-related, 992
shortcut menus, 15–16
Show First Line Only button, 653, 659
Show Formatting button, 653, 656
Show Heading buttons, 390, 653, 662–63
Show/Hide ¶ button, 18, 36, 71, 72, 365
side-by-side columns. *See* columns, table
SIGN function, 809
Size menu (Equation Editor), 816, 818
sizing
    frames, 517–19, 520
    pictures, 539–43
    text boxes, 528
    window panes, 339

sizing arrows, 24, 25
SKIPIF field, 746
slash (/), 803
Smart Cut And Paste, 108
Smart Quotes, 134–35
snaking columns. *See* columns, snaking
Snap To Grid button, 553, 556–57
Snap To Grid dialog box, 556
soft fonts, 584
Sort dialog box, 789
sorting
    alphanumeric, 792–93
    columns, 797–98, 800
    by date, 793–94
    default options for, 790
    numeric, 793
    in Outline view, 794
    overview, 789–92
    tables, 417, 799–800
    tabular lists, 794–98
Sort Options dialog box, 789–92
Sort Text dialog box, 789, 790–91
sound annotations, 338
space characters, 73, 74
spaces
    em, 161–62
    en, 161–62
    non-breaking, 73, 163–64
spacing
    between characters, 246, 247–48
    between lines, 228–29, 231
    between paragraphs, 229–30, 231
    within paragraphs, 228–29, 231
    between snaking columns, 502
    between table columns, 381–84
special characters
    creating, 839–40
    inserting, 157, 161–66
    inserting with keyboard, 165, 166
    nonprinting, 36, 72–73, 311
    replacing, 128–29
    searching for, 115–18
    shortcut keys for, 165, 988–89
    storing as AutoText, 839–40
Spelling button, 17, 180, 185

spelling checker
    adding words to dictionary, 181,
        186–87
    and AutoCorrect, 182
    case in, 184, 187
    default options, 183–85
    dictionaries for, 185, 186–89
    excluding words from dictionary,
        188–89
    ignoring words, 180–81, 184
    (no proofing) option, 189
    overview, 179–80
    selected text, 186
    single words, 186
    suggestion options, 183–84
    turning off in grammar checker, 190,
        194
    undoing changes, 182–83
Spelling dialog box, 180–83
Spelling key (F7), 180, 185
Spike, 151–53
Spike key (Ctrl-F3), 152
split bar, 339
split box, 21
Split Cells dialog box, 396
Split command, 12, 21
split pointer, 21
splitting windows, 21. *See also* panes
spreadsheets, Word tables as, 417,
        812–13
square brackets ([ ]), 114, 336
Standard toolbar
    Format Painter, 17, 25, 27, 249–51
    Help button, 18, 32
    illustrated, 17
    moving, 316–17
    overview, 16–19
    Show/Hide ¶ button, 18, 36, 71, 72,
        365
    turning on/off, 34
    Zoom drop-down list box, 18, 69, 309
"star-dot-star" (∗.∗), 47
starting Word for Windows
    from MS-DOS, 8
    from Windows, 4–8

startup macros, 878
startup templates, 941
statistical fields, 703–7
statistics
  document, 58
  readability, 192–94
status bar, 19, 21–23, 310
straight quotation marks (" "), 134
strikethrough, 354
style area, 311, 457–59
Style dialog box
  applying styles with, 433, 457
  listing styles in, 432–34
  viewing style definitions, 433–34
Style drop-down list, 432–34, 443
Style For Following Paragraph option,
  437–38
Style Gallery, 426, 429–32
Style menu (Equation Editor), 816, 818
style names, 435, 444
STYLEREF field, 835–38
styles
  adding, 441–43
  alias feature, 444
  applying, 433, 443, 454–57
  applying with Formatting toolbar, 457
  applying with shortcut keys, 456
  applying with Style dialog box, 433,
    457
  assigning to shortcut keys, 454–56
  AutoFormat, 420–27
  automatic, 429, 445, 448
  Based-On option, 437, 438–40, 450–53
  built-in, 428, 429, 445–49
  built-in, list of, 446–47
  changing, 443–44
  changing (built-in), 445
  changing by example, 449–50
  changing (custom), 443–44
  changing in templates, 465–67
  character vs. paragraph, 428, 433, 435,
    441, 442, 443, 449, 462–63
  circular, 453
  combining with direct formatting,
    460–62

styles, *continued*
  copying, 462–64, 947
  creating by example, 449–51
  creating from scratch, 441–43
  custom, defined, 428–29
  defining, 434–41
  deleting, 445, 947
  importing, 464–65
  levels of, 453
  listing, 432–34, 443, 446–47
  manually applied, 429, 448
  merging, 462–65
  moving, 947
  naming, 435
  Normal, 428, 445, 447, 448–49
  in Normal template, 445–47
  for outlines, 656, 671–72
  overriding, 460–62
  overview, 419, 427–29
  paragraph vs. character, 428, 433, 435,
    441, 442, 443, 449, 462–63
  previewing, 430–31
  printing list of, 459–60
  related, 453
  renaming, 444, 947
  replacing, 127–28
  restoring to defaults, 467
  saving changes, 445, 466–67
  searching for, 119–21
  shortcut keys for formatting, 990
  storing, 429, 945–47
  Style For Following Paragraph option,
    437–38
  in tables of contents, 764–66
  in templates, 429, 945–47
  types of, 428–29
  viewing definitions, 433–34
  viewing in style area, 457–59
SUBJECT field, 701–2
subscript. *See* Equation Editor
SUBSECTION field, 595
subtraction operator (–), 802, 803
SUM function, 801, 809, 813
Summary Info dialog box, 52–53, 56–59,
  603, 615

summary information
  editing, 615
  fields, 700–702
  overview, 56–59
  printing, 271
superscript. *See* Equation Editor
supplementary templates, 64, 326, 940,
    941, 943–44
support, technical, 31
switches
  for date and time fields, 695
  numeric, 693–95
  overview, 678–79
  for text formatting, 690–92
Symbol dialog box
  choosing bullets from, 481
  Special Characters card, 161, 164
  Symbols card, 157–58, 164
Symbol font, 246
symbols
  as bullets, 480, 481
  creating, 839–40
  inserting, 157–60
  shortcut keys for, 158–60, 988–89
  storing as AutoText, 839–40
synonyms, finding, 153–56
SYSTEM directory, 602

T

tabbed cards. *See* Options dialog box
Tab key, 374, 375, 407
tab leaders, 234, 235
Table AutoFormat, 367–71
Table Borders And Shading dialog box
  Borders card, 407–10
  Shading card, 408
Table button, 364
Table Cell Height And Width command,
    379–81
Table Convert Table To Text command,
    401, 416
Table Convert Text To Table command,
    413, 416

Table Delete Cells command, 390–91, 394
Table Delete Columns command, 394
Table Delete Rows command, 389–90
Table Formula command, 810, 811
Table Gridlines command, 365
Table Insert Cells command, 386, 388–89,
    394
Table Insert Columns command, 391, 393
Table Insert Rows command, 386, 387
Table Insert Table command, 362, 366
Table menu, 13, 14
Table Merge Cells command, 395
Table Of Contents Options dialog box,
    763–64
Table Of Figures Options dialog box,
    771–72
tables
  adding cells to, 394–95
  adding columns to, 391–93
  adding rows to, 386–88
  adding text above, 400
  aligning, 398
  aligning rows in, 399–400
  AutoFit, 371, 380–81
  AutoFormat, 367–71
  as AutoText, 367
  at beginning of document, 400
  borders in, 407–12
  breaking rows across pages, 386
  calculations in, 417, 812–13
  captions for, 825–30
  column width in, 377–81
  combining cells, 395, 396–97
  converting text to, 412–16
  converting to text, 401, 416–17
  creating, 361–71
  cutting and pasting in, 402–5
  deleting, 398
  deleting cells in, 394–95
  deleting columns in, 394
  deleting rows in, 389–91
  editing text in, 401–4
  entering text in, 373–74
  formatting text in, 405–7
  formatting with AutoFormat, 367–71

tables, *continued*
  as go-to destination, 352
  gridlines in, 363, 364–65
  indenting rows in, 399–400
  indenting text, 406
  inserting, 361–67
  inserting cells into, 394–95
  list of shortcut keys, 992
  merging cells in, 395, 396–97
  moving columns, 394
  moving rows, 390
  navigating, 374–75
  paragraphs in, 401–7
  paste area, 402–4
  pictures in, 547
  row height in, 384–86
  selecting text in, 375–77
  shading in, 408
  shortcut keys for navigating, 374–75
  side-by-side, 401, 410–12, 507
  sorting, 417, 799–800
  space around text, 385, 406
  space between columns, 381–84
  splitting cells, 396
  splitting in two, 400–401
  as spreadsheets, 417, 812–13
  tabs in, 406–7
  text in, 401–7
  using ruler with, 371–73
Table Select Column command, 376
Table Select Row command, 376
Table Select Table command, 376
tables of authorities, 783–85
tables of contents
  creating from multiple-file
    documents, 785–86
  creating from outline headings, 762,
    764–66
  creating from TC fields, 762, 767–69
  fields, 762, 764, 766, 767–69, 772
  formatting, 770–71
  in long documents, 785–86
  for master documents, 594–95
  multiple levels in, 765
  numbering pages in, 763

tables of contents, *continued*
  overview, 762
  partial, 769–70
  separate sections for, 763
  TOC field for, 764, 766, 772
  updating, 764, 767
tables of figures
  building, 771–74
  formatting, 774
  using captions, 773–74
Table Sort command, 789
Table Wizard, 365–67
tabs
  as field delimiters, 727–28
  in tables, 406–7
Tabs dialog box, 233–36
tab stops
  adding, 235
  bar-type, 234
  centered, 226
  clearing all, 235
  custom, 234–35
  decimal, 226
  default, 234
  deleting, 235
  editing with Tabs dialog box, 235
  left-aligned, 226
  right-aligned, 226
  setting with ruler, 226
  setting with Tabs dialog box, 234–35
  types of, 226, 234
tabular columns. *See* columns, tabular
TA field, 783, 784, 785
TC field, 767–69, 772
Technical Support command (Help), 31
TEMPLATE field, 706
templates. *See also* forms; wizards
  attaching, 328–29, 939, 940
  AutoText entries in, 146, 148–49, 948,
    949
  changing, 327, 465
  context for, 64
  copying, 936
  creating, 327–28, 929–36
  creating by modification, 935–36

templates, *continued*
creating from documents, 934–35
creating from scratch, 931–34
creating from wizards, 936, 944
default directory for, 930–31
defined, 63
deleting, 938
detaching, 328–29
document, 326, 327, 328–29
editing, 327, 937–38
for file conversion, 637
global, 326, 329, 938, 939, 940, 941,
942, 943–44
macros in, 849–950, 860
naming, 328
Normal, 64, 65, 325–27, 942, 944
Normal vs. global, 326, 938–39, 941,
942, 943–44
overview, 63–65, 325
passwords for, 933–34
for practice, 952–54
previewing in Style Gallery, 430–31
restoring Word defaults, 327
saving, 315, 466–67, 932, 974
startup, 941
storing customizations, 941–43
styles in, 429, 945–47
supplementary, 64, 326, 940, 941,
943–44
types of, 325–27, 938–44
which kind to use, 943–44
with Word 6.0, 944
Templates And Add-Ins dialog box,
326, 328–29, 939–40, 953
text
adding to frames, 513
aligning, 223, 227, 232
aligning vertically, 489–90
blocks, 74, 87–89
boldface, 241–42
borders around, 238
centering, 223, 227, 232
copying, 100–103, 104–6
cutting and pasting, 94, 99–108
deleting, 91–92

text, *continued*
editing, 91–94
elements of, 73–75
entering, 70–71
finding, 109–15
flowing around frames, 520–21
formatting (*see* formatting)
framing, 514
hidden, 119, 127, 271, 311
hyphenating, 198–204
inserting, 91
italic, 241–42
justifying, 223, 227, 232
left-aligning, 223, 227, 232
lowercase, 245
moving, 103–4
multicolumn, 497–509
navigating, 75–84
overwriting, 91, 92–93
replacing, 91, 92–93, 121–27
replacing from Clipboard, 105–6
right-aligning, 223, 227, 232
searching for, 109–15
selecting, 84–90, 303
in tables, 401–7
underlining, 241–42
uppercase, 245
wrapping, 67–68, 312
text area boundaries, 299–301, 302, 310
Text Box button, 526, 551
text boxes
borders for, 529
in frames, 544–45
vs. frames, 525, 526, 527, 530–31, 533
in headers and footers, 533–34
inserting, 525–26
moving, 526
positioning, 528
shading of, 528
sizing, 528
when to use, 530–31
text files
carriage returns in, 624
formats for saving, 633

text files, *continued*
   MS-DOS Text Only With Line Breaks
      option, 633
   MS-DOS Text option, 623–24, 625
   options for importing, 623–25
   Text Only option, 624, 625
   Text Only With Line Breaks option,
      633
   Text option, 623–24, 625
   Text With Layout option, 624, 625
Text Form Field Options dialog box,
   754–55
text form fields, 754–55
Thesaurus, 153–56
Thesaurus dialog box, 154–56
Thesaurus key (Shift-F7), 154
3-D display effects, 313
thumbnails, 276–77, 308
TIFF(Tagged Image File Format) files, 536
tilde (~), 608, 609
time
   formatting, 695, 698–99
   in headers and footers, 172, 173
TIME field, 172, 173, 696–700
timeout, printer, 258
Tip of the Day, 9, 30
title bar, 10–12
TITLE field, 701
titles, in document summaries, 57
TOA field, 785
TOC field, 764, 766, 772
toolbars. *See also* buttons, toolbar;
      Formatting toolbar; Standard
      toolbar
   adding buttons, 318–21
   assigning macros to, 853–54
   changing, 317–20
   creating, 321–22
   customizing, 316–20
   floating, 316–17
   moving, 316–17
Tools AutoCorrect command, 133, 137,
   138
Tools Compare Versions command, 358
Tools Customize command, 954, 965

Tools Envelopes And Labels command,
   282
Tools Grammar command, 190
Tools Hyphenation command, 198, 199
Tools Macro command, 845, 856, 857
Tools Mail Merge command, 717–18
Tools menu, 13, 14
Tools Options command. *See* Options
      dialog box
Tools Protect Document command, 340,
   756
Tools Revision command, 353
Tools Spelling command, 180, 185
Tools Thesaurus command, 154–55
top-down document design, 208
top margin, 209, 210, 218–19
trademark symbol, 164
trigger keys, changing, 960, 962
troubleshooting
   printing, 265–66
   saving documents, 59
TrueType fonts, 582–83
TXT files, 48, 621
typefaces. *See* fonts
typeover mode. *See* Overtype mode
Typing Replaces Selection option, 37, 93,
   105–6

U

undeleting. *See* Undo command
underlining
   character formatting, 241–42
   revisions, 354
Undo button, 18, 94–95
Undo command
   overview, 94–95
   recovering cut text, 102
   using with AutoCorrect, 140
Ungroup button, 553
Unindent button, 225
units of measurement, 212, 313
unlinking fields, 688
Unlock Field key(Ctrl-Shift-F11), 688

unlocking documents, 341
Unspike key (Ctrl-Shift-F3), 152
Update INCLUDETEXT (Ctrl-Shift-F7), 687
Update key (F9), 685–87, 764, 767, 783
updating
    indexes, 783
    links, 313, 644–45
    tables of contents, 764, 767
Upper argument, 692
uppercase characters, 245, 692. *See also* drop capitals
USERADDRESS field, 707
USERINFO field, 707
user information
    default options, 40
    fields for, 707
    searching by, 607, 612
USERINITIALS field, 707
Use Smart Cut And Paste option, 108
Use The INS Key For Paste option, 38
utilities. *See* Options dialog box

V

values, defined, 717
variables, defined, 717
version number, 706
versions, comparing, 358–59
vertical ruler, 218, 278–79, 280–81, 311
vertical scroll bar, 20, 21, 35, 76–77
vertical sizing arrow, 24, 25
vertical split pointer, 24, 25
vertical text aligning, 489–90
View Annotations command, 337–38
View Full Screen command, 304–6
View Header And Footer command, 171, 175, 493
viewing Clipboard contents, 101–2
viewing line numbers, 472–73
View Master Document command, 590
View menu (Word 6.0), 13, 14, 34
View menu (Equation Editor), 816, 817
View mode, 20

View Normal command, 69, 294–95
View (Options) card, 35–36, 300, 310–12, 683, 684–85
View Outline command, 84, 297, 652, 654
View Page Layout command, 298
View Ruler command, 34
views, 69, 293–309, 310–12
View Toolbars command, 34, 317
View Zoom command, 69, 306
voice annotations, 338

W

watermarks, 534–35
While...Wend statement, 908–9
widows and orphans, 220–21, 232
wildcard characters, 47, 113–14, 604, 608
Window menu (Equation Editor), 816, 819
Window menu (Microsoft Graph), 574, 577
Window menu (Word 6.0), 13, 14
windows. *See also* screen display
    list of shortcut keys, 992
    splitting into panes, 21
Windows Application Control menu, 11, 61
Windows Control Panel, 254, 262, 585
WINDOWS directory, 602
Windows environment, starting Word from, 4–8
Windows Metafile format (WMF) , 536
Window Split command, 12, 21
WIN.INI file, 188
WinWord. *See* Microsoft Word 6.0 for Windows
WINWORD directory, 602
WINWORD.OPT file, 327
wizards
    defined, 322
    Fax Wizard, 322–23
    reusing, 324
    using, 322–24
    WORDWIZ.INI file, 324

WMF files, 536
WordArt objects
  borders for, 568
  creating, 562–63
  drop caps as, 571–72
  formatting, 563–68
  framing, 569
  inserting, 562, 568
  inserting as icons, 569–70
  moving, 569
  rotating, 566–67
  shading, 567
WordArt toolbar, 563
WordBasic
  commands, 871, 873, 898–900, 904–8
  defined, 867
  resources for, 926
Word Control menu. *See* Windows
    Application Control menu
Word for Windows. *See* Microsoft Word
    6.0 for Windows
WordPerfect
  blue screen for users, 313
  help for users, 30–31, 36
  navigation keys option, 36
  status bar indicators, 22
WordPerfect Help command (Help), 30
words. *See also* text
  counting, 74
  defined, 73
  deleting, 92
  selecting, 86

Words In CAPS option, 200
WORDWIZ.INI file, 324
wordwrap, 67–68, 312
WPH indicator, 22, 23
WP indicator, 22
WPN indicator, 22
wrapping text, 67–68, 312
Wrap To Window option, 312
write reservation passwords, 54–55, 934
WYSIWYG, 581, 582

X

XE (index entry) field, 776, 778, 779

Z

Zoom dialog box, 69–70, 307–8
Zoom drop-down list box, 18, 69, 309
zoom settings
  in Normal view, 307
  overview, 69–70
  in Page Layout view, 306, 307, 308
  in Print Preview, 277–78

M. David Stone has been working with and writing about personal computers since 1981. He was Computers Editor at *Science Digest* and is currently a contributing editor at *Windows Sources* and at *PC Magazine*, where he writes the word processing section of the Solutions column. His work has also appeared in *Computer Shopper*, *PC Sources*, and *InfoWorld*, among other publications. His other computer-related books include *Getting the Most from WordStar and MailMerge*, *Microsoft Word Power Pack*, and *Getting Online*, which was a primary selection of the Small Computer Book Club.

Alfred Poor writes in his "electronic cottage" in Bucks County, Pennsylvania. As a contributing editor with *PC Magazine* and *Computer Shopper*, he has reviewed hundreds of products, including dozens of word processing programs. His articles have also appeared in *PC Week* and *PC Sources*. He is the author of three other books: *New Life for Old PCs*, *The Data Exchange*, and *The Hewlett-Packard LaserJet Printer Handbook*.

he manuscript for this book was prepared and submitted to Microsoft Press in electronic form. Text files were prepared using Microsoft Word for Windows. Pages were composed by Microsoft Press using PageMaker for Windows, with text in Palatino and display type in Optima Bold. Composed pages were delivered to the printer as electronic prepress files.

Cover Designer
Rebecca Geisler

Cover Illustrator
David Lemley

Cover Color Separator
Color Service Inc.

Interior Graphic Designer
Kim Eggleston

Electronic Artist, Gallery Designer
Lisa Sandburg

Principal Layout Artist
Brett Polonsky

Principal Editorial Compositor
Barb Runyan

Principal Proofreader/Copy Editor
Shawn Peck and Alice Copp Smith

Indexer
Julie Kawabata

Printed on recycled paper stock.

Other Titles from Microsoft Press

Microsoft Press® Computer Dictionary, 2nd ed.
Microsoft Press

More than 5000 entries, written in clear, standard English, go
beyond simple definition to provide useful detail. Includes pronunciation
guides and dozens of new illustrations. Written by a distinguished team
of experts from computer, business, and academic backgrounds.
ISBN 1-55615-597-2   456 pages $19.95 ($26.95 Canada)

Desktop Publishing by Design, 3rd ed.
Aldus® PageMaker® Edition
Ronnie Shushan and Don Wright

A design-oriented sourcebook of project ideas, instruction, and
inspiration that is really three books in one. You'll find coverage of elements
of design, a desktop-publishing portfolio, and dozens of hands-on projects.
Covers PageMaker version 5 for the IBM PC and the Apple Macintosh.
ISBN 1-55615-566-2   512 pages $29.95 ($39.95 Canada)

Windows NT™ Answer Book
Jim Groves

An authoritative, fact-filled guide—in question-and-answer format—
that provides accessible coverage of all relevant topics to help you decide
whether the Windows NT system is right for your computing environment.
Answers all the most commonly asked questions about Windows NT.
ISBN 1-55615-562-X   224 pages $16.95 ($21.95 Canada)

Microsoft Press

Microsoft Press® books are available wherever quality books are sold and through CompuServe's Electronic Mall—GO MSP.
*Call 1-800-MSPRESS for direct ordering information or for placing credit card orders.**
Please refer to BBK when placing your order. Prices subject to change.

*In Canada, contact Macmillan Canada, Attn: Microsoft Press Dept., 164 Commander Blvd., Agincourt, Ontario, Canada M1S 3C7, or call (416) 293-8464, ext. 340.
Outside the U.S. and Canada, write to International Sales, Microsoft Press, One Microsoft Way, Redmond, WA 98052-6399.

Information—Direct from the Source

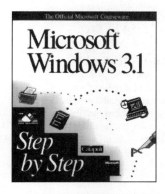

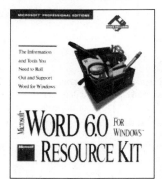

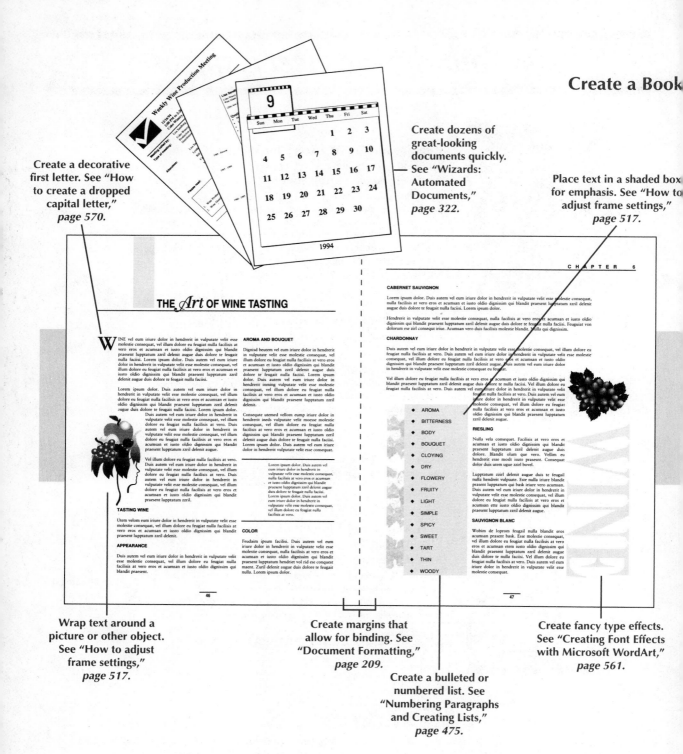

Create a decorative first letter. See "How to create a dropped capital letter," *page 570.*

Create dozens of great-looking documents quickly. See "Wizards: Automated Documents," *page 322.*

Place text in a shaded box for emphasis. See "How to adjust frame settings," *page 517.*

Create a Book

Wrap text around a picture or other object. See "How to adjust frame settings," *page 517.*

Create margins that allow for binding. See "Document Formatting," *page 209.*

Create fancy type effects. See "Creating Font Effects with Microsoft WordArt," *page 561.*

Create a bulleted or numbered list. See "Numbering Paragraphs and Creating Lists," *page 475.*